THEIRS THE STRIFE

To the memory of the uncle I never knew.

Sub-Lieutenant JLT Graham-Brown RN

HMS *Royal Oak*, Scapa Flow, 14 October 1939

THEIRS THE STRIFE

The Forgotten Battles of British Second Army and Armeegruppe Blumentritt, April 1945

John Russell

Helion & Company

Helion & Company Limited
Unit 8 Amherst Business Centre
Budbrooke Road
Warwick
CV34 5WE
England
Tel. 01926 499 619
Email: info@helion.co.uk
Website: www.helion.co.uk
Twitter: @helionbooks
blog.helion.co.uk

Published by Helion & Company 2020
Designed and typeset by Mach 3 Solutions Ltd (www.mach3solutions.co.uk)
Front cover designed by Paul Hewitt, Battlefield Design (www.battlefield-design.co.uk)
Back cover designed by John Russell
Printed by Gutenberg Press, Tarxien, Malta

Text © John Russell 2020
Images © as individually credited
Maps and figures drawn by and © John Russell 2020

Every reasonable effort has been made to trace copyright holders and to obtain their permission for the use of copyright material. The author and publisher apologize for any errors or omissions in this work, and would be grateful if notified of any corrections that should be incorporated in future reprints or editions of this book.

ISBN 978-1-913118-56-3

British Library Cataloguing-in-Publication Data.
A catalogue record for this book is available from the British Library.

All rights reserved. No part of this publication may be reproduced, stored in a retrieval system, or transmitted, in any form, or by any means, electronic, mechanical, photocopying, recording or otherwise, without the express written consent of Helion & Company Limited.

For details of other military history titles published by Helion & Company Limited contact the above address, or visit our website: http://www.helion.co.uk.

We always welcome receiving book proposals from prospective authors.

Contents

List of Illustrations		vi
List of Figures		x
List of Maps		xi
Preface		xiii
Acknowledgements		xvii
Abbreviations		xix
1	From Pillar to Post: 23 March–4 April 1945	23
2	The Rock of Resistance: German Forces on the Weser and Aller	47
3	Forward on Wings of Flame: Second Army April 1945	103
4	Stukas, Tigers and Panthers: VIII Corps' Battles for Weser Bridgeheads 5–6 April 1945	141
5	Fat Cars, Chateau Lafite and the Steel-eyed Boys: 7–9 April 1945	182
6	'Men Who Enjoyed Dying': XII Corps across the Weser 5–10 April 1945	229
7	'A Little Bit of Burma': The Battle for the Aller Bridgehead at Essel 10–12 April	262
8	'One of the Hardest Days': The battles on the roads to Ostenholz and Winsen 13–14 April 1945	303
9	A Most Decisive Victory?: The Battle for Rethem 11–12 April 1945	328
10	Belt-fed Bazookas: 53rd Division across the Aller 11–14 April 1945	362
11	Through the Crust: The Collapse of the Aller Line and XII Corps' Breakout 14–17 April	390
12	Die Stunde Null: 15 April–8 May	434
Epilogue		452
Appendix A		472
Bibliography		478
Index		485

List of Illustrations

The Weser at Petershagen. Photograph taken from the left bank in 2015. (Author)	24
The Aller at Rethem. Photograph taken from the left bank in 2015. (Author)	24
The Leine near Schwarmstedt. Photograph taken from the left bank in 2019. (Graham)	25
Fachhallenhaus. In 1945 the huge roof would probably have been thatched. (Author)	27
Typical scene of a Weser-Aller Plain village: tall oaks and brick buildings with crossed horses' heads in Gross Eilstorf. Photograph taken in 2015. (Author)	28
Industrial building with camouflaged roof at Kampfstoffabrik Leese. Photograph taken in 2015. (Author)	29
Industrial structure with camouflaged roof at Walo I, Bomlitz. Photograph taken in 1982. (Author)	29
Tanks of 5 RTR pause on a main road during the advance to the Weser (Huett).	30
Seekriegsleitung signal allocating 2. Marine-Infanterie-Division to Heeresgruppe 'H' and ordering its deployment to the Osnabrück area. (Mehner)	64
The Weser with the tile factory in the background. Picture taken in 2015. (Author)	145
The demolished road and rail bridge at Stolzenau and the warehouse behind which G Company 8 RB took cover.	153
The railway crossing with Haus Johann beyond on the left. Picture taken in 2015. (Author)	164
The final approach to Bierde, with its buildings visible in the background. The Gehle stream, its course improved since 1945, is on the right. (Author)	167
The grave in Ilvese war cemetery of the three Panther crewmen. (Author)	167
Destroyed engineer transport at Stolzenau. The incomplete Bailey pontoon bridge can be seen on the right with the demolished road and rail bridge beyond.	177
Leutnant Hans Nagel's grave in Essel's *Soldatenfriedhof*. (Author)	186
A NSGr. 1 (Nord) Ju 87 D-5 captured on the ground at Wunstorf. Note the exhaust damper to aid concealment during night operations. (Dupas)	191
The bridge over the Leine at Neustadt. The repaired blown span can just be seen on the left. Photograph taken in 2019. (Graham)	193
2 FF Yeo Comet crossing the Petershagen Class 40 Bailey pontoon bridge. The soldier standing on the bridge is Sergeant Ian Grant, who was filming the crossing. (© Crown Copyright, IWM negative number BU3199)	195
The crossing site from the right bank in 2015. (Author)	195
Under a large Red Cross, surrendered defenders of Leese march off to captivity.	202
Destroyed V-2 on the railway spur line leading through the forest to Kampfstoffabrik Leese.	204
Destroyed V-2 and a *Meillerwagen* rocket transporter/launch trailer.	204
A Challenger of 15/19 Hussars in overwatch as a Cromwell supports infantry from 1 Cheshire advancing across country typical of the area between the Weser and Leine.	206
Captured Hitler Youth of SS-A.u.E.Btl. 12 'HJ' await evacuation to the divisional cage. They are all wearing the Model 1943 service tunic, a shoddy garment made of waste wool and rayon.	211

Steimbke still shelters in its quiet valley, although the roofs are now tiled not thatched. Photograph taken in 2015. (Author)	224
A gravestone in Steimbke churchyard of an unknown member of SS-A.u.E.Btl. 12 HJ. (Author)	226
Hoya road bridge over the Weser with the *Schloss* to its right. Apart from the modern style of bridge, a scene little-changed from 1945. Photograph taken in 2014. (Author)	230
A pre-War postcard of Rethem's bridge.	230
Rethem railway station on its low embankment. Photograph taken in 1992. (Author)	231
Hoya Bailey bridge.	243
Soldiers of 1/5 Welch setting-off into the mist. Ominously, the group of soldiers sitting on the ground looking at the camera are a stretcher-bearer party.	246
The dead-end to the railway station, with the station at the end of the road. Photograph taken in 1982. (Author)	250
1/5 Welch officers observing Rethem from the newly-captured '*Schweinebarth*' strongpoint.	252
Sergeant Jake Wardrop (without shirt), his crew and their Firefly. (Forty)	253
Sergeant Jake Wardrop's grave in CWGC cemetery Becklingen. (Author)	254
Although the course of Reichsstrasse 209 has been modernised, this is the site of the Wardrop ambush. B Company and 11 Troop entered the killing zone from the road on the left of the picture. The log obstacle was positioned where the main road starts to bend out of sight. Photograph taken in 2015. (Author)	257
The fan cowl on Jake Wardrop's Firefly showing the impact of the *Panzerfaust* warhead. (TNA)	258
The Aller at Essel. Photograph taken in 2015. (Author)	262
The Esseler Kanal and its road bridge. The depth of the channel and the cover it afforded played important roles during the battle in the forest. Photograph taken in 2015. (Author)	264
The railway bridge over the Aller. Although the photograph was taken in 2015, the bridge is identical to its 1945 predecessor. (Author)	265
The Aller road bridge taken from the left bank in 2006. The 1945 bridge was almost identical. (Author)	265
The railway bridge from the right bank. Photograph taken in 2015. (Author)	274
Korvettenkapitän Josef Gördes' grave in Essel's *Soldatenfriedhof*. The helmet was found in place when the photograph was taken in 1992. (Author)	281
The raft transporting M16 half-tracks belonging to a self-propelled troop from 172 Battery 58th LAA Regiment. In the foreground, infantry from 4 KSLI are ferried in an assault boat. On the far bank a recovery bulldozer is evident.	296
A blurry shot taken in action of prisoners hurrying down the Ostenholz road. On the right of the photograph is a tree-covered dune, dominant features in the forest. (Peston)	298
Franzen's view down the Ostenholz road as he rounded the bend in Tiger F01. John Langdon's troop were either side of the road near where it runs out of sight. (Author)	298
F01 soon after its destruction. Smoke is still coming out of the commander's cupola and the soldiers of 3 RTR and 4 KSLI lean on the glacis plate, probably discussing the next stage of their battle up the Ostenholz road. A surrendering German soldier can be seen to the rear of F01. (Peston)	308
A toy-like Cromwell of HQ 29th Armoured Brigade bypasses the formidable bulk of F01 blocking the Ostenholz road. The state of the verge indicates that A Squadron 3 RTR had passed through by the time the photograph was taken. (Peston)	308

The fire-damaged F01 after it was pushed off the Ostenholz road. The shot hole from Sergeant Harding's AP round is clearly visible above the sixth road wheel and the main armament is on full recoil after the round 'cooked off'. (The Tank Museum Ltd)	309
The menacing appearance of F01 belies its true, burnt-out state. An unfired *Panzerfaust* lies at the foot of the birch tree. (The Tank Museum Ltd)	309
The Ostenholz road and site of F01's destruction today. Sergeant Harding fired his shot from off the photograph to the right. (Author)	310
The moor today, with the much-improved drainage allowing cultivation. (Author)	312
The entry hole of the 88mm AP round that hit Trooper Bligh's Comet. (TNA)	316
The road through the forest to Winsen. Photograph taken in 2015. (Author)	320
The Flak 41 crew's view to Lance Corporal Chambers' Comet as it emerged from the forest. Photograph taken in 2015. (Author)	326
The Eystrup road after the battle, with the von der Kammer strongpoint among the buildings on the right of the photograph.	331
The burnt-out shell of '*Elfriede*' in a photograph taken after the capture of Rethem. The soldier is peering into a German trench, where at least four helmets and a stick grenade can be seen.	331
Bryan de Grineau's drawing of the alleged massacre. (© Mary Evans Picture Library)	333
4.2-in mortar of D Company 1 Manchester firing in support of the attack on Stöcken.	338
The 'huge arena' and the railway embankment viewed from the start line. Photograph taken in 1983. (Author)	341
Infantry of 2 Mons starting their advance towards Rethem. (Huett)	342
The view from the German positions on the railway embankment of 2 Mons' approach. Panorama photograph taken in 1992. (Author)	344
Sergeant Stimpson (front, left) and Sergeant Lines (right) pose with crew members on a Pak 40 after the fall of Rethem. 'Coldsteel' Pearson is in the leather jerkin (centre, back). (Stimpson)	350
View from the turret of a C Squadron 5 RTR Firefly as it entered Rethem. (Crickmay)	351
Captain Dixon (left) and Major Crickmay (right) of 5 RTR in the centre of Rethem immediately after its capture. German prisoners in the background. (Crickmay)	352
German prisoners on the Eystrup road being marched away to the west. (Huett)	352
C Squadron 5 RTR Cromwells in the centre of Rethem. The second tank is a Cromwell MkVI close support tank of squadron headquarters. As all the vehicles are pointing west, the photograph was probably taken when 5 RTR was about to pull out of Rethem. (Crickmay)	353
Two C Squadron 5 RTR Cromwells and a Stuart of Recce Troop in Mühlenstrasse in the centre of Rethem. (Crickmay)	353
Abandoned Pak 40 in the town centre with smoke from fires still billowing. (Huett)	354
Four of the 10.5cm Flak. The nearest gun has been stacked with sleepers in an attempt to protect the crew and has received a direct hit. Rethem station in the background. (© Crown Copyright, IWM negative number BU3569)	354
The 10.5cm Flak. (© Crown Copyright, IWM negative number BU3591)	355
Pak 40 in a hedge-line. Above the gun's muzzle brake, Denis Huett's Firefly can just be seen on the orchard's far side. (Huett)	355
The wrack of war. Pak 40 with dead anti-tank gunner from Marine-Panzerjäger-Abteilung 2, an unused *Panzerfaust* by his side.	357
Bullet-riddled town sign and burnt-out house provide mute testament to the ferocity of the fighting in Rethem. (Huett)	358

A view of the destruction in Rethem taken from the remains of the demolished road bridge. The tower on the right is the St. Marien Kirche.	358
The FBE at Westen.	367
Vickers machine-gunners of 1 Manchester engaging targets on the right bank. Sticking upright in the field forward left of the gun is a zero post, used to align the gun when firing in the indirect role. A watering can has been appropriated to fill the gun's condenser can.	373
The road to Kirchwahlingen on the Aller's right bank. The road crosses the middle of the photograph, with the hamlet and its church tower visible in the trees right of centre. Photograph taken in 2015. (Author)	393
Bailey pontoon bridge at Rethem with the demolished road bridge lying in the Aller next to it.	394
A 4th Armoured Brigade Sherman crosses the Bailey pontoon at Rethem. The house on the left was where the 2 Mons patrol found the marine OP on 12 April.	396
Shermans of the Scots Greys and Kangaroo APCs carrying 6 RWF wait to cross the Rethem pontoon bridge. (© Crown Copyright, IWM negative number BU3648)	397
The cars of today replace the Shermans and Kangaroos of 1945. (Author)	397
Cromwells moving through the smoking ruins of Vethem.	409
Peter White and his lead section were advancing down the slope towards the camera when the ambush was sprung. Photograph taken in 2015. (Author)	417
Stalag XIB – *Appelplatz* with the camp's main administration building in the background.	425
'…what looked like half a dozen tall warehouses.' Photograph taken in 1982. (Author)	428
Outside Stalag XIB's wire, newly-liberated prisoners enjoy their freedom.	431
A typical scene of the final days. A Ford 3000 series truck laden with surrendered German troops drives past Cromwells of 5 RTR pausing in a street. (Huett)	447
A picture with a dreamlike air. Under a large oak, two surrendered German officers wait with their bicycles and belongings, ignored by the crew of a Cromwell busy adjusting their tank's tracks. (Huett)	447
MG 42 and StG 44 found on the battlefield. (Author)	468
Splinter-damaged *façade* in Rethem. (Author)	468
Rethem's memorial stone. (Author)	468
Soldatenfriedhof Essel in the forest where 3 Cdo and HQ 1st Commando Brigade fought for their survival against the counter-attacks. (Author)	469
The last remaining section of the railway line leading through the forest to Kampfstoffabrik Leese. (Author)	469
Steps in Stalag XIB. Photograph taken in 2015. (Author)	470
CWGC cemetery Becklingen. (Author)	471

List of Figures

1	OB Nordwest – 6 April 1945.	49
2	Armeegruppe Student – 6 April 1945.	50
3	2. Marine-Infanterie-Division – 7 April 194.	58
4	SS-A.u.E.Btl.12 'HJ' – April 1945.	72
5	Minden Sector Weapon Return as at 31 March 1945.	79
6	Kampfgruppen Totzeck and Scherer – 6 April 1945.	81
7	Gruppe Grosan – 6 April 1945.	82
8	Kampfgruppe Schulze – 4 April 1945.	84
9	14.Flieger-Division – 12 April 1945.	90
10	14.Flak-Division – October 1944.	97
11	21st Army Group – 4 April 1945.	104
12	VIII Corps – 4 April 1945.	124
13	11th Armoured Division – April 1945.	125
14	6th Airborne Division – April 1945.	127
15	6th Guards Armoured Brigade – April 1945.	129
16	1st Commando Brigade – April 1945.	130
17	XII Corps – April 1945.	131
18	7th Armoured Division – April 1945.	132
19	Guards Armoured Division – April 1945.	134
20	53rd Welsh Division – April 1945.	135
21	4th Armoured Brigade – 14 April 1945.	137
22	58th LAA Regiment Log – 5 April 1945.	154
23	58th LAA Regiment Log – 6 April 1945.	176
24	5 RTR Tank Casualty Log – 10 April 1945.	259
25	2. Marine-Infanterie-Division strength return – 21 April 1945.	439

List of Maps

1	The Field of Battle.	25
2	Heeresgruppe 'H' situation – 2 April 1945.	41
3	Second Army's Advance to the Weser – 23 March–5 April 1945.	42
4	Defence of the Rivers – April 1945.	51
5	The Northern Wehrkreise.	52
6	2. Marine-Infanterie-Division's Training Locations.	57
7	Armeegruppe Student's Centre on the Aller.	66
8	Armeegruppe Student's Centre on the Weser.	74
9	The Defence of Leese.	76
10	Armeegruppe Student's Left Flank on the Weser.	78
11	Armeegruppe Student's Left Flank on the Aller.	80
12	*Luftwaffe* Bases in North Germany – April 1945.	91
13	*Flak* support to the Weser Line.	100
14	6th Airborne Division across the Weser – 5 April 1945.	143
15	11th Armoured Division Across the Weser – 5 April 1945.	149
16	Stolzenau – 1650 Hours 5 April 1945.	155
17	Situation 1200 hours 6 April 1945.	160
18	The Tiger Group's Attack – 6 April 1945.	161
19	The Panther Group's Attack – 6 April 1945.	166
20	Kampfgruppe Tischler's Attack – 6 April 1945.	171
21	45 (RM) Cdo Crosses the Weser – Night 6/7 April 1945.	174
22	Route of US 3rd Air Division – 7 April 1945.	183
23	6th Airborne Division's Advance to the Leine – 7 April 1945.	188
24	7 Para's Disaster at Neustadt – Night 7/8 April 1945.	192
25	159th Infantry Brigade Group's Advance on the Weser's Right Bank – 7 April 1945.	194
26	1st Commando Brigade's Attack on Leese – 8 April 1945.	201
27	11th Armoured Division's Advance to the Leine – 8 April 1945.	207
28	The Action at Ricklingen Bridge – 8 April 1945.	218
29	11th Armoured Division's Advance to the Leine – 9 April 1945.	222
30	The Battle for Steimbke – 9 April 1945.	225
31	Deployment of Marine-Grenadier-Regiment 5 at Rethem – 9 April 1945.	234
32	6 RWF Crosses the Weser – 9 April 1945.	242
33	53rd Welsh Division's Advance to the Aller – 10 April 1945.	245
34	1/5 Welch Attacks – 10 April 1945.	247
35	Sergeant Moses' *Coup de Main* – 10 April 1945.	249
36	Ambush of 11 Troop 5 RTR and B Company 6 RWF – 1915 hours 10 April 1945.	255
37	The Defence of the Schwarmstedt Area – 10 April 1945.	263
38	159th Infantry Brigade Group's Attack on Schwarmstedt-Essel – 10 April 1945.	270
39	1st Commando Brigade Crosses the Aller – 10–11 April 1945.	276
40	6 Cdo's Assault on the Aller Road Bridge – 1030 hours 11 April 1945.	283
41	B Squadron 3 RTR – 0925 hours 11 April 1945.	287
42	The Germans seal the Bridgehead – 12 April 1945.	292
43	45 and 46 (RM) Cdo Attacks – Morning 12 April 1945.	294
44	1 Troop's Encounter with Tiger F01 – pm 12 April 1945.	300
45	(RM) Cdo's Attack on Hademstorf – 1400 hours 13 April 1945.	304
46	The End of Tiger F01 – 1030 hours 13 April 1945.	307

47	The Ground Beyond the Forest.	313
48	The Action at Half-way Wood – 1400 hours 13 April 1945.	314
49	The Advance to Winsen – 13 April 1945.	319
50	The Advance to Winsen – 14 April 1945.	323
51	1/5 Welch's Dawn Attack – 0445 hours 11 April 1945.	329
52	Plans A and B.	335
53	Trace for Op HATTON fire plan – 11 April 1945.	337
54	Preliminary Operations – Rethem – 11 April 1945.	340
55	2 Mons' Attack on Rethem – pm 11 April 1945.	343
56	The Weser-Aller Triangle and the Aller's Right Bank.	363
57	1 E Lancs crosses the Aller – am 12 April 1945.	365
58	158th Infantry Brigade's Bridgehead on the Aller – pm 12 April 1945.	369
59	71st Infantry Brigade's Advance on the Right Bank – 12/13 April 1945.	371
60	71st Infantry Brigade – pm 13 April 1945.	376
61	The German Counter-Attacks – 13/14 April 1945.	381
62	C Squadron 53rd Recce Regiment under attack – 13/14 April 1945.	383
63	Situation in the Rethem Bridgehead – Midday 14 April 1945.	392
64	4th Armoured Brigade – pm 14 April 1945.	396
65	158th Infantry Brigade's Advance Northwards – pm 14 April 1945.	400
66	4th Armoured Brigade's Attacks on Gr. Eilstorf and Kirchboitzen – 15 April 1945.	403
67	4th Armoured Brigade's Advance Northwards – pm 15 April 1945.	407
68	22nd Armoured Brigade's Advance to Walsrode – 15 April 1945.	410
69	Ambush on 10 Platoon 4 KOSB – 15 April 1945.	415
70	158th and 71st Infantry Brigades and the Capture of Verden – 15–17 April 1945.	419
71	The Relief of Stalags XIB and 357 – 17 April 1945.	426
72	Visselhövede – 2. Marine-Infanterie-Division's Last Stand – 18–19 April 1945.	436
73	The Final Divisional Advances – 15 April–3 May 1945.	440
74	Final Dispositions of 1. Fallschirm-Armee and Armeegruppe Blumentritt – 3 May 1945.	444

Preface

This book tells the story of a series of actions fought 75 years ago between British Second Army and Armeegruppe Blumentritt during the closing weeks of the North-West Europe campaign, a time when the war's result seemed no longer in doubt and, for the Allies, the race nearly won. Compared to other actions they were not momentous and their duration was short, yet in terms of ferocity they equalled some of the fiercest of the campaign and were fought by men who knew that the war must surely soon end. For them fear of death or injury was intense, courage harder to muster, acts of bravery more significant and casualties more poignant, and the book's title, part of a line from Lord Byron's narrative poem 'The Giaour', seeks to reflect the burden shared by the men of both sides as they prosecuted a long war to its bitter conclusion.

As historians of the British part of the campaign have tended to focus on major events such as D-Day, Normandy and the battle for Arnhem, history has largely ignored the final weeks. The few narratives covering the period hurry from the Rhine to the surrender on Lüneburg Heath and at best make only passing reference to the bitter actions fought en route. Though often brief, these actions had to be fought and casualties were inevitable, but to spare an exhausted, war-weary home population, war correspondents tended to gloss over the severity of the fighting. The lack of recognition for those who had to do the fighting was therefore deeply frustrating, as Noel Bell, in April 1945 commanding G Company, 8th Battalion The Rifle Brigade, recalls:[1]

> Reading the English newspapers at that time, one would have thought that fighting had virtually ceased and that all we were doing was to motor along and take thousands of prisoners. This annoyed us to no small degree and…two of our bitterest engagements were yet to be fought. Although things were going very well, yet valuable lives were still being lost daily, and we wished that some of these war correspondents who were sending back these totally inaccurate reports could be up with us to see what was really going on.

As well as the neglect of historians and correspondents, the proximity of powerful events such as the relief of Belsen, Hitler's suicide and then VE Day combined to make the actions even more opaque and once the war was over the British understandably looked to peace and the future. Except in the memories of those who had to fight them, awareness of the actions of the last weeks soon faded so I determined to shed light on this little-known period of history, set straight the record and by making fullest possible use of primary sources, give voice to the soldiers and airmen who had to shoulder the burden.

Chiefly the product of wartime photographs and newsreels, there is a perception that in April 1945 the German Army did little more than surrender. This is profoundly mistaken and many units fought on with courage and resilience. Although British divisional and regimental histories, war diaries and personal accounts reveal the fighting's intensity, their testimony has been overlooked and this, linked to the dearth of contemporary and historical coverage, has given rise to the perception that the advances through Germany and the Netherlands were uncontested formalities, resulting in the final advance being left in the nation's memory as a trouble-free 'swan'. Nothing

---

1 Noel Bell, *From the Beaches to the Baltic, The Story of G Company, 8th Battalion the Rifle Brigade, During the Campaign in North-West Europe* (Aldershot: Gale & Polden, 1947), p.105.

could be further from the truth and in the six weeks from the crossing of the Rhine on 23 March to the war's end on 8 May, Montgomery's 21st Army Group at certain times and places fought an implacable enemy, resulting in some 20,000 casualties, nearly a quarter of the total for the campaign, with 4,009 killed in action, 15,796 wounded and 1213 missing.[2]

In April 1945 Second Army was an organisation of strong contrasts. While it was undoubtedly at its peak in terms of equipment, tactical doctrine and leadership, its combat arms were worn out and extremely casualty conscious, with the infantry in particular close to exhaustion, both quantitatively and qualitatively. The opposing combatants were therefore more equal than might be assumed and both faced the same challenge: summoning up the energy and courage to fight a war to its bloody conclusion. Furthermore, it is easy to forget that in early April 1945 nobody knew that the *Reich* would collapse in a few weeks and there was a strong possibility that the war would need to extend to Scandinavia to defeat the sizeable German garrisons in Denmark and Norway, generating well-founded concerns regarding Second Army's capacity to prosecute an extended campaign.

My interest in this period began in 1981 when I was adjutant of the 3rd Battalion The Queen's Regiment stationed in Fallingbostel, a British Army of the Rhine (BAOR) garrison on the North German Plain mid-way between Hannover and Hamburg. One day, with the in-tray low and the commanding officer away, I was browsing the wartime history of The Queen's Royal Regiment (West Surrey), one of my regiment's forebears, and noticed that the 1st/5th Battalion had fought through the Fallingbostel area in April 1945 and was present at the relief of the large prisoner of war (PoW) camp, Stalag XIB, whose foundations were still visible in the woods close to our barracks. More intriguingly, the history revealed that in the days prior to the camp's relief, bitter fighting had taken place to capture crossings over the rivers Weser and Aller, not far to the west of Fallingbostel. This fighting not only surprised me, as I too thought that the advance across Germany was largely a formality, but the history also mentioned the 2. Marine-Infanterie-Division, an emergency-raised formation consisting of ships' crews and surplus naval personnel destined to be the *Wehrmacht's* last formally established formation to be fielded against Second Army. Intrigued, I started to gather information about the actions that had taken place locally and from this modest beginning the book had its origin, with the naval division's short but violent existence providing the framework on which the book's narrative is hung. So by design it does not describe the entirety of Second Army's advance from the Rhine to the Elbe but concentrates on a 2-week period during which VIII and XII Corps fought to cross three rivers – the Weser, Leine and Aller – against the spirited defence mounted by 2. Marine-Infanterie-Division, SS-Panzer-Grenadier Ausbildungs und Ersatz Bataillon 12 'Hitlerjugend' and other supporting units.

In 1994 part of the book was published as 'No Triumphant Procession',[3] which had as its central theme the actions fought by XII Corps against the naval division. However, as it concentrated on the actions fought by 53rd Welsh Division, 'No Triumphant Procession' told only some of the story and the battles fought by other formations and units were either covered in far less detail or not at all. This book therefore takes a significantly wider view and now includes VIII Corps' involvement by covering 6th Airborne and 11th Armoured Division's battles for their bridgeheads over the Weser at Petershagen and Stolzenau, 11th Armoured Division's demanding advance to the Leine against the young soldiers of the *Hitlerjugend* battalion, and the subsequent battle for the Essel bridgehead and the contested advance to Winsen. It also includes actions in the air. As a subsidiary aim of the book is to record the organisation, equipment and state of the participating British and German forces in 1945, there are two contextual chapters providing background to the

---

2 TNA WO 171/3873, 21st Army Group 'A' SITREP No. 331, 8 May 1945.
3 John Russell, *No Triumphant Procession*, (London: Arms & Armour Press, 1994).

narrative. However, a cautionary word regarding these chapters – in order to keep the background information in proportion to the book's structure, of necessity there are omissions and generalisations, and this may not satisfy everyone; for this my apologies. Other readers less interested in the context, can omit Chapters 2 and 3 or dip into them later as required. Lastly, in the Epilogue, I summarise the British strengths and weaknesses and explore why some German units, in particular 2. Marine-Infanterie-Division, offered such stubborn resistance so close to the war's end.

Since writing 'No Triumphant Procession', a number of developments have greatly increased my sources of material. First and foremost is the internet, in the early 1990s in its infancy and the information and contacts it would make available unimaginable. While considerable care needs to be taken with the veracity of its information – for instance sites can feed each other the same incorrect material, giving an illusion of collateral – the internet has enabled me to access a wide range of material and authorities, allowing me to add new information and greater depth. Additionally, the internet has made me aware that the original book was something of a treasure trove for the war-gaming fraternity and so I hope the additional information in this book will be of particular interest to them. Lastly with regard to the internet, at Appendix A is a list of links to online video sources showing contemporary film of events in the book, adding a fascinating additional dimension to the written word. However, it needs to be noted that most of these sources tend to reinforce the image of the advance being the uncontested 'swan' referred to above and there is little in them that reveals the misery of the closing weeks. Besides the internet, I have been able to make use of books and accounts written in the 1990s by veterans recording their wartime experiences before memories faded, and include Ultra decrypts, a classified source of information previously unavailable but now released by the National Archives at Kew and providing an extraordinary and near tangible impression of the Third *Reich* in its death throes. Lastly, I have benefitted from recently-published academic works covering the last stage of the European war, in particular Professor John Buckley's 'Monty's Men' and Professor Ian Kershaw's 'The End'.

Fully accepting that my use of lengthy and lumbering German unit titles and ranks might grate with some readers, I justify their use in the interests of historical accuracy and avoiding the ambiguity that can creep in when providing equivalent British descriptions. For example, the English translation of both *Heeresgruppe* and *Armeegruppe* is 'Army Group', an inaccurate rendition for what were to the Germans different and distinctive organisations. I do however provide translations of less obvious titles the first time they are mentioned so that the reader is not left completely in the dark. Some other miscellaneous points of detail: all terms, British and German, requiring abbreviation are given first in full, followed in brackets by the abbreviation to be used thereafter; ranks for the men of both sides are those held in April 1945; I considered going metric but decided to leave measurements in imperial and weapon calibres a mix of imperial and metric depending on nation; and 'left' or 'right' descriptions of river banks assume the reader is looking downstream.

Possibly as a result of the costs of production, many military histories suffer from a lack of maps. As there is nothing more frustrating for the reader, and I did not want the book to suffer similarly, using Ortelius® cartography software I have produced a large number of maps to support the narrative. Please note: organisations are shown either using NATO map-marking symbols or merely their title; if the size of an organisation is uncertain, the size symbol is omitted; to aid identification, all map-marking and organisation charts associated with German forces are in grey whereas British units are in white with movement arrows in black; and the quantity and size of the maps' explosion symbols seek to reflect the intensity of a given action.

Any mistakes or omissions are mine alone.

John Russell
Warminster, England
March 2020

For these reasons, friend and foe alike, should respect all those who, with the inescapable outcome in front of them, have sacrificed their lives even to the very end, fulfilling their oath of allegiance and fighting for their country.

Oberst Rolf Geyer, 1a, Oberbefehlshaber Nordwest, April 1945.[4]

---

4   US National Archives B-414, Operational Summary, Heeresgruppe 'H'/OB Nordwest, 10 March – 9 May 1945, p.39.

Acknowledgements

First and foremost, I wish to thank the many individuals, regimental headquarters and museums who have helped me with material, both written and photographic. In particular: Cathy Webbon who allowed me to use extracts from her grandfather John Langdon's account of his war service, which she edited and published as the 'The Sharp End'; Dr Stephen Pannell, who provided me with a copy of 'The Sharp End' and photographs of Tiger F01; Richard Gough, Director of the Shropshire Regimental Museum for giving me permission to quote liberally from Major 'Ned' Thornburn's account of 4th Battalion The King's Shropshire Light Infantry; Ian Martin, archivist of the regimental museum of The King's Own Scottish Borderers, for providing David Ward's account of his time in the commandos, and the Ward family for allowing me to publish extracts from the account; and the Rae family for their agreement for me to use extracts from Colin Rae's unpublished story of his military service.

I am, secondly, very grateful to Duncan Rogers and his staff at Helion & Company, who have been unfailingly helpful to me during the drafting process, and I would like to thank Kim McSweeney of Mach 3 Solutions for her thoroughly professional work in typesetting the book, not an easy task given the large number of photographs and maps. I am also very grateful to all those who responded to my questions posed on the internet forum WW2Talk and to 'Trux' on the website, which supplied much of the information on British equipment and organisations. I am also grateful for the assistance provided by the staff of The National Archives (TNA) at Kew, the Central Library of the Ministry of Defence, the Archive and Reference Library of the Tank Museum and Prince Consort's Library, Aldershot. I would in particular like to express my gratitude to two good friends: Mike Jelf for 'volunteering' to read the manuscript and point out my errors, inconsistencies and oversights, and Anthony Biggs, who tramped the battlefields with me and helped prove the veracity, or otherwise, of the war diaries and regimental histories.

From the outset it was my intention to record the German as well as British participation in the battles. Despite the ruin and turmoil that prevailed in Germany in 1945, it was surprising to find that some German units were still keeping typed, written records and even more surprising that they had survived. Kurt Mehner of Rinteln not only most generously assisted me with their provision but also gave me a copy of his book listing *Wehrmacht* formations and their commanders. My knowledge of the German part in the actions is largely a result of his support. I also received substantial assistance from: Günther Milkau, the former 1a (chief of staff) of Marine-Grenadier-Regiment 6; Hermann Kleinebenne of Petershagen, who gave me a copy of his admirable book '*Die Weser Linie – Kriegsende 1945*'; Philip Graham, who translated Wolfgang Buchwald's book '*Endkampf*', telling the brief history of SS-Panzer-Grenadier Ausbildungs und Ersatz Bataillon 12 'Hitlerjugend', and helped me with photographs; and August Jahns of Rethem, who provided information on Rethem. I also received assistance from Ulrich Saft, whose book '*Krieg in der Heimat*' provided useful, if not always wholly accurate, information on the German participation. Through the website 12oclockhigh.net I had invaluable help on the *Luftwaffe* – uncharted territory for me – from Nick Beale, Michaël Svejgaard and Marcel van Heijkop. My thanks to all of them. The excellent website Sturmpanzer.com provided me with details on German formation-level operations and assessments, all contained in online facsimiles of debriefing papers written in the immediate post-war period by incarcerated German officers and commanders.

Over the years I have accumulated quantities of photographs relating to the account and many appear in the book, with known sources added to the photograph's title. In particular I wish to thank Les Huett for allowing me to use photographs taken by his father Denis of C Squadron 5th Royal Tank Regiment and subsequently published in Denis's book 'The Long Drive'; two of Denis's photographs hold pride of place on the front cover. In mentioning photographs, I would like to record my disappointment at the scale of fees charged by the Imperial War Museum (IWM) for their media licences. These fees have severely limited my use of official photographs, making history the poorer.

Although some of the war diaries included maps, they were eclipsed by an online resource: the War Office, 1944, 1:25,000 Germany series held by the Harold B. Lee Library, Brigham Young University, Utah. This public domain mapping resource allowed me to create accurate maps reflecting the geography – both human and physical – extant in 1945. I was also kindly loaned a bound volume of 1945 era 1:100,000 maps of north-west Europe by the daughters of Brigadier (later Lieutenant General Sir Charles) Coleman, in April 1945 the commander of 160th Infantry Brigade.

Finally, I would like to thank my wife Ginny for her forbearance. I think my near 40-year fascination in a two-week period of long ago has totally bemused her but now, with the book published, I hope she is looking forward to seeing me again.

Abbreviations

A.u.E./E.u.A.	Ausbildungs und Ersatz
AEC	Associated Equipment Company
AGRA	Army Group Royal Artillery
AOP	Air observation post
AP	Armour-piercing
APC	Armoured personnel carrier
APCBC	Armour-piercing, capped, ballistic capped
Ar	Arado
ARV	Armoured recovery vehicle
Bf	Bayerische Flugzeugwerke
BC	Battery commander
CAN	Canadian
Cdo	Commando
CLY	County of London Yeomanry
cm	centimetre
C-in-C	Commander-in-Chief
Coy	Company
CSM	Company sergeant major
CWGC	Commonwealth War Graves Commission
cwt	hundredweight
DAA & QMG	Deputy Assistant Adjutant & Quartermaster General
DCOS	Deputy Chief of Staff
DF	Defensive fire
E	Eisenbahn
FBE	Folding boat equipment
FF Yeo	Fife and Forfar Yeomanry
FH	Feldhaubitze
Flak	Fliegerabwehrkanone
FOO	Forward observation officer
Fw	Focke Wulf
GAF	German Air Force
gem.	gemischte
GPO	Gun position officer
GS	General service
HAC	Honourable Artillery Company
HE	High explosive
He	Heinkel
HEAT	High explosive anti-tank
HLI	Highland Light Infantry
-in	inch
INTSUM	Intelligence summary
IR	Infra-red

JG	Jagdgeschwader
Ju	Junkers
kg	kilogram
KG	Kampfgeschwader
KOSB	King's Own Scottish Borderers
KRRC	King's Royal Rifle Corps
KSLI	King's Shropshire Light Infantry
LAA	Light anti-aircraft
LAD	Light aid detachment
-lb	pound
LCpl	Lance corporal
le.	leichte
LI	Light Infantry
LOB	Left out of battle
Me	Messerschmitt
MG	Machine-gun/Maschinengewehr
mm	millimetre
MP	Machine pistol
NCO	Non-commissioned officer
NSGr.	Nachtschlacht Gruppe
O Group	Orders Group
OB	Oberbefehlshaber
OC	Officer commanding
OKH	Oberkommando des Heeres
OKL	Oberkommando der Luftwaffe
OKM	Oberkommando der Marine
OKW	Oberkommando der Wehrmacht
OP	Observation post
Orbat	Order of battle
Pak	Panzerabwehrkanone
-pdr	pounder
Pi	Pionier
PIAT	Projector, Infantry, Anti-Tank
Pl	Platoon
PW/PoW	Prisoner of war
PWK	Panzerwerferkanone
RA	Royal Artillery
RAC	Royal Armoured Corps
RAD	Reichsarbeitsdienst
RAMC	Royal Army Medical Corps
RAOC	Royal Army Ordnance Corps
RAP	Regimental aid post
RASC	Royal Army Service Corps
RB	Rifle Brigade
RE	Royal Engineers
REME	Royal Electrical and Mechanical Engineers
RHA	Royal Horse Artillery
RHQ	Regimental headquarters
RM	Royal Marine

RMO	Regimental medical officer
ROB	Reserve-Offizier-Bewerber
RP	Rocket projectile
RTR	Royal Tank Regiment
RUR	Royal Ulster Rifles
RV	Rendezvous
RWF	Royal Welch Fusiliers
SAS	Special Air Service
SdKfz	Sonderkraftfahrzeug
SEP	Surrendered enemy personnel
SHAEF	Supreme Headquarters Allied Expeditionary Force
SITREP	Situation report
SP	Self-propelled
Sqn	Squadron
SS	Schutzstaffel
StG	Sturmgewehr
StuG	Sturmgeschütz
StuH	Sturmhaubitz
t	ton
TA	Territorial Army
TNA	The National Archives, Kew
Tp	Troop
TSM	Troop sergeant major
ULK	Unterführer-Lehr-Kompanie
z.b.V.	zur besonderen Verwendung
z.V.	zur Vergeltung

1

From Pillar to Post: 23 March–4 April 1945

The stage on which the events of this account will play out is the North German Plain, part of the vast Great European Plain formed during the frequent invasions of ice sheets of the Pleistocene era and stretching east from the Belgian coast to the lowlands of central Russia. More particularly it concerns that part known as the Weser-Aller Plain, lying in today's state of Niedersachsen (Lower Saxony). Ironically, this part of Germany once had exceptionally close links with England. In 1714 George Louis, the ruler of the Duchy and Electorate of Brunswick-Lüneburg, became by the terms of the Act of Settlement of 1701 King of Great Britain and Ireland and the first sovereign of the British dynastic House of Hannover. Until the succession in 1837 of Queen Victoria, the British sovereigns retained their German titles as electors of Hannover and dukes of Brunswick-Lüneburg and, from George III, as Kings of Hannover. There were also very close military links, forged during war. The English army was active in the area during the Seven Years' War when it formed part of Ferdinand of Brunswick's Anglo-German army, which in 1759 inflicted a decisive defeat on the French at Minden. In 1803, following the next French invasion, many officers and soldiers of the Hannoverian army went to England where they formed the King's German Legion, the only German army to fight continuously throughout the Napoleonic wars, and to this day the white horse of Hannover is worn as a collar dog by the Yorkshire Regiment.

The Weser-Aller Plain is host to the meandering courses of three major rivers: the Weser and its tributaries the Aller and Leine. The three rivers are all features of significance and for centuries have played important roles in the area's social, economic and historical evolution. The Weser, with its source near Kassel, dominates the other two rivers and is formed from the confluence of the Fulda and the Werra. It flows to the great mercantile city of Bremen and thence to the North Sea, some 30 miles away at Bremerhaven, and with an overall length of 280 miles is the longest German river to reach the sea with a course entirely within national territory. The Weser is a major transportation route and in its lower reaches is used by barges up to 1,200 tons deadweight. At Minden the barges can leave the Weser to join the Mittelland Canal, a key west-east route linking the Dortmund-Ems and Elbe-Havel canals.

Two miles north-west of Verden the Weser is joined by the Aller, its largest right-bank tributary. The Aller, rising to the west of Magdeburg in the state of Saxony-Anhalt, has a length of 130 miles and although a sluggish river, particularly in its lower reaches, is navigable as far as Celle. During the 1960s the Weser and Aller were partially canalised to bypass the longer meanders and improve navigation for larger barges, but this was not the case in 1945 and their courses twisted serpentinely across the Plain.

The Leine, flowing for some 170 miles from its source in the state of Thuringia, joins the Aller as a left-bank tributary just to the north of Schwarmstedt. Although not as substantial as the Aller, it is a significant river and flows through two cities: Göttingen and Hannover.

The Weser at Petershagen. Photograph taken from the left bank in 2015. (Author)

The Aller at Rethem. Photograph taken from the left bank in 2015. (Author)

The Leine near Schwarmstedt. Photograph taken from the left bank in 2019. (Graham)

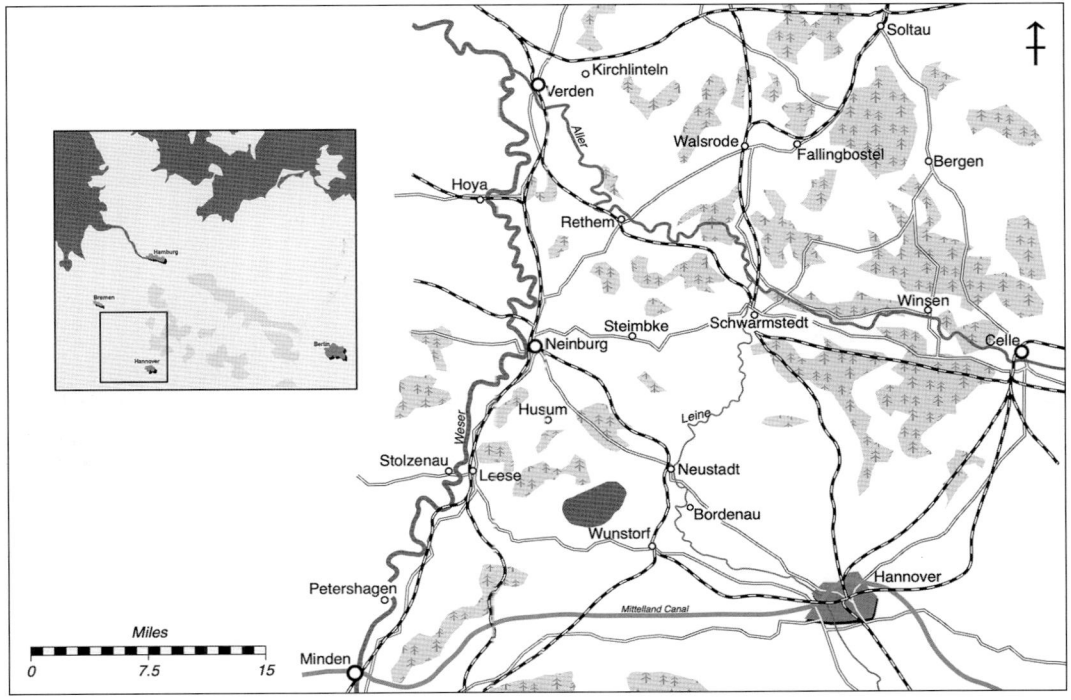

Map 1 The Field of Battle.

In April 1945 the rivers were swollen with melt-water from their upper reaches and although they had not burst their banks were running with smooth, deceptive power. It should be noted, however, that the book's present-day photographs of the rivers do not reflect either their 1945 strength or width.

The ground of the Weser-Aller Plain is typical of the subdued countryside of the North German Plain and is similar to the Thetford area of Norfolk, which has related geology and geomorphology. The surface relief varies from level to undulating, with the lowest points characterised by flat, peat moors, in 1945 poorly-drained, and extensive blocks of pine forest, while on the higher ground the countryside is gently-rolling and has a lighter, more open feel with mixed forests of pine and deciduous trees, particularly oak and sweet chestnut. The Weser-Aller Plain's highest points, only some 200 feet above sea-level, mark the positions of former moraines. Lying on either side of all three rivers are meadows with ox-bow lakes and twisting depressions, echoes of the rivers' former courses, and in the area of the account the right bank of the Aller is dominated by extensive pine forests. To the north-east of the Weser-Aller Plain, towards the Elbe, lies the Lüneburg Heath, a large expanse of moor and pine found on the poor soils of the *Geest*, the name given to this slightly hilly, sandy terrain.

Most of the towns (see Map 1) in the account are situated on the three rivers, where they developed at bridge or ferry sites, and villages and hamlets dotted the countryside. In 1945 there was an extensive railway network as the region had particularly benefited from the nineteenth century building programme of the Prussian State Railways, which favoured the relatively backward agricultural areas. Hannover, the region's major city, was an important railway junction and manufacturing centre and here Continental made tyres for military vehicles and aircraft, Maschinenfabrik Niedersachsen Hannover and Hanomag manufactured guns and tracked vehicles, and Accumulatoren Fabrik Aktiengesellschaft produced batteries for submarines and torpedoes. On the north-east outskirts of the city lay the refinery complex Deurag-Nerag, which produced aviation fuel and oils for the *Luftwaffe*. As a consequence of the railway and playing host to these industries, the city had been very heavily bombed and lay largely in ruins.

Agriculture has always been central to the economy of this predominantly rural area. Wheat, potatoes, sugar beet, rye, and oats as well as cattle, sheep, pigs and poultry have long been the agricultural mainstays and the extensive loess layers provide fertile soils for high-yield farming. However, from 1944 German agriculture suffered extreme productivity decreases. Yields drastically reduced, principally owing to the shortage of synthetic fertilisers as a consequence of the appropriation of nitrogen and phosphate stocks for ammunition production.[1] The loss of skilled agricultural manpower to the *Wehrmacht* and war industries exacerbated the situation and although forced labour helped paper over the cracks, it was insufficient to make up for the loss. Lack of farm machinery, spare parts and horses, most long-since gone to meet the army's demand and replaced for haulage by cattle, compounded the rapidly deteriorating state of affairs.

In 1945, farms and houses tended to be concentrated on the villages and hamlets and there were relatively few isolated buildings. As the last time the area had experienced significant destruction was during the Thirty Years' War of 1618–1648, when it was tramped over by both Swedish and Imperial armies, many fine historic buildings were still in evidence and in the country the farmhouses were typically *Fachhallenhaus*, the great timber-framed, brick buildings combining living quarters, byre and barn all under one roof. Many of these fine buildings, usually set among stands of tall, majestic oaks, still exist and are characterised by a large gateway at the gable end and a vast roof, in 1945 mostly still thatched with reed, sweeping down to just above head height. Over the

---

1   Zdenka Johnson, 'Financing the German Economy during the Second World War', *https://dspace5.zcu.cz/bitstream/11025/26236/1/Johnson.pdf*, p.124, (accessed 9 May 2019).

Fachhallenhaus. In 1945 the huge roof would probably have been thatched. (Author)

gateways are carved, painted panels giving the name of the builder and the year the house was built, and often on the gable ends are crossing wooden boards in the shape of stylised, horses' heads said to represent Hengist and Horsa. Besides agriculture, the area also produced some crude oil, discovered in the 1930s in an area to the east of Nienburg between the Weser and the Aller and providing a small but useful contribution to the *Reich's* besieged fuel situation. Nodding donkeys and wooden wellhead towers poking above the pine trees provided visible evidence of the production.

Spring had come early in 1945, a welcome relief as January and February had been the coldest of the century. While warmer, sunny days had begun to feature, the weather was still unsettled and in the earlier part of April there were days of rain, low cloud and mists. The countryside was, however, beginning to show recovery from the long winter, with fruit trees coming into blossom and forsythia bushes bursting out in bright yellow flower. John D'Arcy-Dawson, a war correspondent accompanying Second Army, describes the scenery:[2]

> The countryside was pleasantly green, the fields full of cattle and the corn well forward. Every farmhouse was in excellent condition, and the farm buildings would have delighted a British farmer. With plenty of slave labour it was no wonder the farms were so well tilled. In parts of the country the houses and outbuildings were similar to the black and white beamed houses of Cheshire except that the main barn and house formed one continuous building with an immense, steeply sloping roof. The soil appeared to be very light and would, I imagine, require careful handling if it were to give bountiful crops. In some places I saw enormous flocks of

---

2   John D'Arcy-Dawson, *European Victory* (London: Macdonald & Co, 1945), p.275.

Typical scene of a Weser-Aller Plain village: tall oaks and brick buildings with crossed horses' heads in Gross Eilstorf. Photograph taken in 2015. (Author)

Industrial building with camouflaged roof at Kampfstoffabrik Leese. Photograph taken in 2015. (Author)

Industrial structure with camouflaged roof at Walo I, Bomlitz. Photograph taken in 1982. (Author)

sheep, while every farm and house had dozens of chickens running about. Except for blown bridges and wrecked vehicles lying in hedges and ditches this part of Germany was untouched by war.

While to D'Arcy-Dawson the landscape may have appeared largely untouched, closer inspection would have revealed otherwise. Numerous slave labour camps dotted the area; guns and emplacements of *Flak* batteries were ugly blots in the fields; and wrecked trains and twisted tracks characterised the railway system. Hidden in the forests of the Weser-Aller Plain were an array of important war industries and materiel sites, particularly fuel and storage depots and factories producing chemicals, explosives and ammunition. Prior to the war the Germans had expended considerable effort dispersing industrial plants and storage facilities to the forests and over the war years these concealed industries had greatly expanded, forming a key part of Speer's vast organisation for the production of materiel. The sites were heavily camouflaged and, to blend in, many of the buildings and structures were given flat roofs on which a deep layer of soil was added to allow planting with grass, shrubs and trees.

Elsewhere were air bases, prisoner of war (PoW) camps, concentration and slave labour camps, army barracks and, carved out of the unproductive soils of the Lüneburg Heath, extensive training areas. Less apparent was the increased size of the rural population, expanded by the influx of refugees from the east and the bombed-out cities.

Despite the flatness of the terrain, this would not be easy country for British tanks as woods, large blocks of forest, boggy heathland, water courses and large drainage ditches were commonplace, restricting or channelling movement. Although many in Second Army pictured the armour being launched on a great sweep across the plain as if it were the steppes, the advance would as normal focus on roads and tracks with cross-country deployment only when in contact with the enemy or contact was expected. The roads, unsurprisingly, allowed the fastest movement and in any case were needed as main supply routes for the logistic tails. The main roads were good but the secondary roads usually had narrow, cobbled surfaces, sometimes with a wide sandy verge, which

Tanks of 5 RTR pause on a main road during the advance to the Weser (Huett).

soon broke up under heavy traffic; tertiary roads were made of gravel. Tracks were generally passable by all types of vehicle but in low ground were liable to collapse if used excessively. Where the roads crossed the rivers, bridges necessarily became key features for the Germans and British alike.

With the stage described, what was the sequence of events that brought Second Army to this area of Germany in 1945?

* * *

The spectacular advance by the Allies following the successful conclusion of the Normandy campaign had by early September 1944 carried them across France and Belgium. The German Army appeared incapable of stopping the flood of armour and men rolling on across the Rhine and taking Berlin and many on both sides thought the war would be over by December. Despite the appearance of imminent victory, the war was in fact far from won and the Allies would face many more months of bitter fighting. Logistically they were severely stressed, for every gallon of petrol, round of ammunition and tin of bully beef still had to be trucked from the Mulberry harbours in Normandy as the port facilities on the French and Belgian coasts were either demolished or still resolutely defended by the Germans. Although in early September Antwerp and its intact port had quickly fallen to the British, it would be many weeks before it could be reached by shipping. Senior Allied commanders are often blamed for committing a strategic error by failing to recognise the importance of the Scheldt estuary, in particular the island of Walcheren dominating the sea-lanes to Antwerp, and also failing to seal 15. Armee's escape route.[3] While this is true, it is also true that in early September, even if they had crossed the Scheldt at Antwerp, the British had neither the numeric nor logistic strength to advance much beyond the city and badly needed to draw breath following the headlong advance of the preceding weeks. There was therefore little likelihood that any advance made in September beyond the Scheldt would have made a material difference to the progress of the campaign.

The Allies' situation was exacerbated by the effort required to mount Operation MARKET GARDEN and the subsequent failure to seize the bridge at Arnhem; this lost them further momentum and it was not until early October that the importance of Antwerp was recognised and the First Canadian Army tasked to begin what became a long, bloody battle to clear 15. Armee from northern Belgium and the Scheldt estuary. Although this was achieved by early November, the requirement to de-mine the estuary and port area resulted in the first ship not reaching Antwerp until the end of that month. The situation for the Americans to the south was no better for they were suffering the same logistic problems and had become embroiled in slogging matches, particularly at Metz and in the forests on Germany's western border, and their advance too had slowed.

The restrictions placed on the Allies by logistics forced them to make headway only when sufficient materiel was available, resulting in the advance dwindling to a series of alternating jabs across the front. This was ideal for the Germans who were able to employ 'fire brigade' tactics with their meagre reserves, preventing the Allies from gaining anything more than limited, localised successes and causing a general loss of momentum. This provided vital time for the Germans to generate forces for the defence of the approaches to the *Reich*, and during the closing weeks of 1944 the German armies in the west under Generalfeldmarschall von Rundstedt were reinforced with newly-raised *Volksgrenadier* divisions allowing them to plug gaps – particularly in the fortifications of the *Westwall* – and force the Allies to fight a gruelling winter campaign as they closed up to the Rhine. Meanwhile, directly supervised by Hitler, far more ambitious preparations were in hand to

---

3   Milton Shulman, *Defeat in the West* (London: Secker & Warburg, 1947), pp.222–227.

mount a counterblow against the Allies using two newly reconstituted armies – 5. and 6. Panzer-Armeen – in an offensive to strike weak US forces in the Ardennes before swinging north-west towards Antwerp to cut off 21st Army Group.

On 16 December the German offensive, code-named *WACHT AM RHEIN* (WATCH ON THE RHINE),[4] was launched. Despite achieving surprise, the offensive lasted only two weeks, by which time the Allies had recovered from the shock and mounted counter-moves. By 16 January the so-called Battle of the Bulge was over and the Germans were back in their original positions having lost some 130,000 men, of whom 19,000 were killed, and 600 armoured vehicles.[5] With the German offensive spent the Allies could look once again to crossing the Rhine, but for this to be successful the remaining German armies west of the river had to be defeated. In early February 1945 Montgomery launched his series of offensives into the Rhineland – Operations VERITABLE, BLOCKBUSTER and GRENADE – and for the next five weeks battles raged of an intensity unknown since the *bocage* battles in Normandy, only this time the fighting took place during the most unpleasant winter for years and produced conditions familiar to the soldiers of both sides who had fought in the First World War. Although the Germans could not hold back 21st Army Group, they fought courageously in defence of their homeland and the battles between the Maas and the Rhine delayed Montgomery a further month and cost him some 15,500 casualties;[6] losses with consequences for this story. However, despite the delay and manpower costs, the offensives essentially destroyed the last German army in the west – 1. Fallschirm-Armee (1st Parachute Army) – and in defeating it in front of the Rhine had eliminated the forces able to pose a far greater threat had they been withdrawn to the right bank and used to counter-attack Allied crossings. Although the German defeat in the Rhineland was inevitable, its totality was largely due to Hitler's refusal to allow any withdrawal.

Allied planning now turned to crossing the great river. Eisenhower's intention was to cross in two areas: 21st Army Group in the north between Emmerich and Wesel, and US 12th Army Group in the south between Mainz and Karlsruhe. The contrast in the character of the two operations could not have been more different. While the Americans looked to bouncing a crossing over the Rhine, Montgomery planned a complex assault only rivalled in scale by the Normandy landings. In broad outline his plan involved the First Canadian Army providing security on the left flank while Second Army crossed between Rees and Wesel and US Ninth Army, under British command, crossed in the Rheinberg area. For Operation PLUNDER, the crossing of the Rhine, and the subsequent advance Montgomery fielded 27 divisions: seventeen infantry, eight armoured and two airborne, reinforced by five independent armoured brigades, a British commando brigade and an independent Canadian infantry brigade, supported by very substantial artillery and aircraft of Second Tactical Air Force and Bomber Command. The operation would start with massive bombing and artillery programmes, followed by crossings at night and supplemented the next day by the two airborne divisions landing in depth. Once the German defences were overcome, Montgomery promised his forces would '…crack about in the plains of northern Germany, chasing the enemy from pillar to post.'[7] His plan for these subsequent operations involved First Canadian Army driving north to cut off German forces in the Netherlands, Second Army striking out across the North German Plain towards Berlin, while Ninth Army headed in a south-easterly direction as the northern hook of the manoeuvre to envelop the Ruhr. On 7 March, however, troops of the US 27th Armored Infantry Battalion captured intact the railway bridge over the Rhine at Remagen and at once the balance of

---

4 Although this is the name by which the offensive is commonly known, its correct code-name was *HERBSTNEBEL* (Autumn Mist).
5 Matthew Cooper, *The German Army 1933–1945* (London: Macdonald & Jane's, 1978), p.525.
6 David Fraser, *And We Shall Shock Them* (London: Hodder and Stoughton, 1983), p.390.
7 TNA WO 171/3949, 2nd Army, Montgomery's Order of the Day for 23 March 1945.

Allied planning swung to the south as Eisenhower looked to exploit this unexpected good fortune.[8] Bradley's 12th Army Group and the southern thrust to envelop the Ruhr now took on a greater degree of importance than activity in the north, where 21st Army Group was still only in the planning stage of its crossing operation. Although the initiative had swung to Bradley, Montgomery would soon directly benefit as the Germans hurriedly switched most of their reserves to south of the Ruhr in order to seal the anticipated American exploitation from Remagen.

* * *

On 11 March 1945, four days after the debacle at Remagen, Oberbefehlshaber (OB) (Commander-in-Chief (C-in-C)) West, the German headquarters responsible for the West Front, underwent a change of command when Generalfeldmarschall von Runstedt was sacked for the third and final time by Hitler and replaced by Generalfeldmarschall Albert Kesselring, formerly the commander of Heeresgruppe 'C' in Italy. Kesselring was expected to repeat the successful delay battles he had fought in Italy at such heavy cost to the Allies in time, men and materiel, but the conditions existing on the West Front bore scant resemblance to Italy and neither Hitler nor the Allies would allow him to fight on his own terms. In his memoirs Kesselring described his situation as feeling '…like a concert pianist who is asked to play a Beethoven sonata before a large audience on an ancient, rickety and out-of-tune instrument.'[9] To achieve his mission he had a nominal 55 divisions, but with a real strength of less than half that number.[10] By this stage of the war most of the German Army's formations were shattered remnants and the use of impressive titles such as *Armee* and *Korps* had little bearing on the size and quality of formations generally comprising handfuls of troops with little or no experience, very few heavy weapons and virtually no armour. Indeed, the continued use of these titles added to the delusion that the army was similar to the formidable fighting organisation of former years. The infantry divisions were severely understrength and made up of sweepings from broken formations joined by raw recruits combed from industry and every imaginable branch of the *Wehrmacht*, while armoured formations had fighting strengths of tanks and assault guns numbered in tens. The parachute formations held their titles in name only and were based on a few veterans bumped up with the remains of *Luftwaffe* field divisions, redundant air and ground crews and any other members of the *Luftwaffe* without a proper role, and bore no resemblance to the highly-trained, elite units that had fought in Crete and at Cassino. Kesselring's problems were compounded by chronic fuel shortages preventing or severely constraining deployments, an air force that had lost control of the *Reich's* airspace allowing Allied bombers and fighters to roam at will, and Hitler's interference in the lowliest of tactical decisions. Richard Bessel provides a succinct description of the state of the German army in early 1945:[11]

> With reports of military catastrophe cascading in after the collapse of the Ardennes offensive and the Soviet breakthrough on the eastern front, the *Wehrmacht* was thrown back on hasty, desperate improvisation. This resulted in some temporary tactical successes as German units sometimes managed to stall the progress of the Allies and, on occasion, even score minor

---

8 The capture of the bridge was of greater propaganda than operational importance as the main crossings were still required elsewhere.
9 Albert Kesselring, *The Memoirs of Field Marshal Kesselring* (London: Greenhill Books, 1988), p.259.
10 Kesselring, *Memoirs*, p.239.
11 Richard Bessel, *Germany 1945 – From War to Peace* (London: Simon & Schuster Ltd, 2009), pp.20–21. Text copyright © Richard Bessel 2009, reproduced by kind permission of Simon & Schuster UK. Ltd. Although when referring to the German army (*Heer*) Bessel's use of '*Wehrmacht*' is incorrect, common usage tends to make them synonymous.

victories, while Allied forces regrouped and amassed supplies for their next offensive. The available documentation of *Wehrmacht* operations in early 1945 reveals the huge increase in losses in soldiers and equipment. The military value of many units, filled with very young or very old recruits lacking combat experience and without internal cohesion, was limited, and consequently they served as little more than cannon fodder. It was obvious therefore that fighting could continue for only a few weeks or, at most a few months, before the inevitable collapse. Consideration was not given to the longer-term viability of the *Wehrmacht* or to the maintenance of a war-fighting capability even for the medium term. Military strategy in the conventional sense had gone completely out of the window. The essence of Nazism had overwhelmed the ethos of the German military. The *Wehrmacht* no longer existed to win military victories but instead to sacrifice its soldiers in an apocalyptic final struggle.

Pointless though this 'strategy of self-annihilation' may have been, it did not mean that the *Wehrmacht* was unable to cause enormous bloodshed; they still proved very effective in defensive tactics. German soldiers remained capable of inflicting serious losses on their opponents and were, despite everything, generally more effective in combat man-for-man than British or American ground troops and, by a greater margin, than their Soviet opponents. Although outnumbered and outgunned, German soldiers were able to inflict more casualties per man on their enemies than Allied soldiers were able to inflict on the Germans…But the fact that the *Wehrmacht* was so completely outnumbered, outgunned and outsupplied, and unable to move effectively, coupled with the determination of its leadership to throw as many men as possible into combat, ensured that there would be astronomical numbers of casualties on all sides until the Germans finally surrendered.

By 1945 the German strategic and operational direction of the war was utterly dysfunctional. This was a culmination of confused division of responsibilities between Oberkommando der Wehrmacht (OKW) (HQ Armed Forces) and Oberkommando des Heeres (OKH) (HQ Army), which was exacerbated by Hitler's direct command of the army and compounded by the unwillingness of Generalfeldmarschal Keitel, Chef des Oberkommando der Wehrmacht (Chief OKW), and Generaloberst Jodl, Chef der Wehrmachtführungsstab (Chief OKW Operations), to challenge any of Hitler's decisions, however insane. Although for some years Hitler had played an increasingly interfering role, with his order of 21 January 1945 – known as the 'Shackling Order' – the Army field commanders finally lost the last vestige of their capacity for independent action, and this extract from an extraordinary document represents the ultimate triumph of the Corporal over the Generals:[12]

I order as follows:

1. Commanders-in-chief, commanding generals and divisional commanders are personally responsible to me for reporting in good time:
(a) Every decision to carry out an operational movement.
(b) Every attack planned in divisional strength and upwards which does not conform with the general directives laid down by the High Command.
(c) Every offensive action in quiet sectors of the front, over and above normal shock-troop activity, which is calculated to draw the enemy's attention to the sector.
(d) Every plan for disengaging or withdrawing forces.
(e) Every plan for surrendering a position, a local strongpoint or fortress.

---

12 Cooper, *The German Army 1933–1945*, p.542.

2. They must ensure that I have time to intervene in this decision if I think fit, and that my counter-orders can reach the front line in time…

General Warlimont, Jodl's deputy, pithily describes the chaotic final weeks:[13]

> So, in this final phase of the war, OKW and its strategy was torn in all directions – between east and west – between attempts at ambitious operations for which neither the forces nor resources were available, and the pitiless march of events which continuously overtook their planning; between the grizzly heroism of a determination not to recognise the approach of catastrophe, and day-to-day activity in a dream world of armies, divisions, and regiments capable of fighting. The determination of one man possessed of the devil governed everything; the machinery of command churned out orders in normal form though there might be no one to receive them…Hitler's leadership was therefore now without object or objective, but the last crazy orders continued to issue forth stamped with his own faults and his own phraseology.

Of course, unknown to Warlimont, through the Ultra decrypts the Allies were fully aware of the chaos and desperation of the collapsing *Reich* and during April 1945 that desperation is tangible, with the high commands sprinkling their signals with phrases such as 'with utmost urgency', 'immediate energetic action', 'act at once', as if the forceful and emphatic phrases could by themselves stem the flood. As an aside, while Ultra provided the Allies with unprecedented insights into their enemy, the very effective German signals intelligence service provided excellent information to the last on Allied orbats, dispositions and intentions. The *Wehrmacht's* deterioration resulted, however, in the Germans being unable to exploit the intelligence, leaving it generally accurate but of little or no use.

While Hitler and his immediate entourage still deluded themselves that the *Wehrmacht* could hold back the Allies, few in OKW and OKH, and even fewer at the fronts, would have suffered similar delusions and it can therefore be assumed that most orders for offensive action were largely issued to appease Hitler, sparing the originators his wrath and the possibility of summary justice. Amazingly, despite the fraught situation, there was no general collapse of the will to resist, and through the continuance of the *Führer* system Hitler maintained his grip on the civilian population and armed forces, with summary execution employed as the principal way to instil steadiness. An order issued on 5 March 1945 by Generaloberst Johannes Blaskowitz, commander of Heeresgruppe 'H', typifies the savagery of the edicts served on the German soldiery, who had already born an immense burden of death and misery for their *Führer*:[14]

> As from midday 10 March, all soldiers in all branches of the *Wehrmacht* who may be encountered away from their units on roads or in villages, in supply columns or among groups of civilian refugees, or in dressing stations when not wounded, and who announce that they are stragglers looking for their units, will be summarily tried and shot…
> Signed: Blaskowitz. Obst.Gen.

As the enormity of the impending defeat sank in, death penalty warnings such as this became increasingly shrill and frequent, and represented a convenient way for the elite to broadcast its loyalty to the *Führer*. The warnings were no vague threats and in the final months thousands of

---

13 Cooper, *The German Army 1933–1945*, p.543.
14 Shulman, *Defeat in the West*, p.309.

German soldiers were 'tried' and summarily executed. However, in contrast to the savagery meted out to lower ranks for failure or perceived back-sliding, most senior commanders not displaying blind obedience to Hitler's orders, however absurd, were usually spared the attentions of the flying courts martial and were instead dismissed to the reserve list.

* * *

In mid-March 1945 the German forces of OB West in the Netherlands and facing the Allies from the right bank of the Rhine in northern Germany belonged to Heeresgruppe 'H'. The *Heeresgruppe* had its origins in Armeegruppe Student formed in late October 1944 but redesignated as Heeresgruppe 'H' in November. Generaloberst der Luftwaffe Kurt Student commanded the *Heeresgruppe* up to 31 January 1945 when he handed over to Generaloberst Blaskowitz, only recently sacked by Hitler from command of Heeresgruppe 'G' following the failure of Operation *NORDWIND* in the Vosges and Alsace. Student was placed in the Führer-Reserve OKH, the reserve pool of general officers, but not for long as will be seen. In late March 1945 Heeresgruppe 'H' comprised General der Infanterie Günther Blumentritt's 25. Armee in the Netherlands and in northern Germany General der Fallschirmtruppe Alfred Schlemm's 1. Fallschirm-Armee. As mentioned, Schlemm's army had suffered severely during the battle for the Rhineland and despite the resolve of its soldiers to defend the Fatherland, with them facing the greater part of 21st Army Group's strength the likelihood of their repelling the impending crossing of the Rhine was distinctly bleak. 1. Fallschirm-Armee's three corps were deployed on the Rhine's right bank from north to south as follows: on the right flank and facing British XII and XXX Corps was General der Fallschirmtruppe Meindl's II. Fallschirm-Korps comprising the three Fallschirmjäger-Divisionen 6, 7 and 8; in the centre facing US XVI Corps was General der Infanterie Straube's LXXXVI. Armee-Korps, consisting of 84. and 180. Infanterie-Divisionen and the various units of Kampfkommandant Wesel; while on the left flank facing US XIII Corps was General der Infanterie Abraham's LXIII. Armee-Korps with two divisions, 324. Infanterie-Division (aka Infanterie-Division 'Hamburg') and 2. Fallschirmjäger. Schlemm's infantry reserve was provided by 190. Infanterie-Division, an exhausted and weak formation, while his very small armoured reserve was provided by General der Panzertruppe Lüttwitz's XLVII. Panzer-Korps, comprising 116. Panzer-Division and 15. Panzergrenadier-Division, held on Schlemm's right flank 15 miles north-east of Emmerich. These two armoured divisions mustered 35 tanks.

Following the demolition it had suffered in the Rhineland, 1. Fallschirm-Armee was in a parlous condition and certainly in no shape to fight and win a major battle. Meindl's II. Fallschirm-Korps was the only formation capable of offering some resistance and it had received reinforcement following its withdrawal across the Rhine, although the reinforcements it received were in the main young, wholly inexperienced and with very few weapons; virtually no replacements had been found to make good the losses in armour and artillery. More significantly Meindl had no reserve to counter airborne landings. All of Straube's and Abraham's divisions were severely understrength and in their ranks were the untrained, the exhausted and the less than willing. On 21 March the Germans suffered a severe setback when the redoubtable Schlemm was seriously concussed during a fighter-bomber attack on his headquarters near Wesel, preventing him from playing a leading role in the battle soon to follow.

* * *

At 1530 hours on 23 March, Montgomery gave the order to mount Operation PLUNDER. At 2100 hours the same day, soldiers of 51st Highland Division and 9th Canadian Infantry Brigade made the first assault crossing of the river, landing in their Buffalo amphibious vehicles south of Rees where they met heavy resistance from 6. and 7. Fallschirmjäger-Divisionen. One hour later the commandos of 1st Commando Brigade crossed in Buffaloes and assault boats to land downstream from the Highlanders. Their objective was Wesel but the commandos stopped short of the town while 200 Lancaster bombers reduced it to rubble; they then moved in to mop up what was left of the defence. Further south, crossings by the 15th Scottish Division and the US 30th and 79th Infantry Divisions from US XVI Corps were achieved against minimal opposition and the subsequent advance by the Americans caused particular problems for the Germans as it struck the boundary between LXXXVI. and LXIII. Armee-Korps. In an attempt to repel the initial lodgements before the main assault began, Blaskowitz ordered Lüttwitz to release 15. Panzergrenadier-Division for a counter-attack in the Rees area conveniently conforming to Montgomery's design for battle, which aimed to keep German forces away from the southern area of the bridgehead.

The next day Operation VARSITY, the airborne landings by the British 6th and US 17th Airborne divisions, followed the river crossing. Despite some heavy losses from *Flak* during the fly-in, the landings were a success and largely eliminated the artillery and service support elements of 84. Infanterie-Division. The day ended with 1. Fallschirm-Armee facing disaster at Rees, Wesel and on its left flank where US XVI Corps was close to achieving a breakthrough south of the river Lippe; all that was available to counter these threats was 116. Panzer-Division. II. Fallschirm-Korps was in a particularly exposed situation as the collapse and near total loss of 84. Infanterie-Division from the neighbouring LXXXVI. Armee-Korps had uncovered its left flank, and the failure of 15. Panzergrenadier-Division to eliminate the bridgehead south of Rees forced Meindl to pull back his forces still remaining on the Rhine. Despite the dire situation, the Germans offered staunch resistance wherever possible.

Blaskowitz now ordered Lüttwitz to despatch 116. Panzer-Division to counter US XVI Corps, believing this to be the greatest threat. As it would take time to obtain the required fuel and with daylight movement suicidal, the earliest the division could move was the night 25/26 March. Although 116. Panzer-Division eventually managed to reach the left flank it had insufficient strength to counter-attack and could only block the Americans. This, however, it did with some success as the difficulties the British were experiencing further north against II. Fallschirm-Korps and 15. Panzergrenadier-Division resulted in a lack of real estate for the Americans to generate Ninth Army's massive superiority in men and armour, allowing the Germans to hold the attackers to limited gains. While for the next two days the Germans fought bitterly throughout the bridgehead, the weight of numbers began to tell and the first major crack in the defence came on 28 March when paratroopers of US 17th Airborne Division, clinging to the decks of Churchill tanks of 6th Guards Armoured Brigade, broke through north of the river Lippe and raced on 17 miles to outflank 116. Panzer-Division. At about the same time the Allies completed their first bridges across the Rhine and 1. Fallschirm-Armee was unable to counter the unleashed flood of men and armour. On the right flank II. Fallschirm-Korps fell back to the north-east, LXIII. Armee-Korps had largely ceased to exist on the left flank, while in the centre LXXXVI. Armee-Korps had received a severe mauling and was forced to retreat in a north-easterly direction, opening a rift in the front rapidly exploited by XVI Corps. The ensuing American advance drove the remnants of XLVII. Panzer-Korps and LXIII. Armee-Korps south into the Ruhr to join Model's Heeresgruppe 'B', creating a gap between the two *Heeresgruppen* that was never to close.

On 28 March Hitler made two major changes in command. As it was clear that Schlemm would not make a swift recovery from his concussion, command of 1. Fallschirm-Armee was transferred to Blumentritt, who was in turn replaced as commander of 25. Armee by General Kleffel. Despite the merry-go-round of generals, the state of the German forces was now beyond repair and all commanders struggled to cope with the deluge of problems, threats and challenges. Blumentritt's views on his new command were pragmatic, if far from sanguine:[15]

---

15 Shulman, *Defeat in the West*, p.311.

I reported to Generaloberst Blaskowitz at Heeresgruppe 'H' and he and his chief-of-staff both agreed that as the Rhine was crossed the situation, with the forces at our disposal, was past repair. But since orders from above were to continue resisting I was to do the best that I could. When I took over my new command on 28 March I found that there were great gaps in the front, that I had no reserves, that my artillery was weak, that I had no air support whatever and hardly any tanks. My communication and signal facilities were entirely inadequate and there was one corps under my command that I was never able to contact. The reinforcements that still came to me were hastily trained and badly equipped, and I never used them so that I could save needless casualties.

Nevertheless, orders from OKW were still couched in the most rigorous terms, enjoining us to 'hold' and 'fight' under threats of court-martial. But I no longer insisted on these orders being carried out. It was a nerve-racking time we experienced – outwardly putting on a bold face on the matter in order to do one's duty as one had sworn to do – while we secretly allowed things to go their own way. On my own responsibility I gave orders for lines to be prepared in the rear ready for a retreat. By 1 April I had decided to direct the fighting in such a way that the army could be withdrawn in a more or less orderly manner and without suffering any great casualties, first on both sides of Münster and then behind the Ems Canal and finally to the Teutoburger Wald.

The last days of March also marked major changes for the British, although for them it affected operations rather than command. By the end of the month's fourth week, the bridgehead had expanded to a width of 40 miles and a depth of 25 miles and within this perimeter Montgomery had concentrated 20 divisions and 1,500 tanks. With the Rhine crossed and the bridgehead established, on 27 March Montgomery issued orders to his army commanders to mount a combined advance to the Elbe, with Second Army directed on the Kiel-Hamburg area and US Ninth Army's right directed on Magdeburg;[16] triumphal final victory seemed within his grasp. But on 29 March, with the great advance underway, Eisenhower announced a revised Supreme Headquarters Allied Expeditionary Force (SHAEF) strategy, taking not only Montgomery but also Churchill completely by surprise.[17] Eisenhower's aim for his strategy was to join up with the Russian armies as soon as possible and so divide Germany and destroy the remaining enemy forces. The most direct axis of advance to achieve this was towards Kassel-Leipzig. Once the operation to encircle Model's Heeresgruppe 'B' in the Ruhr was concluded, Eisenhower required General Simpson's Ninth Army to revert to 12th Army Group when it reached the Paderborn area. 12th Army Group rather than 21st Army Group would then make the main Allied drive eastwards, but not with Berlin as its objective but rather the industrial and political complex of the Leipzig area; Berlin would be left to the Soviet armies. The reasons behind Eisenhower's decision were varied: first, he wanted to mop up Heeresgruppe 'B' to remove a threat to the centre of Allied operations; secondly, with Russian armies already on the Oder and only 40 miles from Berlin he saw no political advantage in a race for Berlin as Germany had already been divided into occupation zones at the Yalta Conference, with any ground the western Allies gained in the future Soviet zone having to be relinquished after the war; thirdly, he was influenced by the supposed threat of German forces massed in the so-called National Redoubt in the Alps and he did not wish to become embroiled in the fight for the ruined capital city when a greater danger could exist to his south. Lastly, and left unstated in the various formal communications of the time, American patience with Montgomery was now in extremely short supply and there was no enthusiasm whatsoever for allowing the junior

---

16   TNA WO 205/688, The Advance Through North Germany, 21 A Gp/20748/8 G (Plans), 13 March 1945.
17   Fraser, *And We Shall Shock Them*, pp.393–394.

partner in the alliance to seize any glory.[18] Eisenhower's decision not to advance on Berlin was militarily correct and undoubtedly spared the lives of thousands of Allied servicemen.

SHAEF issued Montgomery with a new directive on 2 April designed to meet Eisenhower's revised operational objectives.[19] The directive ordered Montgomery to continue the advance without pause to the Leine and Bremen, thereafter launching a thrust to the Elbe in conjunction with the Central Group of Armies and protecting their northern flank; for 21st Army Group this actually represented little change from Montgomery's orders of 27 March. He was also to seize any opportunity to capture a bridgehead over the Elbe and be prepared for operations beyond the river. Soon after the directive's issue, Montgomery was instructed to conduct his advance as fast as possible, not only to prevent the Germans regaining any balance but also to reach Schleswig-Holstein ahead of the Soviets and check them from any move they may make to invest Denmark. Swallowing his bitter disappointment at his relegation to a supposed secondary role, on 2 April Montgomery issued his own directive reflecting the change in operational priorities and anticipating that '…there are no fresh and complete divisions in the German rear and all the enemy will be able to do is block roads and approaches with personnel from schools, bath units, pigeon lofts and so on.'[20] A prediction that would soon prove mistaken.

* * *

By the end of March the battle for the Rhine bridgehead was over and Blaskowitz's forces in north-west Germany reduced to a desperate state. On his right flank 1. Fallschirm-Armee, now commanded by Blumentritt, was receiving a severe mauling as it withdrew. In the centre LXXXVI. Armee-Korps was being pushed back towards Münster and the only reason it did not disintegrate entirely was the fortuitous presence of some tanks from 15. Panzergrenadier-Division, which, although now reduced to little more than a *Kampfgruppe*, had joined LXXXVI. Armee-Korps when the remainder of its parent corps, XLVII. Panzer-Korps, withdrew southwards into the Ruhr. Blaskowitz's left flank was in thin air.

While during the last days of March 1. Fallschirm-Armee and LXXXVI. Armee-Korps fell back, the two regiments of Division Nr.490 from Schleswig-Holstein, the three regiments of 325. Infanterie-Division from Jutland and the two regiments of Division Nr.471 from Hannover were being rushed forward in a desperate attempt to bolster the front. Although all three divisions comprised personnel from all parts of the *Wehrmacht* and still undergoing training, some of their units were soon to put up surprisingly strong resistance. Heeresgruppe 'H' also received useful reinforcement in the form of 25 tanks of Panzer-Ausbildungs-Verband 'Grossdeutschland'. On 31 March Division Nr.471, originally destined for the *Heeresgruppe's* right flank, was diverted to defend the area between the Ems and the Teutoburger Wald, one of a number of heavily-wooded blocks of higher ground in this area of Germany, which rise sharply above the plain. The division's main effort was to defend the approaches to Ibbenbüren.

With increasing impatience, OKW and then Hitler repeatedly ordered Heeresgruppe 'H' to mount a counter-attack southwards from Rheine towards Haltern (see Map 2), but Blaskowitz replied that it was impossible as he had insufficient fuel, ammunition, armour or manpower to undertake it. This pessimistic but entirely accurate response resulted in OKW losing confidence in Blaskowitz and on 31 March Hitler ordered Student's mobilisation from the Führer-Reserve

---

18   Dwight D Eisenhower, *Crusade in Europe* (London: William Heinemann, 1948), pp.433–436.
19   LF Ellis, *Victory in the West, Volume II, The Defeat of Germany*, (Uckfield: The Naval and Military Press, 2004), p.301.
20   TNA WO 205/855, 21st Army Group Directive M563, 28 March 1945.

OKH and his immediate dispatch to Heeresgruppe 'H' to mount the counter-attack,[21] a calculated rebuke for an officer of Blaskowitz's standing. Blaskowitz was told that Student had complete freedom to plan and execute the attack and that he could have any forces he required, regardless of the general situation. The same day, Jodl, quoting the Hitler order, gave Student command of General Schwalbe's LXXXVIII. Armee-Korps, fighting the Canadians in the Netherlands east of the river Ijssel, and II. Fallschirm-Korps,[22] with an improvised headquarters for Student provided by staff extracted from OB West and Heeresgruppe 'H'. The capacity for these forces to participate in the counter-attack was of course totally unrealistic and, within hours of his arrival and following briefings from the staff, Student's initial optimism had completely evaporated. However, to avoid committing the same mistake as Blaskowitz, he sensibly did not tell OKW that the attack was impossible and he seems to have decided to 'play it long'. In his signal sent the evening of 1 April,[23] Student therefore optimistically identified the formations and units that would conduct the counter-attack but warned that the attack would not be possible on 2 April as the available fuel and ammunition were insufficient. At 1600 hours on 2 April he signalled again,[24] this time describing the British advances, the objectives of his counter-attack and even giving an H-hour: 1900 hours on 4 April. However, he once more warned of the precondition that the required fuel, ammunition and forces needed to be brought up by the morning of the 4th and added that the attack towards Haltern would not be possible until Allied forces in the Oldenzaal area had been destroyed (presumably because of the threat they posed to an attack's right flank). Faced with these realities, Hitler instead ordered Student to mount local attacks with his allocated forces, on 4 April grandly titled Armeeabteilung Student.[25] The first of these attacks, mounted against British forces to the west of Lingen, ended in failure, and there were no repetitions. Map 2, a rough sketch drawn by Oberst Geyer, 1a of Heeresgruppe 'H', shows the *Heeresgruppe's* situation on 2 April.[26]

The map formed part of the report he wrote in captivity immediately after the war and shows clearly how the British advance after the breakout from the Rhine bridgehead forced the *Heeresgruppe* northwards to a west-east line. Also of note is the absence of depth formations, particularly on the Weser, the uncertainty regarding XI. Armee-Korps and the yawning gap between Heeresgruppe 'H' and Heeresgruppe 'B' in the Ruhr pocket.

* * *

On 28 March, three days prior to those events and on the other side of the hill, Second Army started its break-out from the Rhine bridgehead, shown on Map 3, and began its long eastward advance: XXX Corps on the left with Bremen as its objective, XII Corps in the centre directed on Hamburg and VIII Corps on the right ordered to seize crossings over the Elbe.

VIII Corps was a late arrival in the advance's plan.[27] Prior to the 29 March SHAEF directive, the corps headquarters had been due to take over British forces in the Rhine bridgehead from HQ US XVIII Airborne Corps, so releasing the US headquarters and US 17th Airborne Division to

---

21 Foreign Military Studies (FMS), Historical Division, US Army Europe, B-354, 1. Fallschirm-Armee (28 March–9 April), p.17.
22 TNA DEFE 3/561, BT 9111, Ultra decrypt of Jodl signal 31 March 1945.
23 TNA DEFE 3/561, BT 9189, Student intentions for Haltern attack.
24 TNA DEFE 3/562, BT 9279, Student signal, 1600 hours 2 April 1945.
25 TNA DEFE 3/563, BT 9714, Ultra decrypt 1348 hours 7 April 1945. The title does not seem to have stuck and changed to Armeegruppe Student almost immediately. Student commanded three *Armeegruppen* bearing his name: the first from 30 October–10 November 1944; the second from 31 March–6 April 1945; and the third from 6–10 April 1945.
26 FMS B-414, Heeresgruppe 'H' (10 March–9 May 1945), Skizze 4.
27 TNA WO 171/4031, GS Branch VIII Corps war diary.

FROM PILLAR TO POST 41

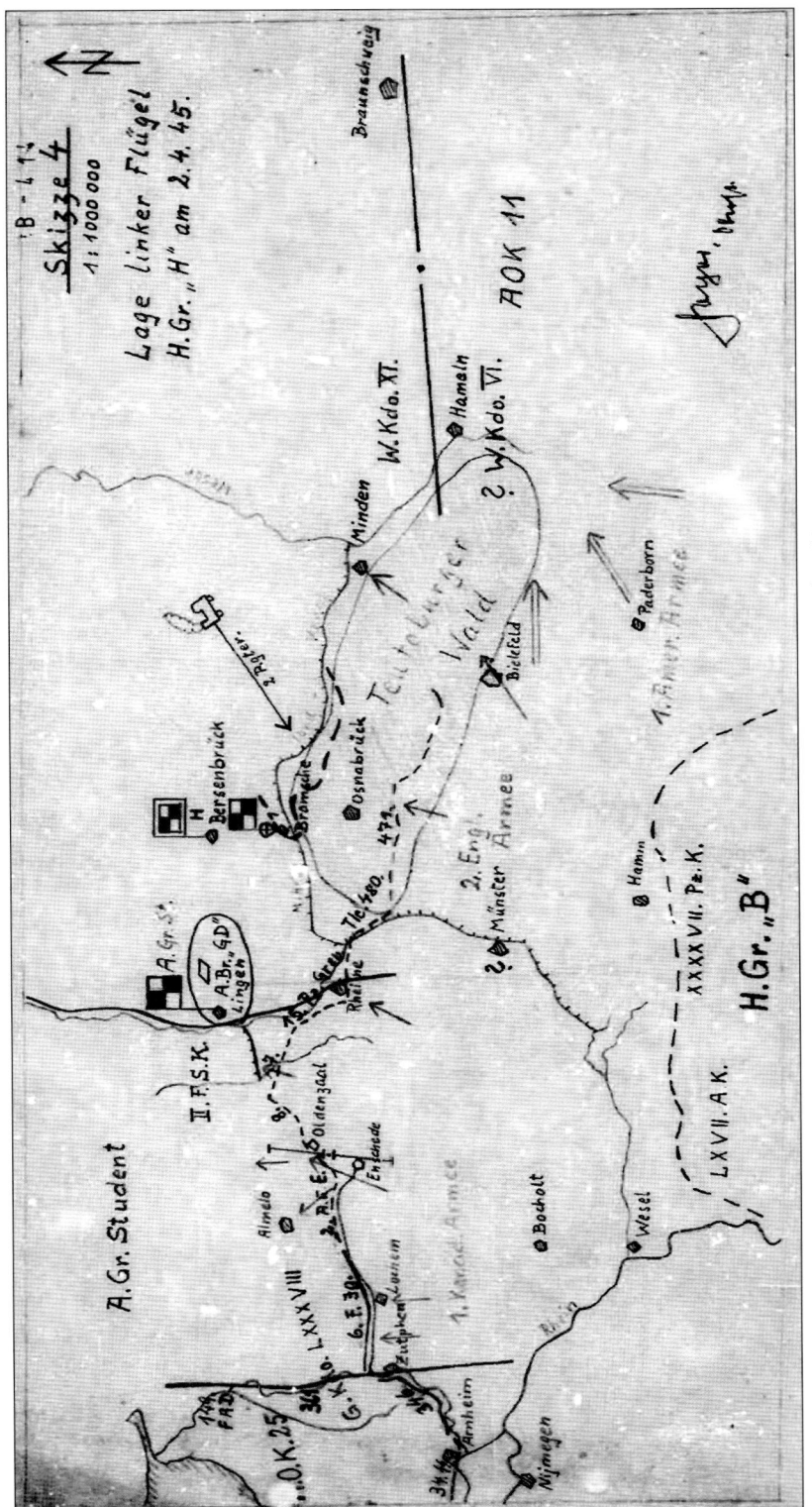

Map 2 Heeresgruppe 'H' situation – 2 April 1945.

42 THEIRS THE STRIFE

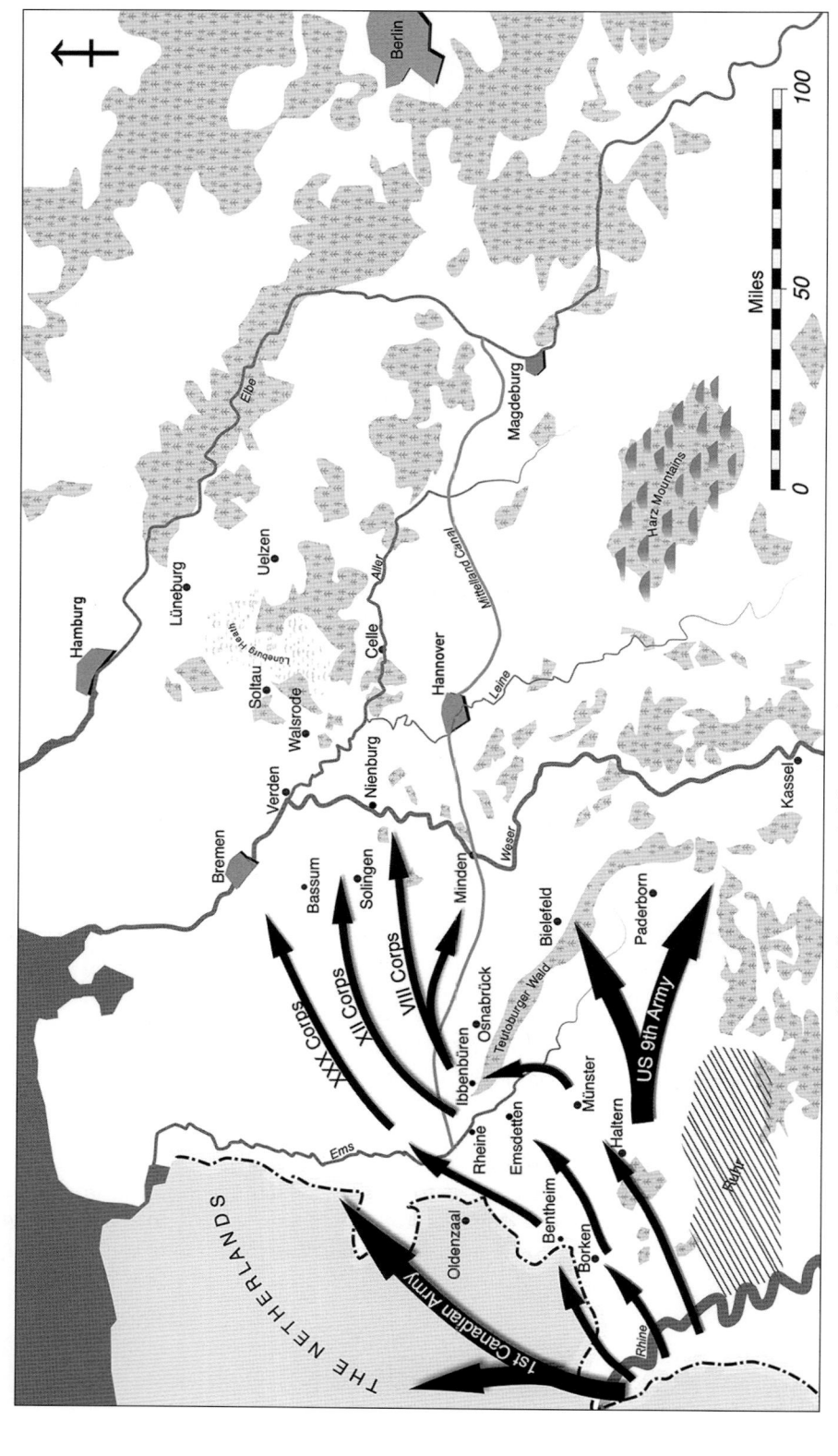

Map 3 Second Army's Advance to the Weser – 23 March–5 April 1945.

take part in the advance. VIII Corps would then handover its sector to US Ninth Army and go into reserve, a role that had not gone down well as it had played only supporting parts since the Normandy campaign and its commanders were eager to be in at the end. On 27 March this plan had begun, with VIII Corps receiving the order to take over British troops in the bridgehead from the airborne corps. But with Eisenhower's revised strategy of 29 March, Second Army not only lost US XVIII Airborne Corps but also now needed a British formation for the right flank of the army's advance, so VIII Corps, the only choice, was promptly warned for operations and allocated 6th Airborne Division, 1st Commando Brigade and the three Churchill tank battalions of 6th Guards Armoured Brigade, all of which were immediately available in the Rhine bridgehead. However, as this orbat was insufficient and lacked armour, Second Army reinforced the corps with 11th Armoured Division, the army's armoured reserve currently moving up from Belgium with its new Comet tanks, and 15th Scottish Division, which would join on 3 April. VIII Corps began its advance on 30 March and by exploiting the vacuum left by the collapsing LXXXVI. Armee-Korps made rapid progress towards Osnabrück. The next day it reached Emsdetten, 50 miles east of the Rhine, and won bridgeheads over both the Dortmund-Ems Canal and the river Ems.

In Second Army's centre XII Corps, consisting of 7th Armoured Division and two infantry divisions, 52nd Lowland and 53rd Welsh, initially faced stiff opposition from 15. Panzergrenadier-Division and its few remaining tanks. 7th Armoured and 52nd Lowland then led the breakout from the bridgehead and although their advance was initially slowed by German parachute units in Borken and Stadtlohn and routes obstructed by damage caused by bombing in the bridgehead area, the two divisions began to make progress and by the start of April had reached the Ems. The corps was then confronted not only by this obstacle but also by the town of Rheine lying at the centre of a ring of well-defended airfields and, not far to the east, the Dortmund-Ems Canal.

While XII Corps began to clear the Rheine area, 11th Armoured Division from VIII Corps crossed the Dortmund-Ems Canal, moved into the sector allocated for the future use of XII Corps and then became involved in very fierce fighting against Division Nr.471 in the area of Ibbenbüren, which dominated the main road where it crossed the low, forested hills of the Teutoburger Wald. Here the ground was particularly advantageous to the defence: the approaches to Ibbenbüren lay in narrow gorges, a small river flowed along the town's southern edge, and woods and broken terrain reduced the British advantage in artillery and air support. Division Nr.471's principal combat power was provided by two *Kampfgruppen*, both led by holders of the Knight's Cross: Oberstleutnant Knaust (complete with prosthetic right leg) commanded a *Kampfgruppe* of infantry and artillery replacements, while Oberstleutnant Lier led the non-commissioned officer (NCO) candidates from Heeres-Unteroffiziers-Schule 11 Hannover. Also present were NCO trainees from the Heeres-Unteroffiziers-Schule für Nebeltruppen Celle commanded by Oberst Hahnke.[28] The concentration of NCOs at Ibbenbüren ensured that the battle would be fierce as the German army believed that thoroughly trained and qualified NCOs were key to the army's effectiveness and even at this very late stage of the war placed emphasis on their development; by definition, these were therefore higher quality men and well-motivated.

Owing to the lack of bridges over the Dortmund-Ems Canal in the Rheine area, XII Corps was unable to advance further so it was decided that 52nd Lowland would take on the clearance of Rheine, freeing the tanks of 7th Armoured to cross the canal via the same bridges as 11th Armoured and then relieve VIII Corps from the Ibbenbüren battle; 11th Armoured could then press on eastwards. Once Ibbenbüren was clear, 7th Armoured would advance to Nienburg, the

---

28 Heeres-Unteroffiziers-Schule 11 was responsible for training infantry NCO candidates. *Nebeltruppe*, as a separate branch of the artillery, operated launchers projecting rocket-propelled high explosive and smoke rounds. Heeres-Unteroffiziers-Schule für Nebeltruppen trained *Nebeltruppen* detachment commanders.

next major town on its axis and situated on the right bank of the Weser 70 miles to the east. On 3 April, 7th Armoured began to move into VIII Corps' bridgehead over the Dortmund-Ems Canal and take on the battle for Ibbenbüren. Events now began to move fast and VIII Corps, relieved of Ibbenbüren, continued the eastward advance against only light opposition. Three bridges on the Mittelland Canal were captured intact and by nightfall on 4 April units of 11th Armoured were only 15 miles from the Weser. Even better progress was made on the corps' right flank where 3rd Parachute Brigade was nearing the outskirts of Minden. On 5 April Montgomery ordered Second Army to secure the line of the Weser, capture Bremen and then advance on the right to the line of the Aller and Leine.[29] Bremen would then be masked while bridgeheads over the Weser, Leine and Aller were secured; thereafter the army was to be prepared to advance to the Elbe. VIII Corps was making such rapid progress, however, that its brigades reached the Weser the day that Montgomery issued this order.

Meanwhile, on relieving 11th Armoured from the battle for Ibbenbüren, 7th Armoured found that quick victory was not forthcoming. The infantry of 131st and 115th Infantry Brigades were committed to an attack on 3 April but made little progress against stubborn resistance. Attacks ground to a halt against numerous snipers, roving machine-gun teams and endless *Panzerfaust* attacks, many skilfully employed by allowing the attacking troops to pass before engaging from the rear. House after house was set on fire but the Germans fought back from the blazing ruins. While the infantry brigades of 7th Armoured fought the defenders of Ibbenbüren, XII Corps decided that 53rd Welsh Division would take on the battle, freeing the armoured division to advance east. 53rd Welsh moved from the corps' left flank to embark on this less than popular task and at 2130 hours on 5 April 71st Infantry Brigade mounted a night attack on the town, meeting stiff resistance. Prior to the handover to 53rd Welsh, 22nd Armoured Brigade from 7th Armoured, had bypassed the town to the south on VIII Corps' axis – a move that took two nights on appalling roads, very badly congested with traffic – and by the evening of 4 April the brigade was ready to push ahead over the high ground of the Teutoburger Wald and relieve 11th Armoured at a captured bridge on the Osnabrück Canal at Halen. The Ibbenbüren battle had delayed XII Corps for three days and it was not until 5 April that General Ritchie was able to direct Major General Lyne,[30] commanding 7th Armoured, to secure as early as possible the area bounded by the towns of Verden, Nienburg, Sulingen and Bassum. Flanks and mopping up were to be disregarded and bridges captured over the Weser.

In summary, by 5 April Second Army had made good progress in its advance from the Rhine: VIII Corps had reached the Weser; although delayed, XII Corps was closing on the river; and XXX Corps was making slow but steady progress towards Bremen. Notwithstanding the general success, the advance into Germany was far from trouble-free. Not only were the fighting troops experiencing resistance but the Germans' extensive use of mines and demolitions caused significant delay and imposed a heavy burden on Allied logistics, in particular tactical bridging by 1945 in short supply. By the war's end an astonishing 29 miles of Bailey bridges, three miles of pontoon Bailey bridges and three miles of folding boat equipment (FBE) bridges would be built between the Seine and the Elbe.[31]

The flavour of the advance is succinctly captured by war correspondent Alan Moorehead, General Sir David Fraser, then a lieutenant in 2nd (Armoured) Battalion Grenadier Guards, and Captain William Steel Brownlie of 2nd Fife and Forfar Yeomanry:

---

29   TNA WO 171/3949, G Ops Branch 2nd Army war diary.
30   TNA WO 205/972C, An account of the operations of Second Army in Europe, p.370.
31   TNA WO 205/1213, Chief Engineer 21st Army Group, *Bridging Normandy to Berlin*.

Alan Moorehead.[32] As soon as we crossed the Rhine we were confronted by a problem almost as big as Germany herself; the millions upon millions of slave workers. With every mile we went into Germany they grew more numerous on the roads: little groups of Frenchmen, then Dutch, then Belgians and Czechs and Poles and Italians, and finally, in overwhelming majority, the Russians in their bright green uniforms…Half the nationalities of Europe were on the march, all moving blindly westward along the roads, feeling their way by some common instinct towards the British and American lines in the hope of finding food and shelter and transportation there. These millions lived a vagabond existence. At every bend of the road you came on another group, bundles on their shoulders, trudging along the ditches in order to avoid the passing military traffic…One began to get a new picture of *Nazi* Germany. What we were seeing was something from the dark ages, the breaking up of a medieval slave state. All the *Nazi* flags and parades and conquests in the end were based on this one thing – slave labour. There was something monstrous about the wired-in workers' compounds and sentry boxes round each factory, something that was in defiance of all accepted norms of civilisation. As yet, in early April, we had only begun to glimpse the extent and depth of the *Nazi* terror system, but already one sensed the utter disregard of the value of human life in Germany. And now the *Reich* was collapsing at its roots because the slaves were melting away. One saw mostly women in the country towns and in the farms as we passed on; nearly all the German men were either at the front or prisoners or dead. And the slaves were on the road. There was no longer anyone to sow the crop, no one to reap the harvest later on.

David Fraser.[33] For their part the Allies advanced with caution. It was inevitable, with the outcome so certain and so imminent, that men did not wish to court death if risk could be avoided. Operations, in many cases, were understandably sluggish. The challenge of earlier days, the exaltation of liberation of occupied territories, was past. The advancing columns would run on to the defences of a village. A few tanks would be hit, a few casualties would be inflicted. The place would be masked while the following echelons deployed to find a way round. A well-placed anti-tank gun on the edge of a wood, probably using its last rounds of ammunition, would take toll from this manoeuvre and withdraw. An artillery programme would be fired, time would be spent, another unit be pushed through to take the lead. A few prisoners would come in, a few of our own dead be hastily buried, a few more miles advanced. Then some route would be found where few defenders were in evidence and a larger leap forward achieved. Acts of heroism in such circumstances – and there were many – are the more meritorious. Casualties – and they were not few – become a little more poignant. The final battles were seldom easy, but to fight them was to engage in a race where the result was already known. The necessity was clear but the stimulus flagged.

William Steel Brownlie.[34] Hopes that the advance would be as swift as that across northern France were however to be dashed. There was no Resistance to round up prisoners or to clear the route ahead. Instead roaming bands of bazooka men – often mere boys – would dismount from their rusty bicycles, set up a road-block, and delay the leading troops by forcing them to deploy after losing their leading tank or tanks. At first each village was entered cautiously, while a couple of troops out-flanked the buildings to one side or the other. Later it was discovered that an inhabited place could be judged clear or otherwise from afar according to

---

32 Alan Moorehead, *Eclipse* (London: Hamish Hamilton, 1945), pp.212–213.
33 Fraser, *And We Shall Shock Them*, p.393.
34 William Steel Brownlie, *'And Came Safe Home'* (Unpublished private memoir, Tank Museum Archive).

whether the 'washing' was out or not. A place that was not defended would often be gay with white flags, sheets, towels or pillow-cases fluttering from the windows as token of surrender, while one in which a rear-guard had been posted would show no such signal. It therefore became the custom in some units to motor straight through any place where the washing was in evidence, although if the Germans had ever thought to take advantage of this habit they might have scored heavily.

It was a period in which emotions were mixed. While the individual knew that speed would hasten the end of the war, he also felt that, having stayed alive so long, he should endeavour to survive till the finish. There was thus a certain caution displayed at times when dash might have been more profitable. There was also a natural tendency to use fire on every possible occasion, not only in self-protection but also out of hatred for the Germans. And yet it sometimes became apparent that the innocent were being made to suffer for the crimes of the guilty. One Yeoman found himself halted outside a thatched cottage, one of a row which were burning fiercely. The owner, an old woman on crutches stood watching her home go up in flames. She turned to him and asked in German: 'Why have you done this to an old woman?' It seemed impossible to give a satisfactory reply.

The 2nd Fife and Forfar Yeomanry regimental history also observed:[35]

> The tenacious resistance by the Germans sometimes came as a surprise to the attacking forces. Everything pointed to an early and crushing defeat for the Fatherland. At every point of the European battle-front the Allies were advancing fast. Yet in many places German troops fought on. Not in any perfunctory way either. They really fought; often with cool heads, often with confidence. Considering that the Allies now enjoyed an overwhelming preponderance in armour, men, aircraft and material, it was impossible not to admire that strange, haunted race, twice ruined in the pursuit of world mastery.

For VIII and XII Corps, their advance during the next two weeks was about to become significantly tougher and, in their operations to cross the three rivers, involve the British in an intensity of fighting that was the equal of anything they had experienced in the campaign thus far. With the scene set, it is now time to look at the organisation and equipment of the German forces they will encounter.

---

35 RJB Sellar, *The Fife and Forfar Yeomanry 1919–1956* (Edinburgh and London: William Blackwood & Sons Ltd,1960), p.235.

2

The Rock of Resistance: German Forces on the Weser and Aller

In the period leading up to the battles on the Weser and Aller, the situation for the *Wehrmacht* in north Germany had become grimmer by the day. On the Heeresgruppe 'H' right flank in Germany,[1] Blumentritt's 1. Fallschirm-Armee was continuing its desperate but effective fighting withdrawal and had fought hard to delay XXX Corps at Bentheim and Lingen. In the centre the last vestiges of Divisionen Nr.471 and Nr.490 were offering only localised resistance to XII Corps' columns advancing rapidly towards the Weser, while on the left flank the collapse of 84. Infanterie-Division left almost no forces to block the advance of VIII Corps, allowing it a clear run to the river. The Ultra decrypt of an OKW message sent on 2 April to Generaloberst Blaskowitz (Heeresgruppe 'H'), Generalfeldmarschall Model (Heeresgruppe 'B') and SS-Oberstgruppenführer Hausser (Heeresgruppe 'G') plainly shows Hitler's mounting desperation as the Western Allies plunged deep into Germany:[2]

For the conduct of operations in the west the *Führer* has ordered:

1. The enemy is operating in the west as though the resistance of the armed forces and the German people had already collapsed. By thrusting ahead with single armoured divisions deep into the hinterland he is not only paralysing the willpower of weak commanders but is destroying the whole command and supply organism and the belief of the people in the possibility of offering any effective resistance at all.
2. An end must be put to such symptoms with the utmost energy and ruthlessness. For this purpose, any means is right that brings success. All strategic measures and every avoidable withdrawal will be ordered by me. It is the task of OB West to get the wobbling fronts to hold, to force his commands to be carried out and to replace every commander who fails to stand firm with his troops or to lead them against the enemy.

Blaskowitz now thought it timely to warn Hitler of the situation he faced on the West Front and three days later an Ultra decrypt reveals him signalling to report that Blumentritt's 1. Fallschirm-Armee was in danger of being outflanked and that he could only protect the northern Netherlands and prevent the enemy advancing into the North German Plain if he received forces capable

---

1   A *Heeresgruppe* was a formally established organisation commanding a number of armies; an *Armeegruppe* was an *ad hoc* organisation formed to meet a special circumstance or to take under command, usually temporarily, an assortment of formations.
2   TNA DEFE 3/563, BT 9588, Hitler order 2 April 1945.

of closing the gap between 1. Fallschirm-Armee and the Weser.[3] Additionally, he sought direction on the three conflicting challenges he was facing: should he withdraw Armeegruppe Student and 1. Fallschirm-Armee to the north-west and restore contact with LXXXVIII. Armee-Korps in the Netherlands but, in so doing, uncover the Emden-Wilhelmshaven area; or should he try to cover that area but in so doing lose contact with LXXXVIII. Armee-Korps and give up the north Netherlands; or should he give up both areas and concentrate on bolstering the weak defence of the Weser. Two hours later Blaskowitz received his reply from General Siegfried Westphal,[4] Kesselring's chief of staff, and was told that, subject to Hitler's approval, his first priority was to prevent further Allied advances towards the ports of Emden, Wilhelmshaven and Bremen, and prevent any crossings of the Weser; maintaining contact with forces in the north Netherlands was, if necessary, to take second place. This reply was not only ambivalent but also failed to give Blaskowitz the additional forces he had requested, effectively ordering him to perform the impossible. Realistic assessments of rapidly disintegrating operational situations and perfectly reasonable requests for direction such as Blaskowitz's were deeply unpopular with Hitler and OKW as they forced them to confront reality; they were therefore rare. Hitler and Kesselring were both infuriated by Blaskowitz's report: the former for his defeatism and for suggesting that he, Hitler, did not grasp the operational situation; the latter for ignoring the chain of command. Blaskowitz was given strict orders never again to make a similar assessment of the situation and get on with holding his sectors with all available means.[5]

Kesselring meanwhile had more than enough of his own difficulties, of which one was exercising command over Heeresgruppe 'H' and *Wehrmacht* forces in the Netherlands and north Germany during the general withdrawal of OB West. The withdrawal was leading to loss of control of these northerly elements and the only solution was to create an additional OB level headquarters under OKW's direct command. Kesselring forwarded this proposal to Hitler, who approved it on 6 April and the next day ordered Blaskowitz's Heeresgruppe 'H' to be subsumed into the new command, entitled OB Nordwest, which was given authority over all army, air force and naval staffs and forces in the Netherlands and north Germany, all duly recorded in an Ultra decrypt.[6] In the Netherlands these forces comprised 25. Armee and various naval units, the latter mainly consisting of static organisations and headquarters under Vizeadmiral Rudolf Stange, Admiral Niederlande; and in north Germany Blumentritt's 1. Fallschirm-Armee and Armeegruppe Student. As a tri-Service headquarters, OB Nordwest was also given authority over Führungsstab Nordküste (North Coast Command), an OKW subordinate headquarters commanded since 14 March by Generalfeldmarschall Ernst Busch. Führungsstab Nordküste was responsible for defence of the coastal waters between Denmark and the Netherlands plus an extensive area of hinterland in Wehrkreis X (see Map 5), and with control of the *Führungsstab* OB Nordwest was able to employ ground forces from two naval commands: Marine-Oberkommando Ostsee (Baltic) and Marine-Oberkommando Nordsee. On the day that it formed, OB Nordwest was also ordered to take under command the once mighty Luftflotte Reich.[7] The *Luftflotte* had previously been

---

3   TNA DEFE 3/564, BT 9801, Blaskowitz signal 2000 hours 5 April 1945.
4   TNA DEFE 3/563, BT 9737, Westphal signal 2200 hours 5 April 1945. As an aside, in 1981 Westphal was the guest of honour at a dinner held by HQ 7th Armoured Brigade to mark the 40th anniversary of the battle of Sidi Rezegh (November 1941), at which Westphal had been Rommel's 1a in Panzergruppe 'Afrika'. I attended the dinner at the brigade officers' mess in Soltau and recall we had roast pheasant, but so tough it was inedible. Perhaps Westphal thought it was deliberate.
5   Kesselring, *Memoirs*, p.257–258.
6   TNA DEFE 3/565, KO 38, 1242 hours 10 April 1945, Hitler order for reorganisation of chain of command in the west.
7   FMS B-414, Heeresgruppe 'H' (10 March–9 May 1945), p.37.

responsible for the air defence of Germany but was now reduced to supporting the army in north Germany from the few air bases still operational, and commanding the *Flak* (anti-aircraft artillery) units in Luftgau XI, the Hannover air region. OB Nordwest's structure following Hitler's order is shown at Figure 1.

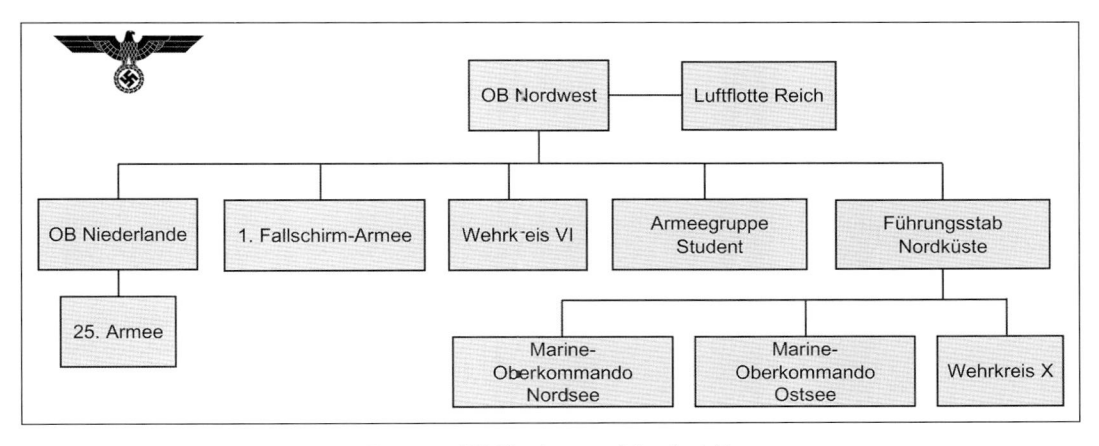

Figure 1 OB Nordwest – 6 April 1945.

Via General Burgdorf, Chefs des Heerespersonalamtes (Directorate of Army Manning), Hitler ordered Busch to handover Führungsstab Nordküste to Admiral Kummetz and, with effect from 7 April, assume command of OB Nordwest.[8] Hitler had previously sacked Busch, an officer well-known for his fanaticism and *Nazi* views, following the annihilation of Heeresgruppe Mitte on the East Front in July 1944, but owing to the now desperate situation his former disgrace was conveniently forgotten. The same day, the deeply unpopular Blaskowitz was moved sideways to command OB Niederlande, now grandly re-entitled Festung (Fortress) Holland.[9]

Armeegruppe Student

Two days prior to these events, with his departure imminent, Blaskowitz had instructed Student to relinquish command of Armeegruppe Student and on 6 April,[10] with authority from OKW, ordered him and his staff to form a new *Armeegruppe* bearing his name with responsibility for the defence of the Weser from Bremen to Hameln and tasked to prevent the British and Americans breaking through this vulnerable sector. Student would command his new *Armeegruppe* for only four days before handing it over to Blumentritt.

On any count, responsibility for the Weser's defence was challenging: the first Allied units had already reached the river the day before, the forces available to Student were woefully thin and generally of low quality, and riverlines, while appearing ideal defensive features are in reality very testing, as a brief look at doctrine reveals. First, prior to the battle for the riverline, forces are needed to delay the enemy's advance, erode his strength, confirm his axes and gain time for the preparation of defensive positions. Secondly, as a defending commander is unlikely to have

---

8   TNA HW 5/690, Burgdorf signal No. 270, 8 April 1945.
9   FMS, B-354, 1. Fallschirm-Armee (28 March–9 April), p.20.
10 FMS, B-414, Heeresgruppe 'H' (10 March–9 May 1945), p.23.

sufficient strength to defend the riverline's entire length he must choose where to concentrate effort or where to accept risk and have fewer defenders, or even none at all, and instead rely on surveillance and mobile reserves to cover the gaps. Thirdly, as the enemy is most vulnerable to counter-attack immediately after crossing, his bridgeheads must be quickly identified and attacked before he can consolidate them. Reconnaissance assets and mobile, capable reserves are therefore key capabilities for the defending commander. Comparing Student's situation to the doctrine: the forces forward of the Weser were not only minimal but also in full retreat, giving the enemy a largely unchallenged run to the river and rapidly eroding what little time remained for defensive preparations; he had extremely limited surveillance resources and, at best, poor communications; he had no reserve, mobile or otherwise; he had three riverlines to defend; and his forces had virtually no mobility. To compound his difficulties, the enemy had excellent tactical bridging allowing the defence to be outflanked and bridgeheads rapidly reinforced with armour and heavy weapons and equipment. The omens for a successful defence were at best inauspicious and Student would have known that all he could hope to achieve was some delay.

On 6 April Student established his small headquarters at Stadthagen, six miles east of Minden, and the next day Heeresegruppe 'H', in its last act before becoming OB Nordwest, ordered him to take command of Stellvertretendes General-Kommando XI. Armee-Korps (aka Korps Hannover) from Wehrkreis XI (the Hannover military district – see Map 5) and 2. Marine-Infanterie-Division.[11] Two days later OB Nordwest also allocated to him XXXI. Armee-Korps z.b.V. (aka Korps Ems) from Wehrkreis X, the military district covering Schleswig-Holstein, Hamburg and Bremen. Collectively, Korps Ems, Korps Hannover and 2. Marine-Infanterie-Division formed the third *Armeegruppe* to bear Student's name.

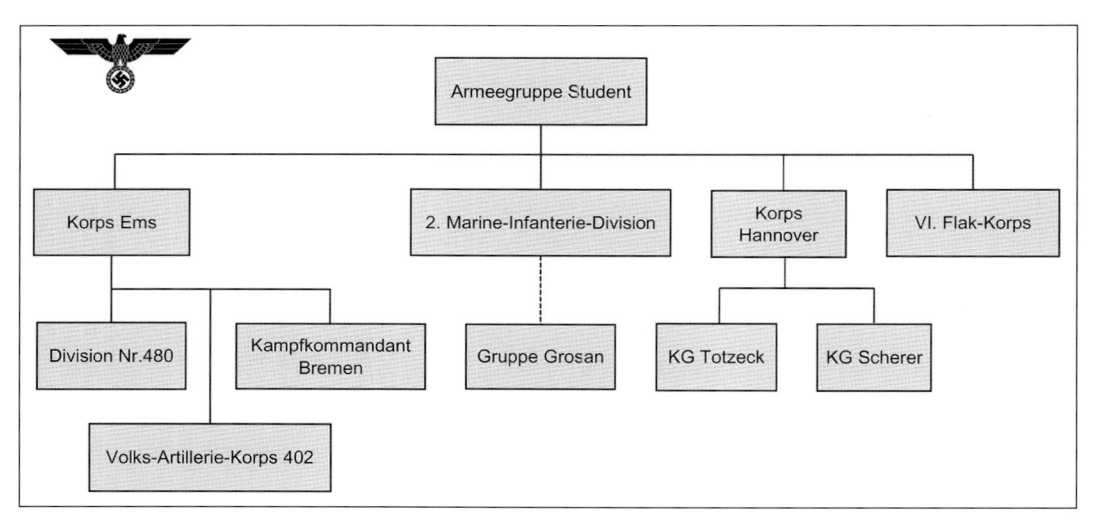

Figure 2 Armeegruppe Student – 6 April 1945.

The deployment of Armeegruppe Student for the defence of the riverlines is shown on Map 4. Korps Ems was responsible for the Armeegruppe's right flank, which included the defence of Bremen and followed the line of the Weser south-eastwards as far as Verden. 2. Marine-Infanterie-Division was responsible for the Armeegruppe's centre, which comprised the line of the Weser

---

11   TNA DEFE 3/564, BT 9816, Heeresgruppe 'H' Instructions effective 7 April 1945.

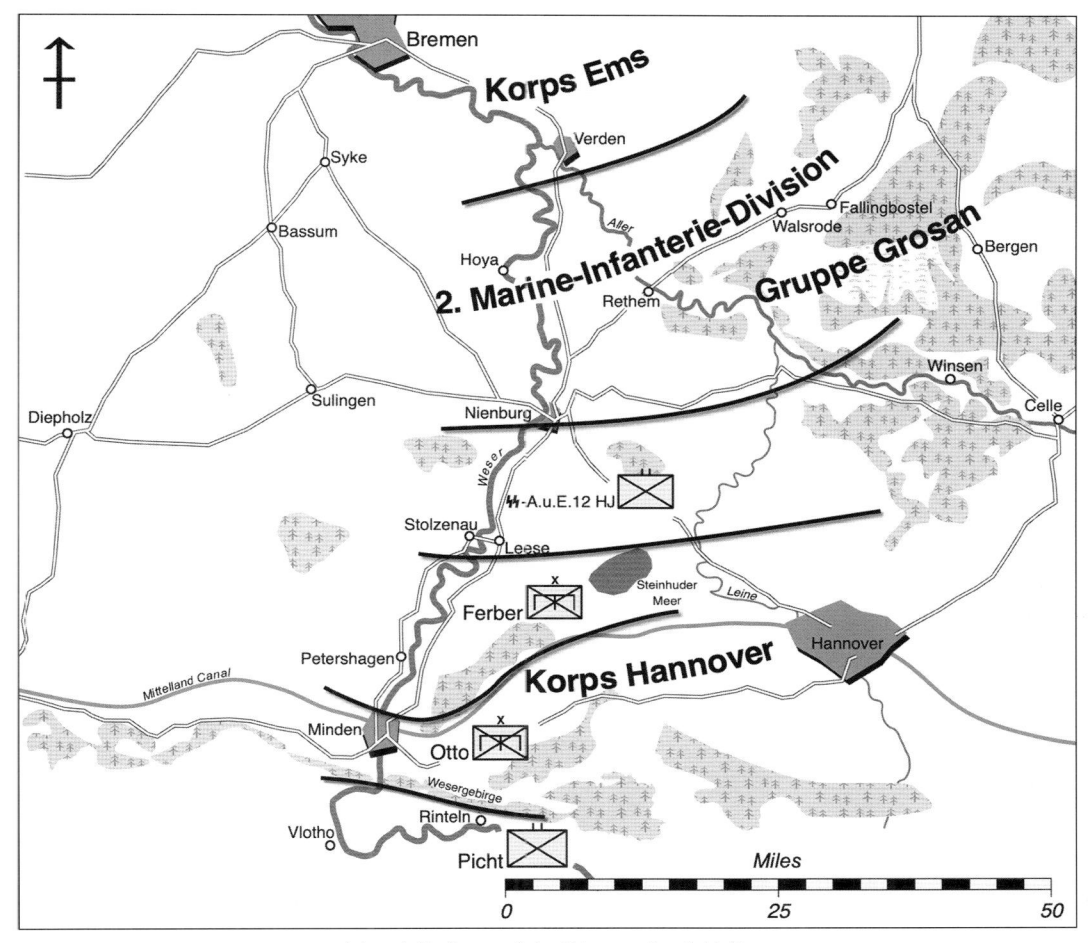

Map 4 Defence of the Rivers – April 1945.

between Verden and Nienburg and the line of the Aller from south of Verden to the Schwarmstedt area, while Korps Hannover was responsible for the Armeegruppe's left flank – the line of the Weser from Stolzenau to Hamelin.

Student was also allocated various elements of Armee-Korps zur Vergeltung (z.V.) ('for retaliation') and, although not mentioned in the Heeresgruppe 'H' signal, Wehrkries VI and what remained of Stellv.Gen.Kdo. VI. Armee-Korps. Armee-Korps z.V. had been responsible for prosecuting the V-weapon campaign and its contribution to Armeegruppe Student is described in more detail later in this chapter. Wehrkreis VI was the military district comprising the then states of Westphalia and Rhineland but by now the forces it had generated had either been eradicated by the Anglo-American advances from the Rhine or bottled-up in the Ruhr pocket and little of its district remained unoccupied. To add to its woes, the location of its headquarters was unknown to HQ Armeegruppe Student despite attempts to establish radio contact and officers being sent to find it.

The naval division besides, Armeegruppe Student's manpower was largely found from the *Ersatz Heer* (Replacement Army), which since 20 July 1944 had been under the command of Reichsführer-SS Himmler as a direct consequence of its role in the failed attempt on Hitler's life. The *Ersatz Heer*, the home-based element of the Germany Army, was regionally organised with

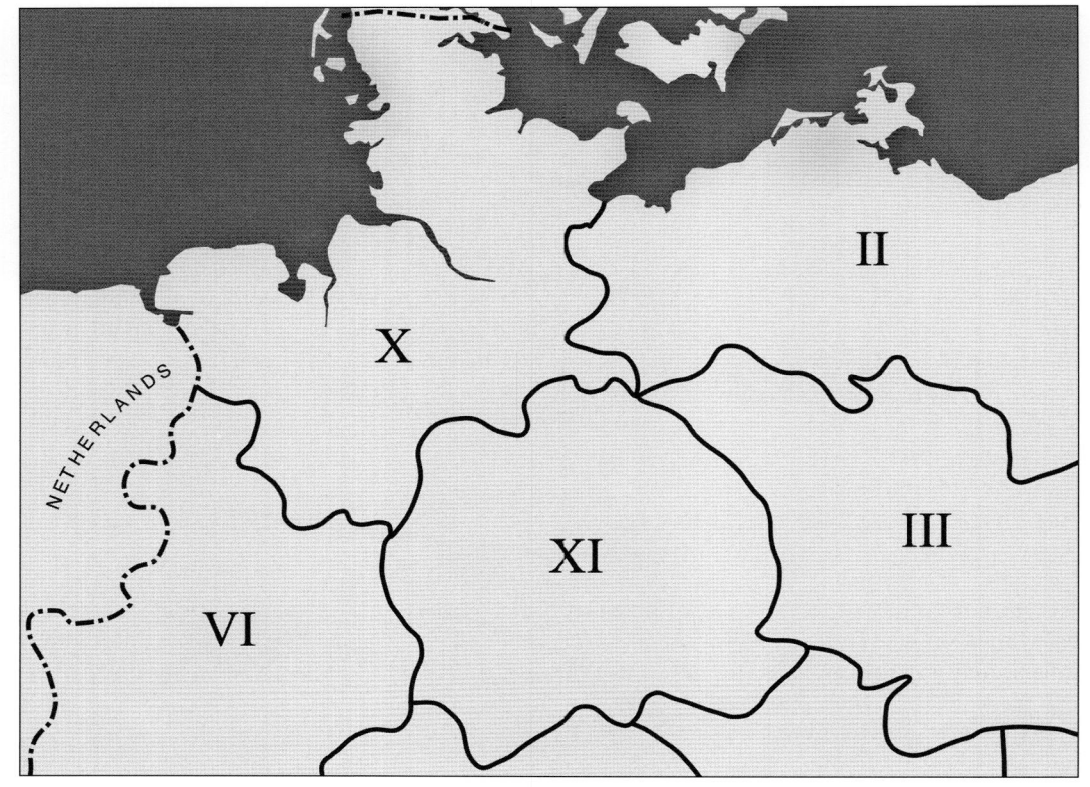

Map 5 The Northern Wehrkreise.

each region under a military district – the *Wehrkreis*. There were 13 *Wehrkreise* within Germany proper, two in Austria and a further four in other areas such as Danzig and Poland; Wehrkreis VI, X and XI will feature in the account and their areas in North Germany are shown on Map 5. The functions of a *Wehrkreis* headquarters were divided between the territorial command of its district and running the training and replacement system for the field units associated with its affiliated *Armee-Korps*, which would be deployed in wartime. In its former capacity the headquarters bore the title *Wehrkreis-Kommando* and in the latter, *Stellvertretendes General-Kommando (Stellv.Gen.Kdo)*.

Stellvertretendes in this context means 'deputy' as headquarters bearing this prefix deputised back in the *Reich* for their deployed first line *Armee-Korps* and both bore the same number. The *Stellv.Gen.Kdo* responsibilities were: conscription; supervising the mobilisation of the waves of infantry divisions; organising new units; conducting military training including the selection and schooling of officers and NCOs; dispatching personnel replacements to field units; controlling training establishments and training areas; local defence; and operating PoW camps in their districts. The *Stellv.Gen.Kdo.* element also controlled the district's *Ausbildung und Ersatz (A.u.E.)* (training and replacement) units through static divisional staffs entitled *Division Nummer (Nr.)* followed by an allocated number (eg Division Nr.490). The *Division Nr.* either directly controlled the *A.u.E.* units or, in the case of infantry, artillery and engineers, delegated control to *A.u.E.* regimental staffs. The deteriorating situation from 1944 onwards increasingly led to the *Division Nr.* staffs being themselves provided with combat units to approximate them to a field division and then deployed to the fronts, with a fresh *Division Nr.* with a new number generated behind them to allow the training and replacement functions to continue. While this was an effective method of creating new formations, the deployed *Division Nr.* divisions were flawed as they had neither anti-tank nor logistic support units.

During 1944 and early 1945 Germany's parlous manning situation had resulted in the deployment to the fronts of most of the *Ersatz Heer*. To mobilise the final elements, on 20 March 1945 Hitler activated a plan of manning desperation codenamed Aktion Leuthen.[12] Leuthen, a town in Silesia, gave its name in 1757 to a battle fought and won by the Prussians under Frederick the Great against a much larger Austrian army. For the Germans of 1945 it would have had resonance as it was a renowned last-ditch battle that had to be won despite numerical inferiority, but there the similarity ends as the 1757 battle was also a classic of manoeuvre in which excellent use was made of ground and well-drilled soldiers. When in receipt of the codeword 'Leuthen', the remaining staff of the *Wehrkries* headquarters would form a field headquarters, be reinforced with all available manpower, regardless of levels of training, and together with any remaining *A.u.E.* units deploy forward, almost certainly on foot, in extemporised battlegroups to establish positions in depth of the front.[13] Aktion Leuthen would not only be the *Ersatz Heer's* swansong as it spelt the end of any capacity to provide either trained replacements or formed units, but it would also be the death knell for much of its manpower, which largely consisted of recent conscripts with at best only a few weeks' training, chronic shortages of weapons and ammunition and virtually no logistic support. Some Aktion Leuthen formations, such as Division Nr.471, were divided between the East and West Fronts, with those destined for the East bearing the title *Ostgoten* (East Goths), or *Westgoten* for the West. Despite their woeful situation, a few training units would fight with great determination and Heeres-Unteroffiziers-Schule 11 mentioned in Chapter 1 resolutely defending Ibbenbüren was one such; as this account unfolds various other training and replacement units will staunchly play their parts.

Let us now look in more detail at the organisation and deployment of Armeegruppe Student. For his right flank Student may have had some confidence in Korps Ems, but he would have had no such confidence in Korps Hannover on his left flank. Here the situation facing Student was far worse than merely lack of confidence for he had little idea of the whereabouts of Korps Hannover's forces, or even of their existence. The reality was that there were virtually none. Furthermore, with LXXXVI. Armee-Korps in the final stages of collapse any hope of defending forward of the Weser was gone and beyond his left flank there existed a void with only General der Infanterie Otto Hitzfeld's 11. Armee, hastily assembling further to the south in the Kassel area, supposedly available to block the Americans; the prospect for successful delay on his left was thus non-existent. His expectations may have been higher for his centre where 2. Marine-Infanterie-Division could win some time on the Weser and the Aller, offering the last opportunities before the Elbe to conduct a defence on major natural obstacles.

Armeegruppe Student's right flank

As mentioned, Student's right flank was allocated to XXXI. Armee-Korps z.b.V., better known as Korps Ems. Korps Ems was activated under Aktion Leuthen and formed around an *ad hoc* headquarters largely made up of the remaining staff of Stellv.Gen.Kdo. X, with combat elements provided from *A.u.E.* and other home-based units in Wehrkreis X. Although the reason for the allocation of the number 'XXXI' is unknown, 'z.b.V.' stood for *'zur besonderen Verwendung'* (for special employment), a description which could cover a variety of circumstances and frequently

---

12 Kunz, Andreas, *Wehrmacht und Niederlage*, (München: R. Oldenbourg, 2007), pp.188–189.
13 TNA DEFE 3/520, BT 8059 and 8164, C-in-C Home Army (Himmler) signals 20 and 21 April 1945.

used by the Germans for describing formations raised for specific purposes or emergency measures. The commander was General der Infanterie Siegfried Rasp, an exhausted man who had recently commanded 19. Armee during its long retreat from southern France and the subsequent failed campaign in Alsace. On formation, Rasp's command consisted only of Division Nr.480, commanded by Generalleutnant Martin Gilbert and based in Verden. This division, also known as Division z.b.V. Gilbert, was formed in autumn 1944 to replace its predecessor, Division Nr.180, which had deployed to the Arnhem area the previous September as part of the emergency response to the airborne landing. The main components of Division Nr.480 were Grenadier-A.u.E. Regiment 22, Grenadier-A.u.E. Regiment 269, Artillerie-A.u.E. Regiment 22, and Pionier-A.u.E. Bataillonen 30 and 34. On 27 March, Division Nr.480 was ordered to deploy and defend the Weser in the area of Verden, its home town.

A few days later Rasp was provided with two further formations – Kampfkommandant Bremen and Division Stab z.b.V. Nr.172 – both cobbled together using an assortment of miscellaneous local units. Kampfkommandant Bremen, commanded by Generalleutnant Fritz Becker, consisted of motley units including six companies of mainly Hungarian *Volksdeutsche* belonging to SS-Panzer-Grenadier A.u.E. Bataillon 18 'Horst Wessel' from Hamburg-Langenhorn, 4. Alarm-Bataillon 'Wesermünde' (an emergency-raised naval battalion from Wesermünde) and Grenadier-Ersatz Bataillon 376. Division Stab z.b.V. Nr.172 under Generalleutnant Richard von Schwerin was formed as a skeleton divisional staff and allocated units such as Polizei-Bataillon 'Ottersberg' (a police battalion from Ottersberg), Grenadier-Ausbildungs-Bataillon 280 (M) (an infantry training battalion manned by soldiers with conditions of the digestive system), three *Nebelwerfer* training battalions and various artillery training units, which, with heavy weapons and ammunition in short supply, were mostly used as infantry.

Korps Ems was supported by Volks-Artillerie-Korps 402. The thirteen *Volks-Artillerie-Korps* (People's Artillery Corps) were brigade-sized artillery groupings created in autumn 1944 from independent, army artillery formations, re-branded with new titles but given no new equipment. They were normally allocated on the basis of one or two per field army and typically comprised five or six battalions with a variety of guns, including anti-tank and anti-aircraft. Volks-Artillerie-Korps 402 had supported the Ardennes offensive and thereafter 1. Fallschirm-Armee but owing to losses was now a shadow of its former self.

Armeegruppe Student's centre on the Aller

2. Marine-Infanterie-Division, responsible for Student's central sector, will play the lead role for much of the account. The division principally comprised naval troops provided in early 1945 by Grossadmiral Karl Dönitz, Oberbefehlshaber der Marine (C-in-C of the Navy), to reinforce the army. By 1945 German ground forces were desperately short of men and the *Luftwaffe*, navy and industry were forced to surrender manpower, even if vital to the war effort, with the topic a standing agenda item during the conferences held between Hitler and his most senior military and civilian leaders. Fortunately, our knowledge of the naval aspects of these conferences is good, though incomplete, as Dönitz or his deputy would take rough notes, later written up as minutes. The minutes, known as the *Führer* Conferences on Naval Affairs, were among a vast collection of German naval archives captured in mid-April 1945 by British intelligence officers from Team 55 of 30 Assault Unit Royal Marines in a daring *coup-de-main* operation mounted on *Schloss* Tambach near Coburg.

During the conferences held in 1945 there was frequent discussion about raising naval units to participate in the land battle. The establishment of private armies was very much *de rigueur* for the leaders of the *Reich*, with Reichsführer-SS Himmler controlling the *Waffen-SS* (by 1945 an organisation over a million strong) and Reichsmarschall Göring sporting a large number of *Luftwaffe* ground combat formations, so with the intense rivalry that existed between the leaders it was inevitable that Dönitz would seize opportunity to create naval ground forces and thereby boost his standing with Hitler. This opportunity came on 18 January and the minutes for the day's conference reveal that during discussion of the situation on the East Front,[14] Dönitz offered Hitler a naval regiment of 3,000 men equipped with standard infantry equipment and ready to deploy at 48 hours' notice. Hitler readily accepted the offer and the deployment area was agreed as the Tilsit sector in East Prussia.[15] Clearly Dönitz began to enjoy the game as just two days later he informed Hitler that in view of the threat in the east he was offering the army 20,000 sailors currently in training; it was subsequently decided that these men could replace 22 army replacement battalions held in Denmark, releasing them for the East Front.[16] On 30 January Dönitz informed Hitler that to assist in the defence of Stettin and Swinemünde,[17] both considered essential to naval operations in the Baltic supporting the East Front, he would also make available the three regiments of Marine-Schützen-Brigade Nord, previously responsible for security of the German coast between Denmark and the Dutch border. With Hitler's permission granted, the brigade was allocated to Heeresgruppe Weichsel (Vistula) and renamed 1. Marine-Division, the first of five naval divisions initially bearing the title '*Marine-Division*' until changed by Hitler on 10 March to '*Marine-Infanterie-Division*'.[18] For the British, the word 'marine' in the title would subsequently cause misunderstanding as some assumed the personnel to be analogous with British marines. However, the German word '*marine*' stands for 'navy' or 'naval' so the division's personnel were in reality naval infantry, making them akin to the sailors of the British naval battalions of the Great War; the account will, however, use 'marine' as shorthand for naval infantry.

Of the five marine divisions, the first fought on the Oder Front where it was largely destroyed in the confused fighting to Berlin's north, with the survivors escaping westwards across the demarcation line in early May. The second division is the subject of this account. The third division was formed in early April 1945 around the residue of 163. Infanterie-Division, decimated the previous month in the battle for Stargard in Pomerania. It took part in the defence of Swinemünde then retreated to the Oranienburg area north of Berlin and was mopped up by the Russians near Kyritz, 25 miles east of the Elbe. 11. and 16. Marine-Infanterie-Divisionen were part of 25. Armee in the Netherlands.[19]

The air of fantasy and misplaced optimism pervading Hitler's conferences and the wholly unrealistic expectations placed on newly-raised formations are evident in a report delivered by Dönitz to the conference of 14 February, in which he gave his impressions of 1. Marine-Division gleaned from an inspection he had conducted two days previously.[20] He smugly informed the conference that he had formed a very good opinion of the division and its readiness for action. Although shortcomings in training were apparent, he felt these could gradually be eliminated. Equipment, particularly heavy weapons, was however still badly needed and he complained that Himmler had withdrawn the assault gun unit that was intended to support the division. In time he expected the marines to adapt themselves well to mobile warfare, although he then contradicted this optimism

---

14   Jak Showell, *Führer Conferences on Naval Affairs, 1939–1945* (London: Chatham Publishing, 2005), pp.425–426.
15   Now Sovetsk in Kaliningrad *Oblast*, Russia.
16   Showell, *Führer Conferences on Naval Affairs*, p.428.
17   Showell, *Führer Conferences on Naval Affairs*, p.434.
18   Showell, *Führer Conferences on Naval Affairs*, p.461.
19   Bernd Bölscher, *Hitlers Marine im Landkriegseinsatz 1939–1945* (Norderstedt: Books on Demand, 2015), p.85.
20   Showell, *Führer Conferences on Naval Affairs*, p.444.

by expressing doubts whether the middle-ranking officers from battalion commanders upwards could cope with the demands of modern warfare. How a non-mechanised formation could participate in mobile warfare was neither explained nor questioned but its unsuitability would soon be brutally exposed with the launch of Zhukov's 1st Belorussian Front in the battle for the Oder-Neisse line, the opening phase of the assault on Berlin. Hitler concluded discussion by asking the Reichsführer-SS's deputy to urge him to return the assault guns and remarked that he believed the naval division capable of great perseverance regardless of its lack of experience in land warfare. At a subsequent conference held on 3 April Hitler asked how well 1. Marine-Infanterie-Division was armed.[21] In stark comparison to his previous upbeat report, Dönitz replied that it lacked artillery and that a recent report from its commander, Generalmajor Bleckwenn, revealed 800 marines were armed only with *Panzerfaust*. No response from Hitler was recorded. Thirteen days later 1st Belorussian Front attacked.

The second division's origin was at the 30 January conference.[22] During the discussion of naval matters Dönitz asked Hitler if the navy, to create a second division, could retain part of the 20,000 men he had recently volunteered; both Keitel and Jodl supported Dönitz's request and Hitler directed that all naval personnel yet to transfer to the army were to be held back to form the division. To provide *Flak* support, Göring offered to equip the division with guns mounted on trucks and trailers. The next mention of the division was made at the conference held on the afternoon of 9 February 1945.[23] At this meeting Dönitz asked Jodl to help supply equipment and arms as the navy could provide almost nothing except personnel and had to depend on the army for everything else. However, as Speer's effort to keep armament production going was now at an end the army was in an equally challenged state, with requirements only being met by the most stop-gap of measures, usually involving robbing 'Peter to pay Paul'. The discussion on naval matters ends with Dönitz stating that the equipping of the division was in accordance with the *Führer's* decision, a dog-eared trump card habitually played at the conferences. Two days later Dönitz again raised the matter of equipping, stating that he could not consent to any arrangements made by subordinate naval representatives with corresponding army headquarters for the navy to supply its own small-arms and vehicles.[24] He then described an example of the navy's shortages in which he had had to order the removal of all small-arms on naval vessels in order to equip an *Abteilung* from 9. Marine-Flak-Regiment in Gotenhafen (now Gdynia) and soon to be thrown into the land battle.

Despite the problems with equipment supply, the establishment order for the second division's three grenadier regiments was issued on 12 February, followed shortly by the order for the supporting arms and services, and the division was allocated to Admiral Förste's Marine-Oberkommando Nordsee pending decisions on its deployment.[25] The division's personnel were gathered from many backgrounds and locations: recent intakes in the 17 to 19 age-group, U-boat crews awaiting new boats, surface fleet crews without ships, and dockyard personnel and men evacuated from bases on the Baltic. The majority had little or no naval training. In recognition of their suspicions regarding the Grossadmiral's motives and their probable sacrificial role, they nicknamed themselves '*Die Dönitz-Spende*', with the English translation the 'Dönitz Donation' having apt alliteration. Initially the personnel concentrated at the training camp at Oksbøl near Esbjerg in Denmark, where they completed basic infantry training before moving to Schleswig-Holstein and the naval barracks at Husum, Glückstadt and Itzehoe; here they were formed into their various units.

---

21 Showell, *Führer Conferences on Naval Affairs*, p.478.
22 Showell, *Führer Conferences on Naval Affairs*, p.435.
23 Showell, *Führer Conferences on Naval Affairs*, p.442.
24 Showell, *Führer Conferences on Naval Affairs*, p.443.
25 Bölscher, *Hitlers Marine im Landkriegseinsatz*, p.368.

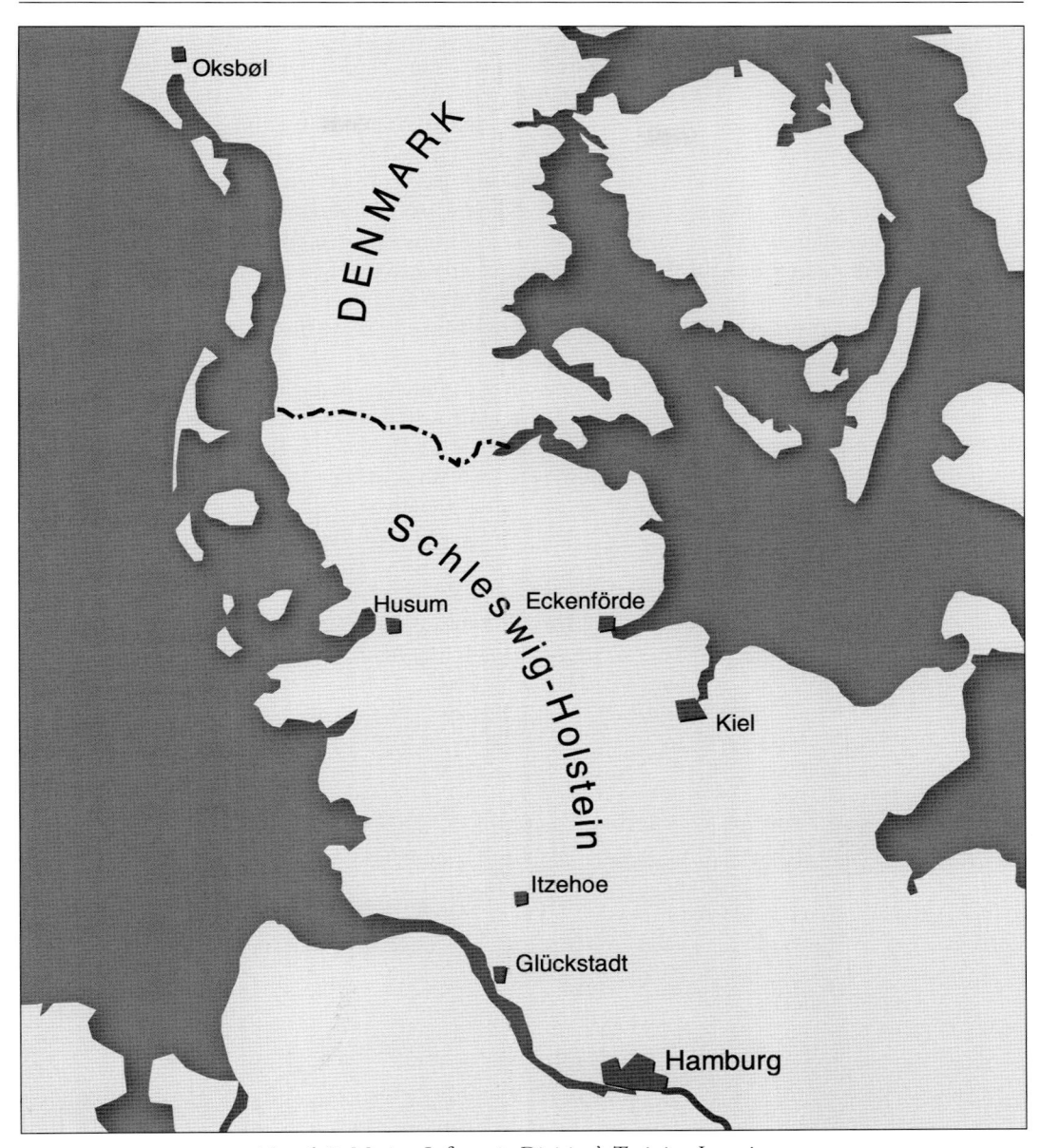

Map 6 2. Marine-Infanterie-Division's Training Locations.

2. Marine-Infanterie-Division's structure is shown at Figure 3. The division followed the Infanterie-Division 45 establishment,[26] which was almost identical to that of the *Volksgrenadier* divisions created by Himmler in the autumn of 1944 as a response to the massive losses on the East Front and the need to make best possible use of limited manpower. Infanterie-Division 45 was the last in a series of wartime establishment revisions conducted to reflect the requirement

---

26 TNA WO 208/2904, Tables Showing Organisation and Equipment of German Divisions, The Infantry Division 1945.

for manpower economies, the strategic change from offence to defence and increases in firepower through greater quantities and types of automatic weapons, factors which combined to allow a manpower reduction to 11,909 from the 17,000 of a 1939 division. On 24 March the division had a strength of 12,372 men and its commander was 50-year-old Vizeadmiral Ernst Scheurlen, plucked in early February from his appointment as Admiral Deutsche Bucht (German Bight) in Cuxhaven. To assist Scheurlen in his new, unfamiliar task he was allocated an army adviser from the General Staff, Oberstleutnant Josef Heck. Scheurlen was an energetic and capable officer, who as a *Konteradmiral* in 1943 had gained distinction commanding Marine-Einsatzstabes Kertsch (Naval Task Force Kertsch) during the significant part it played in resupplying 17. Armee in the Kuban bridgehead, lying on the far side of the Kerch Strait separating the Crimea from the Caucasus. For this work Scheurlen was awarded the German Cross in Gold. 1943 was however a very mixed year for him as his son, Leutnant zur See Hans-Joachim Scheurlen, was on U-469 when she was sunk with all-hands on 25 March 1943 on her first patrol. In June 1943 Ernst Scheurlen was posted from the Crimea to Küstenbefehlshaber (Coastal Command) Deutsche Bucht, thus avoiding any involvement a year later in 17. Armee's difficult and at times disastrous evacuation across the Black Sea following its isolation in the Crimea as a result of Hitler's intransigence.[27]

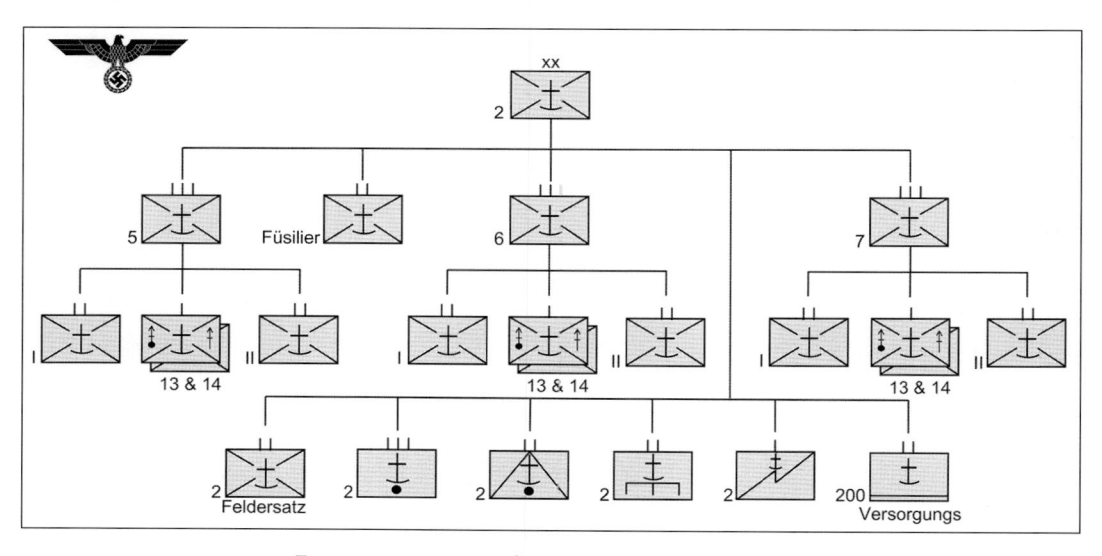

Figure 3 2. Marine-Infanterie-Division – 7 April 194.

In its unreinforced state the division's core combat power was based on three infantry regiments, sequentially numbered Marine-Grenadier-Regiment 5, 6, and 7, and an independent infantry battalion, Marine-Füsilier-Bataillon 2.[28] The three infantry regiments each consisted of two battalions and two regimental heavy weapons' companies, numbered 13 and 14. All battalions, including Marine-Füsilier-Bataillon 2, were identically organised, and comprised three rifle companies and a fourth, heavy weapons' company; each rifle company consisted of three platoons.

---

27 The sinking by Russian aircraft of the ships *Totila* and *Teja* on 10 May 1944 during the Black Sea evacuation of German and Romanian troops is one of the greatest maritime disasters of all time. The exact number of casualties will never be known, but some 8,000 men may have lost their lives.
28 Bölscher, *Hitlers Marine im Landkriegseinsatz*, pp.90–92.

THE ROCK OF RESISTANCE 59

The Germans employed a logical system of unit numbering based on alternating roman and arabic numerals, and this will be used throughout the account. Regiments and companies were denoted by arabic numbers while battalions used roman and by using a slash, affiliations could be created: thus II./5 Bataillon would be the second battalion of the fifth regiment. As a first battalion's companies were always numbered 1–4 and a second battalion's 5–8, parent battalions could be omitted from the description, thus 4./7 Kompanie would be the fourth company (of the first battalion) of the seventh regiment.

Kapitän zur See Hermann Jordan commanded Marine-Grenadier-Regiment 5. Jordan had had a varied military career, initially joining the navy but then transferring to the *Luftwaffe*, in which he reached the rank of *Oberst*. The sole known record of his *Luftwaffe* service is his command from April 1939 to 1941 of Küstenfliegergruppe 106, responsible for air operations over the North Sea. He transferred back to the navy in September 1944 with the rank *Kapitän zur See* and was posted to the Luftwaffenlehrstab in OKM, a staff branch believed to have been responsible for coordinating with the *Luftwaffe* the training required for joint maritime operations such as anti-shipping and long-range reconnaissance. In February 1945 he assumed command of Marine-Grenadier-Regiment 5 when it was forming at Glückstadt.[29]

Kapitän zur See Werner Hartmann, a former U-boat ace and holder of the Knight's Cross with Oak Leaves, commanded Marine-Grenadier-Regiment 6. His seagoing commands had been U-37 and U-198 and while on the latter, a Type IX D2, he completed a 200-day patrol, the war's third longest.[30] In January 1944, following his service on U-198, he took command of U-boat operations in the Mediterranean. This ended in October 1944 when he was selected to play a leading role in setting up the Danzig-West Prussia Volkssturm and assimilating Hitler Youth into its ranks.[31] For this task he was given the honorary rank of *Gau-Führer*, a senior rank in the *Nazi* Party's civilian district structure. The principal reason for his presence was probably to bolster morale as a military hero rather than as an authority on land warfare, for which his knowledge would at best have been slim. Hartmann briefly stars in a section of newsreel from *Die Deutsche Wochenshau No. 741* dated 16 November 1944 featuring among other events the mustering of the Danzig Volkssturm.[32] The *Wochenshau*, *Nazi* Germany's equivalent to the British Pathé News but on steroids, starts with a shot of a newspaper article, possibly from the *Völkischer Beobachter*, trumpeting Hartmann's involvement. This is followed by a clip of Hartmann talking to Albert Forster,[33] the *Gauleiter* of Danzig-West Prussia, followed by the *Volkssturm's* rally through the city where Hartmann can clearly be seen marching in the front rank with Forster and other local *Nazi* and army bigwigs. But despite the banners and swastika flags, the parade has none of the swagger of pre-war *Nazi* rallies and the elderly *Volkssturm* in their flapping overcoats and trilby hats have the look of dead men walking. Fortunately for Hartmann, in February 1945 he was sent to Husum to assume command of Marine-Grenadier-Regiment 6 thus was no longer in Danzig when it fell to Rokossovsky in late March.

Kapitän zur See Karl Neitzel, a former skipper of U-510 and also a Knight's Cross holder, commanded Marine-Grenadier-Regiment 7. When aged 41, Neitzel earned renown as one of the oldest U-boat commanders to take a boat on operations. Prior to Marine-Grenadier-Regiment 7, in 1943 he commanded 25. U-Bootsflottille, a training organisation based in Libau, Latvia, then

---

29   Bölscher, *Hitlers Marine im Landkriegseinsatz*, p. 198.
30   U-37 survived the war at sea and was scuttled in May 1945. U-198 was attacked by aircraft and HMS *Godavari* and HMS *Findhorn* off the Seychelles on 12 August 1944 and sunk with all hands.
31   Bölscher, *Hitlers Marine im Landkriegseinsatz*, p. 180.
32   Die Deutsche Wochenshau No. 741, *https://www.youtube.com/watch?v=jg9onRuHBQk* (accessed 6 June 2016) (Appendix A, Serial 19).
33   Executed by Poland in 1952 for crimes against humanity.

moved with it to Gotenhafen in early 1944.[34] Owing to the threat from the Soviet assault on East Pomerania this unit closed in February 1945 and Neitzel deployed directly to Schleswig-Holstein to take command of Marine-Grenadier-Regiment 7, just starting to form at Itzehoe.

Lastly Korvettenkapitän Josef Gördes, the commander of Marine-Füsilier-Bataillon 2. This battalion was a 700-strong unit and in theory the provider of the division's reconnaissance. However, by this stage of the war reconnaissance was a past memory so *Füsilier* battalions were employed instead as seventh infantry battalions. Gördes was formerly a weapons' engineering officer with responsibility for maintaining and repairing the equipment of coastal artillery batteries, functions conducted in arsenals. He commanded two Marine-Artillerie-Arsenale: from July 1942 to June 1943 the arsenal at Aurich (mid-way between the naval bases of Emden and Wilhelmshaven) and from December 1943 to November 1944 the arsenal at Salamis in Greece.[35] It is not known what position he held from November 1944 to February 1945 when he assumed command of Marine-Füsilier-Bataillon 2. The battalion assembled at Glückstadt that same month but during the first week of March moved to Eckernförde near Kiel, the home of 24. U-Bootsflottille responsible for training U-boat commanders in firing and underwater positioning, and here it received drafts from Marine-Grenadier-Regiment 5 and 6 to form two of its three rifle companies.

Although acute equipment shortages meant that the division could not mirror the Infanterie-Division 45 establishment, compared to many formations of the time it would seem to have received a better than expected allocation. Two platoons in each company were armed with the 7.92mm Sturmgewehr 44 (StG 44) assault rifle, while the third was equipped with the Mauser 7.92mm G98/40 (Kar 98k) rifle. The StG 44 was a revolutionary and reliable selective-fire weapon capable of engaging targets at longer ranges than the MP 40 sub-machine-gun, of more use in close combat than the Kar 98k, and able to provide automatic, suppressive covering fire similar to a light machine-gun. It was largely made from cheap, steel pressings, fired a short-case 7.92mm round to an effective range of 350 yards and provided the post-war design inspiration for Mikhail Kalashnikov. The intention had been for it to replace the Kar 98k but fortunately for Germany's enemies Hitler had interfered in the StG 44 development programme, delaying introduction by at least a year. The Kar 98k was the standard bolt-action rifle with a 5-round magazine and an effective range of 550 yards; by 1945 it was obsolete. Each rifle company fielded nine bipod-mounted MG 42, a general purpose, belt-fed 7.92mm machine-gun with an effective range of 1,100 yards. For those on the receiving end, the MG 42 was a frightening weapon due to its high cyclic rate of fire of 1,200 rounds per minute and the bone-chilling sound this made; it was ideally suited to defensive battles as ammunition could be stockpiled to feed its voracious appetite. In addition to eight MG 42 in the tripod-mounted, sustained-fire role, the battalions' heavy weapon companies were supposedly equipped with four 7.5cm le. IG18 light, infantry guns and six 8cm mortars. The 7.5cm infantry guns had a maximum range of 4,100 yards and fired HE, HE anti-tank (HEAT) and smoke rounds, while the 8cm mortar had a range of 2,700 yards and fired HE, smoke and illumination bombs. An online video (Appendix A, Serial 20) showing the division's sister division, 1. Marine-Infanterie-Division, when it was in the Zehden bridgehead on the Oder Front, gives an impression of the dress and equipment of the marines.

The regimental 13. Kompanie provided indirect fire with artillery and mortars. Under the Infanterie Division 45 establishment it should have had two 15cm s. IG33 heavy, infantry guns and eight 8cm mortars. Although it received the 8cm mortars there is no evidence in either

---

34 Bölscher, *Hitlers Marine im Landkriegseinsatz*, p.250. In 1941, Libau, the German name for Liepāja, was host to a series of appalling massacres of Jews, in which it is believed members of the *Wehrmacht*, including the navy, also participated (source Wikipedia).
35 Bölscher, *Hitlers Marine im Landkriegseinsatz*, p.168.

German or British accounts that it received the 15cm guns. 14. Kompanie had the *Panzerjäger* (anti-tank) role and in theory equipped with fifty-four *Panzerschreck* anti-armour weapons but probably largely replaced by *Panzerfaust*, which were liberally distributed throughout the battalions. The *Panzerschreck* was an enlarged copy of the US 3.5in rocket launcher (aka 'bazooka'); its HEAT, hollow-charge projectile had a range of 200 yards and could penetrate five inches of armour. The *Panzerfaust* was a shoulder-fired, disposable weapon firing a HEAT warhead capable of penetrating eight inches of armour. The weapon had a ferocious back-blast, which instantly revealed the firer's position so few survived to fire a second shot. Four types of *Panzerfaust* were fielded, the most common of which was the Panzerfaust 60 with a range of 100 yards.

Various arms and services supported the division. First the artillery regiment, Marine-Artillerie-Regiment 2, which provided the division's integral artillery support. The regiment was commanded by Major Karl Vogelsang and comprised four *Abteilungen* – three light and one medium – all commanded by army officers. Each *Abteilung* consisted of two batteries, each with six guns. The light batteries were equipped with a mix of horse-drawn 10.5cm le. FH, the standard German army field howitzer, and former Soviet army guns of the same calibre. The 10.5cm le. FH was a reliable gun but its maximum range of 11,675 yards was significantly shorter than its British and Soviet counterparts, the 25-pdr and 76.2mm M1939. The medium batteries should have been equipped with 10cm s. K18 but there is no evidence that these guns existed and in all probability the batteries were equipped with 10.5cm le. FH. To train the marine gunners, an Ultra decrypt revealed that on 25 March Wehrkreis VI ordered Artillerie-A.u.E Regiment 16 in Hamm to provide 35 assorted ranks to instruct the marines at their barracks in Glückstadt.[36] Whether or not this training ever took place is not known. Regardless of the state of the training, as there were no prime movers for its guns Marine-Artillerie-Regiment 2 was unable to deploy in early April with the remainder of the division and had to remain in Schleswig-Holstein until sufficient horses or oxen were acquired; this delay would have consequences for division and regiment alike. As an aside, the propaganda camera's focus on tracks and wheels has led to a misconception that the German army was fully motorised; this was far from the truth and to the end much of the German army remained dependent on horses.

The three companies of Marine-Panzerjäger-Abteilung 2 provided the division's heavier anti-tank and anti-aircraft firepower. The anti-tank company was equipped with twelve 7.5cm Pak 40 anti-tank guns, with the army providing the gun crews as the marines were neither trained in the Pak 40 nor in anti-tank gunnery tactics. Although heavy, the Pak 40 (shown on the front cover) was powerful with a usefully low profile, an effective range of 1,900 yards and an APCBC round which could penetrate all Allied tanks of the period.[37] The *Abteilung's* second company should have been a tank-destroyer company equipped with 14 Jagdpanzer 38(t) tank-destroyers (nicknamed *Hetzer* (Baiter)). Jagdpanzer-Kompanie 1199 was the allocated company but it never made the long journey to the Weser from the *Hetzer* training establishment at Milowitz, 25 miles northeast of Prague, where it was forming. The third company provided *Flak* support and consisted of three platoons each equipped with four 3.7cm Flak mounted on Steyr trucks; these were probably the vehicles and guns offered by Göring.[38]

The divisional engineering unit, Marine-Pionier-Bataillon 2 commanded by Major Rudolf Siegel, an army engineering officer who had served with the navy since 1940, provided limited combat

---

36 TNA DEFE 3/599, BT 8488, Wehrkreis VI order.
37 APCBC – armour-piercing, capped, ballistic capped. This round had a special cap to prevent shattering at oblique impact angles as well as a streamlined ballistic cap to increase velocity and penetration.
38 It is not certain that these vehicles and weapons reached the division. Although a report in an 11th Armoured Division INTSUM states that there was a *Flak* company equipped in this way, no truck-mounted 3.7cm Flak will be reported destroyed or captured by the British.

engineering, such as preparation of demolitions and construction of basic obstacles. Marine-Feldersatz-Bataillon 2 was the divisional manpower reserve comprising some 400 personnel. The role of *Feldersatz* battalions was to give additional training for replacements arriving in *Marsch* (transfer) companies and included a *Kampfschule* (combat school). However, given the short period between the division's formation and its committal to action, the *Feldersatz* battalion would not fulfil its replacement role and will instead be employed as a small infantry battalion. Logistics were the responsibility of Marine-Versorgungs-Regiment 200. A supply regiment would normally have bakery, butchery, repair and transport capabilities, but as there were severe deficiencies in trucks and fuel, the marines it was supposed to support were chiefly forced to live off the land and to move on foot. The establishment of the divisional headquarters was 34 officers, 87 NCOs and 106 other ranks and it was supported by a signal unit: Marine-Nachrichten-Abteilung 2. Little is known about the signal unit other than it should have had a telephone and a signals company and, if available, it would have been equipped with the standard radio transmitter for infantry divisions, the 5WS/24b-104, with a voice range of 10 miles. A *Marine-Küsten-Polizei* (naval shore police) platoon was part of the divisional headquarters.

Despite the marines' inexperience and youth – the average age was 20 – they were enthusiastic, some were still in formed crews and above all they were not battle-weary. They therefore represented a rare commodity in Hitler's Germany of 1945 and there was little comparison between these men and the usual scrapings of boys and old men, invalids and stragglers being swept into the army's ranks. As their knowledge of the tactical skills for land warfare was low, there was a significant distribution of army personnel within the division's structure. For instance, each grenadier regiment and battalion had an infantry adviser and as we have heard Marine-Artillerie-Regiment 2, Marine-Panzerjäger-Abteilung 2, Marine-Pionier-Bataillon 2 and Marine-Feldersatz-Bataillon 2 were commanded by army officers. Embedding seasoned officers and NCOs to bolster inexperienced units was not unique to the division and was normal practice in both the *Heer* and *Waffen-SS*. Despite the quality of the division's personnel, Dönitz issued a crude decree on 7 April to make sure there was no backsliding:[39]

> We soldiers of the *Kriegsmarine* know how we have to act. Our military duty, which we fulfil regardless of what may happen to right and left or around us, causes us to stand bold, hard and loyal as a rock of resistance. A scumbag who does not behave so must be hung and have a placard fastened to him, 'Here hangs a traitor who by his low cowardice allows German women and children to die instead of protecting them like a man.

This was no idle threat and summary execution was a very real prospect for a soldier found away from his unit for any reason, and roving military police and *SS* patrols represented a powerful deterrent to those who considered leaving the front.

In line with a suggestion made by Himmler, who had few days remaining as the incompetent commander of Heeresgruppe Weichsel, Hitler declared at the 1 March naval conference that once the second division's battalions became operational he favoured transferring them to the Angermünde area on the Oder's left bank, but at the same conference he also insisted that the division should deploy to the area of Griefenhagen, south of Stettin on the Oder's right bank.[40] Dönitz, perhaps wisely, said that before giving his opinion he would wait for a report from Konteradmiral Gerhard Wagner, his representative at Hitler's headquarters, who had been dispatched on a visit to 2. Marine-Infanterie-Division in its assembly area in Schleswig-Holstein. The failure to reach a

---

39   Ian Kershaw, *The End* (London: Allen Lane, 2011), p.306.
40   Showell, *Führer Conferences on Naval Affairs*, p.454.

decision at this conference was immaterial as the division's equipping was far from complete and it was still in no fit state to deploy. Two days later Hitler's frustration at the delay in providing equipment is clear when he insisted that it be equipped at once, a futile demand like so many made in the cloud-cuckoo-land of the *Führerbunker*.[41] In reply, Dönitz declared that the division could deploy 10 days after it received its equipment and that according to the divisional commander it must have use of a training area to practise artillery cooperation before moving to the front. Hitler rejected this proposal stating that there was no time for this, but that there was nothing to prevent the division from conducting the required training when it reached the front, without restriction on the use of weapons.

The remainder of March was spent feverishly trying to equip the division, and the time this took led to the focus for its deployment swinging to the West Front, where the British and Americans were becoming increasingly threatening. During the conference of 20 March, Keitel suggested that the division would best be deployed to the Emden area as it was feared a parachute or amphibious landing could take place there. Keitel's concern was not mere personal supposition as OKW was convinced to the last that large formations were available in England for mounting further invasions of northern Europe and Scandinavia, a belief that was a direct outcome of the continuing success of the Allies' strategic deception operation, FORTITUDE NORTH. Originally designed to confuse the Germans with additional threats as part of the D-Day deception plan, the successful FORTITUDE NORTH was sustained as it was in the Western Allies' interest to encourage OKW to keep forces away from their main axes into Germany. Ultra decrypts show how closely the Allies were able to monitor the deception's success, for instance a decrypt of 22 March reveals Führungsstab Nordküste predicting Allied landings in the Ems estuary area,[42] and a decrypt of 12 April shows OB West predicting that 'planned airborne operations (1st British and US 21st Airborne Divisions) in Bremen area will probably be east of the Weser to facilitate 2 Army's progress in Hamburg direction.'[43] It is surprising the Germans considered 1st Airborne, largely destroyed at Arnhem only six months earlier, could be ready for operations and the mention of US 21st Airborne Division reveals the depth of FORTITUDE NORTH's success as this formation did not exist and was part of the elaborate deceit.

Despite OKW's concern about the North Sea coast, no decision on 2. Marine-Infanterie-Division's deployment was taken at the 20 March conference and another 10 days passed before Dönitz raised the topic again by announcing that it was expected to be fully equipped in a week's time and requesting instructions as to where it should deploy for continuation training.[44] Keitel still advocated deployment to the Emden area rather than the Oder front but, with customary indecisiveness, Hitler replied that he would not make the decision whether the division went to the East or West Fronts until just before a deployment became necessary. Two days later his dilemma was resolved when Dönitz suggested that it should deploy to north-west Germany because of the threat posed by the British breakout from the Rhine bridgehead and that the division's comparatively well-equipped units should move immediately.[45] Hitler agreed and on 6 April the signal was transmitted from the Seekriegsleitung (Admiralty) to Marine-Oberkommando Nordsee allocating the division to Heeresgruppe 'H'.[46]

Konteradmiral Wagner was directed to arrange a speedy transfer with the proper authorities so that he could advise the *Führer* of the exact date and area of deployment. The decision taken was

---

41   Showell, *Führer Conferences on Naval Affairs,* p.456.
42   TNA DEFE 3/520, BT 8032, Führungsstab Nordküste appreciation on Allied intentions, 21 March 1945.
43   TNA DEFE 3/565, KO 234, OB West appreciation, 7 April 1945.
44   Showell, *Führer Conferences on Naval Affairs,* pp.473–474.
45   Showell, *Führer Conferences on Naval Affairs,* p.477.
46   Seekriegsleitung 1.Skl Ia 706/45 gKdos/Chefs den 6. April 1945.

> Seekriegsleitung			den 6.April 1945
> 1.Skl Ia 706/45 gKdos/Chefs.
>
> Verteiler: Skl Adm Qu   Pr.Nr. 1
>   Skl Adm Qu II   "   " 2
>   Ib   "   " 3
>
> **Chefsache! Nur durch Offizier!**
>
> Abschrift
>
> Fernschreiben an – KR – Blitz – MOK Nord (hat fernmündl. voraus)
>   nachrichtlich:
>   Mar Wehr Tr, Varel
>   Adm.z.b.V. (Koralle)
>
> Mit OKW/WFSt Op Nr. 88745/45 v. 2.April (Ergänzung zur Führerweisung für Kampfführung im Westen) wird für 2.Mar.Inf.Div. befohlen:
>
> "Zum frontalen defensiven Einsatz gegenüber vordringendem Feind wird die im Raum Glückstadt in der Aufstellung befindliche 2.Mar.Inf.-Div. (zunächst mit den bedingt einsatzfähigen drei Infanterie-Regimentern) der Heeresgruppe H unverzüglich über Bremen in Richtung Osnabrück zugeführt."
>
> Zusatz Skl: Hiermit Div. einsatzmäßig Heeresgruppe H unterstellt. MOK Nord nimmt sofort Fühlung mit Heeresgruppe H auf und regelt alle weitere in unmittelbarem Einvernehmen mit ihr.
>
>   Seekriegsleitung
>   1.Skl Ia 706/45 gKdos/Chefs.

Seekriegsleitung signal allocating 2. Marine-Infanterie-Division to Heeresgruppe 'H' and ordering its deployment to the Osnabrück area. (Mehner)

to deploy it towards Osnabrück as the rapidity of the front's collapse in this area required the division, as the last reserve of any quality, to move immediately to block a breakthrough by the British. However, owing to Hitler's prevarication, the Osnabrück option quickly evaporated as it was clear that the town would fall to the British before the division could reach the area. Another option was to deploy the division to the Netherlands to release more capable troops, but an Ultra decrypt of 6 April reveals that Blaskowitz judged the operational situation prevented this deployment and that he would deploy it instead to reinforce the defence of the Weser between Verden and Nienburg, a virtually undefended area with the bridges over the Weser at Hoya and Nienburg obvious objectives for the British.[47] The very welcome imminent presence of the naval division on the Weser meant that Blaskowitz avoided having to extract a division from elsewhere in his *Heeresgruppe* for this task, as revealed by an Ultra decrypt showing that 245. Infanterie-Division from II. Fallschirm-Korps was ordered on 5 April by an unstated headquarters, presumably Heeresgruppe 'H', to transfer immediately by rail from Löningen to the area Verden-Nienburg-Rethem.[48] The move never happened.

---

47 TNA DEFE 3/563, BT 9591, Blaskowitz signal pm 5 April 1945.
48 TNA DEFE 3/563, BT 9685, Deployment order 1300 hours 5 April 1945.

Owing to the speed of the British advance, getting 2. Marine-Infanterie-Division to the Weser and then having sufficient time to develop a defence was an unwinnable race so Scheurlen was directed instead to deploy the bulk of his division to the Aller. Here its deployment would stretch 25 miles from south of Verden to Schwarmstedt and its dispositions would be based on German positional defensive doctrine tempered by the realities of available weaponry, equipment, manpower and time. This doctrine had been in place since September 1942 and was the result of Hitler's policy *Grundsätzliche Aufgaben der Verteidigung* (Fundamental Tactics of Defence),[49] which essentially, and disastrously, returned German ground forces to the rigid, ground-holding linear defence of the early years of the Great War and ended the flexible defence favoured by his front-line commanders. In accordance with this doctrine, the division established a main line of resistance (MLR) on the Aller's right bank, with the road bridges at Rethem and Essel the points of defensive effort. Although situated on the left bank, Rethem offered an excellent defensive opportunity so here the MLR switched from the right bank to include the town, which became the division's main effort and attracted additional combat power. The division's MLR had two outer layers: advanced positions on the Weser's right bank at Nienburg and Hoya, and outpost positions in villages two to three miles from the Aller on its left bank. The advanced positions would be the first opposition the enemy would contact and their purpose was to confirm his axes, force him to conduct opposed river crossings and buy time before their defenders withdrew along predetermined routes to the Aller. The function of the outpost positions was to disrupt enemy preparations for attacking the MLR, determine his intentions and inflict casualties. Withdrawal would again be via predetermined routes and the outpost positions would be registered for indirect fire for engagement once abandoned. Wherever possible, both types of position would be established in settlements within range of friendly artillery and mortars and occupied by platoon-strength forces with MG 42 as the principal weapon; when available, heavy *Flak* and Pak 40 would be sited in the positions.

Most elements of Armeegruppe Student began to deploy to their battle positions during the latter half of the first week of April, with speed of the essence owing to the rapidity of the front's collapse. The order to 2. Marine-Infanterie-Division to deploy was issued on 6 April and the same day the marines left their barracks to meet troop trains at Husum, Glückstadt and Eckenförde for the journey to the Aller.[50] Despite the enormous damage wreaked on the German railways by Allied bombing, the extensive redundancy in the former Prussian network allowed re-routing to avoid areas of destruction and many lines remained just about functional to the end. The division's deployment was spread over a number of days and nights to avoid the constant threat from Allied fighters, roaming at will and making daylight movement extremely dangerous. The trains managed to reach Verden and Rethem unscathed and the marines then deployed on foot, bicycle or on very limited road transport to their areas of responsibility. The division's subsequent deployment is shown on Map 7.

The first regiment to arrive was Kapitän zur See Neitzel's Marine-Grenadier-Regiment 7, which reached Verden on the same day. He immediately deployed his two battalions to defend the division's right flank: I./7 deploying on a south-easterly orientation between Verden and Neddenaverbergen, while II./7 remained in close proximity to Verden itself. Holding the battalions in this area and not deploying them forward to the Aller to Verden's south-east would have repercussions as the battle unfolded. Some elements of the regiment crossed to the Aller's left bank

---

49 Major Timothy A Wray, 'Standing Fast: German Defensive Doctrine on the Russian Front during World War II', *Combat Studies Institute, Research Survey No.5*, https://www.armyupress.army.mil/Portals/7/combat-studies-institute/csi-books/wray.pdf, p.119 (accessed 19 July 2019).
50 Bölscher, *Hitlers Marine im Landkriegseinsatz*, p.374.

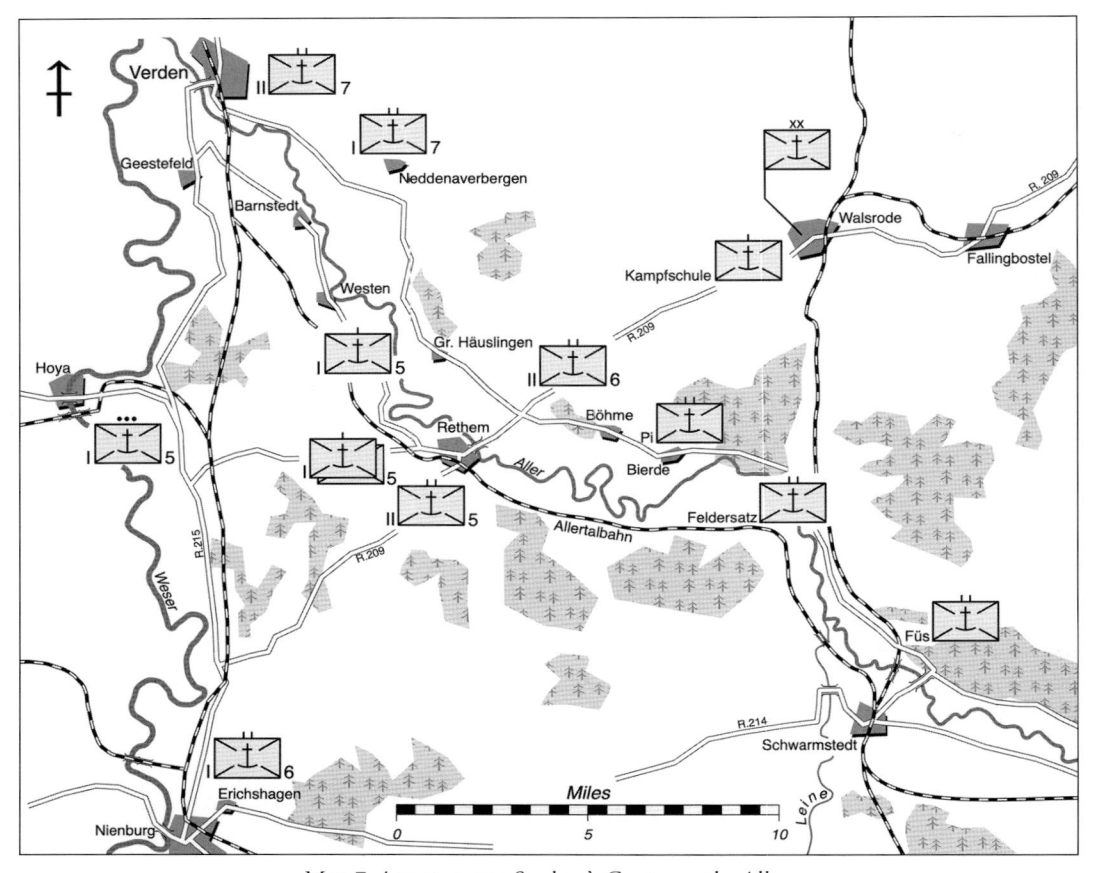

Map 7 Armeegruppe Student's Centre on the Aller.

and occupied outpost positions in the villages of Geestefeld and Barnstedt situated in the triangle of land between the Aller's final reaches and its junction with the Weser.

Next to arrive was Marine-Grenadier-Regiment 6, which left Husum by train in the early hours of 6 April and reached Rethem that night. The regiment's task on the MLR was to defend the sector Gross Häuslingen to Böhme on the Aller's right bank. Kapitän zur See Hartmann was also ordered to provide a battalion to hold a strong advanced position at Nienburg, which would cover two main roads: Reichsstrasse 209 – the road to the Elbe at Lauenburg – and Reichsstrasse 214 – the road to Celle and Brunswick. Leaving behind battalion II./6 to start preparing positions on the MLR, Hartmann, his regimental headquarters and I./6 marched through the night 6/7 April to Erichshagen on Nienburg's north-east outskirts, which they reached at dawn on 7 April. Here Hartmann immediately took command of the Nienburg sector from Oberst Otto Lichtschlag, formerly in charge of Wehrbezirkskommando (recruiting sub-district office) Nienburg. Hartmann and his marines would enjoy the area for less than 24 hours.

Korvettenkapitän Josef Gördes' Marine-Füsilier-Bataillon 2 arrived at Rethem on 7 April then deployed that night on foot, bicycles and a few trucks the 15 miles to the division's left flank and the second point of defensive effort: the road bridge over the Aller to the north of Schwarmstedt. Here the battalion was significantly reinforced, as will be described in Chapter 7.

Kapitän zur See Jordan and the marines of Marine-Grenadier-Regiment 5 were the last to reach Rethem, arriving on 8 April and immediately deploying to the Aller's left bank to defend the

Rethem point of main effort. The town's defence was allocated to battalion II./5 reinforced with the two regimental heavy companies, two companies from I./5 and a company of Pak 40 from Marine-Panzerjäger-Abteilung 2; the remaining company of I./5 was allocated to the villages of Hülsen and Westen, both on the Aller's left bank downstream from Rethem. Jordan also deployed a small force forward to the Weser at Hoya to act as an advanced position and cover the town's road and rail bridges.

The division's support elements moved to cover the remaining frontage of the Aller's right bank: Marine-Pionier-Bataillon 2 deployed as infantry to the area of Bierde to the east of Rethem; the four companies of Marine-Feldersatz-Bataillon 2 went four miles further east to cover the Hodenhagen area, while the Kampfschule was held in depth covering Reichsstrasse 209 from the western edge of Walsrode. Marine-Artillerie-Regiment 2 was of course still plodding its way down from Schleswig-Holstein. Scheurlen and his divisional headquarters established themselves in the village of Ebbingen to the north-west of Walsrode and on 7 April Heeresgruppe 'H' instructed Armeegruppe Student to take the naval division under command.[51]

Armeegruppe Student's centre on the Weser

As mentioned, shortage of time prevented 2. Marine-Infanterie-Division – excepting Hartmann and his battalion I./6 – deploying to the Weser, leaving the line of the river within Wehrkreis X's area very thinly defended, with the few available forces concentrated on the crossing places at Nienburg and Stolzenau. Just to the south of Stolzenau lay the boundary with Wehrkreis XI, and here responsibility for the river's defence changed to Korps Hannover. In the Nienburg area and additional to the marines of I./6, were 400 men of Landesschützen-Bataillon 1020. *Landesschützen* battalions consisted of old men and the medically downgraded and were mostly used for guard duties at vital installations and PoW camps. Their men were very poorly trained and equipped with assorted captured foreign weapons, often with little or no ammunition, and bicycles. Also in the area were 300 engineer officer candidates of Pionier-Reserve-Offizier-Bewerber Bataillon Nienburg (Pi.ROB.Btl. Nienburg). A *ROB* was a reserve officer applicant. Qualified volunteers and suitable conscripts from the ranks were initially designated as reserve officer applicants and attended a 10-month course, usually conducted by the headquarters of the relevant training and replacement unit, to become section or equivalent level commanders. Following training they would transfer to a field unit to prove themselves; if successful, they were appointed *Fahnenjunker* (officer candidates) and sent on an officer course. The men of Pi.ROB.Btl.Nienburg were therefore at the start of their training to be junior commanders and were therefore of reasonable quality.

* * *

There was, however, a significant unit in the Nienburg area, which will play a major part in the account and prove a determined foe for 11th Armoured Division. This unit was SS-Panzer-Grenadier A.u.E. Bataillon 12 'Hitlerjugend' (SS-A.u.E.Btl.12 'HJ'), a *Waffen-SS* training and replacement battalion for 12. SS-Panzerdivision 'Hitlerjugend'. The battalion originally formed in Arnhem in late 1943 to provide trained replacements for its parent division, then assembling at Beverlo training camp south-east of Antwerp. During the battle for Normandy the division sustained very heavy losses and by August 1944 its original training and replacement battalion had been largely consumed as reinforcements. However, it left behind in the Netherlands its permanent

---

51   TNA DEFE 3/564, BT 9816.

staff company and some manpower, which, re-designated as SS-A.u.E.Btl.16 'Reichsführer SS' and with intakes of new recruits, would soon play an important role in the battle for Arnhem as a *Kampfgruppe* under its commander, SS-Sturmbannführer (major) Sepp Krafft.

Following the defeat in Normandy, 12. SS-Panzerdivision 'Hitlerjugend' fought its way back through northern France and Belgium and while it did so its new training and replacement battalion was forming at Kaiserslautern in the Saarland, close to Germany's border with France. The first 170 recruits arrived on 23 August at the Dänner Kaserne, one of three barracks on the town's eastern outskirts, and began eight weeks of basic training delivered by veterans, many of whom were recovering from wounds and injuries. By late September 1944 the heavily-depleted parent division, now only 40 percent of its 6 June strength, had reached the Saarland to reconstitute and the remnants of SS-Panzer-Grenadier-Regiment 26, one of the division's two *Panzer-Grenadier* regiments, joined the nascent SS-A.u.E.Btl.12 'HJ' in Kaiserslautern and occupied both of the town's other two barracks.

Despite being back in the *Reich*, there was no relief from the enemy as Kaiserslautern's railway marshalling yards became a target for Allied bombing and as all three barracks were located only a mile from the yards and lay under the bomb-run for enemy aircraft, the soldiers were at particular risk. The first raid occurred on 28 September 1944 when 217 Lancasters dropped 900 tons of bombs, destroying 36 percent of the town's buildings and killing 144.[52] In the aftermath of this raid, taking place only nine days after the swearing-in ceremony of the battalion's first 400 recruits, the soldiers were deployed to assist in rescue and recovery work, exposing them to the horrors of death, injury and destruction. It seemed, however, that the *Waffen-SS* units in Kaiserslautern would escape further bombing as a few days after the RAF raid, the refitting division was ordered to move from its various locations in the Saarland to north-west Germany and to an area bounded by the towns of Deipholz, Sulingen and Bassum, all to the west of Nienburg, where it would continue to refit. In spite of the order, by 14 October the units in Kaiserslautern had yet to move so were subjected to US Eighth Air Force Mission 676, a raid against the marshalling yards mounted by 117 B-24 Liberators.[53] Although there is no record of military casualties, the soldiers were again severely shaken by the bombing and what they witnessed. Perhaps the raid acted as a catalyst for the movement staff as the next day SS-A.u.E.Btl.12 'HJ' began to prepare for a rail move and on 18 October about 500 young men, their instructors, a couple of *Kübelwagen* (German equivalent of the jeep) and a handful of motorbikes with side-cars were put on two trains and began a tortuous journey northwards to Nienburg, a journey that took place largely at night and included numerous detours to bypass damaged sections of track.

SS-A.u.E.Btl.12 'HJ' was organised and functioned in much the same way as all army and *Waffen-SS* training and replacement battalions and so consisted of a *Stamm Kompanie*, an *Einstellungs Kompanie*, a *Genesenden Kompanie*, a variable number of training companies (hereafter *SS-Kompanie*), four *Marsch* companies, and three companies of the *Unterführer-Lehrgang*. The battalion's total strength was some 1,800 personnel. The *Stamm Kompanie* was the permanent staff company and included the battalion headquarters. The *Einstellungs Kompanie* inducted new recruits and issued them uniforms, *Soldbücher* (the booklet giving personal details such as the soldier's photograph, equipment on issue, service history, training and pay rate), ID tags, personal weapons and so forth. Once inducted, the recruits joined one of the training companies. With training completed, they would join a *Marsch* company to await dispatch to the deployed

---

52 Martin Middlebrook and Chris Everitt, *The Bomber Command War Diaries, An Operational Reference Book* (Harmondsworth: Penguin Books, 1985), p.590.
53 Eighth Air Force Historical Society, 'Combat Chronology July – December 1944', *https://www.8thafhs.org/combat1944b.htm* (accessed 2 July 2017).

Feldersatz-Bataillon 12, where they received final training before joining the division's field units. However, since the retreat from France, Feldersatz-Bataillon 12 had ceased to exist and for the remaining months of the war recruits were fed piecemeal to the division. The *Genesenden Kompanie* rehabilitated previously wounded soldiers and the *Unterführer-Lehrgang* provided further training for those showing potential to be NCOs.

At the time of its move to Nienburg, SS-A.u.E.Btl.12 'HJ' was commanded by SS-Obersturmbannführer (lieutenant colonel) Bernhard Siebken, a recent commander of II./SS-Panzer-Grenadier-Regiment 26.[54] On arrival in Nienburg, Siebken established his headquarters in the station hotel, while the Stamm, Einstellungs and Genesenden companies set themselves up in barracks at Langendamm on the town's south-eastern outskirts. The Unterführer-Lehrgang was initially located in Wunstorf but subsequently relocated to Neustadt am Rübenberge (hereafter Neustadt) a few miles to the north. The Langendamm barracks were built in 1935 as part of the infrastructure supporting Lufthauptmunitionsanstalt 3/XI, a *Luftwaffe* munitions factory and storage depot, and here the Einstellungs Kompanie soon became extremely busy inducting a stream of conscripted recruits arriving daily from areas of the *Reich* still unoccupied by the enemy. Shortages of materiel and clothing resulted in the recruits being issued the bare minimum, for instance they received only one pair of combat trousers, a pair of laces but no boots to put them in and a single ammunition pouch. Uniform without holes was a rarity, ID tags were in short supply – later resulting in soldiers going into action without them – and replacement footwear more often than not clogs. Other than a steel helmet, headwear was virtually non-existent. The flow of recruits continued right up to the time the battalion deployed for action, although it would seem that few volunteered to serve in the *Waffen-SS*, as observed in a late April 1945 British INTSUM on the battalion:[55]

(i) A PoW of Dutch-German parentage, originally registered in Arnhem, moved subsequently to Celle. From there he was sent to Wehrbezirkskommando Ausland in Berlin,[56] where he was informed he had volunteered for the *SS* and that Arnhem had turned him down as he was only 1.63m tall. By a convenient mistake he was now found to be 1.65m (the minimum required for *SS* service), sent home and immediately called up to Nienburg.

(ii) Other men were sent, on completion of Reichsarbeitsdienst [(RAD) (Labour Service)] service, to Nienburg 'by mistake' and then drafted into the *SS*, again 'by mistake'.

(iii) In February, youths awaiting their call-up were collected at Seesen [in the Harz] and harangued for half-an-hour by a *SS* officer. Very few volunteered, but most of the others said they would think it over. Immediately they were congratulated on their decision and in due course received *Einberufung* [conscription order] as *SS* volunteers.

The battalion's seven training companies were distributed among villages in Nienburg's hinterland and here the young soldiers were billeted in schools, inns, civic buildings and barns. The initial journey to their billets was conducted on foot owing to the almost complete lack of unit vehicles, and given that each recruit had to carry all his equipment and possessions on his back and most of the locations were at least eight miles from Nienburg, this was arduous. Furthermore, it was not a one-off journey as over the next few months some activities, such as delousing and the showing of

---

54 The British hanged Siebken in 1949 for his part in the murder of three Canadian PoWs on 9 June 1944. Many believe that his superior, SS-Obersturmbannführer Wilhelm Mohnke, should have hanged instead for this war crime.
55 TNA WO171/4277, 53rd Welsh Division INTSUM.
56 This office dealt with the registration and call-up to military service of German citizens living in occupied and neutral foreign countries.

educational films, were centrally-delivered requiring the recruits to make a return trip to Nienburg in the same day. The physical impact of these marches and the demands of field training needs to be seen in the context of 1945 for these were no longer the fit, sun-bronzed youths of *Nazi* propaganda and the strain of war had taken its toll on the nation's young and adults alike, as Hubert Meyer, former *SS-Obersturmbannführer* and 1a of 12. SS-Panzerdivision 'Hitlerjugend', describes:[57]

> The years of war had not passed by the boys without a trace. Their fathers were soldiers, many dead or missing. Their mothers were working outside the home, their teachers and *Hitlerjugend* leaders were, in most cases, soldiers and had been replaced insufficiently and with difficulty. The bombing raids on the residential quarters of the cities had ripped many of them from their normal environments by destroying their homes and being evacuated. In addition, many of the boys were poorly nourished and had only limited ability to endure more strenuous exertions.

Improving the young soldiers' stamina required rations to be increased in terms of quality and quantity, no easy task in 1945 given the challenges facing agriculture and the transport of foodstuffs, and company staff needed to be resourceful. Most companies reared their own pigs, and all probably followed the example of SS-Sturmscharführer (sergeant major) Grabher-Meyer, the company sergeant major (universally known in the army and *Waffen-SS* as *Der Spieß*, 'The Spear') of 2. SS-Kompanie billeted in Rodewald, who traded the welfare cigarettes of those still under 18 for bread and cakes from the farmers. This illicit trade was a constant source of apprehension for the company commander, SS-Obersturmführer (lieutenant) Marsen, who feared that this and other black-market activities would lead to his court martial. With rations in such short supply, the local people often took pity on the young men providing them with additional food and on Sundays inviting them to meals. Even at this late stage of the war few farmers went without.

The recruits received a short but tough training using the limited weaponry issued to the battalion: chiefly Kar 98k rifles and StG 44 assault rifles, grenades, MG 42 and *Panzerfaust*, but no heavy weapons other than mortars. Particular emphasis was placed on realistic firearms' training using methodology gained from experience on the East Front, which emphasised accuracy and firing under simulated battle conditions. Such training had been a feature of the battalion's parent division since the early days of its formation and members of 1st Commando Brigade would soon discover its effectiveness to their cost. Although by the end of their training they were far from the hardened soldiers normally associated with the *Waffen-SS* and were little more than Hitler Youth in soldiers' uniforms, they were numerous, fired with fanaticism and commanded and mentored by *Waffen-SS* officers and NCOs with considerable combat experience. Substantial effort was put into toughening the youths for the task ahead, as a brutish pamphlet found later on a captured member of the battalion reveals:[58]

> Always shoot first! The man who shoots first lives longer!
> I or you: this is the question that will soon every minute of the day affect you and your opponent. At the front there is no mercy at all. Men fight, shoot, strike, bite, scratch and trample in an orgy of physical destruction. You're ill-prepared for battle if you are not quite

---

[57] Hubert Meyer, *The 12th SS. The History of the Hitler Youth Panzer Division: Volume One* (Mechanicsburg: Stackpole Books, 2005), p.12. Meyer was a committed *Nazi* and after the war the last chairman of *Hilfsgemeinschaft auf Gegenseitigkeit der Angehörigen der ehemaligen Waffen-SS* (HIAG), the extreme right wing association for rehabilitating the *Waffen-SS*.
[58] TNA WO171/4104, Guards Armoured Division War Diary.

clear as to what battle means; it means that you must kill if you want to stay alive! Killing is the Englishman's natural inclination. He pictures war as sport. An old English wisecrack says 'Hunting lions is good, hunting man is better, hunting Germans is best of all.'

And so, as you can understand, it means nothing to him to maul and main women and children with high explosive and phosphorous. This is why fighter-bombers harass you with bomb and cannon. This is why it happens that you alone, a solitary gunner, are engaged by a whole battery of English guns. For your enemy in the west, KILLING IS A SPORT!

We Germans take neither joy nor pleasure in killing.

Perhaps one day, you will catch yourself laughing and rejoicing when the enemy is being shot to pieces, when men are being mown down by the hundred in the fierce fire of your company. That's how it should be – you must overcome your reluctance to kill. Abandon the thought that you not only kill the man, but bereave his mother, wife or children. One second, comrade, just one second of such thoughts can bring death to you or the soldier next to you. And if you die, the enemy's bullet brings the same sorrow to your family or your comrade's. And they are many thousand times more valuable than a bloody bolshevik's flock of brats.

KILLING IS YOUR DUTY!

Prepare for it. Practise it with your weapon and learn to master it. And make your heart very hard! Then you will not shrink from the realities of war. Bleeding, wounded, torn maimed men in frightful death-pangs, stiff corpses; these are the sights you must be accustomed to seeing. If you don't kill, you may soon be lying among these groaning victims. You must realise, that if you lack the courage to look all these horrors squarely in the face before you go into action, you will all suffer all the more in the fury of battle.

If ever weakness threatens to overcome your will to annihilate the enemy, then think of all the thousands of women and children that you, and you alone, must revenge. Our enemies have done them to death with cynical cruelty. War abolishes all laws that forbid you to kill. War brings God and the Earth into unison; it sanctifies the earthly task of killing through the heavenly power of your dedication to yourself.

And so, in the hour of war, the law of the soldier is this: BE READY TO KILL!

On 30 October 1944, soon after its arrival in Nienburg, the battalion despatched 250 trained replacements in *Marsch* companies to join the parent division, now to the west of Nienburg where it was continuing to reconstitute. These young soldiers were joined by some 2,000 reinforcements from the *Kriegsmarine* and *Luftwaffe*, numerically strengthening the division but diluting what remained of its elite character. In early November, for participation in the Ardennes offensive, the division moved to a concentration area west of Cologne, leaving behind SS-A.u.E.Btl.12 'HJ' in Nienburg. Following the offensive's failure, the division briefly returned to the concentration area before deploying to Hungary at the end of January 1945 as part of 6. Panzer-Armee's last ditch attempt to counter the Soviet advance towards the Hungarian oilfields. By March 1945 the battalion's strength had decreased to 700-800 men, the *Marsch* companies and the Unterführer-Lehrgang had shrunk to single companies and that month the battalion provided the division with its last reinforcements, many of whom were recuperated wounded from the Normandy battles. Time had now run out for any further reinforcement of the division and the battalion's final intakes of 17 to 19-year-old recruits faced the prospect of fighting with the battalion in their homeland.

The battalion's orbat in early April 1945 is shown at Figure 4 and command of the battalion, now bearing the nickname Kampfgruppe 'Panzerteufel' (Tank Devil), was in the hands of 29-year old SS-Hauptsturmführer (captain) Heinz Peinemann, a former policeman and member of 1.

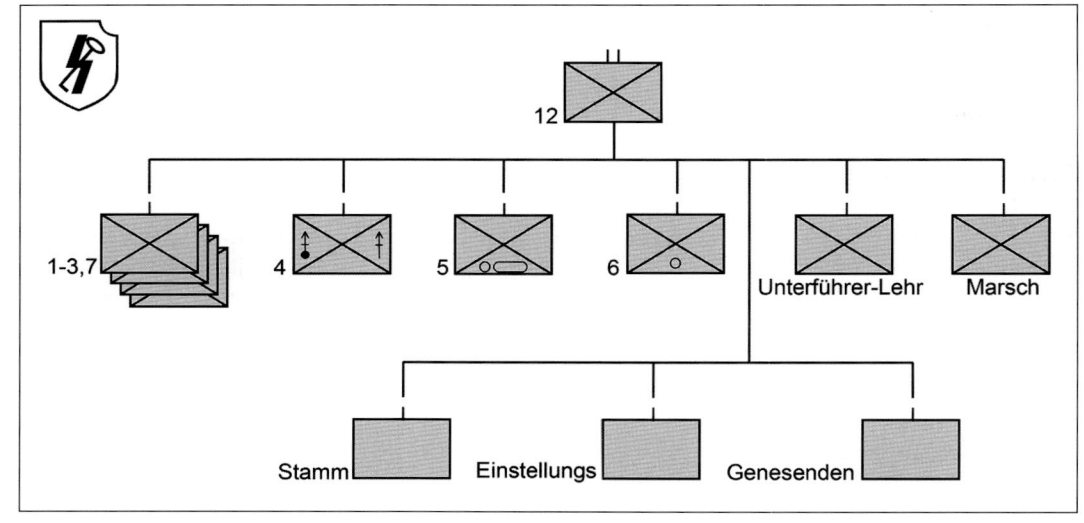

Figure 4 SS-A.u.E.Btl.12 'HJ' – April 1945.

SS-Panzer-Division 'Leibstandarte Adolf Hitler' prior to transferring to 12. SS-Panzer-Division 'Hitlerjugend' when it was at Beverlo. He later commanded 3./I SS-Panzergrenadier-Regiment 25 in Normandy, where he was wounded. The very tall Peinemann would have struck an imposing figure.

Once the Allies had crossed the Rhine, life for the young soldiers became far more serious with uniform worn on a near-permanent basis, live-firing exercises and night route marches frequently conducted and practice call-outs initiated. Defences were dug and constructed in the host villages, much to the consternation of the inhabitants, with emphasis on all-round defence as there was little idea of the enemy's likely direction of approach. Initially the companies remained in their villages, although 3. SS-Kompanie, commanded by SS-Untersturmführer (2nd lieutenant) Greiners and based in Haßbergen to the north of Nienburg, deployed to the Weser's left bank via the Eystrup ferry to guard the approaches to the bridge at Nienburg. Once in position, the company's young soldiers acquired surplus munitions and weaponry from disorganised units trudging back to escape the advancing Second Army and under the impression that their part in the war was ended. On 26 March the swearing-in ceremony of the final cadre of trained recruits took place in a clearing at Erichshagen on Nienburg's northern outskirts; all companies attended, making their way on foot. As the parade would be reviewed by Reichsjugendführer Artur Axmann accompanied by an *SS-Gruppenführer* (major general), the soldiers with the least blemishes on their uniforms were placed in the front ranks and 4. SS-Kompanie, the heavy weapons' company, displayed its machine-guns and mortars.

While the battalion was conducting its final preparations, there was a flurry of orders and counter-orders for its future deployment. An Ultra decrypt of 3 April noted:[59]

> SS Panzer Grenadier Training and Ersatz Battalion One Two on twenty-fifth to be brought up to Operations Staff North Coast for employment as security garrison in second defence line.

---

59 TNA DEFE 3/562, BT 9326, 3 April 1945.

The 'twenty-fifth' referred to in the decrypt was 25 March, while 'Operations Staff North Coast' was Führungsstab Nordküste. This direction to deploy as a security garrison soon changed and a decrypt of an *Ordnungspolizei* communication recorded Amt II (operations department) of the SS-Führungshauptamt (operational headquarters of the *SS*) ordering the battalion on 30 March to deploy immediately by rail to the area bounded by the towns of Friesoythe, Westerstede and Leer,[60] an area forward of the Weser and lying astride a British axis of advance to Bremen. The battalion's advance party was to report immediately to Korps Ems and the battalion on its arrival would be subordinated operationally and for rations to the Korps not Führungsstab Nordküste. However, almost immediately there was another change of plan and on or just after 1 April the battalion was placed under command of Division Nr.480 and ordered to establish defensive positions on the road linking Verden with Ottersberg and centred on the village of Völkersen, 10 miles in depth of the Weser's right bank.[61]

Despite the Völkersen mission, no movement orders were received for this and for the next two days the battalion remained in the Nienburg area. On 1 April, Allied fighters shot up goods wagons carrying ammunition, including V-2 warheads, at Nienburg station. The ammunition detonated and the ensuing massive explosion not only caused widespread destruction but its magnitude meant that it was heard by every company in proximity to Nienburg, serving as a portent for what was soon to come. On the morning of 3 April, the battalion received new orders to concentrate at Mehlbergen railway station, on the Weser's left bank two miles north-west of Nienburg, and board a goods train for a now unknown destination but probably the Sulingen area.[62] It would seem that the order concerned only the training companies, as the Stamm and Marsch companies remained at Langendamm. Without delay, on foot and on bicycles, the companies set off from their host villages for Mehlbergen, with many of the young soldiers pulling handcarts containing equipment and ammunition, while requisitioned tractors and agricultural vehicles towed the field kitchens and carried heavier items of equipment and ammunition. The companies progressively arrived at Mehlbergen station and just before dusk, with the risk of Allied fighter attack diminished, they boarded the train. The final element to be loaded were 18 SdKfz 251 half-tracks,[63] recently appropriated by the battalion while transiting Nienburg to join Panzer-Ausbildungs-Verband 'Grossdeutschland', fighting with 15. Panzergrenadier-Division to the north. Designed as an armoured troop carrier for infantry in the battle area, but not for use in the assault, the SdKfz 251 was a successful vehicle and its versatility made it the basis for a broad range of specialist variants. The half-tracks were just about to be driven onto the railway flats when yet another order was received, ordering the battalion to disembark and immediately deploy to defend the right bank of the Weser south of Nienburg, with the main effort at Leese, a small town opposite Stolzenau and set back about a mile from the river.[64] The probable reason for this abrupt change of plan was the realisation in Armeegruppe Student that the battalion was the only available source of troops to fill the void in the Weser's defences to the south of Nienburg and that it would be far better employed there. No doubt puzzled by the sudden change and amid rapidly spreading rumours, the young soldiers busied themselves unloading the train.

---

60   TNA HW13/205, INTSUMS medium and low-grade communications, ZIP/CIRO PEARL/WJO/W/331, 13 April 1945, p.2.
61   Wolfgang Buchwald, *Endkampf – Das Schicksal des Ausbildungs-und-Ersatz-Bataillons „Kampfgruppe Panzerteufel" der 12. SS-Panzer-Division „Hitlerjugend"* (Privately published, 1977), p.19.
62   Buchwald, *Endkampf*, p.20.
63   'SdKfz' stands for *Sonderkraftfahrzeug* or special purpose vehicle and was a generic descriptor for all military vehicles.
64   Buchwald, *Endkampf*, p.20.

74   THEIRS THE STRIFE

For its new task the battalion's companies deployed in four groups, with their deployment areas shown at Map 8. The first group, 6. SS-Kompanie, was ordered to deploy forward as tank-hunters armed with *Panzerfaust* and the company immediately prepared to head off westwards on bicycles to attack and delay the advancing British armour. The second group, consisting of 1. SS-Kompanie, 2. SS-Kompanie and three platoons of the Marsch Kompanie, was ordered to defend the right bank of the Weser upstream from Nienburg as far as Leese, with 1. SS-Kompanie and the Marsch Kompanie platoons ordered to defend the area of Landesbergen and Estorf, while 2. SS-Kompanie covered Leeseringen, Schäferhof and the remaining stretch of bank to Nienburg. The heavy weapons' company, 4. SS-Kompanie, distributed its mortar and MG 42 teams between the second and third groups.

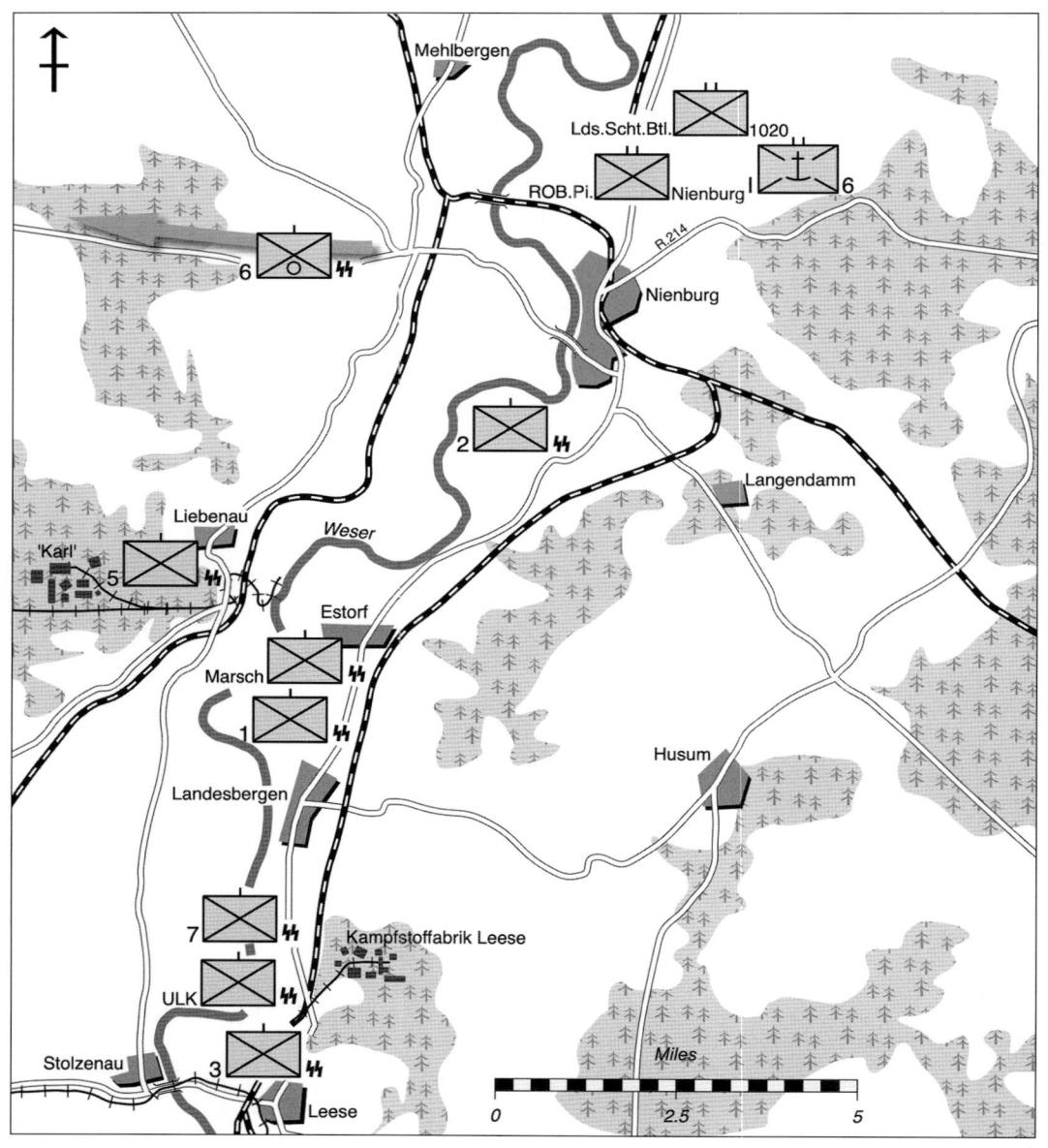

Map 8 Armeegruppe Student's Centre on the Weser.

The third group, comprising 3. SS-Kompanie, 7. SS-Kompanie and the Unterführer-Lehr Kompanie, was ordered to defend the Stolzenau sector, currently commanded by Major Helmig, a *Luftwaffe Flak* officer commanding scant infantry but substantial quantities of *Flak*, soon to be described at the end of this chapter. The Weser at Stolzenau was bridged by a triple-span, steel lattice-truss bridge, which carried not only the road but also on the same deck the Steinhuder Meerbahn, a narrow-gauge railway, which ran from Wunstorf to Uchte. As it would take some time for this third group to reach Leese, two further platoons of the Marsch Kompanie under SS-Unterscharführer (sergeant) Peter Koslowski left Langendamm to act as the advance party for Leese's defence. The three companies duly set off from Mehlbergen, crossed the Weser at Nienburg then tramped south on the road to Leese. On arrival that evening, 3. SS-Kompanie established the command post and the regimental aid post (RAP) in Leese's station buildings while the other companies began to dig positions along a mile of the high embankment on Leese's western edge that carried the Nienburg to Minden railway and provided sufficient elevation to see as far as the roofs of Stolzenau on the Weser's left bank. This was an obvious feature to defend as it not only dominated the meadows bordering the Weser but also overlooked the approaches to Leese from the west. Also prepared was an outpost position near the Weser bridge, from where any enemy movement coming over the levee, which paralleled the river, could be engaged. The initial defensive deployment at Leese is shown on Map 9.

SS-Obersturmführer Wilke's 5. SS-Kompanie, comprising the fourth group, had been allocated the SdKfz 251 half-tracks and was ordered to remain on the Weser's left bank and be prepared to defend the substantial explosives' manufacturing complex, nicknamed 'Karl',[65] concealed in the forest near Liebenau to the south-west of Nienburg. 'Karl' was one of five plants in the Eibia GmbH explosives' production group, which all employed slave labour to produce nitro-cellulose, nitro-glycerine and diethylene-glycol-dinitrate explosives.[66] V-1 flying-bomb warheads were filled at 'Karl' and it is probable that the same process took place there for V-2 warheads.[67] On 4 April, 5. SS-Kompanie was ordered to move to 'Karl', so the company mounted its half-tracks and drove the short distance southwards from Mehlbergen. As they entered Liebenau the inhabitants frantically pulled in the white sheets hung from their windows in expectation of an imminent British arrival. The sudden appearance instead of the *Waffen-SS* must have caused panic as such open displays of defeatism were frequently met with summary executions. Although the inhabitants of Liebenau might not have been aware of it, the day before 5. SS-Kompanie arrived in the village Himmler had issued a Germany-wide decree ordering all males to be shot in any house flying a white flag.[68] Probably because 5. SS-Kompanie had more pressing priorities, the male citizens of Liebenau would seem to have escaped this fate and there is no evidence of executions.

With the four groups now deployed, the teenage soldiers of SS-A.u.E.Btl.12 'HJ' awaited the enemy's arrival. Their wait would not be long.

---

65 'Karl' had an area of 3,000 acres and comprised three hundred buildings, 50 miles of roads and 20 miles of railway. It is estimated that 2,000 slave labourers died there.
66 Eibia GmbH, Anlage 'Karl', Liebenau, *http://www.relikte.com/liebenau/index.htm* (accessed 9 Sep 2015). The other four plants were Waldhof, Walo I and Walo II at Bomlitz and the plant at Dörverden.
67 The V-1's formal title was Fieseler 106. The 'V' stood for *Vergeltungswaffe* or Retaliation Weapon. The V-2's formal title was Aggregat-4 (A-4).
68 Ian Kershaw, *The End*, p.323.

76 THEIRS THE STRIFE

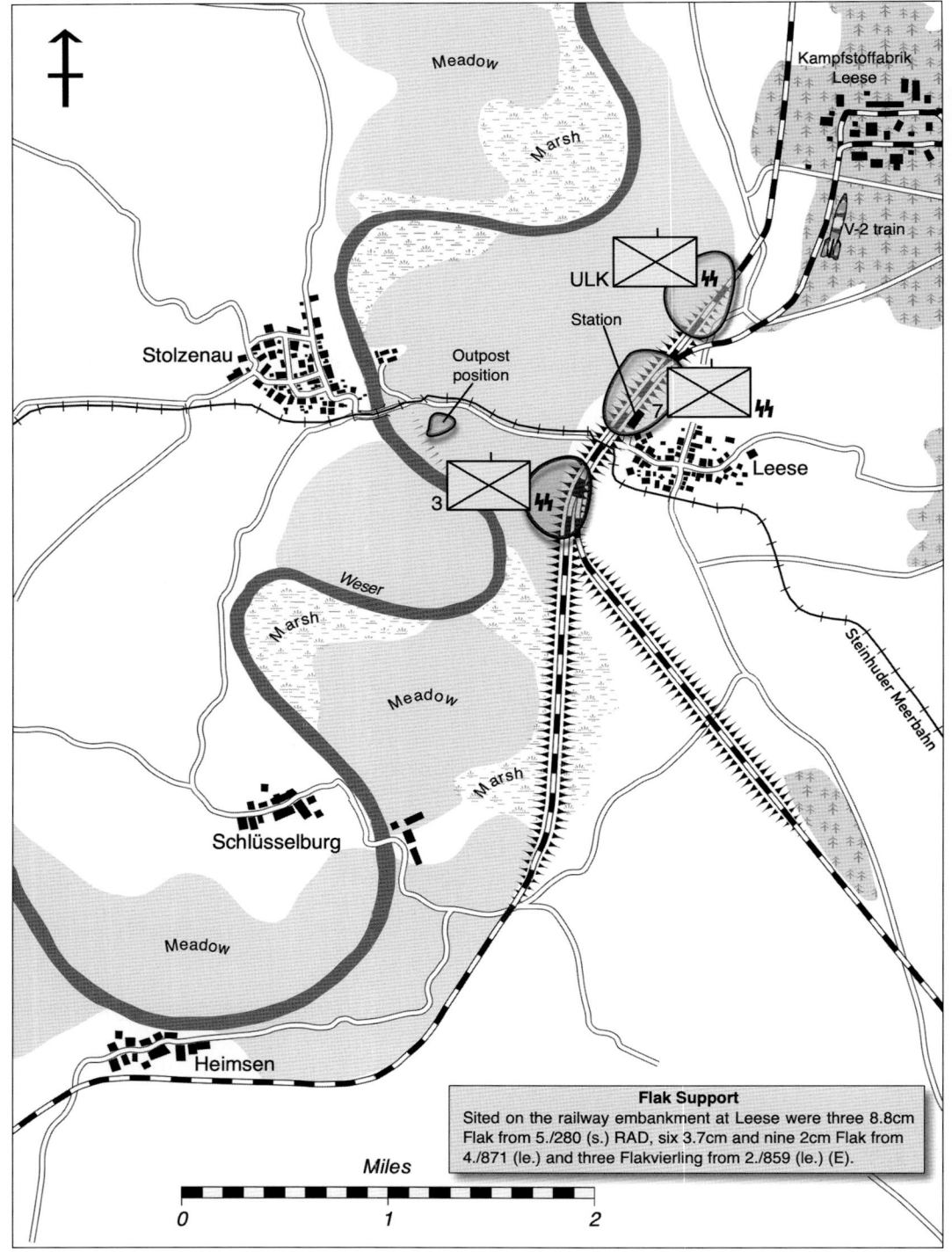

Flak Support
Sited on the railway embankment at Leese were three 8.8cm Flak from 5./280 (s.) RAD, six 3.7cm and nine 2cm Flak from 4./871 (le.) and three Flakvierling from 2./859 (le.) (E).

Map 9 The Defence of Leese.

Armeegruppe Student's left flank on the Weser

For his left flank on the Weser to the south of Stolzenau and beyond, Student would have to rely on General der Infanterie Walter Lichel's Korps Hannover.[69] In accordance with Aktion Leuthen, Lichel, the commander of Wehrkreis XI, had formed Korps Hannover from the scrapings remaining in his *Wehrkreis*. Despite its impressive title, Korps Hannover was woefully weak as the bulk of its training and replacement units had already deployed and the cupboard was now nearly bare. Its last recognised formation had been Division Nr.471, the majority of which had been dispatched in late March to join LXXXVI. Armee-Korps on the West Front (the remainder deploying to the Oder Front) but then, as described in the previous chapter, largely destroyed in the defence of Ibbenbüren.

The left flank was divided into the three sectors shown on Map 10. The northern sector lay within Wehrkreis X and followed the line of the Weser between Stolzenau and the Weser-Mittelland Canal aqueduct in Minden, and was named after the towns of Petershagen and Stolzenau. Its commander was Major Ferber, an engineer officer and chief instructor of the seven officer candidate courses at the engineer Pionierschule II at Dessau-Roßlau near Leipzig in Wehrkreis XI. In late March 1945, the school's remaining trainees and staff were formed into Pionier-Sperr-Brigade 1100 (Engineer Obstacle Brigade) under Major Ferber and deployed to the Weser. The brigade, consisting of two battalions, each of three companies, was tasked to demolish bridges over the Weser and Mittelland Canal and construct obstacles. Responsibility for bridge demolition always carries significant risk but particularly so in 1945, not only from control difficulties owing to the general breakdown in communications and the chaos of retreat, but the recent failure to demolish the Ludendorff Bridge at Remagen had resulted in the execution of two of the officers responsible for its demolition. As a consequence, for the remainder of the war those with demolition responsibilities tended to blow bridges early with little or no reference to the requirements of withdrawing troops or other operations. Once Pionier-Sperr-Brigade 1100's demolition tasks were completed, the brigade deployed as infantry on the Weser's right bank, with two of the first battalion's companies occupying the area of Heimsen to the south of Stolzenau, while the third company was at Lahde opposite Petershagen. Also in the northern sector were elements of Pionier-Ersatz-Bataillon 6 and parts of two companies from Bataillon I./590 of 325. Infanterie-Division, aka Infanterie (Schatten) (Shadow) Division 'Jütland'. *Schatten* divisions only had combat arms and their role was to bring depleted divisions back to strength. Division 'Jütland', mainly comprising former naval personnel, had been largely destroyed in the retreat from the Rhine but remnants had managed to withdraw over the Weser where they were corralled into the riverline's defence.

The left flank's central sector was across the boundary in Wehrkries XI and here the Weser was dominated by Minden and the Wesergebirge uplands, with the Mittelland Canal and the Cologne to Berlin autobahn also running through the area. Oberstleutnant Otto commanded the sector, which was weakly held by engineer training and replacement troops from Pionier-Brücken A.u.E. Bataillon 2, a bridging unit; part of Pionier-A.u.E. Bataillon 6; the second battalion of Pionier-Sperr-Brigade 1100; infantry from Grenadier-A.u.E. Bataillon 159, marines from Grenadier-Regiment I./590, assorted *Landesschützen* and *Volkssturm*, and tank-hunting teams from Panzerjagdverband 'Großer Kurfürst' (see below). While these units mustered some 3,000 men, the weapons' return at Figure 5 from an Ultra decrypt gives us a precise picture of the woeful under-equipping.[70]

---

69 Günter Wegmann, *Das Kriegsende Zwischen Ems und Weser 1945* (Osnabrück: Kommissionsverlag Wenner, 1982), pp.108–114.
70 TNA DEFE 3/561, BT 9248. Strength return by Kampfkommandant Minden, 31 March 1945.

78 THEIRS THE STRIFE

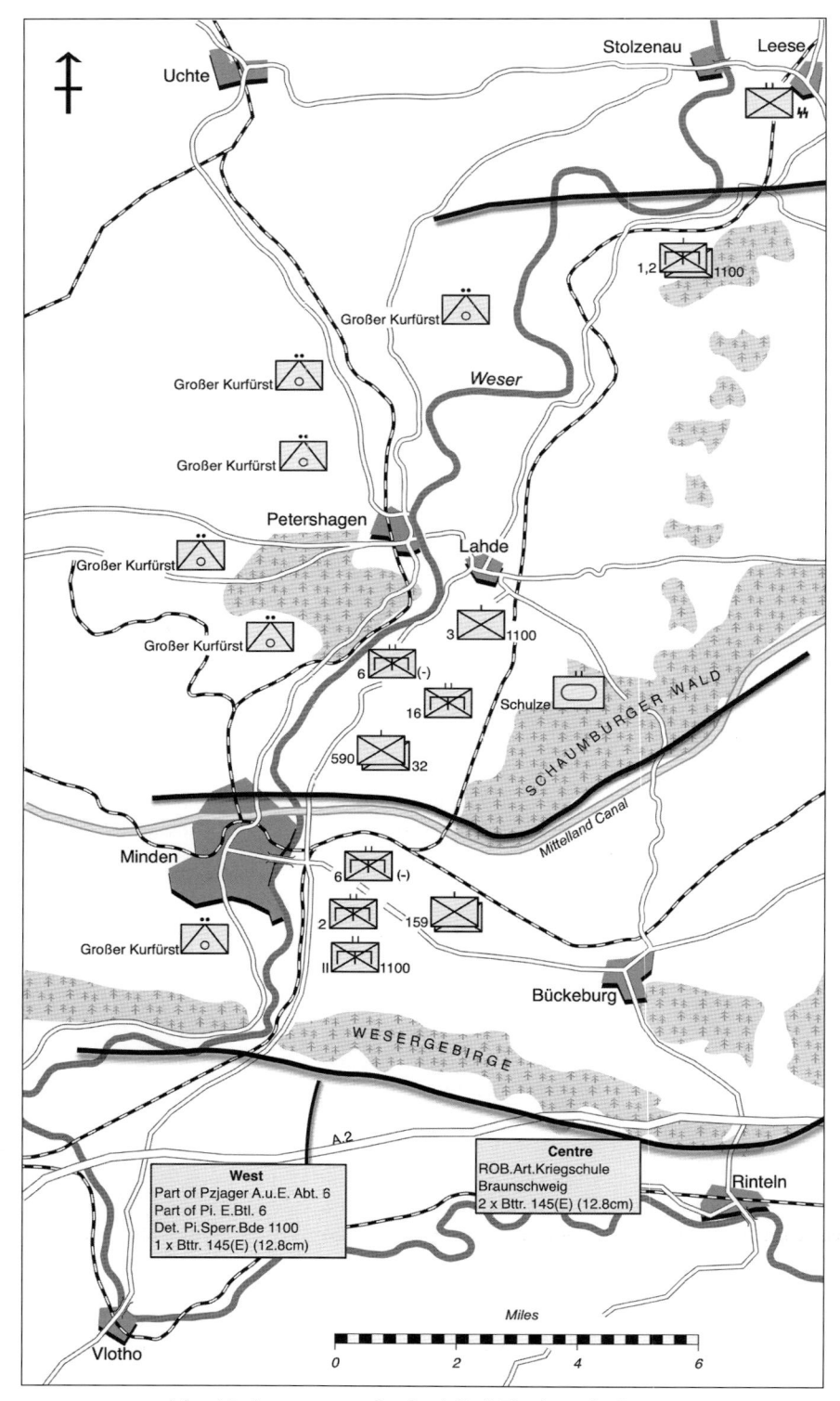

Map 10 Armeegruppe Student's Left Flank on the Weser.

Unit	Officers	NCOs	Men	Rifles	MG	Panzerschreck	Panzerfaust
Grenadier A.u.E Btl. 159	11	87	520	72 K98 82 Danish	8	4	90
Pi.A.u.E.Btl.6	6	157	725	271 K98 581 Danish	3		56
Pi.Brücken A.u.E.Btl.2	1	57	1005	281 K98	2		49

Figure 5 Minden Sector Weapon Return as at 31 March 1945.

Supporting the infantry in the western fringes of Minden were a few StuG IV and Panzer IV/70 (aka Jagdpanzer IV) tank-destroyers. The vehicles probably belonged to Panzer-Ersatz-Abteilung 11, which had fought briefly at Bielefeld on 3 April before being forced eastwards to the Weser. The StuG IV and Panzer IV/70 were both turretless, armoured fighting vehicles based on the Panzer IV chassis. Although the original StuG concept was to give infantry formations an assault gun for providing close support direct fire, as the war progressed the increasing threat from enemy tanks led to the vehicle being up-gunned with the StuK 40 L/48 gun, the same gun as the Panzer IV, and a change in role to tank-destroyer. The Panzer IV/70 was developed as an improved version of the StuG IV. It had a very low height profile of just over six feet, mounted the same 7.5cm KwK 42 L/70 as the Panther and was, when used in the role for which it was designed, a most successful tank-destroyer; it was far less successful when used as a tank substitute.

The southern sector of Student's left flank covered the Weser south of the Wesergebirge forested hills. Here the river flows from the east before taking a 90-degree, northwards turn at Vlotho to pass through an impressive gap it has cut in the ridge before heading north to Minden. The sector was commanded by Major Picht and was divided into east, centre and west sub-sectors to cover the east-west flowing river. To confront US XIII Corps, soon to reach the area, the sector could field only weak, extemporised groupings based on training units supported by mainly static *Flak*. The arrangements for defending Rinteln, the sector's main town, and its important bridge over the Weser reveal the parlous state of the defence. Overall responsibility for Rinteln was vested in the senior officer in the area, one Oberstleutnant Petermann, who as commander of Heeresmusikschule I in Bückeburg would have been deft with the baton but probably a doubtful field commander.[71] To generate additional forces for Rinteln's defence Petermann ordered Oberfeldarzt Dr. Engelhardt of the Reservelazarett (general hospital) Rinteln to contribute wounded soldiers and his medical staff; Engelhardt's reaction to this order is recorded as 'Petermann in Bückeburg is totally mad!',[72] and he ignored the order.

Armeegruppe Student's left flank on the Aller

In addition to Marine-Füsilier-Bataillon 2, Student's left flank on the Aller (see Map 11), was held by Kampfgruppe Totzeck, Kampfgruppe Scherer and Gruppe Grosan, all formed as part of Aktion Leuthen.[73] Beyond these forces to the south and east lay a military void. The two *Kampfgruppen* were generated from staff and trainees of the Nebeltruppenschule at Celle. This school, commanded by

---

71 A famous student of the school was the composer and big band leader James Last, aka Hans Last, who was a cadet at the school in 1943.
72 Wegmann, *Das Kriegsende Zwischen Ems und Weser 1945*, p.114.
73 Ulrich Saft, *Krieg in der Heimat* (Walsrode: Druckerei Gronemann, 1988), pp.69–72.

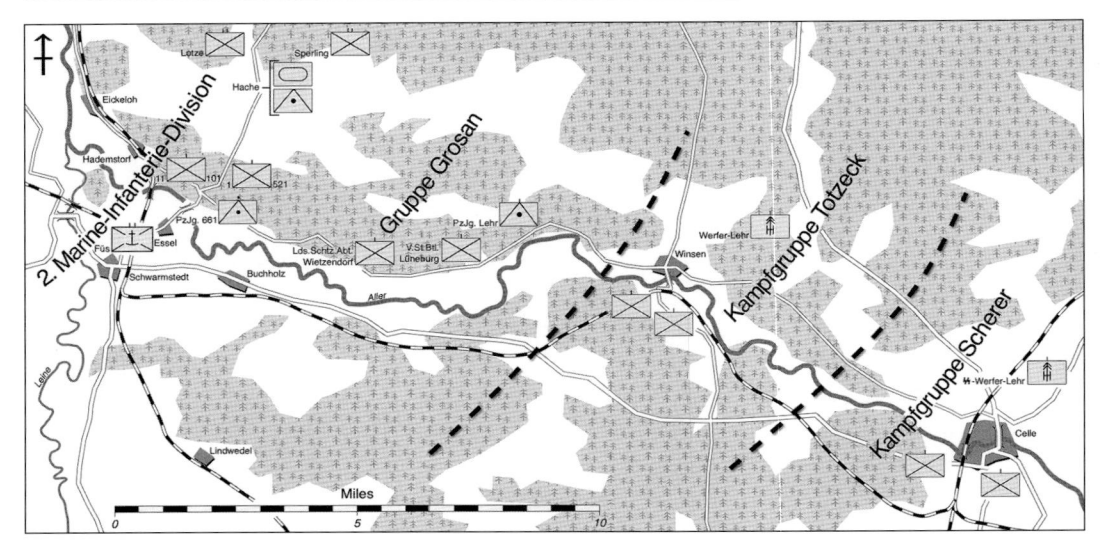

Map 11 Armeegruppe Student's Left Flank on the Aller.

Oberst Stroh, was responsible for training rocket troops in the employment of the various calibres and types of launcher projecting rocket-propelled smoke and high explosive rounds. The school had three training wings, Lehrstab A (officers), B (NCOs) and C (technicians), and a demonstration unit, II./Werfer-Lehr Regiment. The school also contained the Heeres-Unteroffizier-Schule für Nebeltruppen, but this had deployed as infantry as part of Division Nr.471 and, as described in Chapter 1, subsequently destroyed at Ibbenbüren.

Kampfgruppe Totzeck, commanded by Oberst Erich Totzeck, commandant of Lehrstab A, comprised three companies of officer trainees supported by two batteries of *Nebelwerfer* from II./Werfer-Lehr Regiment. The *Kampfgruppe* initially deployed on the Aller's left bank to cover the southern approaches to the road bridge at Winsen, the next major crossing upstream from Essel. Kampfgruppe Scherer, commanded by Oberst Scherer, commandant of Lehrstab B and C, consisted of two companies of *Nebelwerfer* NCO and technician trainees and deployed to defend Celle and its road and rail bridges. The *Nebelwerfer* launchers of the SS-Werfer-Lehr-Abteilung from Lachendorf near Celle supported Kampfgruppe Scherer. Both *Nebelwerfer* units were equipped with various forms of launcher, from SdKfz 4/1 armoured half-tracks (nicknamed *Maultier* (Mule)) mounting 10 tubes for firing 15cm Panzerwerfer 42 rockets, to assorted calibres of towed launchers. All were effective area weapon systems but their capacity to take part in the battles on the Aller would be severely constrained by lack of towing vehicles, mainly owing to fuel shortages, and as a consequence many, particularly the *Maultier*, never deployed and were abandoned near their Celle barracks. The orbats of the two *Kampfgruppen* are shown at Figure 6.

Additional to being the centre for *Nebelwerfer* training, Celle was also home to Heeres-Gasschutz-Schule 1. Although Hitler banned the employment of gas and chemicals in warfare as he feared Allied retribution in kind, training in their offensive and defensive employment continued during the war. As smoke rounds were essentially a chemical munition and most of the *Nebelwerfer* doctrine was based on the techniques for projecting gas or chemicals, it was logical that the Nebeltruppenschule and Heeres-Gasschutz-Schule 1 were co-located. Gasschutz-Schule 1 was, in less stressful times, commanded by Generalmajor Paul Tzschökell but he was now appointed Kampfkommandant Celle and Uelzen with responsibility for the defence of the two towns and their general area. It is probable that the staff from his headquarters deployed with him.

THE ROCK OF RESISTANCE   81

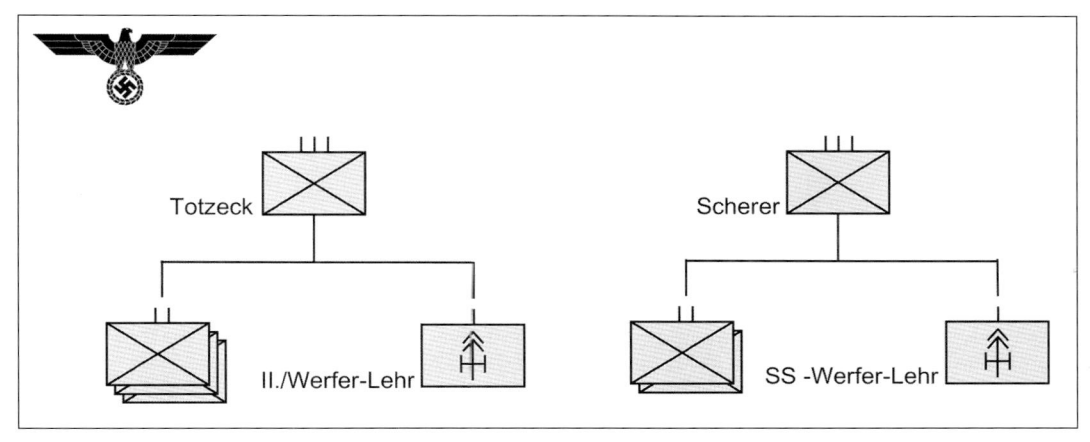

Figure 6 Kampfgruppen Totzeck and Scherer – 6 April 1945.

Gruppe Grosan had its origin in the Panzertruppenschule (School for Armoured Troops) Bergen, situated 40 miles to the north of Hannover. In the mid-1930s the German Army had begun its radical expansion, requiring a corresponding increase in the size and quantity of its training areas. As the sparsely populated Lüneburg Heath was identified as being ideal for this purpose, the few inhabitants were promptly removed and extensive training areas and tank ranges formed, the southernmost being on an area of heath called the Heidmark. To meet the requirement for training two divisions simultaneously, large barrack complexes were built on the Heidmark's western and eastern extremities at Fallingbostel and Bergen-Belsen. By 1943, however, the capacity to raise and train divisions as complete entities was over and the principal role of the barracks changed to providing accommodation for reconstituting depleted formations. The deteriorating operational situation also drove other changes, chief among which was the need to improve armoured training, and a key development in this respect was centralising the training on Bergen. The first move took place in August 1943 when the armoured forces school Panzertruppenschule I Wünsdorf relocated from south of Berlin, where it was in any case vulnerable to Allied bombing, to occupy barracks in Bergen and re-title itself Panzertruppenschule Bergen. The school ran courses for regimental commanders and for battalion and company commanders of tank, *Panzer-Grenadier*, anti-tank and armoured recce units. In October 1944 it was joined by Panzertruppenschule Krampnitz, also from the Berlin area, which moved with its technical and tactics courses and their associated tank and *Panzer-Grenadier* demonstration units to become Panzertruppenschule II Bergen. So, by early 1945, Bergen contained both schools, with their demonstration units based in the barracks at Örbke at the northern end of the Fallingbostel barracks' complex. However, by this stage the demonstration units were heavily run down as much of their capability had been fed to their parent formation on the western front, the Panzer-Lehr-Division.

Although the army's training establishments were part of the Ersatz Heer, the training organisation for armoured forces came under the Generalinspekteur der Panzertruppen, which was independent of OKH and reported direct to Hitler. Hitler established the inspectorate on 28 February 1943 and appointed as its first commander Generaloberst Heinz Guderian, who became responsible for the organisation, technical development, doctrine and training, and replacement system for armoured forces and the command of all armoured schools and their instructional staffs. On 21 July 1944, in the immediate aftermath of the failed attack on Hitler's life, in addition to his duties as the *Generalinspekteur*, Guderian was appointed Chef des Generalstabs des Heeres (Chief of Staff of the Army), a largely figurative post as Hitler had long-since usurped its responsibilities. There then followed for Guderian eight months of extreme difficulty as he attempted to stave off the army's collapse while endeavouring, whenever possible, to stand up to Hitler and his lunatic directions and misjudgements. Guderian was one of the very few generals prepared to argue with Hitler and he consequently trod a dangerously narrow path, from which he finally diverted on 27 March 1945 when he flatly contradicted Hitler in his accusations of incompetence against a colleague. Fortunate not to have been shot, Guderian was instructed instead to take six weeks' sick leave and on 3 April his post as chief of staff passed to General der Infanterie Hans Krebs. No replacement was found for his post as *Generalinspekteur* and it is believed that his duties were assumed by his deputy, Generalleutnant Wolfgang Thomale.

In late March 1945, as part of Wehrkreis XI's contribution to Aktion Leuthen, Generalmajor Oskar Munzel, the commander of Panzer-Truppen-Schule Bergen, was ordered to deploy the armour school's remaining men and vehicles to the West Front. Munzel was not, however, destined to command these forces because Generalleutnant Thomale, or perhaps Guderian in one of his last actions, ordered him to deploy to the Fulda area with the bulk of his headquarters and using training units from central Germany, form an *ad hoc* formation entitled Panzer-Ausbildungs-Verband 'Thüringen'. Munzel duly departed, leaving behind his deputy, Oberst Erhard Grosan, a member of the Panzer-Truppen-Schule since losing a leg in Russia in 1943, to prepare the school's manpower and armoured vehicles for deployment. When Munzel tried a few days later to order Grosan to deploy these assets he could not reach him, with the result that Grosan remained in Bergen awaiting orders. With no further direction forthcoming from Munzel, Grosan decided to contribute the remaining elements of the Panzer-Truppen-Schule to the defence of the local area, an unsurprising decision given his reputation as a forceful personality and determined commander. The grouping, now named Gruppe Grosan and shown at Figure 7, became part of Armeegruppe Student.[74]

During the first days of April Grosan formed his *Gruppe*, principally comprising three infantry *Kampfgruppen* and an armoured group, with the commanders provided by staff and instructors from the various wings of the Panzer-Truppen-Schule. The *Gruppe* had a total strength of between 1,800-2,000 men.[75]

Oberst Heinrich Volker, an experienced combat commander, holder of the Knight's Cross and responsible for the Regimentsführer-Lehrgänge (regimental commanders' course) at Bergen, gave his name to the first of the infantry *Kampfgruppe*. Originally intended to form part of Panzer-Division 'Clausewitz', Kampfgruppe Volker consisted of three rifle companies and a heavy weapons' company equipped with a few mortars. As the most capable and ready of the three *Kampfgruppen*, Grosan ordered it to deploy westwards to the Weser as soon as possible and defend Loccum, in depth of the Hitler Youth companies at Leese. Major Rudolf Kahle, previously an instructor in armoured engineering, commanded Grosan's second infantry *Kampfgruppe*, which consisted of two battalion-sized units – Bataillon Lotze and Bataillon Sperling – manned by former *Luftwaffe* and naval personnel augmented with stragglers corralled at collection points. Unsurprisingly, these men were poorly trained and lacked motivation. Both battalions had four companies, each consisting of two 30-man platoons principally equipped with Italian machine-pistols (probably Beretta Model 38A, commonplace in the *Wehrmacht*), MG 42 and *Panzerfaust*. Major Köhler commanded Grosan's third infantry *Kampfgruppe*. Köhler was an instructor on the *Panzer-Grenadier* company commanders' course and his *Kampfgruppe* comprised two battalions manned with stragglers and Hungarians under training. Köhler's battalions did not deploy but were held at Bergen to await developments and will not play a part in the account.

Additional to these *Kampfgruppen*, Grosan had available to him some very low-quality infantry from Landesschützen-Abteilung 'Wietzendorf' and Volkssturm-Bataillon 'Lüneburg'. The *Landesschützen* unit was probably the guard force from Oflag 83 at Wietzendorf, six miles

---

74 FMS, B-414, Heeresgruppe 'H' (March–May 1945), Anlage 3, p.-d-.
75 Saft, *Krieg in der Heimat*, pp.159–160.

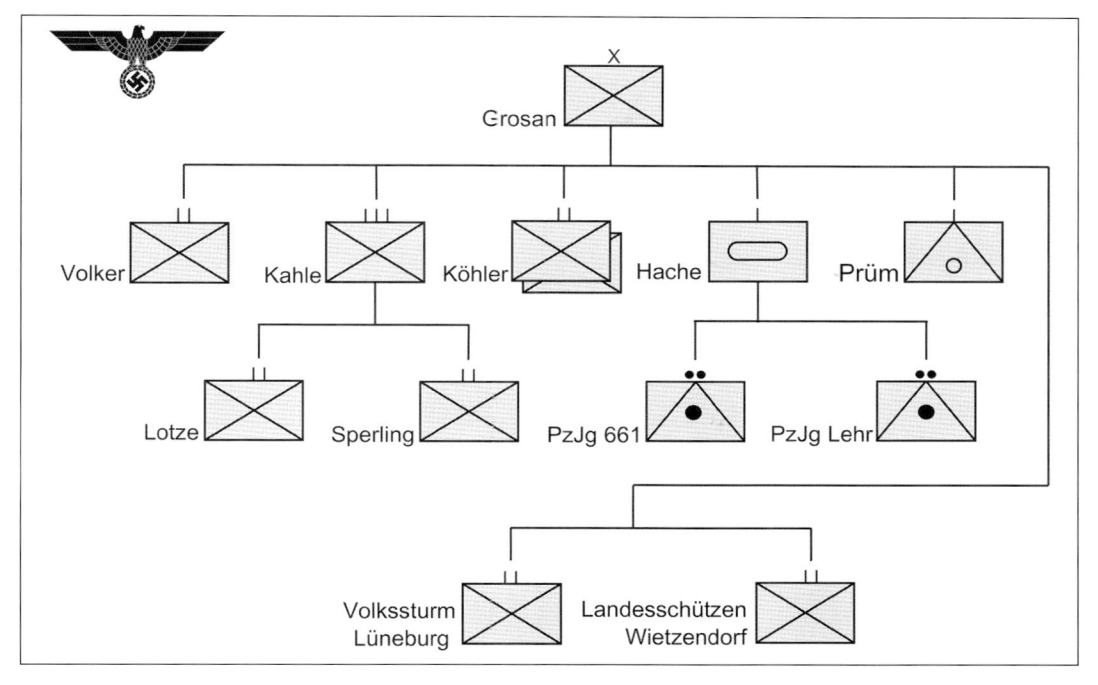

Figure 7 Gruppe Grosan – 6 April 1945.

north of Bergen. By 1945 the camp was holding 3,000 Italian officer prisoners so the removal of the bulk of its guard force to bolster the front further illustrates the terminal state of German manpower. Raised as a National Socialist organisation, the *Volkssturm* was a state militia manned with conscripted males between the ages of 16 and 60; its units therefore consisted of Hitler Youth, the elderly and the infirm. Those for whom arms were available would mostly have carried obsolete foreign weapons, with all the inherent problems of ammunition supply. *Panzerfaust* were however liberally available and unlike many *Volkssturm*, Volkssturm-Bataillon 'Lüneburg' wore uniform. For anti-aircraft defence and direct fire Grosan had sequestered from local *Flak* units two 2cm Flak, one 3.7cm Flak, two 4cm Flak (Bofors) and three 8.8cm Flak 41, all crewed by gunners of the RAD. For bridge demolition and cratering Grosan had some limited engineering support provided by Pionier-Kompanie Golde, an improvised grouping of engineers believed to be from Pionier-Ersatz-Bataillon 6 and Pionier-A.u.E. Bataillon 26.

A number of tanks and tank-destroyers belonging to Panzer-Truppen-Schule Bergen and some vehicles that had formerly been on the strength of the tank training area and ranges at Putlos on the Baltic coast provided Grosan with his armour. From this pool of vehicles he formed two groups, with the first named Kampfgruppe Schulze after its commander, Major Paul Schulze. Schulze was a most courageous and experienced tank officer, who had been awarded the Knight's Cross in December 1943 as a *Hauptmann* (captain) commanding II./Panzer-Regiment 21, and the Oak Leaves in July 1944 as a major commanding Panzer-Abteilung 21. He had been at Fallingbostel since September 1944 when he assumed command of 6. Lehrgruppe (Demonstration Group), which supported Panzer-Truppen-Schule II Bergen, although based at Örbke near Fallingbostel. Örbke had been home to Panzer-Lehr-Regiment 130 but in Spring 1944 the regiment deployed to Normandy with its parent division and by April 1945 all that remained of the Panzer-Truppen-Schule's demonstration capability were remnants of the *Lehrgruppe*. In March 1945 Schulze's

84   THEIRS THE STRIFE

responsibilities changed to command of the Aufstellungsstab-Lehrtruppe, an activation staff for organising new armoured units and providing a residual training and replacement capacity.

Schulze was ordered, probably by Grosan, to form his group from the tanks remaining at Örbke. He gathered up 11 vehicles and divided them into two sub-groups: a six-tank Tiger group commanded by Oberleutnant Rudolf Fehrmann and a five-tank Panther group commanded by a Leutnant Kurt von 'S'.[76] Kampfgruppe Schulze's organisation is shown at Figure 8.

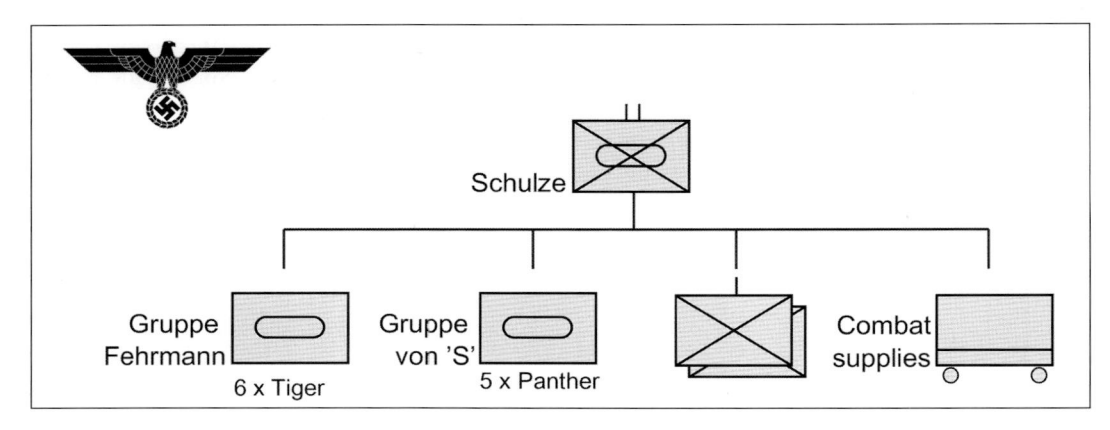

Figure 8   Kampfgruppe Schulze – 4 April 1945.

The Tiger I was the standard, German heavy tank. It was robustly protected by thick, homogeneous nickel-steel rolled armour and although its design premise favoured firepower and protection over mobility, it still had reasonable speed. Its firepower advantage lay in the very effective 8.8cm KwK 36 L/56 gun, firing an APCBC round capable of penetrating four inches of armour at 1,100 yards, and in the precision of its sighting optics. The Tiger I was also armed with three MG 34. Set against these qualities it was over-engineered and took twice as long to build as the Panther, it consumed expensive, scarce and labour-intensive materials, its weight in action placed huge demands on the engine and transmission, both prone to failure, and the turret traverse speed was very slow. Although the Tiger I remained formidable, the latest Allied tanks outclassed it and by September 1944 Tiger I production had ceased in favour of the Tiger II, aka Königstiger. At least three of Kampfgruppe Schulze's Tigers belonged to the Lehrkompanie für Panzer-Fahrlehrer, a tank driver-training company. Two were hybrids, with wheels and commander's cupola from various marks, perhaps reflecting the need for cannibalisation to keep the tanks in service and the lower spares' priority for training vehicles. Contemporary photographs of three of the Tigers show them respectively bearing turret numbers F01, F02 and F13. While some suggest that 'F' stood for Fehrmann, the Germans did not use personalised call-signs, the numbers do not follow their tactical numbering system and it is very unlikely that an *Oberleutnant* would give his name to a grouping within a *Kampfgruppe* commanded by a major. It is more probable that as the Tigers came from the tank driver-training company, 'F' stood for '*Fahrlehrer*' (ie learner driver).

The Panther was an outstanding compromise of mobility, firepower and protection and arguably among the best tanks fielded by any nation during the war. The Ausführung (Ausf.) G was the Panther's final mark and incorporated a wide range of improvements derived from battlefield experience. The Panther had excellent sloped frontal armour, its very effective 7.5cm KwK 42 L/70 gun could penetrate nearly five inches of armour at 1,100 yards, and it was fast with good

---

76   For personal reasons his surname has not been disclosed.

cross-country performance. The Panther was, however, mechanically unreliable and vulnerable to flanking fire as its side armour was thin owing to a compromise on weight. This vulnerability was exacerbated by shortages of critical alloys for armour plate, such as tungsten and molybdenum, resulting in the Ausf. G having lower impact resistance levels compared to Panthers of earlier years. The Panthers belonged to the Panzerjäger-Lehr und Versuchs Kompanie, a trials and development unit which had been trialling infra-red (IR) equipment for night-fighting. In April 1945 it held five Panther Ausf. G tanks and three SdKfz 251 half-tracks, probably the SdKfz 251/20 variant as this mounted 60cm IR searchlights for operating with IR-equipped Panthers. The Panthers and half-tracks had their IR equipment removed before deploying with Kampfgruppe Schulze. Additional to the two tank groups, Schulze formed two companies of infantry using scrapings of manpower. Later British intelligence reports suggest that the companies were supported by two 7.5cm Pak 40, four 7.5cm le. IG 18 light infantry guns and 8cm mortars, although there is no subsequent evidence for these weapons.

With action imminent, there was feverish activity to bring these training vehicles up to fighting standard and provide them with ammunition and fuel. While this was ongoing, on 3 April Schulze received a telephone call direct from OKH, probably from Generalinspekteur der Panzertruppen, ordering him to leave Gruppe Grosan, come under command of Korps Hannover and immediately deploy to the Weser.[77] He was given no further information such as the enemy situation or other friendly forces in the area and neither he nor his commanders had much, if any, knowledge of the ground. The next day, Kampfgruppe Schulze set off on its journey to the Weser and an assembly area in the Schaumburg Forest (see Map 10).

The second of the armour groups formed by Grosan was a combined *Panzer–Panzerjäger* unit commanded by Major Hache, the chief instructor of the Panzer-Truppen-Schule's anti-tank course, the Panzerjäger-Lehrgänge. Hache's unit comprised the Panzer-Truppen-Schule's remaining vehicles, a Panther, a Tiger, two Panzer IV/70 tank-destroyers, a few SdKfz 222 and 223 armoured cars, and some wheeled anti-tank guns. It is possible that the armoured vehicles did not join Kampfgruppe Schulze as they were not ready to deploy on 3 April. The SdKfz 222 was the standard light, four-wheeled armoured reconnaissance car equipped with a 2cm cannon and a co-axial MG34, while the SdKfz 223 was largely the same vehicle but, as the communications variant, mounting a frame antenna. The 222/223 were effective vehicles although lacking range and with limited off-road performance.

In addition to the armoured group, Hache formed two anti-tank companies equipped with the wheeled guns and allocated any manpower surplus to these companies to a *Panzerfaust* unit consisting of 20 teams mounted on bicycles and commanded by a Major Prüm. The first of the anti-tank companies came from the residue of Schwere Heeres-Panzerjäger-Abteilung 661 (Army Heavy Anti-Tank Unit),[78] which had originally been allocated to Panzer-Division 'Clausewitz' (see Chapter 12) but reassigned to Grosan. Although the company only had two 8.8cm Pak 43 anti-tank guns, the Pak 43 was a fearsome weapon and its APCBC round could penetrate all Allied tanks' frontal armour out to a range of 2,100 yards. The second anti-tank company had twelve 8cm Panzerwerferkanone (PWK) 8H63 crewed by anti-tank trainees from the Panzerjäger-Lehrgänge. The PWK 8H63 was a light, smooth-bore gun using the high-low pressure system to fire a fin-stabilised HEAT round (a converted 8cm mortar bomb) able to penetrate five inches of armour out to a range of 800 yards.

---

77 Hermann Kleinebenne, *Die Weserlinie – Kriegsende 1945* (Stolzenau: Weserdruckerei Oesselmann, 2011), p.216.
78 This was an independent anti-tank unit. Its number is not definite as the unit was an amalgam of Abteilungen 661, 683 and 686. Ultra decrypt BT 9284 (TNA DEFE 3/562) mentions Abteilung 683 resting and refitting at Bergen in early February.

During the first week of April Gruppe Grosan deployed to the Aller on 2. Marine-Infanterie-Division's left flank (see Map 11). Not only was this area closest to Bergen for forces that would have to move largely on foot, but Grosan would have known that the road and rail bridges at Essel were likely to be key objectives for the British and, with Korvettenkapitän Gördes having few heavy weapons and no infantry reserve, the marines badly needed his support, and quickly. Grosan allocated Hache's armour group and the two Pak 43 to the marine battalion, and also provided a numerically strong reserve in the form of Bataillon Lotze and Bataillon Sperling, which moved to the area of Ostenholz, in depth of the Aller, where they could await developments. The PWK 8H63 anti-tank guns, *Flak* artillery, tank-hunting teams, and the *Landesschützen* and *Volkssturm* units deployed to the forests to the east of Essel to cover the road to Winsen. Some of the SdKfz 222 armoured cars deployed forward to the area between the Weser and Aller while others patrolled the road to Winsen. Although unconfirmed, it seems likely that Grosan would have been in overall command of the defence of the Schwarmstedt-Essel area as he was both senior to Josef Gördes, the commander of Marine-Füsilier-Bataillon 2, and had infinitely more experience of land warfare. The probable difficulty, or absence, of communications between Gördes and his divisional headquarters at Walsrode makes this command arrangement even more likely.

Grosan's last contribution was to gather the remaining scrapings of manpower at the Panzer-Truppen-Schule and form the impressively titled Panzerjagdverband 'Großer Kurfürst' (Tank-Hunting Unit 'Great Elector'), an infantry tank-hunting group led by Major Kurt Deichen, a Knight's Cross holder and commander of the armoured reconnaissance school at Panzer-Truppen-Schule Bergen.[79] His training staff commanded the *Panzerjagdverband's* companies, which comprised teams of 10 men mounted on bicycles, with each rider armed with a StG 44 assault rifle and two *Panzerfaust* held in clips either side of his bicycle's front wheel. In late March 1945, three hundred surplus soldiers from the SS-Werfer-Lehr-Abteilung supplemented the *Panzer-Truppen-Schule* component, and further reinforcements from the *Waffen-SS* arrived in early April when members of SS-Werfer-Abteilung 500 joined the *Panzerjagdverband*. Once reinforced with the *Waffen-SS* soldiers, the *Panzerjagdverband* grew to its final strength of three companies and, following a week's training at Bergen in anti-tank ambush tactics, on 3 April the teams were despatched westwards on their bicycles to the Weser's central sector between Minden and Stolzenau (see Map 10).

Despite its title, SS-Werfer-Abteilung 500 had not been concerned with the operation of *Nebelwerfer* and there were other reasons why the men of the *Abteilung* were in this area of Germany. The first concerns the V-2 campaign, which had started in early September 1944. Initially the army owned the V-2 programme but Himmler had always seen the V-2 as a way for the SS to gain influence and prestige and had intrigued to take it over. One of his more blatant manoeuvrings was the creation in May 1944 of a *Waffen-SS* V-2 launcher unit formed from *Nebelwerfer* personnel and entitled SS-Werfer-Batterie 500; the battery became operational in mid-October 1944. The concluding act in Himmler's intrigues occurred on 3 February 1945 with the issue of the order creating Armee-Korps z.V. from Division z.V., previously belonging to the army. Himmler's order gave the SS control of the V-weapon programme in its entirety, and the ravenously ambitious SS-Obergruppenführer Kammler was given command not only of the development, production and operations of the V-2 but also of the V-1, previously the responsibility of the *Luftwaffe*, and the production of jet aircraft.[80] To match the inflated ego of the SS, Himmler's order gave title upgrades to the organisation ('*Division*' changed to '*Armee-Korps*', '*Abteilung*' to '*Regiment*' and

---

79   Hermann Kleinebenne, *Kriegstage in Petershagen, April 1945* (Stolzenau: Weserdruckerei Oesselmann, 1994), pp.57–60.
80   He also took control of the V-3 15cm Hochdruckpumpe (high-pressure pump) gun and the V-4 'Rheinbote' rocket but almost immediately cancelled these weapon systems.

'Batterie' to 'Abteilung'), but typically this was not matched by any increases in men and equipment. Kammler's triumph would be shortlived.

Two groups conducted the V-2 campaign's latter missile operations: Gruppe Süd firing from the Eifel on Germany's western borders and Gruppe Nord firing from the Netherlands.[81] By mid-March 1945 advances by the western Allies were threatening to cut off the missile launch areas and on 17 March, owing to the American breakout from the Remagen bridgehead, Gruppe Süd ceased operations against Antwerp and withdrew eastwards. Ten days later, with the Allies across the Rhine and British and Canadian forces advancing into the Netherlands, OKW ordered Armee-Korps z.V. to withdraw Gruppe Nord to Germany with immediate effect. The *Gruppe*, consisting of Artillerie-Regiment z.V. 902, SS-Werfer-Abteilung 500 and, for V-1 operations, the *Luftwaffe's* 5. Flakdivision (W) conducted the move over the period 27-30 March, with the last missile fired at 0849 hours on 28 March against Antwerp (it fell short). Although the withdrawing columns of vehicles were fortunate that low cloud protected them from Allied air attack, command and control problems resulted in a chaotic move and the routes became littered with vehicles, most with their fuel exhausted. Elements of Gruppe Nord eventually reached the Fallingbostel area on 1 April and immediately set about demolishing its equipment and re-roling its manpower, forming infantry companies from the army personnel in Artillerie-Regiment z.V. 902 and four *Nebelwerfer* batteries from SS-Werfer-Abteilung 500; these batteries were ordered to take part in the battle for Berlin and soon disappeared in the confused fighting east of the Elbe. The remaining *Waffen-SS* troops either became tank-hunting teams in Panzerjagdverband 'Großer Kurfürst' or joined SS-A.u.E.Btl.12 HJ at Leese.

With Armee-Korps z.V. in full retreat, the movement chain transporting V-1 and V-2 by rail to the launching areas ground to a halt and trainloads in transit were abandoned, with five such loads left in the Nienburg area. The first load consisted of two trains of V-1 and V-2 stuck on the Weser's left bank at Steyerberg station near Liebenau and partially blown up by V-weapon personnel on 5 April. These loads were later filmed by No. 5 Army Film and Photographic Unit on 9 April and the clip, which is listed at Appendix A, Serial 6, shows that Steyerberg station was also the destination for some of Gruppe Nord's specialised, towed launch-equipment for V-2 rockets and at least sixteen V-2 warheads in their transit drums. Some of the Steyerberg V-2 were transported by road via Stolzenau to the spur line running through the Hahnenberg forest and linking Kampstoffabrik Leese, a heavily-camouflaged chemical plant, to the main railway line. As many as possible were loaded on to waiting stake goods wagons for transportation to an unknown destination, with the remainder dumped on the forest floor. However, probably owing to lack of a locomotive or the extreme risk of rail movement, the wagons never left the spur line and the weapons and launch equipment were unsystematically blown up by members of Artillerie-Regiment z.V. 902 and abandoned. The fourth and fifth trainloads of V-2 were abandoned intact at Landesbergen, on the Weser's right bank three miles north of Leese.

With the German ground forces described, we will now look at the third component of the *Wehrmacht* to feature in the account: the participating air and *Flak* units of the *Luftwaffe*.

The *Luftwaffe*

By 1945 the *Luftwaffe's* once-mighty air arm was incapable of defending the *Reich* and in a terminal state from which there was no hope of recovery. It was ravaged by pilot losses, a dearth of experience and leaders, and fuel was in desperately short supply resulting in thousands of serviceable

---

81 TD Dungan, *V-2. A Combat History of the First Ballistic Missile* (Yardley: Westholme Publishing, 2005), pp.112–113.

aircraft parked with empty tanks in supply airfields and dispersals. Identical to the Army, a frenetic merry-go-round of commanders was taking place in a futile attempt to breathe life into the corpse. Göring, now held in open contempt by Hitler, was no longer invited to his meetings and was instead represented by the most senior *Luftwaffe* officer who happened to be present; Göring will belatedly be replaced on 23 April 1945 by Generalfeldmarschall Robert Ritter von Greim.

Its parlous condition was a combination of strategic errors made in earlier years and the impact of Allied air operations. In the late 1930s Germany's grand strategic plan was to defeat its opponents in the west within three years of the start of the war before turning east to conquer the Soviet Union. The *Luftwaffe* was therefore designed primarily as an army support force, perhaps unsurprising given that its most senior levels were largely staffed by former army officers, who considered the requirement for strategic bombing, maritime air, and air defence capabilities unnecessary. Accordingly, it failed to plan, develop and field a broadly-based, resilient force capable of fighting both offensively and defensively on multiple fronts, and eventual defeat was inevitable. The finale began in 1944 when the US Eighth Air Force turned its attention to the German aviation and fuel industries. The bombers were now protected by long-range fighters causing the *Luftwaffe* irreplaceable losses in seasoned pilots and hapless trainees alike, losses which could not be replaced as the *Luftwaffe* had for some time been saddled with an inadequate and failing training structure. The only bright spot was the continuing supply of aircraft, which, owing to Speer's dispersal of production, carried on nearly to the end. However, even this successful aspect was hampered by the lack of pilots and fuel, resulting in difficulties in deploying replacement aircraft to where they were needed.

The development of impressive and innovative aircraft designs such as the jet-engined Me 262, the Dornier 335 with its push-pull engines, the rocket-powered Messerschmitt (Me) 163 B and the vertically-launched Bachem 349 came too late and were, in any case, produced in such small numbers relative to the threat that there was never any chance of them turning the tide. Although technically interesting, they mostly proved to be evolutionary dead-ends. The *Luftwaffe's* last major effort on the West Front was the disastrous Operation *BODENPLATTE* of 1 January 1945. This operation, a low-level, mass-attack by fighters on Allied airfields in the Low Countries, was intended to cripple enemy air power but resulted instead in the *Luftwaffe's* largest single-day loss of pilots – 217 killed, missing or captured – and a mortally weakened organisation. Many pilots were shot down transiting the Antwerp area as they were unaware of the very high density of Allied light anti-aircraft batteries interdicting the V-1 offensive on the city and its port. Others were shot down by their own *Flak* by straying too close to the V-2 launching sites near The Hague, and *Flak* gunners being generally unaware of the operation owing to its tight security.[82] Despite all these disasters and impediments, the *Luftwaffe* was still, at discrete times and places, capable of wreaking death and destruction and the courage of its aircrew was never in doubt.

Although the *Luftwaffe* kept its basic structure to the end, by 1945 all levels were decidedly skeletal and, matching the army, organisational titles bore little relation to reality. Oberkommando der Luftwaffe (OKL) in Berlin continued to be the strategic level of air command, although during March its staff had started moving to the relative safety of Bavaria. The *Luftflotten*, teetering on collapse, remained the top level of operational command, with beneath them a variety of *Korps* and *Divisionen*, such as *Flieger-Korps* (air corps) and *Jagd-Divisionen* (day-fighter divisions). Next were the *Geschwader*, roughly equivalent to RAF wings, and the largest organisations at the tactical level. They remained the *Luftwaffe's* beating if sclerotic heart and were categorised according to their role, for instance a *Kampfgeschwader* (KG) flew bombers and ground-attack aircraft while a *Jagdgeschwader* (JG) flew day-fighters.

---

82   ER Hooton, *The Luftwaffe, A Study in Air Power 1933–1945* (Classic Publications, 2010), p.243.

A *Geschwader's* basic building block was the *Staffel*, originally comprising some nine bombers or 12 fighters. Three *Staffeln* with a *Stab*, the headquarters flight of about three aircraft, comprised a *Gruppe*, and in theory a *Geschwader* consisted of three to five *Gruppen*. In the war's latter stages, it became rare for all of a *Geschwader's* elements to be operating from the same base or even for all to be in existence. The *Luftwaffe* used the same hierarchical system of alternating roman and arabic numbers as the army, with the *Geschwader* having an arabic numeral, the *Gruppe* a roman, and the *Staffel* arabic. Thus 'I./KG 66' represents the first *Gruppe* of KG 66 and '5./JG 26' the fifth *Staffel* of JG 26.

Luftflotte Reich

The units and aircraft to feature in this account were commanded by Luftflotte Reich, one of four remaining *Luftflotten*. Formed in February 1944 in recognition of the growing threat to Germany's airspace from the western Allies, Luftflotte Reich was commanded by Generaloberst Hans-Jürgen Stumpff and at its height was the strongest of the *Luftflotten*, with responsibility for both the day and night defence of the *Reich*. By April 1945 it was very severely depleted and the majority of its numerical strength lay in night-fighter units, a strength that was largely irrelevant as Bomber Command's night offensive was now nearly at an end.

Since Autumn 1944, air operations on the *Reich's* western borders had been controlled by Luftwaffenkommando West, a subordinate headquarters of Luftflotte Reich formed in late September 1944 following the disbandment of Luftflotte 3, previously responsible for the air defence of France and the Low Countries. After the Allied crossings of the Rhine, the British and American advances began to split Germany in two, forcing *Luftwaffe* units to retreat to the north or south. The split made Luftflotte Reich's command of Luftwaffenkommando West untenable and so on 1 April the *Luftwaffenkommando* was made responsible for air operations in southwest Germany and subordinated to Luftflotte 6, itself a hopelessly stretched force responsible not only for the East Front and southern Germany but also Hungary, Czechoslovakia and north Italy. Luftflotte Reich's responsibilities now shrank to the support of the army in the northern half of Germany and on 7 April its diminished status would result in it being placed under the operational command of OB Nordwest rather than OKL.[83]

While the *Luftwaffe's* higher chain of command was undergoing major revision, day-to-day operations on the West Front were conducted, from north to south, by 14., 15., and 16. Flieger-Divisionen. Between them they fielded four conventional day-fighter *Geschwader* and three night-attack *Gruppen*, supplemented by twin- and single-engined night-fighter units, two battlefield recce *Gruppen* and two *Staffeln* of long-range photo recce aircraft. Day bombing was conducted by two *Gruppen* of bombers, while three *Gruppen* of night bombers could sometimes be called upon. However, none of these units were at full strength for long, if at all, nor would all of them necessarily be in action at any given time owing to the demands of relocating, resting and re-equipping. In the final weeks, headquarters and combat supplies, especially munitions and fuel, struggled to keep pace with the units' frequent eastward moves, and with each move the units became less effective. Disbandments and amalgamations were endemic, serviceability worsened as deliveries of spare parts and replacement aircraft faltered or failed and fuel supplies became intermittent or ceased altogether. These difficulties resulted in escalating confusion and over-crowding on the airfields, compounded by the Russians' westward advance forcing units of Luftflotte 6 to relocate to Luftflotte Reich bases. Squeezed into an ever-diminishing area, command and control boundaries became increasingly irrelevant and units were directed to conduct missions wherever they

---

83 FMS, B-414, Heeresgruppe 'H' (March–May 45), p.37.

were needed. During April Luftflotte Reich's operational efficiency was further degraded by the nomadic existence of its own operational headquarters; for the initial period of the account it was at Stapelburg in the Harz before moving on 9 April to Quassel south-east of Hamburg.

14. Flieger-Division

The *Flieger-Divisionen* provided a variety of aircraft types flying in support of ground forces. Formed from II. Jagd-Korps, 14. and 15. Flieger-Divisionen were created in late January 1945 to support Heeresgruppen 'H' and 'B' respectively and, in the main, comprised army support units of various types. On 4 April the two *Flieger-Divisionen* were subordinated to Luftflotte Reich.[84] 14. Flieger-Division's commander was Oberst Lothar von Heinemann and it is aircraft from his command that will play the principal air role in the account. Map 12 shows the main airfields from which 14. Flieger-Division units, and other *Luftwaffe* units associated with the account, flew during April 1945, although it should be noted that most would be progressively abandoned in response to the Allied advances. During the earlier part of the account 14. Flieger-Division had its battle headquarters in the police barracks in Wunstorf.

Shown at Figure 9 is 14. Flieger-Division's orbat as structured on 12 April,[85] with the numbers indicating the totals of aircraft that were combat-ready, ie battleworthy and with pilots/crews. The orbat is, however, a snapshot in time and the structure would frequently change during the final weeks owing to attrition and the chaos of the withdrawal. Furthermore, the totals give too rosy a picture as lack of fuel meant that many combat-ready aircraft were in reality grounded.

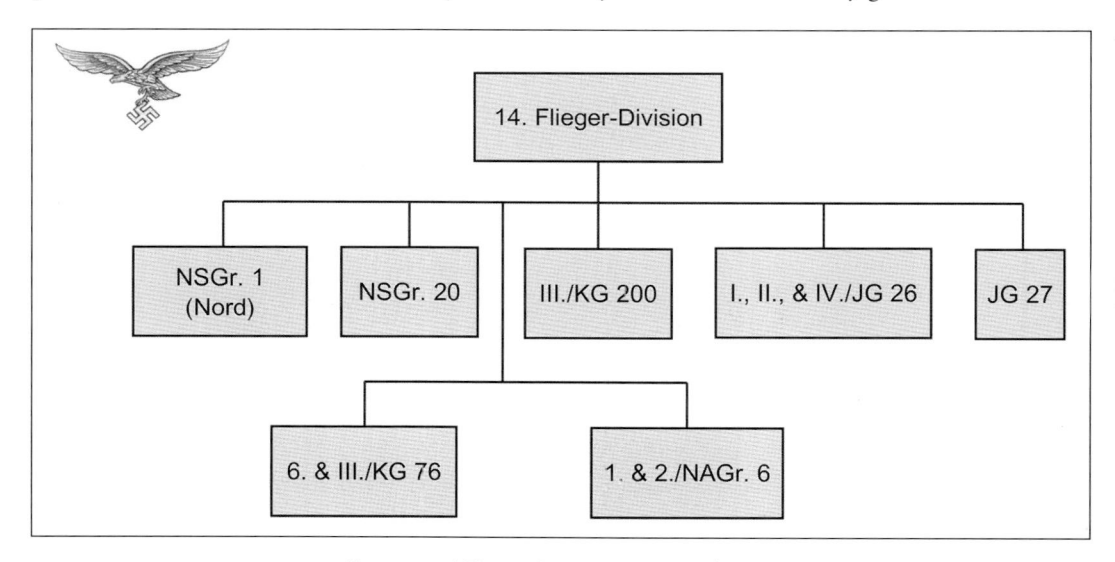

Figure 9 14.Flieger-Division – 12 April 1945.

14. Flieger-Division comprised four categories of units, the first of which specialised in low-level, night-attack missions against targets such as troop and vehicle concentrations, artillery positions

---

84 TNA DEFE 3/563, BT 9570, Luftflotte Reich signal 4 April 1945.
85 …fgruppe Gen.Qu. 529/45 g.Kdos., *Einsatzbereitschaft der flg.Verbände in Bereich Lfl.Kdo.Reich abends 12 April 1945* (Luftflotte Reich strength return 10/11 April 1945).

THE ROCK OF RESISTANCE 91

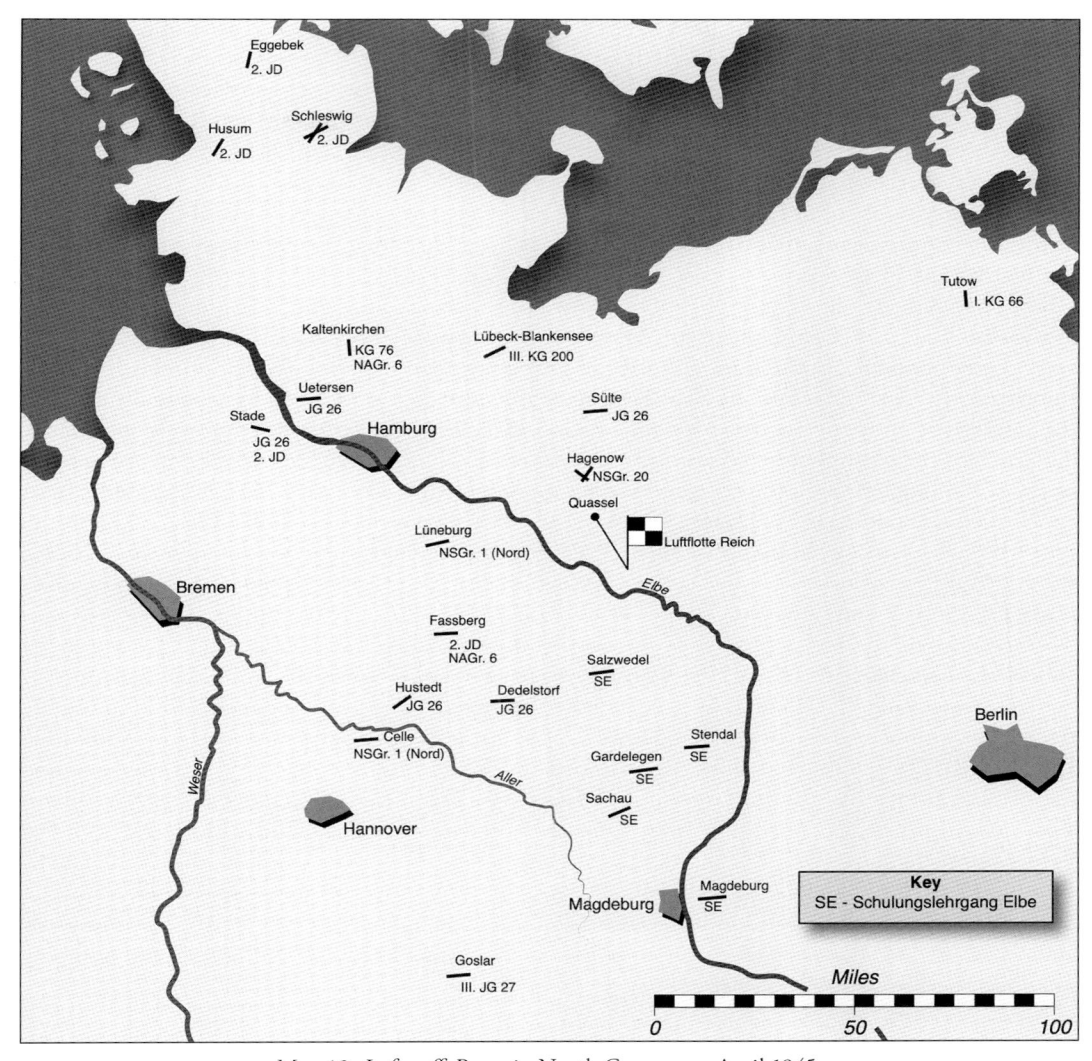

Map 12 *Luftwaffe* Bases in North Germany – April 1945.

and vulnerable points, such as bridges and defiles. Three Gruppen in this first category feature in the account: Nachtschlachtgruppe (NSGr.) 1 (Nord), NSGr. 20 and III./KG 200.

NSGr. 1 (Nord). NSGr. 1 was equipped with the Junkers (Ju) 87 D-5, universally known as the '*Stuka*'. The D variant had an uprated engine and the D-5 extended wings, providing additional lift allowing it to carry a useful bomb-load of up to a 1000kg bomb on its centreline and, mounted under each wing, two 50kg bombs. The aircraft could also carry containers of cluster munitions, effective against troops in the open and unarmoured vehicles, and to improve its ground-attack firepower, in each wing a 20mm cannon replaced the 7.92mm machine-guns. With a maximum speed of only 195mph, the Ju 87 was very vulnerable to enemy fighters and anti-aircraft fire and from 1943 onwards losses from daylight use forced a change to flying dusk to dawn nuisance raids, a tactic copied from the Russians. Fitted with exhaust flame dampers and additional armour, the Ju 87 D-5 proved an effective night intruder, flying low and slow to attack targets close to the front line. It could, *in extremis*, still be used in daylight but this required fighter escort and considerable courage on the part of the aircrew, as will be seen.

In late March 1945, NSGr. 1 was split in two by the Allied advances beyond the Rhine, with one part driven south, the other northward, never to reunite. Hauptmann Müller-Broders commanded the northern element, NSGr. 1 (Nord), which was initially based at Wunstorf airfield 10 miles to Hannover's north west. However, the threat of a British advance beyond the Weser forced it to withdraw in early April to Lüneburg and Celle. The availability return for 1 April shows NSGr. 1 having 23 combat-ready aircraft,[86] although it is not known how this total was divided between the Nord and Süd groups.

NSGr. 20. NSGr. 20, commanded by Major Kurt Dahlmann, flew Focke Wulf (Fw) 190 F-8 and G-8 fighter-bombers. At the start of April the unit was operating from Vörden, some 12 miles to the north of Osnabrück, but the British advance forced it to withdraw to Hagenow 20 miles to the south-west of Schwerin. The Fw 190 F and G variants of the famous fighter were specifically designed for the ground-attack role, with armour added to vulnerable areas and bomb racks fitted to carry a 500kg bomb on the centreline and under each wing either two 70kg bombs, or various types of cluster munition containers. The aircraft was armed with two 20mm wing cannons and two 13mm (.50-in) machine-guns above the engine, making it a useful strafing platform. The G variant could carry underwing fuel tanks to extend its range. On 1 April NSGr. 20 had 36 combat-ready Fw 190 F-8 and G-8.

III./Kampfgeschwader (KG) 200. Formed in January 1945 from the ground-attack unit I./Schlachtgeschwader 5, III./KG 200 was initially used to trial anti-shipping bombs shaped to hold their trajectory after entering water. However, the project was abandoned in early April 1945 and III./KG 200 joined Luftflotte Reich, switching to the fighter-bomber role to fly day and night missions against ground targets. The *Gruppe's* commander was Major Helmut Viedebantt and on 10 April it was operating from Lübeck-Blankensee with 24 combat-ready Fw 190 F-8 fighter-bombers.

The second category of unit in 14. Flieger-Division were two fighter *Geschwader*: JG 26 'Schlageter' and JG 27 'Afrika', both conducting combat air patrols, armed recce, ground-attack and bombing missions.

JG 26 'Schlageter'. In early April 1945 JG 26, commanded by Major Franz Götz, comprised the Stab and I., II. and IV. Gruppen, III. Gruppe having disbanded in March. On 1 April, JG 26 fielded 79 combat-ready Fw 190 D-9 fighters principally operating from Stade and Hustedt airfields, Stade being 10 miles to Hamburg's west while Hustedt lay 4 miles to Celle's north-east. It also had fighters scattered among the airfields at Oldenburg, Uetersen and Dedelstorf and, later in the month, Sülte to the south of Schwerin. The Fw 190 D-9 was arguably the best German fighter of the war. It was designed for the anti-fighter role and was armed with two 13mm machine-guns and two 20mm cannons, all firing through the propeller arc. The aircraft had a stretched aft fuselage and longer nose than the Fw 190 A and was known as the *Dora-9* but nicknamed '*Langnasen-Dora*' ('Long-nose Dora'). I. and IV. Gruppen flew combat air patrols, armed recce and ground-attack missions, while II. Gruppe was used in the low-level fighter-bomber role with its aircraft carrying either 250kg or 500kg bombs, or cluster munitions. Albert Schlageter was a member of the *Freikorps* whose sabotaging activities against French occupying troops after World

---

86 Einsatzbereitschaft Luftflotte Reich, Stand 1.4.1945, abends (provided by Michaël Svejgaard).

War 1 led to his arrest and eventual execution. German nationalist groups, in particular the *Nazi* party, cultivated his death and he was widely commemorated as a national hero and used as an honorific in *Wehrmacht* unit titles.

JG 27 'Afrika'. JG 27 consisted of the *Stab* at Gitter airfield, 2 miles south of Salzgitter; I. and II. Gruppen at Helmstedt, 20 miles east of Brunswick, and Völkenrode, 4 miles north-west of Brunswick; and III. Gruppe at Goslar in the Harz. JG 27, commanded by Major Ludwig Franzisket, was equipped with Bf 109 G and K-4 and had the same roles as JG 26.[87] On 1 April it had 52 combat-ready aircraft. The Bf 109 G was the most numerous version of the famous fighter and was armed with two 13mm machine guns in the engine cowling and either a 20mm or 30mm cannon firing through the propeller boss. It could carry a 250kg bomb. The Bf 109 K was the fighter's final variant, it had a rate of climb superior to nearly all Allied fighters, was armed with an engine-mounted 30mm cannon and two 13mm nose-mounted machine-guns, and could carry up to a 500kg bomb. With a good pilot the Bf 109 was an excellent fighter, but by 1945 the *Luftwaffe* had very few pilots of this calibre. On 8 April JG 27 would be resubordinated to 15. Flieger-Division.

The third category of unit was a bomber *Geschwader*, Kampfgeschwader (KG) 76.

KG 76. KG 76 fought throughout the war and in April 1945 was one of the last true bomber *Geschwader* still operational, although by this late stage comprising only the *Stab*, 6. Staffel and III. Gruppe. On 1 April it fielded just four, combat-ready Ar 234 B-2 jet-engined bombers. Powered by two Jumo 004 turbojet engines, the Ar 234 B-2 was faster than all Allied fighters of the time (less the Meteor III). However, owing to its slim fuselage it had no space for the internal carriage of bombs so the bomb-load had to be carried on the aircraft's centre-line, reducing its speed and limiting the aircraft to single bombs up to 1000kg. Despite its revolutionary design, the small bomb-load and paucity of aircraft in service combined to make the Ar 234 B-2 at best only an irritation to the Allies. On 5 April Second Army's advance forced KG 76 to evacuate Marx airfield (only occupied on 2 April) and that evening it managed to get 17 aircraft airborne and fly them to Kaltenkirchen, north of Hamburg. Commanded by Oberstleutnant Robert Kowalewski, KG 76 was also known as Gefechtsverband (Battle Group) Kowalewski, a grouping of Ar 234, Me 262 and Fw 190 F-8 units formed under Kowalewski in March 1945 to coordinate attacks against the Remagen bridgehead. The name continued in use despite the *Gefechtsverband* disbanding after the failure to contain the bridgehead.

The last category of unit in 14. Flieger-Division was a battlefield photo recce *Gruppe*.

Nahaufklärungsgruppe (NAGr.) 6. The Gruppe comprised Stab and 1. and 2. Staffeln. In theory 1. Staffel would have flown the Fw 190 A-3/U4 photo recce version but it is likely that by April 1945 these specialist aircraft were no longer available and ordinary Fw 190 A fighters would have been used instead, with the pilots providing visual reports. The 2. Staffel flew the jet-engined Me 262 A-1/U3, an unarmed, interim recce version equipped with cameras. With a top speed of 540mph, the revolutionary jet-engined Me 262 was faster than all Allied aircraft. Although an innovative design, such a sophisticated aircraft suffered from its pioneering technologies and its development was particularly delayed by problems with the Jumo 004 engine, which even in its final version had an incredibly short life measureable in hours. Furthermore, the aircraft's construction demanded skilled labour and rare materials, both in very short supply by the fifth year of the war. On 1 April the Stab was at Fassberg, while 1. and 2. Staffeln flew from Kaltenkirchen.

---

[87] 'Bf' stands for Bayerische Flugzeugwerke. After the firm changed its name to Messerschmitt in 1938, models designed thereafter bore the prefix 'Me'. 'Me' was in common use by both the Germans and the Allies.

Also to play a part in the account were two air units that were not part of 14. Flieger-Division but were tasked by it: the former night-fighters of 2. Jagd-Division and the bombers of I./KG 66.

2. Jagd-Division

Formed in 1942 to control night-fighter operations in north Germany and Denmark, 2. Jagd-Division was superimposed on 14. Flieger-Division's area of operations. With its headquarters at Stade airfield, the division was commanded by Oberst Gustav-Siegfried Rödel and belonged to IX. Flieger-Korps (Jagd). In early April it started to take under its command the night-fighters of the disbanding 3. Jagd-Division and by 5 April it comprised the following night-fighter units: Stab, 1., 4., 7., and 10./Nachtjagdgeschwader (NJG) 1 at Husum airfield; Stab, I. and III./NJG 2 at Rotenburg and Schleswig; Stab, 1., 7., and 10./NJG 3 at Grove in Denmark and Stade; Stab, 1., 4., and 7./NJG 4 at Fassberg and Eggebek; and 7./NJG 11 operating from Hamburg-Fuhlsbüttel.

Despite its specialist role, 2. Jagd-Division was thrown into the land battle using some of its twin-engined Junkers (Ju) 88 G aircraft as bombers to carry out nocturnal ground-attack missions. These aircraft were stripped of their airborne interception radars and fitted with bomb or container release mechanisms to supplement their 20 or 30mm cannons. Although 2. Jagd-Division was principally equipped with the Ju 88 G, there were also Heinkel (He) 219 A and Bf 110 G; 7./NJG 11 flew Bf 109 G and K models.

I./KG 66

KG 66 was formed in France in April 1943 as a pathfinder and target-marking *Geschwader*. Although most bomber *Geschwader* were disbanded in autumn 1944, with some converting to fighters as *Kampfgeschwader (Jagd)* units and their surplus air- and groundcrew despatched to fight as infantry, I./KG 66 was retained as pathfinders to drop illuminations for Ju 88 bomber missions and it participated in the Ardennes offensive, mine-laying operations in the Scheldt estuary and trained for a stillborn operation to attack powerplants in the Moscow region. In March 1945 the Gruppe was allocated to Gefechtsverband (Battle Group) Helbig, part of Luftflotte 6 fighting on the East Front. The *Gefechtsverband* comprised elements from a variety of units and specialised in mounting *Mistel* (Mistletoe) operations against bridges across the Oder and Neisse rivers. These courageous but ineffective operations, involving a fighter flying piggy-back on an unmanned, explosives-packed Ju 88 before releasing it to fly to the target, had by April 1945 all but petered out and I./KG 66 was increasingly used as a conventional bomber unit.

The *Gruppe* was commanded by Major Hermann Schmidt and in early April 1945 was operating from Tutow, 70 miles east of Hamburg. I./KG 66 was principally equipped with two types of medium bomber: the Ju 88 S and Ju 188. The Ju 88 S was the fastest and most capable version of the famous twin-engined bomber. To achieve this improvement various drag-reducing measures had been taken, such as removing the ventral gondola and replacing the 'beetle-eye' nose window with smooth glass. The Ju 88 S could carry 3000kg of bombs, considerably more than the Allied medium bombers the B-25 Mitchell, Marauder and Boston III. The Ju 188, also a twin-engined bomber, was developed to replace the Ju 88 but came into service too late to have significant impact. Although its bomb-load remained the same as the Ju 88, it was a popular aircraft to fly as it had a spacious cockpit with good visibility and outperformed the Ju 88 series. On 16 April I./KG 66 fielded 26 combat ready Ju 88 S and nine Ju

188.[88] The *Gruppe* also flew some Ju 88 G night-fighters supplied by disbanded units and with their four 2cm cannons, were useful for strafing missions.

Schulungslehrgang Elbe

One final unit remains to be described, which was both independent and unconventional. This unit stemmed from a radical proposal made in late 1944 by Oberst 'Hajo' Herrmann,[89] commander of the then 9. Flieger-Division (Jagd) and holder of the Knight's Cross with Oak Leaves and Swords. Herrmann, an air defence expert and a former inspector general of air defence, believed the Me 262 to be the only answer to the *Luftwaffe's* inability to strike back decisively against American bombers, but that time was needed to build more aircraft and train their pilots. Time, in the Germany of 1945, was, however, a commodity in extremely short supply so he proposed achieving a pause in the devastating US bombing campaign through the shock effect of a series of mass, ramming attacks conducted by special units manned by volunteers. The ramming aircraft would be high-altitude variants of the Bf 109, the G-10 or K-4, stripped of armour and all unnecessary equipment. As the lightened aircraft were expected to out-perform the American fighters and not require escorting, only single 13mm machine-guns with 50 rounds of ammunition were left for self-defence.

Once a significant enemy bomber formation was identified, the operation would be launched with the fighters climbing to 30,000 feet and massing in selected areas on the bombers' expected route. The ramming tactic would involve each aircraft diving on their selected bomber, either aiming to hit with a wing the enemy aircraft's structure at its weakest point in front of the tail, or to flatten out of the dive and use the propeller as a circular saw against the trailing edges of the tail or control surfaces on the wings. Canopies would be ejected before the attack and the pilot would parachute to safety just before or just after hitting the bomber, with many aircraft having their gun sights removed in order to assist the pilots' bailing out. Herrmann did not underestimate the risk and accepted that probably only 50 percent of the pilots would survive, but he believed the prize was worth it and the *Luftwaffe* was, in any event, losing hundreds of pilots a month. Although undoubtedly high risk and callous, ramming was not designed as a suicide tactic.

Herrmann's proposal was subsequently approved by Göring, who qualified it by ordering that only student pilots from the training schools would fly the ramming aircraft as he needed the experienced pilots to fly the expanding force of Me 262. In February 1945 Göring signed a secret order calling for trainee pilots to volunteer for 'special and dangerous' duties. The operation was named Operation *WERWOLF* and the first (and only) operational ramming *Geschwader* was given the cover name Schulungslehrgang Elbe (Training Course Elbe) and was organised into three *Gruppen* each with 45 pilots.[90] The take-up of the order was immediate and impressive and in early March the volunteers reported to Stendal airbase, the operation's focus, where they were briefed on their mission. Under Major Otto Köhnke, those selected began two weeks' training, which included concentrated periods of indoctrination to motivate the pilots to their mission but minimal flying through lack of fuel. The training ended on 4 April and the pilots were allocated to five airfields: Stendal, Salzwedel, Gardelegen, Sachau and Magdeburg (see Map 12). A force of 188 Bf 109 was allocated to the operation, with the aircraft kept dispersed and only concentrated

---

88   *Einsatzbereitschaft der flg.Verbände in Bereich Lfl.Kdo.Reich abends 12 April 1945.*
89   Herrmann was a prisoner of the Soviets until 1955. He subsequently became a lawyer specialising in defending neo-*Nazis* and Holocaust deniers, including the British historian David Irving, and was active as a speaker for far-Right political parties.
90   Also sometimes known as Sonderkommando Elbe or Rammkommando Elbe.

on the five airfields at the last moment owing to the risk of Allied attacks destroying the operation on the ground. Although Herrmann was dissatisfied with the number of pilots and aircraft as it would not achieve the desired mass effect, with the Allies rapidly advancing into Germany time was running out fast and Schulungslehrgang Elbe would have to be launched at the first available opportunity. It was belatedly decided that once in the air the Bf 109 would be too vulnerable and that Me 262 from JG 7 and I./KG (J) 54, the very aircraft to be garnered for future success, were needed to lure the US escorts away from the bombers, leaving the skies clear for the ramming force; subsequent events would suggest that this intent was not passed to the Me 262 pilots.

Among the leaders of the *Reich*, by now clutching at any straw however flimsy, expectations for Schulungslehrgang Elbe's success were high, as reflected in Minister of Propaganda Joseph Goebbels' diary entry for 31 March 1945:[91]

> The enemy bomber squadrons are now in the air uninterruptedly and they are inflicting the most severe damage on us. Obsolete German aircraft are now to be used as ram fighters against these bomber squadrons. These ram fighters are now to make suicide attacks on the enemy bombers, 90 percent casualties being reckoned with. The ram fighters should be in action in 8 or ten days. Extraordinary success is expected from them. Of our fighter pilots 50 to 90 percent have volunteered, proof that morale among our fighter pilots is extraordinarily high, even though Göring, for transparent reasons, invariably states the opposite.

It is interesting that Goebbels considered the pilots to be on suicide missions as this was certainly not Herrmann's intention since the concept needed pilots to survive in order to conduct repeat attacks. It could be, however, that Goebbels was confusing Schulungslehrgang Elbe with the pilots of 5./KG 200, the so-called 'Leonidas' Staffel, who had volunteered to crash their aircraft onto suitable ground targets. As hyperbole was Goebbels' daily fodder, perhaps it was only to be expected that he would view the ramming attacks in this way. It is also unclear whether he thought the 90 percent casualties would be among the bombers or the German pilots.

Luftwaffe ordnance

There were two basic types of bomb in the *Luftwaffe's* arsenal:[92] the *Sprengbombe Cylindrisch* (SC) general purpose, thin-walled, high explosive bombs which maximised blast and the *Sprengbombe Dickwandig* (SD) thick-walled, fragmentation bombs used where penetration was required. Both types came in a range of weights, with their numerical designation equating to their weight in kilograms. In the account the most commonly used bombs are the SC and SD 250. The maximum bombload carried by a Bf 109 was 250kg bomb, while the Fw 190 could carry a 500kg bomb. Ar 234 B-2, Ju 88 and Ju 188 could carry combinations of 70kg, 250kg, 500kg and 1000kg bombs up to their maximum payloads. The *Luftwaffe* also fielded a range of sub-munitions carried in canisters of various sizes, with the AB 23 and AB 250-2 being the most common. Being smaller, the AB 23 canister was suited to carriage by fighter-bombers and contained twenty-three SD 2 bomblets, while the AB 250 could contain up to 17 SD 10A anti-personnel bomblets or 224 SD 1 bomblets or 144 SD 2 bomblets. Although the SD 2 bomblet or 'butterfly bomb' was the most frequently used, all types of SD munitions were effective against troops in the open and soft-skinned vehicles

---

91 Joseph Goebbels, *The Goebbels Diaries – The Last Days* (London: Secker and Warburg, 1978), p.288.
92 *Luftwaffe* Resource Center, 'Drop Ordnance', http://www.warbirdsresourcegroup.org/LRG/bombs.html (accessed 17 March 2017).

and represent the world's first example of this now infamous weapon system. Night target illumination and marking used the *Licht Cylindrisch* (LC) 50 parachute flare.

The *Flak* Arm

Although the Army, Navy and *Waffen-SS* had their own air defence units, the *Luftwaffe* was by far the greater provider of anti-aircraft firepower, both for the defence of the *Reich* and its deployed field forces, and by 1945 its *Flak* arm was an immense organisation of some 1.25 million personnel. Owing, however, to the fronts' insatiable demand for manpower there was a steady flow away from the *Flak* defending the *Reich* and replacements had to be found from a variety of sources: local factory workers, *Luftwaffenhelfer* (usually Hitler Youth) and *Luftwaffenhelferinnen* (female auxiliaries), Italian and Hungarian volunteers and Russian PoWs. Most of the replacement manpower came however from young members of the RAD, the German labour service in which every German adolescent male had to perform six months' service prior to *Wehrmacht* call-up. As the war progressed hundreds of RAD units were converted wholesale into *Flak* batteries, not only to increase the *Reich's* anti-aircraft defences but also to replace *Flak* personnel swept into the *Luftwaffe* field divisions. In 1945 manning the *Flak* became so challenging that 17-year-olds were called up directly into the *Flak* from civilian life, without any form of artillery training. Known as *Flak-v. Soldaten*,[93] the teenagers replaced experienced gunners sent to the front in *Flak Sturm* regiments, which formed part of the *Flak-Korps* mentioned below. The October 1944 manning figures shown at Figure 10 for 14. Flak-Division,[94] responsible for the defence of the synthetic oil refinery at Leuna and other key installations in southern Germany, provide an example of the significant size and proportions of a static *Flak* formation:

Regular *Luftwaffe* personnel	28,000 (43%)
RAD	18,000 (30%)
Luftwaffenhelfer (male auxiliaries)	6,000 (10%)
Luftwaffenhelferinnen (female auxiliaries)	3,050 (5%)
Hungarians and Italians	900 (1%)
Russian prisoners	3,600 (6%)
Others	3,000 (5%)

Figure 10 14.Flak-Division – October 1944.

For the air defence of the *Reich*, the *Flak* divisions were the top level in the *Flak* arm's structure and came under the control of their local *Luftgau*, the *Luftwaffe* equivalent to the *Wehrkreis*. A *Luftgau* would control one or more *Flak* divisions, which in turn controlled two or more *Flak* brigades, each of between two and four regiments. A *Flak* regiment consisted of between four and six *Abteilungen*, each comprising a number of *Flak* batteries, the basic unit. All levels above battery were controlling headquarters and did not actually possess guns. There were four main categories of *Flak*: *schwere* (heavy – 12.8cm, 10.5cm and 8.8cm guns), *leichte* (light – 2cm and 3.7cm), *gemischte* (mixed calibres) and *Scheinwerfer* (searchlight). A *Flak* unit could be further defined by its

---

[93] '*v.*' was a manning category standing for *Verwendungsfähig* ('employable') as opposed to *Kriegsverwendungsfähig* (*kv.*) ('front line employable').
[94] Dr Alfred Price, *Luftwaffe Handbook, 1939–1945* (London: Ian Allan Ltd, 1986), p.74.

mobility: *motorisiert* (fully-motorised),[95] *verlegbar* (deployable but without organic transport) and *ortsfest* (static). *Eisenbahn* (railway) was a discrete mobility category. The Germans considered the railway *Flak* to be the elite and consequently it attracted the best personnel and the latest equipment.[96] By 1944 the railway *Flak* had become even more important to the anti-aircraft defence of Germany as it was able to respond rapidly to changes in Allied targeting and its movement was not constrained by fuel shortages. Allied bomber crews particularly respected railway *Flak* not only for its power but also for its capacity for rapid redeployment, which challenged the accuracy of Allied *Flak* maps and made the process of selecting routes for the bomber streams chancier. Railway light *Flak* always made low-level attacks by Allied fighters on trains and railway infrastructure risky.

By February 1945 the air battle over Germany was nearing its end and on the West Front the principal threat to the regime had shifted to the Allied armies. Holding them back would need every man and weapon in Germany's inventory, but the collapsing manpower situation and an arms industry in its death throes meant that there was no hope of making good the losses in men and materiel. However, as the German army fell back on the *Reich* it also fell back on large numbers of static and deployable *Flak* and this valuable if stopgap source of artillery could be re-roled to deliver fire support, both direct and indirect. To make this support effective, control of the *Flak* had to change from the rigid *Luftgau* structure to one suited to the fluidity of land operations and this was met by the creation of two additional *Flak-Korps*, the top level of formation associated with controlling *Flak* for the field army but still under the overall control of the *Luftwaffe*. One of the two formations was VI. Flak-Korps, formed in February 1945 to control *Flak* supporting Heeresgruppe 'H' in north Germany and the Netherlands. VI. Flak-Korps was subordinated to Luftflotte Reich and was commanded by Generalleutnant Schilffarth. The *Flak* division and the two *Flak* brigades it originally controlled were subsequently destroyed in the battles for the Rhineland and Rhine bridgehead and VI. Flak-Korps' headquarters was forced back to the north-east where, for the final battle, it established itself in Oldendorf to the west of Hamburg. Here it took under command three existing static *Flak* formations: 3. Flak-Division, 8. Flak-Division and 8. Flak-Brigade, respectively providing the *Flak* defence of the Hamburg, Bremen and Hannover regions. Schilffarth ordered these three formations to support Armeegruppe Student.[97]

On 3 April 8. Flak-Division instructed Flak-Regiment 122(E) to control the batteries provided by 3. Flak-Division and 8. Flak-Brigade.[98] This railway *Flak* regiment, commanded by Major Alfred Majewski, was formed in 1941 as part of Hamburg's air defences and thereafter was the controlling headquarters for a fluctuating number of railway, heavy *Flak Abteilungen* operating in Luftgau XI, the Hannover-Hamburg air district. In early March 1945 it controlled 10 such *Abteilungen* spread across northern Germany. A month later, with most of its own *Abteilungen* destroyed, Flak-Regiment 122(E) was given the mission to command the remaining *Flak* units in the Verden-Nienburg area and support the marine division on the Weser, with concentrations of effort at the Hoya, Nienburg and Stolzenau crossings. This would be vital support for the division given the absence of Marine-Artillerie-Regiment 2, still moving down from Schleswig-Holstein. Some of the batteries allocated to Flak-Regiment 122(E), both static and deployable, were already in situ as part of northern Germany's *Flak* defences and therefore time was spared having to deploy them to their battle positions. However, as Armeegruppe Student would need to fight sequentially

---

95 Fully-motorised *Flak* operated with the field armies and was naturally more suited to participating in land battles. The guns were frequently required to provide fire support against ground targets, particularly tanks.
96 Edward Westerman, *Flak. German Anti-Aircraft Defenses 1941–1945* (University of Kansas Press, 2001), p.157.
97 Lexicon der Wehrmacht, 'VI. Flakkorps', *http://www.lexikon-der-wehrmacht.de/Gliederungen/Flakkorps/Flakkorps6.htm* (accessed 16 May 2018).
98 *Gefechtsbericht des Flakregiments 122(E), 14 April 1945*, p.2.

on the Weser and the Aller, Flak-Regiment 122(E) would at some point need to withdraw the deployable batteries,[99] a challenging prospect given the chronic shortage of prime movers, carriage systems and fuel. Most guns would have to be drawn at walking pace by horses or cattle, and the smaller ones transported in farmers' horse-drawn carts. The *Flak* units supporting the Weser Line are shown on Map 13.

The batteries controlled by Flak-Regiment 122(E) fielded a variety of guns; first the heavy *Flak*. The 8.8cm Flak 37 was the *Luftwaffe's* smallest calibre heavy *Flak* gun but it was abundant and much respected by the Allies in its anti-armour role. For land engagements, it had an APCBC round able to penetrate four inches of armour at 1,100 yards and a HE round with an effective range of 16,000 yards. The 8.8cm Flak 41 was the final development of the Flak 37 and an excellent weapon, although experiencing problems of cartridge extraction owing to a complicated barrel design. It was well-suited to ground action as it had a usefully low profile, it fired HE ammunition and had an AP round able to penetrate nearly eight inches of armour at 1,000 yards. The 10.5cm Flak 39 was a more powerful version of the 8.8cm; its APCBC round could penetrate five inches of armour at 1,100 yards and its HE round had an effective range of 19,000 yards. The ubiquitous 2cm Flak 38 provided the *Wehrmacht's* principal light anti-aircraft firepower, with the gun primarily coming in single and quadruple-barrelled (*Flakvierling*) versions. Although it lacked ceiling, lethality and being fed from a 20-round magazine had a low rate of fire, the 2cm Flak fired HE and AP rounds at a rate of 180 rounds per minute to a range of some 5,000 yards and was effective against personnel and lightly armoured ground targets. The second light *Flak* gun was the 3.7cm Flak 36, which could fire 80 rounds per minute, had a ground range of 7,200 yards and greater hitting power than the 2cm. The rounds for both the 2cm and 3.7cm self-destructed when reaching their maximum effective range, giving a useful air-burst effect.[100]

With his headquarters established near Walsrode, the Flakregiment 122(E) war diary records Major Majewski setting off on 4 April with his adjutant and ordnance officer to make a rapid review of his command.[101] He first visited the three batteries supporting the SS-A.u.E.Btl.12 'HJ' companies at Leese: part of RAD Batterie 5./280 equipped with three 8.8cm Flak; Batterie 4./871 with two troops of 3.7cm Flak (totalling six guns) and three troops of 2cm Flakvierling (nine guns). Additionally, at Leese station, there was a troop from Batterie 2./859(E), belonging to one of Flak-Regiment 122(E)'s own *Abteilung*, with three *Flakvierling* mounted on railway wagons. Majewski immediately identified that the guns of the RAD and the light battery were not sited to engage ground targets so he directed urgent action to move most of the guns onto the railway embankment from where they could fire directly onto Stolzenau, the Weser bridge and the road from Stolzenau to Leese. Although most guns were moved to the embankment, two of 4./871's *Flakvierling* troops were left in depth to provide defence against low-level air attacks. His last direction was that anti-tank and HE ammunition was required and that observer positions were needed to control direct fire. In addition to the *Flak* at Leese, there was one other *Flak* battery in the area under Flak-Regiment 122(E)'s control: RAD Batterie 4./132 with six 8.8cm Flak at Loccum, five miles to the south-east of Leese; Majewski did not visit this battery, either because it would not be in the direct fire role or he ran out of time, and he and his team returned to Walsrode.

The next morning he visited Hoya where there were four batteries: Batterien 4./117 and 4./162 (gem.), both deployed to the Weser from Brunswick on 1 April and each equipped with four 10.5cm Flak and three 2cm Flak; RAD Batterie 2./604 (gem.) with five 8.8cm Flak 36 and three

---

99   Guns could be fitted to a temporary transport frame clamped to two bogies and towed by a suitable prime mover.
100 Ian Hogg, *German Artillery of World War Two* (London: Arms & Armour Press, 1975), pp.142–176.
101 *Gefechtsbericht des Flakregiments 122(E), 14 April 1945*, p.3.

100　THEIRS THE STRIFE

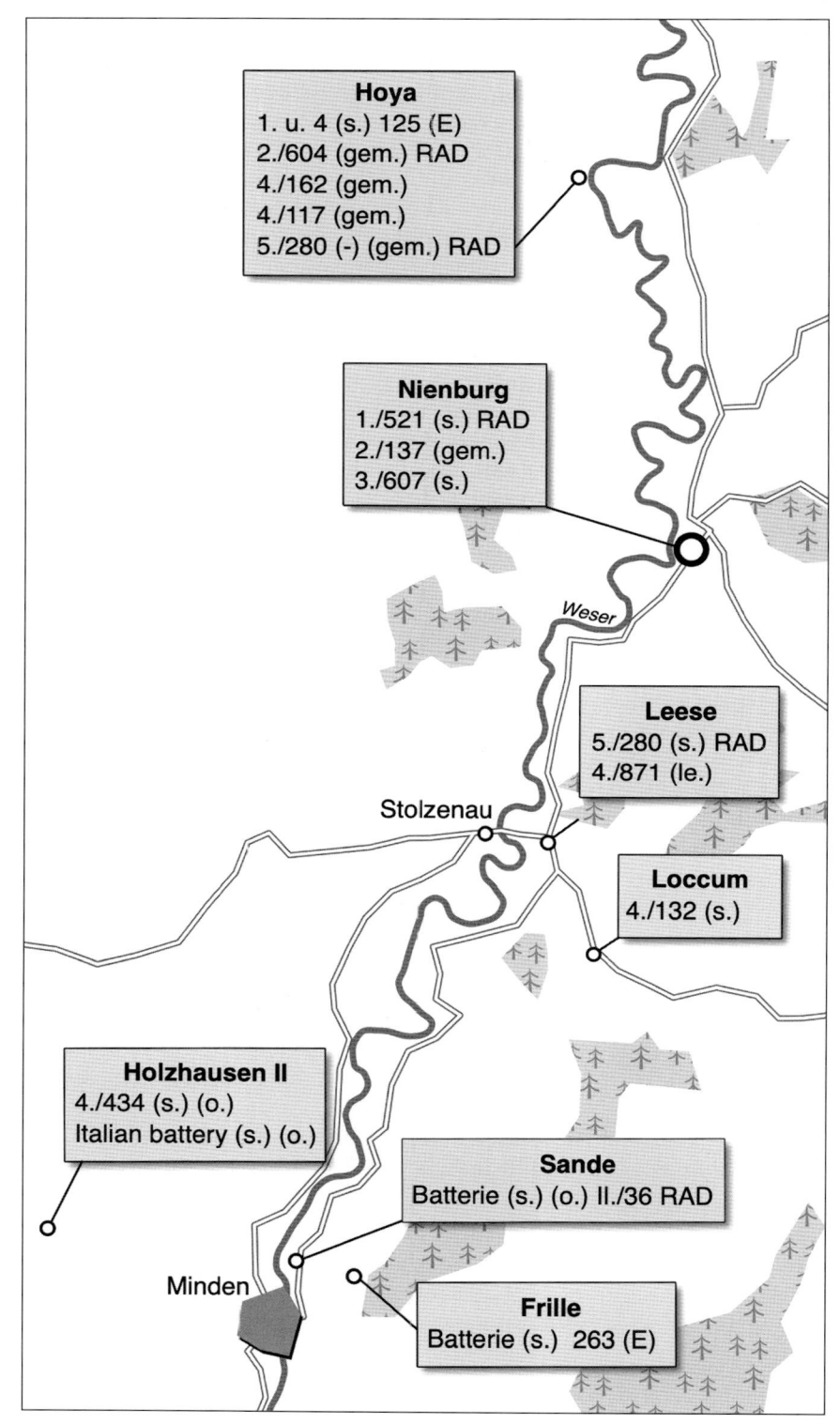

Hoya
1. u. 4 (s.) 125 (E)
2./604 (gem.) RAD
4./162 (gem.)
4./117 (gem.)
5./280 (-) (gem.) RAD

Nienburg
1./521 (s.) RAD
2./137 (gem.)
3./607 (s.)

Weser

Leese
5./280 (s.) RAD
4./871 (le.)

Stolzenau

Loccum
4./132 (s.)

Holzhausen II
4./434 (s.) (o.)
Italian battery (s.) (o.)

Sande
Batterie (s.) (o.) II./36 RAD

Minden

Frille
Batterie (s.) 263 (E)

Map 13 *Flak* support to the Weser Line.

Flakvierling; and the combined heavy batteries 1. and 4./125(E) with five 10.5cm Flak mounted on railway flat-wagons. The first three of these batteries were located in the loop of the Weser to the east of Hoya, but their guns had not been dug-in, could not engage targets with direct fire, and targets had not been predicted. In addition, the railway heavy *Flak* was still on the Weser's left bank where it was very vulnerable to being unable to withdraw in time and dependent for that withdrawal on the railway bridge at Hoya not being blown or captured. This mal-location was possibly the result of confusion over whether or not railway heavy *Flak* could take part in the ground battle, as revealed in a late March Ultra decrypt.[102] The decrypt shows that railway heavy batteries were forbidden from being employed in ground combat as they were considered too vulnerable and, as they were the only moveable reserve of high-quality *Flak*, were essential for air defence. However, four days later another Ultra decrypt reveals that the order was rescinded, allowing railway *Flak* to be used in ground combat when the situation demanded.[103] In nearby Hassel Majewski found the three remaining 8.8cm guns of RAD Batterie 5./280 (the other three guns being at Leese). With all the Hoya *Flak* units found and visited, he ordered the following immediate changes: the railway *Flak* should withdraw without delay to the Weser's right bank and relocate to Rethem; that the remaining guns had to be placed in positions from where they could bring direct fire onto the road leading from Hoya to Hassel; that small bridges over streams should be blown and that all guns needed better camouflage. Majewski then set off for Nienburg, which he reached at midday.

Flak support in the Nienburg area was provided by five batteries under the control of Leichte-Flak-Abteilung 859(E) commanded by Major Helmig of Flak-Regiment 122(E): RAD Batterie 1./521 with four 10.5cm Flak;[104] Batterie 2./137 with five 10.5cm and three 2cm Flak 30; Batterie 3./607 with four 8.8cm Flak; z.b.V. Batterie 6969 with eleven 3.7cm Flak;[105] and the army-owned Batterie 2./902 equipped with eleven *Flakvierling*. This last battery, belonging to Artillerie-Regiment 902 z.V., the provider of low-level air defence for Gruppe Nord's V-2 forces, had withdrawn to the Nienburg area and then been commandeered to support the Weser Line. Flak-Regiment 122(E)'s war diary mentions that Majewski found the command arrangements unclear for the ground defence of the Weser in the Nienburg area.[106] Although the diary does not expand on the reasons, presumably there was confusion between Kampfkommandant Nienburg, Oberst Lichtschlag, and SS-A.u.E.Btl. 12 'HJ'. The only direction Majewski seems able to give was to order Helmig to deploy four *Flakvierling* from Batterie 2./902 to the area of Lemke on the Weser's left bank, where they could support the Hitler Youth of 3. SS-Kompanie and soldiers from Landesschützen-Bataillon 1020.

The left flank of the Weser Line was in Korps Hannover's area and here responsibility for the provision of *Flak* support switched to II./RAD Flak-Regiment 36, which provided thirteen 8.8cm guns and supporting 2cm Vierlingsflak in a static site at Sande, just to the east of Wietersheim, with the guns manned by RAD and Hitler Youth *Flakhelfer* (Flak assistant);[107] a railway *Flak* unit, probably from Flak-Abteilung 263(E), with four 10.5cm *Flak* located near Frille station; and a powerful *Flak* site to the east of Holzhausen II comprising twelve 8.8cm of 4./434 Flak-Abteilung and a battery of eight 8.8cm manned by Italians. All these heavy *Flak* batteries were part of the

---

102 TNA DEFE 3/601, BT 8896, Westphal signal 29 March 1945. OKW direction on employment of railway *Flak*.
103 TNA DEFE 3/566, KO 316, *Flak* snippets – employment of railway *Flak*.
104 Some accounts refer to it as RAD 3./182.
105 High numbered *z.b.V. Flak* units were formed late in the war with ground combat in mind.
106 *Gefechtsbericht des Flakregiments 122(E), 14 April 1945,* p.6.
107 From January 1943 whole classes of older teenagers were drafted into the *Luftwaffe* as *Flakhelfer*. The most famous *Flakhelfer* was Joseph Ratzinger, subsequently Pope Benedict XVI.

defence of the strategically vital viaduct carrying not only the Mittelland Canal over the Weser but also the massive adjoining lock, linking river and canal.

* * *

So, as dawn breaks on 5 April 1945, the scene is set with 2. Marine-Infanterie-Division, Gruppe Grosan, Panzerjagdverband 'Großer Kurfürst' and Kampfgruppe Schulze deploying to the Weser and Aller; the companies of SS-A.u.E.Btl.12 'HJ' are preparing positions in the Leese and Nienburg areas; the *Flak* crews are adjusting their guns' positions; and the aircrew of 14. Flieger-Division and the other *Luftwaffe* units are either already flying missions or are awaiting the next call to action. All knew that contact with the enemy on the Weser was imminent. Despite clear indications that the end of the war was closing fast, morale was remarkably high and most of the Germans preparing to defend the riverlines were determined to acquit themselves to the best of their ability in what must surely be their final effort against the enemy. In the next chapter we turn to the British forces they are soon to confront.

3

Forward on Wings of Flame: Second Army April 1945

The British forces involved in the account were part of Field Marshal Montgomery's 21st Army Group,[1] one of three Allied army groups[2] committed to the North-West Europe campaign and fighting under the command of General Dwight Eisenhower, the Supreme Allied Commander. 21st Army Group comprised two constituent armies: Lieutenant General Sir Miles Dempsey's Second British Army (aka the British Liberation Army) and General Henry ('Harry') Crerar's First Canadian Army. In reality neither of the armies was homogeneously British or Canadian and both included Polish units and small Dutch, Belgian and Czech components, with US forces also periodically attached; the lines of communication units for both armies were however predominantly British. The purpose of this chapter is to provide an overview of the organisation, state and equipment of Second Army in April 1945 and the orders of battle (orbats) of its formations that will play their part in the account. It should be noted, however, that the detail of orbats changed frequently, particularly with regard to attached arms, so those described represent only a snapshot in time during mid-April 1945. Since both air forces will also enter the story, at the chapter's end are short summaries of the Second Tactical and US Eighth Air Forces and their aircraft relevant to the account.

In recent years the reputation of the British Army of 1945 has been denigrated by some military historians, who have also compared it and its commanders disparagingly with the German Army. As a mass conscript army formed from a society short on martial traditions, Second Army lacked the fanaticism present in sections of the German armed forces, and prior to D-Day it had been under-trained as there was neither the time nor expertise to get it to a standard comparable to the German army. For it to be victorious, it would need to rely on materiel rather than men, sustain its morale by avoiding defeats, prevent excessive casualties and grind the enemy down with massive firepower.[3] While German ground forces were acknowledged to excel at close combat, the British Army had recognised this prior to D-Day and rather than trying to match the Germans, sought to play to its own strengths, namely: firepower, logistics, intelligence, command and control, field engineering and medical support.[4] With regard to these aspects it would prove entirely successful. In addition, it displayed an ability to develop and inculcate new tactics and innovate, particularly with regard to specialised armour.

---

1   TNA WO 171/3852, G Branch 21st Army Group war diary.
2   The other two army groups were both provided by the United States: Devers' 6th and Bradley's 12th.
3   Stephen Hart, 'Field Marshal Montgomery, 21st Army Group and North-West Europe, 1944–1945' (PhD Thesis, King's College, University of London, 1995), https://kclpure.kcl.ac.uk/portal/files/2927568/283396.pdf (accessed 8 July 2016), pp.94–103.
4   John Buckley, *Monty's Men, The British Army and the Liberation of Europe* (London: Yale University Press, 2014), pp.14–15.

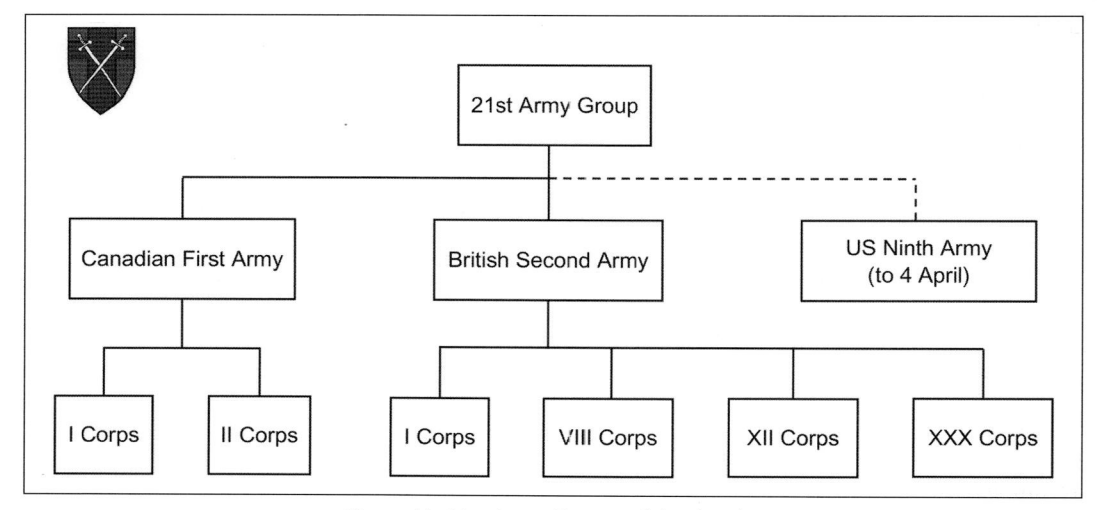

Figure 11 21st Army Group – 4 April 1945.

Despite the success of the campaign thus far, by Spring 1945 Second Army was weary, dangerously short of effective manpower and reserves, and extremely casualty conscious with the end so obviously close. In particular the infantry was near to exhaustion both quantitatively and qualitatively. This situation was no surprise as the manning consequences for Great Britain of fighting a total war had been identified as early as 1942 and it was accepted that it would struggle to replace the casualties generated by the invasion of France and the subsequent campaign to defeat the German armies in the west. By 1944 the nation's manpower barrel was being scraped, there could be no back-up to Second Army and, as a dwindling asset, it would have to be conserved for as long as possible.[5] Furthermore, as mentioned in the Preface, nobody knew that the war would end in May 1945 and there were very real concerns that Second Army might have to go on to defeat the German Army in Denmark and Norway.

Second Army's losses placed such severe demands on the infantry's manpower that in autumn 1944 a crisis point was reached when it ran out of reinforcements.[6] Urgent steps were sanctioned by Churchill to provide manpower: men from Home Forces, the Royal Navy and RAF Regiment were transferred to the army, large numbers from the Royal Artillery's anti-tank and light anti-aircraft regiments were retrained as infantry, and two infantry divisions were disbanded, with their manpower reallocated as reinforcements.[7] While these measures improved manning, the men they provided were poorly trained in infantry tactics, less than keen to join the rough and bloody life of the infantryman and understandably reluctant to become a casualty with the war's end in sight. It was therefore with this brittle weapon that Montgomery and Dempsey had to fight the campaign from D-Day onwards, and the condition of the Army's manning is therefore a key, but overlooked explanation for the oft-criticised, ponderous nature of Second Army operations.

---

5   John Peaty, 'British Army Manpower Crisis 1944' (DPhil Thesis, King's College, University of London, 2000), https://kclpure.kcl.ac.uk/portal/files/2931337/313385.pdf (accessed 3 February 2014), pp.323–332.
6   Peaty, 'British Army Manpower Crisis 1944', pp.6–8.
7   Peaty, 'British Army Manpower Crisis 1944', pp.312–314.

Second Army

In April 1945 the principal formations participating in Second Army's advance into Germany were the three corps: VIII, XII and XXX. The account will, however, focus only on VIII and XII Corps as it is these formations that will confront 2. Marine-Infanterie-Division and the other forces covering Armeegruppe Student's central sector. Second Army also commanded I Corps, previously with First Canadian Army but from 4 April responsible for protecting the Rhine bridges, security of the army's lines of communication, assistance to military government in liberated areas, battlefield clearance and disposal of enemy installations.

The main headquarters of Second Army was a massive organisation with some 3,450 personnel on its establishment, a figure not including attached staff from the RAF, and support staff such as drivers, signals units, defence units and so forth. Dempsey's tactical headquarters was, however, very small with only sufficient staff and communications required for him to command the current battle. It operated under canvas and could be packed up and moved at short notice. Whenever possible, the main headquarters co-located with the RAF's HQ 83 Group, which contributed air reconnaissance and air support cells.

Assigned to HQ Second Army was one of the two squadrons of GHQ Liaison Regiment, known as Phantom. Although the regiment's role was to update HQ 21st Army Group on the current location, operations and state of every organisation down to battalion level, HQ Second Army and the corps also had access to this information, the source of which was the squadron's nine patrols. These patrols were allocated to corps and divisions and fed material direct to the squadron headquarters by encrypted Morse, with the immediacy of the reports often resulting in the staff at corps and army level knowing the situation before it reached them via the normal G reporting chain. Owing to their speed of movement, the armoured divisions were assigned their own liaison troop, J Troop, which gained its information by monitoring the nets rather than co-locating with divisional headquarters; its information was regarded as unconfirmed.

Headquarters

Three staff branches supported all commanders down to brigade level: General Staff (G), Adjutant General (A) and Quartermaster General (Q). Their equivalent functions today are: G staff – G2 (intelligence), G3 (operations), G5 (plans) and G7 (training); A staff – G1 (personnel); and Q staff – G4 (logistics). There was no branch with responsibility for communications (G6), finance (G8) was not the major function it is today but civil affairs (G9) was a significant responsibility owing to the demand for governance in liberated and conquered territories. The function of the headquarters was to provide the means to command its assigned forces, and the staff to coordinate both the deployment of combat arms and the services to support those arms. The duty of the staff was to provide the commander with information for decision-making, issue the orders to implement his decisions and arrange for the supply and maintenance of the troops. At all levels from army group down to division, headquarters were divided into three functional parts: tactical, main and rear. The tactical headquarters was small and mobile and would deploy forward to allow the commander and his key decision-making staff to command operations at critical times and places; the main headquarters contained the G staff, responsible for conducting the current battle and planning future operations; while the rear HQ was the domain of the A and Q staffs, responsible for logistics.

Corps

A corps could contain a variable number of divisions and be task organised for specific operations. A variety of units were however organic to the corps, such as the headquarters staff and the defence company, signals, provost, medical assets and transport. Corps also had combat support assets such as artillery, engineer and reconnaissance, either kept under the control of the corps or, more normally, allocated to its divisions as required. The corps headquarters was tactical in the sense that it was mobile but as it operated out of range of enemy artillery there was no requirement for functioning under armour. At corps level each of the three staff branches was commanded by a brigadier, with the Brigadier General Staff being first among equals. Additionally, the corps commander had a number of one star (brigadier-level) advisers, namely Commander Royal Armoured Corps (RAC), Commander Royal Artillery (RA), Commander Royal Engineers (RE) and Commander Royal Signals. During 1944 Montgomery sacked a number of corps commanders owing to perceived lack of suitability, causing turbulence in command and generating controversy. The challenges and difficulties facing British senior command in 1944 – 1945 were largely an amalgam of Montgomery's personality and way of command, his relationships with Dempsey and the corps commanders, and differing opinions regarding the doctrine for armour and infantry; by April 1945 these matters were, to the greater benefit of the army, more settled.[8]

Divisions

The division was the largest formation with a fixed structure. Taking part in Second Army's advance in April 1945 were three[9] armoured divisions, six infantry divisions and one airborne division. The armoured divisions consisted of a headquarters and two brigades: one tank, the other lorry-borne infantry. Infantry divisions consisted of a headquarters and three lorry-borne infantry brigades, with armour support provided, usually, by an independent armoured brigade. The airborne division comprised a headquarters, two parachute brigades and an airlanding brigade. The principal difference between an infantry division and the airborne division was the latter's two echelons: the first conducted the airborne operation and was therefore light with an emphasis on combat, whereas the second consisted mainly of combat service support elements and materiel and reinforced the first once the corridor to the area of operations was open and secure. Artillery, reconnaissance, engineers, signals and services (eg medical, maintenance and ordnance) supported the divisions and were allocated to the brigades as required. Colonels led the staff branches.

Armoured and infantry divisional headquarters were broadly similar but differed in their vehicles. For armoured divisions the tactical headquarters was small and mounted in cruiser tanks, allowing the commander to function well forward. The headquarters had seven cruiser tanks: one for the divisional commander, one for Commander RA, two for liaison and three for the protection troop. The staff and signallers in the main headquarters could operate from eight AEC armoured command vehicles whenever necessary and key staff officers such as Commander RA, a brigadier, and Commander RE, a colonel, could accompany the tactical headquarters in Staghound armoured cars. The infantry division's headquarters, on the other hand, largely operated from trucks and was therefore unprotected, limiting its capacity to operate forward. The only armoured vehicles in the infantry division headquarters were two Staghound armoured cars, providing a

---

8   Hart, 'Field Marshal Montgomery, 21st Army Group and North-West Europe, 1944–1945', pp.247–254.
9   There was also the specialist armour division, 79th Armoured. This division did not operate as an entity but attached its specialist armour to divisions as required.

limited capability for exercising command under armour. In both types of divisional headquarters, Commander RA worked very closely with the divisional commander, accompanying him at all times and responsible for implementing fire plans for the divisional artillery and any attached artillery units such as medium regiments; he consequently had a substantial staff.

Armour

Armour and its employment was the focus of protracted argument during the pre-war years and indeed for much of the war. The argument had four closely interwoven issues: doctrine for the role of armour; doctrine for operating armour with infantry; tank development, particularly weight of armour and calibre of the main armament; and the organisation of armoured formations. The two doctrinal arguments centred on whether the tank was simply an infantry support vehicle or whether it was for rapid, mobile operations once the enemy's line was broken.[10] Inability to resolve this issue resulted in the development of two distinct types of tank – the faster medium or cruiser tank and the slower infantry support tank – and two types of armoured brigade – the armoured brigade in an armoured division and the independent armoured brigade. Unsurprisingly, the introduction into service of the two types of tank did nothing to resolve the doctrinal arguments, and British tank design then struggled to develop and fit main armament sufficiently powerful to take on the later models of German medium and heavy tanks produced to counter Soviet armour and well-suited to fighting defensive battles; British armour suffered when pitched against them.

In April 1945 most British tanks were the US-built Sherman, a consequence of a range of problems that had affected the British development of armour, including lack of interest in the pre-war years, muddled direction and conflicting ordnance requirements, restrictive turret ring sizes preventing up-gunning to counter German tank developments, tank design hampered by obsolete size and weight restriction criteria, lack of standardisation, and excessive experimentation in evolutionary dead-ends.[11] It took until the arrival of the Comet in December 1944 for the British to have a tank able to compete with its nearest German equivalent, the Panther; a state of affairs attracting this observation in the regimental history of the 15th/19th Hussars:[12]

> The Comet, unlike many previous British cruiser tanks, was reliable and battleworthy from the first…a sorry epitaph on British tank provision before and during the war.

Against the difficulties the British experienced with tank design, there were many successful developments such as the introduction of powered traverse, the 17-pdr and 76.2mm guns, armour piercing discarding sabot (APDS) rounds, and the range of specialised armoured vehicles and wheeled reconnaissance vehicles.

Through hard-won combat experience in North Africa and Italy the importance was belatedly recognised of the need for armour and infantry to fight in concert rather than as separate entities, with the first organisational changes to address this beginning in 1942 when the armoured divisions lost one of their two armoured brigades and gained an infantry one. Despite this change, senior commanders and doctrine still dictated that the two arms should operate separately as it was felt that the infantry would constrain the armour's mobility.[13] No steps were taken to produce

---

10 John Buckley, *British Armour in the Normandy Campaign 1944* (Abingdon: Frank Cass, 2004), pp.70–104. Strongly recommended for those interested in the arguments.
11 Buckley, *British Armour in the Normandy Campaign*, pp.135–159.
12 Major G Courage, *History of 15th/19th Hussars 1939–1945* (Aldershot: Gale and Polden, 1949).
13 Buckley, *British Armour in the Normandy Campaign*, p.73.

mixed brigades of armour and infantry and it was with separate arms that the armoured divisions initially fought in Normandy. In 1944 the armoured divisions were intended for rapid exploitation following the creation of penetrations in the German defences and were therefore only supposed to be unleashed once a break-through was about to happen. However, in the early stages of the Normandy campaign they were often used in the assault, a role for which they were neither designed nor trained, with predictably catastrophic results.

The reality of combat, particularly the need to overcome the threat posed by German infantry using short-range, hollow-charge projectiles in close country, soon drove much closer integration between the armour and infantry and best practice was effectively disseminated.[14] Irrespective of this integration, artillery barrages still dominated planned assaults and as a consequence tactics tended to be inflexible, relatively predictable, slow and overly cautious. Barrages also presented commanders equipped with cruiser tanks with the dilemma of whether to stay with the infantry advancing on foot or risk becoming separated from the infantry by moving rapidly, close behind the barrage in order to reach their objectives before the enemy had recovered from the effects of the shelling and could bring anti-tank weapons to bear.

The eight independent armoured brigades generated additional arguments.[15, 16] The original intention for these brigades was to equip them with the Churchill heavy tank to provide close support for infantry divisions and provide armour to help them create the penetrations referred to above. However, sufficient Churchills were produced to equip only three brigades, with the remainder having to be equipped with Shermans. Argument then raged as to whether the Sherman-equipped independent brigades could provide close support, with Montgomery adding to the argument with his hostility to the infantry tank concept and his strongly held view that all armoured brigades were interchangeable and, furthermore, that there should be a 'universal' tank capable of both roles.[17] In the absence of such a tank he declared the Sherman to be 'universal', which it patently was not.

History has treated British armour harshly and the gruelling experience of Normandy where it was pitted against the Tiger and Panther, both ideally suited to defensive operations, has led to severe criticism. However, the armour's difficulties in Normandy were as much to do with immature tank-infantry tactics as to its physical attributes and once released from the confines of Normandy it performed well, with excellent mechanical reliability being a key attribute. By the closing months of the war, the arguments and problems had to a certain extent been resolved by experience won in the bloody laboratory of battle and reduced relevance owing to the significant decline in the threat posed by German armour. By 1945 tanks and infantry operating combined was standard procedure and the armoured divisions fought with their armoured regiments paired with infantry battalions, with the infantry trained to ride on the tanks and combined arms groupings at squadron and company level also in regular use, even though the infantry operated with flawed low-level tactics and lacked protected mobility unless specifically provided. Despite these improvements, it is interesting to note that more often than not the infantry is rarely mentioned in armoured regiment war diaries and one can be mistaken for believing that the armour was still fighting without infantry.[18]

---

14 Buckley, *British Armour in the Normandy Campaign*, pp.102–103.
15 Buckley, *British Armour in the Normandy Campaign*, p.77.
16 Buckley, *British Armour in the Normandy Campaign*, p.15.
17 Buckley, *British Armour in the Normandy Campaign*, pp.139–140.
18 For instance, in 44 RTR's war diary entries for 15 April 1945 (TNA WO 171/4715) there is no mention of 2 KRRC during the action to clear Gross Eilstorf, an action that was primarily an infantry battle with some tank support.

In April 1945 there were five types of tank in the armoured divisions and independent armoured brigades: for rapid manoeuvre in the advance the M4 Sherman, A27 Cromwell, A30 Challenger and A34 Comet cruiser tanks, and for support to infantry operations the heavier A22 Churchill.

Sherman. The Sherman, procured from 1943 onwards as British industry was unable to produce the Cromwell in time, became the dominant tank in British service, although by 1945 nearing obsolescence. While its main virtue lay in the huge quantity in which it was produced, the Sherman was robust, reliable and most marks were easy to maintain. It was a tank ideally suited to breakout operations. With a crew of five, it mounted a dual-purpose, medium velocity 75mm gun and two 30 calibre machine guns. The 75mm gun could only knock out Panthers and Tigers at extreme close range, and then only in the flank or rear, and the tank was vulnerable to German 7.5cm and 8.8cm guns. Although all types of Sherman suffered notoriety for catching fire quickly, often ascribed to its fuel being petrol, many tanks of the period were petrol-engined and the actual cause was the ignition of propellant charges vulnerably stowed in turrets and hull sponsons, exacerbated by the dangerous habit of crews carrying excess ammunition to reduce the need for resupply during battle.[19] Once steps were taken to address these practices the Sherman's reputation improved, assisted by later variants holding ammunition on the hull floor in wet storage, although regrettably few of these reached British tank regiments. The Sherman was fielded in various marks, the most significant for tank-on-tank engagements being the Sherman VC Firefly. The Firefly was a standard Sherman but mounting a modified 17-pdr gun in a turret with a new mantlet and the hull machine-gun removed to make space for the bulky ammunition, the reduced space cutting the crew to four. Although the Firefly was a stop-gap and the 17-pdr was not without drawbacks, in the right circumstances it allowed British armour to defeat Panther and Tiger at much healthier ranges. By 1945 the 17-pdr also had an effective HE round, increasing the Firefly's utility when targets other than tanks were encountered, which by April 1945 was more often the case.

Cromwell and Challenger. The Cromwell was a successful design, although on entering service in 1944 already over-matched by the latest German tanks. It was fast, reasonably protected and armed with the medium velocity 75mm gun and two Besa 7.92mm machine-guns. It suffered from not having sloped armour and, identical to the Sherman, the tank's 75mm gun placed it at a significant disadvantage in tank-on-tank engagements. Although an attempt was made to fit the high velocity 75mm gun into the Cromwell, this was unsuccessful leading to the development not only of the Sherman Firefly but also the A30 Challenger, which began to be issued to all Cromwell troops in July 1944. The Challenger was a Cromwell variant with an elongated hull and a 17-pdr gun in a large, high profile turret, thinly-armoured to reduce weight. This resulted in the dichotomy of a tank – Challenger – designed to fight it out with enemy tanks having thinner armour than one – Cromwell – which was not. Additionally, the Challenger had reduced manoeuvrability owing to a poor length to breadth ratio and it lacked reliability. By April 1945 the Cromwell's limitations had become increasingly irrelevant with the threat from German armour much-reduced and as most targets were now soft, the Cromwell's 75mm gun firing HE provided effective support to the infantry.

Comet. The Comet was the evolutionary conclusion of the cruiser tank and from December 1944 began to replace the Cromwell, Challenger and Sherman Firefly. In essence it was an up-gunned, up-armoured Cromwell with a new turret mounting a 76.2mm gun (a slightly less powerful version of the 17-pdr), and track return rollers and strengthened suspension to take the increased

---

19   Buckley, *British Armour in the Normandy Campaign*, pp.127–128.

weight. The 76.2mm, firing a version of 17-pdr ammunition with a shorter case, named '77mm High Velocity' in order to prevent confusion over ammunition supplies, was very accurate even if lacking the penetrative power of the 17-pdr. The Comet had excellent sighting equipment and was fast and reasonably well-protected, although still vulnerable to German 7.5cm and 8.8cm guns, and hollow-charge projectiles. Two 7.92mm Besa machine-guns, one mounted co-axially with the main armament the other gimbal-mounted in the hull, completed the Comet's armament. Given the obvious effectiveness of sloped glacis plates evidenced by the Panther and Soviet T34, the Comet's vertical frontal armour was a particular design flaw, but one that would soon be corrected with the arrival of the Centurion in May 1945. The bitter lessons learnt in 1944 of the necessity for good communications with the infantry resulted in the Comet having a No. 38 radio fitted in its turret alongside the No. 19 radio used for the squadron and regimental nets.

Churchill. The more heavily armoured and slower Churchill with its design based largely on trench warfare requirements, equipped three independent armoured brigades and was the source vehicle for a range of specialist tanks in 79th Armoured Division (the main reason for the shortfall for equipping the other five independent brigades). As the independent brigades had been formed from infantry battalions converted to the armour role, infantry co-operation was second nature to the crews and close, effective relationships were more easily created. Although the Churchill's top speed of 12mph suggested that it was unsuited to pursuit operations, and it needed support from Achilles tank-destroyers if enemy tanks were expected, combat experience revealed that it was able to keep up with cruiser-equipped formations owing to its excellent cross-country performance and the time saved by slick drills with the supported infantry. Furthermore, its thick armour and eleven bogies allowed it to sustain greater battle damage before immobilisation than the cruiser tanks. Despite Montgomery's hostility, the Churchill performed well in Normandy, the battles to capture the Channel ports and the bitter fighting when Second Army closed up to the Rhine, and it was popular with its crews and the infantry it supported. In 1945 various marks of Churchill were in service: the Mk IV mounting a 6-pdr gun, Mk V with the 95mm close support howitzer, Mk VI mounting the same 75mm gun as the Sherman, and the up-armoured Mk VII also mounting the 75mm. Despite the Mk VII's six inches of frontal armour, this remained un-sloped so did little to improve protection and Panthers, Tigers and heavy anti-tank guns could still punch holes in the Mk VII at ranges beyond 1,000 yards; its flanks were vulnerable out to 2,000 yards. A variant of the Churchill was the Crocodile flame-thrower, a Mk VII with a 75mm gun but equipped with a flame projector instead of the hull machine-gun and towing an armoured, jettisonable two-wheeled trailer containing 400 gallons of pressurised flame fuel. The battle range for the flame was 80 yards and the trailer contained sufficient fuel for 80 one-second bursts. There were three regiments of Crocodiles, all belonging to 79th Armoured Division and allocated to 21st Army Group's corps as the need arose.

Armoured brigade headquarters. In the armoured brigade headquarters the functions and duties of the staff mirrored those in the division, although posts were ranked lower and the headquarters was considerably smaller than its divisional counterpart. The headquarters was divided into six groups with the first being the brigade commander and his three key staff officers: brigade major, Deputy Assistant Adjutant and Quartermaster General (DAA & QMG) (today's Deputy Chief of Staff), also a major, and the intelligence officer, a captain. The brigade major implemented the orders, issued operational orders and instructions, and passed information to the divisional headquarters and flanking units. He had a deputy, a General Staff Officer Grade 3, with responsibility for operations, organising road moves, distributing maps, and maintaining the log and brigade war diary. The DAA & QMG, supported by a staff captain, was in charge of combat supplies, discipline, PoWs, control of transport, the administrative aspects of operational orders, location selection and layout of the headquarters and recording casualties. The intelligence officer was responsible for identification of enemy units, collating information on the enemy and making deductions on his intentions, supplying maps and aerial photographs to units and coordinating patrol activity. The brigade headquarters could have attached to it a selection of headquarters elements from the arms and services supporting the brigade, such as the commanding officer of the supporting field artillery regiment, the officer commanding the engineer field company or a RAF air liaison officer.

The second group was the headquarter squadron providing the functions and personnel to support the daily needs of the headquarters. The third was the fighting group consisting of two armoured command vehicles providing forward and rear communications for the commander's tactical headquarters, 10 cruiser tanks (two were command variants, the remainder were used by artillery battery commanders (BC) and forward observation officers (FOO)), three Valentine bridgelayers with scissor bridges and ten scout cars. The fourth group was the office and recce group with 4x4 cars, motorcycles, two 3t trucks and a 3t caravan used as the commander's sleeping quarters and office. The fifth was the administrative group with a mix of 4x4 cars, motorcycles, and trucks for stores; while the sixth was the Royal Signals troop running the forward and rear radio links and equipped with motorcycles for dispatch riders and a mix of 3t trucks, 4x4 cars and 15cwt trucks containing radio equipment and communications material.

Regimental organisation. Although all armoured regiments comprised three sabre squadrons, each of four troops, and a headquarter squadron, the types and distribution of cruiser tanks differed significantly between the armoured divisions. In 7th Armoured Division the three armoured regiments and the armoured recce regiment were predominantly equipped with Cromwell. However, owing to limited production of the Challenger and manufacturing effort going into the Cromwell and Comet, the Challenger fielding programme did not extend to 7th Armoured and tank-killing firepower continued to be provided by Fireflies. Sabre squadron headquarters fielded two Cromwell Mk IV or VII, two Cromwell Mk VI close support tanks armed with 95mm howitzers and a Centaur or Cromwell armoured recovery vehicle (ARV).

In December 1944 the three armoured regiments and the armoured recce regiment of 11th Armoured Division had their Shermans replaced with Comets, each troop having four tanks. Sabre squadron headquarters had two Comets, two Cromwell Mk VI and a Sherman ARV, while the troops each had three Comets. In the Guards Armoured Division the armoured regiments were equipped with Sherman V and Fireflies; each troop having two of each type. Sabre squadron headquarters comprised four Sherman V, one of which carried a dozer blade, and a Sherman ARV. Two of the armoured regiments in 4th Armoured Brigade were equipped with Sherman I and II and Fireflies, again on the ratio of two 75mm and two Fireflies per troop, while the third regiment was still equipped with the amphibious variant of the Sherman V, the duplex drive or 'DD'. Tanks in the sabre squadron headquarters were the same as in Guards Armoured.

6th Guards Armoured Brigade was equipped with three regiments of Churchills. In 1945, as the Churchill brigades were being used in a similar fashion to the cruiser tank brigades, their titles had been changed from 'Tank Brigade' to 'Armoured Brigade', although designated Type B as they had no motorised infantry battalion. The regiments had three squadrons each comprising four troops of four Churchill tanks. Sabre squadron headquarters comprised two Churchill Mk V, two Churchill Mk VII and a Churchill ARV. In the troops the majority of Churchills were Mk VII but Mk IV and VI were also present. Regardless of the tank they crewed, all RAC crews wore heavy, khaki-cotton, all-in-one coveralls (known as the 'zoot suit'), beret or when necessary rimless steel helmets, and carried either Browning pistols or Sten guns.

Headquarter squadrons comprised the recce troop, an intercommunication troop and an administrative troop. The recce troop was in theory equipped with 11 US-built Stuart Mk VI tanks, armed with a turret-mounted 37mm gun, two .30-in machine-guns and known to the British as the 'Honey' owing to its reliability. However, due to its light armour, high silhouette and relatively feeble gun the Stuart was of little use and many regiments replaced them with scout cars. Those Stuarts that remained usually had their silhouettes lowered by the removal of the turret and were used as battlefield transports or providers of machine-gun support using their pintle-mounted .50-in machine-guns. The intercommunication troop was used for liaison and the provision of radio-rebroadcast to maintain communications; the troop was equipped with eight scout cars. The administrative troop contained the medical section with the medical officer and two half-track ambulances and provided combat service support using a quantity of 3t 4x4 GS trucks carrying combat supplies (ammunition, rations, fuel and lubricants, and water).

Armoured personnel carrier (APC) regiment. To support Second Army's infantry, the RAC was also responsible for a regiment equipped with Kangaroo APCs. This regiment was originally the Territorial Army (TA) 49th Royal Tank Regiment (RTR), which in January 1942 took on the role of operating Grant tanks equipped with searchlights, known for deception cover as 'canal defence lights', for dazzling enemy positions during night attacks and providing movement light. Although the regiment deployed to Normandy as part of 79th Armoured Division, the lights were never used and in autumn 1944 the regiment converted to the APC role by equipping its four squadrons with Kangaroos and renaming to 49th APC Regiment. The Kangaroo was an obsolete Canadian Ram tank with the turret and 75mm ammunition storage removed to create space for infantry. With comparable manoeuvrability to cruiser tanks, it enabled armour and infantry to manoeuvre for the first time in concert rather than as separate entities and allowed the infantry to be rapidly delivered close to their objective, and with a measure of protection. Although a very major step forward, the vehicle was far from ideal as the transmission shaft and battery boxes produced a cluttered interior, the men had to kneel or crouch on the floor, dismount over the top and, as there was no overhead protection, the occupants were vulnerable to indirect fire and shrapnel. The vehicles were also extremely noisy. The infantry commander and his APC opposite number moved in adjacent Kangaroos with control vested in the APC commander, though the infantry commander retained the right to shout: 'Stop! This is where we get out.' The regiment's three squadrons were each able to lift an infantry battalion's four rifle companies, with a Kangaroo lifting a section of infantry.

Divisional reconnaissance

In the armoured divisions reconnaissance had been the responsibility of an armoured recce regiment organised and equipped identically to an armoured regiment. However, combat experience during the Normandy campaign soon proved armoured cars to be stealthier than tanks and so armoured car regiments were re-assigned from corps troops to the divisions, with the armoured recce regiments they replaced becoming the divisions' fourth tank regiments. The tasks of the armoured car regiments were to gather information on the enemy, going and bridges and obstacles; exploit once a breach or bridgehead was opened; control traffic at choke points such as cross-roads and river-crossing sites; and provide a limited infantry capability. The regiments each fielded four recce squadrons. Although their internal organisation during the campaign was fluid, the squadrons generally comprised five light troops each equipped with two Daimler Dingo scout cars and two Daimler armoured cars armed with 2-pdr guns and Besa machine-guns; a heavy troop equipped with a Dingo and two AEC Matador heavy armoured cars armed with 75mm guns; and a support troop with a Dingo and two or three International Harvester M14 half-tracks or White armoured trucks. Squadron headquarters was equipped with a Dingo, three Staghounds and a Daimler armoured car. Some regiments retained the anti-aircraft troop with five Staghounds mounting twin .5in machine-guns.

In the infantry divisions, recce was the responsibility of the Reconnaissance Corps, which was formed in 1941 owing to the then shortage of RAC recce regiments. The corps was originally an infantry organisation but as it employed cavalry tactics and nomenclature in January 1944 it was formally absorbed into the RAC, where it joined the remainder of the recce community; the regiments' titles continued to be numbered, however, in accordance with the number of their parent infantry division. A recce regiment consisted of a regimental headquarters, three recce squadrons and a headquarter squadron. Regimental headquarters was equipped with a Humber Mk IV armoured car, a scout car and two White 4x4 trucks or M14 half-tracks. Each recce squadron consisted of three scout troops and an assault troop. The scout troops had a headquarters with a Humber Mk IV armoured car and a Universal carrier, a recce section with a Humber Mk IV armoured car armed with 37mm guns and two Humber or Daimler scout cars, and two carrier sections with a total of six Universal carriers. The assault troop of 32 dismounts was carried in five M14 half-tracks and comprised a headquarters and four assault sections. The headquarter squadron provided a signals troop, a mortar troop with six 3-in mortars, two anti-tank troops fielding eight, rarely-used 6-pdr guns, and an administrative troop with 3t trucks. The tasks of the recce regiment were the same as the armoured car regiment but its greater combat power enabled it to perform additional tasks such as flank protection, seizure of key points, provision of signals communications, pursuit, infantry tasks and convoy protection. In the advance the squadron could operate with its three troops on separate roads or with two forward and one in reserve. A scout troop would initially operate with the cars moving ahead of the carriers. The carriers would form a strongpoint as a base for the cars and move by bounds from firm base to firm base. The assault troop was used for reconnaissance on foot where armoured cars could not go or employed as an infantry platoon. By night the carrier crews would dismount and lead the advance supported by the cars moving closely behind them. Squadron headquarters moved a mile or so behind the lead troops, but the squadron leader would normally be found forward in his scout car.

In 6th Airborne Division an armoured recce regiment of three squadrons – two recce and one support – provided the reconnaissance capability. Each of the two recce squadrons comprised an armoured troop of four tanks and three carrier troops each equipped with two Universal carriers. Eight airportable M22 Locust light tanks provided the tanks for the airborne phase. As these light tanks would have neither the firepower nor protection to fight for information once the airborne phase was over, it was recognised that heavier armour was needed so Cromwell Mk VII tanks formed part of the sea-borne element and the Locust crews would simply swap vehicles. During VARSITY the Locusts were found to be ill-suited even for the airborne phase as they suffered significantly from accidents and enemy action and never appeared again. The third squadron, support squadron, contained a Vickers troop with eight machine-guns carried in Universal carriers, a heavy mortar troop with four, trailer-borne 4.2-in mortars towed by Jeeps and an infantry support troop mounted on motorbikes. Once the airborne phase was over, the independent parachute squadron – the division's pathfinders for airborne operations – reinforced the armoured recce regiment with a three-platoon, lorry-borne rifle company.

For the final weeks of the war, men from 1st and 2nd Special Air Service (SAS) regiments were deployed as two reinforced squadrons to supplement the advance's reconnaissance effort. Under the title Operation ARCHWAY, 1 SAS provided 146 men and 2 SAS 120 men, with each producing a squadron of three troops. The SAS force, known as Frankforce after Lieutenant Colonel Brian Franks, commanding officer of 2 SAS, deployed to the right bank of the Rhine on 25 March and initially the 1 SAS squadron supported 6th Airborne Division while the 2 SAS squadron supported 6th Guards Armoured Brigade. The troops were sub-divided into sections, each equipped with three armed Jeeps: two mounting front and rearward-facing Vickers K .303-in machine-guns while the third carried a gimbal-mounted Browning M2 .50-in machine-gun and a pair of rearward-facing Vickers K. The weapons were ideal for SAS operations: the Vickers K was very reliable and had a 100 round drum magazine to feed its high rate of fire, while the powerful Browning M2 was effective against infantry, lightly armoured vehicles and buildings. Although the driver and front-seat gunner were protected by an armoured panel and had semi-circular, armoured glass screens, the unarmoured jeep and its crew depended for their survival on their firepower, and the vehicle's speed and manoeuvrability. For additional support, the troops could call on the 3-in mortar section in squadron headquarters.

Infantry

The infantry was (and still is) the principal combat arm and the other arms were there to support it. In 1945 the doctrinal role of the infantry remained unchanged from 1942, namely to attack organised enemy defensive positions, fight by night or in country unsuitable for armour, hold ground gained, and occupy defensive positions.[20] Tellingly, even at this stage of the war there was still no mention of fighting in concert with armour. The pre-war development of the infantry's tactical training for its role had been as contentious and protracted as that for armour and in 1939 it had gone to France with its skills barely developed from 1918.[21] Two years later, little had been done to rectify the situation with the infantry's poor state compounded by its commitment to homeland defensive tasks and supplementing civilian labour. Despite War Office indifference, a few evangelists recognised the woeful state of platoon and section tactical training and in 1942 set up battle schools to teach drill-based tactics to junior leaders, with fire and movement and the flanking attack as core skills.[22] The intention was for the drills to be adaptable and promote the use of initiative when encountering the unpredictability of the battlefield. Unfortunately, this did not eventuate and the drills were passed down as 'gospel', leading to stereotypical tactics and reluctance to use initiative.

While battle drills were wholly laudable, they were set in a single-arm context and neither took account of attacking behind timed, artillery fire plans nor the likely involvement of supporting armour, medium machine-guns and mortars. During the campaign, the infantry was continually encouraged to keep as close as possible to barrages as the consequences of not doing so were seen to be dire. However, this advice was not always followed or was impractical under the realities of battle, and there was in any case general mistrust in the artillery's effectiveness to neutralise the enemy. The infantry received little training in the tactics required if the barrage failed in this respect and in particular they did not address the tactics needed for the assault's final 200 yards, the distance the infantry had to cover without artillery support as the fire had to lift to let them reach the objective. Though an attempt was made via the lane method to address the tactics for the final 200 yards, it was far too complex and rarely used in battle. As a consequence, infantry assaults frequently struggled and in the attacks on Rethem on 10 and 11 April we will see the consequences of this gap in doctrine and training, a gap exacerbated by the infantry's tactical development suffering from the RAC's infantry tank versus cruiser tank doctrinal arguments. Keeping close to the artillery barrage, although an incomplete solution, was the only tactic.

---

20 Military Training Pamphlet No. 23, Operations. General Principles, Fighting Troops and Their Characteristics. Part 1, 1942.
21 T Harrison Place, *Military Training in the British Army, 1940–1944* (London: Frank Cass Publishers, 2000), p.170.
22 Harrison Place, *Military Training in the British Army, 1940–1944*, p.51.

Reliance on artillery firepower tended to make British infantry tactics predictable and plodding, and inhibited the development of other tactics such as infiltration. In contrast, the German approach saw all low-level tactical situations as largely unique, men were required to perform at least two ranks above their own and the use of initiative and rapid responses were demanded. As a consequence, most German units functioned even with high losses, although it needs to be remembered that the German soldier operated under a draconian system with the firing squad never far away.

As mentioned, by April 1945 the infantry's manpower was in a parlous condition. Platoons operated at about half their established strength, exacerbated by the 'leave out of battle' (LOB) system whereby a NCO and about six privates per platoon did not go into action in order to form a nucleus for rebuilding the platoon if it suffered significant loss. The heavy fighting in late 1944 and early 1945 in the Low Countries, the Reichswald and on the Rhine's left bank bore heavily on the infantry and the loss of experienced junior commanders and soldiers had a telling effect on many battalions' leadership and battlefield skills. By April 1945 most units were nearing the end of their tether and this description of 1st Battalion The East Lancashire Regiment describes the state of a typical infantry battalion:[23]

> Signs of prolonged strain had already begun to appear. Slower reactions in the individual; a marked increase in cases of 'battle exhaustion'; and a lower standard of battle efficiency – all showed quite clearly that the limit was fast approaching. And it applied particularly to the more seasoned veterans, whose personal example and steadying influence was so essential. At home there seemed to be a widespread impression that the resistance had ceased on the Rhine and that the sweeping advance across Germany had become just a triumphal procession. How far the idea deviated from the truth requires no emphasis, but what was not sufficiently realised was the fact that experienced reinforcements were no longer forthcoming, so that each new casualty amongst the junior leaders at that late stage threw an ever-mounting strain on the few who remained. There were, in any case, not enough battle-trained and experienced NCOs in the rifle companies.

All varying to a greater or lesser extent in their organisation, five types of infantry battalion will feature in the account: the battalion in an infantry division, the battalion in the infantry brigade of an armoured division, the motor battalion in an armoured brigade, parachute and air-landing battalions, and the commando, with the last three types operating in the account as conventional infantry rather than in their special roles. Additionally, the infantry also provided medium machine-gun and heavy mortar battalions and companies.

Infantry brigade headquarters. Infantry brigade headquarters were functionally structured in the same way as the armoured brigade headquarters although there were some additional posts, such as a transport officer responsible for organising the large quantity of vehicles in the B echelons. Mobility was provided by a selection of 4x4 cars, Jeeps, and 3t trucks.

The infantry battalion in the infantry division. An infantry division comprised three brigades, each of three battalions. Although the brigades contained a mix of Regular and TA battalions, by 1945 their origin was immaterial and the battalions virtually indistinguishable. The infantry battalion had a strength of 845 all ranks and was organised on the basis of four rifle companies,

---

23   Brigadier Burden, *History of the East Lancashire Regiment in the War, 1939–1945* (Manchester: Rawson & Co Ltd, 1953), p.287.

a support company and a headquarter company. In action, the commanding officer would form a small tactical headquarters consisting of himself and his three operations officers: adjutant and the signals and intelligence officers. The rifle company had a strength of 127 all ranks and consisted of three platoons, each comprising a platoon headquarters of six and three sections of ten men. When out of contact, the rifle companies would be carried in 3t trucks supplied by a Royal Army Service Corps (RASC) troop-carrying platoon. In terms of its firepower the rifle platoon was arguably less powerful than its 1918 predecessor and this played a significant part in precluding the development of more imaginative and effective tactics. In short it lacked weight of fire, exacerbated by the rifle company's smaller manpower establishment compared to other armies. The rifleman's weapon was the .303-in No. 4 rifle with a 10-round magazine, a spike bayonet and a range of 600 yards. Although a solid performer it was obsolete when compared with the semi-automatic M1 Garand or the selective fire StG 44 assault rifle with its 30-round magazine and optimised for engagements out to 300 yards, the range at which the majority of infantry actions take place. Each section also had a .303-in Bren light machine-gun and NCOs carried the 9mm Sten Mk II submachine-gun. The Bren was reliable and accurate but its magazine contained only twenty rounds and as a magazine-fed weapon it could not produce the sustained weight of fire needed to suppress the enemy during the assault. The Sten was cheap and mass-producible but tended to jam and was dangerous owing to lack of a safety catch. The excellent No. 36 grenade was widely distributed. The platoon had a 2-in mortar able to fire HE, smoke and illumination bombs, but only to a range of 500 yards, and the HE bomb lacked punch. Platoon anti-tank firepower came in the form of a PIAT (Projector, Infantry, Anti-Tank), which launched a 3-lb hollow-charge bomb 120 yards in the direct fire role or 350 yards in the indirect. The PIAT had a two-man team: firer and No. 2, who carried six bombs in two containers. Although an unpopular weapon because of its weight and awkwardness to load, the PIAT could be operated by one man, fired from within hard cover as it had no back-blast and in theory its bomb could penetrate four inches of armour. However, it was inaccurate and suffered from faulty fuses.

The infantryman wore 1942 pattern serge battledress, hobnailed boots, webbing anklets and carried his fighting and immediate living requirements in 1937 pattern web equipment. Although issued with an entrenching tool, he probably carried an unwieldy GS spade as the experience of German mortar fire had taught him the benefit of digging-in as fast as possible. By now he probably wore a Mk III helmet, the recently-introduced replacement for the iconic earlier pattern, and a leather jerkin, a hard-wearing, practical and warm garment. Although in late 1944 he might have been issued with a camouflaged, windproof smock, unlike his German opponents camouflaged uniforms were a rarity. At night he slept under a blanket (sleeping bags were still in the future) and out of contact wore a GS cap, a large, unpopular beret-like head-dress known as 'Cap, Ridiculous'. In summary, his clothing, weapons and equipment were unsophisticated and outdated but robust.

Support company comprised a carrier platoon, a mortar platoon, an anti-tank platoon and a pioneer platoon. The carrier platoon had four sections, each with three Universal carriers and had a variety of tasks, including reconnaissance, casualty evacuation, mobile firepower reserve and supply. The Universal carrier, as a general-purpose design, replaced a range of earlier carriers, including the Bren gun carrier. It was a simple but versatile vehicle with a top speed of 30mph and able to carry either men or materiel, although its thin armour and absence of overhead protection made it unsuitable as an assault vehicle. The sections had a 2-in mortar and a PIAT, and each carrier was equipped with a Bren gun. Many battalions also had six carriers converted to carry the Wasp Mk II flame-throwing equipment and its associated fuel tanks, pressure bottles and piping; the flame could be projected about 100 yards. The anti-tank platoon had three sections each with two detachments of 6-pdr anti-tank guns towed by Loyd carriers, a larger version of the Universal and able to carry an eight-man section in addition to the crew of three. The 6-pdr fired an effective APCBC round, although unable to penetrate the frontal and turret armour of the Tiger. By 1945 there was a 6-pdr APDS round, which could defeat the Tiger but suffered accuracy problems, was in limited supply and the disintegrating sabot was a threat to infantry forward of the gun. The mortar platoon consisted of six 3-in mortars transported in modified Universal carriers; the 3-in mortar had a crew of three, a maximum range of 2,750 yards and fired HE, smoke and illumination bombs. The pioneer platoon had two assault sections and a tradesman section.

The administrative platoon provided limited supply and maintenance for the battalion. It principally comprised the 3t trucks carrying each company's immediate combat supplies – controlled by the company quartermaster sergeant – a recovery truck, butcher, REME armourer, post NCO and two trucks carrying ammunition. The signals platoon was responsible for communications between battalion headquarters and the companies. It could communicate by wireless, line or the use of signaller orderlies, similar to dispatch riders but not provided by the Royal Signals. The main radio for short-range communications from rifle company to battalion headquarters was the No. 18. This radio required two men: one to carry and one to operate. Although in theory platoons were equipped with the No. 38 radio, shortages resulted in the runner remaining the main means of communication both within the platoon and from platoon to company headquarters. Communication rearward to brigade headquarters was provided by Royal Signals personnel using the No. 22 radio. Critically, the infantry company could not communicate with supporting tanks other than by the telephone fitted to the rear of most tanks.

Infantry battalion in the armoured division. Each of the three armoured divisions had a lorry-borne infantry brigade consisting of three battalions. Their role was to secure and hold the start lines for attacks, occupy and hold ground captured by the armour, protect the armour when in harbour and lead it in close country or built-up areas. Although the doctrine made no mention of fighting in concert with armour, the experience of Normandy forced change and the armoured divisions unofficially reorganised to create combined arms brigades with each battalion operating with a particular armoured regiment, allowing the development of close understanding. It became common practice for the armoured squadrons to carry the infantry on their tanks' decks, enabling the advance to continue apace and give the tanks a measure of immediate infantry protection. Although essentially identical to a battalion in an infantry division, a battalion within an armoured division had two differences: the battalion headquarters was mounted in White 4x4 armoured trucks or M14 15cwt half-tracks, providing improved protection and the mobility to keep up with the armoured regiment headquarters, and No. 19 radios were widely issued to provide communication with the tanks.

Motor battalion. Each armoured brigade equipped with cruiser tanks had a motor battalion. The role of the motor battalion was to restore mobility to their armoured units held up by anti-tank defences, mop-up by-passed enemy and protect the armour at night, in poor visibility and close country. Although, again, there is no mention of fighting in concert with armour, Normandy forced change for the motor battalion also and it too began to operate in close concert with the brigade's tanks. The motor battalion comprised three rifle companies mounted in M14 half-tracks. The half-tracks were a great improvement on the trucks they replaced, but they were not APCs as their armour was thin, they had no overhead protection and they had restricted off-road mobility. In addition to their three rifle platoons, each company had a recce platoon mounted in Universal carriers and a mortar detachment with two 3-in mortars, similarly carried. Support company comprised three anti-tank platoons equipped with a total of twelve 6-pdr guns towed by Loyd carriers, and two medium machine-gun platoons equipped with a total of eight .303-in Vickers transported in Universal carriers. Despite having only three rifle companies rather than the four of a standard infantry battalion, the motor battalion's mobility and the additional firepower of the machine-gun platoon made it the most powerful infantry organisation fielded by the British.

Parachute battalion. A parachute battalion had the following differences from a standard infantry battalion: there were only three rifle companies rather than four; the rifle sections were commanded by sergeants and included a sniper; there was no support company but headquarter company had two mortar platoons (one with four 3-in mortars and the other able to field either four 3-in mortars or four Vickers) and an anti-tank platoon equipped with ten PIAT and two Brens for anti-aircraft use (something of a gesture in terms of effectiveness). Sten Mk V sub-machine-guns were widely issued, as were Jeeps and motorcycles. All airborne soldiers wore the camouflaged Denison smock and the rimless airborne helmet, although the maroon beret was worn whenever possible.

Airlanding battalion. The role of the glider-borne airlanding brigade was to provide additional infantry strength to support the two parachute brigades. An airlanding battalion mirrored a standard infantry battalion, with the following differences: there were three mortar platoons, each with four 3-in mortars; every rifle company had four platoons and a Bren detachment with five guns; the support company fielded eight Vickers and eight 6-pdr anti-tank guns; and there were large numbers of Jeeps and motorcycles. They were stronger than the parachute battalions by several hundred men and were equipped with twice the number of anti-tank guns, mortars, and Vickers machine-guns.

Commando. A commando consisted of a small headquarters group, five fighting troops, a heavy weapons' troop, a signals troop and administrative support troop. The total strength was 546 all ranks, significantly smaller than an infantry battalion. The fighting troops, commanded by captains, were the equivalent of rifle companies but only consisted of 65 men divided into two sections of 30, subdivided into three sub-sections, each of 10 men. The heavy weapons' troop comprised three mortar sections each with two 3-in mortars and a Vickers section of four guns. The administrative support troop comprised thirty-four Jeeps and trailers, 10 motorcycles, eight 15cwt trucks and six 3t trucks. This provided sufficient vehicles to lift a commando's headquarters, two fighting troops and the heavy weapons' troop. By 1945 the commandos had adopted the Denison smock but resolutely continued to wear their green berets, even when sound reasons of self-preservation suggested they should wear helmets.

Medium machine-gun battalions and companies. Infantry divisions were supported by divisional machine-gun battalions, each comprising three machine-gun companies equipped with a total of 36 Vickers in three platoons, and a heavy mortar company with sixteen 4.2-in mortars divided into four platoons of four mortars each. Independent machine-gun companies, each consisting of three Vickers machine-gun platoons and a 4.2-in mortar platoon, supported the infantry in armoured divisions, generally by detaching a platoon to each battalion. The Vickers machine-gun was a battle-proven design, utterly reliable and extremely popular with the infantry it supported. It was tripod-mounted and its water-cooling system, though heavy, enabled the gun to keep firing for extended periods, with a condenser helping to reduce water resupply issues and prevent steam giving away the gun's position. The Vickers had a range of 2,100 yards but in the indirect fire role it could reach 4,300 yards; this produced very effective plunging fire and, similar to artillery and mortars, allowed predicted shoots. Each Vickers had a dedicated Universal carrier. The 4.2-in mortar originally equipped RE chemical companies but on their disbandment in mid-1943 the mortars were allocated to the divisional machine-gun battalions to form mortar companies. The 4.2-in mortar fired HE and smoke bombs to a range of 4,100 yards, very short by today's standards, with the weapon transported in trailers towed by Loyd carriers. Retaining the Vickers and 4.2-in mortars in specialist battalions did little to increase tactical effectiveness and often resulted in them being unavailable when most needed.

Artillery

The Royal Regiment of Artillery (RA) was created in 1924 by amalgamating the Royal Field Artillery and the Royal Garrison Artillery, and included two smaller regiments, the Royal Horse Artillery (RHA) and the Honourable Artillery Company (HAC). The role of artillery was to cause the enemy casualties and reduce his morale, prevent him using his weapons effectively and destroy his structures and materiel. As mentioned, during the war Britain invested heavily in artillery as a means to save lives and compensate for increasing shortages of manpower and by the late war the RA was arguably the best-trained and led part of the British Army, as succinctly described by Shelford Bidwell:[24]

> According to Marshal Zhukov, it was only in 1945 that the Russians...even thought of attempting to coordinate movement with fire: their techniques were roughly equivalent to the British methods of 1915–16. The American artillery was admirable, well-organised and with the best equipment on the whole of any; but it was slow, prone to indulge in 'artillery preparation' of the type the British gave up after the Somme and Third Ypres, and all decisions to engage even at battery level were referred back to command posts far in the rear and out of sight of the battle. The British system, so simple, so obvious, so flexible and which had taken so long to be accepted rested on (1) reserve of control at a high level, like the Americans; but (2) off-setting this with intimate trust and liaison at each level of command: no one was ever denied fire when he wanted it as a result of centralisation; (3) concentration of fire; (4) giving the right to take decisions to the man at the front; (5) an obsession with speed in reply to calls for fire; and above all (6), on maintaining an elaborate system of radio communications linking every user, every agency, and every battery together.

The British system was greatly enhanced by the speed and accuracy of its survey, allowing it to produce an accurate grid, known as the theatre grid, and orientation which in turn enabled multi-unit concentrations of fire. These concentrations, for instance 'Mike' (regiment) and 'Uncle' (division), could simultaneously bring to bear up to one thousand guns and the effect at the receiving end was awesome, giving rise to a German urban myth that the British had developed belt-fed artillery. However, the shells of the two standard artillery pieces, the 25-pdr and the 5.5-in medium gun, lacked destructive power and heavy fire density was required to achieve significant results. As a consequence, artillery doctrine sought instead to achieve suppression and psychological effect, although this demanded rapid manoeuvre by assaulting forces if full advantage was to be taken of the enemy's temporary incapacity.

For planned fire support the artillery would employ programmed shoots, which could take the form of either concentrations or barrages, or a combination of the two. A concentration was aimed at a specified target area whereas a barrage had no specified target areas but was put down on successive lines across an area. Barrages were either creeping for infantry assaults or rolling for armoured assaults. In a creeping barrage fired by a field regiment, two batteries could cover a line 400 yards wide while the third battery engaged the full width of the next line. In a rolling barrage the artillery units' fire leap-frogged each other. The principal challenges for the field regiment commander were planning the timing for engaging each line in relation to the expected rate of advance of the infantry and delivering sufficient intensity (rounds per 100-yard square per minute) of fire, a combination of density (rounds per 100-yard square) and duration. In a barrage this meant allocating the appropriate rate of fire (intense, rapid, normal, slow and very slow) onto each line

---

24 Shelford Bidwell, *Gunners at War* (London: Arms & Armour, 1970), p.201.

for sufficient time, generally considered to be at least two minutes. The challenge for the infantry was to keep close to the barrage and maintain the rate of advance as it was impossible to modify a barrage once it had begun. As we have heard, for the infantry the last 200 yards of the assault were critical and the artillery would employ deception measures, such as varying the barrage's pattern, to try to keep the enemy off-balance. While FOOs were trained to deal with unexpected targets, this depended on reliable communications between the FOO, the supported infantry and the guns. Radio technology of the time was however far from reliable and the infantry invariably had to assault behind the original fire plan regardless of changed situations.[25]

When deployed for action, battery gun positions were normally 1,000 to 2,000 yards apart, troops a few hundred yards apart and the guns about 20 to 30 yards apart. In action, a regiment deployed as two main groups: the regimental headquarters and the batteries. When supporting a brigade, the commanding officer would co-locate with the brigade headquarters as the brigade commander's artillery adviser. The second-in-command at regimental headquarters would site, allocate and subsequently control the battery gun areas; the signals officer would set up communications between command posts, batteries and observers; and the survey officer established a zero line (centre of arc to the expected target area). Each battery had four groups. First was the BC's party, which provided the battery's tactical headquarters and normally co-located with the headquarters of the supported arm. His command post officer was responsible for the battery's deployment and selecting troop positions so that the guns could be oriented as soon as they arrived, and for the technical control of the battery. Secondly were the FOOs, found from the troop commanders and tasked to observe and report on the tactical situation, maintain close contact with the supported arm, provide fire support at the earliest moment and direct and control the fire of the allocated guns. FOOs would routinely control the fire of their battery and regiment and, if given authority, could employ all guns in the division, plus any other guns within range. The guns and their tractors comprised the third group. The guns were not sent for until the gun position was ready in all respects as they were expected to be capable of opening fire immediately on arrival. Once the guns were positioned, their tractors withdrew to the wagon lines. Each troop had a gun position officer (GPO) responsible for orienting the guns, maintaining the troop's parallelism and for the production of firing data. The last group was the ammunition group, which normally travelled with the guns and carried a first reserve of ammunition. Ammunition was normally dumped at the gun position but the tractors, towing limbers, could run loops to ammunition resupply points in the rear.

Field regiments. Field regiments were numbered and bore one of three titles: RHA, HAC RHA or simply Field Regiment. All field regiments, regardless of nomenclature, consisted of three batteries, each of two troops equipped with four 25-pdr guns. Two regiments of field artillery provided an armoured division's integral artillery; one regiment was equipped with a total of 24 Sexton self-propelled 25-pdr guns, a very successful design marrying the gun to a Canadian-built Sherman chassis, while the second regiment was equipped with 24 towed 25-pdr guns. In the armoured brigades the artillery commanding officers, BCs and FOOs could draw on the eight OP tanks held in the brigade headquarters; these tanks were the same type used by the brigade and had RAC drivers. Three regiments of towed 25-pdrs supported an infantry division, with each regiment allocated to a brigade. Towed guns had a crew of six and Morris Quad tractors pulled the guns and their limbers. BCs would move in half-tracks, while FOOs and their OP parties used Universal carriers. The 25-pdr, towed or self-propelled, was the workhorse of the army's field artillery and an

---

25   Nigel F Evans, British Artillery in World War 2, *http://nigelef.tripod.com*. An excellent site for the detail of British gunnery.

excellent gun able to fire HE and smoke rounds to a range of 13,000 yards at a high rate of fire. However, the gun's lightness resulted in it firing a lighter shell than its 10.5cm competitors and as the shell only contained 1¾lb of HE (compared to 3lb in the German 10.5cm) its round was less effective.

Airlanding light regiment. The artillery support for 6th Airborne was provided by the three batteries of the airlanding light regiment equipped with a total of twenty-four 75mm pack howitzers towed by Jeeps. The US-designed and built pack howitzer was an effective weapon with a range of 8,750 yards. Although capable of breaking down into a number of parts, the British deployed it complete. The airlanding light regiment did not provide FOO parties, a task done instead by a specialised observation unit.

Mountain regiment. The three batteries of 1st Mountain Regiment RA provided the artillery support for 1st Commando Brigade. The regiment was equipped with twenty-four 3.7-in howitzers, a gun developed many years before to support operations on the North-West Frontier. The 3.7-in was light, accurate and fired HE, smoke, illumination and shrapnel rounds. Despite having a range of only 6,000 yards, the 3.7-in was ideal for supporting assault operations as it could be towed by jeep, man-handled into positions or even broken down into component parts. In addition to its excellent howitzer and batteries tempered by action, 1st Mountain developed very effective FOO parties by employing the fittest and most determined men to carry and use the heavy No. 22 radio. This radio was more reliable than the No. 38 usually carried by FOOs, ensuring 1st Mountain's FOOs were permanently available and calls for fire got through.

Medium regiments. Medium regiments were equipped with either 4.5-in or 5.5-in guns, which were virtually identical as they used the same carriage. The regiments consisted of only two batteries, each of two troops, with each troop having four guns. The 4.5-in/5.5-in guns had crews of ten and provided the principal counter-battery capability. The 4.5-in fired a 55-lb shell to a useful range of 20,500 yards but the round lacked lethality. The 5.5-in fired either a 100-lb shell to a range of 16,200 yards or an 80-lb shell to a range of 18,100 yards. The AEC Matador tractor towed both calibres of gun.

Army Groups RA (AGRA). Additional artillery support was provided by the AGRAs. By early 1945 21st Army Group had seven British and two Canadian AGRAs. The AGRAs, as *de facto* artillery brigades, were under HQ Second Army command but were allocated as required to supported corps for the provision of additional, particularly medium and heavy, fire support. They did not have a fixed structure but by 1945 would typically total five regiments: a field regiment, three medium regiments and a heavy regiment with US 155mm M2 guns, known as 'Long Tom', which fired a 45kg shell to a range of 25,000 yards and was towed by either Scammell Pioneer or Mack NO 6x6 tractors.

Anti-tank artillery. RA anti-tank regiments provided artillery for defensive deployment and to boost the anti-tank firepower for Churchill regiments. The regiments consisted of two batteries of self-propelled 17-pdr guns mounted on tracked tank-destroyers – Achilles (M10) in the armoured divisions and Archer in the infantry divisions – and two batteries of towed 17-pdr guns. The towed 17-pdr guns were pulled by former Crusader tanks with a box superstructure instead of a turret. By April 1945 the defensive role for anti-tank regiments was very significantly diminished owing to the predominance of offensive operations, and in any case the large number of Fireflies and Comets proportional to the threat made them largely redundant. As a result, the tracked batteries were used in quasi-armour roles while the wheeled batteries had their guns mothballed and their manpower employed for infantry-type tasks such as guarding key points on the lines of communication and assisting military government in occupied territory.

Low-level air defence. Light anti-aircraft (LAA) regiments, each comprising three batteries, provided low-level air defence. Their principal role was to protect mobile columns, supply dumps and vulnerable points such as bridges. By 1945 the *Luftwaffe's* decline was such that aircraft targets were relatively rare and so the guns were found other tasks such as thickening artillery fire, engaging soft targets with direct fire, and marking axes with tracer for advancing troops; anti-aircraft personnel were also released to become infantry. In the armoured divisions the batteries were all self-propelled and comprised two troops each with four M16 half-tracks mounting quadruple .50-in guns in Maxson mounts and two troops each with four self-propelled 40mm Bofors mounted on Morris C-9 trucks. In the infantry divisions, the Bofors were towed and there were six guns to a battery. The 40mm was an excellent gun able to cover the sky with a 90-degree elevation and a 360-degree traverse, and an automatic feed able to fire 120 rounds a minute (faster than the crew could load the clips of ammunition) to a maximum effective ceiling of 10,000 feet.

Engineers

An armoured division's engineers provided two field squadrons, a field park squadron and a bridging troop; entitled 'companies' and 'platoons' in the infantry divisions. In 1945 there were no RE regiments and the organisations and assets were controlled by a lieutenant colonel and his engineer staff in divisional headquarters. In addition to general engineering tasks the field squadrons were trained in bridge-building, laying and lifting mines, creating obstacles, conducting demolitions and route denial and, if need be, could be used as infantry; there were, however, usually too many engineer tasks to make this anything but an emergency option. The field park squadron provided a reserve of skilled personnel and specialised equipment, such as bulldozers and assault boats, and a pool of basic engineering stores. The bridging troop held Bailey bridging on 3t trucks for construction by the field squadrons. For river crossings, the principal items of equipment were 48 Mk IV assault boats, each capable of carrying 15 fully-equipped men, and FBE Mk III for Class 5 or 9 (the Class number referred to the tonnage weight restriction of the bridge) decked rafts, which could be linked to make a Class 9 pontoon bridge with the use of Bailey bridge panels. While the Class 9 FBE could carry most of the vehicles in an infantry division, the heavier vehicles and equipment in an armoured formation required Class 40 Bailey pontoon bridges or rafts. Bailey bridges were constructed where circumstances allowed and could be built to take loads up to Class 70.

Divisional combat service support

A range of combat service support organisations provided logistic and administrative support to a division's combat arms. Each was commanded by a colonel in divisional headquarters.

Communications. The Royal Corps of Signals provided personnel down to unit level for the combat and combat support arms as well as the rear link communications at all levels from unit to army group. Divisional signals regiments had standardised organisations and there were few differences between regiments supporting armoured and infantry divisions. An armoured divisional signals regiment comprised four squadrons: No. 1 Squadron provided communications for the division's headquarters and included a command vehicle troop, a wireless troop with 15cwt trucks, a cable troop and a dispatch rider troop; No. 2 Squadron supported the artillery; No.

3 Squadron provided communications for the infantry brigade and the battalion headquarters' rear nets, Commander RE and the armoured recce regiment; and No. 4 squadron supported the armoured brigade headquarters, the armoured regiments and the motor battalion. In 1945 signalling was a simple affair and information technology was limited to teleprinters, typewriters and Roneo duplicators for printing orders, intelligence summaries and so forth. The most common radios used by the Royal Signals were the No. 19, the main vehicle set and used in particular by the armour, and the No. 22, used in vehicles or dismounted.

Transport and combat supplies. The RASC was responsible for the provision of combat supplies, the transport for these supplies and lift for marching infantry, tanks and heavy bridging equipment. Each brigade was allocated a RASC company providing transport for 2nd Line scales of ammunition and troop-carrying 3t trucks; there were also companies to support divisional troops and divisional transport companies. The RASC companies were, with minor adjustments, capable of operating in a variety of roles and could use any type of vehicle, although the mainstay was the 3t truck.

Supply. The Royal Army Ordnance Corps (RAOC) provided an ordnance field park responsible for the supply of stores in frequent demand such as vehicle spares, batteries and clothing, all kept on 3t trucks. Originating from their role for clothing decontamination, the RAOC was also responsible for the provision of an organisation traditionally the butt of much humour but utterly vital: the field mobile bath and laundry unit.

Medical. The most basic medical support was at individual level and all soldiers were trained in simple first aid and the use of morphine, plus they carried a first field dressing and a shell dressing for immediate use. Some vehicles also carried a boxed medical kit. Every infantry battalion and armoured regiment had a Royal Army Medical Corps (RAMC) regimental medical officer (RMO) (usually a captain), a sergeant and a medical orderly. While infantry battalions did not have ambulances, each motor battalion company had a half-track ambulance; an armoured regiment had two half-track ambulances. Infantry wounded were collected by stretcher-bearers (a battalion would have about twenty infantrymen acting as stretcher-bearers) and taken by jeep or carrier to the RAP where the RMO and his orderly would give immediate treatment. The next level was provided by the fully mobile, field ambulance, which supported infantry and armoured brigades with advanced dressing stations and Austin K2 wheeled ambulances for evacuating wounded from RAP to dressing station; their headquarters staffs formed main dressing stations where wounded could receive further treatment prior to evacuation to a field hospital. A third field dressing station provided a reserve medical capacity and surgical teams to reinforce the other dressing stations.

Maintenance. Repair of vehicles and equipment was conducted by the Royal Electrical and Mechanical Engineers (REME) and organised on a number of lines depending on the complexity of the work. At 1st Line, within the units, vehicle crews and drivers were responsible for routine maintenance such as checking water, oils, tyre pressures and track tensioning and serviceability. The unit light aid detachment (LAD), manned by REME personnel and unit fitters, was responsible for recovery, carrying out replacement of minor assemblies, light running repairs and maintenance, and servicing using the tools and skills available within the unit. Recovery was a key REME capability as vehicles left on the battlefield soon became total write-offs but could often be rapidly returned to service if promptly recovered; consequently, each squadron had an ARV. Repairs beyond the capacity of 1st Line were back-loaded to the brigade-level 2nd Line, where REME workshops would carry out the work. The workshops could reinforce LADs when circumstances allowed or dictated.

Minor services. The division was further supported by an array of minor but no less important services such as the Intelligence Corps, Royal Army Chaplains' Department, and the Corps of Military Police. The Intelligence Corps provided each divisional headquarters with a major and a captain and a 12-man field security section responsible for tasks such as interrogation, seizure and examination of documents and registration of civilians. All infantry battalions, armoured regiments and artillery regiments had a chaplain, who would usually be found working in the RAP offering succor to the wounded and, more sorrowfully, conducting services at field burials. In addition to its policing role, the provost company provided six sections to control access at main and rear headquarters, provide traffic control on main divisional routes, route signing, control at dumps and refilling points, and PoW handling and guarding.

With the functions and equipment of the arms and services described, let us now look at the British orbats to feature in the account.

VIII Corps

In 1945 VIII Corps was commanded by Lieutenant General Evelyn 'Bubbles' Barker, who prior to assuming command of the corps in early December 1944, had commanded 49th (West Riding) Division in Normandy and during the breakout. The corps had taken part in all the major set-piece operations during the Normandy campaign, playing a major role in Operations EPSOM, JUPITER, GOODWOOD and BLUECOAT; it was then reduced in size and moved into reserve prior to the breakout, subsequently fighting only in supporting roles. Following the Rhine crossing, as we have heard the corps was reactivated and allocated the army's right flank for the advance into

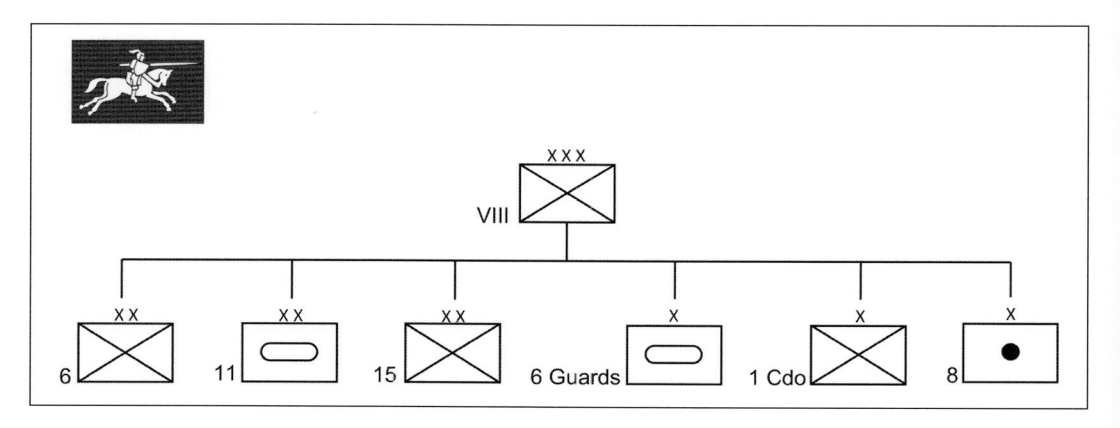

Figure 12 VIII Corps – 4 April 1945.

Germany. In early April 1945, its principal formations were 11th Armoured Division and 6th Airborne Division, reinforced by 6th Guards Armoured Brigade and 1st Commando Brigade; 15th Scottish Infantry Division, joining the corps on 4 April, was also a significant component but plays only a fleeting part in the account. The corps was supported by VIII Corps Troops. The artillery component within corps troops was 6th and 25th Field Regiments (from 3 AGRA), 63rd Anti-Tank Regiment, and 109th and 121st LAA Regiments, reinforced by 8 AGRA's 61st, 63rd, 77th and 146th Medium Regiments. Other corps troops' units were A Squadron Westminster Dragoons (Flail), C Squadron 7th Battalion RTR (Crocodile) and the three flights, each with four Austers, of 659 Air OP Squadron, which provided artillery target indication, observation and liaison for the corps. VIII Corps Troops RE provided three field companies (100, 101 and

224), 508 Field Park Company and 106 Bridging Company RASC. VIII Corps Signals provided communications for the corps headquarters and rearward to HQ Second Army.

11th Armoured Division

11th Armoured Division, with the snorting black bull as its badge, was formed in 1941 in response to the success of the *Panzer* divisions. Three years later on 13 June the division began landing in France to fight throughout the Normandy campaign and the subsequent breakout. It played a supporting role for MARKET GARDEN, took part in operations to counter the Ardennes offensive and some of its infantry were used in the operations to clear the Rhineland. In December 1944 the division was re-equipped with Comet tanks. However, as there were insufficient to equip 11th Armoured in its entirety, 15th/19th King's Royal Hussars (15/19 Hussars) became a hybrid regiment with two squadrons equipped with Comets while regimental headquarters and the third squadron retained their Cromwells and Challengers.

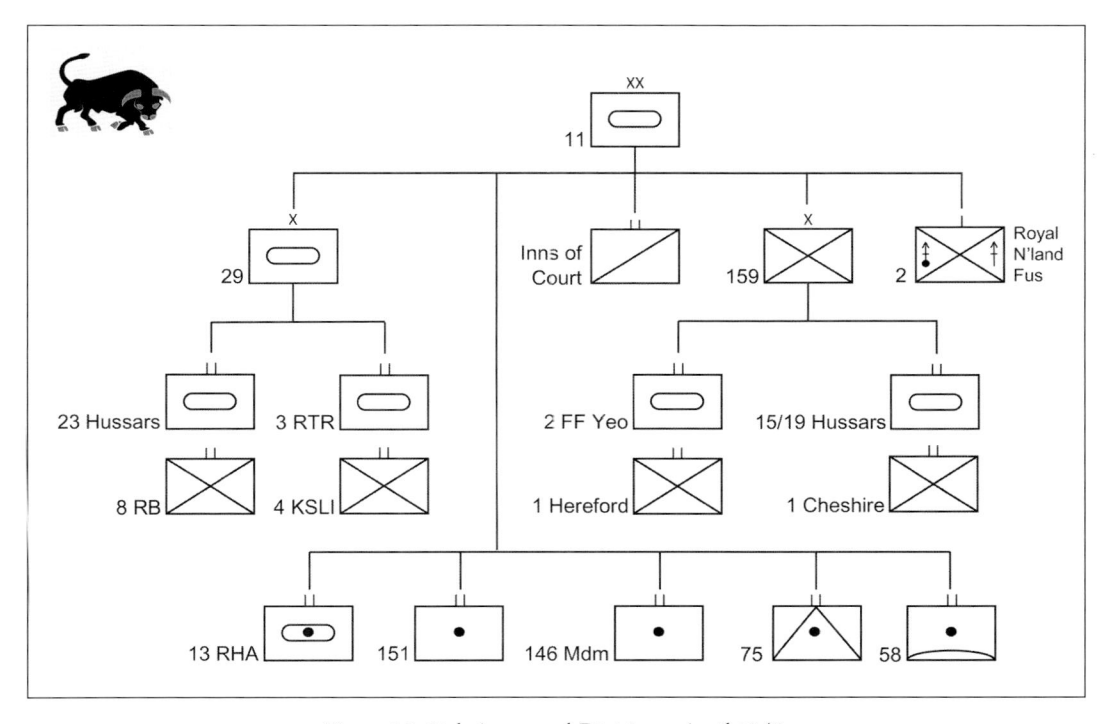

Figure 13 11th Armoured Division – April 1945.

When it crossed the Rhine on 28 March, 11th Armoured was Second Army's reserve formation but, as we have heard, it was allocated to VIII Corps when the corps became part of the advance. The division was subsequently embroiled in the tough fighting for Ibbenbüren before breaking out to the Weser. In April 1945 11th Armoured was commanded by Major General 'Pip' Roberts and comprised two brigades, 29th Armoured and 159th Infantry. Since Normandy, both brigades operated in paired groupings of armoured regiments and infantry battalions with their squadrons and rifle companies similarly paired. The Inns of Court Regiment, a yeomanry armoured car regiment raised from barristers, clerks and others working around the Law Courts, was allocated from

Corps Troops to provide the division with its principal reconnaissance capability, freeing 15/19 Hussars, the armoured recce regiment, to be the division's fourth armoured regiment. On 4 April a squadron from 1 SAS consisting of C, M and T Troops and commanded by Major Harry Poat, was allocated from Frankforce to operate with The Inns of Court.

Two 25-pdr-equipped field artillery regiments supported the division: 13th (HAC) Regiment RHA (13 RHA) with Sexton, and 151st (Ayrshire Yeomanry) Field Regiment with towed guns. 146th Medium Regiment and a battery from 63rd Medium Regiment provided additional firepower. Although 75th Anti-Tank Regiment still supported the division, by early April 1945 the guns of its two batteries of towed 17-pdrs had been backloaded and their gunners formed into two weak infantry companies, which operated with the two self-propelled batteries (117 and 119) of Achilles to form a quasi-battalion group called Todforce after its commanding officer. Low-level air defence was the responsibility of 58th LAA Regiment, comprising two self-propelled batteries (172 and 173) and a towed battery (174). 2nd Independent Machine-Gun Company (Royal Northumberland Fusiliers) provided Vickers and 4.2-in mortar support.

The division's engineers consisted of two field squadrons (13 and 612), a field park squadron (147) and a bridging troop (10). The division was supported by 11th Armoured Divisional Signals, 18 and 179 Light Field Ambulances and 7 Field Dressing Station, two brigade workshops, two RASC companies and 11th Armoured Divisional Ordnance Field Park.

29th Armoured Brigade. 29th Armoured Brigade was commanded by Brigadier Charles 'Roscoe' Harvey and consisted of three armoured regiments equipped with Comets, and a motor infantry battalion. The armoured regiments were 23 Hussars, 3rd Royal Tank Regiment (3 RTR) and 2nd Fife and Forfar Yeomanry (2 FF Yeo). 23 Hussars was a war-raised regiment formed from cadres supplied by 10th Royal Hussars and 15/19 Hussars; 3 RTR was a pre-war Regular regiment and as a West Country regiment bore the fine nickname 'Armoured Farmers'; 2 FF Yeo was a TA regiment with a long lineage. All three regiments had fought in the North-West Europe campaign since Normandy. The motor battalion was 8th (Motor) Battalion The Rifle Brigade (8 RB), a London-based TA battalion. However, to create a balanced combined arms' structure, the brigade detached 2 FF Yeo to 159th Infantry Brigade and in return was allocated 4th Battalion The King's Shropshire Light Infantry (4 KSLI). The subsequent combined arms' grouping was known as 29th Armoured Brigade Group and operated in two pairings: 23 Hussars with 8 RB (23 Hussars Group), and 3 RTR with 4 KSLI (3 RTR Group).

159th Infantry Brigade. 159th Brigade was a pre-war TA brigade originally belonging to 53rd Welsh Division but allocated to the forming 11th Armoured in 1942. The brigade had fought with the armoured division since Normandy and in April 1945 Brigadier Jack Churcher was its commander. The brigade originally comprised three TA, lorried-infantry battalions: 3rd Battalion The Monmouthshire Regiment (3 Mons), 4 KSLI and 1st Battalion The Herefordshire Regiment (1 Hereford). However, as a consequence of the mauling it received at Ibbenbüren, 3 Mons was withdrawn from the brigade's orbat and on 6 April was replaced by 1st Battalion The Cheshire Regiment (1 Cheshire). As mentioned above, 4 KSLI was detached to 29th Armoured and 15/19 Hussars and 2 FF Yeo were attached to allow the brigade to operate as 159th Brigade Group, with two pairings: 2 FF Yeo and 1 Hereford (2 FF Yeo Group) and 15/19 Hussars and 1 Cheshire (15/19 Hussars Group). A and C Squadrons 15/19 Hussars were equipped with Comets.

6th Airborne Division

6th Airborne came into being on 23 April 1943 with its manpower provided by line infantry battalions converted to the parachute role via airborne forces' selection and training. On 6 June 1944, 6th Airborne took part in the invasion of Normandy, thereafter holding the bridgehead's vulnerable left flank until the breakout to the Seine in early September 1944, when it was withdrawn to the UK and reformed. The division deployed to Belgium in late December 1944 as part of the measures to counter the Ardennes offensive, then moved north to the Netherlands to hold the area on the river Maas between Venlo and Roermond. It returned to the UK in February 1945 to prepare for Operation VARSITY, the airborne phase of the Rhine crossing. On 24 March, in concert with US 17th Airborne Division, the division was dropped on the right bank of the Rhine, with its mission the depth disruption of German manoeuvre and the capture of areas of key terrain. While VARSITY was a success, the division suffered heavily with 347 killed, 731 wounded and 319 missing.[26] Following VARSITY and with bridges and rafts across the Rhine available, the sea-tail element married up and as part of VIII Corps the division joined the eastward advance.

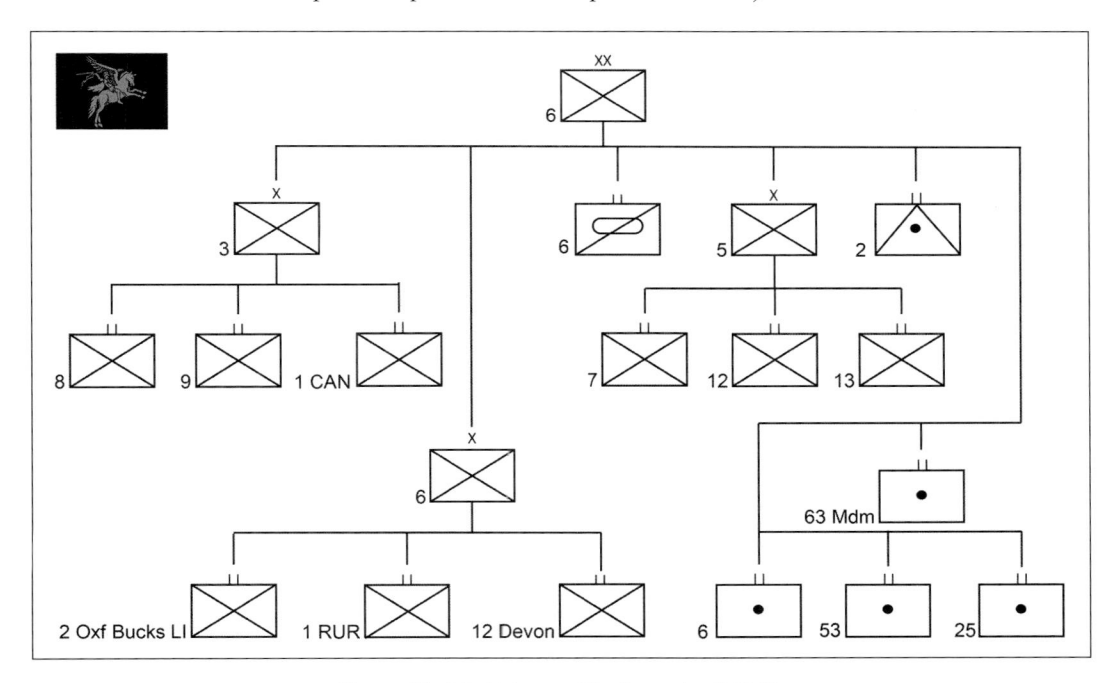

Figure 14 6th Airborne Division – April 1945.

6th Airborne was commanded by Major General Eric Bols and consisted of three brigades: 3rd Parachute, 5th Parachute and 6th Airlanding. For the advance, the division operated with 1st Commando Brigade and the three battalions of Churchill tanks from 6th Guards Armoured Brigade. As the division could undertake a variety of missions, the combat support and combat service support elements were task organised depending on the requirements of the supported organisation. This organisational flexibility was greater than in armoured and infantry divisions and was particularly evident after VARSITY, when the division had to refocus from an airborne

---

26 http://www.pegasusarchive.org/varsity/frames.htm (accessed 23 October 2016).

operation to the demands of a rapid, ground advance. The Cromwells of 6th Airborne Armoured Recce Regiment reinforced by 22nd Independent Parachute Squadron provided the division's reconnaissance, while three batteries (210, 211 and 212) of 53rd (Worcester Yeomanry) Airlanding Light Regiment equipped with twenty-four 75mm pack howitzers provided indirect fire. No. 2 Forward Observation Unit RA provided the FOO parties for the airlanding regiment. 6th and 25th Field Regiments and 63rd Medium Regiment from 8 AGRA reinforced the division's artillery. 2nd Airlanding Anti-Tank Regiment provided three batteries fielding a mix of 48 towed 17-pdr and 6-pdr anti-tank-guns. The division was reinforced with a self-propelled battery of Achilles tank-destroyers from 146 (Argyll and Sutherland Highlanders) Battery 63rd Anti-Tank Regiment, detached from corps troops.

The division was supported by 3 and 591 RE Parachute Squadrons, 249 Field Company and 286 Airborne Field Park Company; 6th Airborne Divisional Signals; 224 and 225 Parachute Field Ambulances and 195 Airlanding Field Ambulance; 716 Light, and 63 and 398 Composite Companies RASC; 6th Airborne Divisional Workshop; 6th Airborne Divisional Ordnance Field Park; and 6th Airborne Divisional Provost Company. The lack of troop lift in the division during the advance could have made for difficulties but was overcome by a phenomenal capacity for improvisation and the pressing into service (aka theft) of civilian transport.

3rd Parachute Brigade. The brigade was formed in England on 7 November 1942 and was initially allocated to 1st Airborne Division. In April 1943, it was reassigned as the nucleus brigade for 6th Airborne, then forming in anticipation of D-Day. The brigade jumped into the area of the flooded river Dives in Normandy during the night of 5/6 June 1944 and was responsible for the assault on Merville Battery. It participated in the heavy defensive fighting around Ranville and Breville then withdrew to the UK after the August breakout. The brigade took part in operations to counter the Ardennes offensive and the subsequent defensive deployment to the Netherlands. The brigade commander was Brigadier James Hill and his command consisted of three battalions: 8th (Midlands) Parachute Battalion (8 Para), 9th (Eastern and Home Counties) Battalion (9 Para) and 1st Canadian Parachute Battalion (1 CAN Para). 3 Parachute Squadron RE and 224 Parachute Field Ambulance supported the brigade.

5th Parachute Brigade. 5th Parachute Brigade was formed in England in June 1943 and in April 1945 was commanded by Brigadier Nigel Poett. The brigade first saw action on D-Day and remained in Normandy until September 1944. It then took part in 6th Airborne's deployment to the Ardennes, suffering significant casualties in early January, and operations in the Netherlands. During VARSITY the brigade again suffered casualties but secured all its objectives. The parachute battalions in the brigade were the experienced 7th (Light Infantry) Parachute Battalion (7 Para) and two new parachute battalions, the 12th (Yorkshire) Parachute Battalion (12 Para) and the 13th (Lancashire) Parachute Battalion (13 Para). 591 (Antrim) Parachute Squadron RE and 225 Parachute Field Ambulance supported the brigade.

6th Airlanding Brigade. 6th Airlanding Brigade was formed in May 1943 as a glider-borne formation and first went into action on the night of 5/6 June 1944 when forces from the brigade mounted the famous *coup de main* assault on the bridges over the Caen canal and the river Orne, giving it the accolade of some of the first troops to land in occupied Europe. The brigade then fought on the left flank of the Allied bridgehead until withdrawn to the UK with the remainder of 6th Airborne in September. The brigade was the divisional reserve during the Ardennes deployment and it participated in the division's operations on the Maas. 6th Airlanding Brigade suffered heavily during VARSITY owing to its slow-moving gliders' vulnerability to anti-aircraft and machine-gun fire and during the landings the brigade had more fatalities than during its 10 weeks in Normandy. In April 1945 its commander was Brigadier Hugh Bellamy and the brigade consisted of three glider-borne battalions: 2nd Battalion The Oxfordshire and Buckinghamshire Light Infantry (2 Oxf Bucks LI), 1st Battalion The Royal Ulster Rifles (1 RUR) and 12th Battalion The Devonshire Regiment (12 Devon). Other assigned units were 249 Field Company RE and 195 Airlanding Field Ambulance.

6th Guards Armoured Brigade. The brigade was formed in 1941 as a response to the threat of invasion and originally belonged to the Guards Armoured Division.[27] It left Guards Armoured in October 1942 when armoured divisions reduced from two armoured brigades to one and it became an independent tank brigade.

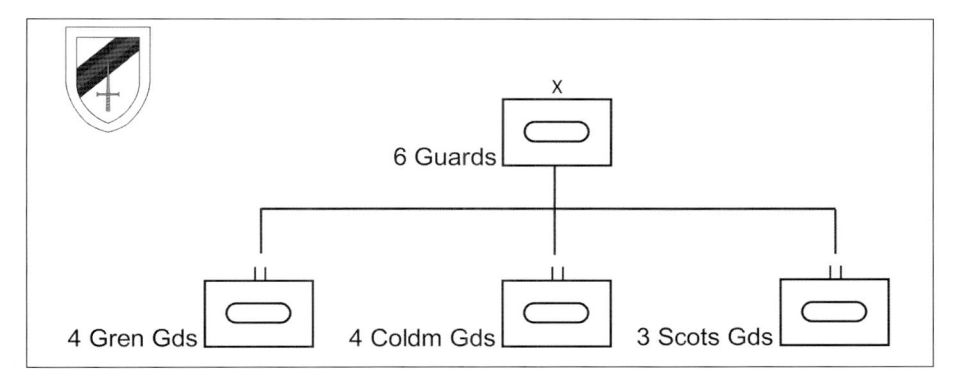

Figure 15 6th Guards Armoured Brigade – April 1945.

In 1945 Brigadier Douglas Greenacre was the commander and the brigade consisted of 4th (Armoured) Battalion Grenadier Guards (4 Gren Gds), 4th (Armoured) Battalion Coldstream Guards (4 Coldm Gds) and 3rd (Armoured) Battalion Scots Guards (3 Scots Gds), all equipped with Churchill tanks. From 27 March the brigade was reinforced with Achilles tank-destroyers from 144 Battery 63rd Anti-Tank Regiment, the second of the regiment's self-propelled batteries.

1st Commando Brigade

1st Commando Brigade had its origins in the dark days of 1940 when Churchill ordered the formation of raiding forces to take the fight to the enemy. The army formed the first commando units but additional commandos raised by the Royal Marines joined them during 1942. During 1940–44 commando forces took part in a series of raids against targets on the enemy's coast; the largest and best known being the raids on the Lofoten Islands, St Nazaire and Dieppe. But by 1943 the operational requirement was shifting from raiding forces to a need for heftier groupings able to play their part in large-scale seaborne landings, leading to the formation of four commando brigades known as Special Service (SS) brigades. 1st SS Brigade took part in OVERLORD where it fought with 6th Airborne on the left flank. The brigade returned to UK in September 1944 before hastily returning to the continent in January 1945 to hold a stretch of the river Maas as part of the reinforcement to counter the Ardennes offensive. In December 1944 the hated abbreviation 'SS' was dropped and the 1st and its sister brigades were re-designated as numbered commando

---

27 TNA WO 171/4321, 6th Guards Armoured Brigade war diary.

brigades. 1st Commando Brigade subsequently took part in Operation BLACKCOCK to clear the Roer triangle and played a full part in Operation PLUNDER, when it was responsible for capturing the town of Wesel; thereafter it joined 6th Airborne for the advance into Germany and played a major part in the capture of Osnabrück. As we will hear, it will soon fight under the command of 11th Armoured Division.

The brigade was commanded by Brigadier Derek Mills-Roberts and in 1945 consisted of four battalion-equivalent units: No. 3 and No. 6 (Army) Commandos (3 Cdo, 6 Cdo) and 45 and 46 (Royal Marine) Commandos (45 (RM) Cdo, 46 (RM) Cdo). The brigade included a detachment from 3 (X) Troop, No.10 (Inter-Allied) Commando. No.10 Commando had eight troops, each specific to soldiers from other nations. To make use of their geographical knowledge and their language skills for interpreting and interrogation, on operations small numbers of No. 10 Commando were attached to British commando forces. No. 3 (X) Troop, also known as the Miscellaneous Troop, was particularly unique as it consisted of men with German, Austrian or eastern European backgrounds; these men were mainly political or religious refugees from *Nazi* Germany and all had adopted British names and false personal backgrounds.

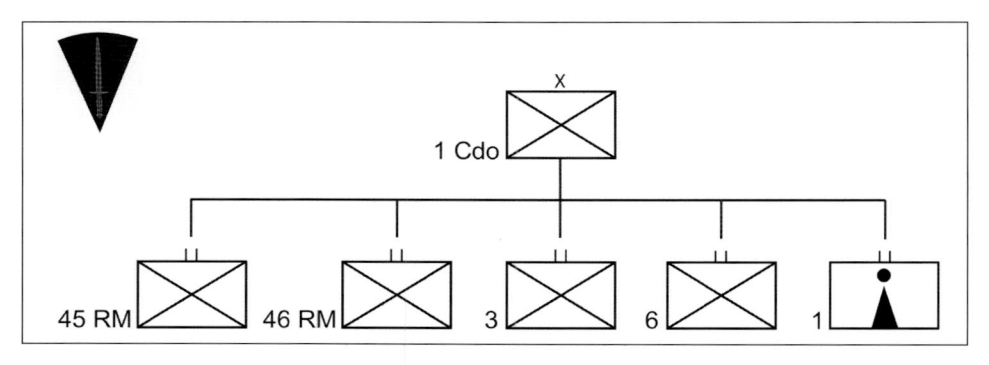

Figure 16 1st Commando Brigade – April 1945.

The three batteries (451, 452 and 474) of 1st Mountain Regiment RA provided the brigade's direct support artillery. This regiment had its beginning in 1940 when the British Army started the development of light artillery to support airborne operations and operations in difficult terrain. Continuously deployed since the assault on Flushing (known as Vlissingen to the Dutch) in November 1944, the regiment was allocated to 1st Commando Brigade in late February 1945 and remained with the brigade until the end of the campaign.

XII Corps

Lieutenant General Neil Ritchie commanded XII Corps. Ritchie had been removed in 1942 as commander of the Eighth Army but was given command of XII Corps in time for Normandy, and then commanded the corps throughout the North-West Europe campaign. XII Corps' active role in the war began in early July 1944 when as part of the follow-on forces for Normandy it assumed responsibility for the Odon Valley area. Here it took part in diversionary actions prior to Operation GOODWOOD and the fighting to close the Falaise pocket. In August and early September, it advanced on Second Army's left flank during the breakout through northern France and Belgium and subsequently fought to expand the left shoulder of XXX Corps' advance to link-up with the airborne forces at Nijmegen and Arnhem. In the autumn of 1944 it fought in southern Holland and was responsible for the prosecution of Operation BLACKCOCK. For the

Rhine crossing XII Corps commanded the assaults by 15th Scottish Division in the Xanten area and 1st Commando Brigade's operation to capture Wesel.

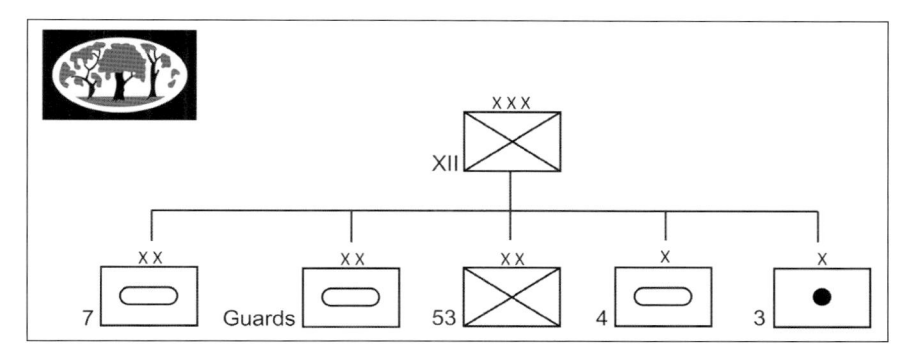

Figure 17 XII Corps – April 1945.

With the Rhine bridgehead secure, XII Corps became the centre corps for Second Army's advance to the Elbe and was reconfigured to two divisions, 7th Armoured and 53rd Welsh, although other divisions and brigades will be attached at various stages as situation demanded. The corps was supported by 3 AGRA, consisting of 13th, 67th and 72nd Medium Regiments and 59th Heavy Regiment, and the various components of XII Corps Troops, comprising: 86th Anti-Tank Regiment, 112th LAA Regiment and 7th Survey Regiment; XII Corps Troops RE with three field companies (262, 263 and 280) and a field park company (106); while XII Corps Signals provided communications for the corps headquarters and rearward to HQ Second Army. 653 Air OP Squadron supported the corps.

7th Armoured Division

7th Armoured Division had its origins in the Mobile Force, formed in the late 1930s from the Cairo Cavalry Brigade. This organisation, irreverently known as the 'Immobile Farce' owing to the antiquity of its vehicles and equipment, changed its title in 1940 to 7th Armoured Division and at the same time adopted a red desert rat as its symbol. The division fought every major battle in the North Africa campaign before taking part in the opening phases of the Italian campaign. It was withdrawn to the United Kingdom over the winter of 1943 to prepare for operations in north-west Europe, primarily by equipping it with Cromwell Mk VII and Firefly tanks. Although not involved in the assault phase, the division began to land in Normandy on the afternoon of 6 June and then fought throughout the Normandy campaign, with the battle of Villers-Bocage and Operation GOODWOOD its most significant, if ill-famed, actions. The division took part in the subsequent advance to the Seine and the breakout through France and Belgium, and in late October 1944 it advanced to secure the line of the Maas. During the period from June to November the division's reputation suffered and two divisional commanders and a quantity of officers were removed from post. Some have suggested that the stress and fatigue of four years of near continual action had led to excessive caution and reluctance to close with the enemy. However, there is little evidence to support this and other equally active formations, such as 4th Armoured Brigade, did not display such suggested failings. Rather than weariness of the soldiery, it is more likely that weaknesses in command and lack of vision to meet the changed tactical circumstances in Normandy resulted in the division's lacklustre battlefield performance. In November 1944 Major General 'Lou' Lyne took command of the division and for the remainder of the war it performed well.

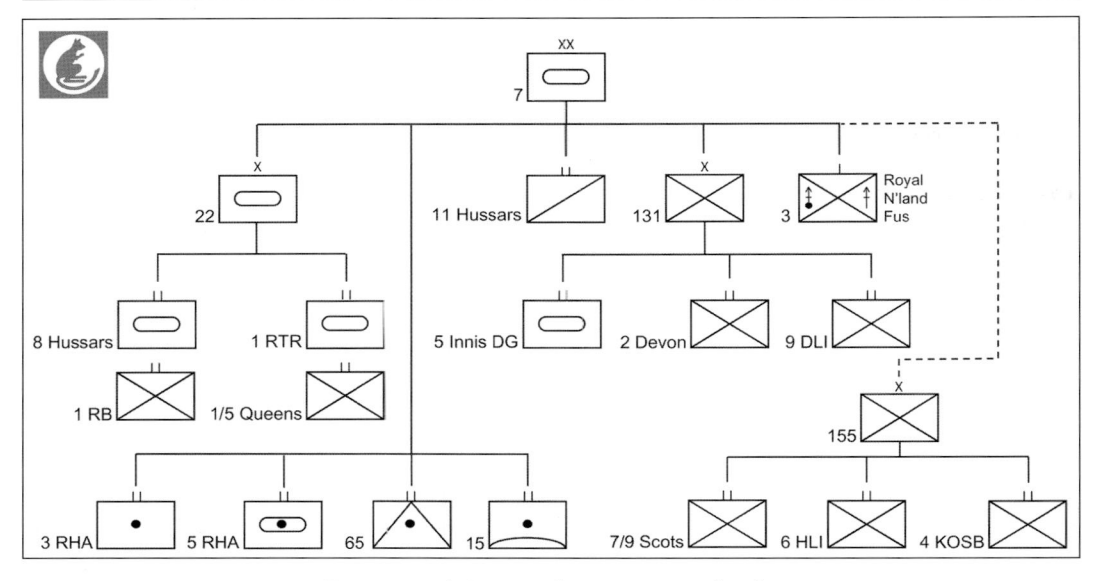

Figure 18 7th Armoured Division – April 1945.

7th Armoured comprised 22nd Armoured Brigade and 131st Infantry Brigade; 155th Infantry Brigade will join during the account. 11 Hussars, the corps armoured car regiment, provided the division's reconnaissance and was equipped and organised on the same lines as Inns of Court in 11th Armoured Division. 8th (King's Royal Irish) Hussars (8 Hussars), the armoured recce regiment, operated as a conventional armoured regiment and was equipped with Cromwells, with each troop including a Challenger. 8 Hussars' recce troop had a mix of Stuart VI and seven, recently issued, M24 Chaffee light tanks. 3 RHA equipped with towed 25-pdrs and 5 RHA equipped with Sextons provided indirect fire support. Two batteries (117 and 119) of 65th Anti-Tank Regiment supplied anti-tank artillery, each equipped with twelve Achilles 17-pdr self-propelled guns; the regiment's two towed batteries (118 and 338) had been converted to infantry companies. Low-level air defence was the responsibility of 15th LAA Regiment with three self-propelled batteries (172, 173 and 174), and 3rd Independent Machine-Gun Company, The Royal Northumberland Fusiliers provided Vickers and 4.2-in mortar support. The division's engineers comprised two field squadrons (4 and 621), 143 Field Park Squadron and 7 Bridging Troop. 7th Armoured Divisional Signals was responsible for the communications infrastructure and 2 Light Field Ambulance, 131 Field Ambulance and 29 Field Dressing Station the medical support. RASC and REME provided companies and workshops to support their affiliated brigades and the RAOC provided 7th Armoured Divisional Ordnance Field Park.

22nd Armoured Brigade. 22nd Armoured was formed in September 1939 and originally comprised three yeomanry regiments. The brigade fought throughout the desert campaign and was affiliated to 7th Armoured from the battle of El Alamein (October 1942) onwards. After D-Day, 22nd Armoured suffered significantly at Villers-Bocage during the failed attempt on 13 June 1944 to bypass Caen. In April 1945 it was commanded by Brigadier Tony Wingfield and consisted of three Regular armoured regiments and a motor battalion. The armoured regiments were: 1 RTR, 5 RTR and 5th Royal Inniskilling Dragoon Guards (5 Innis DG). Both RTR regiments had served in 22nd Armoured since September 1942; 5 Innis DG joined the brigade in Normandy in July 1944. All three regiments were equipped with Cromwells, with Fireflies providing the fourth tank in each troop. 1st Battalion The Rifle Brigade (1 RB) was the brigade's motor battalion. During the account 5 RTR will be detached from the brigade and allocated to 53rd Welsh Division; it will be replaced by 8 Hussars. 1/5th Battalion The Queen's Royal Regiment (West Surrey) (1/5 Queens) mounted in Kangaroos will be attached to the brigade from 131st Infantry Brigade.

131st Infantry Brigade. 131st Brigade was a TA infantry brigade originally entitled 131st (Queen's) Infantry Brigade but renamed in December 1944 when two of the Queen's Royal Regiment battalions were swapped out owing to heavy losses. The brigade fought in France in 1940, the Western Desert, Tunisia, the Italian Campaign up to the crossing of the Volturno, and in north-west Europe from Normandy onwards. 131st Brigade was a standard, lorried infantry brigade within an armoured division and in April 1945 was commanded by Brigadier John Spurling. During the period of the account, the brigade will consist of 2nd Battalion The Devonshire Regiment (2 Devon) and 9th Battalion The Durham Light Infantry (9 DLI), reinforced by 5 Innis DG.

155th Infantry Brigade. 155th Brigade was one of 52nd (Lowland) Infantry Division's three infantry brigades. The brigade was in France in 1940 but did not deploy again to the Continent until October 1944, when it took part in 52nd Lowland's operations to clear the area of the Scheldt. In January 1945 the brigade was attached to 7th Armoured to provide additional infantry for Operation BLACKCOCK, and again from 3 April for the advance into Germany. To support the brigade, 80th Field Artillery Regiment, equipped with towed 25-pdrs, was also allocated to 7th Armoured. 155th Brigade comprised 7th/9th Battalion The Royal Scots (7/9 Scots), 6th Battalion The Highland Light Infantry (6 HLI) and 4th Battalion The King's Own Scottish Borderers (4 KOSB). Brigadier JFS McLaren was the brigade commander.

Guards Armoured Division

During the account the Guards Armoured Division, consisting of 5th Guards Armoured and 32nd Guards Infantry brigades, will operate with XII Corps. The division was formed in 1941 by converting Household Division infantry battalions to the armour role and it went into action in Normandy in June 1944. It then fought throughout the campaign in north-west Europe under the command of Major General Sir Allan Adair. In Normandy Guards Armoured converted its two brigades to combined arms' groups, based as far as possible on regimental affiliations. The armoured regiments were equipped with Shermans while 2nd Battalion Welsh Guards, the armoured recce regiment, was equipped with Cromwells and Challengers and operated as the fourth armoured battalion. The infantry battalions, less the motor battalion, were lorried.

2nd Household Cavalry Regiment (2 HAC) was allocated to the division to provide armoured car reconnaissance. 55th (Wessex) Field Regiment equipped with towed 25-pdrs, 86th (Hertfordshire Yeomanry) and 153rd (Leicestershire Yeomanry) Field Regiments equipped with Sexton, and 64th Medium Regiment with 5.5-in guns provided the division with its artillery support. 21st Anti-Tank Regiment formed two, quasi armour-infantry groups by converting its two towed 17-pdr batteries into infantry companies and combining them with the two Achilles batteries. 94th LAA Regiment provided the division's air defence. Engineering support came from 14 and 615 Field Squadrons and 148 Field Park Squadron, and medical support from 128 and 19 Light Field Ambulances and 8 Field Dressing Station. Guards Armoured Divisional Signals was responsible for the communications infrastructure. 224 and 310 Companies RASC and two REME workshops supported their affiliated brigades and the RAOC provided the Guards Armoured Divisional Ordnance Field Park.

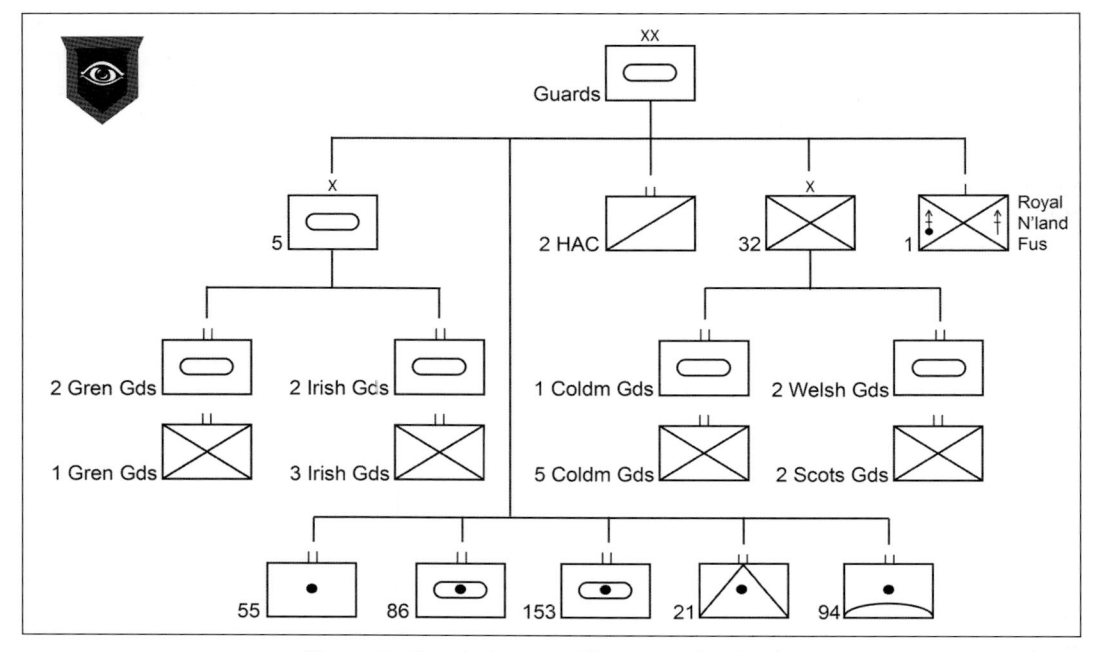

Figure 19 Guards Armoured Division – April 1945.

5th Guards Armoured Brigade. 5th Guards Armoured was commanded by Brigadier Norman Gwatkin and in its tactical orbat comprised the Grenadier Group consisting of 1st (Motor) Battalion Grenadier Guards (1 Gren Gds), equipped with M14 half-tracks, and 2nd (Armoured) Battalion Gren Gds; and the Irish Group consisting of 2nd (Armoured) Battalion Irish Guards and 3rd Battalion Irish Guards. The motor battalion provided Vickers machine-gun support.

32nd Guards Infantry Brigade. Brigadier George Johnson commanded 32nd Guards Infantry and its tactical orbat consisted of the Coldstream Group comprising 1st (Armoured) Battalion Coldstream Guards (Coldm Gds) and 5th Battalion Coldm Gds; and the Scots-Welsh Group consisting of 2nd (Armoured Recce) Battalion Welsh Gds and 2nd Battalion Scots Gds. The 1st Independent Machine-Gun Company, The Royal Northumberland Fusiliers provided Vickers machine-gun and 4.2-in mortar support.

53rd Welsh Division

53rd Welsh was the original Welsh Territorial division created when the TA formed in 1908. Between the wars the division, similar to the rest of the armed forces, entered the doldrums of defence spending with dummy equipment substituting for the real thing and the horse remaining largely unreplaced by vehicles and it was only in the late 1930s, with the likelihood of war greatly increased, that it began to catch up on the years of neglect. On 1 September 1939 the order to re-embody the TA was issued and the division mobilised in its home area of Wales and west central England. 53rd Welsh did not deploy to France with the British Expeditionary Force and during the early part of the war it combined the tasks of training itself, assisting its second line division, the 38th, and anti-sabotage duties. After Dunkirk it played a part in the anti-invasion preparations and deployed to Northern Ireland on internal security. In November 1941 the division returned to England and spent the next two and a half years preparing for D-Day. On 28 June 1944 53rd Welsh disembarked in Normandy as part of XII Corps. The division's baptism of fire was far from pleasant and in a four-week period during July – August 1944 it lost 32 officers and 269 other ranks killed, 75 officers and 1,326 other ranks wounded and 17 officers and 218 other ranks missing. The casualties were so heavy in August that the battalions in the two regimentally-organised brigades (158th and 160th) had to be redistributed within the division to overcome the difficulties of concurrently reinforcing three battalions of the same regiment.

53rd Welsh fought throughout the Normandy campaign and took part in the breakout. In October 1944 it played the lead role in the capture of the Dutch town, s'Hertogenbosch. It formed part of the deployment to reinforce the Allied effort to defeat the Ardennes offensive and was fully committed to Operation VERITABLE to clear the Rhineland. This operation, fought in appalling conditions, saw some of the bitterest fighting of the campaign and in the period from 8 February to 10 March the division suffered 1,695 battle casualties, more than any other infantry division over the same time period and creating a high demand for reinforcements.[28] After VERITABLE, 7th Battalion The Royal Welch Fusiliers, for instance, required 13 officers and 346 other ranks, a nearly 50 percent turnover, with clear implications for its future effectiveness. Twenty-one percent were termed 'exhaustion' (psychiatric) casualties and it was noted that a large proportion of these men had either been wounded before or were young, immature youths in their first action, with poor combat temperament and often below average intelligence.[29] The majority of the casualties inevitably fell on the division's rifle companies, leading to many gaps in every unit, and the impact of this attrition was compounded by disproportionate losses of experienced leaders. The consequences of these losses would soon become starkly apparent during the actions against 2. Marine-Infanterie-Division.

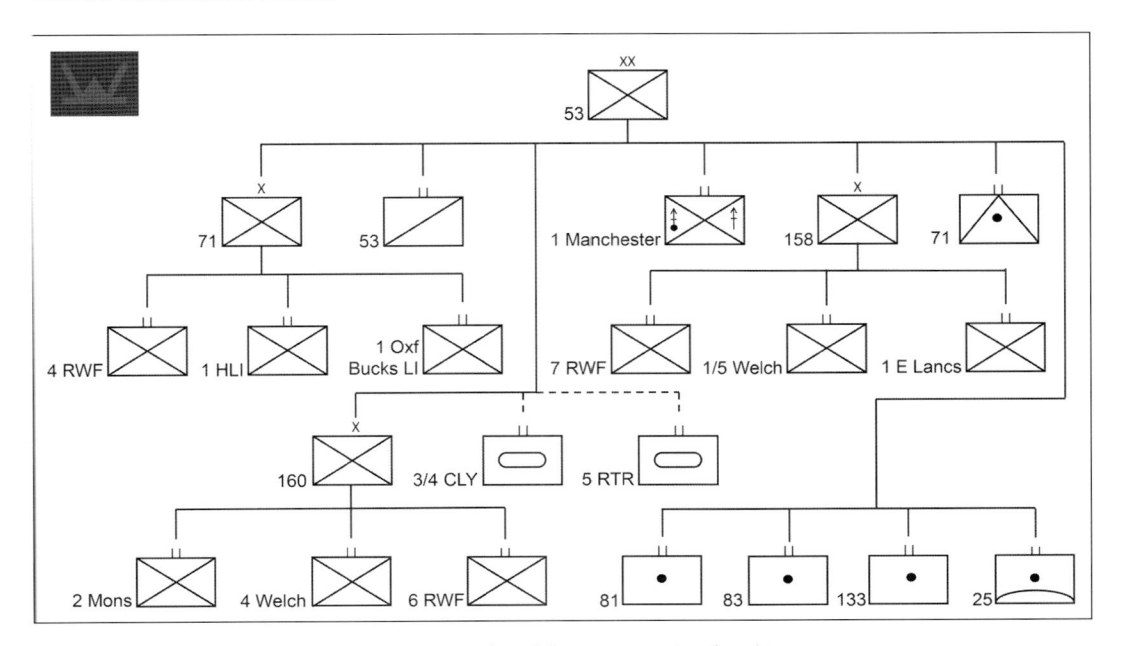

Figure 20 53rd Welsh Division – April 1945.

---

28 Francis Crew, *Official History of the Second World War, The Army Medical Services, Campaigns, Volume IV: North-West Europe* (HMSO: 1962), p.555.
29 Crew, *Official History of the Second World War, The Army Medical Services, Campaigns, Volume IV: North-West Europe*, p.555.

Major General 'Bobby' Ross commanded 53rd Welsh, a unique formation with English, Scots and Welsh battalions and arguably the most British division fighting in north-west Europe. The division consisted of three lorried-infantry brigades, 71st, 158th and 160th, and during the account it will have 4th Armoured Brigade and 5 RTR under its operational control. 53rd Recce Regiment, 25th LAA Regiment and 71st Anti-Tank Regiment supported the division and three field artillery regiments, 81st, 83rd and 133rd, all equipped with towed 25-pdrs, supplied the integral artillery, with the three regiments allocated in ascending numerical order to the three infantry brigades (ie 81st Field Regiment RA supported 71st Infantry Brigade). The Vickers and 4.2-in mortars of 1st Battalion The Manchester Regiment (1 Manchester) provided additional firepower. 244, 282 and 555 Field Companies, 285 Field Park and 22 Bridging Platoon delivered engineering support while 147, 202 and 212 Field Ambulances and 13 and 26 Field Dressing Stations were responsible for the division's medical support. 53rd Welsh Divisional Signal Regiment Signals provided communications and RASC and REME companies and workshops supported their affiliated brigades; the RAOC supplied the 53rd Divisional Ordnance Field Park.

71st Infantry Brigade. 71st Brigade was not originally part of the division but joined in October 1943 to fill the gap resulting from 159th Brigade's transfer to the forming 11th Armoured Division. The brigade commander was Brigadier Maxwell Elrington and the brigade consisted of 1st Battalion The Oxfordshire and Buckinghamshire Light Infantry (1 Oxf Bucks LI), 1st Battalion The Highland Light Infantry (1 HLI) and 4th Battalion The Royal Welch Fusiliers (4 RWF). Both 1 Oxf Bucks LI and 1 HLI were Regular battalions that had fought in France in 1940 and joined 71st Brigade in 1942. 4 RWF was a TA battalion originally belonging to 158th Infantry Brigade but transferred to 71st Brigade in August 1944 when the division restructured its brigades.

158th Infantry Brigade. 158th Brigade was formerly the Royal Welch Fusiliers brigade but following the August 1944 restructuring was reconfigured to comprise the TA battalions 7 RWF and 1st/5th Battalion The Welch Regiment (1/5 Welch) (formerly of 160th Brigade), and the Regular 1st Battalion The East Lancashire Regiment (1 E Lancs) (formerly of 71st Brigade). Brigadier John Wilsey commanded the brigade.

160th Infantry Brigade. 160th Brigade, commanded by Brigadier Charles Coleman, was originally the South Wales brigade comprising three battalions of the Welch Regiment. Following the August 1944 restructuring, the brigade consisted of three TA battalions: 2nd Battalion The Monmouthshire Regiment (2 Mons), 4th Battalion The Welch Regiment (4 Welch) and 6 RWF (formerly of 158th Brigade). 6 RWF will be detached to 4th Armoured Brigade on 14 April.

4th Armoured Brigade

4th Armoured Brigade will come under command of 53rd Welsh on 13 April 1945.[30] The brigade was formed in Egypt in 1938 as part of the Mobile Force and fought throughout the desert campaign either as a brigade in 7th Armoured Division or, from autumn 1942, as an independent armoured brigade, and sported a black desert rat to mark its desert service. The brigade subsequently fought in Sicily and Italy until January 1944 when it returned to England to prepare for D-Day. It landed in Normandy on 7 June 1944 and thereafter served throughout the North-West

---

30 TNA WO 171/4314, 4th Armoured Brigade war diary.

Europe campaign. As an independent armoured brigade its affiliation changed frequently and, from landing in Normandy to coming under 53rd Welsh, it did so 26 times.

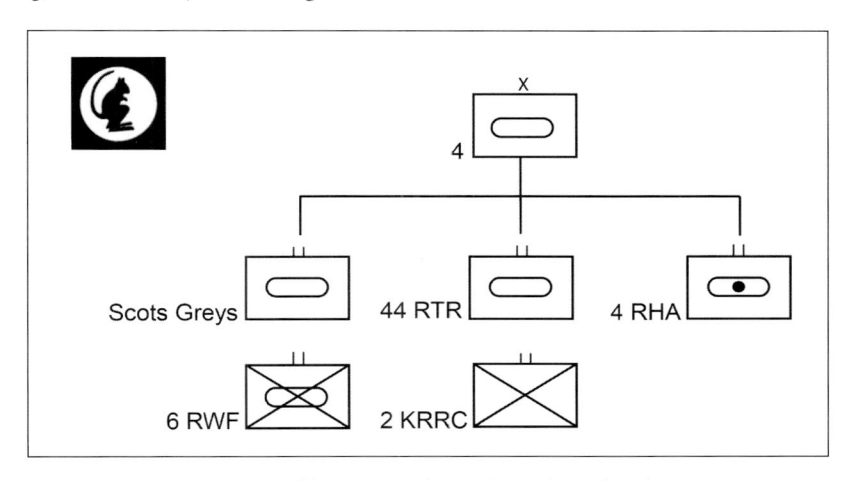

Figure 21 4th Armoured Brigade – 14 April 1945.

The formidable Mike Carver, at 29 the youngest brigadier in the Army, commanded the brigade, which comprised three armoured regiments The Royal Scots Greys (Scots Greys), 3rd/4th County of London Yeomanry (3/4 CLY) and 44 RTR, and a motor battalion, 2nd Battalion The King's Royal Rifle Corps (2 KRRC). In the account 3/4 CLY will be detached from the brigade to support the 53rd Welsh infantry brigades; in its place 6 RWF, with two companies carried in F Squadron 49 APC Regiment's Kangaroos, will be attached allowing 4th Armoured to fight with balanced pairings of armour and infantry: Scots Greys with 6 RWF and 44 RTR with 2 KRRC. The Scots Greys and 3/4 CLY fielded the Sherman 75mm and Fireflies, while 44 RTR was equipped with the amphibious Sherman V 'DD'. Integral artillery support was provided by 4 RHA, a Sexton regiment.

Second Tactical Air Force

Second Tactical Air Force, formed on 1 June 1943 from Army Co-operation Command as part of the preparations for OVERLORD, provided 21st Army Group with its air support. While most of the constituent units came from Fighter Command, Bomber Command provided the medium and light bombers and Army Cooperation Command the Auster IV/V liaison and fire control aircraft. The task of Second Tactical Air Force was to provide air defence, bombing, photographic and visual reconnaissance, ground attack by fighters armed with cannon, bombs or rocket projectiles (RP), and meteorological support. Two of these tasks – air defence and ground attacks – will feature in the account. Air Marshal Sir Arthur Coningham, an officer with considerable experience of supporting ground operations as a result of his command of the Desert Air Force and then First Allied Tactical Air Force in Italy, commanded Second Tactical Air Force. But despite its power all was not perfect and many senior RAF officers still considered that the close battle was the army's responsibility and that the air force's role was to support the army by depth interdiction of the enemy and his logistics. This doctrinal hostility was compounded by poor relationships, not only between Coningham and Montgomery, with the latter seeing the RAF staff as advisers rather than equals, but also between senior RAF and army commanders. Despite these high-level difficulties, at low levels relations were good, and the sheer quantity of air power and the much-reduced threat from the *Luftwaffe* papered over the relationship cracks.[31]

Second Tactical Air Force's first airstrips were established in Normandy by D+4 and for the remainder of the campaign it supported British and Canadian ground forces from the soil of continental Europe. Second Tactical Air Force was organised on three principal groups: No. 2 Group provided the medium and light bomber support using Mitchell II and Mosquito VI aircraft, while No. 83 and No. 84 Groups flew Spitfires, Typhoon 1B, Tempest V and Auster IV/V. Additionally, No. 83 Group flew a squadron of Meteor III jets. No. 83 Group supported Second Army and No. 84 Group supported First Canadian Army. In April 1945 No. 83 Group, commanded by Air Vice Marshal Harry Broadhurst, comprised a recce wing of Spitfires, seven Spitfire, Typhoon 1B and Tempest V wings, and four Auster IV/V squadrons. The basic flying unit was the squadron, usually consisting of 30 aircraft, of which 24 were operational with six held in reserve. Squadrons contained only aircraft and aircrew and operated as part of a wing, usually comprising three to four squadrons all flying from a single airfield. Aircraft operated from three types of base. The most austere were the refueling and rearming strips, where only essential servicing and repairs could be conducted. Next were the advanced landing grounds; these were fully equipped, usually had runways made of pierced-steel planking but were not capable of operating a complete wing. Last were the fully operational airfields with metalled runways and hard-standing. In early April the squadrons were still flying from advanced landing grounds west of the Rhine as there had not been sufficient time to move to new locations to the east. This significantly increased the time needed to reach the vans of the rapidly advancing corps, resulting in reduced air cover; this will have fatal consequences for troops in 11th Armoured Division in particular.

In April 1945 the principal air defence tasks were patrols and sweeps. Patrols usually comprised four aircraft allocated to patrol sectors by their parent squadrons. A group control centre used radar to track the patrols and enemy aircraft, vectoring the patrol towards the target. While the patrol was operating, other squadrons were on stand-by either to relieve the patrol or to reinforce it if necessary. Sweeps were aggressive patrols to maintain air superiority and consisted of a larger formation of aircraft flying over enemy territory with the aim of destroying the *Luftwaffe* either on the ground or in the air. Opportunity ground targets other than the *Luftwaffe* were the focus of armed reconnaissance missions and involved squadrons flying over enemy territory to attack trains, road convoys and military installations with cannon, bomb or RP. When the target was in close proximity to forward troops, experienced fighter controllers travelling in a leading tank or an armoured contact car would direct attacks; specific ground targets were the subject of programmed ground-attack missions. The main threat to armed reconnaissance missions, particularly when engaged in low-level attacks, was the widespread and still effective German *Flak*.

The principal British aircraft in the account are the Typhoon 1B and Tempest V. The Typhoon was originally designed to replace the Hurricane and although it had some success as a low-level interceptor, its powerful engine and stability fitted the RAF's requirement for a ground-attack aircraft. That it did not meet the army's is a moot point and while an adequate stop-gap, it was not designed for the role so lacked necessary features, such as additional armour, inevitably leading to increased attrition. The Typhoon was armed with four 20mm cannon and could carry either bombs or RP, although in practice Typhoon wings specialised in one or the other. The RP aircraft carried eight RP3 60-lb HE or HE fragmentation rockets. The RP was a simple device consisting of a warhead screwed on the front of a cast-iron tube filled with a cordite propellant and fitted with

---

31 Wing Commander P Rait, Advanced Command and Staff Course No. 17, 'Me, myself and I: How important were personality, ego and personal relationships to British Air Land Integration in the Western Desert and Normandy?' *shorturl.at/dhoA8* (accessed 23 October 2017).

four large tailfins. Tactical doctrine for a RP attack involved the Typhoon formation approaching the target at 8,000 feet. With his wingman close behind, the leader would normally make the first attack to mark the target and assess the threat from *Flak*; other aircraft would then follow in close succession. If the target was defended, the pilots would attack in a dive angle of 60 degrees and fire all eight rockets in a single salvo at an altitude of about 4,000 feet and a range of about 1,600 yards. Only one attack would be attempted. If the target was lightly defended, pilots would make a shallow dive of 25 degrees and fire the rockets in pairs at an altitude of about 1,500 feet and a range of 1,100 yards. Squadrons also developed their own tactics, one of which was to fly down to low level in a shallow dive, aim at about 600 yards then fire cannon and rockets together at close range, sometimes as close as 250 yards. While improving accuracy, this tactic not surprisingly brought added dangers from trees, cables, and the detonations and debris thrown up from the attacks. Whatever the tactic, and the enemy apart, rocket attacks required considerable skill as the pilot had to compensate for variables such as wind speed and direction, rocket fall and deflection. The RP was therefore very much an area weapon and was at its most effective as a means of reducing the morale of those on the receiving end. During the account, the following Typhoon 1B squadrons will feature: 137, 181 and 182 Squadrons flying from B.106 strip at Enschede (Twente) and 184 Squadron flying from B.100 strip at Goch.

The Tempest V was a development of the Typhoon 1B that gave the aircraft a thinner wing, a four-bladed propeller and increased tail surfaces, improving its performance sufficiently to allow its use as a low and medium altitude fighter. Because of the aircraft's increased speed and stability, the Tempest V squadrons were kept back in England to combat the V-1 offensive and so did not transfer to Second Tactical Air Force until late September 1944, when 122 Wing moved to B.80 strip at Volkel in the Netherlands. Thereafter the Tempest squadrons played a significant role in the offensive against German jet aircraft, mounting patrols and armed reconnaissance missions. The Tempest mounted four 20mm cannon and the principal patrol formation was the 'fluid six' where the aircraft operated in pairs and echeloned both in height and front to rear. Despite the aircraft's qualities, losses to the *Luftwaffe* and ground fire were not insignificant and there was an enduring threat from US pilots confusing the Tempest with Fw 190. No. 56, 80 and 486 Squadrons flying from Volkel will all play a part in the account.

The third aircraft to feature is the Auster, a high-wing monoplane used in the air observation role for artillery fire direction, information gathering and liaison flights. The normal strength of an Auster squadron was 12 aircraft with the personnel a mix of RA and RAF; all 19 pilots were RA officers. The squadrons were allocated to the corps, with each division allocated a flight. Aircraft were fitted with the No. 22 radio, which was an HF set providing two-way voice communications with artillery units and formations on the ground.

US Eighth Air Force

The US Eighth Air Force was formed in January 1942 and began to deploy to the United Kingdom in the summer of the same year to fulfill its mission: the mounting of strategic daylight bombing operations against the enemy's war effort in western Europe. By 1945 the Eighth Air Force was a formidable organisation capable of dispatching from its airfields in eastern England more than 2,000 four-engined bombers and 1,000 fighters to multiple targets in a single mission. In 1945 it comprised three air divisions of heavy bombers, the VIII Fighter Command and the VIII Air Support Command.

Each air division contained a total of four combat bombardment wings comprising a total of 12 bombardment groups. A bombardment group would occupy a single air base and would generally consist of four squadrons each of 12 bombers. 1st and 3rd Air Divisions provided the Boeing B-17

Flying Fortress combat bombardment wings and 2nd Air Division provided the Consolidated B-24 Liberator wings. By 1945 the bombardment groups were flying the B-17G Flying Fortress and the B-24J Liberator, the final variants of these famous bombers. The B-17G had a crew of 10, a ceiling of 35,000 feet, a top speed of 280mph and could carry its bombload 2,000 miles. It was defended by thirteen .50 in M2 Browning machine guns and was renowned for its capacity to accept punishment. The B-24J Liberator flew faster and could carry a heavier bombload to a greater range but was more vulnerable to battle damage and tended to catch fire. The B-24J had a crew of 10 and was armed with eleven .5in machine guns. To make best use of their defensive firepower and to concentrate the bomb pattern, bomber squadrons flew in combat boxes with the aircraft staggered in plan, profile and front elevation views. North American P-51 Mustang and Republic P-47 Thunderbolt fighters escorted the bomber formations. The Mustang was an excellent aircraft with a very large fuel capacity allowing it to escort bombers to their targets deep inside Germany, and with performance at altitude outmatching most *Luftwaffe* fighters. The heavy Thunderbolt did not have the range of the Mustang and was less maneuverable, but was a powerful aircraft armed with eight .50-in machine-guns.

* * *

With both opponents described and the operational scene set I will turn the calendar to 4 April 1945 and move to the Weser, about to be reached by units of 6th Airborne Division from VIII Corps.

4

Stukas, Tigers and Panthers: VIII Corps' Battles for Weser Bridgeheads 5–6 April 1945

Once relieved by XII Corps from the Ibbenbüren battle, VIII Corps made such rapid progress against light opposition from 325. Infanterie-Division that the advance began to outstrip the production of orders from 21st Army Group and Second Army. On 5 April Montgomery ordered Second Army to secure the line of the Weser,[1] capture Bremen and then advance on the right to the line of the Aller and Leine. The same day General Barker issued his instructions to his divisions, which were as follows: 6th Airborne Division was to advance to the Weser and capture bridges at Minden, secure a bridgehead at Petershagen and protect the corps' right flank; 11th Armoured Division was to advance to the area of Stolzenau and secure a bridgehead over the Weser sufficiently large to protect construction of a bridge; 15th Scottish was to complete its concentration in the Lengerich area and be prepared to move up on 6 April to a concentration area close to the Weser; and 1st Commando Brigade was to finish clearing Osnabrück and be prepared to send a commando forward to 6th Airborne and take over and hold Lübbecke. As it was apparent that operations to cross the rivers would soon demand additional infantry, particularly for 11th Armoured, 77th Medium Regiment was ordered to move forward as quickly as possible to assume 1st Commando Brigade's security duties, freeing the commandos for infantry operations to the east.

On the other side of the hill, the Germans braced themselves to defend the riverlines. On 4 April demolition teams from Panzer-Pionier-A.u.E. Bataillon 16 and Pionier-Sperr-Brigade 1100 destroyed the ferry at Petershagen and on 5 April demolished the bridges at Minden as well as the road and foot-bridges at Nienburg. There was, however, no requirement to demolish the railway bridge near Nienburg as 617 Squadron RAF had, as part of the effort to prevent reinforcements reaching the Rhine, done the job for them on 22 March with hits by a Grand Slam and two Tallboy bombs.[2] With the demolitions complete, the scene was set for Armeegruppe Student's defence of the Weser.

---

1 TNA WO 171/3952, 2nd Army G Ops Main war diary.
2 Middlebrook and Everitt, *The Bomber Command War Diaries,* p.686. Both types were deep-penetration, 'earthquake' bombs. The Grand Slam weighed 22,000-lb, the Tallboy 12,000-lb.

Thursday 5 April

6th Airborne Division on the Weser

The opening shots of the battle for the Weser were fired on the afternoon of 4 April when units of 6th Airborne began to close up to the river. The first action involved 6th Armoured Reconnaissance Regiment,[3] which for the advance from Osnabrück had allocated its A Squadron to 6th Airlanding Brigade and B Squadron to 3rd Parachute Brigade; C Squadron the support squadron, and 22nd Independent Parachute Company provided a guard for the division's open left flank. Shortly before 1430 hours, B Squadron reported that C Squadron, which was following, was being engaged by heavy *Flak* guns. These guns, firing from the Holzhausen II *Flak* site and belonging to Batterie 4./434 and the Italian battery, had allowed the recce squadrons to pass before coming into action to engage C Squadron. With C Squadron pinned down by the fire, B Squadron Cromwells had to be sent back to extract their comrades, who had insufficient firepower to counter the 8.8 cm *Flak*. The regimental war diary records that during the action a White scout car and four mortar Jeeps were destroyed, and a Vickers troop was missing. With supporting fire from the Cromwells, the Holzhausen II *Flak* site was subsequently cleared by a platoon from 22nd Independent Parachute Company supported by C Squadron's assault troop and 200 prisoners taken.

While the recce troops were dealing with the *Flak*, 3rd Parachute Brigade was closing on Minden.[4] Followed by 6th Airlanding Brigade, the brigade had led the division's advance on a single brigade frontage, while 5th Parachute Brigade remained in Osnabrück to help 1st Commando Brigade secure the town. The advance, led by No. 1 Squadron 4 Gren Gds with its Churchill tanks carrying A Company 8 Para,[5] was largely uneventful until the early afternoon when, as they neared the outskirts of Minden, they saw a Panther and four assault guns hastily withdrawing into the built-up area. Soon after they encountered a blocking position, probably manned by men from Pionier-Ersatz-Bataillon 6, and at 1430 hours as the lead Churchill commanded by Lieutenant Minnette-Lucas closed on this position a StuG IV (possibly belonging to Panzer-Ersatz-Abteilung 11) suddenly appeared and fired at the Churchill. Normally the 75mm AP round fired by a StuG would not have posed a threat to the heavily-armoured Churchill but tragically this round hit the turret ring, penetrated the armour and killed Minnette-Lucas and two of his crew. 8 Para tried to outflank this opposition but came under intense machine-gun fire and without artillery support was unable to make headway.[6] Although the battalion was held-up, Brigadier Hill guessed that the enemy probably had few reserves and he decided to capture Minden by night. However, this attack was destined never to take place as two US officers, accompanied by a major from 9 Para, drove into the town at 1900 hours under the cover of a white flag to deliver an ultimatum, which was on the lines of 'surrender the town or it will be shelled out of existence!'[7] At 2345 hours 8 Para and 1 CAN Para,[8] accompanied by Churchills of 4 Gren Gds, entered the town and by 0230 hours on 5 April it was reported clear, although the bridges were found demolished. 3rd Parachute Brigade remained in Minden until ordered to withdraw at mid-day on 5 April to allow US 5th Armored Division to occupy the town as it lay in US Ninth Army's area.

While 3rd Parachute Brigade was involved in Minden, 6th Airlanding Brigade, led by 2 Oxf Bucks LI and Churchills from No. 2 Squadron 4 Gren Gds, had moved up on the division's

---

3   TNA WO 171/4161, 6th Airborne Division Recce Regiment war diary.
4   TNA WO 171/4306, 3rd Parachute Brigade war diary.
5   TNA WO 171/5146, 4 Gren Gds war diary.
6   TNA WO 171/5135, 8 Para war diary.
7   TNA WO 171/5135, 9 Para war diary.
8   TNA WO 171/4536, 1 CAN Para war diary.

STUKAS, TIGERS AND PANTHERS 143

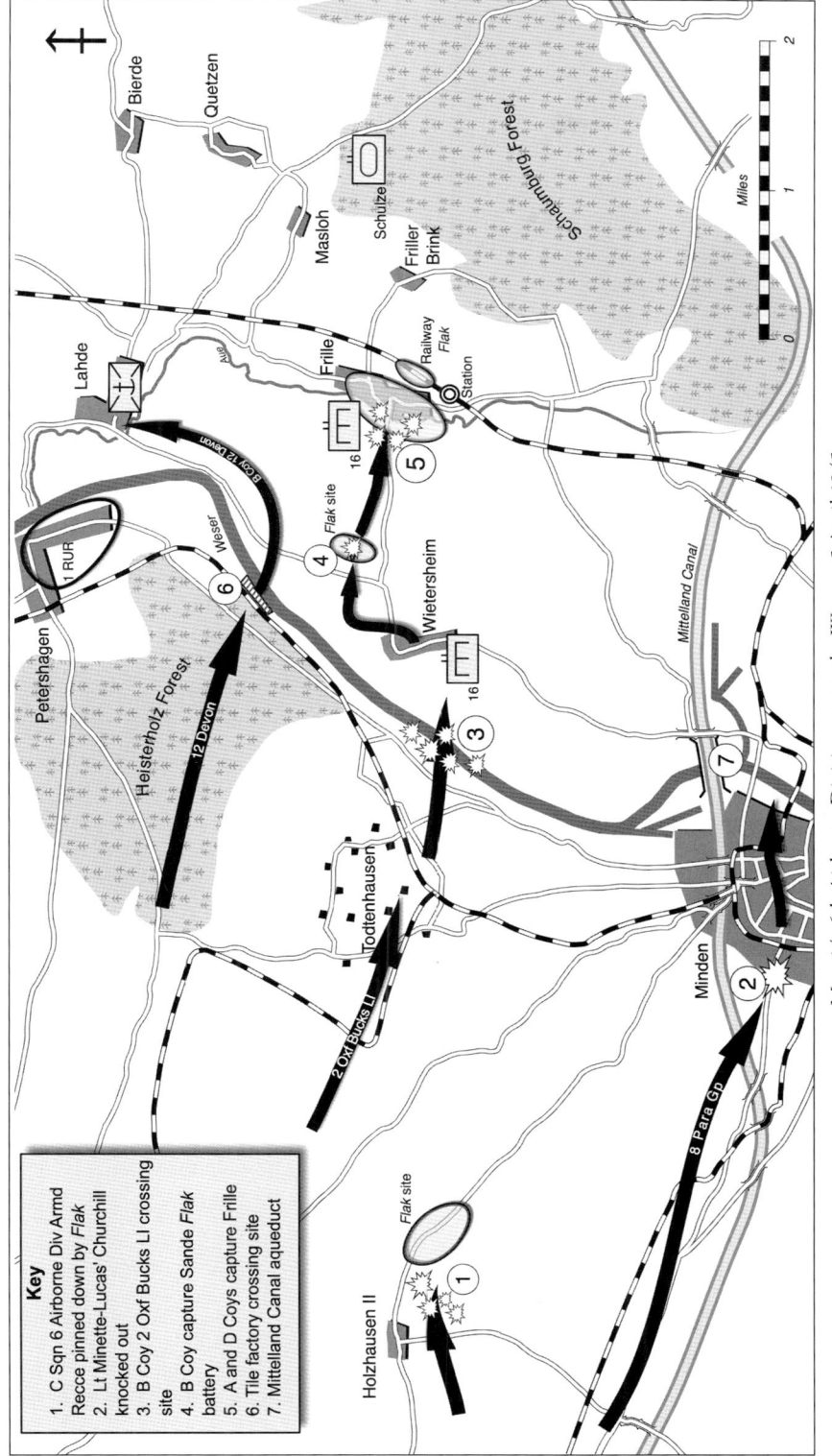

Map 14 6th Airborne Division across the Weser – 5 April 1945.

Key
1. C Sqn 6 Airborne Div Armd Recce pinned down by *Flak*
2. Lt Minette-Lucas' Churchill knocked out
3. B Coy 2 Oxf Bucks LI crossing site
4. B Coy capture Sande *Flak* battery
5. A and D Coys capture Frille
6. Tile factory crossing site
7. Mittelland Canal aqueduct

left flank and fought its way forward against enemy artillery and roving *Panzerfaust* teams from Panzerjagdverband 'Großer Kurfürst'. Considerable opposition was met in the area of Kutenhausen[9] and two Churchills were hit by *Panzerfaust*, but by mid-afternoon on 5 April the battalion had reached the Weser at Todtenhausen, although an immediate crossing was not possible owing to frequent shelling and air-bursts. As evening fell a slackening in the enemy's fire allowed a platoon from B Company to cross in assault boats under the cover of an artillery barrage fired by 53rd Airlanding Light Regiment,[10] supported by a medium battery and the battalion's mortars. The successful lodgement on the right bank was soon reinforced by the remainder of B Company and the complete company then advanced to Wietersheim, where it cleared opposition from Panzer-Pionier-A.u.E. Bataillon 16 and mopped up the Sande RAD *Flak* battery. A and D Companies promptly followed and began to exploit the two miles to Frille. Reaching the village in the late afternoon of 5 April, they found it stoutly defended by further engineers from Bataillon 16 and it took until 2000 hours and a stiff fight to clear it. Meanwhile, back on the Weser's left bank, the battalion's pioneer platoon and 591 Para Field Squadron were building a raft to ferry the battalion's 6-pdr anti-tank guns and 3-in mortars over the river.[11] This was no easy task as the Germans were engaging the site with fire from *Nebelwerfer* and the 10.5cm railway *Flak* at Frille station; while generally inaccurate, with most rounds falling upstream of the rafting site, the fire was distinctly uncomfortable. Ferrying got underway but eventually a salvo landed close to the raft, which at the time was carrying Lieutenant Clift and part of the mortar platoon, tipping them into the river; amazingly none of the party drowned and even the 3-in mortars were recovered. Other troops, however, were not so fortunate and a later salvo killed three and wounded many more. Ferrying continued through the night regardless of the artillery fire and by dawn on 6 April two 6-pdr guns and all the battalion's mortars were across the river and able to support the three rifle companies.

12 Devon, commanded by Lieutenant Colonel Gleadell, had meanwhile advanced on 2 Oxf Bucks LI's left through the Heisterholz forest to reach the area of a roofing tile factory on the Weser's bank and here they could cross the river in assault boats.[12]

Colonel Gleadell's plan was for D Company followed by B Company to cross during the early part of the night 5/6 April and seize a bridgehead then, in order, A Company, the R Group, C Company and battalion headquarters would cross the following day. The battalion's war diary makes light of D Company's crossing: 'D Coy crossed at 1930 hours and quickly established themselves in a small hamlet on the other side of the river…' But for those taking part it was far from easy, and even before they crossed Private Arthur Taylor, a 2-in mortarman in D Company, had severe misgivings about both the assault boats and the impending operation:[13]

> The general direction of our advance was north-east and we were soon confronted with the river Weser. It was nothing like as formidable as the Rhine, not very wide, perhaps 60 or 70 yards, but it was quite deep and very fast flowing. We knew that there would be no airdrop over this little obstacle, and my company was ordered to cross it. How? Using army issue 'Assault boats, Infantry, for the use of'. These boats had a plywood floor with sides that telescoped down flat in the collapsed position. They could be transported in this position, about seven to eight in a 3t lorry. When delivered by the RASC drivers to the destination where they were to be used, they could be unloaded, and the sides, which were canvas, would be pulled upward from the floor to their fullest extent which was about 18 or 20 inches and held in place

---

9   Here, on 1 August 1759, an Anglo–German army defeated the French at the Battle of Minden.
10   TNA WO 171/4762, 53rd Airlanding Light Regiment RA war diary.
11   TNA WO 171/5582, 591 Para Field Squadron RE war diary.
12   TNA WO 171/5172, 12 Devon war diary.
13   AW Taylor, *Shine Like a Glow-Worm* (Darlington: Serendipity, 2002), pp.114–115.

The Weser with the tile factory in the background. Picture taken in 2015. (Author)

by wooden struts. Plywood paddles were handed out, and there was your water transportation for one infantry section of eight men and all their weapons, ammunition and kit.

In ideal conditions, it was military policy that the users of these rather primitive craft would have time to get practice in using them. The NCO, the section leader, would be in charge and become the helmsman and call out the timing of the paddle strokes, synchronising the efforts of everyone and so controlling the boat as it made its passage. In fact this seldom happened, and it did not happen on this occasion either. It was the first time that most of these big, hairy, tough airborne soldiers had seen these boats let alone handled them. We turned pale and cringed at the thought that eight heavily laden men with weapons, ammunition and equipment could possibly be loaded and moved in such frail boats; why, they were just a bit of plywood and canvas! We would have faced anything rather than the escapade we were about to embark on. Even the very good swimmers among us were terrified at the thought of capsizing. If one went overboard, the weight of one's equipment would carry the unfortunate down like a rock, straight to the bottom, and the not so good swimmers were petrified, goggle-eyed and frightened, many believed their end was near. We were called together behind the raised banks of the river and given advice on how to use our boats. Most of us were landlubbers and would have preferred some practical tuition, but our hard-hearted masters were intent on getting across the river regardless of the potential casualties we might sustain.

We had not been meeting a great deal of resistance from the enemy since the Rhine operation, but we knew that they were over the other side of that river. We also knew that the only anti-tank weapon that we could carry with us was the PIAT, a small weapon that might offer some protection, but which was useless against the thick armour of the Tiger and Panther class tanks held by the enemy. There were no bridges and it would be some 36 hours before the engineers could put a bridge across capable of carrying anti-tank guns and reinforcements to relieve us. So we were setting out across a deep, fast-flowing river, never having handled these boats before. We had no idea what enemy force would be waiting for us, and we might easily be destroyed during the crossing. If by some miracle we did get across, we had no weapons capable of destroying enemy heavy tanks, so if there were any in the vicinity, we would be unlikely to survive. Charming.

Finally, to put the icing on the cake, it was almost twilight; our crossing was to be made in total darkness.

During the early evening the assault boats were delivered to the unloading point and then carried forward to just short of the river by the men of D Company. Arthur Taylor recalls the events that unfolded:[14]

> Talk about a recipe for disaster! To this day I can hardly believe our luck. We crouched behind the riverbank preparing our boats and discussing how we should actually make the crossing. We learned that it was to be a silent attack without the support of artillery or machine-guns from our side, the element of surprise supposedly giving us a better chance of success. If a boat was lost, or ended up somewhere it should not be, we knew where we had to make for to find our unit. We were wished good luck and we settled down behind our cover to wait.
>
> At the appointed hour, 7.30 pm on 5 April 1945, near the small town of Petershagen we carried our boats over the bank to the riverside where we were supposed to load our boats and await the order to cast off. As we arrived at the water's edge we were horrified to see that there was no gentle slope, but a sheer drop of between four and five feet to the river. There the water was racing past just as fast as it did midstream. This meant that the boats had to be dropped over the edge of the river bank and held by one man lying flat on the ground with one arm hanging down over the bank holding a small painter in one hand and holding on for dear life to the grass tufts on the bank to keep himself from falling in with the other. This inadequate painter being very short, even at full stretch, held the front of the boat out of the water, and the back end almost under.
>
> Pandemonium, chaos and sheer panic took over as men tried to lower themselves into the boats. Thankfully quite a number of sections were successful in getting loaded, only to turn even paler if that were possible, when they realised just how little freeboard there was, just six or seven inches. They were convinced that the river would slop over the gunwales and sink the boat, but their confidence increased with time, and they accepted the situation albeit with a faint heart.
>
> I never heard the order to go. Some boats were already out of control, some with only one or two men on board had broken away prematurely and were hurtling away downstream into the black night with white-faced panic-stricken men, helpless and frightened, calling for help which was unavailable. Suddenly we were on our way, heading supposedly to the far bank. In reality it was more like into the unknown; the men cursing and swearing as only soldiers can, gradually made their way, fearfully at first, but with more confidence as they became more proficient. Skill was either acquired quickly, or control was lost.
>
> Just over half the force managed to get across without serious mishap. Even and regular paddle strokes by three men each side of the boat, time being called by the section leader, enabled reasonable control to be maintained, in-out, in-out, desperate voices calling in the dark, in-out, in-out. Many and varied were the courses of some of the craft. I saw one turning in a continuous circle speeding away, carried by the fierce current down the centre of the river making no headway toward either bank. Lord knows where they finished up. One or two boats were actually heading back for the starting bank; try as they might, they just could not control their craft.
>
> An estimation of the time factor involved and the speed of the current enabled a rough estimate of where the landing area should be, and also the assembly point on the opposite bank.

---

14   Taylor, *Shine Like a Glow-Worm*, pp.115–117.

However, no allowances had been made for the lack of handling experience and other numerous errors that occurred and contributed to the general cock-up which, when one thinks about it, was only to be expected. The eventual landing area was well spread out along the opposite river bank for several miles, and it was well into the next morning before the stragglers found their way back up to the unit. A few men never did make it back and had disappeared forever it seemed. Probably into enemy hands somewhere downstream. It would not have surprised me if one or two boats had actually reached the sea and were still sailing on like the Flying Dutchman, forever doomed to wander the ocean.

Because the enemy had been retreating, and I presume the surprise of the action, we reached the far bank without a shot being fired. We were very lucky again that night: had there been just one enemy machine-gun post on the far bank, and with the scene brightly lit with flares, there would have been such a slaughter, and we would undoubtedly have been destroyed. Still, there it was, we had made it across, but I would not want another experience like it. Those safely across could now crack jokes and treat it as if it had been a piece of cake, full of bravado now; it was in sharp contrast with the fearful terrified men of a few hours before. Still, the war had to go on. The planned landing area having been very badly misjudged, we moved back upstream, finally reaching our original intended area, still without discovery by the enemy, and several hours late we took up positions around a group of farm buildings.

Although Arthur Taylor records that the crossing was silent, according to the 12 Devon war diary the battalion's Vickers fired from the top floor of the factory to support D Company's assault boats while they crossed the river; perhaps the confusion, noise and fear experienced by the men blocked out the steady thump of the Vickers. Though delayed by a communication problem with the supporting artillery, B Company crossed the Weser just after midnight and advanced north towards Lahde,[15] eventually reaching the village's western edge some four hours later. With the initial bridgehead secure, 249 Field Company began work to throw a Class 9 FBE across the river,[16] which started well but soon became plagued by equipment faults, such as badly twisted anchor cables and unserviceable outboard motors. To add to the sappers' difficulties, rain and mist came down blotting out all light and the railway *Flak* at Frille station started shelling again, fortunately few shells fell in the bridging area. Through the night these problems were compounded by the strength of the current, which was unexpectedly strong owing to the demolition of the aqueduct carrying the Mittelland Canal over the Weser, with the additional water increasing the river's speed to over five knots, its depth by 16 inches and its width by some 20 yards. The state of the river not only prevented 591 Para Field Squadron from getting a cable across but also from operating the rafts that 249 (Airborne) Field Company needed to get their equipment to the right bank and prepare its approach.

While events at the tile factory site unfolded, 1 RUR closed on Petershagen and by 2100 hours had secured the undefended town, providing the division with a useful bridging site in the area of the ferry. The battalion was not however the first British troops in the town as a 15/19 Hussars reconnaissance patrol from 11th Armoured Division had entered it that afternoon, but not without loss as the lead scout car was destroyed in the main street by a *Panzerfaust* fired by a member of Panzerjagdverband 'Großer Kurfürst', killing Trooper Sayers. With Petershagen clear of enemy, the plan for 1 RUR was to move to the tile factory FBE, cross the Weser then return north up the

---

15   Lahde was the site of an *Arbeitserziehungslager*. Eighty-four of these penal camps were established in Germany to deal with anti-social slave labourers and were in most respects worse than concentration camps. They were administered by the *Gestapo*.
16   TNA WO 171/5523, 249 Field Company RE war diary.

right bank and secure a bridgehead opposite the town to provide security for 100 Field Company's construction of a Class 40 Bailey pontoon bridge.[17]

The Stolzenau bridgehead

Further north, on the corps' left axis, 11th Armoured was advancing with 29th Armoured Brigade Group left and 159th Infantry Brigade Group right,[18] both with Stolzenau and its bridge over the Weser as their objective. Captain William Steel Brownlie, second captain in A Squadron 2 FF Yeo, describes how 11th Armoured's regimental groups advanced:[19]

> Within the division the usual double centre line was adopted, with a mixed brigade group on each. Within the leading regiment the usual formation was as follows: the forward squadron was 'loose', that is, unencumbered by infantry, and advanced up its road or track with its point troop spraying the hedges, woods and buildings with machine-gun bullets among which was included a good proportion of incendiaries. A HE shell would occasionally be put into any nasty-looking undergrowth at the next bend. The gunner OP tank was invariably with squadron HQ, just behind the leading troop…Then came regimental HQ with the infantry CO in attendance, and behind them the remaining two squadrons carrying two companies of infantry on their backs, with A1 echelon bringing up the rear. Some way behind, the batteries would leapfrog along, at least one being ready on the ground when required. This businesslike arrangement required few alterations and proved itself many times over as the most powerful and yet the most flexible that could be devised.

159th Infantry Brigade Group's advance on 5 April from the Diepenau area was nearly incident-free, but this was soon to change.[20] 2 FF Yeo,[21] commanded by Lieutenant Colonel Scott, was leading the brigade and as the first Comets of A Squadron were exiting Harrienstedt on the road to Glissen, south-west of Stolzenau and some two miles from the river, a tank-hunting party from Panzerjagdverband 'Großer Kurfürst' consisting of 10 men commanded by Obergrenadier Joachim Stiehler lay in wait in ditches on either side of the road at the village's southern exit. William Steel Brownlie describes the events that followed:[22]

> Approaching Glissen, still at full speed, Frank Fuller's troop was in the lead. His corporal [Corporal Bush] was first tank and the operator reported on the air 'no washing' (ie no white flags) in the village ahead. Therefore they slowed down. The corporal reported enemy in the ditches on both sides of the road. Frank reported that he had been hit and then was silent. His corporal reported that he seemed to have gone right through the enemy pocket and was told to stay where he was. The squadron deployed off the road, myself going left into the fields looking for a position to fire on to the road or into the village. The following troops unloaded the infantry who were travelling on the back of the tanks to start a clearing action. Meantime Frank's tank sat alone and silent, round the bend in the road.

---

17 TNA WO 171/5455, 100 Field Company RE war diary.
18 TNA WO 171/4184, G Branch 11th Armoured Division war diary.
19 William Steel Brownlie, 'And Came Safe Home', (Unpublished private memoir, Tank Museum Archive).
20 TNA WO 171/4426, 159th Infantry Brigade war diary.
21 TNA WO 171/4700, 2 FF Yeo war diary.
22 William Steel Brownlie, 'And Came Safe Home'.

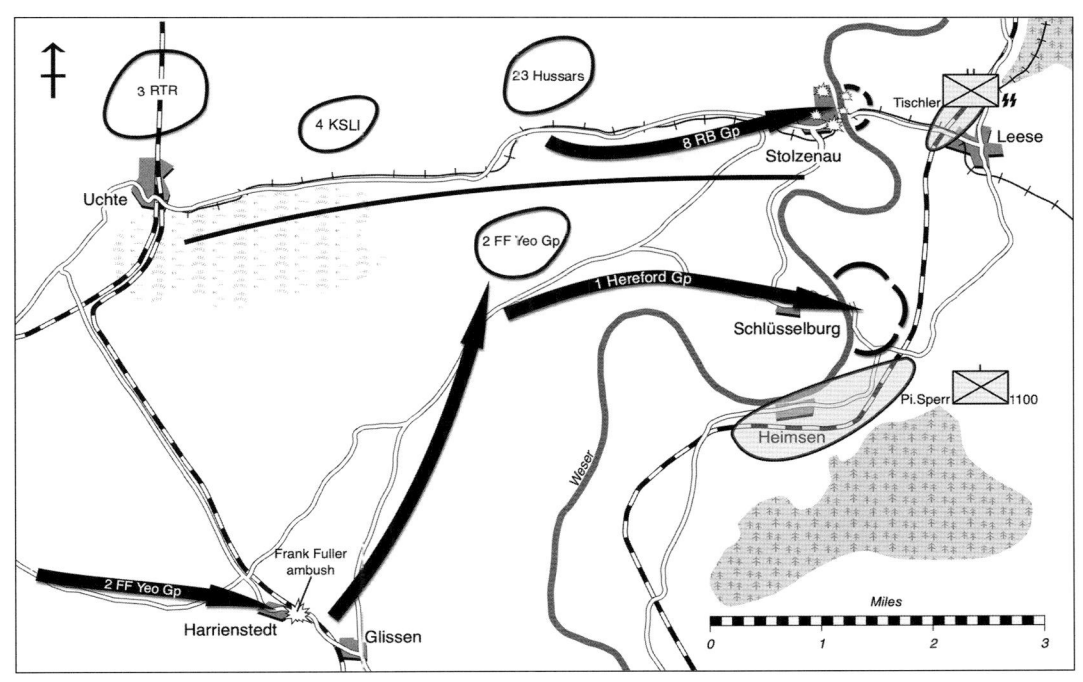

Map 15 11th Armoured Division Across the Weser – 5 April 1945.

Suddenly his operator, Trooper Oxley, came on the air and said very quietly that the rest of the crew were dead, that the enemy were all around, and he proposed to lie doggo till he could escape. He was told to do that. I found a good fire position and saw our infantry deployed and advancing. I fired in front of them to help them forward, but they went to ground. Maybe they mistook my stuff for enemy fire. More of our tanks came up, a few prisoners were taken and casualties inflicted on others trying to escape. I shot at some crossing open ground to my left and Glissen was taken without much trouble: more prisoners. They were from 12 SS Panzer [sic], very young, blubbering and weeping as they ran back along the dusty road urged by the boots of our infantry. I helped by brandishing my pistol from the turret and shouting, '*Schneller, schneller!*'. We found bicycles and *Panzerfaust* in the ditches. Obviously the enemy were now scraping the bottom of the barrel but they could still kill people.

The troops were sent on separately to find a crossing over the Weser, now only a mile or so away. I stayed with squadron HQ. I was taking the first mouthful of a meal when I was sent back several miles to contact an infantry unit. En route I met some of our echelon where Frank's tank had been hit and pieced together the story. I tell it in memory of him and of many like him whose luck ran out.

His tank was hit in the front by a *Panzerfaust* and halted in the midst of the enemy party. He got no reply from his driver or co-driver on the intercom so got out of the turret to climb down and perhaps get in on top of the driver and try to drive out of danger; perhaps better than sitting still and being finished off but a hard decision. He was at once riddled with MG fire and blown off the tank by another *Panzerfaust*. His gunner lost his nerve and jumped out: killed. I think the three dead were Lance Corporals Axtell, Grossmith and Marris. Frank was one of the few juniors who was married (he was 33-years-old). When I arrived back at the scene the tank had been shoved off the road and Frank's just recognisable body was in the ditch.

The two *Panzerfaust* projectiles that hit Fuller's tank were fired from the front at a range of 20 yards producing scoops on the mantlet and near the hull machine-gun, but neither causing sufficient damage to force the crew to evacuate. According to the report on tank casualties the squadron leader later stated that after the first hit the driver got out to investigate and was killed by small-arms' fire from the road block;[23] Frank Fuller then got out to see what had happened and met the same fate, as did the gunner and co-driver who followed Frank. With the benefit of hindsight, they would have survived had they stayed inside the tank, but they presumably thought that it was about to be finished off and decided their chances of survival were better outside. As clearing a village was not an operation for armour on its own, D Company 1 Hereford, carried on A Squadron's tank decks, was rapidly deployed to mop up the enemy. The situation was soon brought under control by the infantry and nine prisoners captured. Stiehler escaped but was later hit by tank machine-gun fire and severely wounded. The loss of A Squadron's Comet not only marked the start of 10 days of heavy fighting for the division but also the circumstances of the loss were typical of the advance through Germany; being lead vehicle was an unpleasant and risky task and the views and descriptions in this extract from 23 Hussars' history would have been widely familiar:[24]

> Rumbling along in a tank, frequently halting and then moving on, it was possible to sum up in one's mind the impressions gained since we had crossed the Rhine. It must be admitted that uppermost was a slight feeling of disappointment. Surely we should be going faster. But every day seemed to produce something to check us, something to prevent us achieving success equal to the dash across the Somme and the overrunning of defenders on that memorable advance to Antwerp. Just when we appeared to be gaining momentum, just when the Germans appeared to be most disorganised before us, and we were beginning to look for the next map to put on our boards, 'Bang' would go a bazooka, and then we would be involved in the slow process of rooting out a determined enemy, with the riflemen bearing the brunt. We had looked forward to cruising down the *Autobahns*, but instead we found twisty country lanes, innumerable woods and many streams and rivers, where dash and the speed of our Comets availed us nothing. Perhaps we had been optimistic. After all, the Germans were now fighting in their own country. But we could not be blamed for hoping for a chance to show what we could do, and unfortunately it had never really come. What had been most amply shown, however, was the courage and skill of the tank crews, for the leading tank was virtually certain to have at least one bazooka fired at it before it went very far.

However, courage was not just the preserve of tank crews and using a *Panzerfaust* also required significant bravery on the part of the firer. Although somewhat sensational and describing an action on the East Front, Guy Sajer's description of engaging tanks with *Panzerfaust* gives a sense of what it must have been like:[25]

> I can still see those tanks, blotting out everything else. I can also see the metal plaque, and the nose of my first *Panzerfaust*, and my hand, stiff with fear, on the firing button. As they rolled

---

23 TNA WO 205/1165, 2 FF Yeo, Serial D.46, Wright, HB, Captain RAMC and Harkness, RD, Captain RAMC, *A Survey of Casualties Amongst Armoured Units in North-West Europe*, January 1946. These two officers belonged to a Medical Research Council team attached to No. 2 Operational Research Section and their report analysed data obtained on 330 armoured fighting vehicle casualties and 769 personnel casualties sustained by 19 armoured regiments between 24 March–5 May 1945.
24 Various, *The Story of the 23rd Hussars 1940–1946* (Germany: 1946), p.224.
25 Guy Sajer, *The Forgotten Soldier* (London: Cassell, 1999), p.447.

toward us, the earth against which my body pressed transmitted their vibrations, while my nerves, tightened to the breaking point, seemed to shrill with an ear-splitting whistle. Once again I understood that one could wear out one's life in a few seconds. I could see reflected yellow lights on the front of the tank, and then everything disappeared in the flash of light which I had released, and which burned my face.

My brain seemed paralysed and made of the same substance as my helmet. To the side, other flashes of light battered at my eyes, which jerked open convulsively wide, although there was nothing to see. Everything was simultaneously luminous and blurred. Then a second tank in the middle distance was outlined by a glow of flame. It had not been able to take the three projectiles we had lobbed toward it with a considerable degree of precision. We could hear the noise of a third tank crossing a hillock just beyond our position. It had accelerated, and was no more than 30 yards from us, when I grabbed my last *Panzerfaust*. One of my comrades had already fired, and I was temporarily blinded. I stiffened my powers of vision and regained my sight to see a multitude of rollers caked in mud churning past in a dull roar of sound some five or six yards from us.

While 159th Brigade Group closed up to the Weser on the division's southern axis, to their north 29th Armoured Brigade Group,[26] with 23 Hussars and 8 RB in the lead, advanced rapidly during the morning to Stolzenau. However, at 1030 hours, just as the carriers from F Company entered the town, the steel, lattice-truss bridge carrying the combined road and narrow-gauge railway was blown up and collapsed into the river.[27]

Despite the disappointment of not capturing the bridge intact, the town was quickly taken and as it appeared that there was very little opposition on the right bank, and it looked as if the bridge's masonry piers could support a Bailey bridge. the decision was taken to make a rapid crossing to secure a bridgehead. Assault boats were quickly brought up and H Company was selected to make the first crossing, upstream from the demolished bridge. At 1300 hours H Company's lead platoon began crossing under a smoke screen, kneeling in the flimsy wood and canvas boats and paddling them American Indian style. Some civilian boats, moored nearby, were employed to ferry the 6-pdr anti-tank guns. While the first platoon paddled across, the second platoon began to cross using the girders of the demolished bridge, but this soon became very slow and risky so the platoon was called back and ordered to cross by boat. As they started to launch the assault boats, 2cm fire splattered the area killing Captain May, second-in-command of H Company, and wounding a rifleman. Although the crossing was supported by 13 RHA and Comets from B and C Squadrons 23 Hussars in fire positions along the river,[28] artillery and armour alike experienced great difficulty in locating the enemy guns and it proved almost impossible to hit them. With H Company lodged on the right bank, 23 Hussars pulled back to leaguer but left B Squadron in Stolzenau to support the infantry.[29] During these opening events at Stolzenau, the other two regiments in the brigade – 3 RTR and 4 KSLI – were held back from the river to await construction of a bridge and keep the division's left flank secure in the Uchte area.

The enemy barrage came from the *Flak* on the western edge of Leese, which, alerted to the British activity, engaged Stolzenau with 8.8cm airburst and fire from 2cm guns – the opening rounds of a bombardment to continue day and night for the next few days. There was no shortage of *Flak* and following Major Majewski's direction there were now located on the railway embankment

---

26   TNA WO 171/4345, 29th Armoured Brigade war diary.
27   TNA WO 171/5257, 8 RB war diary.
28   TNA WO 171/5084, 13 RHA war diary.
29   TNA WO 171/4693, 23 Hussars war diary.

three 8.8cm guns, six 3.7cm guns, nine 2cm Flakvierling, and three 2cm Flakvierling mounted on railway flat-wagons. The guns were well-camouflaged and from their elevated position able to produce very effective harassing fire on Stolzenau and its surrounding area. Indirect fire was also available, provided by the five 8.8cm guns of RAD Batterie 4./132 at Loccum, five miles to the south-east of Leese.

With the area of the demolished bridge clearly under observation, Lieutenant Colonel Hunter, commanding officer 8 RB, ordered G Company and the remainder of H Company to cross the river downstream from the bridge and then form a bridgehead to provide security for bridge construction work on the right bank. The sappers had moved up to Stolzenau during the morning to begin the engineering effort to cross the Weser, which required 240 feet of Class 40 Bailey pontoon bridging. 224 Field Company from VIII Corps Troops provided the assault boats and unloading parties, 13 Field Squadron was tasked to construct rafts and far-side approaches,[30] and 612 Field Squadron the landing bays and end floating bays.[31] Work began at 1640 hours. Waiting its turn to cross, G Company had taken cover behind a 10-foot high bank just short of the river but now left its safety to cross the river, as Major Noel Bell, commanding G Company, recalls:[32]

> It seemed that we lay behind the bank for a century while we received our final briefing, checked our portable radio sets and waited, waited, waited. A few 88mm HEs burst in the fields behind us to relieve the monotony of the airbursts overhead. The colonel arrived and gave us some words of encouragement, which were much appreciated. Years passed. We knew H Company were having a tough time and that did not help. Finally, an order was received that G Company would cross on the northern side of the bridge, owing to the state of the opposition on our immediate front, and we made preparation to move. A high piece of ground separated our present position from the one selected as our new crossing place and in order that we should not be observed crossing such an obvious hump, it was necessary to make a detour through some marshy undergrowth about hundred yards back. As we made our way through the bushes crouching low, aerial rods, rifles, spades and all the 'panoply of war' became entangled in the masses of briar and thorn, which coupled with the sloping and slippery ground made progress slow and awkward. We had no material cover between the enemy and us and it was necessary to rely on the camouflage of the foliage and providence. This finally accomplished without incident, we took cover behind a warehouse that backed down to the river. No sooner had we gained this position than a hail of 20mm tracer swept down over the marshy ground at waist level from which we had just emerged. We had been spotted – too late.
>
> We had another wait here while the final preparations were made for the crossing during which shelling by airburst persisted, punctuating the Spandau fire which, directed at H Company still establishing themselves, chattered away with regularity. The atmosphere was tense – as tense as it always was during those minutes of waiting before action. At last we received the command to make our way down to the riverside, a platoon at a time. We emerged from our cover of the warehouse and turned right down what must have been the main street. After a 50-yard sprint the river was swirling, black and menacing at our feet. It was a good spot to cross 'as good spots went' for we were completely out of sight of the enemy, who were holding positions some hundred of yards back across the water, owing to a ridge on the far side similar to the one on our own.

---

30 TNA WO 171/5747, 13 Field Squadron RE war diary.
31 TNA WO 171/5750, 612 Field Squadron RE war diary.
32 Bell, *From the Beaches to the Baltic*, p.107.

The demolished road and rail bridge at Stolzenau and the warehouse behind which
G Company 8 RB took cover.

The Weser was wide and flowing fast – too fast to be pleasant. We knew that unless we could gain the opposite bank before the current had carried us too far down, the game was well and truly up, for the bridgehead was only a hundred or so yards in width. The bridge itself, was on our immediate right, and lay sprawled across the water, making the river swirl and eddy as it washed its way across the twisted girders. There were with us a RE officer and some sappers, already making plans for the building of a new bridge. The assault boats lay to our left in a small inlet. There were not many of them and it was apparent that a ferry service would be necessary to transport all of us across. 12 Platoon went over first, one of their boats being carried well down the river by the strong current before finally touching down on the other bank. 10 Platoon followed, with elements of 9, then 11, and company HQ brought up the rear. The whole company was across, and no casualties so far.

By 1530 hours both companies were across and digging-in to establish a defensible perimeter. Some 10 minutes later, much to everyone's surprise, the *Luftwaffe* appeared over the Weser, heralding the start of a series of damaging air attacks to last on and off for the next two days.

The first aircraft seen by the British was a Ju 87 Stuka, a menacing and instantly recognisable shape. Noel Bell describes this opening encounter:[33]

> As the last member of company HQ made the far side, a *Stuka* appeared from behind some trees on the southern side of the bridge at about 50 foot. Some Brens opened up on it from our side, and several Brownings mounted on our vehicles, on the other; but the *Stuka*, unruffled and kestrel-like, seemed to hover over the bridge quite patiently, apparently impervious to the hail of lead being directed at it. Then the pilot, having presumably seen all he wished to, made off as suddenly as he had come. We guessed that the *Stuka* was carrying out a reconnaissance and we thus expected a more forceful visit some time later. It was not long in coming.

---

33 Bell, *From the Beaches to the Baltic*, p.107.

About an hour later a pair of *Stukas*, again at 50 feet but this time on an attack run, flew in to release their bombs on the bridge area, causing casualties to 10 Platoon of G Company on the right bank. These aircraft came from NSGr. 1 Nord and probably flew from Celle airfield, only some 10 minutes flying time away even for an aircraft as slow as the *Stuka*. The company headquarters looked after the wounded as best they could, knowing that the continual shelling and the strong possibility of further air attack would make evacuation in assault boats across the river a slow and risky business. They were correct in their expectation of further air attacks, but could not have imagined their scale and that a variety of some 70 aircraft would arrive over the next two hours to attack targets in the Weser area in general and the Stolzenau bridging site in particular and that they would be on the receiving end of the *Luftwaffe's* last major effort against the British Army. Locations at the start of the air attack are shown on Map 16.

The air attack was complying with an OKL order for maximum effort in an attempt to buy time for the army to prepare defensive positions. The order was retransmitted by Luftflotte Reich to its formations on 4 April and duly decrypted by Ultra:[34]

> To engage Anglo-American columns and tanks especially on *Reich Autobahns*, all possible *Luftwaffe* forces are to be employed by day and night. By ceaseless operations Allied advance must at all costs be halted finally so that Army has chance of creating a concentrated defence line. Besides employment of day fighters with bombs and aircraft armament, all available night ground attack and night fighter units to be included in these operations. Even slightly suitable weather to be fully used. Employment of all units in closest collaboration with competent Army headquarters, who will report currently to HQ Luftflotte Reich the areas in which full freedom has been granted to *Luftwaffe* units to attack.

58th LAA Regiment's log for the afternoon and evening of 5 April, shown below at Figure 22,[35] clearly reveals the effort mounted by 14. Flieger-Division, and the intensity of activity and variety of aircraft types show that the *Luftwaffe* still had the ability to coordinate attacks and pass targeting information. In line with the Luftflotte Reich direction, the attack on Stolzenau formed part of a general attack on enemy transport and armoured vehicles closing up to the Weser from the west.

1650	H Tp 174 Bty at MR 8533 engaged 2xJu87B – bombs dropped.
1655-1830	B Tp 172 Bty at MR 856355 engaged 3xJu87B, 2xMe262 and 6xMe109. No specific claims or damage, but several a/c were smoking heavily.
1700-1730	E Tp 173 Bty at MR 795315 engaged 1xJu87B and 2xMe109. No claims.
1705	H Tp 174 Bty at MR 8533 engaged 1xAr234.
1720-1735	H Tp 174 Bty at MR 8533 engaged 1xMe109 – bombs dropped.
1800-1900	E Tp 173 Bty at MR 847345 engaged 2xJu88, 12xMe109 and 4xFw190. No claims.
1800-1900	F Tp 173 Bty at MR 9035 and 8533 engaged 4xJu87, 8xJu88, 4xMe109, 6xFw190, which made anti-personnel bombing attacks at heights varying from 300 to 3,000 ft. Claims – Nil.
1845-1910	H Tp 174 Bty at MR 8533 engaged 6xJu188, 10xMe109 – HE and AP bombs dropped. Claims – one Cat II

Figure 22 58th LAA Regiment Log – 5 April 1945.

---

34 TNA DEFE 3/563, BT 9576, 6 April 1945.
35 TNA WO 171/4945, 58th LAA Regiment war diary.

STUKAS, TIGERS AND PANTHERS 155

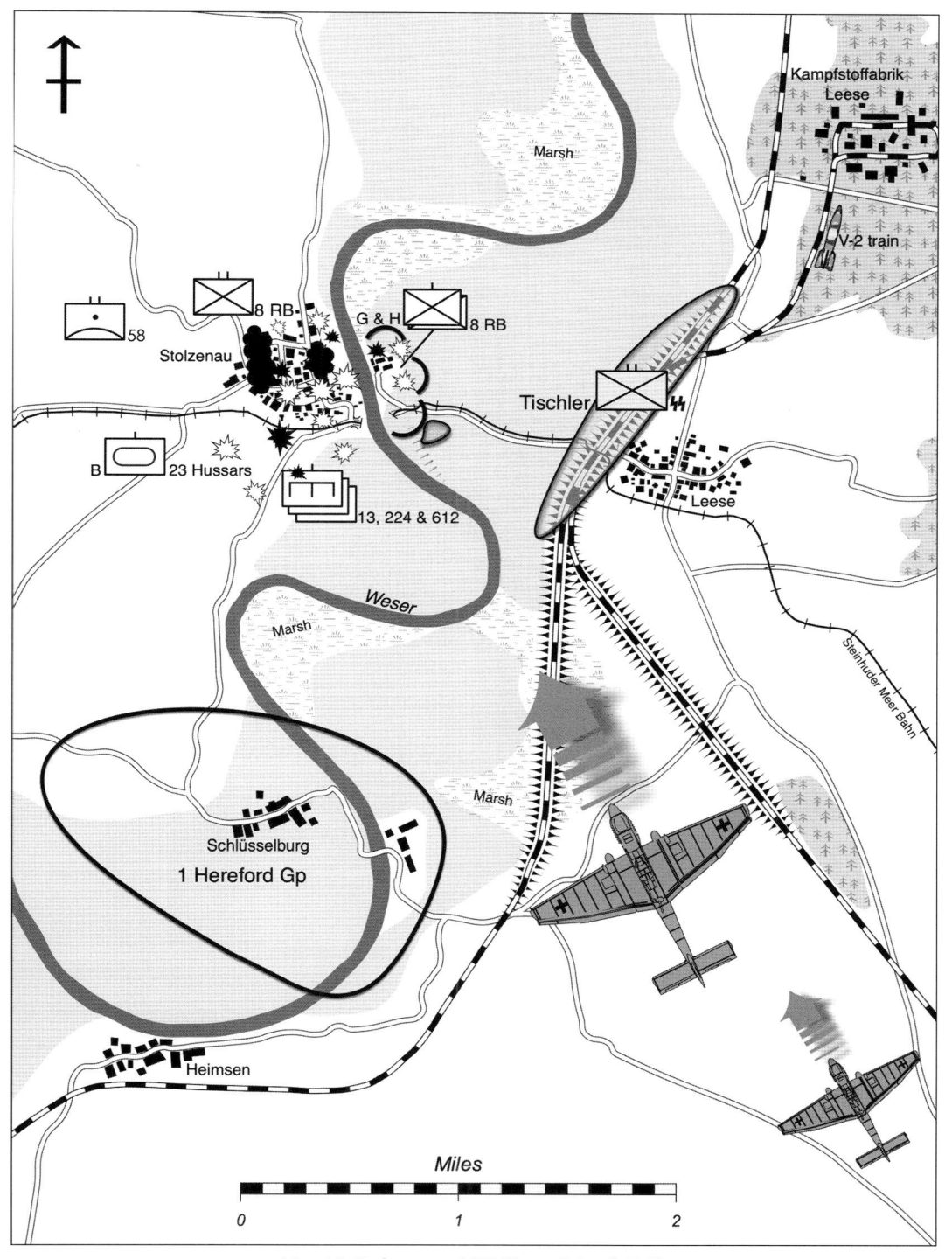

Map 16 Stolzenau – 1650 Hours 5 April 1945.

Analysis of the aircraft types reveals participation by approximately nine units. First, the two Me 262 were probably from NAGr 6, 14. Flieger-Division's battlefield recce group. The fact that there was a pair of jets possibly relates to an Ultra decrypt, which details a 15. Flieger-Division proposal of 5 April recommending that Me 262 recce flights should consist of two aircraft: a Me 262A-5a recce aircraft accompanied by a Me 262A fighter.[36] The somewhat doubtful premise for the proposal was that the fighter would provide protection for the unarmed recce jet and could attack Allied fighters, causing the Allies 'extreme uneasiness and uncertainty thus with luck some respite might be obtained for using orthodox [ie not jet] recce aircraft.' The Bf 109 seen throughout the evening belonged to I. and III./JG 27 and would have been tasked to strafe targets with their onboard cannon and machine-guns. The Ar 234 engaged at 1705 hours was part of a 10-aircraft sortie from III./KG 76, all carrying 500 kg bombs. The Ju 88 engaged between 1800 and 1900 hours were part of a 15-aircraft sortie of former night-fighters from 2. Jagd-Division, tasked to mount a twilight attack on road targets in the area between Stolzenau and Minden. The Ju 88 were carrying AB 250 canisters loaded with SD 10 anti-personnel sub-munitions and were escorted by twelve Bf 109, probably from 7./NJG 11. The Fw 190 attacking during the same period were from III./KG 200 and NSGr. 20, which launched a combined total of 44 aircraft to conduct bombing and strafing attacks against targets on the Weser's left bank. The six Ju 188, which concluded the evening's attacks, probably belonged to II./KG 200, with the ten Bf 109 escorts provided by JG 27. Not seen by the gunners but also taking part in the mission were nine Fw 190D fighters led by Leutnant Söffing of I./JG 26 and tasked to strafe roads in the area.

British troops subjected to the attacks found them thoroughly unpleasant and an experience to which they were far from accustomed, as evidenced by HQ 11th Armoured's SITREP reporting 'abnormal' enemy air activity over its area. During one of the attacks Frank Fuller and his three crew members were being buried in an orchard near the site of the ambush at Glissen.[37] Although no bombs fell close, all but one of those present felt inclined to take cover. This one person was Captain Welsh, the regimental padre, who despite the noise neither wavered nor looked up at the aircraft and concluded the burials with due dignity. The final attack of the day strafed 15/19 Hussars in its harbour area at Harrienstedt, resulting in the destruction of a scout car and three wounded troopers.[38] Fortunately for the British, the 40mm Bofors of 58th LAA Regiment were deployed in point defence of the bridging site and prevented the German pilots having an unopposed run to their target, although no enemy aircraft are recorded as being shot down. However, an Ultra decrypt of a 14. Flieger-Division message probably destined for Luftflotte Reich,[39] reveals losses of one aircraft destroyed and 13 missing from the sorties flown over north Germany on 5 April. Although not all of these missing aircraft would have been involved in attacking Stolzenau, perhaps the gunners of 58th LAA Regiment had more success than they believed.

Unfortunately for the British, the speed of the advance east of the Rhine meant that the RAF had not had time to establish advanced landing grounds or occupy former *Luftwaffe* airfields and Coningham had warned Montgomery that Second Tactical Air Force might not be able to provide full support until new forward air bases were captured and made operational. This was not to be achieved until 12 April and so for the first part of the account Second Army was operating without its customary levels of air support. Great efforts were made to provide extended cover by aircraft using long-range tanks but the transit time from the bases in the Netherlands inevitably led to gaps in cover, allowing the *Luftwaffe* opportunities to mount attacks. In its INTSUM for 5 April, 83 Group rather sniffily recorded:[40]

---

36 TNA DEFE 3/563, BT 9693, 7 April 1945.
37 Frank and his three crew members now lie in Hannover CWGC cemetery.
38 TNA WO 171/4692, 15/19 Hussars war diary.
39 TNA DEFE 3/565, KO 75, 10 April 1945.
40 TNA AIR 37/366, 83 Group RAF INTSUM 250.

There is a tendency to think that the GAF [German Air Force] is impotent in attack and that it is perfectly safe for ground forces, to use a technical term, to swan into areas at the limit of or beyond the range of effective fighter cover. The fact is that German aircraft will always attack when they can do so with reasonable chance of success. They are now beginning to get that chance as our armies advance into areas within easy range of enemy bases, whereas we have the utmost difficulty in covering their extended flanks and distant spearheads from bases now far in the rear. Until forward airfields become available, this state will continue.

While 29th Armoured Brigade units were active in the Stolzenau area, units of 159th Infantry Brigade Group had reached the river two miles upstream and during the early afternoon Lieutenant Colonel Turner-Cain, commanding officer of 1 Hereford, put B and C Companies across the Weser near the village of Schlüsselburg and established a small bridgehead some 400 yards deep and 800 yards wide.[41] To support the bridgehead, B Squadron 2 FF Yeo was positioned in overwatch on the left bank, two sections of Vickers from 2nd Independent Machine-Gun Company deployed to the right bank and a platoon of 4.2-in mortars established a baseplate on the left. As the Weser's left bank to the south of 159th Brigade was neither covered by 11th Armoured nor 6th Airborne Division, 15/19 Hussars was ordered to patrol the river bank between Langern and Petershagen. This task was conducted by B Squadron, reinforced by the regimental reconnaissance squadron (which subsequently lost the scout car in Petershagen as we have heard), and its tanks busied themselves engaging movement in the buildings and on the roads of the right bank. The artillery also engaged targets and during the afternoon the 25-pdrs of 151st Field Regiment were used against German transport seen moving in the east.[42] It is possible that these were the supply trucks of Kampfgruppe Schulze making best use of the low cloud cover and absence of Allied fighters to complete the final stage of their move to the Schaumburg Forest.

On 11th Armoured's northern flank Inns of Court pushed patrols down the Weser's left bank and during the morning met opposition at Liebenau from enemy infantry equipped with *Panzerfaust*.[43] Although unrecorded, these would have been Hitler Youth of 5. SS-Kompanie. This company had been despatched on 4 April to guard the 'Karl' explosives complex near Liebenau and were in the area until the afternoon of 5 April, when it was ordered to return to the Weser's right bank and join the other companies preparing the defence of Leese. The Inns of Court described the fighting as being very stubborn, further evidence that in all probability it involved 5. SS-Kompanie. C Squadron Inns of Court was given the mission to recce bridges over the Weser at Landesbergen, Leeseringen and Nienburg. The first bridge was found not to exist. The route to the second bridge took them near Liebenau, which they bypassed as the fighting was still in progress, and although the bridge was found intact it was unusable as the tracks that led to it petered out. In the afternoon the squadrons were ordered to pull back to harbour in the area west of Stolzenau as it was decided that the bridges to the north were no longer of importance and heavier forces were needed to deal with the opposition at Liebenau.

Having offered resistance in Liebenau, at dusk 5. SS-Kompanie departed in its half-tracks, crossing the Weser to reach Nienburg by night-fall. Here the vehicles had to be refuelled and the young soldiers rolled 200-litre fuel barrels into a warehouse where, as there were no pumps available, the precious fuel was decanted into everything from buckets to watering cans to allow it to be poured into the fuel tanks. Not only was this exhausting and inefficient but it filled the air with petrol fumes leaving many soldiers wandering around as if drunk. Once the vehicles

---

41 TNA WO 171/5201, 1 Hereford war diary.
42 TNA WO 171/4849, 151st Field Regiment RA war diary.
43 TNA WO 171/4701, Inns of Court war diary.

had refuelled, the company headed off to Leese, some 12 miles to the south, where in the early morning of 6 April it joined the other companies to form a group known as Kampfgruppe Tischler. SS-Obersturmführer Tischler is believed to have been the commander of the Unterführer-Lehr-Kompanie and, as the senior commander present at Leese, gave his name to the *Kampfgruppe*. Also ordered to pull back to the Weser's right bank on 5 April was 6. SS-Kompanie, previously dispatched westwards on their bicycles to attack the advancing British armour. It had to carry out this move as fast as possible as the demolition parties from Pionier-Sperr-Brigade 1100 had been ordered to destroy Nienburg's bridges. However, 6. SS-Kompanie, moving slowly on foot and on bicycle, were still well to the west when the time came to blow the bridges, leaving the company temporarily stranded on the Weser's left bank.

With initial crossings of the Weser achieved, VIII Corps' intention was for 6th Airborne to consolidate its bridgehead at Petershagen, 11th Armoured to join together its two bridgeheads at Stolzenau and Schlüsselburg and then for 15th Scottish to pass through in the south and 11th Armoured in the north and advance to the Leine. It was already apparent however that the Germans would continue to resist the northern bridgehead strongly, and equally apparent that 11th Armoured was not well placed to expand and join its bridgeheads owing to lack of infantry. VIII Corps therefore decided to reinforce 11th Armoured with 1st Commando Brigade, still back in Osnabrück, and its commander, Brigadier Mills-Roberts, was ordered to provide a commando as soon as possible to support 8 RB's bridgehead.[44] Consequently 45 (RM) Cdo was released and at 0430 hours on 6 April started moving by truck to Stolzenau.

Friday 6 April

The Kampfgruppe Schulze counter-attack

On 4 April Kampfgruppe Schulze had left Fallingbostel on the long road move to the Weser. Accompanied by trucks carrying fuel and ammunition, its route took it via Rethem where it crossed the Aller. Despite losing a Tiger with gearbox problems near Rethem, the *Kampfgruppe* reached Nienburg without further incident and then moved south-eastwards on the final leg of its journey to its hide location, the Schaumburg Forest. Arriving on the evening of 5 April, the tank crews concealed their vehicles in the forest's western fringes while Schulze reported to Major Ferber, the commander of the Petershagen-Stolzenau sector, who had established his command post in the Spiekerberg brickworks on the edge of Quetzen; here Schulze and Ferber discussed options for using the armour the next day. Although it is not known what these options were, 6th Airlanding Brigade's war diary mentions,[45] with information probably gleaned from a PoW, that Kampfgruppe Schulze's mission was to hold the low ridge running north-south between Bierde and Masloh. Subsequent events show the armour being used more aggressively than this but there is nothing to suggest in its future manoeuvres that the *Kampfgruppe* was given the two British bridging sites as its objectives.

6 April dawned foggy with low cloud and rain would persist all day. On VIII Corps' right flank, 6th Airborne Division had spent the night 5/6 April in feverish activity getting troops across the Weser at the Todthausen and tile factory crossing sites. As we have heard neither crossing was easy, but despite the state of the river and frequent shelling of the Todthausen rafting site, 2

---

44 TNA WO 218/73, 1st Commando Brigade war diary.
45 TNA WO 171/4320, *HQ 6th Airlanding Brigade, April 1945*, Appendix, Report – Op VARSITY, (C) – Brief account of battle until R Elbe (D+5 to D+27).

Oxf Bucks LI, commanded by Lieutenant Colonel Darell-Brown, made good progress with C Company getting across the river to join the other three companies.[46] The shelling, directed by an observer in the tower of Frille's church, increased in intensity during the early part of the morning, forcing suspension of further crossings, and it was not until 0915 hours that rafting the battalion's transport could start. This progress was possible because at first light A Company had exploited from Frille to attack the four guns of the *Flak* train positioned at the station, resulting in the rapid capture of four 10.5cm guns and 30 prisoners. Although the battalion's loss of four killed in action on 6 April appears small, this figure is additional to the 121 killed since landing at Hamminkeln some 13 days previously. Grievous losses. Despite the majority of the shelling ceasing with the capture of the railway *Flak*, the rafting site was still subjected to harassing fire from a self-propelled gun in the Friller Brink area.

At 12 Devon's crossing site at the tile factory, A Company crossed in assault boats before dawn followed by C Company and the remaining elements, allowing the complete battalion to begin enlarging the left flank of the bridgehead. Although the rifle companies had successfully crossed, attempts to raft the battalion's mortars and 6-pdr anti-tank guns failed owing to the continuing strength of the current. Why rafting was more of a problem for 12 Devon than 2 Oxf Bucks LI is unknown but the absence of the anti-tank guns would soon place the battalion in serious jeopardy. Once across, A Company advanced down the Weser's right bank to its objective south-east of Lahde, followed closely by the recce platoon. Lahde was, however, far from secure and both B and C Companies were having considerable trouble with marines from I./590 defending houses in the central and eastern parts of the village and it took until mid-morning for the companies to secure these areas. By now three companies of 1 RUR had crossed the Weser in assault boats and were advancing north to relieve 12 Devon, which was completed by 1045 hours. 1 RUR then moved off to secure the area opposite Petershagen to provide protection for the sappers of 100 Field Company, who had started to build the pontoon Bailey bridge at 0730 hours. With Lahde cleared, 12 Devon's task was now to expand the left flank of the bridgehead with the companies' tasks as follows: A Company to occupy a firm base on the south-east edge of Lahde, B Company to secure Quetzen, C Company to secure Bierde, and D Company to cross the railway line and advance eastwards to secure Masloh. At 1310 hours 12 Devon reported that its battalion headquarters was established on the eastern edge of Lahde.

Major Ferber at the Spiekerberg brickworks was made aware during the early part of the morning that enemy infantry were advancing on the right bank of the Weser and subsequent events indicate that he decided to launch Kampfgruppe Schulze against this threat rather than using the tanks to hold the Bierde–Masloh ridge. He probably assessed that at this stage only infantry were across and that the enemy was vulnerable with the bridgehead unconsolidated and, with the bridges not yet complete, unsupported by tanks and possibly also anti-tank guns; this favourable situation would soon end. His concept would seem to have been to launch his two tank groups on separate attacks against the enemy infantry: on the left Oberleutnant Fehrmann's group of five Tigers would attack in a westerly direction via Quetzen and Masloh, while on the right the four Panthers commanded by Leutnant von 'S' would advance from Quetzen to Bierde. A handful of tank-hunting infantry from Panzerjagdverband 'Großer Kurfürst' would accompany the Panther group in three SdKfz 251 half-tracks.

Tiger group. At about 1030 hours the *Kampfgruppe* left its hide in the Schaumburg Forest and moved the short distance to Masloh, where the group divided with the Panthers continuing north to Quetzen while the Tiger group drove through Masloh and moved to the crest line of the ridge.

---

46 TNA WO 171/5254, 2 Oxf Bucks LI war diary.

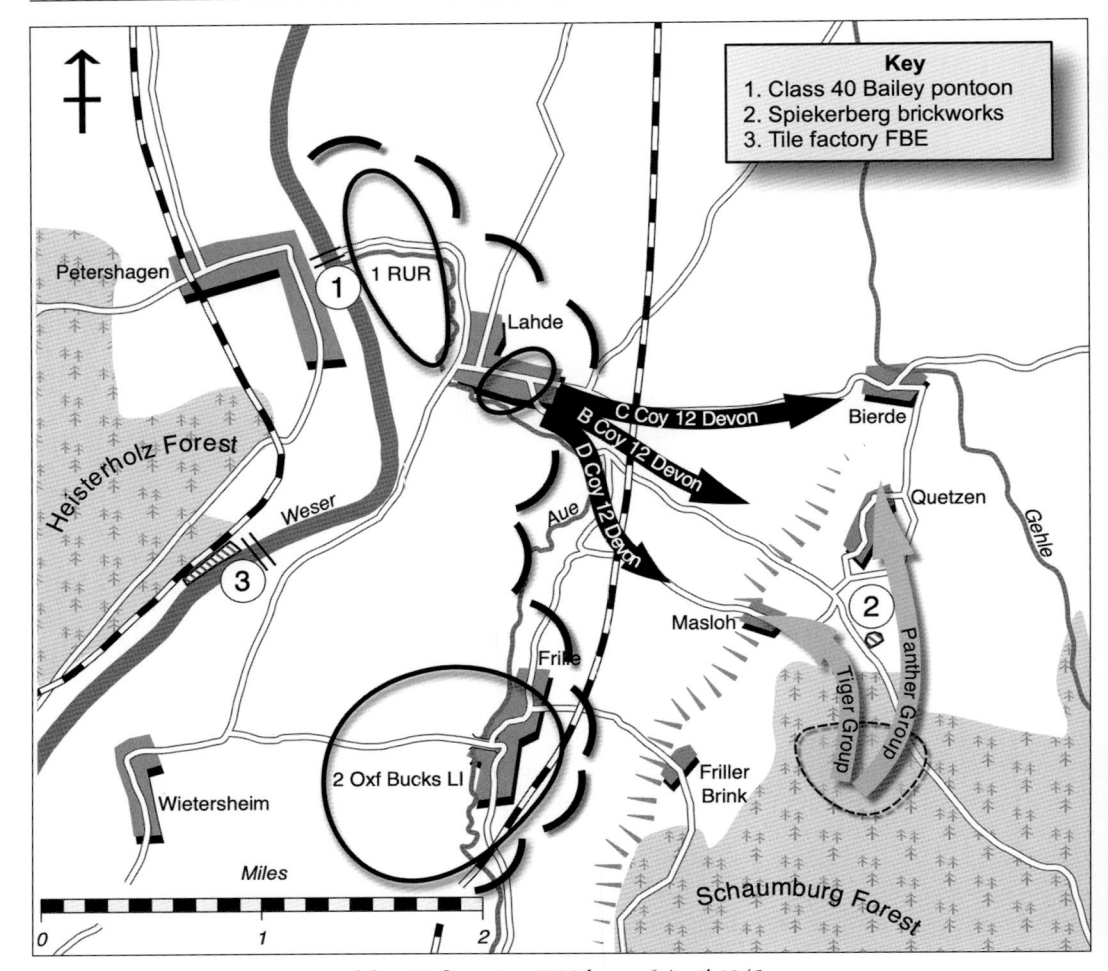

Map 17 Situation 1200 hours 6 April 1945.

Here the tanks took up overwatch positions from which they could look across the fields to Timpen, a hamlet of scattered farmhouses, and the open ground across which the British would have to advance. At approximately 1330 hours they saw the first soldiers of D Company 12 Devon advancing towards them on the road from Timpen. The appearance of enemy infantry would have been a perfect target and one can imagine the buzz of excitement the sight would have caused the tank crews. With the lead British soldiers nearing the foot of the ridge, Fehrmann gave the order to open fire with the tanks' machine-guns and to advance. The drivers engaged gear, let out the clutches and with revs increasing on their Maybach engines the five Tigers trundled down the gentle slope.

At the moment D Company and the Tiger group met, D Company commander, Major Palmer, his headquarters and 20 Platoon, the lead platoon, were nearing the bottom of the ridge, while the other three platoons were following but still in the area of Timpen and the fields to the west. Captain Ralph Hartland, second-in-command of D Company, describes the events that followed:[47]

---

47   WJP Aggett, *The Bloody Eleventh* (Exeter: The Devonshire and Dorset Regiment, 1995), p.466. The tanks Hartland saw were of course Tigers.

STUKAS, TIGERS AND PANTHERS 161

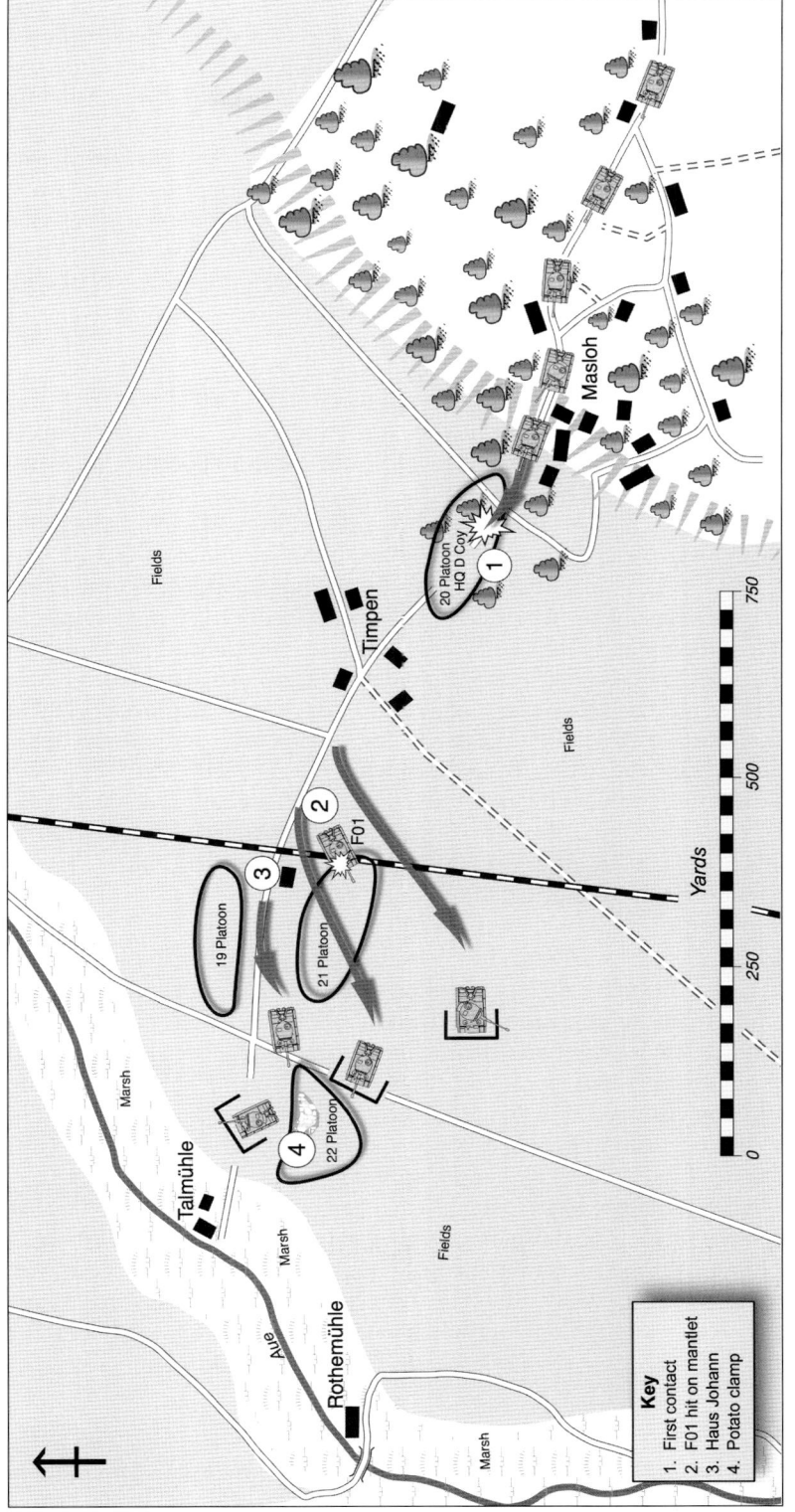

Map 18 The Tiger Group's Attack – 6 April 1945.

> Crossing the open ground we experienced the awesome sight of a number of Panther [sic] tanks breasting the slope in front of us. We were fairly caught on the hop but the tank commanders had their turrets closed and didn't, I think, spot us at first. The only shelter was a pair of isolated houses. My company commander ordered us to seek cover there and miraculously we did. While the rest scrambled into the building a corporal and I stood guard. Then I heard my companion grunt and realised he had been hit so I got him into the house and down to the cellar where everyone was huddled. With the trap door closed we waited as the noise of the approaching tank stopped and we heard footsteps and German voices in the rooms overhead. Then after an interminable time we heard the tank start up and move away. One grenade through that trapdoor would have been enough. I have always wondered how the Germans failed to find us. Perhaps they were even more scared than we were.

As soon as he saw the Tigers heading down the ridge towards them, Major Palmer managed to warn battalion headquarters, and at 1355 hours the battalion alerted HQ 6th Airlanding Brigade that four enemy tanks, still incorrectly identified as Panthers, were in the Timpen area. Now aware of the threat, Brigadier Bellamy immediately ordered anti-tank guns to have first priority for movement over the tile factory site FBE. The bridge, however, was still incomplete and the infantry would have to rely on their PIATs until the guns could reach them. At 1500 hours, just as 249 Field Company introduced the last two rafts into the bridge and the required extra trestle was being brought forward, the report of enemy tanks in the brigade bridgehead reached the sappers at the bridge. Why it took an hour for this critical information to reach them is puzzling, however they immediately started man-handling 12 Jeeps towing 6-pdr guns over the uncomplete bridge. Meanwhile to the east, D Company headquarters and 20 Platoon had managed to scatter into the woods and buildings on Masloh's western edge and so were fortunate in being able to avoid the Tigers and their machine-gun fire; other platoons, in the open fields and initially oblivious to what was taking place to their front, would be less fortunate.

Once they reached the bottom of the ridge the Tigers roared westwards down the road to Timpen shooting up any targets as they appeared. Corporal Dudley Anderson, a section commander in 21 Platoon commanded by Lieutenant Guy Reakes, for obvious reasons nicknamed 'Stinker', describes how events rapidly unfolded:[48]

> The front half of the company were already in the village [Masloh], and we in the rear half were still advancing in Indian file strung out on either side of the road when we came under fire. At the same moment came a loud, mechanical roar that sounded just like a tank engine starting up. It was followed by a massive rumbling of tracks, and from their hiding-places in the village five German tanks appeared. Four of them were giant Tigers and the fifth was a Mk IV. 21 Platoon was trapped in flat, open countryside without even the cover of houses to fight from. Our only anti-tank weapon was Leslie Meeks' PIAT, its eight bombs carried by various members of the platoon. We had walked into a perfectly sprung ambush.
>
> 'Get all the PIAT bombs to Meeks, and then take cover in the slit trenches,' yelled Lieutenant Reakes. The Germans had dug the slit trenches but now they would serve us. I dashed around, collected all the bombs and got them to Leslie Meeks before dropping into the nearest trench. We crouched as low as we could as the tanks rumbled down the road towards us. The PIAT, we had been taught, was capable of knocking out any known tank. Now we would see.

---

48 Dudley Anderson, *Three Cheers for the Next Man to Die* (London: Robert Hale Ltd, 1983), pp.160–161. Although aliases are used in Anderson's book, I have used the correct names for Lieutenant Reakes and Private Meeks. Leslie Meeks was later awarded the Military Medal for his part in this action.

> As the first Tiger came within 50 yards, Reakes ordered Meeks to fire. Leslie scored a direct hit and the tank stopped. The engine faded out and we were jubilant, preparing to take on the tank crews with small arms. Suddenly the engine started up again and the monster began to lumber forward. Leslie Meeks hit the same tank some seven times but it came remorselessly on. This was the last of our PIAT ammunition. We had nothing but rifles and bayonets.

Dudley Anderson properly identifies the tanks as Tigers. It is likely that the Tiger hit by Meeks with his PIAT was callsign F01 commanded by Oberleutnant Fehrmann as this tank was struck on the mantlet during the counter-attack, damaging it and preventing elevation of the main armament. Despite this small success, the PIAT was ineffective against the heavy tanks and Private Arthur Taylor describes the weapon's futility as well as the terror of being on the receiving end of the tanks' machine-guns:[49]

> If we had been armed with pea-shooters we would have created just as much effect on those tanks. The PIAT rounds just bounced off the armour plate. Even direct hits had no effect, most exploded leaving a white blast mark on the tank but they had no other effect than to alert the crews that we were there, and that we were without effective anti-tank weapons. In other words, sitting ducks. Opening up with their machine-guns they began firing at us as we flattened our bodies, forcing them down and digging with broken fingernails into the earth hoping that we were not going to die. It was another of those occasions when I should have been killed. I have to believe in luck, or fate, or call it what you will. Why is it that comrades either side of me were killed, some terribly wounded, yet I was left untouched? I saw the ugly bullets raking the ground just inches in front of my eyes. One of my mates, the lower part of his face missing and pouring blood, looked up at me for comfort and help, and then his head fell forward.

The unequal battle between heavy armour and lightly-armed infantry could have only one outcome, as Dudley Anderson recalls:[50]

> With no more bombs being fired at them, the panzers now slewed across the road into the fields and began shooting us up in our slit trenches. We kept our heads down – there was no point putting your head up to fire a rifle at a 60-ton tank. On the other hand, the tank crews were not going to show themselves for fear of getting shot, so they lowered their sights as far as possible and tried to kill us in our trenches. But they could not get low enough. In the end they won the completely uneven contest by sheer weight. As the giant tanks towered over the trenches, the soil started to crumble and bury the occupants. One by one 31 Platoon was forced to surrender…Lying in the bottom of the trench, I buried the German flag I had captured in Hamminkeln and the German officer's Walther pistol and *SS* dagger in loose earth at the bottom of the trench. Then I lay low and waited, hoping I would not be noticed. I thought I had a chance as the German crews were, quite sensibly, still not prepared to leave their tanks.
>
> The sound of rumblings increased and I could feel vibrations at the bottom of my trench as the tanks started to move off. The column of captured Red Devils was near enough for me to

---

49 Taylor, *Shine Like a Glow-Worm*, p.117. The soldier shot in the face was captured alive and subsequently had his face rebuilt in a German hospital. Arthur met him at a London station after the war and was amazed at the surgeon's skill.
50 Anderson, *Three Cheers for the Next Man to Die*, pp.161–162.

The railway crossing with Haus Johann beyond on the left. Picture taken in 2015. (Author)

see them as they were marched away along the side of the road. Unfortunately, as they passed my trench they all leaned over and glanced down, presumably to say a last farewell thinking I was dead. Their action did not pass unnoticed. The last tank in the column stopped. The tank commander climbed down, walked across to my trench and leaning over pointed a Luger pistol at me. In perfect English he said, 'For you, the war is over'…It was the classic statement of capture, almost a *cliché*.

While the rear platoons were being mopped up, which resulted in 51 members of the company, including Dudley Anderson and three officers, being taken prisoner and herded into Haus Johann near the railway crossing, Major Palmer and his group escaped and made their way to the firm base position occupied by A and B Companies in Lahde.

Dudley Anderson believed that the German officer who captured him was the commander of the tank group. The Tiger was in fact commanded by Feldwebel Bellof, who had advanced in his Tiger over the railway line and caught the hapless enemy infantry taking cover in the area of a potato clamp near the Talmühle mill on the Aue stream. Arthur Taylor, who was also captured, describes the end of the fight against Fehrmann's Tigers:[51]

> Those of us still unhurt scattered. I rolled away from the danger, and quickly moved behind a wall of a farmhouse, which gave cover from the murderous machine-gun fire. The damn tanks were still advancing, but now of course they knew where we were. We were helpless against such superior force and could not defend ourselves, we had no weapons that could stop those tanks; armed only with rifles and light machine-guns, our bullets struck that enemy armour with about as much effect as a fly landing on an arm.

---

51 Taylor, *Shine Like a Glow-Worm*, p.119.

There was an awful feeling of helplessness and fear as we realised that this was finally it. We could run away, but the tanks would catch up with us at the river. We could surrender and hope to escape later, or we could continue to put up a pointless resistance until we were all dead. Common sense pointed to the surrender option and about 60 of us put up our hands and were rounded up. We were herded back to enemy territory and imprisonment. Unknown to the enemy and us their prisoners, over half the unit remained free; they had hidden in cellars, which were not searched and they remained undiscovered.

Those of us that were prisoners were ordered to give up our weapons, which we did, however none of the tank crew searched us and most of us carried hand grenades in our smock pockets, which gave some of us the idea of dropping one down the tank hatch if we got the opportunity.

Having dealt with D Company and incarcerated the prisoners in Haus Johann, the Tigers pushed on into the fields where they fanned out to take up fire positions. Here we will briefly leave the Tiger group and D Company and follow the Panther group's attack on C Company.

Panther group. In the late morning the four Panthers, accompanied by the three SdKfz 251 half-tracks carrying troops from the *Panzerjagdverband*, left Quetzen and drove north across the pastures of the Quetzer Heide towards the next village, Bierde. A move that was in reaction to sightings of British infantry advancing eastwards from Lahde. At 1100 hours, while the Panther group was approaching Bierde from the south, C Company 12 Devon, having recently finished helping B Company mop-up Lahde, was nearing the village from the west. As the company closed on Bierde, the FOO from A Troop 2nd Forward Observation Unit supporting the company,[52] spotted four tanks in the vicinity of the village and at 1115 hours called for fire, which was provided by 61st and 63rd Medium Regiments, 6th Field Regiment and 53rd Airlanding Light Regiment. The storm of shells damaged one of the Panthers and forced the group to beat a hasty retreat.

At about mid-day, C Company reached the village and quickly began preparing defensive positions in and among the houses of this forward-most point on the bridgehead line. The company was distinctly vulnerable with no 6-pdr anti-tank gun support and since that morning's first report of enemy tanks in the bridgehead, a race was taking place between the tanks' next attack and making the FBE at the tile factory site sufficiently negotiable for Jeeps towing 6-pdrs. By 1530 hours, although still incomplete, the sappers had managed to man-handle Jeeps and 6-pdr guns across the FBE and the guns were rushing to A and B Companies in Lahde and C Company in Bierde. At 1550 hours 12 Devon reported to HQ 6th Airlanding Brigade that four enemy tanks were again visible in the Bierde area and at much the same time two 6-pdr anti-tank guns reached C Company and were immediately deployed to cover the southern and eastern approaches to the village.

Although the Panthers were observed in the mid-afternoon, Leutnant von 'S' did not advance again on Bierde until the early evening when, shortly before 1900 hours, his Panther group again headed north. Why there was such a long delay – about six-hours – is a mystery. However, the delay would prove disastrous for the Panther group as it provided C Company with the time to prepare defensive position in the village and for the anti-tank guns to arrive. As the Panthers neared Bierde they fanned out across the pastures with the left-hand Panther on the Kleiberg lane and the *Leutnant's* command Panther advancing 250 yards behind it. When the tank on the lane reached Bierde's first house, a civilian flagged it down and shouted a warning to the commander that the British had occupied the village. This information was passed to Leutnant von 'S', who

---

52   TNA WO 171/4762, Appendix F, 53rd Airlanding Light Regiment RA war diary.

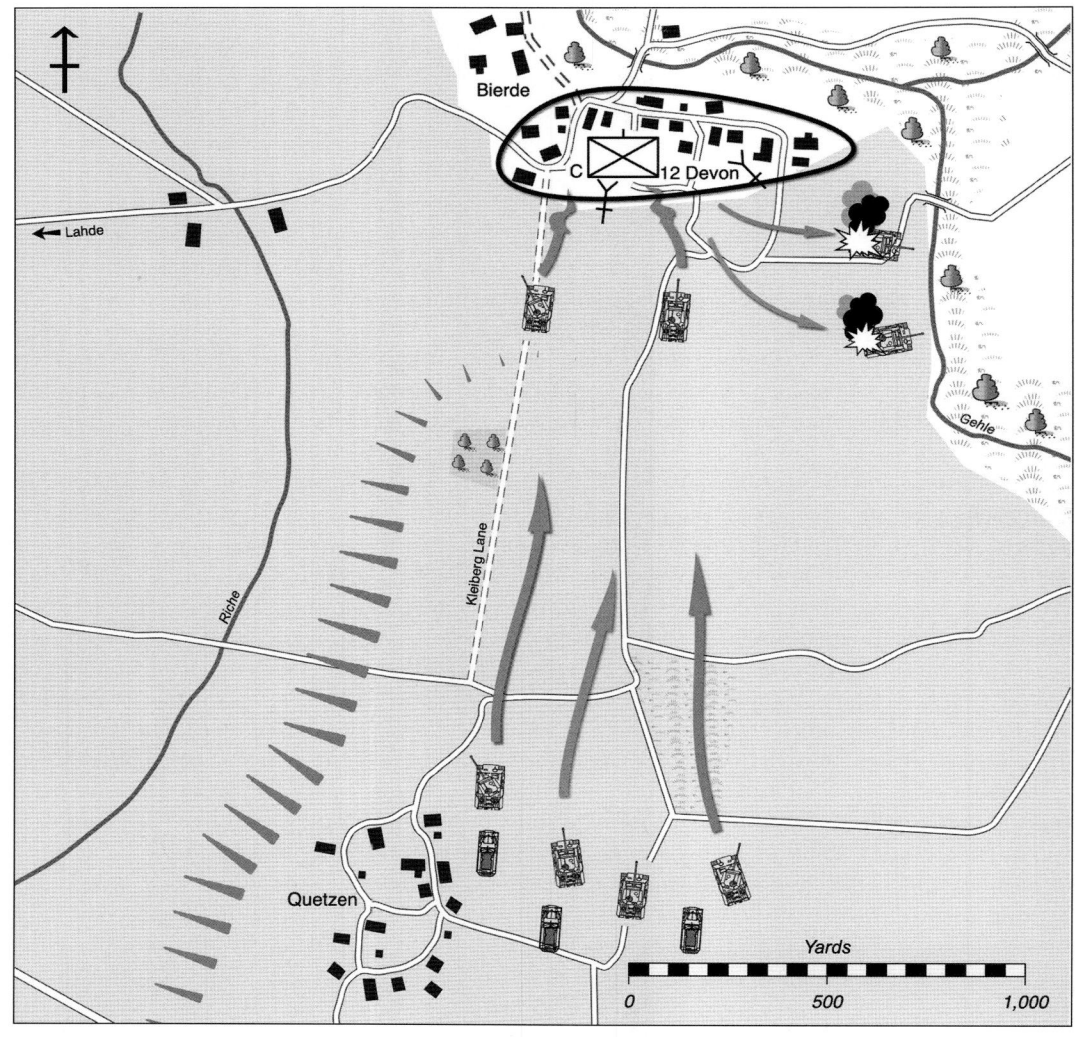

Map 19 The Panther Group's Attack – 6 April 1945.

immediately ordered the group to attack. At 1900 hours 12 Devon reported C Company being attacked by tanks from three directions.

C Company, concentrated on the village's southern perimeter, engaged the Panther group with its two 6-pdrs and with small-arms' fire from slit trenches and from windows in the houses. The Panthers returned fire using both main armament and machine-guns and in his command tank, Leutnant von 'S' drove towards the eastern side of the village where he tried to break in. As he did so he identified a 6-pdr near a tall electricity transformer building, which he engaged with a HE round, collapsing the building onto the gun and its crew. However, during the fighting his Panther had taken hits, killing a crew member, Obergefreiter Held, and leaving a shot lodged in the turret ring, jamming the traverse but leaving the tank mobile. The fight to break-into the village was fierce but with insufficient infantry it soon became clear to the Germans that they would not be able to overcome the British and Leutnant von 'S' ordered his group to break-off and withdraw. Disaster now overtook two of the Panthers, which swung away to the open ground east

STUKAS, TIGERS AND PANTHERS 167

The final approach to Bierde, with its buildings visible in the background. The Gehle stream, its course improved since 1945, is on the right. (Author)

The grave in Ilvese war cemetery of the three Panther crewmen. (Author)

of the village where they were soon checked by the Gehle stream and became easy targets for a 6-pdr. Both tanks were rapidly hit in their turrets by APCBC shots and destroyed, with three crew members of one Panther burning to death in their tank.

Lieutenant Hargreaves, a very recent reinforcement who had joined the battalion after the Rhine crossing, knocked out one of the Panthers despite never before having fired a 6-pdr. In the failing light the two surviving Panthers withdrew south-eastwards to an area of woods, where they were spotted and heavily engaged by artillery. They then made their back to the Schaumburg forest, although the command Panther diverted via the Spiekerberg brick works where the crew used a crane to lift the turret in an attempt to release the shot; this was, however, unsuccessful so the unrepaired tank moved off to join the other Panther in the forest.

Tiger group. We will now return to the Tiger group, which we had left fanning out in the fields beyond the railway line. Following his success against D Company, it is curious that Fehrmann did not then order his Tigers to manoeuvre out of the fields and continue their advance to the Weser and the tile factory bridging site. We do not know the reasons why he did not do so but perhaps neither of the two bridges over the Aue could take the weight of a Tiger, or the Tigers were running low on machine-gun ammunition or fuel, or the defence of the ridge line, now half a mile to his rear, remained his principal task. For whatever reasons, the group advanced no further and held its positions on the line of the Aue for about an hour engaging opportunity targets. In the open fields the Tigers were, however, very obvious targets and from 1355 hours onwards they came under sustained artillery fire, directed by a CANLOAN officer, Captain Sid Mooney, detached from No. 2 Forward Observation Unit to act as FOO to 2 Oxf Bucks LI. Mooney had remained hidden north of Frille when the infantry pulled back from the threat posed by the Tigers and although the tanks were very close and the artillery concentrations were falling around him, Mooney remained in position to direct the fire; he was later awarded the Military Cross for his bravery and resolve. Eventually Fehrmann decided that there was nothing further to be gained from remaining where he was so ordered his Tigers to pull back, taking with them the prisoners from D Company. Arthur Taylor recalls the withdrawal:[53]

> We were told to get on the tanks and we were driven several miles back into Germany. We saw no enemy troops, but we passed through two or three small villages and the people came out of their houses to take a look at what for most of them was their first sight of the enemy. Strangely, they were mostly silent, but gazed at us with sullen eyes as we drove by, I must admit to having thought that we might have got some rough treatment from them, but not so. Perhaps the realisation that the war was lost had knocked the stuffing out of them. Anyway they showed no sign of hostility toward us.

The Tigers withdrew via Masloh to the area of Friller Brink, which sits on the same ridge as Masloh, and here they joined a StuG IV, which had played no part in Schulze's attack but had earlier been engaging 2 Oxf Bucks LI in the Frille area. At 1530 hours the FOO from B Troop 2nd Forward Observation Unit spotted four tanks at Friller Brink carrying the prisoners and called down a regimental fire mission by the 25-pdrs of 25th Field Regiment.[54] There is no indication in the war diary of any pangs of conscience at shelling their own men nor, oddly, does Arthur Taylor make any mention of the artillery fire! What he does mention is a pair of low-flying Typhoons, which swooped low over the area causing the Tigers and prisoners to scatter for cover. Once the

---

53   Taylor, *Shine Like a Glow-Worm*, p.119.
54   TNA WO 171/4814, 25th Field Regiment RA war diary.

aircraft had passed, the prisoners were herded up and ordered to remount the tanks. However, during the confusion Arthur Taylor and another soldier had remained hidden in the ditch where they had taken cover and as the guards had no idea how many prisoners they had and Fehrmann was keen to reach the cover of the Schaumburg Forest as soon as possible, they were not missed and the tanks with their charges rumbled away to the east while Arthur and his companion remained hidden. With Lieutenant Reakes, who also escaped, they rejoined the battalion two days later.

The Kampfgruppe Schulze counter-attack was a missed opportunity to create mayhem in the shallow 6th Airborne bridgehead. Had the two tank groups fought as a single unit and been given one or other of the bridging sites as their objective, they could have posed a significant threat. Although the Tiger group mopped up the best part of a rifle company, the attack in general was a half-hearted affair which achieved little. With not much knowledge of the ground and what they were supposed to achieve, perhaps the commanders' hearts were not in it.

Fehrmann now decided that further withdrawal was the only option and ordered his group to pull back into the Schaumburg Forest, taking with it the captured members of D Company. Once the Tigers reached the forest, Fehrmann swapped his damaged F01 with Unteroffizier Franzen's Tiger and Franzen, the youngest of the Tiger commanders, was ordered to take F01 back to Fallingbostel to exchange the gun mantlet. Franzen duly set off on the long journey to the rear and he and a battleworthy F01 will reappear in the account in six days' time. When the two surviving Panthers reached the forest, they married up with the Tigers and the depleted Kampfgruppe Schulze withdrew through the Schaumburg Forest to cross the Mittelland Canal near Rusben, transiting the British and US army group boundary as they did so.

What precisely happened thereafter is not known, but photographs taken in 1946 show two Tigers (one bearing the callsign F13), a Panther and two SdKfz 251 half-tracks in a field close to the railway line at Achum, north of Bückeburg. Some have suggested that the vehicles were destroyed in battle with US 5th Armored Division, but this is mistaken for three reasons: the division did not advance through the Bückeburg area, the 1946 photographs show no sign of battle damage to the tanks' armour and none of the vehicles are tactically deployed. Moreover, for April 1945 this was a significant enemy grouping and would certainly have featured in the after action reports of 334th Infantry Regiment (of the 84th US Infantry Division) and Company C, 638 Tank Destroyer Battalion,[55] which jointly captured Bückeburg and cleared the surrounding area on 8 April. While 334th Infantry's history mentions German self-propelled guns in action at Bückeburg,[56] no mention is made of other German armour by the recce elements and tank-destroyers, which bypassed the town via the left flank (ie the Achum area). This suggests the Kampfgruppe Schulze armour was either not seen (unlikely) or irrelevant (more likely) and it would seem that on 7 April, having passed through Rusben, Kampfgruppe Schulze reached the field at Achum where the vehicles were abandoned, probably owing to lack of fuel or becoming bogged, and then destroyed by their crews. However, the armour in the field was possibly not the end of Kampfgruppe Schulze and it is probable that a Tiger and a Panther encountered on 8 April on the Leine by 1 CAN Para and a force from 15th Reconnaissance Regiment belonged to it. US 5th Armored Division[57] recorded the destruction of a Tiger and a Panther on 9 April and these were more than likely the same two vehicles.

---

55 After Action Report, 638th Tank Destroyer Battalion, November 1944–May 1945, *http://cgsc.cdmhost.com/cdm/ref/collection/p4013coll8/id/3605* (accessed 15 April 2017).

56 Corporal Perry S. Wolff, *Fortune Favored the Brave, History of the 334th Infantry* (Mannheim: Mannheimer Großdruckerei, 1945), p.110.

57 5th Armored Division After Action Report, April 1945, *http://www.5ad.org/04_45.html* (accessed 11 April 2017).

During the course of the Schulze counter-attack the British misreported seeing various types of enemy armour including a 'Ferdinand',[58] Panzer Mk IV tanks and self-propelled guns. Although Dudley Anderson correctly identified the tanks as Tigers, surprisingly there is no mention of Tigers in any of the war diaries as they were routinely, and usually incorrectly, reported whenever German tanks were encountered. From the tenor of the war diary entries, Schulze's attack does not seem to have unduly worried the British at either brigade or divisional level and the entries for HQ 6th Airborne on 6 April only briefly mention stiffening enemy resistance and that counter-attacks were mounted in the Bierde area. This insouciance was certainly not shared at battalion-level and 12 Devon had a stressful day with six killed, 12 wounded and 48 missing, losses additional to the 72 men already killed in action since the battalion landed at Hamminkeln 13 days previously. However, 6 April ended well for 6th Airborne with the bridgehead secure and the enemy armoured counter-attack defeated, and the division would soon be poised to exploit to the east. At 1730 hours 249 Field Company finally completed the Class 9 FBE at the tile factory site and 17-pdr guns from 3 Battery, 2nd Airlanding Anti-Tank Regiment were manhandled across,[59] although the manpower needed to move the guns significantly delayed preparation of the approach on the right bank where the ground was very soft and this work was not finally completed until 2000 hours. 249 Field Company's war diarist recorded the company as the proud builder of the first British bridge across the Weser, but that working against the clock to build 320 feet of bridging had exhausted the sappers. Meanwhile, construction of the Class 40 Bailey pontoon bridge at Petershagen by 100 Field Company supported by 2 Troop 3 Para Squadron also continued without let-up during Schulze's counter-attack. This bridge was vital for the projection of armour across the Weser but its construction was no easy task as the seven knot current caused great difficulty for ferrying engineer stores and connecting the bridging.

An interesting side note to the day is an entry made by HQ 3rd Parachute Brigade recording the first sighting of British jet aircraft over the front.[60]

Stolzenau and the bridgehead

While solid progress was being made on 6 April in 6th Airborne's sector, further north operations by 11th Armoured were significantly more challenging. Despite the night 5/6 April passing relatively quietly, with the coming of dawn action in the Stolzenau bridgehead began to hot up and the British infantry on the right bank now came into direct contact with Kampfgruppe Tischler, dug-in on the railway embankment and an outpost position near the demolished Weser bridge. Although short of infantry heavy weapons and without tanks, the *Kampfgruppe* was numerically strong and, as we have heard, supported by quantities of *Flak*.

The first contact on the right bank came when the forward-most section of H Company 8 RB, covering the road embankment leading to the bridge, was rushed in the half-light of dawn by a group of about 40 Hitler Youth, who had sallied forth from the outpost position. Not only was the section captured but the enemy gained a foothold in the middle of the platoon position. Movement thereafter became extremely dangerous and both sides spent the remainder of the day sniping at

---

58 Nicknamed after Ferdinand Porsche, the vehicle's designer, this was the initial nickname for the SdKfz.184 heavy tank-destroyer; by 1945 it had changed to 'Elefant'. SdKfz.184 did not operate on the West Front and this was probably a mis-identified StuG IV or Panzer IV/70.
59 TNA WO 171/4756, 2nd Airlanding Anti-Tank Regiment RA war diary.
60 The two Gloster Meteors were from 616 Squadron flying from Nijmegen. Although before the war's end there were no air-to-air combat engagements by Meteors, owing to a ban on their operating in the depth of enemy territory, they mounted some successful ground attack missions.

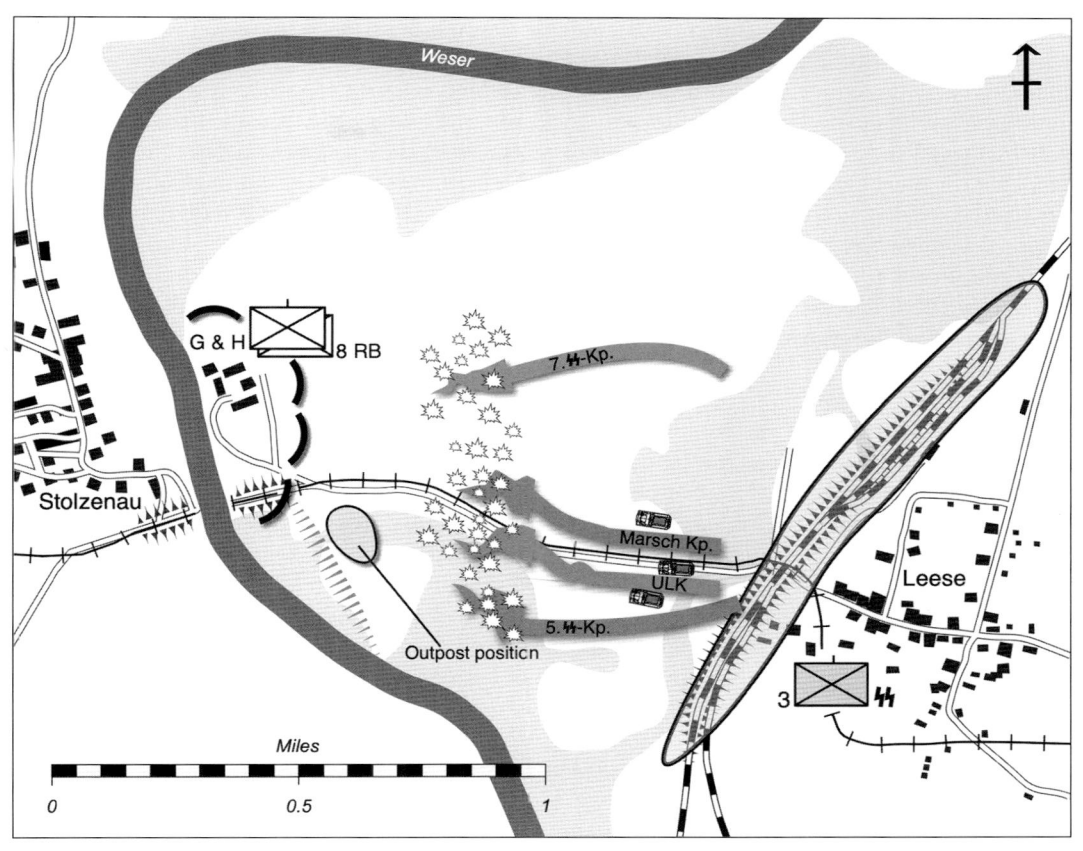

Map 20 Kampfgruppe Tischler's Attack – 6 April 1945.

each other. This was not a one-sided matter and H Company lost a platoon commander, a platoon sergeant, two corporals and two riflemen during the course of the day.

During the early part of the morning Kampfgruppe Tischler mounted a concerted attack against the British lodgement on the right bank. 7. SS-Kompanie and the recently-arrived 5. SS-Kompanie moved forward from their positions on the railway embankment and fanned out in the meadows either side of the road leading to Stolzenau, with 7. SS-Kompanie on the road's northern side and 5. SS-Kompanie on the southern. Meanwhile soldiers of the Unterführer-Lehr-Kompanie and the Marsch Kompanie mounted SdKfz 251 half-tracks at a forming up point behind the railway embankment and at about 0900 hours, using the road as the axis, the four companies began to advance towards the 8 RB bridgehead, with the dismounted companies plodding their way over the soggy meadows and the companies in the half-tracks following on the road. Initially all went well and the attack seemed to achieve surprise.

11 Platoon was the first to see the enemy and alerted company headquarters that infantry were advancing in waves across the open ground. Given the precarious nature of 8 RB's bridgehead this attack posed a significant threat but fortunately DF targets had been registered on this approach to deal with just such a contingency. In the open ground the Hitler Youth companies were extremely vulnerable to the fire from 8 RB's 3-in mortars and the 25-pdrs of 13 RHA and 151st Field Regiment, which soon rapidly fell on the meadows, stopping the attack in its tracks as the young soldiers sought whatever cover they could find. This was the first time they had been in action and the fire, which swept the meadows, must have been terrifying. Pinned down, any movement was

met by small-arms' fire and as there was absolutely no prospect of withdrawal in daylight, those who could dug-in while others hugged the ground to try to survive until nightfall. Losses began to mount and respite only came hours later with the coming of darkness when the exhausted, filthy and hungry Hitler Youth were able to pull back under the cover of a barrage fired by the *Flak*, which allowed the badly mauled companies to withdraw to the area of the train station, the start point for the morning's attack. The darkness was also used to bring in the wounded and to salvage desperately needed weapons and munitions from the fallen. 11th Armoured's SITREP sent to VIII Corps that night reported that a counter-attack had been beaten-off and that it had resulted in 30 enemy dead and 10 prisoners from SS-A.u.E.Btl.12 'HJ' and Pionier-Sperr-Brigade 1100.

Despite the failure of the attack, there was no let-up in the Germans' resistance and this un-named *SS-Oberscharführer* from Kampfgruppe Tischler describes the fighting from the German viewpoint:[61]

> I was an instructor in the battalion. My own service had been with the Leibstandarte in Russia. Usual decorations, Iron Cross, Infantry Assault, Close Combat and Wound Badge in Silver. I lined my platoon along the railway embankment, which stands 5 metres above the ground between the Weser and the village of Leese. The first British probes were easily repulsed – our field of fire was excellent. We could see every movement that the tommies made. I had my mortars behind the embankment with the reserve sections and three, tripod-mounted MG 42 firing on fixed lines. The battalion had ammunition enough. We had been ordered to hold to the last. We did not know it then but there was a V-2 assembly plant [*sic*] about a mile behind the railway line, just north of Leese, and it was our task to hold until the civilian scientists had got away.

By early morning, 45 (RM) Cdo was complete at Stolzenau and plans were drawn up for the commando to cross the Weser then advance to attack Leese from the south in order to relieve pressure on the bridgehead.[62] During the late morning the commando successfully crossed in assault boats, but this operation was not as smooth as the war diary suggests, as David Ward, commanding a section (equivalent to a platoon) in E Troop, recalls:[63]

> There was a lot of noise as the Germans were shelling the sappers who were trying to drop the old blown bridge before running a new Bailey bridge in its place. The shelling was coming from an 88mm firing airburst plus a lot of 20mm airburst flak. There were a few folding assault boats lying about. We put the men into houses in the village [Stolzenau] and Ian [Major Ian Beadle, officer commanding E Troop] took the SNCO and myself off on an O Group. It seemed that there was a Rifle Brigade platoon on the other side of the river and we had to get across and relieve them. Fair enough it seemed but there was rather a lot of nasty 20mm *Flak* popping off around us. Ian lost part of an ear lobe about then as we went back to brief the men and get on with things. It was fortunate that the 88mm crew could not see us when we were down by the river.
>
> Imagine my feelings when on turning out the troop I discovered that the majority were tight – totally pissed – and tottering about and rather bellicose towards life in general. I went and told Ian what was on and he took over. It was so simple; we, the officers and sergeants, opened up the boats and ran them down to the water's edge. We then persuaded the men

---

61   James Lucas, *Last Days of the Reich* (London: Arms & Armour Press, 1986), p.184.
62   TNA DEFE 2/51, 45 (RM) Cdo war diary.
63   Lt Col DCR Ward, 'My Time with 45 RM Commando' (KOSB Regimental Museum, T1.36).

down to the boats and encouraged them to embark and row over to the other side. This they did and the remainder of us came over in our own boat. Those incapable, occupied the already dug slits and those capable expanded the position. We then had to search the sleeping beauties and recover any bottles they had on them. These turned out to be German Army issue. I think that if the men had had breakfast before leaving the last place [Osnabrück] there would not have been a problem.

By midday 45 (RM) Cdo, including the worse for wear E Troop, had completed its crossing of the Weser and by 1700 hours had formed a narrow bridgehead about half a mile upstream from the demolished bridge and the two 8 RB companies. At 1345 hours, under the cover of artillery fire from 1st Mountain Regiment and a battery of 146th Medium Regiment,[64] the commando began to infiltrate up the right bank as the first part of the manoeuvre for its attack on Leese. However, this manoeuvre exposed them to Kampfgruppe Tischler's outpost position and the further they reached the greater the volume of fire they attracted from machine-guns, *Panzerfaust*, mortars and small arms, and by late afternoon, having managed to advance only some 200 yards, it was clear that further advance was impossible against the enemy's concentrated fire; the commandos were forced to dig in as fast as possible to hold what they had and link their left flank with 8 RB at the bridge, which they had achieved by 1800 hours. David Ward describes these events:[65]

> The rest of the commando turned up just after midday and started off upstream on the enemy side and we followed and a damnably bedraggled lot we were. The forward troop bumped the enemy who were *Jugend SS* and a nasty bunch. Several of our men were killed when they looked over the bank but the spit between the water and the bank was clear and the commando advanced and we moved into the place where the men were killed. It was obvious that to look over the bank would be fatal so we engaged in a grenade-throwing match. The next troop forward was able to snipe into the German position and it seemed that there were not more than 10 of them.
>
> Meanwhile the fighting in the bridgehead had become nothing short of desperate. The *SS* were sniping at us with deadly accuracy, and our casualties were steadily mounting in consequence. Able Troop, feeling their way forward amongst the hedgerows on the edge of the bridgehead, ran into a small party of Germans, and a furious hand-to-hand struggle resulted. It was during this short, sharp engagement that Captain Dudley Coventry – Able Troop's commander – was credited with striking a German soldier dead with one blow of his fist.
>
> The German soldier, a young boy in the *SS*, came at Captain Coventry from behind a hedgerow. The latter, to use his own words, was 'very annoyed' by this time, and before the startled German could do or say anything he had felled him to the ground with one mighty blow to the jaw. When our padre reached the body some minutes later, thinking that he would have to give first aid, he found that it was lifeless.

With progress impossible without incurring heavy casualties, Brigadier Mills-Roberts describes the circumstances he faced and his thoughts for future action:[66]

> This was the situation I found when I myself reached the divisional HQ – the rest of the brigade was following up as fast as it could. Having got the full situation from the general [Pip

---

64 TNA WO 171/5011, 1st Mountain Regiment RA war diary.
65 Ward, 'My Time with 45 RM Commando'.
66 Derek Mills-Roberts, *Clash by Night* (London: William Kimber, 1956), p.174.

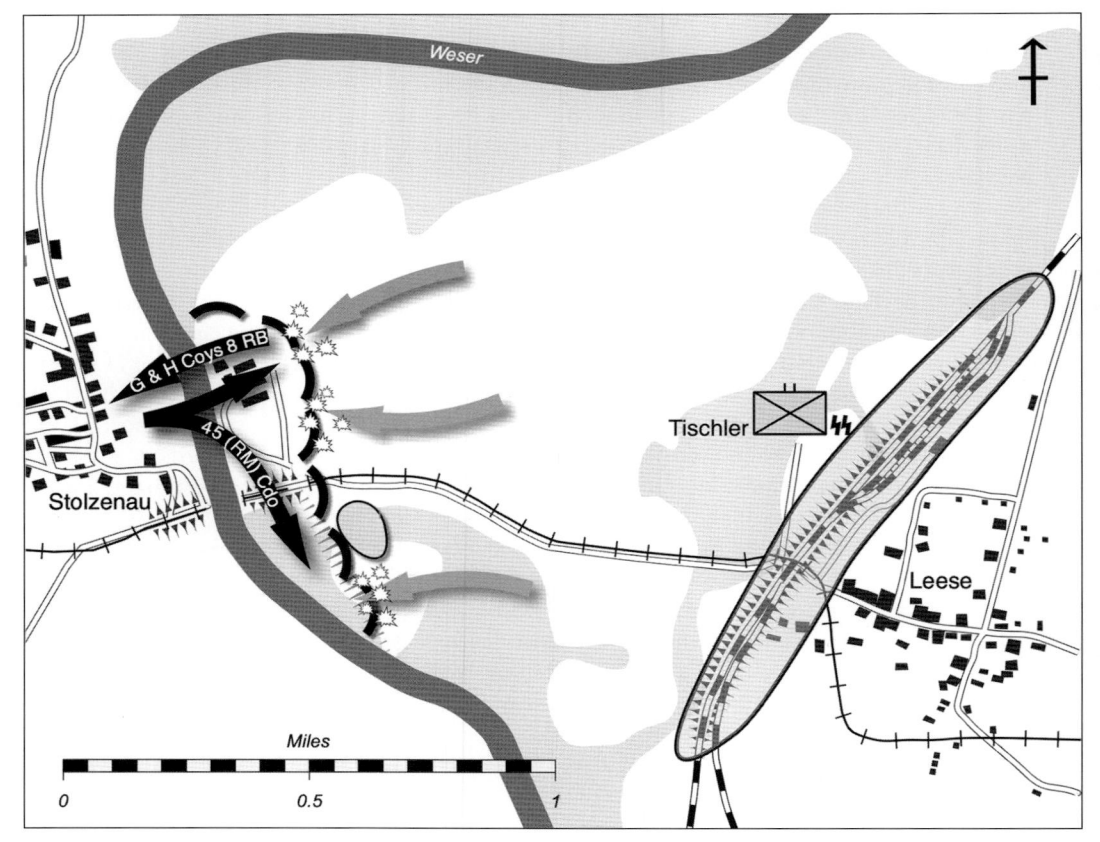

Map 21 45 (RM) Cdo Crosses the Weser – Night 6/7 April 1945.

Roberts] I went down to have a look myself. No doubt the Germans were fighting a delaying action and their most determined resistance would probably be on the various riverlines. The sooner a strong force was across the river and pushing on the better. The situation would deteriorate with delay.

I took Corporal Walkley, my driver, and Corporal Smith and drove to Stolzenau. The main street leading down to the river was under 20mm fire from the opposite bank. We left the car and walked down the street – the racket was terrific, but the 20mm shells were going high. Down by the river itself the divisional sappers were trying to build a bridge but over 40 planes were attacking them…the bridge was damaged and there were many casualties. We found a small canvas boat and paddled across to 45 (RM) Cdo. Things were not good: the whole of the bridgehead was under mortar and 20mm fire as well as a few overs from the aircraft attacking the bridge. The noise was intense and it was difficult to hear oneself speak. Major Blake had things well in hand but it was clear that the situation was too tough for one commando to deal with alone.[67]

In the attack on Leese they had met determined opposition and it was obvious that the enemy had been considerably reinforced. In the ensuing dog-fight with rifles and grenades

---

67 Blake was the acting commanding officer substituting for Lieutenant Colonel Gray, who had been wounded during the Rhine crossing.

prisoners had been taken and identified as 12 Panzer SS Training Battalion [sic] – their shooting was above average. On our way back across the river we found that our boat had several bullet holes in it. Corporal Smith dealt with one of these…by plugging it with an indescribably dirty handkerchief. I got back quickly to divisional HQ and told General Roberts that I would like to get the whole brigade over as soon as possible and deliver Leese a sharp blow from the flank. He told me that there was a factory in the woods north of Leese, which required investigation and that this would also be part of our objective.

The accuracy of the Germans' shooting referred to by Brigadier Mills-Roberts was no understatement and the quality of the young men's training in shooting and fieldcraft from their veteran instructors was paying dividends. 45 (RM) Cdo suffered four further fatalities of men shot through the head when they raised their heads above the bank, of which Lieutenant Peter Caspar's was particularly tragic, as recalled by Captain John Day:[68]

At one of our brief pauses while we moved along the river bank I found myself crouching beside a young subaltern, Peter Caspar, whose men were endeavouring to provide us with some covering fire. During a lull in the firing we heard shouting from the German positions. Peter said, 'They want to surrender,' leapt to his feet, took off his beret, and waved it at the enemy. Two or three bullets cracked at us and Peter Caspar fell dead at my feet.

Despite the difficulties in the bridgehead all was not gloom as a large store of excellent wines and spirits had been discovered in a cellar in Stolzenau. Such was the popularity of the cellar it was called 'Hockpoint' and controlled by HQ 29th Armoured Brigade as if it were issuing combat supplies. Brigadier Mills-Roberts takes up the story:[69]

As I was waiting for the brigade to come up I decided to go down to the river again. I saw a familiar figure coming up the road – it was Captain Philip Dunne of the Blues.[70] This debonair Household Cavalryman always got a lot of fun out of life… 'You want to be quick,' he said, 'The local Justerini & Brooks has just fallen.'[71] And out of his battledress blouse he produced a bottle of brandy – from its label it appeared to have been the brand most favoured by the Crown Prince of Serbia. The German commandant of Stolzenau had apparently been unable to remove his forcibly acquired wine cellar across the river when he had hurriedly left earlier.

Despite the threat to the Stolzenau bridgehead, it was decided the hard-pressed 8 RB companies, by now having suffered some 50 casualties, needed to be relieved at the earliest opportunity. Brigadier Mills-Roberts therefore planned a crossing operation for the night 6/7 April that would simultaneously extract the 8 RB companies and get his other three commandos over to the right bank. The complete commando brigade would then mount a night, flanking manoeuvre using a lengthy approach to the south of Leese and attack the village from the rear at dawn.

Regardless of the harassing fire on the bridging site, during the night 5/6 April the sappers of 13 and 612 Field Squadrons and 224 Field Company had made progress and by 0800 hours 6 April the bridging work was some 60 percent complete, bringing the very welcome deployment of

---

68   John Day, *A Plain Russet-Coated Captain* (Dorking: Self-published, 1993), p.145.
69   Mills-Roberts, *Clash by Night*, pp.174–175.
70   Nickname of the Royal Horse Guards.
71   Fine wine merchants still very much in business at 61 St. James's Street, London.

tanks to the right bank much closer. The operation seemed to be going well. However, during the early afternoon the *Luftwaffe* resumed its attacks with a vengeance and a succession mounted by nine *Stukas* of NSGr. 1 (Nord), twenty Fw 190 from III./KG 200 and Bf 109 from JG 27 came swooping in at heights from tree-top level to 5,000 feet.[72] 58th LAA Regiment's log for 6 April clearly shows the intensity of the *Luftwaffe's* attacks:[73]

06-Apr	Enemy a/c very active during afternoon and evening making attacks on bridge-building at STOLZENAU
1400-2000	172 Bty at STOLZENAU engaged at frequent intervals numbers of Ju87B,[1] Fw190, Me109 flying at heights of zero feet to 5,000ft. Bombs dropped and bridging material damaged by hits obtained by 3xFw190 flying height 50ft.
1445	F Tp 173 Bty at STOLZENAU engaged 6xFw190 flying at zero feet making bombing attack, one bomb caused damage to bridging eqpt.
1725	E Tp 173 Bty at MR 882357 engaged 1xMe109 and claim it Cat I.
1707	174 Bty at MR 8433 (Gun Area) engaged 3xJu87 which dropped bombs. Enemy a/c weaved the whole time in and out of clouds. No claims.
1735	174 Bty at MR 8533 engaged 6xMe109 making bombing attack.
1745	174 Bty at MR 8533 engaged 2xMe262.
1800	F Tp 173 Bty at STOLZENAU engaged 4xJu87 flying at 5,000ft which dropped bombs outside town.
1935	174 Bty at MR 8533 engaged 4xMe109 – bombs dropped, damage unknown.
1945	174 Bty at MR 8533 engaged 2xJu87 – bombs dropped, damage unknown.
1950	E Tp 173 Bty at MR 887354 engaged 1xJu87B which made attack on bridge-building at STOLZENAU. Hits obtained on a/c but no claim.

Figure 23 58th LAA Regiment Log – 6 April 1945.

The bridge, still under construction, was severely mauled when Fw 190s scored hits on an end floating bay and both approaches, destroying half its length. By now a large amount of pontoon equipment and engineer transport had been destroyed and insufficient undamaged components remained for the bridge's completion. Worse soon followed when a lone *Stuka* scored a direct hit on the toiling sappers of 13 Field and 612 Field, killing 13 and wounding as many. 13 Field's squadron headquarters also suffered as the officer commanding, Major Astles, was wounded in one of the air attacks and Captain Robins, his second-in-command, had already been killed by an airburst shell during the morning. 612 Field's war diary recorded 6 April as one of the bleakest days in the history of the squadron, during which it suffered three killed and 17 wounded.

Because of the intensity of the air attacks and shelling, their casualties and continual damage to the vehicles, work on the bridge was suspended and at 1830 hours 13th Field and 612 Field pulled back from the river.[74] Later a low-flying aircraft dropped a bomb in the area of 23 Hussars regimental headquarters; fortunately the tank crews were already in their slit trenches, but it shook up a group of officers in a nearby house who were enjoying supplies from the 'hockpoint' and killed Captain Rolt, a 23 Hussars' officer serving in HQ 29th Armoured, who was visiting the regiment at the time. The shelling also took its toll and among the targets hit was the 23 Hussars' RMO's half-track, seriously wounding the doctor, Captain McBeath, mortally wounding his batman and putting the RAP out of action. Although the air attacks were grim for the British, they were

---

72 TNA DEFE 3/564, BT 9959, 14. Flieger-Division operations report for 6 April 1945.
73 TNA WO 171/4945, 58th LAA Regiment RA war diary.
74 TNA WO 171/4187, HQ RE 11th Armoured Division war diary.

Destroyed engineer transport at Stolzenau. The incomplete Bailey pontoon bridge can be seen on the right with the demolished road and rail bridge beyond.

fortunate they were not attacked around the clock as the pilots of NSGr. 1 (Nord) and NSGr. 20 specialised in night attacks; the cessation of the attacks at night-fall was probably a result of exhausted pilots and fuel shortages.

But unlike the attacks the day before, the *Luftwaffe* now no longer had free rein and the RAF had begun to mount patrols over the Weser and surrounding area. On one such patrol of the Dummer See and Steinhuder Meer area during the late afternoon of 6 April, six Tempest V of 80 Squadron led by Squadron Leader Mackie were vectored by forward contact car callsign 'Scalwag' on to five enemy aircraft approaching Stolzenau at 1,500 feet from the south-east.[75] After a short chase Flight Lieutenant Cooper closed to 300 yards behind a Fw 190D-9 and with 30-degree deflection gave the enemy aircraft two, one-second bursts. He observed strikes on the cockpit and the canopy flew off, forcing Cooper to take violent evasive action. A few moments later the German aircraft was seen burning on the ground. Flying Officer Smith followed another Dora-9 and as it climbed into cloud gave it a 3-second burst from below at a range of 330 yards, obtaining strikes along the fuselage and cockpit. Although the Dora-9 entered the cloud it soon emerged on its back and dived vertically into the ground with its pilot seen to parachute clear. Both aircraft were from IV./JG 26 flying from the grass airstrip at Dedelstorf, north of Brunswick, and their pilots, Unteroffizier Alois Horner and Unteroffizier Wolfgang Schneider, survived bailing out and were captured; Dedelstorf airfield was overrun by US forces some eight days later.

Later the same afternoon, Squadron Leader MacKichan of 56 Squadron was leading a patrol of eight Tempest V along the line of the Weser when they saw a number of Fw 190F-8 bombing the Stolzenau area. The German aircraft were flying very low owing to the cloud level and did not see the Tempests until too late. However, to close with the *Focke Wulfs*, the Tempests had to fly through heavy British ground fire and the aircraft of Warrant Officer Freeman and Flying Officer Dennis were both hit; Freeman made a forced landing on the left bank of the Weser and was seen to walk away while Dennis managed to return safely to B.80 strip at Volkel. The remaining Tempests closed on the *Focke Wulfs* and one was swiftly sent crashing in flames; two more were

---

75   TNA AIR 50/34, 80 Squadron RAF combat reports.

178 THEIRS THE STRIFE

chased away to the east and subsequently destroyed. All three Fw 190F-8 came from 10./KG 200: Fähnrich Walter Hassel was killed flying Black 4, Unteroffizier Ludwig Stimmler was killed in Black 2 and Leutnant Hans Gering was killed in Black 7. Squadron Leader MacKichan's combat report of the action reads as follows:[76]

> I was leading Nalgo Squadron on a patrol of the forward troops on the River Weser between Nienburg and Minden.[77] As the weather was very bad we flew low and when flying north at about 200 feet saw aircraft ahead bombing the bridgehead near Stolzenau. I called up and we closed up behind them at 100 feet. They were strung out roughly in line astern, turning to port for the execution of another attack. Closing on the last two I identified them as Fw 190s. Picking the one to starboard I opened fire at 100 yards, angle of 10–20 degrees and saw strikes in the region of the cockpit. The one to port swung across towards me, so allowing 30 degree deflection at 150 yards. I obtained strikes on the starboard wing root and forward fuselage. The Fw 190 started to smoke, flames appearing later. It continued turning to starboard, diving into the ground and broke up in flames. The first aircraft had turned to starboard so I swung back and saw him well out of range. I waited until my No. 2 had finished firing without success, then gave chase roughly in an easterly direction. I caught it up after about 4 minutes, the Hun's only evasive action was to dive and climb making no use of cloud cover. As he was pulling up I fired from 250 yards line astern and obtained strikes. He started to turn to port and I closed in to about 150 yards at approximately 20–30 degrees off and obtained further strikes. The Fw 190 went down with the inside of the cockpit a mass of flame and crashed below me. I was getting intense, accurate light flak so pulled up for cloud cover. The remains of the Fw 190 were burning on the ground near the gun positions, the location of which I could not identify except as being in the Hannover area. The enemy aircraft were camouflaged a grey colour and had bomb racks under each wing. No long-range tanks were fitted. I claim two Fw 190 destroyed.

MacKichan's destruction of the first Fw 190F-8 is captured in a seven second clip from his gun camera (Appendix A, Serial 1),[78] which shows the burning aircraft plunging into a field with its wings vertical to the ground and immediately blowing up. It would have been a mercy if the pilot was already dead. A further Fw 190F-8 was shot down near Nienburg and the pilot, Unteroffizier Hans Schmidt from 9./KG 200, killed.

On 6 April it was not, however, only Fw 190 that suffered and the *Stukas* from NSGr. 1 (Nord) also came into the sights of the RAF pilots. At 1820 hours Flying Officer Sheddan of 486 (New Zealand) Squadron flying a Tempest V took off from B.80 strip and at 2000 hours, just before dusk, made the following attack:[79]

> I was flying Pink 3 on a patrol in the Dummer and Steinhuder Lakes when, near Stolzenau, we were advised by forward contact car 'Scalwag' that Ju 87 were attacking the bridge over the Weser at Stolzenau. We were orbiting at about 2,500 feet and guided by ack-ack, which was reported firing at Ju 87s. I broke up into wispy cloud. At about 4,000 feet I spotted a Ju 87 flying due east. I opened fire from about 200 yards' range in dead line astern and saw some strikes on the fuselage. I maintained fire until within approximately 10 yards and broke

---

76 TNA AIR 50/22, 56 Squadron RAF combat reports.
77 The derivation of 'Nalgo' is unknown.
78 IWM OPE 90.
79 TNA AIR 50/160, 486 Squadron RAF combat reports. The *Stukas* would have been D-5 variants rather than B.

violently to port to avoid ramming the Ju 87. This took me into cloud and the last I saw of the Ju 87 was it pulling up into cloud and almost stalling. Pink 4 (Flying Officer Ross) who was flying on my starboard during the whole of the attack reports seeing two parachutes going down just after the Ju 87 went into cloud. After breaking into cloud, I flew due east for about two minutes – broke cloud and saw another Ju 87 on my port and about a mile in front of me. I manoeuvred into line astern and opened fire from about 200 yards and gave three short bursts down to 10 yards but observed no strikes. I pulled out to port and made a further attack following this with another from starboard. While positioning for a fourth attack I saw a parachute open and saw the Ju 87B commence a gliding turn. It spiralled slowly towards the ground – at 500 feet I saw the second parachute open – and the Ju 87B hit the ground and blew up just north of Steinhuder Lake. During the attack on the second Ju 87B the gunner of the enemy aircraft was firing the whole time but I was not hit. I claim two Ju 87B destroyed.

It must have taken singular courage for the *Stuka* pilots to fly their lumbering aircraft in daylight as they were extremely vulnerable to enemy fighters. The name of only one of the *Stuka* pilots is known: Leutnant Heinz Köhler of NSGr. 1 (Nord). Köhler's aircraft was hit by anti-aircraft fire on the evening of 6 April and subsequently crashed; his body was later found in a meadow near Leese and today he lies in the town's war cemetery.

From his position on the right bank David Ward of 45 (RM) Cdo watched the attacks by the *Stukas*:[80]

A group of *Stukas* proceed to bomb behind the village [Stolzenau] we had recently left. A large cloud of smoke rose and it looked as if something had been badly hit. We found later that it was the brigade's RASC transport all closed up in one lump. The Stukas did a couple of circuits above us and then went off. They would certainly have seen us, and this fact sank into the most hung-over member of E Troop. What used to be known as 'improving the position' began at once. They did return in a short time but were received by some Tempests who got amongst them in good style. Several *Stukas* were hit and the crews bailed out. Certainly I saw three white parachutes come out and drift with the wind behind the enemy positions.

Returning to action on the ground, activity on 6 April was not confined to the Stolzenau bridgehead and elements of Kampfgruppe Tischler also attacked the Schlüsselburg bridgehead, held by B and C Companies 1 Hereford and in proximity to the *Kampfgruppe's* left flank. During the day 3. SS-Kompanie moved to seal the Hereford's bridgehead from the north-east and south-east, and subjected the British to volleys of 2cm and small-arms' fire. Patrols from the Hereford companies encountered numerous Hitler Youth and the bridgehead line was sufficiently hard-pressed to require support from the 25-pdrs of 151st Field Regiment, which fired DF tasks directed by the FOO, Captain Lucas, who had deployed to the right bank with the infantry. While the small bridgehead was not seriously threatened, it was decided that it was superfluous owing to the proximity of 45 (RM) Cdo's bridgehead and the decision was taken to withdraw the two companies during darkness to the left bank. Furthermore, 1 Hereford was required for operations planned for the next day, which would start with crossing the Weser at Petershagen. By 2115 hours the rifle companies and all equipment had returned to the Weser's left bank without incident, although the battalion had lost two dead and five wounded during its time in the bridgehead.

---

80   Ward, 'My Time with 45 RM Commando'.

Away from the Weser, 1 Cheshire moved up during the day and en route took over from 3 Mons the additional vehicles it needed to operate as an infantry battalion in an armoured division.[81] By evening the battalion had reached Harrienstedt, three miles west of the Weser, where it harboured and came under command of 159th Brigade. During the war's remaining weeks 1 Cheshire will operate with 15/19 Hussars, the three rifle companies moving on the tank decks and the fourth, in reserve, following up in trucks.

For VIII Corps 6 April ended with mixed results. On the left flank at Stolzenau the casualties and failure to bridge the Weser forced a change of plan. Although the effort to build a bridge at Stolzenau had had to be abandoned, the single Class 40 bridge at Petershagen would be wholly insufficient for a corps and, as a single point of failure, its damage or loss would have severe impact on operations. While a second Class 40 Bailey pontoon bridge was therefore essential, and it was decided that the best site for it would be the Schlüsselburg ferry upstream from Stolzenau, construction could only start once 1st Commando Brigade had secured the right bank. With 11th Armoured's engineers both exhausted and depleted from their efforts at Stolzenau, the sappers of 279 Field Company from 15th Scottish Division were warned to build the Schlüsselburg bridge.[82] But this field company would not be available for at least another two days so for initial operations east of the Weser, 11th Armoured would have to depend on the bridge at Petershagen. Also, 3 Cdo and 45 (RM) Cdo would have to weather the storm in the bridgehead for another day until joined by the remainder of 1st Commando Brigade during the night 7/8 April; the brigade could then take Leese and capture Kampfstoffabrik Leese. Despite their failed attack, for the German defenders of Leese 6 April had generally been a successful day and an Ultra decrypt of a Heeresgruppe 'H' signal sent early on the 6th to OB West has an air of quiet confidence, although clearly showing concerns about force availability:[83]

> A PG *ersatz* and training battalion of Wehrkreis VI being sent in against alleged Allied crossing place Stolzenau. Available *Volkssturm* and emergency defence units had been alerted by Führungsstab Nordküste. Bridge destroyed in good time. Führungsstab Nordküste could make no other troops available to area there, nor could *Heeresgruppe*.

Interestingly, the *Heeresgruppe* was unable to name SS-A.u.E.Btl.12 'HJ' correctly and that on the second day of the fighting at Stolzenau the British crossing was still 'alleged'; both indicating the poor situational awareness that existed.

On VIII Corps' right flank the situation was far better. A secure bridgehead was in place opposite Petershagen and the German armoured counter-attack had been repelled. The Class 9 FBE was up and running at the tile factory site and 100 Field Company had made steady progress on the Class 40 Bailey pontoon bridge, now nearing completion at Petershagen. During the night 6/7 April, VIII Corps received 'most immediate' orders from HQ Second Army instructing it to push on at once to the next river, the Leine, and secure bridgeheads in the area of Wunstorf and Neustadt. Accordingly, VIII Corps' orders for the next day directed 6th Airborne to advance south of Steinhuder Meer, with the Mittelland Canal as the division's right boundary, secure Wunstorf airfield and seize bridges over the Leine at Bordenau and Neustadt. 11th Armoured was directed to advance north of Steinhuder Meer and seize bridges over the Leine at Mandelsloh and Niedernstöcken. If bridges could not be seized, both divisions were ordered to assault across the Leine and secure bridgeheads to provide security for the construction of Class 40 bridges. To

---

81 TNA WO 171/5169, 1 Cheshire war diary.
82 TNA WO 171/5540, 279 Field Company RE war diary.
83 TNA DEFE 3/563, BT 9689, Heeresgruppe 'H' signal.

be in position to cross the Weser via the Petershagen bridge early in the morning of 7 April, 5th Parachute Brigade concentrated in Petershagen during the afternoon of 6 April and that night 11th Armoured's 159th Infantry Brigade Group moved south to the Petershagen area; it was intended that 29th Armoured Brigade Group would cross later the same day. Meanwhile, 15th Scottish Division with 6th Guards Armoured Brigade were moved up to a concentration area west of Petershagen to be poised to cross the Weser and exploit either 11th Armoured's or 6th Airborne's success. In the next chapter we will see how the events of the next three days unfolded.

5

Fat Cars, Chateau Lafite and the Steel-eyed Boys: 7–9 April 1945

US Eighth Air Force and Schulungslehrgang Elbe

Saturday 7 April dawned bright, sunny and, on the ground, visibility was good. While 6 April was dominated by low-level air action against 11th Armoured Division on the Weser, 7 April would feature action over the heads of the men of VIII Corps but at much higher altitudes and not targeted against them. It would also be an action unique in the experience of both the *Luftwaffe* and the US Eighth Air Force. The US operations for the day were initiated by Field Order 1914A and involved the three air divisions mustering a total of some 1,300 bombers escorted by 850 fighters to attack targets in north Germany (see Map 22).[1] This would be the 931st raid of the war and considered something of a 'milk run' with German fighters a spent force and the routes to the targets avoiding the remaining *Flak* zones. The targets included airbases, particularly those hosting jet aircraft, oil storage facilities and ordnance depots. The route for the majority of the bombers would track them over Amsterdam and thence to the north of Hannover, where the bomber stream would split to take the combat wings to their various targets. 2nd and 3rd Air Divisions, comprising 25 bombardment groups with a total of 529 B-17 and 340 B-24 bombers, would pass directly over VIII and XII Corps.

The bombers began to take-off from their bases in East Anglia during the morning and had an uneventful flight across the North Sea. The signal traffic generated by such large forces and the reports by weather and route scouts were intercepted by the remaining *Luftwaffe* monitoring stations, giving 'Hajo' Herrmann the indication he needed that a suitably large target for the ramming aircraft of Schulungslehrgang Elbe was inbound. In the morning he accordingly issued the order to activate the Bf 109 formations. Hauptmann Roman Pesch, a Schulungslehrgang Elbe pilot, describes the early stage of the operation:[2]

> We received orders at 8 o'clock in the morning. Then readiness until just before 12. Damn, the engine on my Bf 109 Nr. 21 would not start and I was to lead the *Staffel*! Five minutes before take-off my machine becomes serviceable and I climbed aboard. Death candidates! The airfield (Stendal) was crammed with airwomen and soldiers. The commanding officer stands by the *Reichskriegsflagge* [*Reich* war flag] and salutes each machine as it takes off. At precisely 11.30 I commence my take-off run with my *Staffel*. We are in radio contact with the ground. Orders: climb to 11,000 metres. The British and Americans generally flew at 10,000 metres and, as we

---

1   Mission 931, *http://www.8thafhs.com/missions.php* (accessed 8 May 2016).
2   Boiten and Bowman, *Battles with the Luftwaffe* (London: HarperCollins, 2001), p.214. 'Fat car' was *Luftwaffe* slang for a heavy bomber.

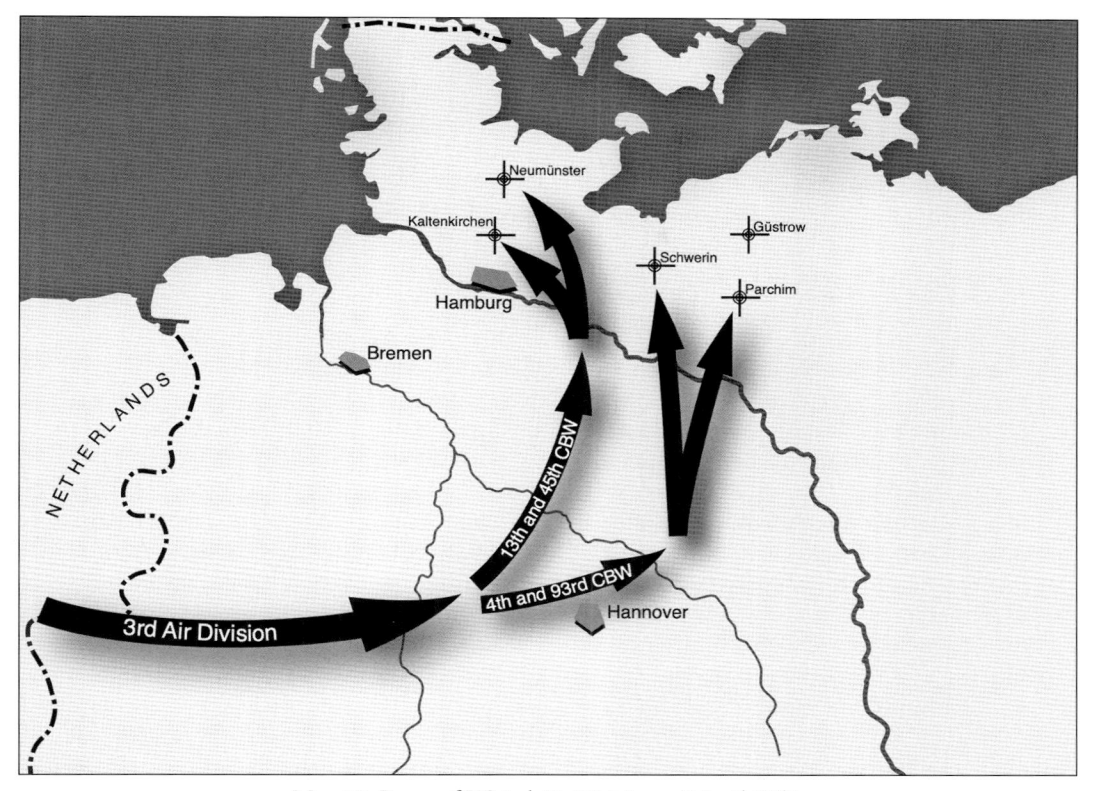

Map 22 Route of US 3rd Air Division – 7 April 1945.

carried no guns, we were to be well above them. I keep my men closed up within sight of each other, we do not speak. It takes three quarters of an hour before we are at 11,000 metres. We jettison our drop tanks over the Harz mountains. A female voice kept repeating over the radio: 'Comrades, think of your wives and children lying under the ruins, think of them and try to do justice through your efforts!' Exhortations to the last. Once in the air our anxiety evaporates. Before Hannover we get a report: 'Fat cars have crossed the Rhine. Get ready!'

But confusion, late arrival of aircraft from the satellite airfields and mechanical problems resulted in only 120 fighters taking to the air, well below the number required by Herrmann to achieve the intended mass result. And the problems did not end there. The temperature fell dramatically with height and at 30,000 feet, the altitude for launching the fighters' attacks, it was minus 48 degrees Centigrade causing icing problems and intense discomfort for the pilots, exacerbating the problems the inexperienced men were already having in keeping formation. Patches of thick cloud compounded their difficulties and by mid-day the force, by now well-dispersed, had shrunk to 70 aircraft.[3]

Contact was first made at about 1155 hours when US fighter escorts shot down two Bf 109. With the bomber routes now firmly identified Herrmann launched the Me 262 of JG 7 and I./KG (J) 54 to draw-off the enemy escorts and leave the bombers vulnerable to the ramming aircraft. This intent, however, does not seem to have been passed to the Me 262 pilots, who as normal attacked the bombers, resulting in the US escorts remaining largely in place. This first contact

---

3   Adrian Weir, *The Last Flight of the Luftwaffe* (London: Cassell & Co, 1997).

between the escort fighters and the Me 262 force took place over Nienburg, with the jet fighters soon joined by Bf 109 from Schulungslehrgang Elbe and an intense battle now took place. The US escort pilots were not only surprised by the large number of German aircraft, not seen for some months, but also by the reluctance of the Bf 109 to engage in air-to-air combat. While the US escorts immediately began to shoot down the German fighters, inevitably others were able to make their ramming runs and the first strike on a bomber was probably against a B-24 from 93rd Bombardment Group, hit on the wing. While this bomber was fortunate and limped home, others were less fortunate and a few devastating incidents took place as the ramming aircraft found their targets; the destruction of B-17 'Candy's Dandy' was one such:[4]

> In the sky to the north of Steinhuder Lake the battle around the 100th Bombardment Group continued…In one of the older Fortresses Lieutenant Arthur Calder and his crew of eight were flying *'Candy's Dandy'* of the 418th Bomb Squadron and was positioned in the lower formation of the 100th's lead squadron. With the battle raging around them, the crew were already on a high state of alert, the gunners firing at any fighter that posed a threat.
>
> The attack on 'Candy's Dandy' came from above, a lone Bf 109 plunging through the upper formation from a 5 o'clock position. Having avoided the prowling escorts the *Luftwaffe* pilot pushed his fighter into a steep dive. Unable to approach his target in the prescribed manner, he passed the upper Fortresses without inflicting any damage. However, the speed of the fighter's dive and the position of the bombers of the lower formation placed the Bf 109 on a collision course with Lieutenant Calder's bomber. Whereas other aircraft on this day suffered a protracted death, the end of *Candy's Dandy* was sudden and brutal. Both aircraft were consumed in a massive explosion as fuel and bomb-load ripped them apart…

Although the German pilot who destroyed *'Candy's Dandy'* remains unknown, this is not the case for a ramming attack mounted on a B-17 flown by 1st Lieutenant Carrol Cagle of the 490th Bombardment Group, which had launched thirty B-17s to attack JG 7's airfield at Parchim, north-west of Berlin. Sergeant James Lee Hutchinson, the radio operator/gunner on another 490th B-17, witnessed the attack on Cagle's B-17:[5]

> Lieutenant Templeton gave the alert over the intercom just before the formation reached the Initial Point to start our bomb-run. 'Bandits at twelve o'clock high!' I looked out the top hatch and saw two Me 109 above as they came diving down on our formation with machine-guns blazing. Our gunners were returning the fire with a hail of 50 caliber slugs and tracer bullets zoning in on the attackers. The enemy fighters shot down a bomber out of our high squadron on the first pass. I saw the B-17 to the left of us slide out of the formation with an engine on fire. The pilot held it level as the crew bailed out. I tried to count the chutes as they popped out of the stricken plane. Our formation gunners concentrated on the two fighters as they circled and came in for another pass. Being the lead bomber, our gunners had a good crack at them as they swooped down on us. Bert Allinder left waist gunner and Roddy in the top turret were sure they hit one as it burst into flames and it dived into our squadron. The fuselage was burning off the fighter and its frame looked like a flaming orange crate. I saw the pilot's lifeless body in the cockpit as the plane missed us and rammed into another bomber on our right, bounced off and fell to earth. The badly damaged Cagle plane dropped out of formation, but managed to stay aloft…

---

4   Weir, *The Last Flight of the Luftwaffe*, p.127.
5   Hutchinson, James Lee, *The Boys in the B-17* (Bloomington: AuthorHouse, 2011), p.202.

The pilot of the Bf 109 that hit Cagle's B-17 was Leutnant Hans Nagel. Nagel, perhaps as an older, more experienced pilot, flew an armed fighter and he had already made two attacking passes on the 490th and had shot down the high squadron B-17 before starting his ramming dive. Sergeant Colby Le Neve, the ball-turret gunner on Cagle's B-17, was unpleasantly close to events:[6]

> Around mid-day the intercom rattled with the dreaded news that bandits were in the area. Indeed there were, within seconds Me 109s came blazing in, head-on. On the second wave, one of the enemy fighters tried to close in on our tight formation and was knocked out of control. It had no place to go but down, in between B-17s stacked wing to wing. We were in the wrong place and the inevitable was about to happen – we were going to be rammed. My eyes closed and words of the 23rd Psalm parted my lips…at that instant our B-17 was rocked by the impact of the Me 109 as it hit and started a half roll around our ill-fated bomber – the fighter struck the rear of our left wing where it joins the fuselage. Luckily that is the very backbone of a B-17. Had the impact been several inches behind this point we surely would have been sliced in two.
>
> The fighter continued to spin around and under the belly of our ship, badly damaging the ball turret, which I occupied. The impact of the fighter had caused the right trunnion of one of my 50 calibre machine-guns to break loose and the MG slammed across my right arm, snapping it like a matchstick. The gun casing continued on to smash my Sperry gunsight just inches from my head. The turret entry and escape hatch was sprung open and carried away by the slipstream – leaving me with nothing but my safety belt to keep me in the turret! However, with the escape hatch missing, several crew members were able to grasp my para harness and pull me free from the turret and back into the bomber.
>
> The collision ripped off the Number 3 engine supercharger and broke a prop blade on Number 4 engine. A great deal of skin was stripped from beneath the right wing and a hole as large as a door was added to the radio room. At first we in the back were not sure if we were headed down out of control, but the ship was being skilfully manoeuvred by our pilot, Lieutenant Carrol Cagle, and the co-pilot, Lieutenant Robert Barnard, who were fighting the controls while salvoing the bombs at the same time. Again we were blessed, for the pilots found some cloud-bank cover to level off into as enemy fighters chased behind trying to finish us off.
>
> Our navigator, Tony Belzer, plotted a course to get us out of enemy territory as fast as possible, because no-one knew the real extent of the damage we had sustained or how long the plane could remain airborne. The starboard engines were creating a great deal of drag and the port engines had to be boosted to maintain flight – the guys at the controls certainly had their hands full.

Despite serious damage the immensely robust B-17 flew on and eventually landed at Merville[7] in northern France:[8]

> Our pilot tried to assure us that the plane was under control and that it should hang together for one more landing. Old '058' had survived 84 missions and she settled down gracefully despite a partially deflated main landing gear wheel and the unstowed ball-turret dragging at

---

6 Hutchinson, *The Boys in the B-17*, pp.202–203.
7 Not the famous battery of D-Day but a former French airforce station to the west of Lille used by the *Luftwaffe* as a fighter base. In September 1944 it became RAF advanced landing ground B-53 and was used by the USAAF for the Rhine crossing.
8 Hutchinson, *The Boys in the B-17*, p.203.

Leutnant Hans Nagel's grave in Essel's *Soldatenfriedhof*. (Author)

least one gun-barrel as we swallowed up the runway. A flare had been fired to alert the ground that an injured person was on board and an ambulance was there to spirit me off to hospital.

Nagel was not so fortunate. He plunged to earth in the wreck of his aircraft crashing near the village of Berkhof, east of Schwarmstedt. The villagers, who had witnessed the overhead battle, identified Nagel and buried him in their cemetery.[9]

Schulungslehrgang Elbe's action continued until the surviving German pilots broke-off owing to exhaustion or lack of fuel and returned to their bases. Despite the action's intensity and shock effect, only a very small proportion of the US bombers were targeted and the bulk of the three air divisions flew serenely on to their targets and delivered their tonnages. Kaltenkirchen airbase, home to the Ar 234 of KG 76, was the target for four bombardment groups; the airfield was heavily cratered but no damage was done to the dispersed Ar 234. The daily OKW press communiqué covering 7 April made no specific mention of the ramming attack, but stated that American bombers had suffered heavy losses from the *Luftwaffe's* fighters.[10] Perhaps the tactic of resorting to ramming was deemed more than the German public could stomach and, unsurprisingly, the OKW report made no mention of their pilot losses. The US assessment was that approximately 10 bombers were rammed, of which seven were lost; a further 12 were lost to *Flak* and conventional fighter attack. It would seem 53 German fighters were destroyed during the operation and between 25–40 pilots lost. Roman Pesch, mentioned at the start of the chapter, succeeded in ramming a

---

9 Nagel was later reinterred in the German war grave cemetery at Essel where he lies today.
10 Günter Wegmann, (ed.), *"Das Oberkommando der Wehrmacht gibt bekannt…" Der deutsche Wehrmachtbericht, Band 3, 1944–1945* (Osnabrück: Biblio Verlag, 1982), p.526. The *Wehrmachtbericht* was the daily OKW communiqué and a key element of *Nazi* propaganda. It covered the military situation and was broadcast daily by the Reichs-Rundfunk-Gesellschaft (*Reich* Broadcasting Corporation).

bomber and parachuting to safety despite a wound to the thigh and a broken shin. He received medical treatment at Schwarmstedt hospital and on 11 April was awaiting evacuation to hospital in Hannover when he was captured by the British. For the Eighth Air Force the losses represented an increase over recent raids but it was only 2 percent of the bomber force; in comparison, the loss rate for the notorious second Schweinfurt raid of 14 October 1943 was 26 percent of the attacking force. Although in numerical terms the operation's effect was negligible, it did have some psychological impact and US pilots who had witnessed the ramming attacks were ordered not to discuss what they had seen. While the results could have been greater had Herrmann assembled his full force, Germany's situation was now so desperate that any result would have been nugatory. Goebbels, ever one to find excuses and put a positive spin on events, recorded in his diary on 8 April:[11]

> The first use of our suicide [sic] fighters has not produced the success hoped for. The reason given is that the enemy bomber formations did not fly concentrated so that they had to be attacked individually. In addition, our suicide fighters encountered such heavy defensive fire that only in a few cases were they able to ram. But we must not lose courage as a result. This is only an initial trial, which is to be repeated in the next few days, hopefully with better results.

The reasons he describes for the lack of success are spurious and contradictory, and lack of concentration of the bomber formations should have made targeting easier as it thinned the bombers' defensive fire not made it heavier. Despite the willingness of the pilots, owing to a combination of fuel shortages, Allied ground advances and lack of resolve in the higher echelons of the *Luftwaffe* there was no repeat of the 7 April operation. Schulungslehrgang Elbe's mission therefore exists as an interesting but unique oddity in the air campaign over Europe. Strangely, there are only two mentions in VIII Corps' war diaries of crashing fighters and none of bombers; attention, understandably, was fixed on the ground. Although Enigma messages regarding Schulungslehrgang Elbe were intercepted, the first one,[12] a *Luftwaffe* message dated 24 March, was not disseminated by Ultra until 7 April, the day of the attack. The decrypt mentions that pilots called up but not yet despatched to 'Training Course Elbe' were to remain with their units. The associated prescient Bletchley comment said that the significance of the message was not known but that there was a possible connection with Göring's appeal for volunteers for a near-suicidal undertaking and that although this was unlikely it had to be borne in mind.

6th Airborne Division advance to the Leine

On 7 April, while air battles raged thousands of feet above them, 6th Airborne supported by the Churchills of 4 Gren Gds started its advance to the Leine;[13] it was to be a day of achievement but also of great tragedy.

5th Parachute Brigade, held in a concentration area since moving up from Osnabrück on 5 April, would play the lead role in the divisional advance.[14] The brigade plan involved it breaking out of 6th Airlanding Brigade's bridgehead and advancing on minor roads south of Steinhuder Meer to capture the bridges over the Leine at Bordenau and Neustadt, 35 miles to the east. As

---

11   Hugh Trevor-Roper (ed.), *The Goebbels Diaries*, p.323.
12   TNA DEFE 3/564, BT 9756, Parts 1 and 2.
13   TNA WO 171/4157, G Branch 6th Airborne Division war diary.
14   TNA WO 171/4307, 5th Parachute Brigade war diary.

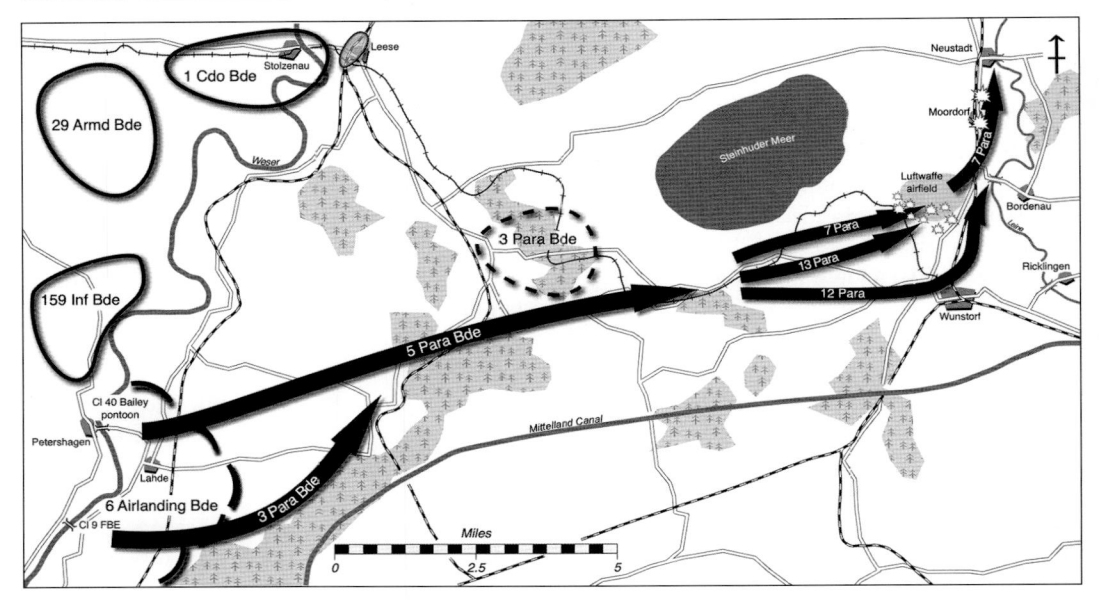

Map 23 6th Airborne Division's Advance to the Leine – 7 April 1945.

6th Airborne Reconnaissance Regiment had lost many tanks during the advance from the Rhine it could no longer operate effectively so the division's advance would be headed by two squadrons from 15th (Scottish) Reconnaissance Regiment: B Squadron would lead 5th Brigade's advance on the left while C Squadron provided flank protection on the right and contacted US forces. Following in the wake of B Squadron, the brigade's vanguard comprised the Churchills of No. 3 Squadron 4 Gren Gds carrying soldiers of C Company 12 Para on their decks, with the remainder of the battalion following in trucks; their objective was the bridge at Bordenau. Once the vanguard had captured this bridge, 13 Para would cross, advance north on the Leine's right bank and seize the bridge at Neustadt; 7 Para would follow 13 Para and be prepared to assist. 3rd Parachute Brigade would advance after 5th Parachute Brigade, with its objective the bridge at Ricklingen and its vanguard, 1 CAN Para, carried on the Churchills from No. 1 Squadron 4 Gren Gds. 6th Airlanding Brigade would continue to hold the bridgehead on the Weser, finish mopping up any remaining enemy then head east to join the two parachute brigades.

Operations for the day started at 0400 hours with A and B Companies 12 Devon capturing Masloh and Quetzen – the villages where D Company had suffered so heavily at the hands of Kampfgruppe Schulze the previous day – to expand the bridgehead line prior to the divisional breakout. Construction of the Petershagen Class 40 pontoon Bailey bridge was completed also at 0400 hours and the recce squadrons were the first to cross, followed by 5th Parachute Brigade's vanguard and the remainder of the brigade. The force made good progress against very little opposition, taking a broadly eastwards route via the villages to the south of the Steinhuder Meer and it was not until early afternoon that the vanguard had its first significant contact with the enemy when it became involved in a fire-fight with the defenders of Wunstorf airfield. Links to two online videos of the brigade's advance to the Leine are at Appendix A, Serials 2 and 3.

As the likelihood of the demolition of Bordenau's bridge increased with every minute that passed, delay at the airfield was very unwelcome so Lieutenant Colonel Ken Darling, commanding officer of 12 Para, ordered B Squadron to keep the enemy occupied while C Company and the tanks bypassed the airfield and pressed on to the bridge as fast as possible. Ken Darling describes the advance's final stage:[15]

> This time the tanks led and with their whips out set a cracking pace. It was like Derby Day. On the way a column passed through a large number of Frenchmen lining the road who gave a cheer. As the column rounded the last corner the stone bridge could be seen intact; this seemed to make the Churchills go more quickly. A Hun lorry with a man on his feet could be seen on the near side of the bridge. As he was obviously up to no good, the lorry was engaged by every Besa and all weapons which could be brought to bear as the column rapidly neared the bridge. Then round the last corner and in a twinkling of an eye the vanguard was across, into the village shooting up, and the charges removed and thrown into the river.

With 12 Para securing a bridgehead at Bordenau, 7 Para was ordered to capture the bridge at Neustadt, but from the left bank. Why the plan was changed from the right bank operation by 13 Para is not known but it was to have disastrous consequences. 7 Para duly moved up and passed through Wunstorf town but then hit opposition as it neared the airfield, still defended by the Germans. Lieutenant Colonel Geoffrey Pine-Coffin, commanding officer of 7 Para and known to all as 'Wooden-Box', was leading the advance in his scout car:[16]

> After passing Wunstorf the road swings due north and passes over an airfield. At [grid reference] there was a bit of badly churned up mud and after crossing it myself, I slowed up considerably to see if the 3-tonners could get over it all right. When I saw that they could I sped up again and had myself just reached the edge of the wood when I spotted two Germans at the side of the road about 50 yards in front of me. They were not behaving like the other Germans we had met and could be seen to jump into a slit trench. The scout car unhappily did not mount a Bren gun and all the occupants of it were pistol armed. Expecting a burst of MG fire at any moment, I stopped the car and ordered everyone out of it, this was accelerated by the expected burst of MG fire and then by a loud explosion close to the car. This latter was a *Panzerfaust* which passed just to the rear of the car and was clearly seen in the air by the 2IC (Major Taylor), who had been travelling just behind my car in his jeep and had run up to see why the scout car had stopped. A ditch beside the scout car provided cover for the whole party.
>
> All this happened very quickly and while it was happening the leading four trucks of B Company were all on the stretch of road between the muddy patch and the scout car and had come under fire from both flanks (afterwards found to be from two MGs, one on each side of the road, and a *Flak* gun somewhere on the right, or east, of it). Their casualties amounted to six killed and 11 wounded with the leading platoon commander (Lieutenant Pape) amongst the killed.
>
> For a time it was a most unpleasant situation because the 2IC and myself were much too far forward to control the battle and anyway were pretty securely pinned ourselves. The scout car became the target for the *Panzerfaust* enthusiast; he was an extremely bad shot though and, despite the range being only about 30 yards, he missed it continuously, but his overs came uncomfortably close to the ditch we were using for cover. Finally he did hit it and this put the wireless set out of action. Lance Corporal Mundy (Royal Signals) worked his way back to and into the car, and confirmed that the set was completely dead. Excellent work was also done by

---

15   TNA WO 171/5137, 12 Para war diary, Appendix 2.
16   TNA WO 171/5134, 7 Para war diary, Annex.

Private Strudwick, Major Taylor's batman, who ran back across the open to the four trucks of B Company with my orders for Major Reid, the company commander.

Major Reid had very quickly grasped the situation and had in fact started, on his own initiative, to carry out what turned out to be my orders to him. He was to work up the right of the road, which would bring him past our ditch, and clear two houses close to the scout car. He put down smoke with his 2-in mortars and led the first wave himself; I was able to tell him as he passed me to continue as far as the east-west road at the cross roads where I had intended to debus. This he duly did and as his company rushed past, I found myself in a position to observe some truly great leadership by his officers and NCOs. It was then necessary for me to get to my normal place in this column before I could clear up the situation properly; this had to be done on foot and was very unpleasant. I found that the bulk of the column was in dead ground behind a spur and that the brigade commander [Brigadier Poett] himself was with them and had ordered up the tanks. These went into action as I was running back and started to lace the wood to the east of the axis road, they did not know that B Company had entered these woods – fortunately they caused no casualties and their fire was of great assistance.

Although endangering B Company, the Churchills' fire eased the pressure on the battalion and allowed C Company to move up and clear the left of the road then, with the help of the tanks, advance across Wunstorf airfield itself, which was subsequently cleared by 13 Para.[17] A subsequent search of the hangars and airfield produced a haul of six Ju 88 night-fighters, one Ju 87 *Stuka* D-5, twenty-nine Bf 109, three Fw 190, a Siebel 204 light transport/trainer aircraft and a Fiesler 156 *Storch* liaison aircraft. A link to an online video of Wunstorf airfield shortly after its capture is at Appendix A, Serial 4.

As the airfield was a maintenance base, most of the aircraft were in various states of disassembly, repair or destruction, but the most exotic discovery was not the aircraft but a brothel furnished with women from Lithuania. This institution naturally attracted attention as Private Alfred Draper of C Company 13 Para recalls:[18]

> There were several three-storey barrack blocks and on the edge of the airfield there was a single storey building with young women lounging outside. This turned out to be a brothel and by lunchtime the next day, half the battalion was there! Bob [Private Bob Giles] and I had gone exploring (looking for loot) and had not been involved. The CO had seen what was going on and ordered the place to be closed down and a guard put on to stop anyone going in. Bob and I got the job because we hadn't been involved. It was a hot sunny afternoon, the girls were lying on the ground, flaunting themselves and several of the lads were trying to bribe their way past us.

While 13 Para was clearing the airfield, 7 Para advanced north towards Neustadt, with A Company in the lead. As the company approached Moordorf there was a huge explosion caused by the detonation of three 250kg bombs buried in a culvert beneath the road. Fortunately, at the instant of detonation, the company was taking shelter in roadside ditches and only one man was killed, but the crater blocked the road for the tanks. Two further culverts containing 250kg bombs were discovered at 50-yard intervals up the road, but luckily the one that detonated was the furthest from A Company. Had this linked device functioned as intended, the casualties in A Company

---

17 TNA WO 171/5138, 13 Para war diary.
18 Andrew Woolhouse, *13 – Lucky for Some. The History of the 13th Parachute (Lancashire) Parachute Battalion* (Amazon Createspace, 2013), p.540.

A NSGr. 1 (Nord) Ju 87 D-5 captured on the ground at Wunstorf. Note the exhaust damper to aid concealment during night operations. (Dupas)

would have been very severe and the brigade commander, who at the time was with 7 Para, possibly killed. Following its capture, Wunstorf airfield was found to be littered with dumps of bombs of various sizes and these had clearly provided the Germans with a local source of powerful ammunition. 7 Para had a lucky escape at Moordorf, but the battalion will soon be drastically less fortunate in its next encounter with *Luftwaffe* bombs.

Following the incident at Moordorf, A and C Companies pushed on to Neustadt and by early evening entered the town, encountering no opposition. The battalion plan for these two companies was to secure the greater part of the town on the left bank while B Company infiltrated down the Leine's river bank to capture the bridge, then cross to secure the buildings on the right bank and form a bridgehead. B Company initially made good progress and German voices could be heard as it neared the bridge, but then the Kleine Leine, a watercourse looping off the main river, forced it to swing westwards when still 400 yards from the objective; this was most unwelcome as it added delay and the company would now have to capture two bridges instead of one.

When they reached Neustadt's main east-west road a civilian was encountered and Major Reid, a German speaker, questioned him about the bridges and the presence of German troops. The man told him the Leine bridge was prepared for demolition and stressed the need for speed if it was to be captured intact. This will not be the only example of German civilians, with an eye to their post-war future, being unhappy to see their bridges blown. The civilian's information confirmed to Major Reid his original plan to rush the bridge and trust to getting across in time to prevent it going up. He therefore ordered his men to charge and, led by the company second-in-command Captain Woodman, the two leading platoons under Lieutenant Gush and Sergeant McIver rushed the bridges. The first bridge, over the Kleine Leine, was crossed without difficulty, but laid across the road on the first span of the second bridge were a number of aircraft bombs linked nose to tail with detonating cord. As they dashed forward the men jumped over the bombs and Captain Woodham managed to kick free several of the fuses; he and this first group reached the right bank and cleared the bridge's guard force, who fled after firing a few shots. At approximately 0015 hours on 8 April, while the third platoon was crossing, the remaining armed bombs detonated with devastating results, demolishing the first span and causing heavy casualties not only to the platoon crossing but also among those already crossed, with 19 soldiers killed instantly and six never

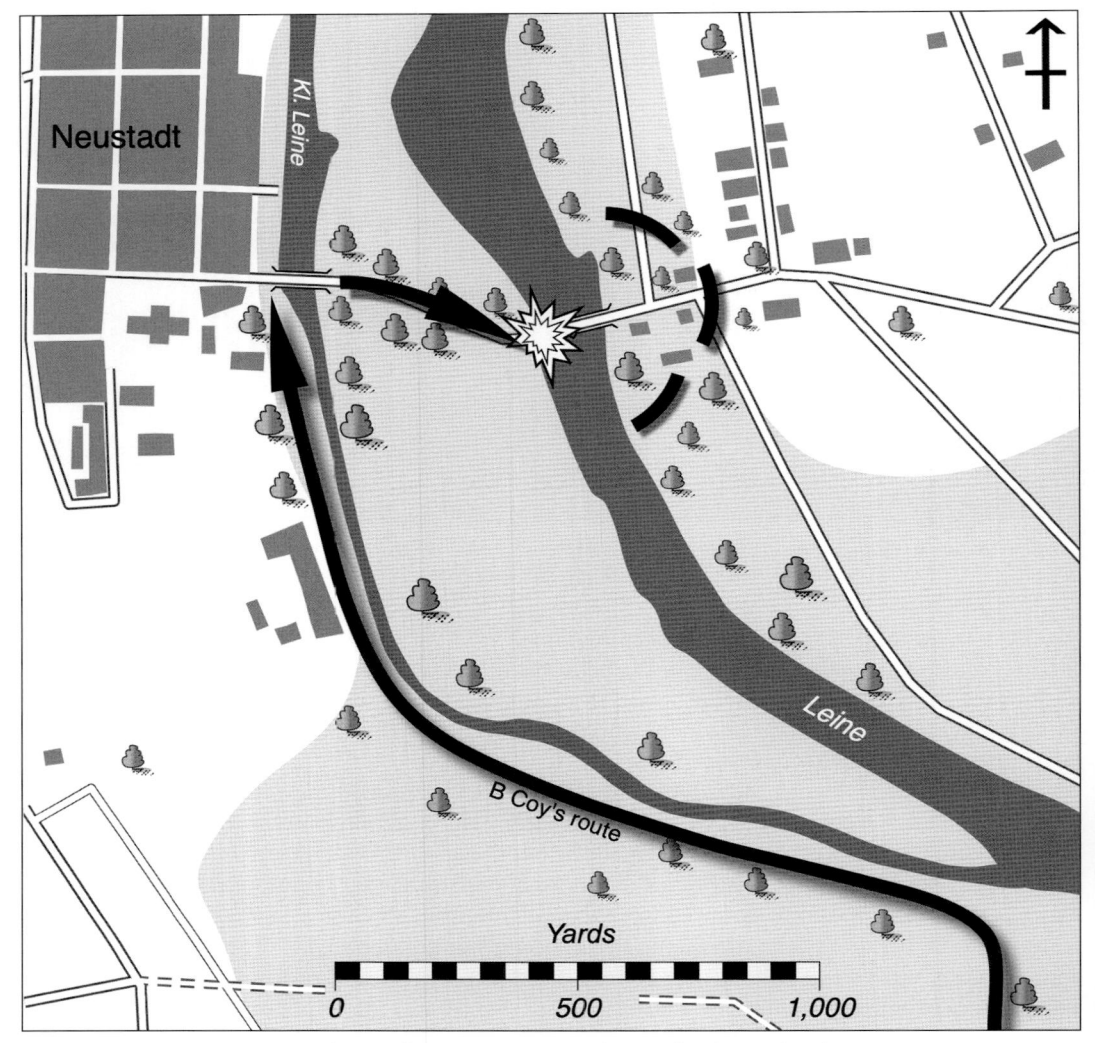

Map 24 7 Para's Disaster at Neustadt – Night 7/8 April 1945.

found; 19 were wounded. Despite the shock of the disaster, the two officers and 10 men surviving on the right bank held their bridgehead until reinforced by A Company the next day. Investigation at daylight revealed that although the bridge's first span was gone, much of the rest of its structure was intact and the gap could easily be spanned by Bailey sections. Notwithstanding the horror of the night, compassion was not absent and in the aftermath of the incident the wounded were evacuated to a nearby house where Erika Najork, helped by Ursula her 20-year-old daughter, cared for their country's enemies. In his account of the disaster Geoffrey Pine-Coffin singled out the efforts of the RMO, Captain Wagstaff, his medical orderlies and the padre, Captain Beckenham; for these men, 8 April 1945 must have been particularly terrible.

While 5th Parachute Brigade was in the final stage of its advance to the Leine, 3rd Parachute Brigade crossed the Weser via the Class 9 FBE at the tile factory site and struck off east on foot. The brigade met little opposition during its advance and later concentrated for the night in the Münchehagen area, approximately half way between the two rivers. With 6th Airborne making

The bridge over the Leine at Neustadt. The repaired blown span can just be seen on the left. Photograph taken in 2019. (Graham)

good progress, we will now step back in time to the early morning of 7 April and follow 11th Armoured Division.

11th Armoured Division breakout from the Petershagen bridgehead

Major General Roberts' plan for his division's advance to the Leine and beyond was for 159th Infantry Brigade Group to advance on the right axis, with the Leine bridges at Mandelsloh and Niedernstöcken as its objectives, and for 29th Armoured Brigade Group to advance on the left with the bridge at Bothmer and then the bridge over the Aller to the north-east of Essel as its objectives (see Map 29). B Squadron Inns of Court, supported by Frankforce patrols, would operate on the division's left flank but would not cross the Petershagen bridge until the evening of 7 April. The ground for the advance was flat agricultural land with large blocks of forest and a network of villages, typically situated at the hubs of the roads.

2 FF Yeo and 1 Hereford of 159th Brigade Group began to cross the Petershagen bridge at 0930 hours and then advanced north-east towards Loccum.

Its advance met no opposition until entering Loccum, where it was met by heavy fire from Kampfgruppe Volker and other defenders. Two rifle companies of 1 Hereford, with each company supported by a squadron, launched an attack with C Squadron and B Company directed to clear the north-west side of the town while A Squadron with C Company cleared the centre. A Squadron

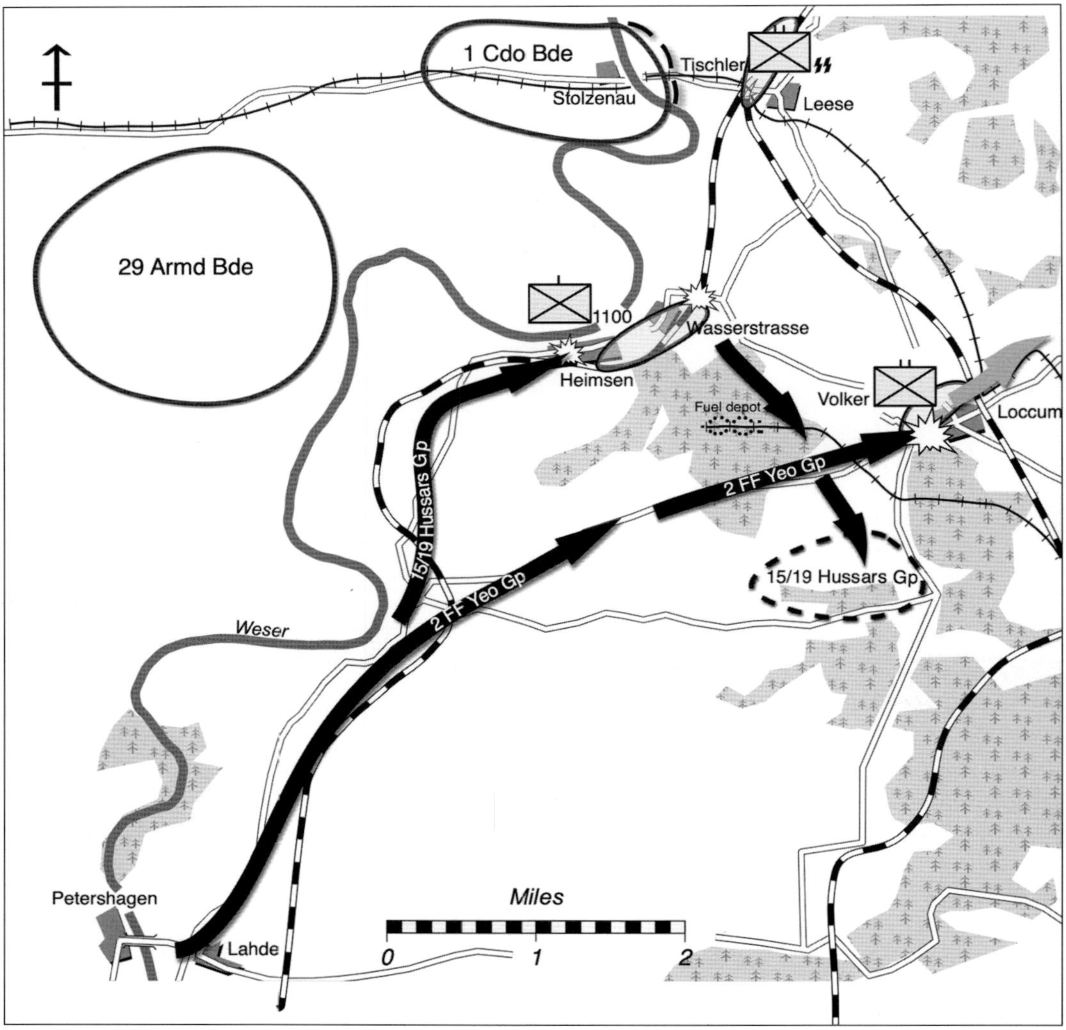

Map 25 159th Infantry Brigade Group's Advance on the Weser's Right Bank – 7 April 1945.

met little resistance and Captain Steel Brownlie describes how he dealt with the only obstacle his tank encountered during Loccum's clearance:[19]

> I was going so fast that even if I had wished I could not have avoided the huge chest of drawers that some civilians had moved on to the street from their burning home. I hit the thing at about 30mph with 45 tons of Comet and without a tremor the tank smashed it into a thousand pieces. Underwear and clothing of all sorts were caught in the tracks and they whirled round and round as we went roaring down the street looking like some fantastic part of a gala celebration.

---

19 Sellar, *The Fife and Forfar Yeomanry 1919–1956*, p.234.

2 FF Yeo Comet crossing the Petershagen Class 40 Bailey pontoon bridge. The soldier standing on the bridge is Sergeant Ian Grant, who was filming the crossing. (© Crown Copyright, IWM negative number BU3199)

The crossing site from the right bank in 2015. (Author)

Other tanks moving via the back gardens did not advance in such dramatic fashion, with the soft ground resulting in many bellying-in and a troop from B Squadron having to be brought forward to replace them. Despite these difficulties, progress was made through the village and as A Squadron, now with D Company, neared the group's final objective, the railway station on the eastern edge of the town, it engaged a large number of Germans as they tried to escape to the east. By attacking from the south-west 2 FF Yeo Group would seem to have caught the defenders of Loccum by surprise as the German defence was concentrated along the north-west edge of the village. The Germans had presumably heard the sound of fighting from the area of Heimsen and Wasserstrasse (see below) and assumed that the next British advance would be from the north-west towards Loccum. Although A Company was not committed to the battle, Robert Price recalls a sad incident, which could have had tragic consequences:[20]

> We were advancing across a rather rough ploughed field when three German soldiers about two hundred yards in front of us dropped to the ground and lay still. I turned to Simo our Bren gunner, who was walking alongside, and said, 'Give them a burst.' Although he fired from the hip, he was bang on target; two of them immediately sprang to their feet, hands high in the air, the third lay still. I don't think any of us were quite prepared for what we found when we reached them. The first thing we noticed was a pair of white silk knickers – the unlucky soldier was a woman. She was wearing a skirt and dark silk stockings instead of trousers. Simo's fire had blown her kneecap off; it looked pretty bad. She never made a sound, not a murmur, although she must have been in terrible pain. The two men were wearing Red Cross armbands, but they were also carrying pistols. This annoyed me; I pointed to the Red Cross symbol, then the gun, and thumped him in the chest with my fist. He was very lucky he was not shot on the spot. After the losses of 1 April the mood of the company had changed. One individual who had lost his mate in that battle went berserk and it was sometime before he could be left with prisoners on his own.

Had he shot the medics, Price would have committed a war crime. Article 9 of the Geneva Conventions 1929 stated that personnel engaged exclusively in the collection, transport and treatment of the wounded…had to be respected and protected under all circumstances.[21] The medics were entitled to carry pistols as Article 8(1) stated that protected status of medical personnel did not cease if they were equipped with light individual weapons solely to defend their patients or themselves against acts of violence.

By late afternoon Loccum was cleared with a haul of 150 prisoners taken from Kampfgruppe Volker, Panzerjagdverband 'Großer Kurfürst' and RAD *Flak* personnel, together with three 8.8cm Flak from RAD Batterie 4./132, three 2cm Flak, two half-tracks and five trucks. The twenty-seven German soldiers who were killed lie buried in Loccum war cemetery. No members of 1 Hereford were killed during the battle but 10 men were wounded and three members of an attached Vickers team from 2nd Independent Machine-Gun Company, The Royal Northumberland Fusiliers were killed. Despite the capture of Loccum, the day had great sadness for 2 FF Yeo. Late in the battle when B Squadron was preparing to push eastwards to the narrow-gauge railway, its squadron leader, Major Arthur Loram, went forward to contact his detached troop. Tragically, he drove too far down the road and his scout car was hit by an 8.8cm round, killing him and Trooper Evans his driver. A saddened 2 FF Yeo Group harboured for the night just to the village's east.

---

20   Robert Stanley Price, *Just a 'Walk in the Sun* (London: Nivello, 2011), p.107.
21   Convention Relative to the Treatment of Prisoners of War, Geneva, 27 July 1929, *https://ihl-databases.icrc. org/ihl/INTRO/305* (accessed 17 February 2013).

While 2 FF Yeo Group was advancing towards Loccum, at 1000 hours 15/19 Hussars Group crossed the Petershagen bridge and headed north along the Weser's right bank to clear the ground between the Petershagen and Stolzenau bridgeheads, before linking-up with 1st Commando Brigade and jointly capturing Leese. The advance was trouble-free until A Squadron, leading the group, neared Heimsen, where it met stiff resistance from tank-hunting teams, principally members of Panzerjagdverband 'Großer Kurfürst' but joined by anyone who could handle a *Panzerfaust* or rifle. C Company 1 Cheshire was rushed forward on C Squadron's Cromwells and dismounted to help A Squadron clear the houses. 3 Troop led the attack and was allowed to pass through the village but when 1 Troop followed, it was ambushed. Lance Corporal Chamber's Cromwell was engaged from a range of 20 yards by four *Panzerfaust*; all projectiles fortunately missed, allowing Chambers, commanding a tank for the first time, to fire his Sten from the cupola killing the inexperienced *Panzerfaust* firers. Heimsen was cleared by C Company and the advance pushed on to the next village, Wasserstrasse, which was undefended. However, when the lead tank from 4 Troop reached a level-crossing, about a mile further on, it was hit by a *Panzerfaust* fired from a slit trench close to the road; the hollow-charge warhead detonated on the centre of the sloping, front section of the turret, brewed up the tank and killed the commander, Sergeant Crump, and Troopers Beard and Powell, the operator and gunner. Other tanks in 4 Troop dealt with this enemy and 2 Troop, followed by A Squadron headquarters, passed through to take the lead. The headquarters then found themselves surrounded by numerous groups of well dug-in Germans. However, these groups, probably engineers from Pionier-Sperr-Brigade 1100, neither fought nor surrendered and a number of rounds of HE were fired to encourage them to give up. 2 Troop meanwhile advanced further up the road but then met more positions dug-in on the railway embankment and here resistance stiffened. The advance had struck the left flank of Kampfgruppe Tischler and the 15/19 Hussars' history records that the occupants of these positions were more concerned with shooting at the surrendering soldiers than engaging the British. With light fading, radio communications difficult and the enemy numerous it was decided to break off the advance and for the group to pull back into a harbour area to the south-west of Loccum. Despite 159th Brigade Group's progress, 29th Armoured Group was unable to follow as planned onto the right bank because congestion at Petershagen and lack of space in the bridgehead forced it to remain in the Stolzenau area.

The Stolzenau bridgehead and the Steyerberg vintage wines

Back in the Stolzenau bridgehead, as the preliminary part of Brigadier Mills-Roberts' plan to attack Leese, 45 (RM) Cdo received orders at 0105 hours to withdraw from its positions and pull back to relieve the hard-pressed 8 RB companies in their small bridgehead. His intention thereafter for the night 6/7 April involved simultaneously extracting the 8 RB companies to the left bank and getting his other three commandos over to the right. The complete brigade would then mount a night, flanking manoeuvre using a lengthy approach to the south of Leese and at dawn attack the village from the east.

The Hitler Youth got wind of increased activity in the bridgehead and mounted an attack on 45 (RM) Cdo's right hand troop at 0130 hours. Although the attack was beaten off, it yet again showed the enemy's determination and aggression. At 0200 hours the brigade advance parties crossed the Weser into 8 RB's bridgehead and as soon as 3 Cdo, the first commando, arrived it too was ferried across. During the subsequent relief of H Company 8 RB's sector, the Hitler Youth attacked once more resulting in the death of several riflemen and at 0440 and 0535 hours the guns of 151st Field and 146th Medium Regiments were called on to fire DFs to keep the enemy at bay.[22] There was now growing realisation that the delay caused by the enemy counter-attacks and a shortage of assault boats would prevent the generation during the hours of darkness of the remainder of the commando brigade to the Weser's right bank and that there was therefore no chance of successfully conducting the manoeuvre on Leese that night. 45 (RM) Cdo, and now also 3 Cdo,[23] would consequently have to spend another day of sniping, mortar fire and airburst in the confined bridgehead. Despite this set-back, during the early morning the two 8 RB companies were relieved by the commandos and by 0815 hours were back on the left bank. Noel Bell described a feeling of considerable relief to be once more on the comparatively friendly side and here the riflemen climbed aboard their own vehicles, ankle-deep in spent cases from engaging the *Luftwaffe*, and pulled back to Niendorf, three miles behind the river, where they washed, shaved and had their first decent meal for three days. The respite was not to last long.

In the very restricted bridgehead, 7 April would prove a most uncomfortable day for 3 Cdo and 45 (RM) Cdo and their men had to endure continual sniping and fire from German light and heavy *Flak*. To try to reduce pressure on the bridgehead, Leese was attacked twice during the day from the air. In the morning Squadron Leader MacKichan with seven Tempests from 56 Squadron was instructed by forward contact car 'Scalwag' to attack guns and mortars in Leese. Although the village was duly rocketed and shot-up, against such small targets the Tempest attack had little effect and in the late afternoon another six Tempests from the squadron repeated the attack, but again with no apparent result. Despite the lack of success from the air, David Ward describes a memorable event on the ground:[24]

> We reverted to chucking the odd grenade and abuse at the SS above the river bank and received the same in kind. With three dead comrades beside us who had tried to look over the bank there was no possible way we could have mounted an attack from our position. There arrived with us a small angry man who called us all the cowards under the sun. He then took up one of our Brens, ran up the bank and belted off the whole magazine in one long burst – then fell at our feet in a heap. The one round that the enemy had managed to return had hit inside the flash hider at the end of the barrel, split into two pieces and one had removed his front teeth and the other hit his eye. We picked him up and dusted him down and I sent him back down the river with one of the section. Who he was I never found out until a reunion on 27 April 1996 when an angry old gaffer with a black eye patch came up to the 45 table and proceeded to tell the same tale in reverse! (This was Ian Harris of No. 10 Cdo and 45 (RM) Cdo) I am delighted to tell that he was astounded to be told that the QM was still looking for him with a bill for a new barrel!

Ian Harris was a remarkable man.[25] Born Hans Hajós in 1920 to mixed Jewish and gentile parentage in Vienna, he was the only child of an officer in the Austro-Hungarian cavalry twice decorated for gallantry in the Great War. Hans was in the Vienna Boys' Choir and educated at a military boarding school where all his classmates were in the Hitler Youth. He fled to England after the *Anschluss* and later became a non-combatant soldier in the Pioneer Corps. In order to strike back at the *Nazis* he subsequently joined the German-speaking exiles of 3 Troop, No. 10 (Inter-Allied) Commando and with a changed name landed on D-Day with 46 (RM) Cdo, and was wounded. On recovery he was assigned to 45 (RM) Cdo for the Rhine crossing. The incident described by

---

22 TNA WO 171/5042, 146th Medium Regiment RA war diary.
23 TNA WO 218/83, 3 Cdo war diary.
24 Ward, 'My Time with 45 RM Commando'.
25 Daily Telegraph obituary, 8 May 2012, *https://www.telegrah.co.uk/news/obituaries/military-obituaries/army-obituaries/9252940/Ian-Harris.html* (accessed 17 September 2015).

David Ward won Harris the Military Medal as his action saved Major Blake, commanding officer 45 (RM) Cdo, and his tactical headquarters group from an imminent counter-attack.

While 3 Cdo and 45 (RM) Cdo were fully occupied on the right bank, activity was still ongoing on the left. Todforce was tasked to clear northwards to Lemke, some three miles to the north-west of Nienburg.[26] On their way, the former divisional anti-tank gunners now acting as infantry cleared Liebenau but then met enemy armed with *Panzerfaust* near Bühren. These were members of 6. SS-Kompanie stuck on the left bank. After a brisk fight the youths were mopped up and the force pushed on up the main road. However, after about half a mile they met a much stronger group of about 50 Hitler Youth, who blocked the road preventing any further advance. Todforce remained in the Bühren area for the remainder of the day but withdrew at last light to Liebenau. Meanwhile a patrol from A Squadron Inns of Court reached Steyerberg, to the south of '*Karl*' in the Liebenau forest, where it found the two trainloads of V-1 and V-2, including undamaged specimens. Also found ground-dumped in Steyerberg station yard were 20 or so V-2 warheads in transit drums, boxes of V-2 warhead ignition assemblies, and operational equipment including a V-2 transporter/launch trailer (*Meillerwagen*) and a liquid oxygen bowser (*A-stoff Betriebstoffanhanger*). The presence of these launch-associated items indicate that Steyerberg was a destination for Gruppe Nord's withdrawal from the Netherlands. A link to an online video of the Steyerberg V-1s and V-2 parts and equipment is at Appendix A, Serial 6.

Accompanying A Squadron was the war correspondent Alan Moorehead, who recorded finds far more interesting than V-weapons:[27]

> The villagers and passing refugees were wholly concentrated upon a warehouse in the main street. Inside was a store of the most beautiful wine I have ever seen, all of it cased, and almost certainly loot the Germans had taken from France and brought out here from Bremen to escape the worst of the bombing. Germans and foreigners were milling round the boxes. An innocent child lurched past carrying a case of Château Yquem of a very good year. Her father and mother and several uncles had gone for the more serious stuff: Margaux 1929 and Haut Brion of the same year, all of it bottled at the château. These they were loading on to a wheelbarrow, and no one seemed to mind when they dropped a bottle or two on the floor; there were plenty more. The sherries were mostly Amontillado 1911, the Chablis and Rieslings perhaps a little young, but all of it vintage. And now it was all posting down the street on the backs of the villagers, in hand-carts and trolleys. Half-demented children were romping among the really great prizes of the place – a Rothschild Château Lafite 1891 – and this was in the magnum, the jeroboam and the rehoboam which is the most beautiful kind of bottle in the world and on account of its size very easily dropped and smashed...That evening the floor was awash with the Lafite and the other clarets. A friend of mine who visited the place the following morning said that he walked almost ankle deep in slush and nothing remained in the broken cases.

Such is war.

---

26 TNA WO 171/4777, 75th Anti-Tank Regiment RA war diary.
27 Moorehead, *Eclipse*, p.214. A bottle of Rothschild Château Lafite 1891 auctioned at Christie's in 2011 realised £5,980.

Sunday 8 April

1st Commando Brigade attack on Leese

The night 7/8 April would see the start of the conclusion to the troublesome Leese bridgehead. At 2330 hours on 7 April men of 46 (RM) Cdo,[28] crewing 40 assault boats, started to paddle the commando's troops across the Weser, followed by 6 Cdo and brigade headquarters, to join their exhausted comrades in the bridgehead. By midnight the brigade was complete on the right bank and soon after, led by 6 Cdo, it set off on the operation to take Leese, leaving behind in the bridgehead the brigade's heavy weapons' troops to give the impression it was still held. For the remainder of the night 7/8 April, in single file the brigade conducted a very difficult encircling manoeuvre across areas of marshland to get into position to attack Leese from the east at dawn.

Brigadier Mills-Roberts describes the manoeuvre and the attack that followed:[29]

> Our wide sweep round to the right followed the river bank for two miles and then we swung inland. The hard ground by the river-bank suddenly gave way to a wet, soggy swamp but we pushed on making what speed we could. We again used our trail of thick, four-inch tape, which indicated the route like a paper chase to the following single file of troops. It was over rotten country – over streams, hedges and wide ditches full of water – and the oozing bog slowed up the pace.
>
> Donald [Donald Hopson, the Brigade Major] and I were in front with 6 Cdo. The going seemed to be getting even worse but still 6 Cdo struggled on seeking the firmest ground they could find in the line of our general direction. In the darkness the whole column came to an abrupt halt. There was no sound apart from the ominous sucking noise when many pairs of legs tried to make progress. We were then up to our knees in thick mud. I went forward and found that the leading men were bogged down. I had been told that the ground far round to the right was impassable but I did not believe it. Whatever happened we had to be right round this flank before daylight and attack the Germans at first light or the chaos would be indescribable.
>
> We halted the column and Tony Lewis [commanding officer of 6 Cdo] sought firmer ground away to the left. After 15 minutes' hard labour the men seemed to be able to feel their feet on something solid at last. It was still a foul bog, which stank like a midden but we could at least make some progress. Suddenly out of the darkness loomed the railway embankment we expected to find. It was so wet and slimy that one had to dig one's fingers in to get across. I lent a hand to Ted Ruston, the Gunner, [BC 451 Battery 1st Mountain Regiment] who had a heavy wireless set on his back. Once over the railway embankment we hoped for better going – but it was another patch of that infernal bog. In less than half a mile we should reach another railway embankment. Patience was running low and it had taken a long time to cover the last three or so miles. We pushed on like rats wading through the main sewer. At last we crossed the second embankment. It would be dry now. But no – there was more swamp. Then suddenly we hit the good hard earth. It was like waking up from a bad dream. We were mobile again and well round and slightly behind Leese. I only hoped that the enemy were not down wind of the brigade or they would smell us coming. It would not be long before daylight and Tony Lewis spurred 6 Cdo to every effort possible.

---

28 TNA DEFE 2/977, 46 (RM) Cdo war diary.
29 Mills-Roberts, *Clash by Night*, p.177.

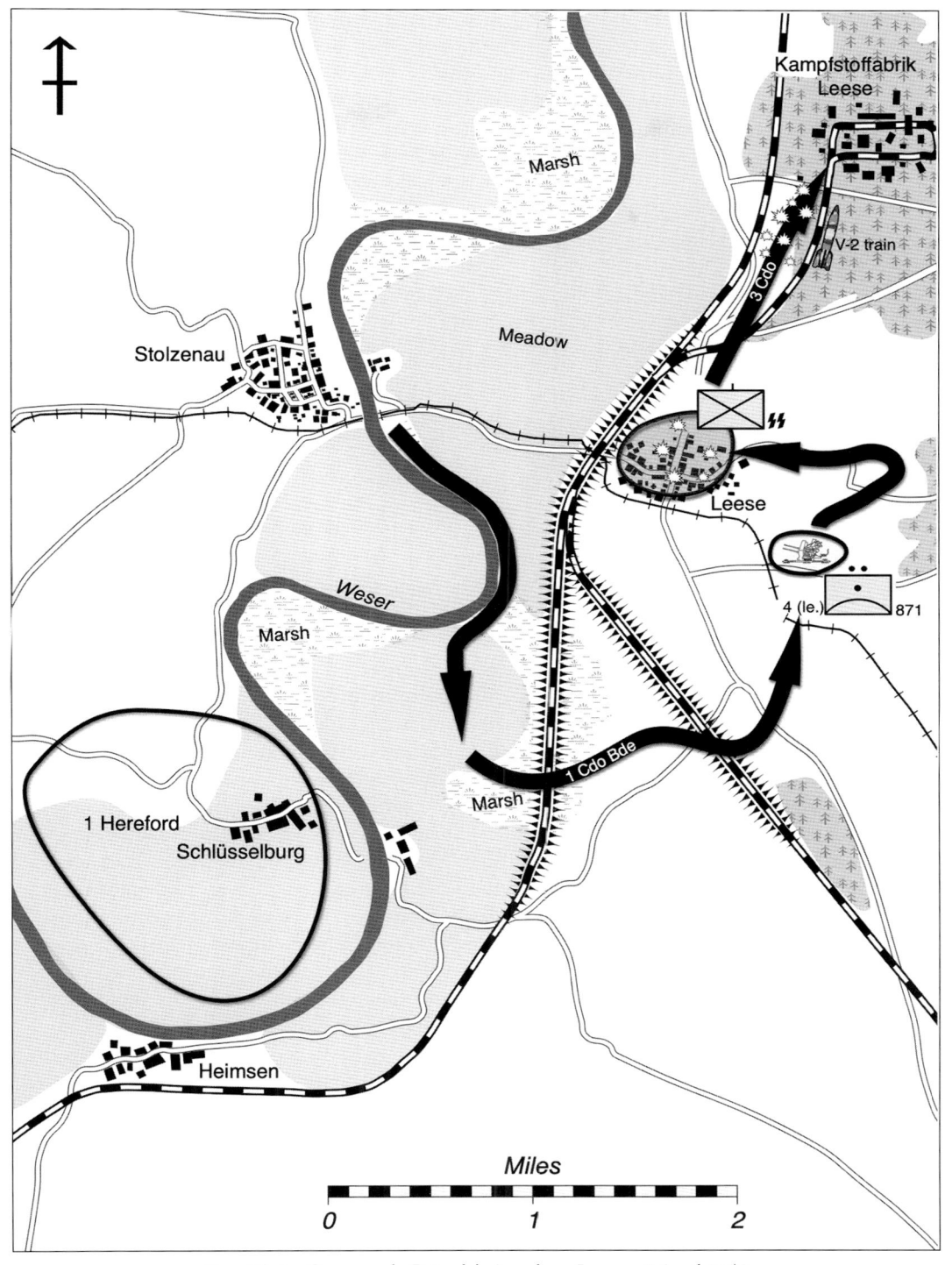

FAT CARS, CHATEAU LAFITE AND THE STEEL-EYED BOYS 201

Map 26 1st Commando Brigade's Attack on Leese – 8 April 1945.

Under a large Red Cross, surrendered defenders of Leese march off to captivity.

As the brigade neared Leese the countryside was lit-up by burning houses and this showed an opportunity to take a short-cut, but Mills-Roberts ordered 6 Cdo to stick with the planned route as he did not wish risking any loss of surprise.[30] Nearing its forming-up point for the attack, 6 Cdo's lead troop came across four 2cm guns from RAD Batterie 4./871. These were some of the guns deployed in depth of the railway embankment to provide defence against low-level air attacks. A group commanded by Captain Peter Cruden promptly rushed the guns and two officers were captured, but the crews vanished into the half-light. The brigade moved on, stealthily approached the town from the east and by 0620 hours 46 (RM) Cdo had established a bridgehead on its edge. At 0700 hours 45 (RM) Cdo started to sweep through to its objective, the railway embankment on Leese's western edge. The assault appeared to catch the Germans by surprise, meeting only sporadic resistance from the occasional *Panzerfaust*, rifle and machine-gun, and by 0930 hours Leese was secure. Thirty prisoners were taken and about the same number found dead or wounded; also captured were three 8.8cm Flak, and five 3.7cm and 2cm Flak.

On the railway sidings the commandos found three undamaged and five damaged locomotives and sundry rolling stock. Although Flakregiment 122(E)'s war diary records that the three 8.8cm Flak belonging to RAD Batterie 5./280 (gem.) were blown up by their crews before they withdrew,[31] David Ward tells a different story, confirming at least two of the guns at Leese station were not destroyed:[32]

---

30   TNA WO 218/86, 6 Cdo war diary.
31   *Gefechtsbericht des Flakregiments 122(E), 14 April 1945*, p.8
32   Ward, 'My Time with 45 RM Commando'.

We were sent to clear the railway yard and the station. There was a little skirmishing with the enemy rearguard but they had left the station, complete with a couple of 88mm guns and ample ammunition. Ian and a wandering gunner immediately turned round one of the guns, raised it to maximum elevation and belted off a couple of rounds into Germany. I was not allowed a shot. The enemy having departed we went into minimum security and fed for the first time in 48 hours. That night I occupied a double-bed in the station master's house, sharing with four other members of my section. No one seemed to object sharing a bed though we must have stank like a flock of randy billy goats. Buried in the station yard was a *SS* lieutenant colonel – no cross, just a marker and a couple of other unmarked graves.[33]

While 1st Commando Brigade was nearing the end of its long infiltration, at 0600 hours C Squadron 23 Hussars crossed the Petershagen bridge and began moving down the right bank to link up with the commandos and provide armour support and assistance in enlarging their bridgehead northwards. The squadron reached Leese soon after the village's capture and married up with the commandos. A troop was detached to 3 Cdo and the force then swept north to capture Kampstoffabrik Leese, heavily camouflaged in the Hahnenberg Forest and lying just to the north of Leese. The plant, believed by the British to be assembling rockets, was actually a chemical production site comprising two firms: Riedel-de Haën AG[34] manufacturing tear gas and liquid oxygen, a constituent of V-2 fuel, and Lonal-Werke AG (Berlin) producing arsine gas, a precursor for the production of gases resistant to cold. As the commandos approached the forest they began to draw fire from Hitler Youth still in the area and at 0845 hours, leading his men across the open ground, Captain John Alderson, commanding 6 Troop, was hit; he was evacuated in a captured ambulance but later died of his wounds. Seeing the lead troop in difficulty Lieutenant Colonel Peter Bartholomew, commanding officer of 3 Cdo, climbed onto a Comet to direct the tank's fire; this was a brave act as German resistance was heavy and his runner, Corporal Joe Court, was shot through the lung (he survived) as he sat beside him. With Peter Bartholomew's intervention restoring the attack's momentum, 3 Cdo entered the forest and pressed on to Kampfstoffabrik Leese, which it cleared by 1600 hours, capturing some Hitler Youth and civilian staff in the process. The commandos were amazed at the sophistication of the Germans' concealment of the facility, in particular the buildings' flat, concrete roofs bearing feet of soil and well-established fir trees and bushes. On the spur line to the site was a trainload of V-2 rockets on railway flat-wagons, some destroyed but others intact and still in their camouflaged transit covers, with one marked '*Nach ENGLAND*', a slogan destined to remain unfulfilled.[35] Additionally, in the forest adjacent to the spur line was a large quantity of demolished launch equipment and further V-2 rockets.

Kampfstoffabrik Leese was not the only industrial site hidden in the area's forests and about three miles to its south was the *Luftwaffe's* Loccum fuel depot consisting of 18 storage tanks and large quantities of barrels containing, inter alia, methanol and smoke-generating chemicals for screening targets from daylight bombing raids. The depot was linked to the railway system and would have stored and distributed production from the Deurag-Nerag refinery near Hannover, which specialised in the production of *Luftwaffe*-associated fuels and oils. Although the depot was

---

33 A *Waffen-SS* lieutenant colonel would have been an *SS-Obersturmbannführer*. As *SS-Oberscharführer* (sergeant) is the most senior *Waffen-SS* rank buried in Leese's war cemetery, Ward probably misread the field grave marker.
34 Now Honeywell Riedel-de Haën with a broad manufacturing portfolio but no longer at Leese. The principal occupier of the Leese site is Raiffeisen Agil, a bioenergy products and fruit-growing company.
35 Although the spur line has been removed, its route can still be discerned and one very small section is evident where it crosses a patch of cobbled road. Many of Kampfstoffabrik Leese's flat-top buildings are still in use, with their vegetation camouflage intact.

Destroyed V-2 on the railway spur line leading through the forest to Kampfstoffabrik Leese.

Destroyed V-2 and a *Meillerwagen* rocket transporter/launch trailer.

captured on 8 April, the war diaries do not reveal which unit found and secured it. Links to online videos of surrendered German soldiers at Leese, the V-2 rockets, Kampfstoffabrik Leese and the fuel depot are at Appendix A, Serials 7, 8 and 10.

The lack of opposition to the commando brigade's night move and the ease with which Leese was captured was a consequence of Kampfgruppe Tischler having withdrawn from the town. Stepping back to 7 April, it must have become clear to Peinemann that the British crossing in the Petershagen area had serious implications for his forces on the Weser, with the presence of enemy armour on the right bank at Loccum a particular threat. Consequently, he ordered the battalion and all other forces capable of moving to withdraw that night in a generally north-east direction towards Rethem. Once over the Aller it is believed that the intention was for the battalion to form a new defensive position in the Walsrode area. Making use of the remaining hours of darkness, Kampfgruppe Tischler's exhausted young soldiers pulled back from their positions on the railway embankment and at about 0430 hours they departed Leese, two hours before the arrival of 1st Commando Brigade, leaving behind a small rearguard and any *Flak* guns unable to be moved. Although Tischler's robust defence imposed three days' delay on 11th Armoured Division, it was of course futile. All his companies at Leese suffered heavily, with 3. SS-Kompanie and the Unterführer-Lehr-Kompanie reduced to remnants. Today 51 Germans, mostly members of Kampfgruppe Tischler, lie buried in Leese's war cemetery.

The threat posed by 11th Armoured at Petershagen not only affected SS-A.u.E.Btl.12 'HJ' but also forced the withdrawal of Hartmann and the marines of I./6 Marine-Grenadier-Regiment at Nienburg. The foot-sore marines, who had arrived on the Weser only the day before, were now ordered to withdraw immediately to the Aller's right bank in depth of Rethem. One can only imagine the effect this must have had on morale. In addition to the infantry, the *Flak* artillery also received orders to pull back and during the night 7/8 April Flak-Regiment 122(E) started to withdraw its batteries supporting the Weser Line. RAD Batterie 1./521 managed to withdraw two of its 10.5cm guns at Nienburg to join Marine-Füsilier-Bataillon 2 at Essel and Batterie 3./607 eventually reached Marine-Feldersatz-Bataillon 2 in the area of Ahlden. At least two of the 8.8cm Flak at Leese were hitched to SdKfz 251 half-tracks and towed off to the east, others were abandoned as we have heard.

The last action on 8 April for 1st Commando Brigade was to extend the Stolzenau bridgehead as far as Landesbergen. 46 (RM) Cdo and C Squadron 23 Hussars were ordered to carry out this task and duly set off down the right bank of the Weser. When they reached Landesbergen they found the village held by significant numbers of enemy. This opposition came from 1. SS-Kompanie, which had not yet withdrawn, joined by members of 5. SS-Kompanie and the Unterführer-Lehr-Kompanie, withdrawing northwards from Leese. After a brisk action, 46 (RM) Cdo and the tanks cleared Landesbergen by 1000 hours, taking prisoners from all three companies and finding two further trainloads of V-2; they then remained there for the rest of the day and the night 9/10 April. Those Hitler Youth that escaped withdrew through the forests to the north-east and when they reached Langendamm dispatched parties to look for food at the barracks formerly occupied by the Einstellungs Kompanie, and a supply depot in Erichshagen. All they found were bottles of advocaat, a bitter disappointment for the young soldiers, who had not eaten anything substantial for days and were extremely hungry. A link to an online video of the remains of the V-2 rockets at Landesbergen is at Appendix A, Serial 15.

11th Armoured Division advance to the Leine

While 1st Commando Brigade was clearing the Leese area, the two brigade groups of 11th Armoured Division – 159th Infantry Brigade and 29th Armoured – prepared to advance to the Leine. The next two days, studded with bloody clashes against SS-A.u.E.Btl.12 'HJ' withdrawing to the Aller,

A Challenger of 15/19 Hussars in overwatch as a Cromwell supports infantry from 1 Cheshire advancing across country typical of the area between the Weser and Leine.

would be eventful for the two brigade groups. Despite the confusion and their exhaustion, during the withdrawal the battalion's young soldiers were to confirm their reputation for obstinacy and courage. Initially the armoured division's advance would be led only by 159th Infantry Brigade Group as the armoured brigade group was still delayed in crossing the Petershagen bridge owing to lack of space for its vehicles in the bridgehead on the right bank. 29th Armoured would therefore have to wait until the infantry brigade had moved eastwards. B Squadron Inns of Court and patrols from 1 SAS would recce forward of the advance.

159th Infantry Brigade Group. The day, which would feature the leapfrogging of 159th Infantry Brigade Group's two regimental groups, started at 0700 hours with the 2 FF Yeo Group advancing a mile beyond Loccum to its objective: the road crossing over the Steinhuder Meerbahn narrow-gauge railway. Prisoners were taken from RAD Batterie 4./132, Kampfgruppe Tischler and 325. Infanterie-Division. 15/19 Hussars Group then passed through 2 FF Yeo Group and took up the brigade's advance on the axis Rehburg, Schneeren, Eilvese and finally Hagen.[36]

Rehburg was cleared with little difficulty and B Squadron, with two 1 Cheshire companies, stayed to secure the village and protect the axis while C Squadron advanced to the high ground to the north-east of Mardorf, where many prisoners, mainly medical personnel, were taken. C Squadron was then relieved by A Squadron on the high ground and advanced through Schneeren to another area of higher ground to its east. Meanwhile back at Rehburg, B Squadron had met some resistance just to the north of the village from soldiers of the Stamm Kompanie and 5. SS-Kompanie and the Cheshires suffered a few casualties mopping them up.

---

36   TNA WO 171/4692, 15/19 Hussars war diary.

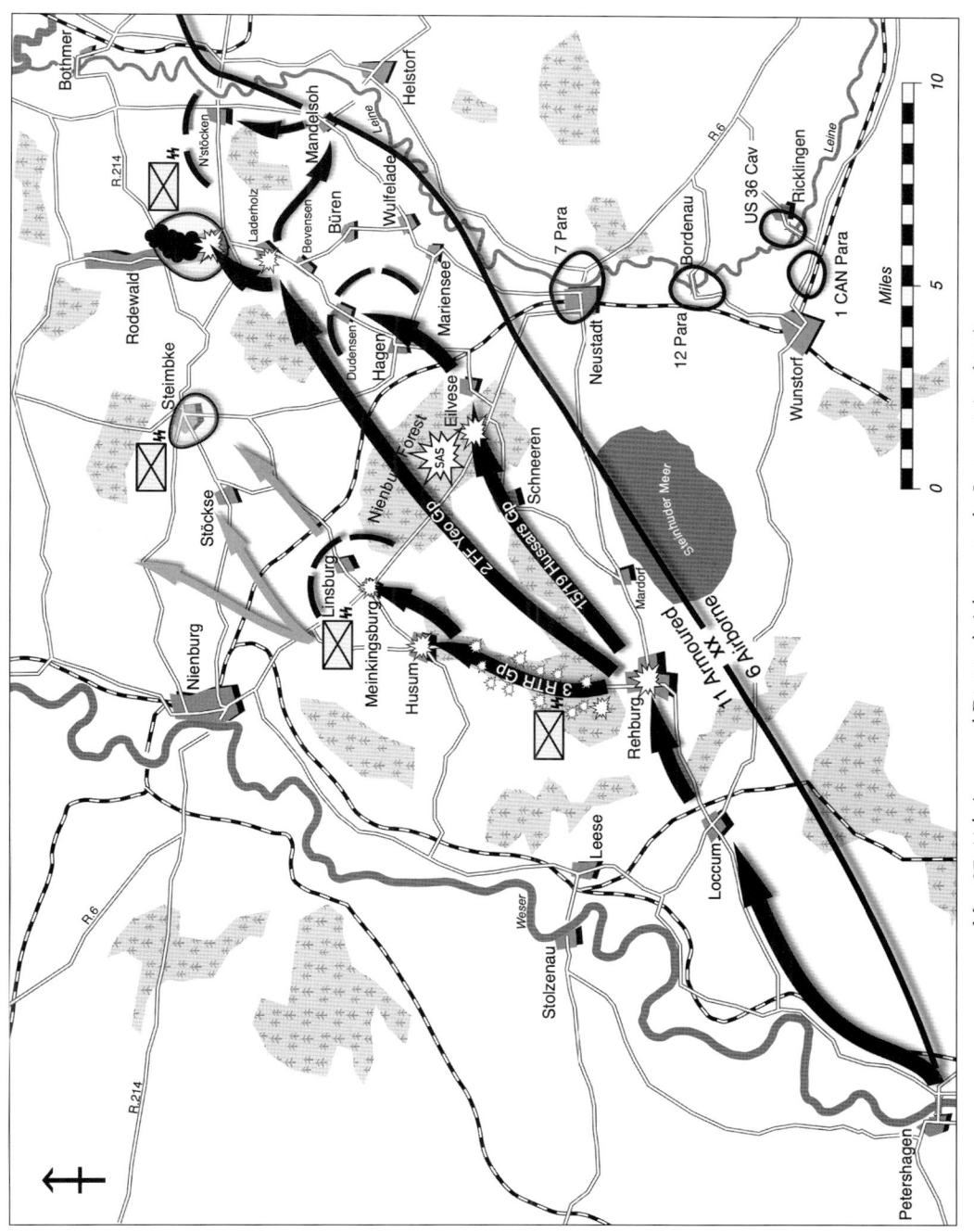

FAT CARS, CHATEAU LAFITE AND THE STEEL-EYED BOYS 207

Map 27 11th Armoured Division's Advance to the Leine – 8 April 1945.

The 2 FF Yeo Group, advancing eastwards from the area of the railway crossing, soon relieved B Squadron Group in Rehburg. This allowed the stretched 15/19 Hussars Group to concentrate near Schneeren before starting to advance eastwards through an extension of the Nienburg Forest to its next objective, Eilvese. While waiting for B Squadron to catch up, Comets of 4 Troop, C Squadron, 15/19 Hussars sat on the high ground to the east of Schneeren and were surprised to see a SdKfz 251 half-track suddenly heading fast down the road towards them from the east; the vehicle was promptly engaged and destroyed. With the group reunited, C Squadron led the advance and initially all was quiet. Unknown to the 15/19 Hussars Group this part of the Nienburg Forest contained considerable numbers of the withdrawing 7. SS-Kompanie. Although this company was without its commander, as SS-Untersturmführer Zeidler had been killed at Leese, its junior commanders were more than capable of organising the Hitler Youth to offer an effective defence against the enemy armour and as the first tanks entered they closed in on them. The lead Comet, commanded by Corporal Miles, was destroyed by a *Panzerfaust* followed swiftly by the destruction of Corporal Walker's Comet; fortunately, the casualties were only minor but it was clear that this was an unhealthy place for armour without infantry protection and the squadron pulled back out of the trees. While 3 Troop kept the Hitler Youth at bay with fire from the turret Besas, B and C Companies 1 Cheshire were brought forward to clear the resistance and a fierce action ensued among the trees. The forest was eventually cleared but with the loss of three members of 1 Cheshire and many Hitler Youth, with the survivors escaping northwards deeper into the forest. With the route cleared, C Squadron advanced again and was soon met by the *Bürgermeister* of Eilvese appearing with a white flag to surrender his village. As an insurance policy the lead tank invited him to sit on its glacis plate and the squadron then moved off to Eilvese, which was captured unopposed. The 15/19 Hussars Group concluded a successful day by reaching Dudensen. During the group's advance, the recce squadron checked the roads leading south-east to Neustadt, contacting here elements of 6th Airborne, and then patrolled up the Leine's left bank clearing the villages of Empede, Mariensee, Wulfelade, Evensen and Büren as it did so.

The recce squadron was not the only reconnaissance assets in the area. Since crossing the Weser on 7 April, three troops from A Squadron 1 SAS had been attached to 11th Armoured from 6th Airborne as it was assumed that the armoured division would make faster progress. Nine Jeeps of Captain Ian Wellsted's C Troop were ordered to support patrols from B Squadron Inns of Court, which were advancing north-eastwards toward the Nienburg Forest. As they entered the forest they were unaware that it contained quantities of withdrawing Hitler Youth. Major Harry Poat, A Squadron commander, wrote an after-action review on 12 April to describe the events that unfolded:[37]

> Wellsted's troop was sent with one armoured car and two scout cars[38] to act as flank guard on the left and northern flank of the main advance. They advanced through the large wood up the track from the south to a crossroads and along west till they were fired on by bazooka and heavy small-arms' fire. The enemy had let the armoured vehicles through, a fierce battle lasting 10 minutes took place, we lost one Jeep, one man killed but took two prisoners, it was absolutely impossible to see the enemy as the woods were too thick.
>
> We were at a terrible disadvantage standing up high on the road firing our Vickers while the enemy were lying in the undergrowth. We then, plus the armoured vehicles [from B Squadron Inns of Court], withdrew to the cross-roads and prepared to make a stand, as it was

---

37 Operation ARCHWAY, Major Poat letter, 12 April 1945, *http://ww2talk.com/index.php?threads/battle-of-rethem-1945-aller-river-crossing.76984/* (accessed 12 June 2019).
38 The armoured car would have been a Daimler and the scout cars Dingos.

now known that our line of withdrawal to our own lines was cut off, the enemy closed in on three sides, his main attack coming from the south. We still could not see him but were suffering casualties from his small-arms' fire. After about 15 minutes he launched three armoured vehicles up the track [possibly SdKfz 222 from Gruppe Grosan]. It was not until the leading vehicle was within 50 yards did it fire and we could definitely say it was enemy. Then I got our armoured car to come up and bolt it with its 2-pdr, which it did with great success. It knocked out one and damaged another, the crews baled out into the woods. The third vehicle turned out to be a troop carrier, and a large number of troops got out into the woods, and tried to close in on us. The chaps fought like devils, firing everything they had. After about 10 minutes I saw we were outnumbered and positioned, and the casualties mounting rapidly, so I gave orders for us to form a body in all the Jeeps still serviceable, got the wounded on board, and made a dash for it, turning down the track which would bring us to our own lines.

This was done. I sent Johnny Cooper off with the wounded first at top speed, then made a dash with the rest later. The Jerry was about 30 yards away when we left, and believe me I never thought the old Jeeps were so slow, 50 mph seemed a snail's pace. The first vehicle we met in our lines was an ambulance, which was lucky, so we got the wounded straight aboard…We are fairly well, and the men in good form, the fighting is very hard and we have mixed it many times with the Hun, and they are all *SS*, the real thing and no doubt about it, although they no longer have an organised defence they are fighting cleverly in a guerrilla role, and I can assure you they are far better at it than our friends the Maquis.

This sharp action left three SAS dead, one missing and five wounded. The next day, SAS patrols carried on the advance and pushed on in a north-easterly direction to Ahlden to investigate whether the bridges on the Alte Leine and Aller had been blown, and in a northerly direction to recce the area to the north of Rodewald. 1st SAS went on to be among the first troops to enter Belsen concentration camp and subsequently ended the war in the area of Kiel.

With 15/19 Hussars Group secure in the Dudensen area, to keep up momentum 2 FF Yeo Group overtook them and advanced to Laderholz. Robert Price describes the events that followed:[39]

We then passed through them [15/19 Hussars] and captured the small town of Laderholz whose defenders, mainly determined bazooka men concealed at the side of the road, gave us the most trouble. Usually the first four tanks in the column carried no infantry for obvious reasons. On this occasion the bazooka man fired at the third tank from a house situated near the road. Fortunately for the tank the bazooka hit the toolbox mounted on the side of the tank doing no serious damage. The tank immediately stopped, swung the turret round and stuck the 77mm gun through the window and fired, killing everyone in the room. I think at this stage of the campaign the majority of tank casualties we were getting were from the bazooka. In the hands of determined men they were very effective weapons, even though the bazooka man was invariably killed afterwards. Their philosophy was simple; it was well worth the loss of one man and a very cheap weapon for a very costly weapon like a tank, and possibly the crew as well.

With Laderholz cleared and A Squadron in the lead, the 2 FF Yeo Group advanced north towards Rodewald. The southern extremity of this 5-mile long, north-south orientated village contained 2. SS-Kompanie, commanded by SS-Obersturmführer Marsen, which either by accident or design had withdrawn to the village that had previously hosted them. The company had escaped action on

---

39   Price, *Just a Walk in the Sun*, p.108.

the Weser and made good progress down Reichsstrasse 214 and then via the Alte Celler Heerstraße to Rodewald, managing to avoid contact with the advancing 11th Armoured Division groups. The company was probably drawing breath in the village before heading north across the Lichten Moor to Rethem when the young soldiers heard British armour approaching from the south and took up positions in the gardens and buildings in the vicinity of the junction at the southern end of the village. The commander of the first A Squadron Comet to approach the junction was Lieutenant Miller. Fortunately, Miller had a suspicion that all was not well, halted his troop and ordered his Comets to back away. His timing was extremely fortuitous as the reversing tanks managed to avoid a storm of *Panzerfaust* fired at them by the young soldiers of 2. SS-Kompanie. With Rodewald clearly held by a determined enemy, Lieutenant Colonel Scott, commanding officer of 2 FF Yeo, planned a quick attack, which would be implemented as soon as the infantry of B Company 1 Hereford had closed up with the tanks. While awaiting the infantry's arrival, the tanks shot up the buildings on the southern edge of Rodewald.

The attack opened with B Company assaulting the area of the junction and soon a lively fight was in progress with smoke from burning buildings adding to the confusion. Hitler Youth holding a strongpoint in the Wiebusch wood to the north of the junction supported their comrades in the houses and they had to be suppressed by the Comets to allow B Company to fight its way into the village. Although with nightfall the fighting in the southern part came to a halt, the enemy was still present in the wood so Lieutenant Colonel Scott decided to withdraw and plan a deliberate attack for the next day. The 2 FF Yeo history describes the village as not merely a hard nut to crack but rather a 'chunk of granite.'[40]

With A Squadron Group engaged at Rodewald, C Squadron and C Company cut south-east to Mandelsloh, close to the Leine, where they found the village undefended but the bridge linking it to Helstorf on the right bank demolished. The group then headed north to capture Niedernstöcken. Seventy prisoners, mainly from SS-A.u.E.Btl. 12 'HJ', were captured during this advance, but here also the bridge over the Leine was found demolished. The quantity of prisoners presented a challenge in terms of guarding, only solved the next morning when the remainder of the 2 FF Yeo Group joined them in the Niedernstöcken area.

29th Armoured Brigade Group. Turning the clock back to the morning, once 159th Brigade Group was clear of the Petershagen bridgehead there was space for 29th Armoured Brigade Group to cross to the right bank of the Weser and at 0830 hours 3 RTR Group rumbled over the Class 40.[41] However, continuing traffic congestion on the right bank delayed the group's advance and it took until mid-day to reach Loccum. After Loccum the group then set off towards Rehburg with B Company 4 KSLI, supported by a squadron of Comets, in the lead.[42] Although the route to Rehburg had by now been used with little problem by both of 159th Infantry Brigade's regimental groups, as B Company passed the wood to the south of the road it came under fire from a machine-gun and *Panzerfaust* from a group from 5. SS-Kompanie. The brigade commander had just ordered that all woods be properly cleared regardless of the effort it took and so Major Edwards, commanding B Company, mounted a quick attack on the enemy positions with two platoons up; heavy casualties were taken by the right-hand platoon and it took the personal intervention of Major Edwards, who crawled forward to kill two men in the position giving the most trouble, to force the enemy to surrender. While B Company was busy mopping-up, the remainder of 3 RTR Group by-passed to the north of the road, entered Rehburg then took the road leading

---

40 Sellar, *The Fife and Forfar Yeomanry, 1919–1956*, p.236.
41 TNA WO 171/4708, 3 RTR war diary.
42 TNA WO 171/5220, 4 KSLI war diary.

Captured Hitler Youth of SS-A.u.E.Btl. 12 'HJ' await evacuation to the divisional cage. They are all wearing the Model 1943 service tunic, a shoddy garment made of waste wool and rayon.

northwards to Husum, the group's next objective, five miles away. A link to an online video of 3 RTR Group in action in the Rehburg area is at Appendix A, Serial 5.

To reach Husum there was only the one road, running through extensive forest and containing youths of 5. SS-Kompanie and the Stamm Kompanie. Both these companies had fought at Leese then withdrawn in an easterly direction to Rehburg, where they fought the 15/19 Hussars Group before being forced to withdraw northwards up the road to Husum. 5. SS-Kompanie had been severely battered at Leese and now consisted of just two platoons, commanded respectively by SS-Oberscharführer Dargel and SS-Hauptscharführer Polzer. Although the forest was ideal infantry ground, for the Hitler Youth the road to Husum was far from ideal as it headed north rather than north-east but they were forced to take it with 159th Infantry Brigade Group advancing on the roads leading north-east.

C Squadron 3 RTR with B Company 4 KSLI mounted on the Comets led the advance on the road to Husum and as the tanks neared the forest edge German soldiers were seen among the trees. Despite the risks inherent in moving armour through close-country with enemy infantry present, Lieutenant Colonel Mitford, commanding 3 RTR, was under pressure from HQ 29th Armoured to make progress and so he ordered the group to force a passage by driving through the forest as fast as possible. Captain Corbett, B Company second-in-command, describes the fight that ensued:[43]

---

43 Major 'Ned' Thornburn, *After Antwerp – The Long Haul to Victory* (4 KSLI Museum Trust, Shrewsbury, 1993. By kind permission of Shropshire Regimental Museum), p.104.

It was decided to try and crash our way through this enemy crust rather than mount a set-piece attack, with one section of tanks leading and the remainder plus ourselves following at maximum speed. Covered by tanks on the left we raced off and, as we entered the forest, bazookas whizzed past the front and rear of our vehicles, and there was also some small-arms' fire which caused some casualties. Private Ince, one of the company's cockneys, unfortunately was killed.

We must have advanced the best part of a mile in this fashion before the leading tank came to grief and we were forced to take to our feet, No. 10 Platoon going right of the road, No. 11 left with No. 12 in reserve. There was quite a lot of inaccurate fire coming our way and No. 10 Platoon was unlucky enough to encounter some fanatical Germans who held their fire until our fellows were only a yard or two away. Private Newman was killed and Corporal Elvin seriously wounded by these methods. Private Smith was outstanding in dealing with these individuals. It now became necessary to advance through the woods, firing at every bush etc as we went along. It was slow going but paid a dividend as we came across a few abandoned bikes and bazookas. On the road a handcart of abandoned mortar bombs blew up just as company HQ were going by and CSM Baker received a very nasty graze on the side of the head but being Baker he refused any aid other than a field dressing.

By now the centre of the column was in difficulties and we were forced to halt for a while. The advance was continued with No. 12 Platoon right and No. 10 Platoon left, No. 11 Platoon being in reserve.

The lead Comet mentioned by Corbett was hit by a *Panzerfaust*, knocking out the tank and killing the commander, Sergeant Duff, and one of his crew. At one stage of the battle, elements of the group were fighting running battles with the Hitler Youth at the forest's entry, centre and exit and it took the committal of all four of 4 KSLI's rifle companies to make progress against a very aggressive enemy. Although the fighting reduced the Stamm Kompanie and 5. SS-Kompanie to uncoordinated groups struggling to escape through the forest, 4 KSLI's history records that the youths, who were to continue to harry the battalion for the next few days, fought like fanatics, were well-camouflaged and used no tracer ammunition, making identification very difficult. The battle lasted two and a half hours and took until 1530 hours for 3 RTR Group to overcome the opposition and press on to Husum, now only a mile away from the forest's northern edge. Among the prisoners taken was an officer with a marked map showing that the withdrawal route SS-A.u.E.Btl. 12 'HJ' was taking was the same as 29th Armoured Brigade Group's axis of advance; this did not bode well.

Two German accounts allege that the British murdered 17 members of SS-A.u.E.Btl.12 'HJ' near Rehburg. According to the first account,[44] two Hitler Youth positioned in a house shot a British tank commander standing in his turret while approaching Rehburg, and that the two men were captured and shot as a reprisal. The account then states that 17 PoWs were held in a carpenter's shop in Rehburg prior to being taken to a spot on Rehburg Moor, which the British had ordered the carpenter to find, and here members of 4 KSLI bludgeoned them to death with rifle butts, then buried them; allegedly the bodies were subsequently re-buried at Husum. In the second account,[45] the allegation is repeated but with added details: the tank commander is named as Major Loram and that he was killed on the road from Rehburg to Husum; the carpenter revealed the story on his death-bed and that he acted as the driver for the British under threat of being killed; the 17 were bound, driven to the massacre location where, in a hollow on the moor to the

---

44　Buchwald, *Endkampf*, p.30.
45　Ulrich Saft, *Krieg in der Heimat* (Walsrode: Druckerei Gronemann, 1988), pp.42–43.

north-east of the Krähenberg feature, members of 1 Cheshire (rather than 4 KSLI) beat then shot them; and the carpenter later transported the bodies in a farm cart to Rehburg, where they were initially buried. There are seven reasons and inconsistencies that strongly contradict the allegation:

1. There is no British record of a tank commander being killed by small-arms' fire in the Rehburg area.
2. Major Loram belonged to a different regimental group to either 4 KSLI or 1 Cheshire and it is most unlikely that riflemen in a third regimental group would either have heard of his death or necessarily been affected by it.
3. It makes no sense for the British to demand a German civilian (the carpenter) to drive what would, presumably, have been a British Army vehicle. It is implausible that they would have used a German vehicle.
4. To commit the atrocity, members of 4 KSLI would have had to break off from their intense battle in the forest, collect the prisoners from the carpenter's shop then drive to the massacre site before rejoining the battle. All highly improbable.
5. It is incongruous for the British to require a civilian to find a spot for a massacre and then leave him as a witness.
6. B Squadron 15/19 Hussars and the two companies of Cheshires were soon relieved in Rehburg by the 2 FF Yeo Group so there was insufficient time for a party of Cheshires to commit the atrocity.
7. The first German account states that the 17 were killed with blows from rifle butts, while the second says they were shot.

While we will soon come across a British admission of prisoners being shot, this will be in the heat of battle rather than a calculated massacre out of contact. Assuming that 17 dead German soldiers were indeed found on the moor, the most likely explanation is that they were killed during 3 RTR Group's battle through the forest and that after the fighting the bodies were collected and placed in the hollow, where they were later found by the carpenter, who, for his own reasons, concocted the story of a massacre. The Germans, however, were not alone in creating false accounts of massacres and a fabricated British account will feature in Chapter 9.

Returning to 3 RTR Group's advance to Husum, as yet unknown to the group, in Husum and its immediate area were Hitler Youth from 3. SS-Kompanie, ready to fight despite the strain of the Leese battle and the withdrawal. Assuming it to be held, Husum was softened up with artillery and at 1730 hours 3 RTR and most of 4 KSLI advanced into the village. Although the majority of the group passed through the village unopposed, the absence of German reaction was deliberate as 3. SS-Kompanie remained concealed in order to ambush the rear of the advance and cut the enemy column into more manageable portions. Captain Corbett describes what befell B Company, the last company to enter Husum:[46]

> We reached the edge of the forest and in front lay Husum. No white flags were flying and we entered quite peacefully. No. 12 Platoon went right through without trouble. No. 10 Platoon on the left had two casualties and reported Germans on the left. As company HQ moved to the centre of the village they came under fire from snipers and CSM Baker was killed. He had given very loyal service to the battalion…especially as CSM B Company. His loss at that time was a very grievous one.

---

46 Thornburn, *After Antwerp – The Long Haul to Victory*, p.105.

After our own squadron and vehicles and the main body of the battalion had passed through the village the snipers, who had kept out of sight, now started to work in earnest and we suffered more casualties at their hands. Corporal Pembleton, Lance Serjeant Houston, Riflemen Wright, Saville, Bridge, Moore, Eyre, Hampson and Hartley were all killed.

2nd Lieutenant Brecknell's platoon, which was ordered to clear a street running off to the left of the main street, met stiff resistance and was held up after its platoon commander had been mortally wounded. We asked for flame-throwers to help us to clear the resistance, but even this did not prove successful.[47] During this hold-up I crossed a courtyard in search of the company commander, who had gone forward to where Brecknell's platoon was held up and was lucky when a sniper, covering the courtyard from several blocks away, only scored a near miss. I took shelter in a house and was trying to locate the sniper when to my horror Major Edwards walked into the courtyard through some double doors at the far end. I shouted to warn him but as he turned his head in my direction the sniper shot him and he dropped like a stone. Believing him dead I was just debating the wisdom of risking further lives in getting him inside when an armoured ambulance, which had been sent forward to evacuate 2nd Lieutenant Brecknell, drove into the yard. Fortunately, we were able to lift Major Edwards in under cover of the vehicle, but it was not until next day that I heard that he was still alive. The ambulance, alas, was little use to poor Brecknell who died just before it arrived.

It was not only the infantry that found the going tough in Husum. Commanding 1 Troop A Squadron 3 RTR was Lieutenant John Langdon:[48]

A Squadron had entered Husum and were in the process of finding positions covering the roads in from the north. I was leading 1 Troop and we were moving slowly along a street of houses, just when I thought everything was quiet there was an almighty explosion, which seemed to rock the tank. We literally came to a grinding halt, Trooper Charlton shouted up from the driving compartment that he was unable to move the tank and had the presence of mind to immediately switch off the engine. I gave the order to bale out and realised we had been hit by a bazooka. We quickly searched the immediate area but found no one, wisps of smoke were coming from the engine compartment with the odd flame coming up through the engine deck, but this was nothing like the serious brews experienced with the Shermans. I ran back to Sergeant Elstob's [the troop sergeant] tank which, all the time, had been covering mine 40 yards to my rear, got up on his turret and got a message through to Scotty telling him what had happened. I said I would take over Corporal Redpath's tank complete with my crew and that I would send Redpath and his crew back to echelon, as my tank appeared to be a write off, certainly as far as the engine was concerned. This I did and, as the enemy seemed to have disappeared, we were able to get our personal belongings, maps etc from the turret and driving compartment, also our bed rolls which were strapped onto the rear of the engine deck and had appeared to have escaped damage. We then stowed everything we wanted onto Redpath's tank while he and his crew with their possessions boarded a convenient vehicle that had come up and was returning to echelon. I was now down to three tanks, which I always considered easier to handle than four. I could not help thinking how lucky we had been that we had no casualties.

---

47 These would have been Wasps belonging to the battalion's carrier platoon commanded by a CANLOAN officer, Captain Harold Henry. The CANLOAN system was established in 1943 to allow a surplus of 623 Canadian officers to fill a deficiency of junior officers in British infantry regiments. They fought with great bravery; seventy-five percent were killed, wounded or captured.
48 John Langdon, 'The Sharp End – A Personal Account of Life in a Tank Regiment in the Second World War', (Stationery Kate: Monmouth, 2003), p.142.

Eventually the fighting died down and as it appeared that German resistance was over, the Comets of A Squadron were able to follow-up behind C Squadron.

While B Company 4 KSLI was fighting in Husum, A, C and D Companies had pressed on with 3 RTR towards Linsburg, the next village. When the tanks reached the hamlet of Meinkingsburg at the cross-roads mid-way between Husum and Lindsburg, they suddenly encountered stiff resistance. What the British did not know was that they had surprised not only significant numbers of Hitler Youth from a variety of companies but also the commanding officer of SS-A.u.E.Btl. 12 'HJ', SS-Hauptsturmführer Peinemann, and some of his company and platoon commanders, called together for orders at Meinkingsburg's inn. The sudden arrival of British armour and infantry took the Germans completely by surprise and mayhem ensued as they rushed to find cover. Soon bullets, grenades and *Panzerfaust* began to fly, with SS-Untersturmführer Greiners hitting two Comets with *Panzerfaust*, although only damaging the tanks. The Germans resisted strongly and a section of Wasp flame-throwers commanded by Sergeant Walpole was called forward to help dislodge the tenacious enemy. The Wasps proceeded to flame but with little success and eventually an attack by A Company and D Company was required to clear the hamlet. Although many Germans were able to get away during the confused fighting, it was not until the next day, and in some cases the day after, that the SS-A.u.E.Btl.12 'HJ' commanders caught up with their companies and platoons. When Captain Corbett passed through Meinkingsburg the next day he observed:[49]

> Here a platoon of Hitler Youth had been caught by our tanks when only partly dug-in and there were dead Germans everywhere. We were surprised to find three nurses so near to the front. They were looking after about a dozen wounded Germans in a house and would not be parted from them when we evacuated them but went with them.

While 3 RTR and most of 4 KSLI were at Meinkingsburg, the fighting to their rear in Husum flared up again in the evening when some remaining Germans decided to mount a final stand. B Company 4 KSLI was by now acutely feeling the strain of battle and the commanding officer requested that 3 RTR send some tanks back to help the infantrymen. 2 Troop of A Squadron, commanded by Lieutenant Dennis Sullivan, was ordered to support B Company and with the tanks' assistance the opposition was soon overcome. Captain Corbett describes the final act of the battle for Husum:[50]

> We were extremely grateful to the CO when he sent a troop of tanks to help us and, as reports had come in that civilians were also using firearms, they had no mercy on the buildings when they did a combined attack with Lieutenant Jimmy West's platoon. Soon many of the houses were blazing as a result of their tracer. Even so, darkness was upon us before we were really sure that we had cleared all enemy from the village. I established what was left of Company HQ in a café in the centre of the village and spent a very uncomfortable night, most of which was taken up with visiting the two remaining platoon commanders, Lieutenants West and Wiltshire.

B Company suffered severely in Husum as Private Dalton, a Bren gunner in 12 Platoon, poignantly describes:[51]

---

49 Thornburn, *After Antwerp – The Long Haul to Victory*, p.106.
50 Thornburn, *After Antwerp – The Long Haul to Victory*, p.105.
51 Thornburn, *After Antwerp – The Long Haul to Victory*, p.106.

> My section commander was Alf Pembleton, a really fine NCO and an old TA man. Like most TA men he had been in many tight spots until he was shot through the head at almost point-blank range in house-to-house fighting in Husum. I recall with great sadness removing the section's tea, sugar and butter from his small pack shortly afterwards. But even sadder was the fate of poor 2nd Lieutenant Brecknell who lasted less than a day when he too, leading from the front, bought it in a similar fashion. I was not in his platoon but earlier that morning he had spoken to me about my PIAT, to which I was quite attached, and I had welcomed him to B Company. These German snipers were deadly – their victims rarely got away with a bullet wound.

Once resistance had ceased at Meinkingsburg, 3 RTR Group, less B Company 4 KSLI which had remained at Husum to secure the brigade's axis, pressed on to Lindsburg, which they reached at 2030 hours. An hour later it was captured, although by this time well alight, and after a hard day, 3 RTR Group harboured for the night in the area of the village. The Hitler Youth survivors of the day's running battles fought between Rehburg and Lindsburg retreated northwards with their walking wounded over the fields to Stöckse, where 5. SS-Kompanie had been billeted during training. Fearing for their village, the inhabitants received them with mixed emotions but as the young soldiers were so exhausted from battle and sleep deprivation the construction of defences was beyond them so their previous hosts gave them places to sleep and the opportunity of a good wash. This respite would not last long and in the small hours of 9 April they set-off for Steimbke, two miles to the north-east.

4 KSLI estimated that 80 Hitler Youth were killed and 120 wounded during the actions in the advance from Rehburg to Linsburg. Today, 42 lie buried in Husum and 23 in Linsburg, among them an unnamed *SS-Obersturmführer* (senior lieutenant). 11th Armoured's INTSUM for 8 April noted that the fighting quality of the Hitler Youth was very good and it was during the bitter skirmishes of this period that the youthful *SS* troopers were given the nickname 'Steel-Eyed Boys' by the soldiers of 11th Armoured.[52] The British advance to Linsburg had, however, succeeded in blocking one of their principal withdrawal routes to the Aller and many Hitler Youth were killed and captured, with only small groups escaping eastwards. With the British now dominating much of the area between the Weser and the Leine, trapped groups of Hitler Youth had to resort to desperate means of escape. For instance, an SS-Unterscharführer Komische and his men from the Marsch Kompanie obtained civilian clothing in order to slip through to their own lines, hiding their *soldbuches* in their boots so that they could prove they were soldiers if captured and hopefully avoid being shot as partisans. Nonetheless, very few reached the Aller.

8 April was also a tough day for 4 KSLI with 13 killed in action, and Major Edwards and 29 other ranks wounded; Edwards being the third company commander in five days to become a casualty. Ned Thornburn reflects on their casualties, particularly the officers, and the German resistance:[53]

> I was always conscious after Normandy that infantry were in short supply on the battlefield. We could not afford to write off anyone at all except for a good reason, and although the morale of our officers and men was terrific I suspect that it needed guiding a little in the right direction. We old stagers had learned the hard way in Normandy not to expose ourselves unless we had to, and as company commanders I preferred to get my whole company onto its objective a few minutes late rather than arrive on time with only half my men. I had also learnt early on

---

52 TNA WO 171/4184, 11th Armoured Division INTSUM.
53 Thornburn, *After Antwerp – The Long Haul to Victory*, pp.101–102.

at [Operation] GOODWOOD what a shattering effect the loss of a platoon commander, with whom the men identify themselves, can have on a sub-unit. A company commander, above all, has no permit to write himself off in front of his men...I get the feeling that the normal rapid advances may have engendered an optimism which bordered on recklessness. Clearly we had the Germans by the throat. What we may not have remembered was the capacity of the Germans for retrieving desperate situations and the stubbornness with which they would defend the most hopeless positions. Opposition might not be frequent, but whenever met it needed to be reconnoitred properly before the leading troops were committed.

While 3 RTR Group was fighting its way forward, 23 Hussars Group was forced to wait on the Weser's left bank as the continuing congestion on the right bank still prevented it crossing the Petershagen bridge. Eventually the situation improved allowing 8 RB to cross the bridge at 1100 hours, followed at 1730 hours by 23 Hussars; the group then rapidly moved via Loccum and Rehburg to Schneeren before being ordered to head north to clear the woods and the main road as far as the Meinkingsburg cross-roads, where later it would harbour for the night.

6th Airborne Division on the Leine

We will now return to 6th Airborne Division on the corps' right axis. With 5th Parachute Brigade consolidating its bridgeheads at Neustadt and Bordenau, at 0900 hours 3rd Parachute Brigade started to advance on its objective, the bridge at Ricklingen. The objective was very close to Second Army's boundary with US Ninth Army and it was recognised that US forces would need this crossing as the demolition of the nearby bridge carrying the *Autobahn* over the Leine was already impacting on their operations to capture Hannover.

In addition to 1 CAN Para advancing on Ricklingen from the west, to hasten the bridge's capture a force from B Squadron 15th Reconnaissance Regiment would be launched from the bridgehead at Bordenau on a *coup de main* operation involving an advance up the right bank, which had the twin advantages of avoiding German armour believed to be in Luthe and the possibility of gaining surprise by approaching the bridge from the rear. A mixed force commanded by Lieutenant Buck and consisting of parts of two carrier troops and the assault troop supported by mortars and a 6-pdr anti-tank gun duly set off at 0900 hours. Thirty minutes later they reached Bordenau, rushed the bridge, captured the demolition party, ordered it to cut the wires and withdraw the charges, and an hour later Buck reported the bridge secure. However, there was no sign of 1 CAN Para, the relief force, and in the early afternoon some shells began to fall around the area of the bridge; Buck and his force were becoming anxious as they had been in place for nearly four hours and the sound of heavy fighting was coming from Luthe, half a mile to the west. Unknown to Buck, this was 1 CAN Para's vanguard force which had made rapid progress towards Ricklingen but had then become involved in confused fighting with German forces, including a Panther, in the area of Luthe, a mile short of the bridge. Lieutenant Buck describes the events that unfolded at Ricklingen:[54]

> Another hour passed. Sergeant Matthews and I looked around the village. I asked some children if they had seen any of their soldiers and tanks. Apparently, they had seen one big tank and a few 'little tanks with no tops but big guns', which I assumed were self-propelled guns. These had gone along the road – the road from which the firing came – before we arrived in

---

54 Kemsley and Riesco, *Scottish Lion on Patrol* (Bristol: White Swan Press, 1950), pp.234–236.

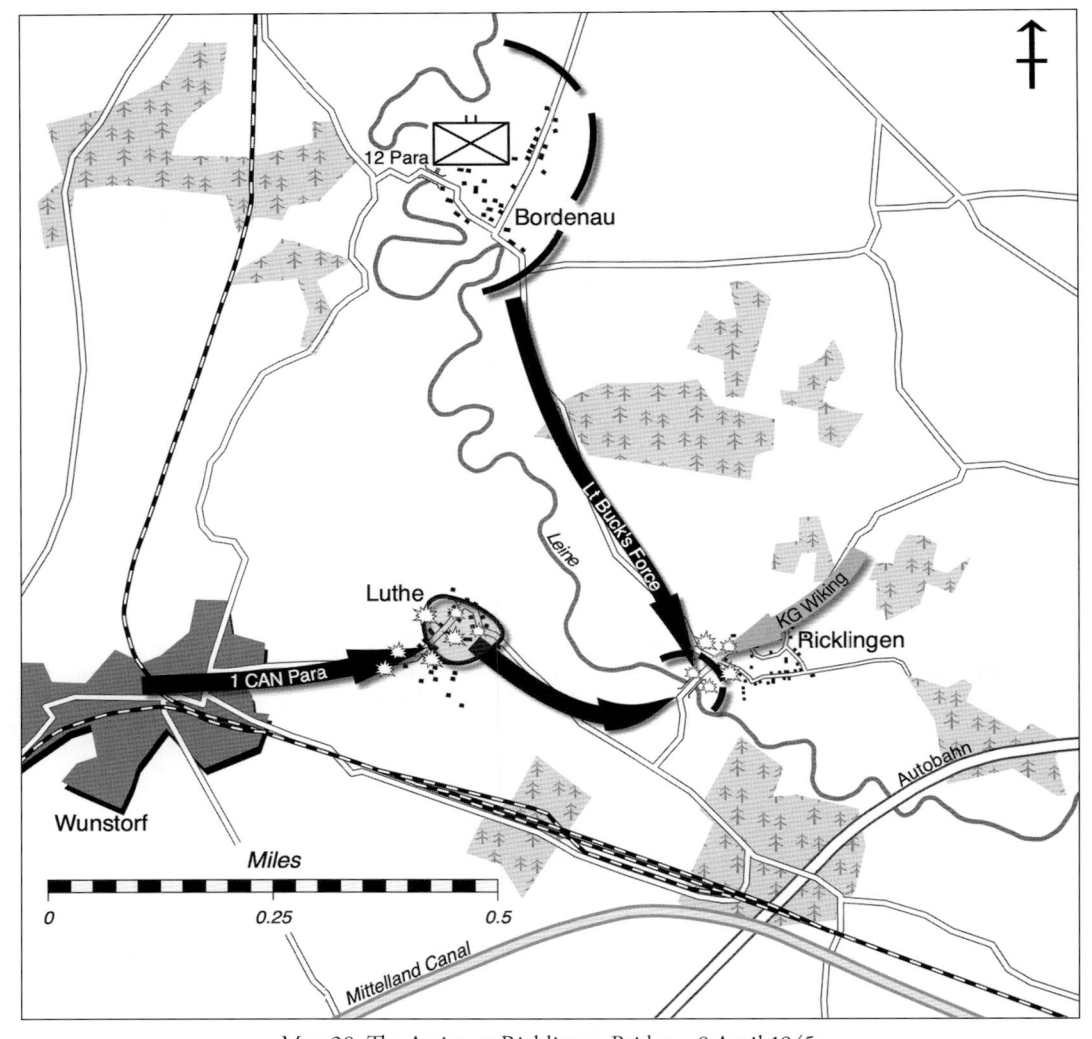

Map 28 The Action at Ricklingen Bridge – 8 April 1945.

the village. Matthews and I felt a little uncomfortable as we had found track marks on the road. From their width, the distance between them and the depth of the imprint we could only draw one conclusion – Tiger. I made the village policeman put everyone in the village into cellars, as I expected trouble.

Sure enough it came!

About 2 o'clock I was sending a wireless report to squadron HQ from my carrier, which was about twenty yards along from the crossroads in the village, when I heard the clanking of tank tracks. Sergeant Matthews ran up and, pointing behind me, said, 'Don't look now, but I think that's a tank.' I looked round quickly. About 40 yards away, just coming around the corner was a terrible looking monster with Tiger written all over it. The 88 was pointing right at us and the muzzle-brake looked the size of a railway engine. The back of my throat felt parched.

My PIAT firer got two or three shots off but was over-keen and missed the vulnerable parts. The tank blazed away and we did not see the poor lad again.

I ran along to the next wireless carrier, out of the line of fire and made a desperate request for tanks to be sent up to support us. I felt sure we would stand a good chance of bagging this Tiger if a couple of Churchills could be sent up. 'No tanks are available,' came the reply. We were on our own; the PIAT was out of action and the 6-pdr was covering a different road.

The Tiger fired its 88 at point blank range into the carrier from which I had come and the old carrier met its end in a shower of sparks, flames and a cloud of white smoke. The tank slewed round and I was again in the line of fire. I ran to the next wireless carrier and asked for artillery to lay a concentration on Ricklingen. We were prepared to risk being hit ourselves just to have the enemy hit too, so that the bridge we had held on to so long might be saved. For various reasons the concentration could not be given, and in a way we were relieved. By now the Tiger was shooting up our vehicles one by one, and in its wake came two self-propelled guns – the ones which had already shelled us from a distance – and three or four half-tracks. I went to one of my half-tracks behind some houses to wireless a report to squadron HQ. All the time my chaps were valiantly firing off everything they had – Brens, Stens, rifles anything to keep the enemy at bay. I was proud to be in command of such grand men. The fire held-off the enemy half-tracks and the self-propelled guns and made the Tiger keep its lid closed. As I spoke on the wireless at the rear of the half-track there was a blinding flash and a noise of tearing metal. The engine had received a direct hit. We hurriedly abandoned the vehicle and flames took possession.

The Tiger reached the bridge and tried to make it unusable by firing its 88 at the parapet. This proved ineffective and it withdrew into the village followed by a renewed burst of small-arms from my party on the left bank.

We got on the road by which we had arrived – the road where the 6-pdr was sited. The Tiger saw us and gave chase. It seemed a good idea to try to manhandle the 6-pdr round and deal smartly with the Tiger at almost point-blank range. We heaved at the gun, one of the gunners nursing an AP shot. But the Tiger opened fire and we had to abandon the gun as we could not turn it in time. The Tiger trundled up and ran over the gun, leaving it useless.

With still no sign of 1 CAN Para and ammunition running low, Lieutenant Buck decided he had to warn his squadron headquarters of the situation and so, with the wireless destroyed, he took a party from his group on the right bank and set off on foot at the double back to Bordenau, leaving the group on the left bank to await the Canadians. Not long after Buck departed they arrived, having managed to work their way forward under cover of smoke and fire from supporting Churchills, and crossed the Ricklingen bridge just in time to see a *Jagdpanther* and three other armoured vehicles pulling out. While the Canadians consolidated in the area of the bridge, the B Squadron crews, who had retreated to the comparative safety of nearby woods, began to emerge and count the cost of the action at Ricklingen: four men missing and seven carriers and three half-tracks destroyed, but the bridge was intact. During the battle a variety of armoured vehicles were reported: a Tiger, a Panther, a Ferdinand (reported by 1 CAN Para) and self-propelled guns. The Tiger and Panther were probably correctly identified and it is probable that these were the vehicles remaining from Kampfgruppe Schulze. While the Ferdinand was a mis-identification, the reports of self-propelled guns were accurate as Kampfgruppe Wiking, an improvised grouping from 5. SS-Panzer-Division 'Wiking' commanded by SS-Hauptsturmführer Nicolussi-Leck and consisting of seven *Jagdpanthers*, 13 SdKfz 251 and 150 men, was active on the western approaches to Hannover area at this time. The involvement of Kampfgruppe Wiking is corroborated by an entry in the 5th Parachute Brigade log,[55] which recorded civilians reporting three tanks with infantry, apparently *Waffen-SS*, moving north on the Leine's left bank.

---

55 TNA WO 171/4307, 1430 hours 8 April 1945.

While B Squadron 15th Reconnaissance Regiment was involved at Ricklingen bridge, during the afternoon C Squadron was ordered to contact US forces. The squadron subsequently reported that the Americans intended switching their left axis northwards to use the Ricklingen bridge as all others over the Leine in their sector were blown. However, the accounts of events at Ricklingen written by the participating units of the two nations are contradictory. On the British side the 3rd Parachute Brigade war diary records that following the bridge's capture on 8 April, it was handed over to the 'American Cavalry Corps' [sic] and notes that the Americans lost one tank and some other vehicles to shelling during the handover while 1 CAN Para war diary simply records the bridge's handover to US 9th Army taking place just before dark. The 'American Cavalry Corps' was the US 11th Cavalry Group and its history states that the Ricklingen bridge was captured by the 44th Cavalry Recon Squadron on 7 April, ie the day before B Squadron's action at the bridge.[56] The history records that as most of the 44th's strength was committed to its flank mission, in the aftermath of the bridge's capture it could only be lightly held and the group's second squadron, the 36th, had to be directed to assist, reaching the bridge late on 8 April under heavy shell and mortar fire. A and B Troops were pushed across the river, 'routed' the enemy on the right bank, secured a bridgehead and in so doing captured eleven 8.8cm guns and a '75mm SP gun.' None of the British accounts make any mention of US forces at the bridge when they arrived on 8 April, while conversely the 11th Cavalry Group history makes no mention of the British handing over the bridge to them that day. As the British war diaries are contemporary primary sources they are arguably the more credible, whereas the 11th Cavalry Group's history was written after the war, possibly with an eye to posterity. The 11th Cavalry's history mentions that the commanding general of 84th Infantry Division, Major General Bolling, was 'highly appreciative of the seizure of the Ricklingen bridge and commented that he fully expected to be delayed in crossing the river while a pontoon bridge was built.' To admit that the bridge was handed over on a plate by their allies was possibly not in 11th Cavalry Group's interest and a spiced-up version was given to the general and history!

At the same time as the parachute brigades were securing crossings on the Leine, the airlanding brigade spent the morning clearing the former bridgehead line, in particular the northern part of the Schaumburg Forest as it was suspected that the German armour was holed up there. 12 Devon and 2 Oxf Bucks LI, supported by two 25-pdr batteries and a medium battery, began the clearance operation at 0900 hours but other than a bogged-in Panzer IV/70 found in the Friller Brink area, there was no sign of any German forces and by 1230 hours the operation had concluded. The brigade then moved east to harbour to the south-east of Rehburg.

Monday 9 April

9 April dawned a fine spring day. VIII Corps issued orders to 6th Airborne Division to continue to hold its bridgeheads over the Leine at Bordenau and Neustadt and operate energetically on the Leine's right bank. By 1215 hours the sappers had bridged the demolished span of Neustadt bridge with a Class 40 Bailey section, providing a second crossing for the corps to exploit eastwards, and 6th Airborne, led by 3rd Parachute Brigade, rapidly advanced beyond the Leine. A link to an online video of the brigade's advance beyond the Leine on 10 April is at Appendix A, Serial 9.

Despite its progress, the airborne division was ordered to concentrate and allow 15th Scottish Division to take over the advance to Celle and beyond. Although we will now leave 6th Airborne

---

56 Lieutenant George Haynes, *11th Cavalry Group from the Roer to the Elbe, 1944–1945* (Nuremburg: Entwurf, Druck Union-Werk, 1945), pp.63–65.

as it plays no further part in the battle for the Aller Line, there would be no let-up for the division during the final weeks and it will play a major role in Operation ENTERPRISE (the Elbe crossing) and the advance to Wismar on the Baltic, which it will capture on 2 May and where it will be at the war's end. 15th Scottish duly passed through the airborne division and took Celle against negligible resistance from Kampfgruppe Scherer on the morning of 12 April. The division also captured Celle airfield, used by NSGr. 1 (Nord), and an online link of film of the historic town and captured airfield is at Appendix A, Serial 11.

11th Armoured Division advance to the Leine

On the corps' left axis, 11th Armoured Division was ordered by VIII Corps to secure a divisional bridgehead and construct a Class 40 bridge over the Leine as a preliminary to advancing to the Aller. With all road bridges in its area blown, the quickest way for 11th Armoured to achieve this would be to use 6th Airborne's captured bridge at Bordenau (the Neustadt bridge still being under construction) then head down the Leine's right bank. Accordingly, Major General Roberts ordered 159th Infantry Brigade, with both its groups now on the Leine, to secure the bridgehead and then exploit to Schwarmstedt and the Aller. In the early morning, 15/19 Hussars Group set off from its harbour near Dudensen and crossed the Bordenau bridge. The group then advanced to Helstorf, meeting no resistance on the way, and here 1 Cheshire dug-in to provide security for 612 Field Squadron to begin building a bridge. Construction started at 1600 hours and from then on, working round the clock and alternating with 13 Field Squadron, the sappers strove to complete a bridge as soon as possible for 11th Armoured's use. Although the original intention was to build a Bailey pontoon bridge, the scarcity of pontoon equipment forced a change of decision and a 170-foot, DT Bailey bridge was built instead.[57]

While 15/19 Hussars Group was moving to Bordenau, the members of 2. SS-Kompanie still holding out in the wood at Rodewald were subjected to a barrage of HE and smoke rounds fired by A Squadron 2 FF Yeo's Comets. Under this choking cover, the infantrymen of B Company 1 Hereford were able to reach the wood and mop-up the remaining resistance with little trouble. With the southern end of Rodewald secure, 2 FF Yeo Group concentrated in the area to await orders for operations on the Leine's right bank. The surviving members of 2. SS-Kompanie withdrew across the Lichten Moor to Rethem, leaving behind eight dead and many wounded comrades, and the exhausted young soldiers were surprised not to be attacked while they headed north. The reason was twofold: 11th Armoured's attention was fixed on its next task, the seizure of crossings over the Leine and Aller, and the Lichten Moor was free of British troops as it was in XII Corps' area and the corps had yet to cross the Weser.

Although the youths of 2. SS-Kompanie were able to escape the British, others were less fortunate, as SS-Oberscharführer Dargel of 5. SS-Kompanie describes:[58]

> We were on the outskirts of the village as it started to get light. I believe it was Bevensen, which was already occupied by the British. We crept quickly into the woods to the left of the village and posted four sentries, while the rest enjoyed the opportunity to catch up on some sleep. In the wood we discussed our position, we being three *Unterscharführer* and 28

---

57 DT stood for 'double truss, triple storey' and comprised two trusses or panels alongside each other in three storeys. Depending on width of gap to be crossed and maximum weight to be carried, Bailey bridges could be expanded as necessary and by use of a simple matrix formula the make-up of the bridge required could be calculated. The matrix shows that a 170-foot span with a Class 40 restriction required a DT bridge.
58 Buchwald, *Endkampf.*

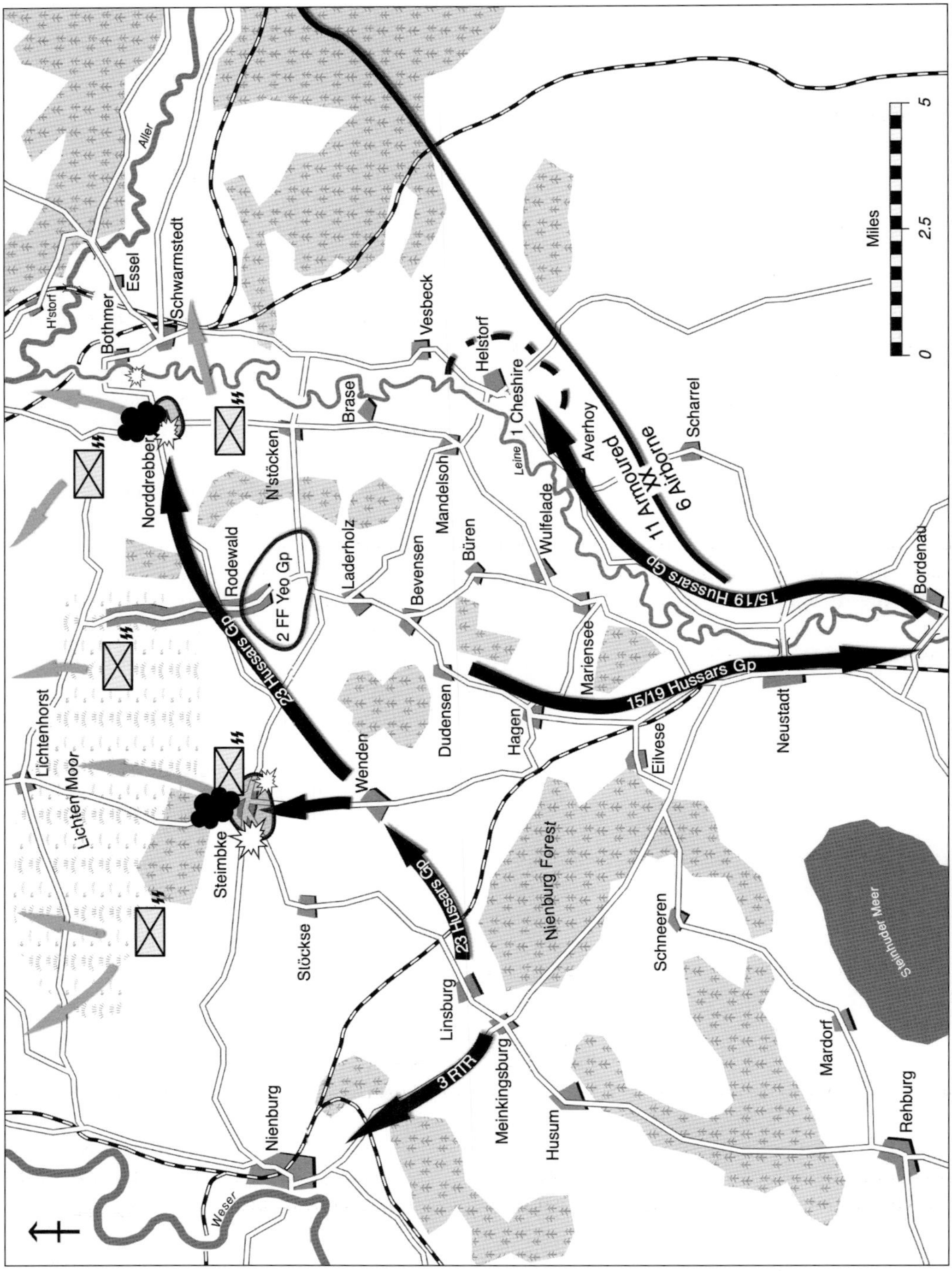

Map 29 11th Armoured Division's Advance to the Leine – 9 April 1945.

grenadiers. Through binoculars we observed the British tank attack on Steimbke. Tragically the defenders no longer had anti-tank weapons. As darkness closed in we broke away towards Lichtenhorst. In the next village we were compelled to beg for bread, but nobody could nor would feed 30 men. British military traffic was heavy on the road [Reichsstrasse 214] but despite the noise the British became aware of our presence and fired at us. The group then became separated as we attempted to escape over the moor and, when it grew light, the British combed through the area, surrounding us and taking us prisoner.

Owing to the distances to be covered during the Germans' withdrawal, the walking wounded and injured soldiers caused particular problems, slowing progress and imposing an emotional drain on their comrades. For those wounded who reached the Aller at Rethem, the medical orderlies of 2. Marine-Infanterie-Division provided rudimentary treatment, after which those who were no longer able to fight were evacuated to the *Reservelazarett* (general hospital) in Walsrode. Other less taxing problems arose during the withdrawal, for instance, some of the young soldiers lost their mess tins and cutlery, not only did this infuriate their commanders but also resulted in them struggling to eat their rations on the rare occasions that they received any. Fortunately for the miscreants, the noodle-soup tended to arrive in milk churns so the lids could be used as bowls, although the noodles had to picked out by finger. Groups that did not manage to cross the Aller at Rethem were faced with greater challenges than lack of mess tins. At Brase, 20 soldiers of 6. SS-Kompanie tried to cross the Leine using a barn door as a makeshift raft. Their efforts were ineffective and resulted in their being tipped into the river and then, to avoid hypothermia, having to rush to the nearest farmhouse to dry themselves and their clothes. The female farmer took pity on the young men and also tried, unsuccessfully, to find them some civilian clothing. With the British closing on the Leine, early on 10 April this group made its escape down the left bank of the river under cover of fog.

On 29th Armoured's axis there was still fighting to be done. At 0700 hours 23 Hussars Group left Meinkingsburg and with A Squadron and G Company 8 RB leading moved north to Linsburg, where 3 RTR Group had fought the day before. Noel Bell describes some final mopping-up in Linsburg:[59]

Like all villages the regiment 'liberated' it was ablaze from one end to the other, only a few houses being spared. As we approached, we could see flames leaping in the darkness and smouldering pieces of thatch drifting aimlessly through the air like slow-motion tracer. Our friends [3 RTR] had not had time to clear the village properly before their departure, as we soon found out for ourselves. Prisoners were brought out from all sorts of odd places, like under beds and wood-piles and, more conventionally, from the cellars. Three separate searches over the same ground were necessary to account for all prisoners, so well were they concealed.

With Linsburg clear the group headed north-east to Wenden. At 0730 hours, as they emerged into some open country to the west of Wenden, tanks from A Squadron spotted two half-tracks towing 8.8cm Flak pulling out of a wood. The German crews appeared oblivious to the British presence and it took only three shots to destroy both targets. The guns probably belonged to Batterie 4./132, as this battery disappears from the Flak-Regiment 122(E) record during the withdrawal from the Weser, and the half-tracks were probably SdKfz 251 from SS-A.u.E.Btl. 12 'HJ'. With the targets destroyed, A Squadron Group pressed on northwards, passing through 3 RTR Group to close on Steimbke, at first sight very tranquil as Noel Bell of G Company describes:[60]

---

59   Bell, *From the Beaches to the Baltic*, pp.110–111.
60   Bell, *From the Beaches to the Baltic*, p.111.

Steimbke still shelters in its quiet valley, although the roofs are now tiled not thatched. Photograph taken in 2015. (Author)

Steimbke looked peaceful enough sheltering in a quiet valley under a warm morning sky. The small cottages with their thatched roofs, and a small pretty church presented a picture of complete tranquillity.

Soon this picture violently changed. At 0840 hours 4 Troop of A Squadron accompanied by 12 Platoon and a section of carriers closed on the village but were met with a storm of small-arms' and *Panzerfaust* fire. The defenders of Steimbke, which had reached the village shortly before the arrival of 23 Hussars Group, principally comprised members of the Marsch Kompanie and a platoon from 2. SS-Kompanie commanded by SS-Unterscharführer Chales de Beaulieu, and some exhausted soldiers of 5. SS-Kompanie. The Marsch Kompanie, probably now commanded by twenty-three year-old SS-Standartenoberjunker Bruno Szvdlowski,[61] had been ordered to hold Steimbke for as long as possible to cover the northwards withdrawal of the remainder of the battalion.

Although the Comets and 12 Platoon were able to break into the village, it was soon apparent that it was much too strongly held and their move down the main street made them increasingly vulnerable to being cut-off. During the latter part of the morning the small force was therefore ordered to pull out and plans were made for a two-company attack, preceded by a fire plan from 13 RHA and the battalion's mortars. During this initial engagement Szvdlowski received a gunshot wound to the stomach and was evacuated by villagers to the shelter of a cellar. Severely wounded and in urgent need of medical care, they moved him back onto the street and covered him in a white blanket in the hope that he would receive attention from medical staff from either side. Szvdlowski was later found dead with his skull broken open.

Prior to the deliberate attack, Steimbke was encircled on three sides by the tanks of A Squadron: 3 Troop covered the west part of the village, 2 Troop the east and squadron headquarters the south; 1 Troop provided protection further to the west in case other Germans, withdrawing to

---

61 A *Waffen-SS* senior, officer candidate.

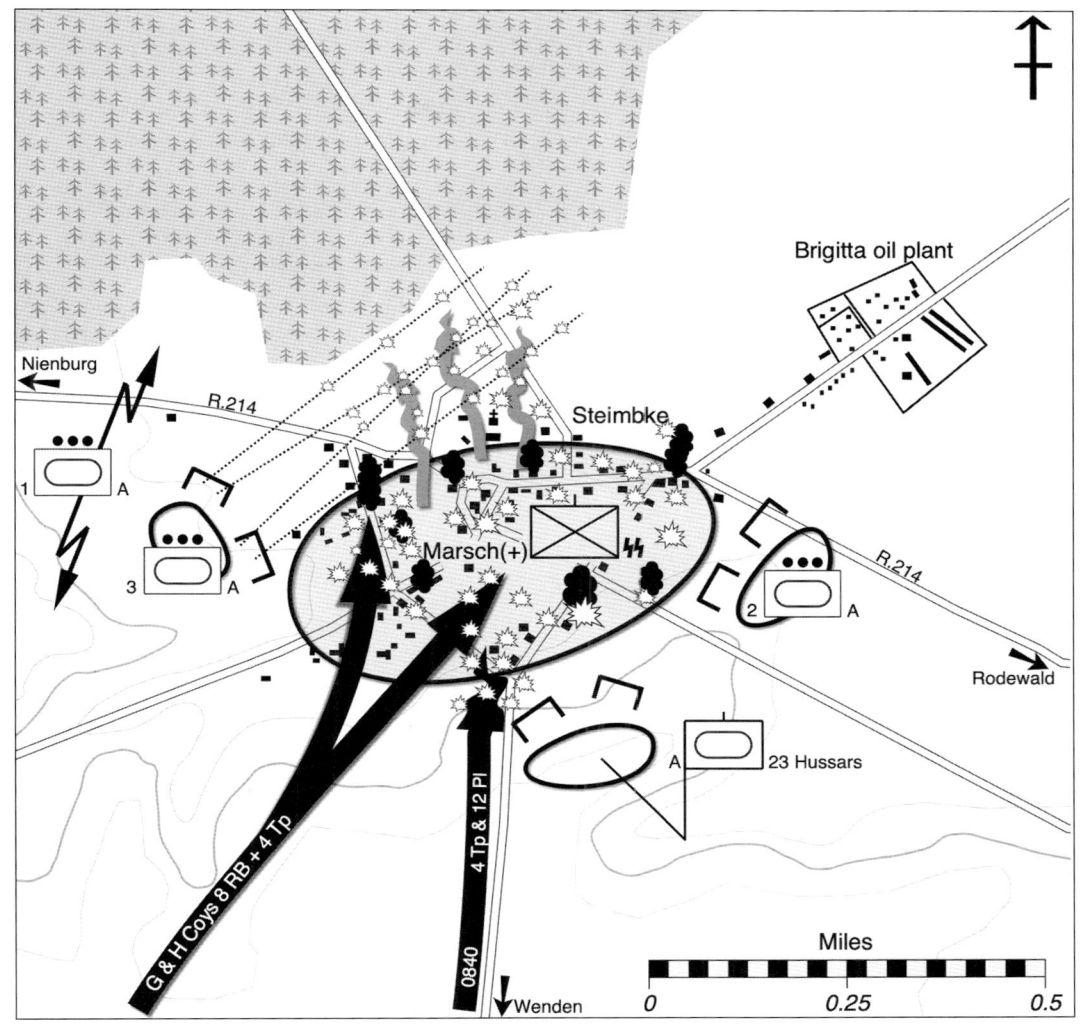

Map 30 The Battle for Steimbke – 9 April 1945.

the Leine, caught A Squadron Group's attack in the left flank. After a pause, the indirect fire dropped on Steimbke; once it lifted it was followed by the Comets engaging the doomed village with HE and Besa fire to cover the move of G and H Companies 8 RB supported by 4 Troop. The battle for Steimbke now began in earnest and raged throughout the afternoon. Despite the firepower ranged against them, the Hitler Youth fought tenaciously and the companies had to clear the village house by house with liberal use of grenades. At 1745 hours a Comet from 4 Troop, commanded by Corporal Anderson, was brewed. The 23 Hussars' history describes how it was hit by a *Panzerfaust*, but the regimental radio log records a message at 1745 hours from F Company: 'One big boy brewed. I think that was caused by small-arms' fire catching petrol on back.' It is questionable why a tank was carrying pack fuel on its decks when action was likely, and the loss seems sufficiently embarrassing for the history to doctor the account. Eventually the young German soldiers were forced to the northern perimeter of the village but here they were faced by open ground, which they would have to cross before they could reach the relative safety of the woods beyond. As they broke cover the Comets engaged them, resulting in many being killed or wounded. With a pressing need for the 23 Hussars Group to reach the Leine, the group did not conclude the battle for Steimbke and it departed eastwards, leaving the village's final clearance that evening to become, as we will shortly hear, the responsibility of 3 RTR Group.

8 RB's diarist recorded that no quarter was asked or given during the fighting and there was no sympathy for the young soldiers of the *Waffen-SS*, as 23 Hussars' history recounts:[62]

> From the village, sullen greasy-looking striplings with the *SS* flash came running, hands raised, their faces contorted with pain whenever the heavy boot of a rifleman was applied. Steimbke, smoking and wrecked, was clear after a model operation, which cost the enemy 150 casualties.

Twenty-one Germans were killed during the fighting of 9 April and are buried in Steimbke's war cemetery next to its church. Fifteen are from SS-A.u.E.Btl. 12 'HJ', with their gravestones bearing the inscription 'SS.PZ.GR.BATL.12', the only cemetery in the area acknowledging the presence of the *Waffen-SS*.

Also buried at Steimbke are a *Flakhelferin* and Dr Ernst Linka,[63] a *Marine-Stabsarzt* (naval doctor). Why a naval doctor was present at Steimbke is unknown, but perhaps he belonged to 2. Marine-Infanterie-Division, recently arrived on the Aller, and had been sent forward to help the many wounded Hitler Youth. 8 RB also sustained casualties, among them Lieutenant Eric Yetman, the commander of 12 Platoon and holder of the Military Cross, who was mortally wounded. From the British perspective the 'model operation' involved razing 53 buildings to the ground. In 1945 this was commonplace against villages offering resistance and few British had much compunction in destroying them if it reduced casualties. Additionally, the presence of *Waffen-SS* in Steimbke would have done little for either the village's or its defenders' chances of survival. Battles against the *Waffen-SS* had always been bitter and, despite their age, the Hitler Youth of SS-A.u.E.Btl.12 'HJ' would have been seen as no different to any other members of the *Waffen-SS*. The organisation's reputation for aggression and brutality led to few chances being taken with those wearing the twin lightning bolts on their collars. Additionally, the frequent arrogance of captured *Waffen-SS* did little to endear them to their British captors and declarations that they were happy to die for the *Führer* often resulted in them doing so. 23 Hussars' regimental history pulls no punches in its description of the Hitler Youth and the regiment's attitude to fighting them:[64]

A gravestone in Steimbke churchyard of an unknown member of SS-A.u.E.Btl. 12 HJ. (Author)

---

62 Anon., *The Story of the 23rd Hussars 1940–1946*, p.228.
63 A *Flakhelferin* was a female auxiliary in the *Flak* arm. Originally office staff, as manpower shortages bit, females were increasingly employed as crews for searchlight, sound-locating and radar units and for duties on *Flak* battery sites. They served in *Flakwaffen-Helferinnen* units.
64 Anon., *The Story of the 23rd Hussars 1940–1946*, p.220.

These young thugs fought true to their tradition, savagely, and absolutely without any code of honour or fair play, which made their opponents feel they were not killing other men, but exterminating vermin.

The regimental headquarters would have fuelled the loathing when it told the squadrons early that morning that: '12 SS [sic] had been shooting ambulances and medical officers and that no mercy was to be shown.' The reference to attacks on medical staff is reflected in an entry in 6th Airborne Division's HQ RAMC war diary, which recorded that on 8 April an ambulance car had been destroyed by a *Panzerfaust* and another captured in an ambush,[65] and it is possible that the news of these losses generated the savage reaction.

While the majority of 23 Hussars Group was committed at Steimbke, B Squadron and F Company 8 RB were sent eastwards on Reichsstrasse 214 to seize the bridge over the Leine at Bothmer. The group was followed by C Squadron, now back with the regiment following its attachment to 1st Commando Brigade at Leese. When B Squadron Group reached Norddrebber it had a sharp clash with *Panzerfaust* teams from Marine-Füsilier-Bataillon 2, operating as an outpost position for their defensive positions in the Schwarmstedt area. The leading carrier from F Company was knocked out and an anti-tank gun engaged 4 Troop from B Squadron as it neared the river. 2 Troop tried to provide support but Lieutenant Vickers' Comet was hit by a 7.5cm round low on the right-hand side of the hull between the engine and turret. The crew baled-out sufficiently quickly to avoid becoming casualties when a second round penetrated the right side of the Comet's turret in its dead-centre. 23 Hussars' war diary describes the marine defenders of Norddrebber as 'fresh troops and full of spirit.' These marines were probably the first from 2. Marine-Infanterie-Division to be encountered by Second Army and for the next two weeks the division's marines would dominate events and British operations in this area of Germany. Once this contact was concluded, with many of Norddrebber's buildings reduced to ashes, the recce troop and B Squadron advanced to the bridge carrying Reichsstrasse 214 over the Leine at Bothmer, only to see it blow up in front of them. Later they joined the remainder of the regimental group to harbour in the area between Rodewald and Norddrebber.

Slipping back a few hours, at mid-day on 9 April 3 RTR Group was ordered to exploit to Nienburg. Although the town was in XII Corps' area of responsibility, as the corps was not yet across the Weser 11th Armoured's left flank, and progressively its rear, were becoming increasingly open as its brigades pushed on to the east so the decision was taken to capture Nienburg without further delay. C Squadron 3 RTR was ordered to move to the town from its harbour area near Linsburg and by 1200 hours the Comets were nearing Langendamm, former home of the administrative companies of SS-A.u.E.Btl. 12 'HJ'. Thirty minutes later Major Jock Balharrie, the squadron leader, sent a troop down the main road towards the town centre and at a road-block on the outskirts the troop leader met the *Bürgermeister*, who declared Nienburg an open town in no position to offer resistance. The *Bürgermeister* clearly felt safe from fanatics and summary execution; other civilians attempting to do the same elsewhere in Germany were not so fortunate. Major Balharrie, by now on the scene, accepted the town's surrender and that of the large *Luftwaffe* ammunition depot, Lufthauptmunitionsanstalt 3/XI Nienburg in the nearby woods, and with no sign of resistance he and two troops of tanks drove to the town centre. With Nienburg clearly not a threat, they soon departed to rejoin the regiment. At 1600 hours 3 RTR Group was ordered to relieve 23 Hussars Group, still mopping-up the Steimbke area, to allow it to press on to the area of Norddrebber on the Leine eight miles to the east. By 1830 hours the handover was complete and 23 Hussars Group headed off eastwards. Steimbke was finally cleared later that evening and

---

65 TNA WO 17/360, HQ RAMC 6th Airborne Division war diary.

found at the east end of the village was the Brigitta oil facility, the focus for crude pumped from the Steimbke-Rodewald field. 3 RTR Group then spent two quiet days in the area of Steimbke and the nearby village of Wenden awaiting the next call to action; it would not be long in coming.

As the Aller would require an assault crossing, and beyond it lay significant areas of forest, Major General Roberts recognised he had insufficient infantry and so once again asked VIII Corps to place 1st Commando Brigade, currently catching its breath following the tough fighting in the Stolzenau bridgehead, under his command. The brigade was duly warned to prepare for operations and at 1500 hours ordered to move immediately to Helstorf. 3 Cdo and 46 (RM) Cdo were trucked forward during the late afternoon, crossed the recently-completed Neustadt bridge and concentrated on the Leine's right bank in the area of the villages of Averhoy and Vesbeck. 45 (RM) Cdo and 6 Cdo would follow the next day once they had completed the clearance of the Nienburg Forest, bypassed by 11th Armoured during its eastward advance.

While the British closed up to the Leine, the companies and platoons of SS-A.u.E.Btl.12 'HJ' had become increasingly fragmented as their withdrawal progressed, not only as a result of clashes with 11th Armoured Division but also from the effects of a multitude of difficulties ranging from the going to exhaustion. Knowledge of their movements during the latter stage of the withdrawal is sketchy, particularly with regard to where and how they crossed the Leine and the Aller, but what is known is that the speed of 11th Armoured's advance forced the bulk of the battalion to retreat in a north-easterly direction across the Lichten Moor to Rethem and its bridge over the Aller. On 10 April groups were still heading across the moor and a patrol from A Squadron Inns of Court clashed with Hitler Youth in strength in the woods north of Lichtenhorst and had to pull back. Owing to the demolition of the bridges at Niedernstöcken and Bothmer, the groups withdrawing in a more easterly direction crossed the Leine using civilian boats or improvised rafts, methods which would have been very slow and, as we have heard, meeting with varying degrees of success. The Aller was then crossed using the Eickeloh ferry or over the lock gates near Hademstorf.

With 11th Armoured preparing to secure a bridgehead over the Aller, we will now leave VIII Corps, turn the calendar back four days and look northwards to XII Corps and its operations to cross the Weser and Aller.

6

'Men Who Enjoyed Dying': XII Corps across the Weser 5–10 April 1945

From the outline of 2. Marine-Infanterie-Division's deployment to the Weser and Aller described in Chapter 2 and depicted on Map 7, it will be recalled that Marine-Grenadier-Regiment 5 was allocated the defence of the Rethem sector, including forces deployed forward to Hoya. Hoya has an ancient lineage and gives its name to Grafschaft Hoya (County of Hoya), originally a state of the Holy Roman Empire but annexed by Prussia during the unification of Germany in 1866. The Weser dominates the town, which in 1945 was equally divided between the two banks but with the town hall and *Schloss* (manor house) on the right.

Hoya's two bridges are only some 200 yards apart and are important crossings for rail and road traffic. The town's principal association with the *Wehrmacht* was the presence on the right bank of a *Luftwaffe* base with a grass runway, which over the war years had hosted a variety of units but most recently night-fighters. An Ultra decrypt recorded that twelve Bf 109 of IV./JG 300 left Hoya on the morning of 29 March for Alperstedt airfield near Erfurt,[1] thus avoiding part of a US Eighth Air Force mission on 4 April, which involved thirty-seven B-17 bombers attacking Hoya airfield as a secondary target, densely cratering the southern part but leaving the town largely unscathed.[2]

Some 10 miles east of Hoya is the town of Rethem, situated on the left bank of the Aller and the marine division's point of main effort for the defence of the Aller Line. In 1945 the town consisted of two distinct parts: first the Old Town close to the Aller bridge and comprising historic brick and timber buildings laid out in a grid of streets and, secondly, the nineteenth century developments, collectively known as the New Town, which spread along three roads radiating from the town centre. Rethem is an important crossing point of the Aller and its steel girder-arch road bridge carried a major trunk road, Reichsstrasse 209.

This road originates in Nienburg and after Rethem makes its way in a generally north-easterly orientation via Walsrode, Fallingbostel, Soltau and Lüneburg to Schwarzenbek, its destination in Schleswig-Holstein; Reichsstrasse 209 would clearly be a major axis for the British. Rethem was on the locally important Allertalbahn railway,[3] connecting Gifhorn and Verden, and the proud owner of a station and sidings situated on a low embankment on the western edge of the town. In addition to its importance as a crossing point of the Aller, the town was the local centre for the outlying villages and hamlets on both banks of the Aller. In 1939 its population was 1,586.

---

1. DEFE 3/562, BT 9297. JG 300 was a fighter *Jagdgeschwader* with its origins as a specialised night-fighter unit flying *Wilde Sau* missions. By 1945 it had become a standard, defence of the *Reich*, day-fighter unit.
2. TNA AIR 40/836, USAAF Operation 926, Hoya (and other airfields).
3. The railway was closed in 1995 and is now no more.

Hoya road bridge over the Weser with the *Schloss* to its right. Apart from the modern style of bridge, a scene little-changed from 1945. Photograph taken in 2014. (Author)

A pre-War postcard of Rethem's bridge.

Rethem railway station on its low embankment. Photograph taken in 1992. (Author)

Although at the start of the war life in Rethem altered little, the town was gradually affected, with the issue of ration cards for food and clothing and the imposition of the blackout being early measures. Soon its men were called up for *Wehrmacht* service, and following the successful conclusion of the Polish campaign they were replaced in the local agricultural workforce by PoWs. Each night after work the Poles had to return to their camp established in the hall of Gasthof Hillmann near the Aller bridge. In the summer of 1940 French prisoners joined the Poles and following the invasion of the Soviet Union in 1941 an influx of Russian prisoners swelled the number of agricultural slave labourers. The civilian population was given strict instructions not to fraternise with the prisoners and they were forbidden to eat at the same tables; these orders were however seldom followed. By the latter war years the quality and quantity of the nation's food had declined markedly, but in the rural areas there was always sufficient and there was none of the privations experienced by the city dwellers. The inhabitants were called upon to help the war effort by providing raw materials and on 19 February 1941 the bells of its church, the St. Marien Kirche, fell victim to one such drive. Between December of that year and January 1942 large-scale collections of materials useful to the war effort and clothing for the troops on the East Front were made. During these drives, conducted by Hitler Youth, the young people chanted as they went from house to house: 'Rags, bones, iron and paper. We collect everything, everything.'[4]

The inhabitants first came into contact with their army in 1939 when troops were quartered in a hutted RAD camp built before the war near the Aller. The RAD labourers left in 1938 to work

---

4   Wilhelm Richter, *Aufzeichnungen zu den Kriegsereignissen im April 1945 an Weser, Aller und im westlichen Teil der Lüneburger-Heide unter besonderer Berücksichtigung der Kampfhandlungen im Gebiet von Rethem/ Aller* (Unpublished, 1967), p.74.

on the West Wall, leaving the camp empty until 1940 when, after the fall of France, the need to quarter troops back in the homeland reached a peak and several companies stayed in the camp while others were billeted in the town. During the summer of 1942 a 200-strong *Waffen-SS* unit occupied the huts and quartering then continued irregularly until 1943, when the need for extra accommodation in the *Reich* ended owing to the fronts' limitless demand for manpower. By 1945 the town's population showed a strong bias towards women, the very young and the very old as most of the male inhabitants of fighting age had gone to war. Despite the change to its population, the pattern of rural life altered little and it was the war in the air that brought the town closest to the fighting.

The air war had started timidly enough with British leaflet raids in March 1940, but by 1942 it had gathered pace and in that summer the townsfolk experienced their first direct involvement when a British bomber was shot down in flames over Rethem. The plane crashed near the Fährsee on the Aller's right bank and the Australian pilot was captured by soldiers of the Marine-Kraftfahrzeug-Abteilung, a naval transport unit in Hülsen, the next village downstream from Rethem. This unit came to Hülsen in 1941 and was responsible for moving ammunition, principally mines and torpedo warheads, to the naval bases in the north from magazines established in the local worked-out potash mines. On 9 November 1942 the area suffered its first damage when incendiaries and HE bombs, probably jettisoned, hit Hülsen destroying three houses and damaging more. A year later, with the air war intensifying, Sahlberger, the mayor of Rethem and also an air-raid warden, had issued a reminder to a local population he deemed insufficiently obedient to air-raid warnings:[5]

> Rethem (Aller), 20 Oct 1943
> Subject: Behaviour on Air-Raid Warnings
>
> It has been noted that a large part of the population behaves irresponsibly during air-raid warnings. Therefore more severe measures to adhere to air-raid discipline and to protect the population have been ordered. The Reichsluftschutzbund (RLD) has explained hundreds and hundreds of times what is to be done and to be avoided during an air-raid warning, ie on hearing the alarm take cover, take children to a safe place, clear roads, stop and park vehicles of any kind, close shops until hearing the all-clear signal.
>
> In future anyone met on the streets during an alarm will have to expect to be fined.
>
> After receiving construction material, the completion of slit trenches is to be carried out as fast as possible. Until then you have to look for adequate cover yourself. The largest part of the air-raid shelter in the Bünte can now be used and is available to anyone who has not got adequate cover.
>
> The orders of the holders of the blue RLD arm-band have to be obeyed implicitly. As of today the security service, wearing a white arm-band, will be on patrol during every air-raid warning and will report anybody who violates air-raid orders for punishment.
>
> Signed: Sahlberger

The threat from the air drove other changes and Rethem posted two men, one to the Old Town and one to the New, to act as night-time air-raid wardens; the town also received its own anti-aircraft defence when a light *Flak* gun was mounted on a wooden tower built near the Aller. The wardens were also tasked to observe enemy air activity and check suspicious people and from June 1944 were supplemented by two Hitler Youth to run messages. The inhabitants witnessed

---

5   Wilhelm Richter, *Aufzeichnungen zu den Kriegsereignissen im April 1945*, pp.77–78.

in awe the glow on the night horizons from the great incendiary fires burning in Hannover and Bremen and by day watched the American bomber streams battling their way to and from their targets deep in the *Reich*. In May 1944 they accepted into their homes the first evacuees from the devastated cities, and during the summer jettisoned incendiaries set fire to the local moors. From the second half of 1943 the enemy's air attacks began to have a far more direct effect on local life as Allied fighters now began to sweep across Germany attacking opportunity targets. On 2 November 1944 an Allied fighter straffed the Verden to Schwarmstedt train as it was passing Wohlendorf on the Allertalbahn, killing one woman and wounding six other passengers. Eight days later another train on the line was treated similarly at Wahnebergen and 20 passengers and station staff were killed and 40 wounded. While this was a calamity, it was dwarfed by an attack which took place locally on 15 October 1944. At 0930 hours a train carrying torpedo warheads was stationary alongside a passenger train at Lindwedel station to the south-east of Schwarmstedt (see Map 10) when they were attacked by Allied fighters. The attack detonated the warheads, completely destroying eight carriages, blasting a crater 80 yards long and 40 feet deep, and killing hundreds of passengers, villagers and slave labourers from Stalag 357. It caused serious damage to many buildings in Lindwedel over half a mile from the station and the explosion was heard 20 miles away. To this day a steel pipe remains embedded high in an oak tree as a testament to the ferocity of the explosion. Throughout the remainder of 1944 and on into 1945 the air war raged overhead and there was a steady toll of bombers and fighters crashing in the area.

In November 1944 all men aged between 16 and 60 were ordered to join the *Volkssturm*. This, however, was largely a superficial exercise as there were neither weapons nor uniforms for them, training was negligible and when the battle came to the Aller they would be of no use at all. In January 1945 the townsfolk accepted evacuees from the eastern territories who, in appalling conditions, had fled the vengeful Soviet Army. These people came from East Prussia, Pommern and Mecklenburg and their stories must have brought a deep gloom to the town.[6] The first indication of impending battle in the area occurred on Wednesday 4 April when the tanks of Kampfgruppe Schulze rumbled across the Aller bridge and headed off to the south-west. Four days later, the marines from Kapitän zur See Jordan's Marine-Grenadier-Regiment 5 began arriving in strength and immediately started to prepare battle positions. With their arrival the inhabitants' role as spectators of war changed irrevocably, and soon violently, to that of participants.

Deployment of Marine-Grenadier-Regiment 5 in the Rethem sector

Once the enemy had crossed the Weser, the two most likely approaches to Rethem were from the south-west using Reichsstrasse 209 from Nienburg, and from the west on the road from Eystrup crossing the moors and forests of the Hämelheide; there was also an approach from the south across the Lichten Moor but this was less likely. To achieve maximum delay, Kapitän zur See Jordan had to create as much depth to his defence as possible so he based his plan on three layers: an advanced position at Hoya, outpost positions in settlements to the west of Rethem, and a main defensive position at Rethem, denying its bridge. The town would be the point of main effort. The depth of Jordan's defence was increased by I./6 Bataillon, which had deployed to Nienburg to cover the starting point of Reichsstrasse 209.

Jordan deployed men from Kompanien 2./5 and 14./5 to the advanced position at Hoya, where they came under the command of Major Döll, a *Luftwaffe* officer from Flak-Regiment 122(E).

---

[6] Of Rethem's 2,230 inhabitants in 1953, 450 were evacuees. Their presence is reflected by street names in the New Town such as Ostpreußenstrasse and Pommern Weg.

234　THEIRS THE STRIFE

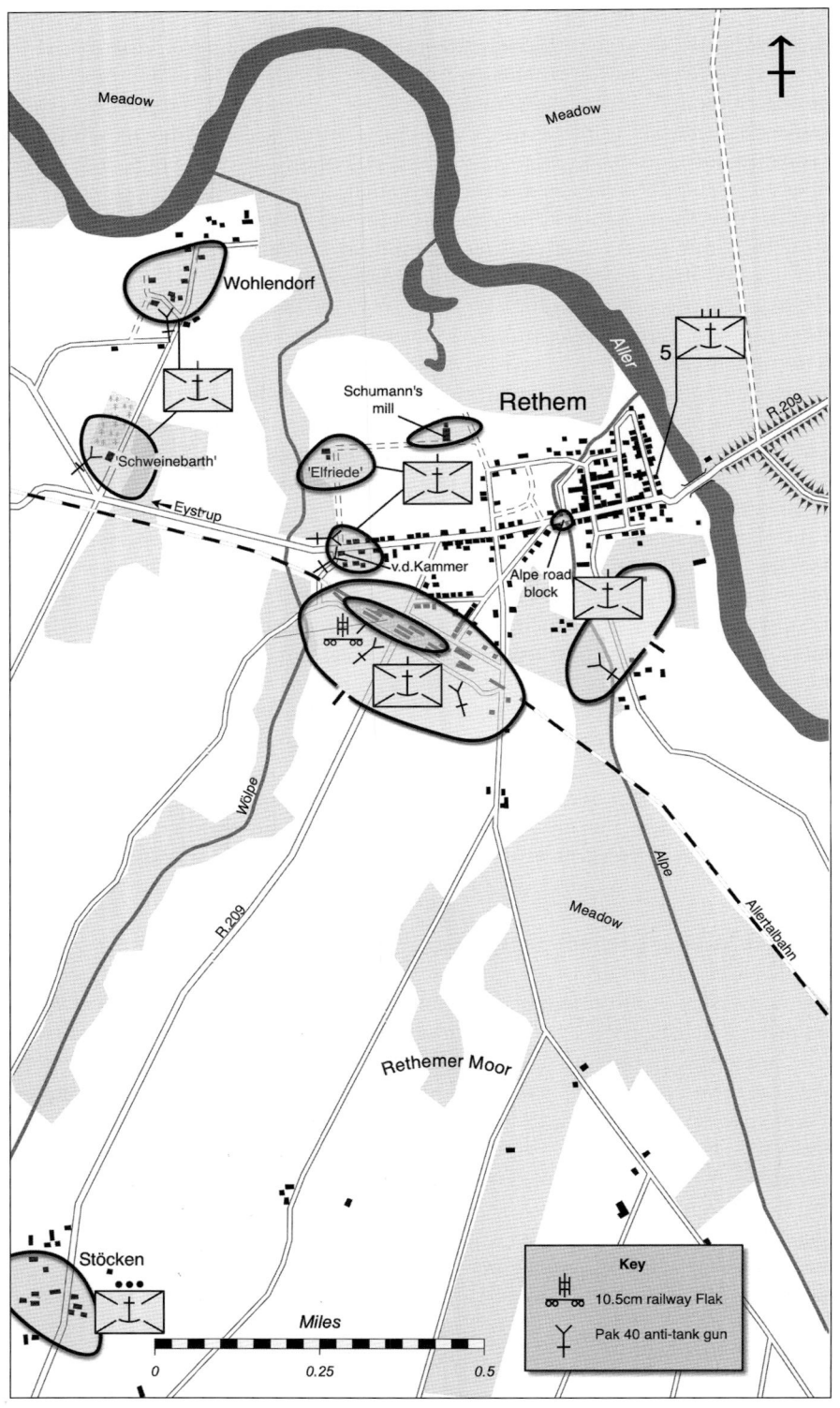

Map 31　Deployment of Marine-Grenadier-Regiment 5 at Rethem – 9 April 1945.

The advanced position was expected to make the enemy's assault crossing of the Weser as difficult as possible, buying time for the development of the main defensive position at Rethem. At Hoya the marines occupied positions in buildings on the right bank, primarily in the area of the *Schloss*, which dominated the area of the two bridges, and in buildings in Hinterstrasse covering the river downstream from the road bridge. The marines were joined, reinforced would be too strong a word, by some middle-aged soldiers from 65 Bataillon of Grenadier-A.u.E. Regiment 269, about 50 equally-old transport drivers and a party of engineers, who immediately prepared the bridges for demolition. Also present in the Hoya area and able to provide limited indirect fire support were some *Flak* assets: Batterien 4./117 and 4./162 (gem.), each equipped with four 10.5cm Flak and three 2cm Flak, were positioned south of the road to Hassel, while RAD Batterie 2./604 (gem.) with five 8.8cm Flak 36 and three *Flakvierling* was near Hassel. Also in the Hassel area was RAD Batterie 5./280 (gem) with three 8.8cm Flak. The fire control necessary for these guns to support ground action effectively would have been suspect at best.

Once the enemy had crossed the Weser and advanced across the ground between the two rivers there were four approaches for attacking Rethem itself, and Jordan established outpost positions to cover the three most likely. The first approach was from the south via Rethemer Moor but, as the least likely, it was not allocated an outpost position. The second approach was from the southwest on Reichsstrasse 209. For this approach an outpost position based on a platoon was sited in Stöcken. The third approach was from the west on the road from Eystrup, and for this an outpost position was established as a strongpoint in the farmhouse named 'Schweinebarth' (probably the owner's surname) near the junction of three roads half a mile to the west of Rethem. The last approach crossed the meadows to Rethem's north-west and to cover this approach an outpost position occupied the hamlet of Wohlendorf. The *'Schweinebarth'* strongpoint and Wohlendorf were held by 3./5 Kompanie commanded by Oberleutnant zur See Jäckle.

The defence of Rethem itself was the responsibility of Korvettenkapitän Burkel's II./5 Bataillon reinforced by two companies from I./5 Bataillon, the two regimental companies 13./5 and 14./5 and a battery of Pak 40 from Marine-Panzerjäger-Abteilung 2. Doctrinally, the Germans encouraged fighting from built-up areas as they provided a ready supply of strongpoints and anti-tank positions, and their neutralisation by the enemy required considerable infantry and artillery effort. As the perimeter of towns were generally considered vulnerable to artillery fire the Germans would normally site a town's MLR well within the built-up area. However, Jordan defended Rethem from its perimeter as the enemy would have to attack over approaches largely bereft of cover and dominated by excellent fields of fire, allowing him to reap maximum damage. In addition to favourable ground, Jordan had another advantage over an attacker: he could fight the battle for Rethem on interior lines, allowing him to supply and move his forces quicker than the enemy. In accordance with German doctrine, counter-attacks would be mounted as soon as positions were on the point of capture.

Although the south-eastern sector faced the least likely approach, as the cover provided by hedgerows and coppices could allow an enemy to close on his perimeter largely unseen, Jordan allocated to it a company with a Pak 40 anti-tank gun. To cover Reichsstrasse 209 and an enemy advance from the south-west, he sited a company along the railway embankment and in the fields forward of it. Slit trenches for machine-gun teams and individual weapon pits for *Panzerfaust*-armed riflemen were dug, with trenches kept flush to the ground and, where possible, sited along natural lines such as hedges; camouflage was afforded a high priority.

Jordan allocated the third company of II./5 Bataillon to cover the approaches on the Eystrup road and across the meadows from the north-west. Here, rather than a single company position, he would defend the town's perimeter with platoon-strength strongpoints, the purpose of which was to break-up attacks before they could enter the town's built-up area. The strongpoints were based on prominent buildings, which had their entrances blocked, windows left open to conceal the origin of fire, roof tiles removed to provide loopholes, and machine-guns sited in cellars to provide better grazing fire. The first strongpoint, sited on the Eystrup road where it entered the town's perimeter, was centred on the von der Kammer farmhouse. In addition to the marines allocated to the strongpoint, three Pak 40 anti-tank guns from Marine-Panzerjäger-Abteilung 2 were also sited in this area. The next strongpoint was established to the north of the von der Kammer farmhouse in an isolated house nicknamed 'Elfriede', possibly after the strongpoint commander's wife or girlfriend. This building, belonging to Heinrich Wohlke, lay just to the east of the Wölpe, a sluggish stream flowing across the fields to the Aller some 350 yards to the north. From 'Elfriede' the marines could dominate any attempt to approach Rethem down the Eystrup road or across the meadows from the area of Wohlendorf and could mutually support both the von der Kammer strongpoint and the third platoon's strongpoint, which was sited in the area of Schumann's Mill on Rethem's northern edge and covered an attack across the meadows. II./5 Bataillon's fourth company, the heavy weapons' company, distributed its MG 42 teams among the positions and deployed its 8cm mortars to a baseplate on the Aller's right bank.

With the majority of his forces allocated to the perimeter Jordan had few resources for the interior of the town. The sole defensive structure was an anti-tank obstacle of vertically-set logs constructed near the town centre where the Eystrup road joined Reichsstrasse 209; the obstacle was covered by a Pak 40. These log obstacles were commonplace in Germany in 1945 but were largely ineffective and the Germans nicknamed them '61 Minute Barriers' as the enemy would laugh at them for 60 minutes before destroying them in one. Teller mines were attached to trees, allowing them to be blown to create obstacles, and the Aller bridge, a robust steel cantilever set on concrete piers, was prepared for demolition. Jordan established his headquarters in the cellar of the Wehland house on Junkernstrasse in the Old Town, close to the bridge, and it is probable that an OP was established in the tower of the St. Marien Kirche. Although Korvettenkapitän Burkel and his II./5 Bataillon provided the majority of the forces for the defence of Rethem, the regimental commander was in overall command of the Rethem sector so Burkel would have played second fiddle to his superior.

The regiment had a plentiful supply of *Panzerfaust* and Pak 40 for anti-tank defence but it lacked artillery support and this would remain the case until the horse-drawn guns of Marine-Artillerie-Regiment 2, plodding down from Schleswig-Holstein, reached the Aller. As these guns were unlikely to reach the Aller before battle was joined, Jordan was reliant on the successful withdrawal of the Hoya *Flak* to positions on the Aller's right bank. However, some heavy *Flak* support was already in place at Rethem. Following *Luftwaffe* Major Majewski's direction,[7] the five 10.5cm Flak of combined batteries 1. and 4./125(E) had been moved from Hoya on 5 April and the guns on their railway flat-wagons were repositioned on the sidings at Rethem station where, from the low embankment, they dominated the western approaches to the town. Although the 10.5cm Flak were powerful guns, the absence of a protected superstructure made them and their crews vulnerable to direct fire, blast, splinters and small-arms' fire so the crews attempted to reduce their vulnerability by stacking railway sleepers in front of the flat-wagons.

Jordan's other battalion, I./5 commanded by Kapitänleutnant Emil Thoren, now with only a single rifle company, deployed on II./5 Bataillon's right to defend Westen and Hülsen and cover any moves to outflank Rethem from the north. In this area also was a three-company Hungarian artillery training battalion, entitled Ungarisch Artillerie-Ausbildungs-Bataillon 7, undergoing training in Verden with Artillerie-A.u.E. Regiment 22 and deployed as part of Aktion Leuthen. This Hungarian battalion, also known as Bataillon Kolotay after its commander, was allocated to 2. Marine-Infanterie-Division as infantry but was of dubious quality and reliability, as events will soon prove.

---

7   *Gefechtsbericht des Flakregiments 122(E), 14 April 1945*, p.9.

7th Armoured Division advance to the Weser

While VIII Corps on 5 April was gaining its initial bridgeheads over the Weser, XII Corps was still engaged in the battle for Ibbenbüren,[8] far to the west. However, by the morning of 6 April the enemy was exhausted and depleted and the British were at last able to take the town, despite the continued presence of snipers that needed mopping up. While the infantry were completing the job, 22nd Armoured Brigade had meanwhile broken out in a north-easterly direction and advanced to a bridge over the Osnabrück canal at Halen,[9] captured earlier by 11th Armoured Division; the brigade then advanced either side of the Dummer See to reach 12 miles beyond the lake by last light. By the evening of 6 April, the brigade had captured Diepholz and Major General Lyne, seeking to reinforce this success, directed 22nd Armoured to push on and capture crossings over the Weser. The brigade began a rapid advance towards its objective, the road and rail bridges over the Weser at Hoya, and through the night of 6/7 April and against negligible opposition 1 RTR and 2 Devon travelled as fast as starlight permitted,[10] with the infantry clinging to the pitching tank decks. But when the column was only two miles from the river, over the noise of the tank engines a tremendous explosion was heard: the German demolition teams had fired their charges, dropping into the Weser the railway bridge and demolishing two spans of the road bridge. The tanks and infantry, although disappointed at having come so close to their prize after a 60-mile night advance, spent the morning of 7 April reorganising in the Hoya area, capturing 40 prisoners in the process. For the corps' infantry divisions, the pace of operations was less rapid: 52nd Lowland on the left flank was making slow progress against elements of Panzer-Ausbildungs-Verband 'Grossdeutschland', and 53rd Welsh was still disengaging from the Ibbenbüren area and preparing to push eastward once more.

With the Hoya bridges no more, 8 Hussars made for the next bridge over the Weser, located two miles to the north-west of Verden. However, any plan to rush the bridge had to be abandoned as it was strongly protected by infantry and artillery, and it was clear that a crossing of the Weser was not possible until much larger forces were brought forward. With a move on Verden postponed, the division consolidated its gains until, early on 8 April, 22nd Armoured Brigade was ordered to advance northwards to cut 1. Fallschirm-Armee's withdrawal routes to Bremen. However, before this advance could start, the brigade needed to be relieved from its positions on the left bank of the Weser in the Hoya area. It was therefore decided that 160th Infantry Brigade from 53rd Welsh would come under command of 7th Armoured and move up to Hoya as quickly as possible to relieve the armoured brigade.

Sunday 8 April – Monday 9 April

On 8 April, with the sound of battle clearly audible to the west, Ortsgruppenleiter Meinecke ordered the evacuation of Rethem.[11] Some civilians fled to the forests near Stöcken, to Hämelsee, to Rethemer Moor or to holes they had dug in the grazing land near the river; many, however, decided to stay put and see things out. For those who stayed, and in particular the owners of the strongpoints, the following days would be fraught with danger. According to Karl von der

---

8 TNA WO 171/4055, GS Branch XII Corps war diary.
9 TNA WO 171/4340, 22nd Armoured Brigade war diary.
10 TNA WO 171/4707, 1 RTR war diary.
11 *Ortsgruppenleiter* was a political rank and the holder was the senior *Nazi* party official within the municipal structure. As the party had generally subsumed the traditional structure, an *Ortsgruppenleiter* was often one and the same as a *Bürgermeister*.

Kammer, the defenders of the strongpoint bearing his name and commanded by a young *Leutnant zur See* were full of optimism and believed the bulk of the British forces were still held on the Rhine and that they would only be facing light advance guards. A resident of '*Elfriede*' was less sanguine:[12]

> We were christened strongpoint '*Elfriede*' when the first defenders occupied our house. The establishment of the defences telegraphed no good. The house was 300m in front of the first houses near the Alpe and we would experience everything a strongpoint could experience in war. We would receive no quarter.

Before 2. Marine-Infanterie-Division had barely fired a shot in anger it suffered a severe blow. On 8 April, Vizeadmiral Scheurlen, accompanied by an Army adviser, Major Wechsmann, left his headquarters in Walsrode in an open-top Horch staff car to visit the battle positions being prepared on the Aller. As they sped westwards down the tree-lined Reichsstrasse 209, the noise of the air rushing by drowned the noise of a number of Allied fighters, which had spotted the lone car and were closing for a low-level attack. The car had just passed the village of Sindorf when the driver and his passengers were caught totally unawares by the first burst; although it missed, the driver's emergency stop led to a skid and the car becoming stuck in the roadside ditch. The passengers in the stationary vehicle were now helpless and the burst from the second aircraft hit the car killing Wechsmann and leaving Scheurlen very severely wounded; the driver managed to escape. Scheurlen was evacuated to the military hospital in Walsrode but he died the next day and command of the division passed to Kapitän zur See Hartmann until a new commander from the army,[13] Oberst Werner Graf von Bassewitz-Levetzow, could arrive from his appointment with the Divisionsführer-Lehrgang (divisional commanders' training course) at Hirschbergin, Lower Silesia,[14] a journey which would take him two days.

160th Brigade assault crossing of the Weser at Hoya

General Ritchie's plan for his corps was for 53rd Welsh to secure crossings over the Weser at Hoya, then move rapidly to seize the important bridge over the Aller at Rethem. Once a bridgehead was secured on the Aller's right bank, the infantry division would sidestep northwards and advance on the axis Verden-Rotenburg-Tostedt, making space for 7th Armoured Division to advance to Hamburg and the Elbe. As yet unknown to XII Corps, 2. Marine-Infanterie-Division was deployed across the corps' future axis and readying itself for battle.

In the early hours of 8 April, Brigadier Coleman, commander 160th Infantry Brigade,[15] was ordered to relieve units of 7th Armoured Division at Hoya and start preparations for an assault crossing of the Weser. As the situation on the Weser was fluid and the brigade somewhat out of touch with operations at the van of the corps' advance, the brigadier visited commander 53rd Welsh Division,[16] Major General Ross, at divisional headquarters at Westerkapeln to get updated and hear from him the details of the divisional plan to cross the Weser and Aller. He was told that the plan involved his brigade conducting the assault crossing of the Weser, 158th Brigade would

---

12 Hans-Heinz Schulze, *Halb Rethem lag in Schutt und Asche*, (Walsroder Zeitung, 16 March 1985).
13 Scheurlen is buried in the military section of Walsrode cemetery.
14 Now Jelenia Góra in Poland.
15 TNA WO 171/4429, 160th Infantry Brigade war diary.
16 TNA WO 171/4277, 53rd Welsh Division war diary.

then form the divisional bridgehead,[17] after which 71st Brigade would pass through to take the bridge at Rethem, the next objective.[18] As a preliminary, 160th Brigade would take-over the Hoya area from units of 22nd Armoured Brigade and deploy a battalion on the loop of the Weser at the town and one on either flank of the loop. Investigation of the river further to the south would be carried out by B Squadron 53rd Recce Regiment, which would join the brigade as it passed through Westerkapeln. Brigadier Coleman was ordered to start planning an assault crossing of the Weser as soon as his battalions reached it, and to assist in this task 282 Field Company would supply 45 assault boats.[19]

By dawn, 160th Brigade had begun its 85-mile move to the Weser, a move enlivened by the streams of liberated PoWs and displaced persons of many nationalities streaming west. Although some were in misappropriated German vehicles, on bicycles or liberated farm carts and horses, by far the majority were on foot and trudging along, tired but happy. The German population in contrast stood sullen but interested as the Welsh drove through their villages. The weather was good and the countryside amazed the troops with its beauty and absence of war damage. The faint green haze of leaves was appearing on the trees and the only signs of war were occasional road blocks of logs and white flags, pillow slips and sheets hanging from windows. By dusk the brigade was nearing the end of its long move and the battalions moved into the sectors allocated to them on the Weser's left bank: 2 Mons the area south of the Hoya loop and occupying Stendern, Holtrup and Schweringen; 6 RWF the centre area from Hoya to Altenbücken; and 4 Welch the area north of the Hoya loop and occupying Hingste, Ubbendorf and Wienbergen.

Once released from Hoya, 22nd Armoured and 131st Infantry Brigade led 7th Armoured Division's northward advance and by 9 April they had captured the towns of Riede and Syke. Thereafter opposition began to stiffen considerably and it was clear that the battle for Bremen would be long, hard and one ill-suited to an armoured formation. Moreover, General Dempsey's intention was for Bremen to be XXX Corps' objective and as XII Corps' decisive direction was eastwards to the Elbe, 7th Armoured would be needed to spearhead the corps' advance. So, to allow 7th Armoured to disengage from Bremen's approaches, 3rd Infantry Division temporarily came under command of XII Corps and began to relieve the armoured division of its responsibilities and release it to move south-eastwards to a concentration area on the Weser's left bank opposite Nienburg.

Meanwhile, back at Hoya, Brigadier Coleman selected 6 RWF to make the assault crossing of the Weser.[20] When the battalion reached the ridge overlooking the river it was ominously quiet and the rumour went around the battalion that the war had ended but nobody had bothered to tell them! 6 RWF's war soon began again when the noise made by 1 RTR's withdrawing tanks drew heavy shell-fire, mostly air-burst, from the *Flak* on the right bank. Despite the shell-fire, because of the largely unopposed advance of the last few days some seemed to forget that there was still an enemy to be faced. 282 Field Company was tasked to bridge the Weser once 6 RWF had secured the right bank and the squadron commander, Major Kent, with his recce officer, moved forward to the river by jeep to recce the proposed crossing-site. Unfortunately, the major was either unaware of the Germans' presence or was somewhat over-confident as he was shot in the legs while sat studying a map in his jeep. He was fortunate to escape with his life and he was probably the first of many in XII Corps to be surprised by a new-found aggressiveness in the enemy. Any movement

---

17 TNA WO 171/4423, 158th Infantry Brigade war diary.
18 TNA WO 171/4384, 71st Infantry Brigade war diary.
19 TNA WO 171/5542, 282 Field Company RE war diary.
20 TNA WO 171/5283, 6 RWF war diary.

near the river was now met by small-arms' fire from the buildings on the right bank occupied by the marines.

The decision was taken that the assault crossing of the Weser would be made by two rifle companies downstream from the road bridge. Once the companies had made an initial lodgement the remainder of the battalion would cross and establish a bridgehead to protect the construction of Class 40 Bailey sections to replace the road bridge's demolished spans. Although the intention was for the crossing to be made during the night 8/9 April, once the men of the companies had marched back to the assembly area, drawn the assault boats and then lugged them forward they were very tired – each boat was a six-man lift – and it was decided to postpone the operation to the hours before dawn on 9 April. With all three battalions on a very extended frontage and in contact only by radio, a busy patrol programme had to be arranged to give security, recce the lie of the land and discover enemy dispositions on both banks. The battalions' patrols subsequently reported that the right bank appeared to be held but apart from 10 members of the *Feldgendarmerie* (military police) captured by 2 Mons, only a few stragglers were found on the left bank. An Ultra decrypt strongly suggests that the military police would have belonged to Feldjägerkommando I, ordered by Kesselring to establish a number of blocking lines to round up stragglers.[21] One such line was ordered for the Weser, with the decrypt ominously ending with the instruction that the *Feldjägerkommando* agree boundaries with the 'SS Police Authority', the regional *SS- und Polizeiführer* with responsibility for security, and summary justice, in the rear areas. Beyond the battalions' patrol areas, 53rd Recce Regiment covered the flanks and the recce troops discovered Drakenburg on the Weser's right bank occupied by the enemy.[22]

While the brigade prepared for the crossing, 83rd and 133rd Field Artillery Regiments were hurriedly moved up to occupy gun positions for supporting the operation. The procedures for such moves were by now second nature and some time before the regimental road moves began the advance parties had already reached the gun areas and begun to plot in the gun positions, placing flags to mark the location of each gun so that no time would be wasted. 133rd Field was the first to move and by 2210 hours on 8 April the regiment reported to 160th Brigade that all guns had come into action in the Hohenholz area.[23] In addition to the field regiments, 53rd Welsh also had available to it the 5.5-in guns of 72nd Medium Regiment.[24] This regiment had driven 85 miles during the course of the day, completing the longest road move it had conducted thus far in the war, and by 1830 hours it was in action with 14 of its guns firing a number of missions in support of 160th Brigade.

During the remainder of the night 8/9 April the battalions continued to mount patrols and, to make a show of force on what was still a very thinly-held front, fired mortar barrages at any German movement identified on the right bank. B Company 4 Welch was ordered to send two fighting patrols across the Weser under cover of darkness to find out if the opposite bank was held by the enemy and in what strength.[25] The first patrol never launched its boats as they were dumped too far from the river and the patrol ran out of hours of darkness in which to cross the river. The second patrol launched its assault boat but when they were mid-stream they were seen and shot-up. With the boat sinking the patrol commander, by now wounded, gave the order to swim for it; only he and one soldier returned from the 15 who set out. With the rivers nearly in flood, the missing were among the many from both sides who over the following days would drown in the swirling waters of the three rivers. Another task during the night involved D Troop 25th LAA Regiment

---

21   TNA DEFE 3/562, BT 9272, Kesselring signal 1 April 1945.
22   Drakenburg was later home to the British Army Weser Sailing Club; I learnt to sail there in 1982.
23   TNA WO 171/4845, 133rd Field Regiment RA war diary.
24   TNA WO 171/5033, 72nd Medium Regiment RA war diary.
25   TNA WO 171/5286, 4 Welch war diary.

moving two Bofors to positions on the Weser's bank to provide direct fire support for the assault river crossing.[26]

As the Germans recognised that they could not prevent the British crossing the Weser and that the *Flak* at Hoya would soon be vulnerable to capture, they were also making use of the hours of darkness to extract as many guns as possible and withdraw them to locations where they could support the main battle on the Aller. RAD Batterie 2./604 managed to withdraw four of its five 8.8cm guns and all three of its 2cm guns, dropping off one 8.8cm gun to support the marines preparing to defend Stöcken on Reichsstrasse 209; the battery then crossed the Aller at Rethem and occupied positions in the area of Timpenberg, an area of glacial sand dunes in the forest three miles to the east of the town. Batterie 4./162 successfully withdrew its full complement of four 10.5cm Flak and three 2cm Oerlikons, but Batterie 4./117 was less successful and owing to the shortage of prime movers or carriage systems had to abandon its four 10.5cm Flak, and only by using improvised carrying frames managed to move its three 2cm guns. For unknown reason the gunners of Batterie 4./117 made no attempt to destroy their guns and a subsequent report by 4 War Material Recce Team stated that at Hoya they found four 10.5cm guns, with 100 rounds of ammunition and an undamaged height-finding apparatus, all in good condition.[27] Batterie 4./117's redundant gunners were formed into *ad hoc* infantry companies and withdrew on foot to take up positions covering Reichsstrasse 209 at Schneeheide, just to the west of Walsrode, where in due course we will briefly meet them again. RAD Batterie 5./280 (gem.) remained at Hassel to support the marines in Hoya.

The coming of dawn on Monday 9 April brought further difficulties for the British. The crossing operation's delay led to D Troop's Bofors being caught in the open and the marines were quick to take advantage of the gunners' predicament, opening fire on the guns and the ammunition heaped next to them. Seventeen-year-old Matrose Rolf Fuchs was one of the marines:[28]

> The exploding ammunition damaged the gun; we could not believe it and were ecstatic. We then turned our fire on the second gun, which we also commenced to destroy. A short while later we came under heavy artillery fire from the other side so we took cover in the cellar.

Despite the difficulties of the night and the coming of daylight, 160th Brigade was ordered to press on with the operation to cross the Weser as speed was of the essence. In addition to the artillery engaging targets on the right bank, a deception plan was required to take the Germans' attention away from the crossing site while the two assault companies paddled their vulnerable assault boats across the river. This plan began at 0900 hours and involved a smoke and mortar barrage fired 1,000 yards upstream of the crossing site. H-hour was set for 0945 hours and 15 minutes later A Company on the right, commanded by Lieutenant Dufty, and C Company on the left, commanded by Captain MacHenry, launched their boats and began to cross. Although the banks made entry and exit difficult, both companies were across by 1015 hours with very few casualties and it appeared that the Germans had been successfully pinned down by the artillery fire. In reality, the marines' inexperience of fighting a land battle was the reason for their lack of reaction as they had not realised the quickening of the artillery programme heralded the crossing and most were still in cellars taking cover as the boats crossed. Rolf Fuchs was one of a party of 13 marines in the cellar of the courthouse and when the artillery lifted they left its shelter via a window to take up fire positions. By the time they emerged it was too late and machine-guns engaged them, instantly killing three of Fuchs's party.

---

26 TNA WO 171/4939, 25th LAA Regiment RA war diary.
27 TNA WO 171/8252, 4 War Material Recce Team war diary.
28 Saft, *Krieg in Der Heimat*, p.105.

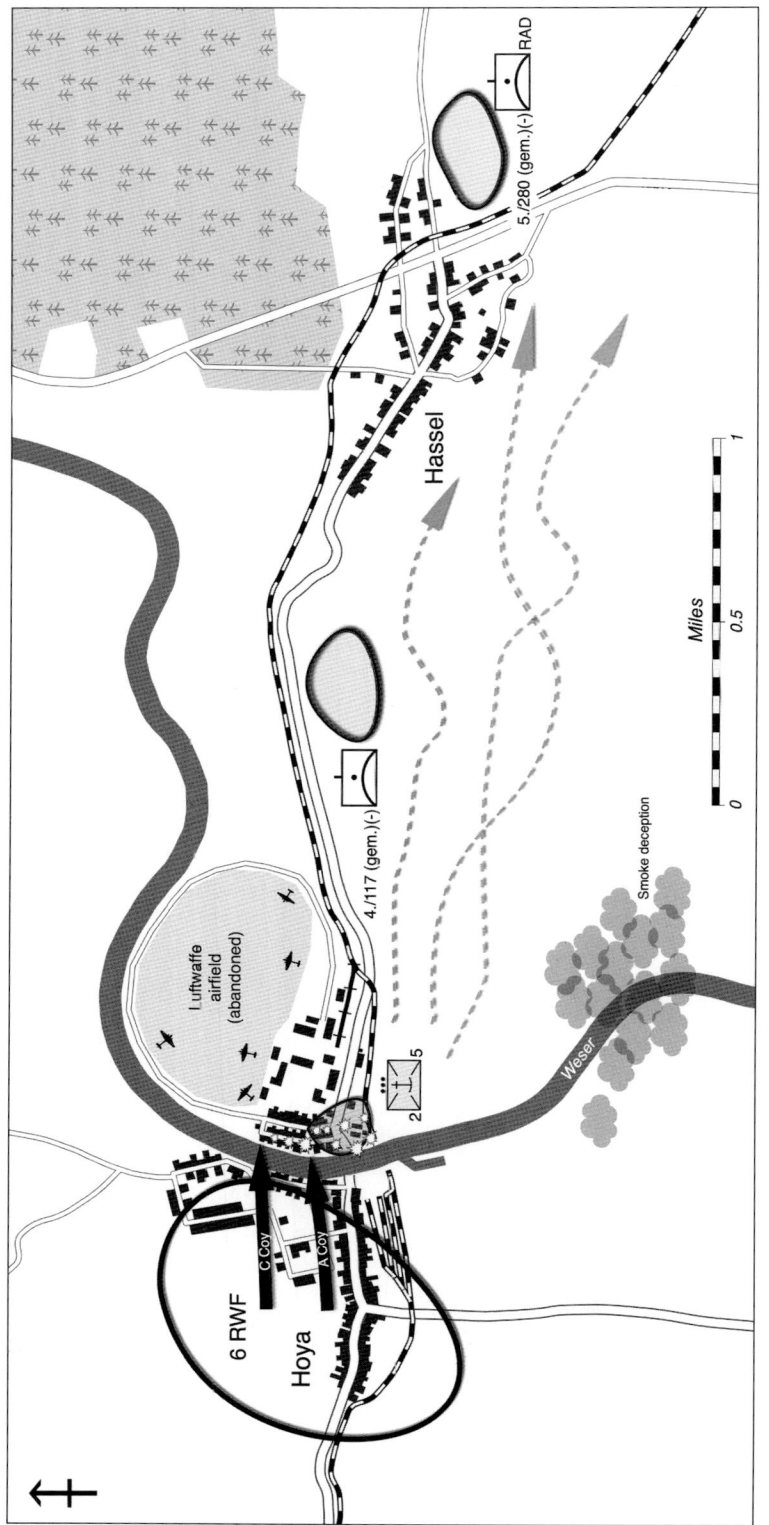

Map 32 6 RWF Crosses the Weser – 9 April 1945.

Although the crossing was largely unopposed, fighting on the right bank was short but bitter as houses had to be cleared. The opposition by the marines from Kompanien 2./5 and 14./5 was fierce and 6 RWF's history recorded they were: 'a very difficult lot of young men who seemed to have nothing to live for and who seemed to enjoy dying!' Despite their resistance there were too few to hold back 6 RWF and the marines were gradually forced out of the buildings, some managing to get away by moving along hedgerows. By 1100 hours the Welsh were firmly lodged on the right bank, having lost eight killed and 17 wounded. Eight marines and four *Flak* gunners from RAD Batterie 5./280 (gem.) were captured; the number found dead is unknown. Once the houses on the right bank were clear, one of the companies exploited to Hoya's airfield where sixteen Ju 52 transport aircraft and nine Fw 190 were found abandoned, probably with empty tanks. At this stage, 6 RWF's commanding officer, Lieutenant Colonel Hutchinson, was ordered by brigade headquarters not to put more troops across and the sappers of 282 Field Company were given the order to start bridging. Fortunately, the German engineers' demolition of the road bridge was not sufficiently thorough and although the first span had dropped, the second was only damaged, the third was intact and the bridge's two substantial masonry piers stood complete in the river. Starting at 1400 hours, 282 Field Company was therefore rapidly able to construct a 100-foot TS Bailey bridge linking the left bank to the first pier,[29] followed by 244 Field Company, which patched up the damaged centre span to create a Class 40 bridge.[30] By 2330 hours the bridge was opened to traffic, allowing 53rd Welsh to start the exploitation to the Aller at Rethem. The next day the BBC reported 7th Armoured Division had bridged the Weser. Although technically correct as 160th Brigade was under 7th Armoured command for the Hoya crossing, this announcement did not go down well with 53rd Welsh and its sappers!

Hoya Bailey bridge.

---

29 TNA WO 171/5542, 282 Field Company RE war diary. 'TS' stood for 'triple truss, single storey' so comprised three trusses alongside each other in one storey.
30 TNA WO 171/5520, 244 Field Company RE war diary.

While the crossing operation was in progress the other two brigades of 53rd Welsh – 71st and 158th – had moved up to the Weser and at 1600 hours 160th Brigade reverted from 7th Armoured to come under its parent division once more. As the brigade had crossed the Weser and formed a bridgehead with relative ease, the divisional plan was now amended and 158th Brigade, instead of merely expanding the Hoya bridgehead, would now pass through and exploit to the Aller. A rapid follow-up to the successful crossing was considered essential to prevent any German reinforcement or consolidation. Prisoners from Kompanien 2./5 and 14./5 taken during the fighting in Hoya revealed not only the presence of a fresh formation but also one that was prepared to fight. Although this new-found aggression surprised the British, they were wholly unsuspecting of the tough fighting which lay ahead and a 53rd Division INTSUM mentioned that although little on the marine division was gleaned from the prisoners: 'what had emerged so far does not create an awesome picture.'[31] A view that was shortly to change. 53rd Division was not alone in having trouble assessing the opposition as a day later the last entry in XII Corps' intelligence log reported the presence in Rethem of a unit entitled: '5 Infantry Mining Regiment'.[32] Little wonder perhaps that 53rd Welsh would soon be caught unawares.

In the early afternoon Brigadier Wilsey, commanding 158th Brigade, gave his orders and detailed how the next phase would be conducted. The brigade group, with 4 Welch under command, would cross at Hoya as soon as the bridge was finished, pass through 6 RWF's bridgehead, advance to Rethem during the night 9/10 April and establish a bridgehead over the Aller, hopefully having captured the bridge intact. The battalions' tasks were as follows: 7 RWF would be first across and clear Hassel, lying three miles to the east of Hoya; 4 Welch would follow, clear Eystrup to the south of Hassel and provide right flank security; 1/5 Welch would advance through 7 RWF to seize Rethem and its bridge; 1 E Lancs would cross last, clear the Memsen state forest then advance to capture the area of Hohenholz and Hämelhausen, roughly half-way between the two rivers. To reinforce the infantry's advance, XII Corps allocated 5 RTR (from 22nd Armoured Brigade) to 53rd Welsh, a decision that was not popular with the tank crews. 5 RTR was very experienced but war-weary and its members not keen to operate with a new infantry formation. Although its squadrons were accustomed to working and fighting with infantry, this was usually with 7th Armoured's own infantry, in particular 22nd Armoured Brigade's motor battalion, 1 RB.

While the British were planning the next phase of their advance, the surviving marines from Kompanien 2./5 and 14./5 were withdrawing to Rethem and making maximum use of the cover of dark and the woods to avoid the threat from enemy aircraft. They were fully prepared, however, to mount immediate ambushes if the opportunity arose and were soon to do so with effect. In Rethem on this Monday morning, Jordan announced to the frightened population that their town would be defended to the last and, in the knowledge that the enemy would soon be on them, the marines in the outpost positions and the town's perimeter continued to prepare their defences as fast as possible.

Tuesday 10 April

Advance to the Aller and 1/5 Welch attacks on Rethem

At 2330 hours on 9 April 7 RWF, the leading battalion of 158th Brigade, began crossing the Bailey bridge at Hoya on foot and then made good progress towards its objective, Hassel.[33] When the lead

---

31 TNA WO 171/4277, 53rd Welsh Division war diary.
32 TNA WO 171/4054, XII Corps GS.
33 TNA WO 171/5284, 7 RWF war diary.

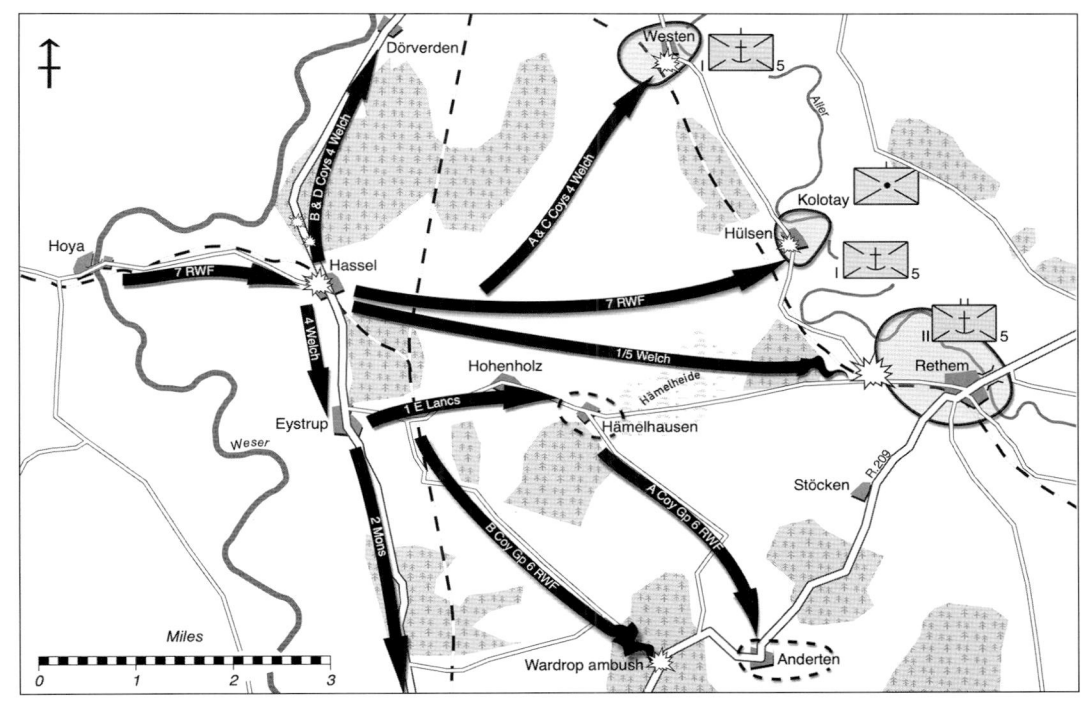

Map 33 53rd Welsh Division's Advance to the Aller – 10 April 1945.

company reached Hassel it met opposition from marines withdrawing from Hoya, but this was quickly overcome and the village was in battalion hands by 0300 hours on 10 April. In clearing some woods to the north of the village B Company had a skirmish with about 20 soldiers from SS-A.u.E.Btl. 12 'HJ'. These young soldiers were possibly from 3. SS-Kompanie as this company had been billeted in Haßbergen, a village just to the south of Eystrup, prior to taking part in the battle at Leese; in the action with B Company two of the youths were killed, one was captured and the rest fled. The next battalion to cross the Hoya bridge was 4 Welch, which moved through 7 RWF and by 0400 hours had captured Eystrup and was providing flank protection from the south. During the evening of 9 April, 1/5 Welch, waiting in an assembly area near Memsen four miles west of the Weser, was called forward to the Hoya bridge and shortly after midnight the battalion crossed to begin the 10-mile advance to Rethem.[34] For the remainder of the night the 1/5 Welch companies threaded their way on sandy tracks through the pine woods and across the moors of the Hämelheide and at 0830 hours, as they neared the end of their advance, they heard shells fired by the 25-pdr guns of 133rd Field Regiment passing overhead to land in Rethem; with these shells the battle for the town began. So far the operation could not have gone smoother.

C Company led 1/5 Welch's advance accompanied by a detachment from the anti-tank platoon with two 6-pdr guns towed by Loyd carriers, and a section of assault pioneers. The leading platoon advanced with its sections in single file on alternate sides of the road followed by company headquarters and the other two platoons, similarly deployed. The commander of the assault pioneer section was Corporal Jack Mulhearn:[35]

---

34 TNA WO 171/5287, 1/5 Welch war diary.
35 Letter to the author.

As we progressed along the road I noticed on the grass verge on the right-hand side what appeared to be land communication cables. I brought this to the attention of the company commander and asked his permission to cut them, which he willingly gave. I cut them as per procedure, which involved removing a section of some length to prevent a speedy reconnection, and carried on, still without contact with the enemy.

My next recollection is of approaching a bend in the road with high hedges on both sides. Just before the bend there was a level crossing with some form of hand-operated barrier. The lead section had crossed and were just approaching the bend when we heard the sound of engines, similar to tanks, and the cry of 'Tanks!' went up. We immediately sought shelter in the woods alongside the road and we turned our vehicles off the road.

The anti-tank commander reacted very quickly to get his guns into position. You can imagine how tense the atmosphere was when around the bend came a large enemy charcoal-burning truck! The lead section commander dealt very smartly with the situation and quickly captured the vehicle and its occupants. It was a ration truck delivering food to the enemy forward troops, confirming our suspicions about having crossed into enemy-held territory.

The situation was secure and we were ready to advance when again we heard the sound of a machine approaching and around the bend came a German despatch rider. Again the section commander was quick to react, he fired two or three bursts from his Sten gun as the rider tried to turn and escape. As a result of the gun-fire he lost his balance and fell off, he then got up and surrendered unhurt. I have since wondered if his journey was the result of my cutting the cables.

These minor contacts were followed at 0900 hours with more serious encounters when the leading companies, still about two miles short of the town, were engaged by marines hidden in the woods. For a while the battalion was able to brush aside this light opposition, but when C Company neared the '*Schweinebarth*' strongpoint it was met by a torrent of small-arms' and machine-gun fire and the advance ground to a halt. In addition to the small-arms' fire the guns of RAD Batterie 2./604 on the Aller's right bank and the railway *Flak* of 1. and 4./125(E) joined in and the battle for the strongpoint now raged for most of the rest of the day. One of the early German casualties was Oberleutnant zur See Jäckle, the strongpoint's commander, who was shot in the lower jaw and evacuated to Rethem.

Soldiers of 1/5 Welch setting-off into the mist. Ominously, the group of soldiers sitting on the ground looking at the camera are a stretcher-bearer party.

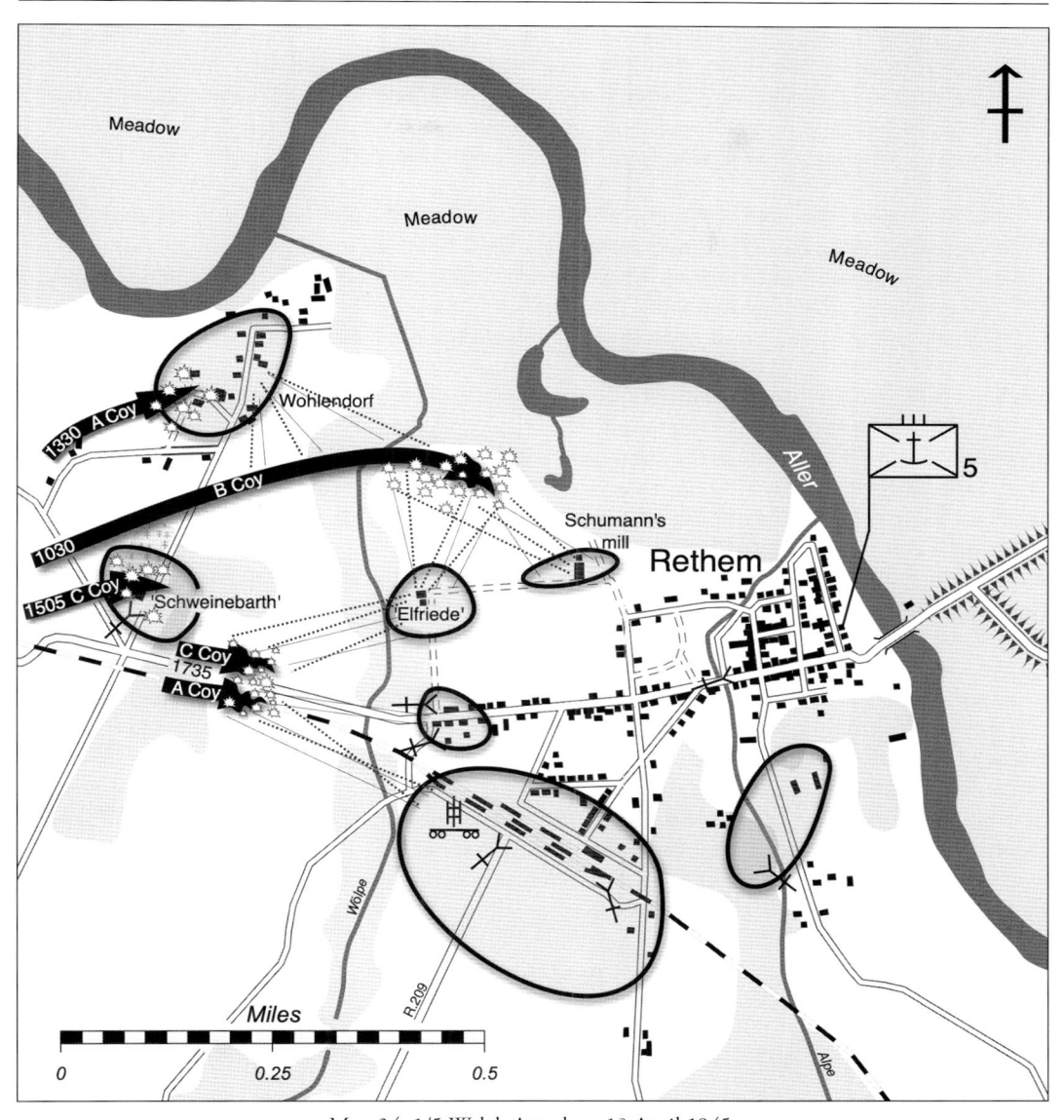

Map 34 1/5 Welch Attacks – 10 April 1945.

While C Company was attacking '*Schweinebarth*' the rest of the battalion moved up and at 1030 hours the commanding officer, Major Bowker, who had commanded the battalion since the previous commanding officer, Lieutenant Colonel Morrison-Jones, was killed when his jeep ran over a mine near Ochtrup on 2 April, ordered B Company to move round the left flank of C Company and enter Rethem from the north. B Company's manoeuvre could be made under the cover of a prevailing ground mist, which it was hoped would provide a screen.

Initially all went well and the company crossed the flat, open meadows to pass to the southwest of the small ox-bow lake just north of the town. At the critical moment, when the company was only 300 yards short of the edge of Rethem, the mist lifted leaving the Welsh without cover and in broad daylight. The marines took full advantage of this turn of events and opened up on B Company with all available weapons, initially from strongpoints '*Elfriede*' and Schumann's Mill but soon with additional fire from marines in Wohlendorf. The company was subjected to a withering cross-fire, made even more unpleasant by shelling from *Flak* and 8cm mortars firing from the right bank. The attack was soon completely bogged down with the Welsh unable either to advance or withdraw. Among those caught in the open was Captain Davies, B Company second-in-command, who found protection from an unexpected source:[36]

> On our approach we took a prisoner who then accompanied us during the remainder of the manoeuvre. As we neared the town the mist suddenly lifted leaving the company in full view of the enemy, with no cover whatsoever and in brilliant sunshine. We were immediately engaged by fire and my prisoner was shot in the arm. Fortunately for me he had provided me with a measure of protection without which I would surely have been killed.

With two of his companies committed and little progress made, Major Bowker decided to launch a direct attack on the bridge. At 1100 hours a force commanded by Sergeant Moses and comprising a section of three Universal carriers and two Wasp flamethrowers was despatched on a *coup de main* mission straight down the Eystrup road. The carriers clattered off down the avenue at full speed reaching the perimeter of the town with hardly a shot fired in their direction.

But when the force entered the town and were passing the von der Kammer strongpoint the marines, by now fully alert, engaged the carriers with *Panzerfaust*. They were, however, so inexperienced at handling the weapons that none hit their targets and some even exploded in the barn they were occupying, identifying their position to Moses's force. In the subsequent return of fire, the youthful *Leutnant* commanding the strongpoint, so mistakenly optimistic the day before, was fatally wounded and the crews of the Pak 40 in the area were killed or wounded. With the von der Kammer strongpoint behind them, the carriers pressed on into the town firing flame and Brens against targets on both sides of the road. Four hundred yards short of the bridge they came to the log road-block on the Alpe and here one of the Wasps took a direct hit from a *Panzerfaust*, destroying the vehicle. The *Leutnant* in charge of the road-block had a lucky escape when the second Wasp doused him in flame fuel, which failed to ignite. With their route blocked, the carrier force managed to swing about and head back on the road down which they had come. However, in the confusion, one of the carriers and the remaining Wasp took a wrong turning and found themselves at the railway station.

Here the two vehicles took a right turn and managed to find their way to the main road, encountering a Pak 40 when they reached it. This they immediately flamed, turned left and drove as fast as possible back to the battalion under heavy fire all the way. Although Moses's force regained friendly lines, losses and casualties in this courageous but abortive attempt were three men missing presumed captured, three wounded and one Wasp destroyed.

With the carrier attack unsuccessful, Major Bowker ordered A Company to clear Wohlendorf as the village had to be taken before any further attacks could be mounted from the north-west, and its capture would take some pressure off the beleaguered B Company still marooned in the fields. A Company's attack began at 1330 hours but the marines resisted strongly and fighting went on in the hamlet until the mid-afternoon. Even when Wohlendorf was eventually cleared at 1500 hours and the battalion's left flank secured, the soldiers of B Company were unable to extract themselves from their desperate situation owing to the fire raking the fields. Although smoke was fired, withdrawal was still impossible and they were forced to endure their bleak predicament for many hours to come. Relief only came as dusk fell, allowing the surviving members of B Company

---

36 Letter to the author.

'MEN WHO ENJOYED DYING' 249

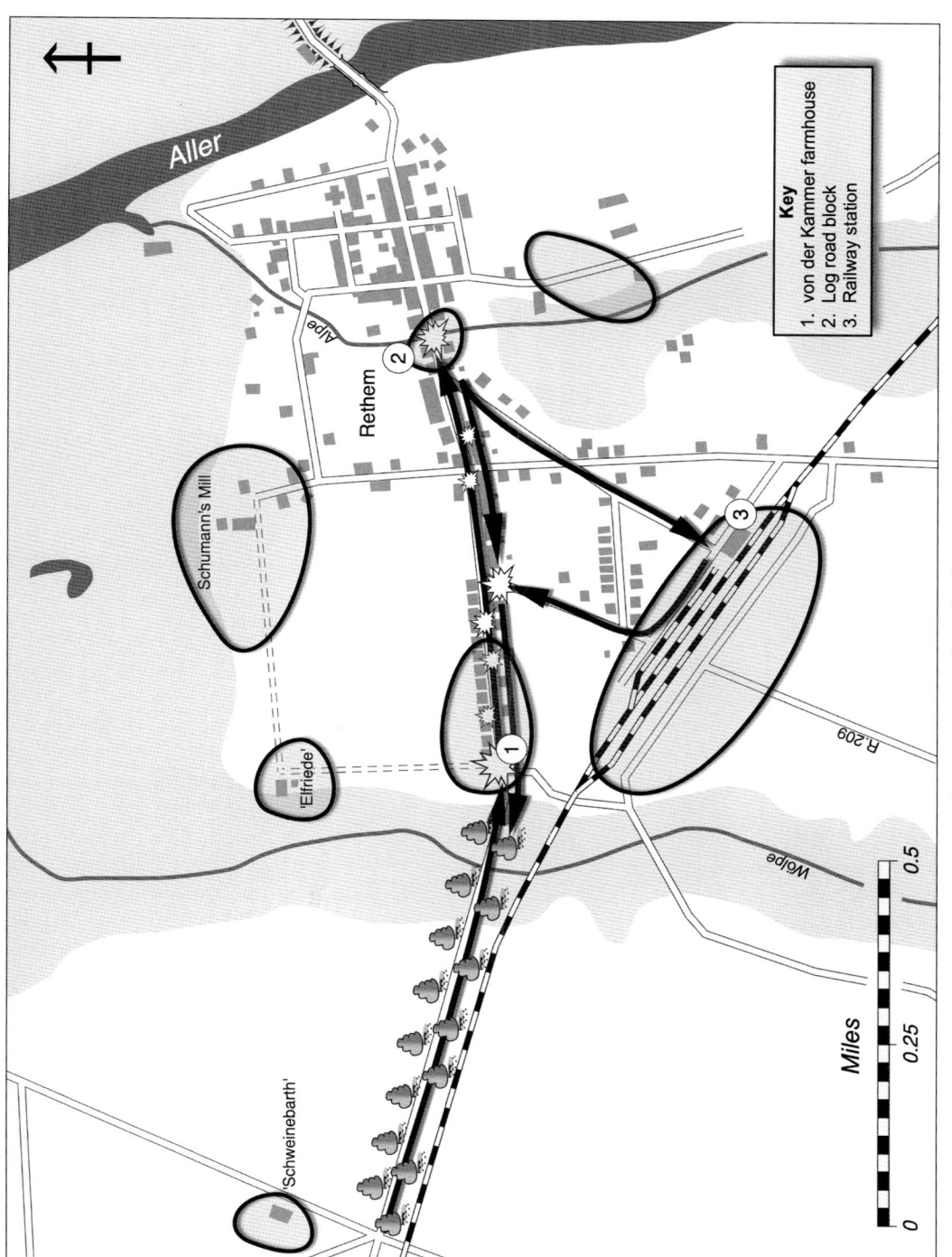

Map 35　Sergeant Moses' *Coup de Main* – 10 April 1945.

The dead-end to the railway station, with the station at the end of the road. Photograph taken in 1982. (Author)

to work their way back to safety. The roll call revealed barely 24 men had returned from the attack mounted that morning with such high expectations.

During 1/5 Welch's attacks on Rethem the other two battalions of 158th Brigade were pushing eastwards from the Weser. 1 E Lancs moved by truck via Hoya and Hassel and cleared Hämelhausen to be close behind 1/5 Welch.[37] The battalion then spent the remainder of the day in a concentration area waiting to hear whether it would take part in the battle for Rethem. Meanwhile, during the morning, 7 RWF cleared the woods to the north of the brigade axis. However, there were still marines in the area and they were prepared to attack whenever the opportunity arose, resulting in HQ 158th Brigade suffering a severe blow. Major Lemon, the brigade's DAA & QMG (DCOS in NATO terminology), was visiting 53rd Division when the brigade headquarters moved to Hämelhausen so a despatch rider, Private Smith, was sent to the old location to escort him to the new. Tragically, for some reason they overshot the junction, which would have taken them to the right place, and ran into a group of marines that had sallied forth from Hülsen and cut the axis being used by 1/5 Welch; Lemon and Smith were ambushed and killed. A Company 1 E Lancs was immediately tasked to re-clear the route, which it accomplished by 1645 hours. While these events were taking place, Lieutenant Colonel Tyler, commanding officer of 7 RWF, was called to brigade headquarters and ordered to advance and capture Hülsen, situated on the Aller downstream from Rethem. The 7 RWF companies spent the afternoon alternately advancing and establishing firm bases as the battalion cautiously moved towards its objective.

---

37   TNA WO 171/5225, 1 E Lancs war diary.

While 7 RWF was directed on Hülsen, 2 Mons from 160th Brigade was ordered to capture Nienburg.[38] As resistance on the Weser's right bank seemed so weak it was decided to risk a rush down the main road. Every vehicle in the battalion was filled with troops and a 40mph dash was launched, ending in the capture of the town. The regimental history proudly announced this was achieved without a shot fired; perhaps unsurprising as Marine-Grenadier-Regiment 6 had withdrawn on 8 April and, as we have heard, the town had surrendered to C Squadron 3 RTR on 9 April. The soldiers of 2 Mons were however justified in thinking they had captured the town as it was in XII Corps' area of responsibility and there were no other British troops in sight. Once the town was secure, 2 Mons established defensive positions to protect the construction of a Bailey pontoon bridge by sappers from 7th Armoured Division. 2 Mons would not enjoy Nienburg for long.

4 Welch, which had returned to its own brigade (160th) when 1/5 Welch set off for Rethem, was ordered to advance north from the battalion's concentration area in woods near Hassel, where it had been since mid-afternoon, and clear the ground between the Weser and the Aller as far as the rivers' confluence nine miles away to the west of Verden. With the help of A Squadron 5 RTR, the battalion's first task was to clear and occupy Westen and Stedorf. The commanding officer, Lieutenant Colonel Frisby, ordered A and C Companies to capture Westen, and B and D Companies Stedorf, clearing Dörverden on the way. A and C Companies struck off to the north-east towards Westen, held by marines from I./5 Bataillon reinforced with Hungarians from Bataillon Kolotay. The companies reached the village without incident and as they started to attack the Hungarians immediately surrendered or swam to the Aller's right bank. The marines, however, resolved to fight it out and in the ensuing action seven were killed, with a further four dying of their wounds in captivity the next day; the remainder were taken prisoner. During the action a Cromwell crew had a lucky escape when a *Panzerfaust* was fired at their tank. Fortunately, the firer's aim was too low as the projectile hit the road under the centre front of the tank, with the resulting explosion bending the floor plates and bursting some hydraulics. Although their tank was immobilised, the crew were unhurt and the hull gunner shot the *Panzerfaust* firer before he could re-engage the motionless Cromwell. Westen's capture not only drove a wedge between the German troops on the Aller's left bank but also provided 53rd Welsh with a potential crossing site if required. B and D Companies had a less active time and by 1900 hours they had accomplished both their tasks, meeting only minor opposition in the northern part of Stedorf.

During the early afternoon 53rd Welsh requested an Auster to check whether the Rethem bridge was blown. The pilot from A Flight 653 Squadron reported back at 1325 hours that it was still intact so planning began for another attempt by 1/5 Welch to break into Rethem and seize the bridge.[39] Brigadier Wilsey contacted Major Bowker by radio at 1545 hours and ordered him to launch a maximum effort, direct attack on Rethem and allocated to him one medium and two field regiments. Major Bowker's plan for the attack involved A and C Companies assaulting from the west astride the Eystrup road under the cover of an artillery barrage designed to neutralize the German defences while the attacking infantry crossed the open ground. By now the '*Schweinebarth*' strongpoint had been captured by C Company, so with Wohlendorf and the strongpoint both in British hands, A and C Companies' attack could go ahead; H-hour was set for 1735 hours.

While the Welsh companies prepared for the attack marines, following German tactical doctrine, sallied forth from Rethem at 1615 hours and mounted a counter-attack against A Company; the attack was repulsed but did little for 1/5 Welch's morale. As H-hour neared the two companies formed up and made final preparations while they lay waiting for the start of the artillery

---

38 TNA WO 171/5245, 2 Mons war diary.
39 TNA WO 171/4750, 653 Air OP Squadron war diary.

1/5 Welch officers observing Rethem from the newly-captured '*Schweinebarth*' strongpoint.

bombardment. The thunder of exploding shells signalled the start of the assault and the soldiers of the two companies got to their feet and began to move towards the town. But as soon as they revealed themselves they were met by a torrent of small-arms' fire, principally from MG 42, stopping the attack in its tracks before it had barely crossed the start line. By 1800 hours it was clear to Major Bowker the attack was doomed and he ordered the assaulting companies to withdraw under cover of an additional artillery barrage and take up defensive positions for the remainder of the night. 1/5 Welch's war diary recorded one officer and 47 other ranks were killed or wounded during the day's actions. Despite the difficulties it had faced, the battalion's part in the battle for Rethem was not over and at 2300 hours Major Bowker was called to brigade headquarters and ordered to mount yet another attack on the town, to be mounted before dawn on 11 April.

The Wardrop ambush

1/5 Welch was not the only battalion in 53rd Welsh to receive an unpleasant surprise at the Germans' aggression. Following its successful assault crossing of the Weser on 9 April, 6 RWF had remained in the bridgehead waiting for its next task. Although warned to take part in the capture of Nienburg, the rapid occupation of the town by 2 Mons made this unnecessary and the battalion enjoyed a night's sleep. On the morning of 10 April it was ordered to move north towards Verden and join the operations to clear the triangle of ground between the rivers. By mid-afternoon the battalion, plus a squadron of tanks from 5 RTR, was on the move and nearing Hassel when orders were received to halt. The commanding officer was called to brigade headquarters where he was ordered instead to clear the area between the Weser and the Aller south of the line Eystrup – Rethem. The plan was simple and involved A and B Companies advancing south-east from Eystrup down two parallel routes to capture Anderten, located on Reichsstrasse 209. C Company would follow B Company and exploit to Rethemer Moor while D Company advanced direct to Stöcken; the three companies were each allocated a tank troop from C Squadron 5 RTR. To prevent the Germans consolidating, the company commanders were ordered to push on quickly and accept risks. With battalions heading off into unknown territory it may seem odd that divisional reconnaissance was not allocated to lead their advances. Unfortunately, the recce troops from 53rd Recce Regiment were not available as the regiment had conducted an 85-mile move during the night 9/10 April and was still at Vilsen, five miles west of Hoya, where it was resting and replenishing; later on 10 April the squadrons began operating on the division's flanks on the Weser's left bank and reported on blown bridges, dumps found and so forth. Perhaps a measure of over-confidence and the desire for speed overcame any concerns that the advance was not being led by the recce regiment.

At 1815 hours the tanks and infantry companies married up: 10 Troop supporting A Company for the left route and 11 Troop supporting B Company for the right, and, shortly after, they set off. The tank troops, each consisting of three Cromwells and a Sherman Firefly, led, with the tanks carrying a section of infantry on their decks; the bulk of the rifle companies followed in trucks a tactical bound behind. 11 Troop clattered off through Eystrup, crossed the railway line then headed south-east on the Eystruper Bruchweg, a ruler-straight lane running across flat pastures and through woods. The troop leader, Lieutenant Crocker, was in the lead tank, a Cromwell, followed by his troop sergeant, Jake Wardrop, in the Sherman Firefly, then came the second Cromwell commanded by Corporal Richardson and the third Cromwell brought up the rear. Jake Wardrop was a brave and resourceful soldier. He joined 5 RTR in 1937 and had fought with the regiment in France in 1940, the Western Desert, Tripolitania, Tunisia and Italy, and in Europe from D-Day onwards.

Sergeant Jake Wardrop (without shirt), his crew and their Firefly. (Forty)

Sergeant George Stimpson, the troop sergeant of 10 Troop and a longstanding friend of Wardrop, recalls the events that unfolded:[40]

---

40 George Forty (ed.), *Tanks Across the Desert* (London: William Kimber, 1981), p.182. Throughout his war service, strictly against regulations, Wardrop kept a graphic record of his experiences and it is this that

At the briefing we were told that the infantry had already patrolled into the wood that morning and that it could therefore be considered as being clear of enemy. With this in mind, the first few miles through the wooded area would be carried out at the double, with the infantry on the backs of the tanks…At Zero hour, both troops advanced along their allotted centre lines and 11 Troop was soon well inside the wood, while 10 Troop, which had more open ground to cross was still clear of the trees. We suddenly saw a number of friendly fighter aircraft clearly shaping up for an attack with us as their targets, so we took the prudent course of stopping and displaying our recognition panels. 11 Troop, unaware of this delay, continued on into the wood. There was really no reason why they should not have done so, after all, it was already reported as clear. Eventually they came to a track junction, and slowed down to check the map, when all hell broke loose! They were right in the middle of an ambush with enemy dug-in around the crossing. It was later discovered that the enemy were marines.

The last two tanks in the troop managed to pull back and from their reports it soon became clear that a terrific and bloody battle had been fought at the cross-roads [sic], with considerable losses to our side, including Jake's Firefly…As soon as I was able I went to the squadron commander and asked for permission to go back into the wood to look for the two missing tanks from 11 Troop. This was granted on condition that I took only those members of my own crew who volunteered to come with me. There were no second thoughts given to this and we set off down the road back into the wood. It was rather quiet and frightening, but there were no signs of the enemy and we eventually came to the place where the battle had taken place. The two tanks were still and quiet and there were bodies of British soldiers everywhere. I found Jake's body at the side of his tank, which was in the middle of the cross-tracks. He had been killed by machine-gun fire. I then inspected the tank and found that it had been hit by a bazooka which had struck the armoured cover over the forward extractor fan, just at the side of the driver's head, but had done very little permanent damage to the vehicle. It was obvious, however, that enough chaos and confusion had been created to make the crew think they had been hit badly and that they must bale out. They were gunned down as they tried to escape.

It was at this time that I took Jake's diary into safe-keeping. I was well aware where he had kept it. Later I was able to start the tank and we drove it back to the squadron, where a new crew took it over.

Sergeant Jake Wardrop's grave in CWGC cemetery Becklingen. (Author)

---

formed the basis of George Forty's book.

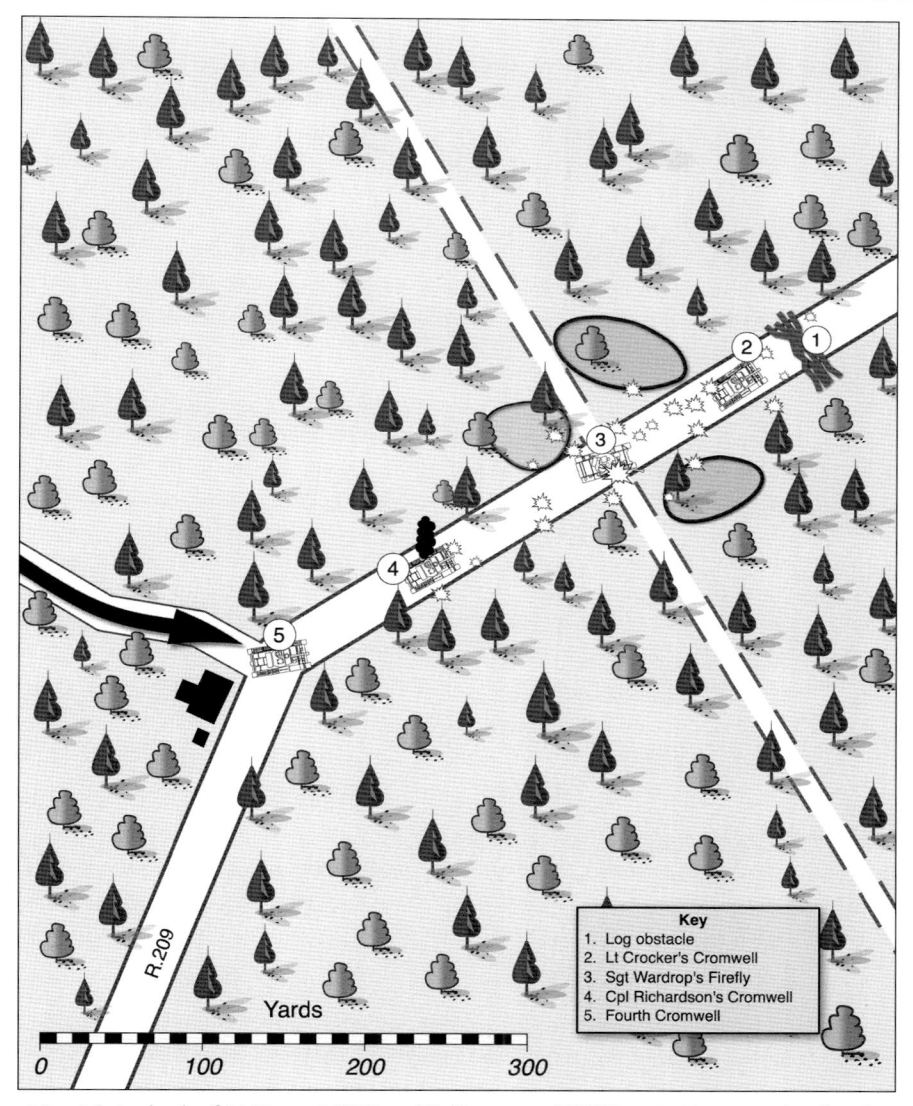

Key
1. Log obstacle
2. Lt Crocker's Cromwell
3. Sgt Wardrop's Firefly
4. Cpl Richardson's Cromwell
5. Fourth Cromwell

Map 36 Ambush of 11 Troop 5 RTR and B Company 6 RWF – 1915 hours 10 April 1945.

The infantry had a different perspective of the ambush, particularly the part played by the tanks, as an un-named fusilier from B Company 6 RWF wrote in this graphic account:[41]

> We set out travelling at high speed, all tanks in sight of each other. A house was situated at a T-junction and as we turned the corner one of the section spotted two of the enemy. He jumped off the tank, which pulled round a corner 100 yards away. The tank commander looking through his glasses spotted a road block, and, pulling in to the side of the road, told the rest of the section to dismount. The second tank [Jake Wardrop's Firefly] came along and

---

41 Anon., *The History of the 6th Battalion The Royal Welch Fusiliers – Europe 1944-45* (Unknown publisher, 1946), p.168.

was knocked out by the enemy. We did not see the third and fourth, but from the noise and explosions in their area it seemed hardly possible that they could have escaped. The enemy fired all he had at us, and we did the same keeping their heads down while we obtained good fire positions. The only support we received was from our tank, which fired one burst as it turned round and retired the way we had come, instead of putting up a fight with us as we had hoped. We were left by ourselves. Underneath the knocked-out tank was one of the dead crew and another badly wounded.

We thought at first we might be able to hold Jerry off until support came. No support did come, however, and more of our boys were killed and our platoon commander, Lieutenant Castles, was wounded in the face, shot through the shoulder and again through the wrist. He was bleeding badly as was the fellow by the tank, but we could do nothing for them. Anyway, they held on, the platoon commander telling me to take charge if anything else happened. Luckily nothing did and he kept us under control. The enemy crept around us on all sides. Knowing we did not stand a chance, we decided to surrender, which I think was the best thing for otherwise we would all have been shot up.

The Jerries took us into a wood, stripped us of all equipment, turned out our pockets and all the while we still thought we would be liberated by the other two platoons in the company. If only they had come then. We were marched on through the wood, being joined by another company of Jerries who were pulling out in some sort of order. As we came out into the open some more Typhoons came overhead, so we were made to go back into the wood until they had passed over. When we pulled out again we ran into one of our artillery barrages and it was anything but pleasant to be on the receiving end this time.

Another fusilier present during the ambush was William Haley, aged 19 and a No. 2 on one of the section's Bren guns:[42]

My main memory is of travelling very fast and grimly hanging on top of the light, fast tanks through the forest road. We stopped briefly to question a civilian walking towards us. Everything appeared to be OK so we travelled on. When approaching a T-junction I observed movement on the right-hand side of the junction but it was not possible to communicate to the tank commander owing to all the noise.

We turned left at the junction and up ahead we could see a tree blocking the road about 100 yards away, maybe less. We approached slowly, still aboard the tanks. We dismounted – I was on the right-hand side of the tank – and moved up to the obstruction following in line. Suddenly a lance corporal doubled back towards me shouting, 'There are Jerries up there!' and kept going. Then the action started. *Panzerfaust* knocked out the second tank, blocking the first against the obstruction; this tank must also have been hit as I immediately dropped flat in the shallow, roadside gulley and was joined by the first tank's crew. My first reaction was alarm that I appeared to be the only one armed in this little group. I took up a firing position and the face of a young German popped up just a couple of yards in front of me. I fired and didn't see him again – if I had had a grenade I would have made sure.

My position in the shallow gulley was not conducive to observe and fire without showing my position. I cleared the empty round and bolted another, ready to fire, but then my rifle jammed and I was unable to clear this without exposure. In the meantime, the noise of action was all around, sniper fire from the tree tops was pinging about while I'm worrying about being separated from the rest of the platoon and having the spare barrel and ammo for the

---

42 Kemp and Graves, *The Red Dragon*, p.229.

Although the course of Reichsstrasse 209 has been modernised, this is the site of the Wardrop ambush. B Company and 11 Troop entered the killing zone from the road on the left of the picture. The log obstacle was positioned where the main road starts to bend out of sight. Photograph taken in 2015. (Author)

Bren gun, which was somewhere with my mate Norman Kent, the No. 1, on the other side of the road.

After a while – it seemed an eternity – I heard our officer shouting: '*Kamerad, Kamerad*'. I shouted to the tank crew in the ditch: 'Get up, it's all over,' then walked down the road where the remainder of the platoon and our wounded officer were gathered. The Germans took over. They seemed a mixed bag: young and old, some sailor types, possibly marines. We were taken through the forests and one wounded tank crew member was left in the forest cottage to be looked after by civilians. After a few rests we eventually came to a small town [Rethem] where we received the usual hostile welcome for PoWs. After a few kicks etc we were told to empty our pockets into our helmets and wait for interrogation.

I went in before two officers, one of whom spoke good English. Having taken some of my personal bits and pieces he told me my division's number and said: 'Why are you fighting?' and I replied: 'For freedom,' but I must admit I felt a little foolish. He got angry and said: 'Bloody Englishman, get out!' We were then marched to Stalag XIB.

6 RWF's log records that the ambush was sprung at 1915 hours and that at 1930 hours the two rear platoons counter-attacked and were moving forward slowly.[43] This manoeuvre was clearly unsuccessful as B Company reported at 2005 hours that the enemy were still holding out and another tank had been knocked out. A second attack was mounted at 2023 hours and a few minutes later the area of the ambush was secured, perhaps unsurprising as the marines and their British

---

43   TNA WO 171/5283, 6 RWF war diary.

The fan cowl on Jake Wardrop's Firefly showing the impact of the *Panzerfaust* warhead. (TNA)

prisoners had by then withdrawn into the gathering gloom. It is strange that with the rest of the company following only a tactical bound behind the lead platoon, the ambush was not rapidly mopped up. In their accounts, neither the un-named fusilier nor Haley indicate that the marines were under any pressure from the rest of B Company, indicating that the counter-attacks took too long to be mounted and were half-hearted.

The ambush is believed to have been commanded by Oberleutnant zur See Helmut Vollmers, and German accounts state he personally knocked out a tank during the action. 6 RWF reported five killed, three wounded and 15 missing as a result of this short but bloody action. The two abandoned tanks, Sergeant Jake's Firefly and Corporal Richardson's Cromwell, were included in the survey of RAC casualties compiled by the two RAMC captains.[44] They recorded that Sherman Vc WD No. 212700 was struck at a range of 30 yards by a hollow-charge warhead, damaging

---

44 TNA WO 205/1165, 5 RTR, Serial B.17, Wright and Harkness, *A Survey of Casualties Amongst Armoured Units in North-West Europe.*

Date	Location	Tank Type/No	How Lost	Crew	Cas	Remarks
10 April	Stöcken	Sherman Vc 212700	Hit by bazooka but did not brew and is a runner	Sgt Wardrop Tpr Wood Tpr Forrest Tpr Colton	KIA Missing KIA OK	By MG fire on evac Believed PW By MG fire on evac
10 April	Stöcken	Cromwell 75 188494	Undamaged	Lt Crocker Tpr Skidmore Tpr Smart Tpr Orpwood Tpr Rands	OK KIA OK OK OK	Hit in head by sniper
10 April	Stöcken	Cromwell 75 121768	Hit by bazooka in road wheels and explosion in turret. Did not brew and is a runner	Cpl Richardson Tpr Wilson H Tpr Butler Tpr Kinvig Tpr Hennessey	Missing Missing Missing Missing Severe head wounds; evac to RAP RWF. Since DOW	Believed PW Believed PW Believed PW Believed PW

Figure 24 5 RTR Tank Casualty Log – 10 April 1945.

the fan cowl on the hull top just behind the co-driver's hatch but not a penetrating hit. The explosion caused no internal damage, and although fragments wounded the driver, who had his head exposed, he was able to move the tank out of the killing area. Two of the turret crew – Jake Wardrop and Trooper Forrest – were subsequently killed by small-arms' fire after dismounting.

For Cromwell V WD No. 121768, the survey recorded that as a result of a hollow-charge explosion on the road wheels a small fire had started in the tank's fuze box. The smoke caused the crew to bale out, except the gunner who stayed firing the machine-gun until the ammunition was expended and he was captured; sadly the identity of this brave crew member is not known. Trooper Hennessey was shot in the head and killed after escaping from the tank. The death of Jake Wardrop was keenly felt throughout his regiment and the formal recording of the fate of 11 Troop in 5 RTR's casualty log,[45] extract below at Figure 24, conceals the sadness that existed.

By the time the ambush was over it was almost dark and 6 RWF was in an exposed situation in thick woods possibly containing many Germans so Lieutenant Colonel Hutchinson ordered A Company to close on B Company and push on into Anderten. Although the village had been captured by 2215 hours without difficulty and the remainder of 6 RWF had joined the two companies, the battalion and C Squadron were now out of physical contact with all other British forces and vulnerable. All-round defence was therefore taken up and vigorous patrolling continued through the night, with a patrol from C Company reaching as far as Stöcken, two miles to the north-east. The patrol reported that the hamlet was held and that an 8.8cm Flak covered Reichsstrasse 209.

While 6 RWF was in action on the division's southern flank, further north its sister battalion 7 RWF had made good progress advancing towards the Aller and by about 2200 hours was ready to attack Hülsen, with B Company tasked to mount the initial assault. The attack was allocated substantial artillery support from 81st and 83rd Field Regiments and 72nd Medium Regiment, which each fired 50 rounds per gun in a pre-H-hour bombardment. Despite this fire, German reports mention that the shelling caused little damage as it landed away from the village falling instead on the area of the railway station to the south-west. The *Flak* batteries in the Rethem

---

45 TNA WO 171/4711, 5 RTR Tank Casualty Log. Corporal Richardson and his three surviving crew members were liberated from Stalag XIB six days later.

area fired harassing missions in an attempt to break up the assault, adding to the general rain of shells. As B Company began to enter Hülsen the platoons met stiff opposition from numerous snipers, and as the effort of fighting from house-to-house caused the attack's momentum to flag, A Company had to be ordered forward to assist and it took until 0300 hours on 11 April to clear the village. Twenty-eight prisoners were taken but many Germans attempted to flee by swimming the Aller; there were losses among these men not only from drowning but also from small-arms' fire and the graves of 40 marines in the cemetery in nearby Westen bear testimony to the ferocity of the battle for this small village. Two fusiliers of 7 RWF died in action at Hülsen.

Back in Rethem Jordan took advantage of the lull in the fighting to visit his marines in the forward positions. He did this riding on the back of a motorbike driven by a marine named Hermann Pieper. Pieper was a member of the Marine-Kraftfahrzeug-Abteilung at Hülsen but had managed to escape on his bike to Rethem when the village was attacked by 7 RWF. On reaching Rethem he was placed at the disposal of the regimental commander and that night he drove Jordan around the positions, weaving through the debris now strewn about the town's streets. He had particular difficulty negotiating the many cables drooping from their poles, a task not made any easier by Jordan shouting at him to go faster. Pieper completed the mission with his commander but his bike would be written-off by shell splinters the next day.

Tuesday 10 April thus came to a close and for XII Corps it had been a mixed day. Although the Weser bridgehead at Hoya was established with ease, Nienburg captured and the Aller reached in places, all attempts to capture Rethem and its bridge had been soundly repulsed. Ominously 2. Marine-Infanterie-Division had shown that it would resist whenever confronted and its defiance did not bode well. On this day Hitler ordered Student and Blumentritt to swap commands, with Blumentritt taking over Armeegruppe Student, which was re-titled with Blumentritt's name, and Student moving to takeover 1. Fallschirm-Armee, still hotly contesting XXX Corps' advance on Bremen.[46] The reason for the swap is not known but perhaps Hitler considered Student better-suited to the command of the fighting withdrawal on the right flank; it is equally possible that it was just another purposeless act of desperation with no rationale. Blumentritt had enjoyed a distinguished war record and had built a reputation as a thorough planner. From 1941–42 he served as Chief of Staff of 4. Armee during the early period of the war on the East Front and this was followed by a two-year appointment as Chief of Staff of Heeresgruppe 'D', where he served von Rundstedt then von Kluge and Model during the Normandy battles and the retreat from France. Appointments then followed fast and furious with his command of XII. SS-Armeekorps in the Aachen area during the winter of 1944, 25. Armee in the Netherlands during February and March 1945, and then 1. Fallschirm Armee for barely two weeks before taking over Armeegruppe Student. While for Blumentritt the command would be his last of the war, Student would experience one further change of command. On 28 April Hitler ordered him to take over Heinrici's Heeresgruppe Weichsel, falling back in disorder from the Oder, and organise the defence of Mecklenburg. He had barely assumed command before the British overran what remained of the *Heeresgruppe* in Schleswig-Holstein. Student was later captured, tried at Nuremburg for condoning atrocities in Crete and received a five-year sentence, which he never served. How ironic it must have been for Student, who had played a leading role in the development of airborne forces, to combat the Allies with the grounded 1. Fallschirm-Armee.

On the morning of 10 April Blumentritt drove to the *Armeegruppe's* headquarters at Celle, where he received a briefing from Student. The situation facing him could not have inspired much optimism. Korps Ems, on his right flank defending the Bremen area, was numerically strong but comprised low-grade troops of suspect effectiveness. In his centre, the enemy was across the Weser

---

46   FMS, B-361, Final Operations of Army Blumentritt (10 April – 5 May 1945), General Blumentritt, p.1.

but 2. Marine-Infanterie-Division and SS-A.u.E.Btl. 12 'HJ' had shown they would resist to the best of their ability and he probably had some confidence that they would put up a fight on the Aller at Rethem and Essel. On his left flank in the Winsen and Celle areas, Gruppe Grosan and Kampfgruppe Totzeck were moving forward to the Aller to fill the gap on the marine division's left flank, but here the enemy was already across the Leine and it was only a matter of time before they were threatening the Aller. To his south the area was virtually undefended and Blumentritt was uncertain about the existence of German forces. He thought that General der Panzertruppe Wenck was forming 12. Armee in the Harz but, as he had no evidence for this, as far as he was concerned it was rumour.[47] With air reconnaissance very limited and ground reconnaissance non-existent, Blumentritt was hamstrung by his inability to discover enemy locations and the situation facing his forces. He was reduced to the humbling expedient of *Fernsprech-Aufklärung* or recce by telephone, involving his staff telephoning village postmistresses and the like and asking them what the situation was in their local area. Furthermore, as his headquarters was supported by an improvised signals battalion with few transmitters and insufficient telephone equipment, he was forced to find his commanders by touring in his staff car and giving orders when and if he found them; a risky method as Scheurlen had found to his cost. Despite his abilities as a commander, Blumentritt was in a hopeless position as the battle for the Aller Line got underway.

With battle joined at Rethem, we will now return to VIII Corps, which we left on 9 April with 1st Commando Brigade closing up to conduct the assault crossing of the Aller in the Essel area.

---

47   FMS, B-361, Final Operations of Army Blumentritt, p.3.

7

'A Little Bit of Burma': The Battle for the Aller Bridgehead at Essel 10–12 April

Deployment of Marine-Füsilier-Bataillon 2 on the Leine and Aller

The defence of the Aller in the Schwarmstedt-Essel area on 2. Marine-Infanterie-Division's left flank was the responsibility of Marine-Füsilier-Bataillon 2, commanded by Korvettenkapitän Josef Gördes. Gördes and his battalion reached the flank on or about 8 April, the same day as 11th Armoured Division started its eastwards advance from the Weser. Both the Leine and Aller flowed through Gördes' allotted area and he knew that he would have to fight the British not only sequentially on the two riverlines but also on two distinctly different areas of ground. The first area, the triangle between the two rivers, was mainly open, agricultural land but with extensive meadows, which, as they neared the rivers, became increasingly soft. The area also hosted some blocks of forest. The Leine, flowing northwards on the triangle's western side, is about 80-foot wide and in its final reaches before its confluence with the Aller near Hademstorf, at the triangle's apex. The Aller, some 120-feet wide, forms the triangle's eastern side.

The Aller at Essel. Photograph taken in 2015. (Author)

'A LITTLE BIT OF BURMA' 263

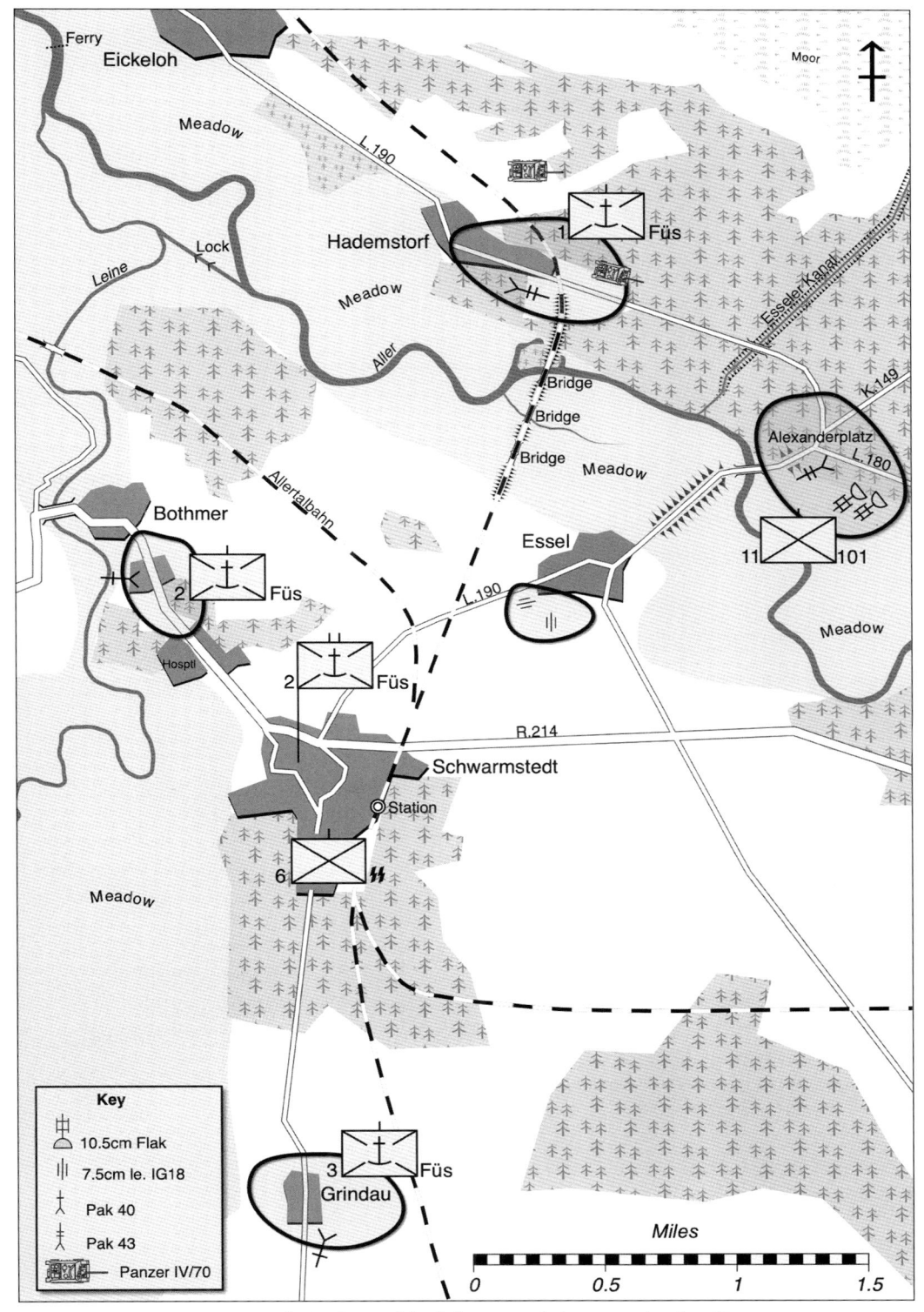

Map 37 The Defence of the Schwarmstedt Area – 10 April 1945.

There are four settlements in the triangle: the largest, Schwarmstedt, and Bothmer and Grindau are on the western side, while Essel lies roughly in the centre. Schwarmstedt and Bothmer lay on Reichsstrasse 214 linking Nienburg and Celle, and to cross the Leine in 1945 the road detoured north of Schwarmstedt to a bridge at Bothmer.

The second area was the right bank of the Aller. Here the terrain was dominated by an extensive forest of Scots pine about a mile in depth, which provided good cover and confined vehicle movement to the roads and tracks. The forest contained areas of ancient, glacial sand dunes, which, with their slightly raised elevations, offered better observation and fields of fire and were therefore obvious defensive positions. Backing the forest was a broad area of poorly-drained moor some four miles in depth and cut by numerous streams and ditches. Only the road to Ostenholz crossed this moor and in 1945 off-road movement by tracked or wheeled vehicles was impossible. A deep drainage channel, the Esseler Kanal, formed a significant part of the moor's drainage system and this man-made feature, about 12-foot deep and 40-foot wide, cut in a south-westerly orientation straight through the forest to join the Aller. The channel was a most effective vehicle obstacle and, where it ran through the forest, was crossed by just one road bridge.

The Hannover to Buchholz in der Nordheide (15 miles south-west of Hamburg) railway runs through Schwarmstedt then heads north-east across the triangle to the Aller. Before crossing the river the line runs for half a mile on a high embankment, taking it across a broad area of meadow. On this section two steel-truss bridges carry the line over a lane and a stream, after which it crosses the Aller on a further steel-truss bridge.

Once on the Aller's right bank, the railway runs through the forest on a gradually reducing embankment to Hademstorf. In 1945 the line had two branches, both now no longer in existence: on Schwarmstedt's northern edge it branched to produce the Allertalbahn, which ran

The Esseler Kanal and its road bridge. The depth of the channel and the cover it afforded played important roles during the battle in the forest. Photograph taken in 2015. (Author)

'A LITTLE BIT OF BURMA' 265

The railway bridge over the Aller. Although the photograph was taken in 2015, the bridge is identical to its 1945 predecessor. (Author)

The Aller road bridge taken from the left bank in 2006. The 1945 bridge was almost identical. (Author)

north-westwards before crossing the Leine near Bothmer and heading to Rethem and beyond, while on the town's southern edge it branched eastwards to Celle.

One thousand yards upstream of the railway bridge Landesstrasse 190, an important local road, crosses the Aller. In 1945 the road bridge was a steel girder construction with a curved top chord and a span of 140 feet.

On the Aller's right bank, at a junction area known as the Alexanderplatz, an advancing enemy has a choice of three routes: first, continue north-westwards on Landesstrasse 190 to Walsrode and then on main roads to Hamburg; secondly, take the minor road Kreisstrasse 149 – the Ostenholz road – and head north-east across the moor to Ostenholz and thence to Fallingbostel or Bergen-Belsen; or, thirdly, head east on Landesstrasse 180 to Winsen and thence to Celle and Uelzen. Any of the three routes provide options for advancing to the Elbe, some 70 miles distant. However, all three were initially dominated by the forests on the Aller's right bank, strongly favouring the defence. After the battle a member of 1st Commando Brigade would glumly describe the Essel forests as 'a little bit of Burma in the midst of the bloody *Reich*.'[1]

Gördes deployed his forces on the reasonable assumption that the British would attack from the west, crossing the Leine in the area of Schwarmstedt before advancing across the triangle to the road bridge over the Aller, their principal objective. His plans were, however, complicated by having to defend successively two riverlines in close proximity to each other. His first defence would be on the Leine, which would conclude with a withdrawal across the triangle to the Aller and thence to the right bank for the second defence and the main battle. The withdrawal had two significant challenges: first, breaking clean from fighting on the Leine and carrying out a rapid withdrawal, probably in contact, across the narrow triangle of land; and secondly, keeping the Aller bridges intact so that he could cross before demolishing them to prevent their capture by the pursuing enemy. Gördes' second defence would be fought in the forest on the Aller's right bank where he would have to counter enemy crossings and prevent a breakout. While fighting in the forest would favour the defence, it would dissipate his limited manpower and give the enemy opportunity to outflank his positions by infiltration.

With the battalion's arrival on 8 April, Gördes established his headquarters in the Gasthof Heuer in Schwarmstedt. He deployed 2./Füs. Kompanie forward to Bothmer to cover the bridge and engage enemy movement on the Leine's left bank. 3./Füs. Kompanie deployed to Grindau, a hamlet to the south of Schwarmstedt, to cover the Leine. A pair of 7.5cm le. IG18 light, infantry guns supported these two forward deployed companies from positions on the southern edge of Essel. 1./Füs. Kompanie, the third rifle company, remained on the Aller's right bank in the Hademstorf area, to act as a reserve. A detachment from Marine-Panzerjäger-Abteilung 2 provided 7.5cm Pak 40 anti-tank guns to support the two forward companies and tank-hunting teams of marines armed with *Panzerfaust* also deployed to Norddrebber on the Leine's left bank (the action between these teams and B Squadron 23 Hussars and F Company 8 RB on 9 April was described in Chapter 5).

Assuming the successful withdrawal of his two forward-deployed companies, for the Aller's defence Gördes probably intended holding the forest on the line of Landesstrasse 190 between Hademstorf and the Alexanderplatz. To support his isolated battle removed from the divisional main effort at Rethem, Gördes was reinforced by a variety of units. Infantry came in the form of 120 men from 11./101 Festungs-Pak-E.u.A. Abteilung (Fortress Anti-tank Replacement and Training Unit) from Fallingbostel. Despite its grandiose title, the unit comprised former sailors from the Kiel area equipped only with small-arms and *Panzerfaust*, who had, since 5 April, been responsible for guarding the bridges in the Essel area but remained in situ when the marines of

---

1   Ward, 'My Time with 45 (RM) Commando'.

Marine-Füsilier-Bataillon 2 arrived; they were more fortunate than the remainder of the *Abteilung* which was despatched to contribute to the defence of Berlin.

With support from Oberst Grosan, Gördes also received some armour and heavy weapons, rare resources at this stage of the war. Grosan had recognised that the defence of the Essel bridges would need as much muscle as possible so he allocated Gördes his three Tigers, a Panther, a Panzer Mk IV, two Panzer IV/70 tank-destroyers, both of which were very low on fuel even before reaching Gördes, and a few SdKfz 222 and 223 light armoured cars. The tanks were moved to Ostenholz to be in position to influence developments, while the tank-destroyers were positioned in the Hademstorf area to cover an enemy breakout on Landesstrasse 190. At least one of the armoured cars was given the task of patrolling eastwards along Landesstrasse 180 to report any enemy crossings, while others deployed westwards beyond the Leine and it is likely that these were the vehicles that clashed with 1 SAS in the Nienburg forest on 8 April. Grosan provided two heavy 8.8cm Pak 43 from Heeres-Panzerjäger-Abteilung 661; the first of these powerful anti-tank guns was sited on the edge of the forest just to the east of the road bridge from where it could cover the road from Essel, while the second was sited on the edge of the wood at the eastern end of Hademstorf where it covered Landesstrasse 190 as the road emerged from the forest. Two 10.5 cm Flak from RAD Batterie 1./521, previously in the Nienburg area but successfully withdrawn to the Aller, were deployed to defend the road to Engehausen and provide some artillery, with the battery's surplus gunners employed as infantry. In the late afternoon of 10 April a SdKfZ 251 half-track towing a 10.5cm le. FH howitzer arrived from Bergen. The gun was sited by its crew near the road bridge and the half-track was commandeered by Gördes as his command vehicle. Since enemy vehicles could only cross the Esseler Kanal via its sole bridge, to provide better targets for *Panzerfaust* attack *Volkssturm* had built an obstacle on the bridge, comprising a chicane of caissons filled with cobble-stones ripped from the road. Engineer teams prepared the rail bridges and the road bridge for demolition, but left intact the foot crossings up and downstream from Essel. The Leine road bridge at Niedernstöcken and the road and railway bridges near Bothmer were all blown on 9 April before the British reached the river.

While Gördes' forces were moving into position, the various elements of Gruppe Grosan were moving forward to the Aller from Bergen and their deployments are shown on Map 11. Bataillon Lotze and Bataillon Sperling under the command of Major Rudolf Kahle were moving on foot towards Ostenholz. Similarly, the anti-tank trainees of the Panzerjäger-Lehrgänge were deploying with twelve 8cm Panzerwerferkanone (PWK) 8H63, with the light guns almost certainly being manhandled by their crews as suitable towing vehicles and fuel would have been very hard to come by. Landesschützen-Abteilung 'Wietzendorf' and Volkssturm-Bataillon 'Lüneburg' were being gathered together and, probably less than enthusiastically, moved towards the Aller. Also deploying was Kampfgruppe Totzeck, which had deployed from Celle to the Winsen area to defend the town's road bridge over the Aller. On arrival, Totzeck positioned his two companies forward of the Aller to meet the expected thrust from the south-west and sited his two Nebelwerfer batteries in depth on the Aller's right bank. At the same time as Totzeck's forces were moving to Winsen, a very different type of march was moving through the area. Between 7–10 April a 'death march' of 4,000 inmates from the Misburg concentration camp, which provided slave labour for the Deurag-Nerag refinery near Hannover, passed through Winsen, with Neuengamme concentration camp near Hamburg as their intended destination. The march, on which hundreds died, mostly shot, only got as far as Belsen, where the survivors were incarcerated.

In its defence of the Aller crossings at Essel, Marine-Füsilier-Bataillon 2 will soon be joined by some four companies of Hitler Youth from SS-A.u.E.Btl.12 'HJ'. Although the young soldiers had escaped destruction at the hands of 11th Armoured Division, they were mostly exhausted and the battalion no longer a coherent force, with its command structure severely degraded by the fighting on the Weser and the subsequent withdrawal. The battalion's situation on 10/11 April was as follows:

Battalion headquarters. The headquarters was established in a farmhouse between Eickeloh and Hademstorf on the Aller's right bank. However, SS-Hauptsturmführer Peinemann, was not present. Although he had been at Meinkingsburg on 8 April, following the battle at the hamlet he disappears from the record until 16 April.[2] In his absence, SS-Obersturmführer Marsen of 2. SS-Kompanie took command of the four companies that reached Marine-Füsilier-Bataillon 2, with an *Oberleutnant* from the *Luftwaffe* taking his place as a company commander; this officer was soon to vanish.

1. and 2. SS-Kompanie. Although 1. SS-Kompanie had not seen much action, 2. SS-Kompanie had fought in the Rodewald area. Both companies had withdrawn across the Lichten Moor before crossing the Aller at Rethem. They were then ordered, probably by 2. Marine-Infanterie-Division, to move south-eastwards to join Marine-Füsilier-Bataillon 2. The companies were moving to a battalion assembly area at Ostenholz.

3. SS-Kompanie. The company was largely destroyed at Leese and Husum. Any remnants would have been incorporated into the other companies.

4. SS-Kompanie. The heavy weapons' company's teams had been allocated to the other companies before battle was joined and its members were sharing the fate of the companies to which they were attached.

5. SS-Kompanie. The company had taken heavy casualties at Leese and Steimbke and its remnants had withdrawn across the Aller via the Eickeloh ferry. Once on the right bank, the company reorganised and recuperated in the forest between Eickeloh and Hademstorf. It is unlikely that any of the company's SdKfz 251 half-tracks were in existence by this stage.

6. SS-Kompanie. Following action on the Weser's left bank, the company had crossed the river by improvised means in the Nienburg area then withdrew due east, frequently skirmishing with 11th Armoured Division. Those soldiers managing to reach the Leine's right bank were incorporated into the defence of Schwarmstedt and Grindau.

7. SS-Kompanie. The company had taken heavy casualties at Leese and in the Nienburg Forest and was still withdrawing via Norddrebber to Rethem. It will reappear on 16 April in the area between Walsrode and Fallingbostel.

Unterführer-Lehr-Kompanie, Marsch Kompanie and Stamm Kompanie. These three companies all took heavy casualties at Leese. After Leese, the Unterführer-Lehr-Kompanie ceases to be mentioned in Buchwald's account; the last of the Marsch Kompanie was destroyed at Steimbke; while the Stamm Kompanie was demolished during the running battles between Rodewald and Lindsburg. Any remnants would have joined the other companies.

So, shortly, 1. and 2. SS-Kompanien will be at Ostenholz, four miles in depth of Marine-Füsilier-Bataillon 2, 5. SS-Kompanie will be a mile to the north-west of the marine battalion in the vicinity

---

2   Buchwald, *Endkampf,* p.43.

of Eickeloh and elements of 6. SS-Kompanie will be in Schwarmstedt; all their young soldiers were exhausted by the demands of the withdrawal and for a while in no fit state for battle. At midnight on 9 April 11th Armoured Division estimated the companies' strengths as follows: 1. SS-Kompanie – 90 percent, 2. SS-Kompanie – 100 percent, 5. SS-Kompanie – one percent and 6. SS-Kompanie – 70 percent. As 1. SS-Kompanie had seen little action the estimate is probably correct; the figure for 2. SS-Kompanie is doubtful as the company had taken casualties in the Rodewald area; 5. SS-Kompanie, while heavily degraded, was not completely destroyed and was, as we will see, still capable of action; and the figure for 6. SS-Kompanie is probably correct. In addition to its losses and exhaustion, the battalion's situation was of course further weakened by the absence of its commanding officer.

Tuesday 10 April

On 10 April Second Army ordered VIII Corps to secure, without delay, Celle and the line of the Aller within boundaries and then, with no reference to advances by XII Corps on its left, secure Uelzen, but keeping contact with US Ninth Army on its right. The same day, VIII Corps ordered 15th Scottish Division to advance on the corps' right flank and capture Celle, construct a Class 40 crossing over the Aller, then advance and secure Uelzen. 11th Armoured Division was ordered to advance on the left flank with maximum speed and secure Bergen-Belsen. The division was given the axis: Helstorf, Schwarmstedt then, via either the Aller's left or right bank, advance to Winsen before swinging north to Bergen-Belsen; a Class 40 crossing over the Aller was required at either Essel or Winsen.

The Capture of Schwarmstedt

11th Armoured tasked 159th Brigade Group to clear the triangle of ground between the Leine and the Aller and at 0800 hours 2 FF Yeo Group moved off to cross the 6th Airborne Division bridge at Neustadt to start this operation. Once on the right bank the group then headed north towards Schwarmstedt. Initially, only limited opposition was encountered and Esperke was captured without difficulty but this changed as the force approached Grindau, occupied by marines from 3./Füs. Kompanie and Hitler Youth of SS-Obersturmführer Stephan's 6. SS-Kompanie. The first indication of stiffening resistance was the destruction of B Squadron's lead tank, which was knocked out by a *Panzerfaust*. The tank's loss was briefly mentioned in the regimental war diary, but the true horror experienced by the crew is revealed in the survey of tank casualties, which gives a detailed description of the tank's destruction. The survey recorded that a hollow-charge projectile hit Comet WD No. 335037, penetrating the visor plate in front of the co-driver, who was also the Besa gunner. The hollow-charge's jet then set off a single HE round in the bin behind the co-driver, causing injuries to the turret crew and triggering the subsequent fire. The jet of molten metal probably hit the co-driver, with other crew members injured by fragments from the HE round. Their fates were recorded as:[3]

---

3 TNA WO 205/1165, 2 FF Yeo, Serial D.40, Wright and Harkness, *A Survey of Casualties Amongst Armoured Units in North-West Europe.*

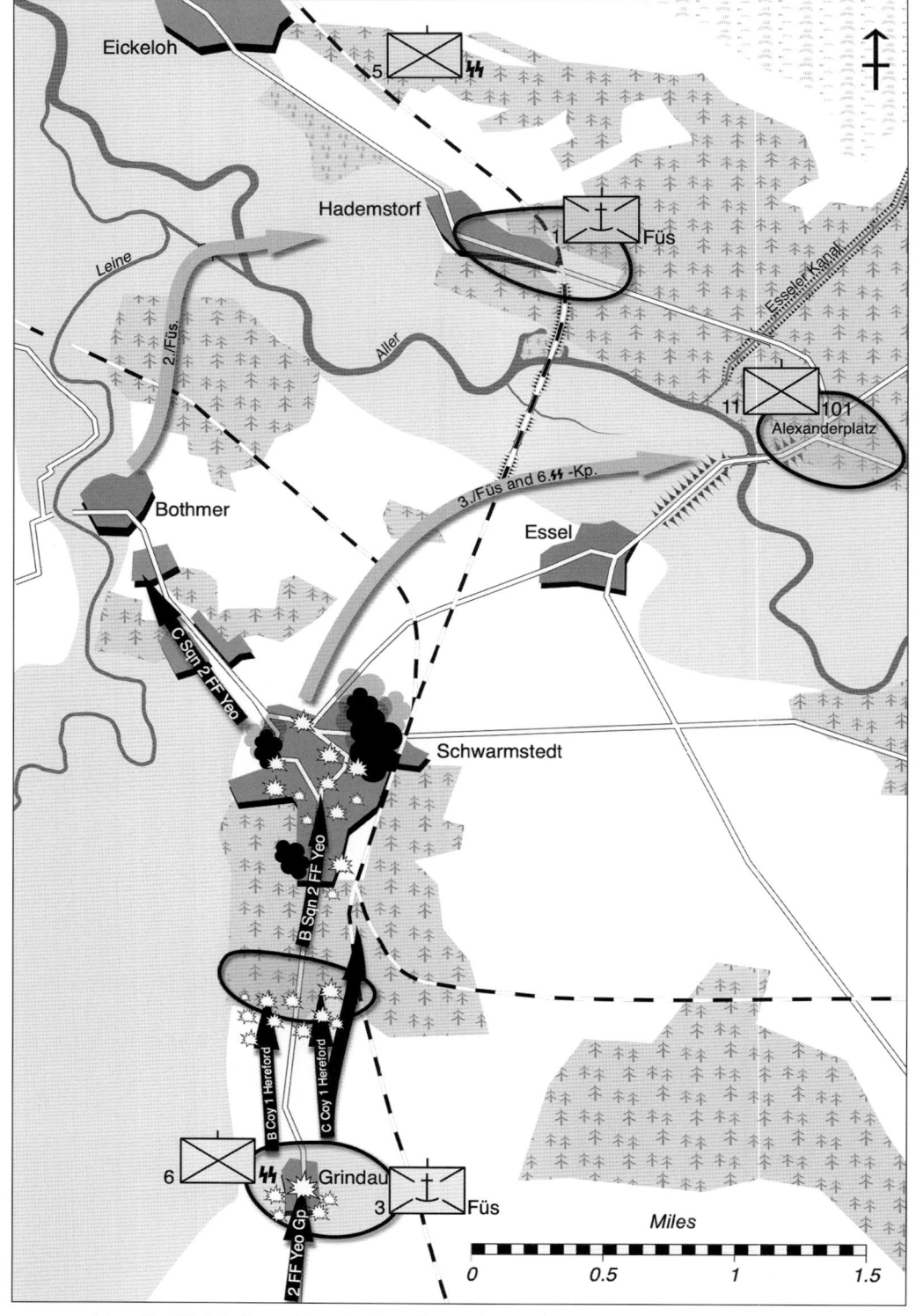

Map 38 159th Infantry Brigade Group's Attack on Schwarmstedt-Essel – 10 April 1945.

Commander: Minor burn left eye. Returned to duty in two months. Category A.1.

Gunner: Wounded and burnt. Extensive 2, 3 and 4 degree burns of buttocks, and inner sides of thighs. Compound fracture of head of right tibia and penetration wound to knee joint. Still in hospital 22 September 1945.

Operator: Burns of hands. Compound fracture left tibia and fibula. Still in hospital 22 September 1945.

Driver: Wounded and burnt. 1 degree burns face. Superficial wounds left scapula region and left buttock. Wounds healed in six weeks but under psychiatric treatment for a further five months. Category C.1 for psychiatric reasons.

Co-driver: Killed. Severely mutilated.

With Grindau plainly defended, the advance's lead changed from the tank regiment to the infantry – 1 Hereford. Despite the Comet's loss there was little delay in the assault on Grindau by A and D Companies 1 Hereford supported by B Squadron, although during the course of the action further fatalities occurred when a *Panzerfaust* hit D Company's radio vehicle, probably an armoured 15cwt truck, killing the operators. Despite these losses, Grindau was cleared and the group pushed on northwards to Schwarmstedt. The surviving marines of 3./Füs. Kompanie and Hitler Youth withdrew northwards from the village to join their comrades already occupying defensive positions on the edge of the wood to Schwarmstedt's south.

As 1 Hereford approached Schwarmstedt, with B and C Companies on either side of the road and each supported by a troop of Comets from B Squadron, they came under heavy small-arms' fire. Marines and Hitler Youth firing from well dug-in positions in the woods to the south of the village engaged B Company advancing on the left and the squadron leader, Captain Ryde, and the company commander were both wounded. On the right of the road progress was equally slow, but by using the line of the railway further to the east the attack was able to make some progress. The overall defence was so determined, however, that A Company, supported by C Squadron firing HE and smoke, had to be brought up to reinforce the attack. The additional infantry enabled 2 FF Yeo Group to exploit to the centre of Schwarmstedt and by 1700 hours the village was clear. Its capture was at a cost of six killed including a platoon commander, Lieutenant Hancox, and 11 wounded. Robert Price recalls the final phase of the battle:[4]

> The defenders of this large village had fought a stubborn battle but had been crushed by sheer power, consequently the whole village was now burning furiously; not many houses would be left standing by nightfall. The smell of the burning flesh of the dead cattle and the smoke from the houses cast a thick cloud over the whole area, making visibility no more than a few yards in places. During the battle we were clearing some out-buildings to a farm when I had to climb over what I thought was a pile of debris. But under that debris was a dead cow and my leg suddenly broke through the animal's rib cage right up to my knee. What a bloody mess, my boot and trouser leg were covered in blood. I wiped off what I could with handfuls of straw, but it still looked a mess. Our new platoon commander thought I had been shot in the leg when he saw it! I thought I shall smell very nicely in a few days' time.

The surviving members of 3./Füs. Kompanie and 6. SS-Kompanie pulled out of Schwarmstedt and headed in a north-easterly direction across the triangle to the Aller road bridge and then joined the defenders in the forest on the right bank. Meanwhile, with Schwarmstedt captured, C Squadron advanced further to Bothmer, where there was no sign of the enemy but the road and railway

---

4   Price, *Just a Walk in the Sun*, p.109.

bridges over the Leine were found demolished. To avoid being trapped in the triangle, Bothmer's defenders, 2./Füs. Kompanie, hearing the fighting to their south and increasingly to their rear, had withdrawn to the Aller's right bank by way of the lock over the Leine and the barrage over the Aller and had then joined the remnants of 3./Füs. Kompanie in depth of the Aller road bridge.

The events of 10 April would have been a blow to Gördes. He had expected the British to come from the west rather than the south and 2 FF Yeo Group's northwards advance down the Leine's right bank to Schwarmstedt had caught his defence in the flank and in the ensuing battle a company's worth of the battalion was destroyed, significantly depleting Gördes' strength before the main battle on the Aller's right bank was joined. Fifty-nine Germans, principally from Marine-Füsilier-Bataillon 2 and 6. SS-Kompanie were killed defending Grindau and Schwarmstedt and the British took 60 prisoners. Today the German dead lie in Schwarmstedt's war cemetery.

To free-up Schwarmstedt and the divisional axis for units taking part in the assault on the Aller, 2 FF Yeo Group now pulled back to Esperke, leaving in the Grindau area A and D Companies, B Squadron, the Vickers platoon – from the divisional machine-gun company – and 1 Hereford's 3-in mortars. Although for 2 FF Yeo the day had been successful, it would end in tragedy. On arrival in the harbour area, a regimental headquarters' tank accidentally fired its main armament; the HE round hit a tree and exploded, killing an A Squadron driver, Trooper Smith, and wounding Major Gilmour, A Squadron commander, and Captain Adams, the adjutant.

1st Commando Brigade assault on the Aller

While 159th Brigade Group had been able to roll up the German defence of the Leine from a flank, a similar tactic would not be possible for the Aller and its bridges, which would require a direct assault. The capture of the Schwarmstedt area now made the Essel road bridge, rather than the one at Winsen, the best option for 11th Armored's subsequent operations on the Aller's right bank, and in the division's Operation Order No. 20 Major General Roberts directed 1st Commando Brigade to capture the Essel bridge that night.[5] If the bridge was captured intact 29th Armoured Brigade Group would exploit to Ostenholz and beyond. While the commandos and 29th Armoured conducted operations on the division's left flank, 159th Infantry Brigade Group would clear the Aller's left bank from Schwarmstedt to Neuwinsen, opposite Winsen, and then be prepared to return, cross the Aller at Essel before advancing to clear the Aller's right bank to Winsen. The brigade was ordered to support the commandos with an armoured squadron positioned on the Aller's left bank ready to engage targets across the river. The operation order, not surprisingly, was vague about the enemy, merely noting the Germans still seem determined to resist and were capable of occasionally producing good fighting formations, as shown by SS-A.u.E.Btl.12 'HJ' and the marines they had encountered in Schwarmstedt.

During the late evening of 10 April, 1st Commando Brigade was trucked to Grindau where the commandos dismounted and moved forward on foot to Schwarmstedt, passing through 1 Hereford's positions near Grindau, as Robert Price recalls:[6]

> After the capture of Schwarmstedt we dug in across the main road and consolidated our position. Tom and I dug our trench in the grass verge giving us a good field of fire up the road towards the river…After dark I was on guard, all the fires had burnt themselves out, but visibility still wasn't very good, when I heard something coming up the road. It was a muffled

---

5   TNA WO 171/4184, 11th Armoured Division Operations Order No. 20, 10 April 1945.
6   Price, *Just a Walk in the Sun*, pp.109–110.

sound but I couldn't identify it, so I woke Tom. We turned the Bren gun round and waited. Out of the mist and smoke loomed a tall figure in a beret. 'Halt!' I called out. The figure stopped and called out his rank and name. '1st Commando Brigade.' The column slowly continued up the road towards the Aller. I then realised why I hadn't recognised the sound; commandos' boots had thick rubber soles, not the standard issue leather and studs like us. We wished them luck.

While the move up was taking place, Brigadier Mills-Roberts went forward to the Aller to see the ground and decide how he would tackle the river crossing. His recce convinced him a direct assault on the road bridge would not succeed as it was the only road crossing of the Aller for miles up or downstream and would therefore be guarded and demolished at the first indication of a threat. It was for this reason 2 FF Yeo Group, having cleared Marine-Füsilier-Bataillon 2 from the triangle between the two rivers, was not moved up to clear Essel as it was believed this would automatically result in the demolition of the Aller road bridge. Mills-Roberts looked instead to using the rail bridge, which might, with German attention focussed on the road bridge, be only lightly guarded. As speed was of the essence, he decided on an infiltration across the railway bridge that night followed by a manoeuvre through the forest to seize the road bridge from the rear. Although the chance of success was low, even if the road bridge was blown he expected to be well-placed to secure the bridgehead needed to provide security for bridge-building.

At his O Group at 1700 hours Mills-Roberts explained to his four commanding officers and the commanding officer of 1st Mountain Regiment that the assault on the railway bridge would start with patrols dealing with the enemy sentries prior to the engineer troop removing the demolitions. The whole brigade would then cross as fast as possible to establish the bridgehead, with a strong fighting patrol moving ahead of the main body to try to seize the road bridge from the rear. Very little was known about the enemy. The order of march would be 3 Cdo followed in turn by 45 (RM) Cdo, 6 Cdo and 46 (RM) Cdo, and to keep direction the brigade would employ the white tape method successfully used on the night attack on Leese. 1st Mountain would be in direct support of the night assault using an on-call fire plan, with 13 RHA and 146th Medium Regiment firing a timed programme at three grid references to distract the enemy during the final stage of the move to the railway bridge. The two lead commandos would each have a battery in support plus two FOOs and a liaison officer, who would call for fire. Particular emphasis was placed on the need for maintaining communications. Geoffrey Tudor, a battery GPO, describes the preparations to provide support, soon to be put to the sternest of tests:[7]

> No comfortable well-lit cellar to work in this time. More like one of those schemes in the Scottish mountains – the pine trees all around added to the illusion. Working by torchlight they sprawled on the ground with planks for tables. Signallers moving around reeling out cable, connecting field telephones: 'Through to battery, Sir!' Radio operators linking with the FOO parties. And in the midst of the hurly-burly, the two 'acks' [assistants], working steadily away, plotting the targets as they came in, writing out the gun programmes. Thank God for the tannoy relay! Saved a lot of shouting and running around, helped to create a gun position that worked with quiet efficiency.

The start line for the infiltration was the station at Schwarmstedt, giving rise to inevitable jokes about tickets to Berlin. It was a partially moonlit night and the rain, a feature of the day, had

---

[7]   Geoffrey Tudor, *Hoofprints in the Clouds – Jeep Tracks in the Mud* (Brighton: Pen Press Publishers, 2008), p.226.

The railway bridge from the right bank. Photograph taken in 2015. (Author)

stopped. At 2200 hours, when it was fully dark, the brigade moved off following the line of the railway and initially all went well. 6 Troop, leading 3 Cdo, crossed the first and second bridges, which carried the railway over the lane and the stream, and without any enemy reaction was nearing the railway bridge over the Aller. However, at 2350 hours when only 200 yards short of the Aller the still of the night was split by a series of loud explosions. The Germans had seen the commandos and initiated the demolition charges, successfully dropping the first bridge but leaving the second unscathed and, more significantly, only damaging the main bridge over the Aller, leaving it crossable.[8]

The noise of the explosions was the cue for the Germans to open up with a machine-gun firing tracer on a fixed line down the railway. Colin Rae, adjutant of 3 Cdo, describes the events that followed:[9]

> As we approached the span of the railway bridge there was a massive explosion and the span disintegrated. We moved on cautiously and then saw that the span over the actual river was still intact. James Griffith from brigade HQ volunteered to swim the river and cut any demolition wires that he could find on the other bank while we went across the span, hoping for the best.[10]

---

8   There is an anecdote that local German civilians, with a post-war eye, had interfered with the demolition charges.
9   Colin Rae, 'Playing at Soldiers, 1939–1946' (Unpublished).
10 Captain James Griffith was a member of No. 3 (X) Troop, No.10 (Inter-Allied) Commando. He was born Kurt Glaser and had served with his father – Dr Willy Glaser, a Jewish doctor – with the International

There was a stream of machine-gun tracer coming across the bridge span but it seemed to be fairly high so I and Arthur Wardle (OC 3 Troop) and the leading section of 3 Troop clambered onto the railway track and started to run across the bridge keeping as low as possible. Our boots seemed to make an awful noise on the gravel and when we were about halfway across the machine-gun opened up again and five men were wounded. We ran as fast as we could and when we got to the end we opened up with rifle and Tommy gun fire in the direction the tracer was coming from. Luckily the firing stopped and it was fortunate that it must have been on a fixed line or we would have had more casualties. James Griffith, soaking wet, joined us. He had found and cut some wires leading to one of the caissons, which may have been demolition wires as there were no further explosions. Gordon Pollard (OC 1 Troop) appeared and said, 'Come and charge the edge of the wood!' and firing our weapons we did. There were some screams and the German shots stopped.

Wednesday 11 April

1st Commando Brigade battle for the Aller's right bank

With the railway bridge damaged but passable, 6 Troop crossed, destroyed the machine-gun post and by shortly after midnight had formed a small bridgehead on the right bank. Sporadic small-arms' fire crackled through the forest as the remaining troops of 3 Cdo crossed the bridge and 3 Troop now took the lead in the manoeuvre to take the road bridge from the rear. Although the shortest route was through the forest, the quickest would be via Landesstrasse 190 so the road was the troop's initial objective. Colin Rae describes his part in the early stage of this manoeuvre:[11]

> There was no time to waste and, as there were others to mop up, Arthur and I, with No. 3 Troop behind us, set off on my bearing. We started off through fairly thick wood running as fast as we could because we had a couple of miles to go; we wanted to attack while it was still dark and most of the German soldiers, if they were nearby the bridge, would be asleep. My bearing took us up a track and as this was in the right direction we ran down it, keeping on the grass verge to avoid too much clattering of army boots. The track improved and suddenly, in the moonlight, I saw ahead what looked like a bridge and blockhouse [probably the caissons of the road block] on either side, so calling on No. 3 Troop to follow me, and for once switching off my Tommy gun safety catch, I charged up and over the bridge firing bursts with my weapon. As I got level with the blockhouse three or four German soldiers emerged firing at us. I let off half a magazine at them and then something like a cart-horse's kick hit my right knee and down I went. I called on No. 3 Troop behind me to span out 100 yards ahead and to tell the next troop to go half right towards the main road bridge and try to stop it being blown.
>
> I felt nothing and knew I had lost a leg. I remember looking at my watch and it was just 4 am and beginning to start to get a bit lighter. By then the rest of 3 Cdo were following through and doubling ahead firing as they went. There was a lot of shooting going on and then a large explosion, which I guessed was the bridge being blown. I remember taking out a field dressing, opening it to clamp on to the stump and trying to remember how to do some

---

Brigade during the Spanish Civil War. He joined the commandos as a medic but by April 1945 was serving as an intelligence officer in HQ 1st Commando Brigade.
11 Rae, 'Playing at Soldiers, 1939–1946'.

276   THEIRS THE STRIFE

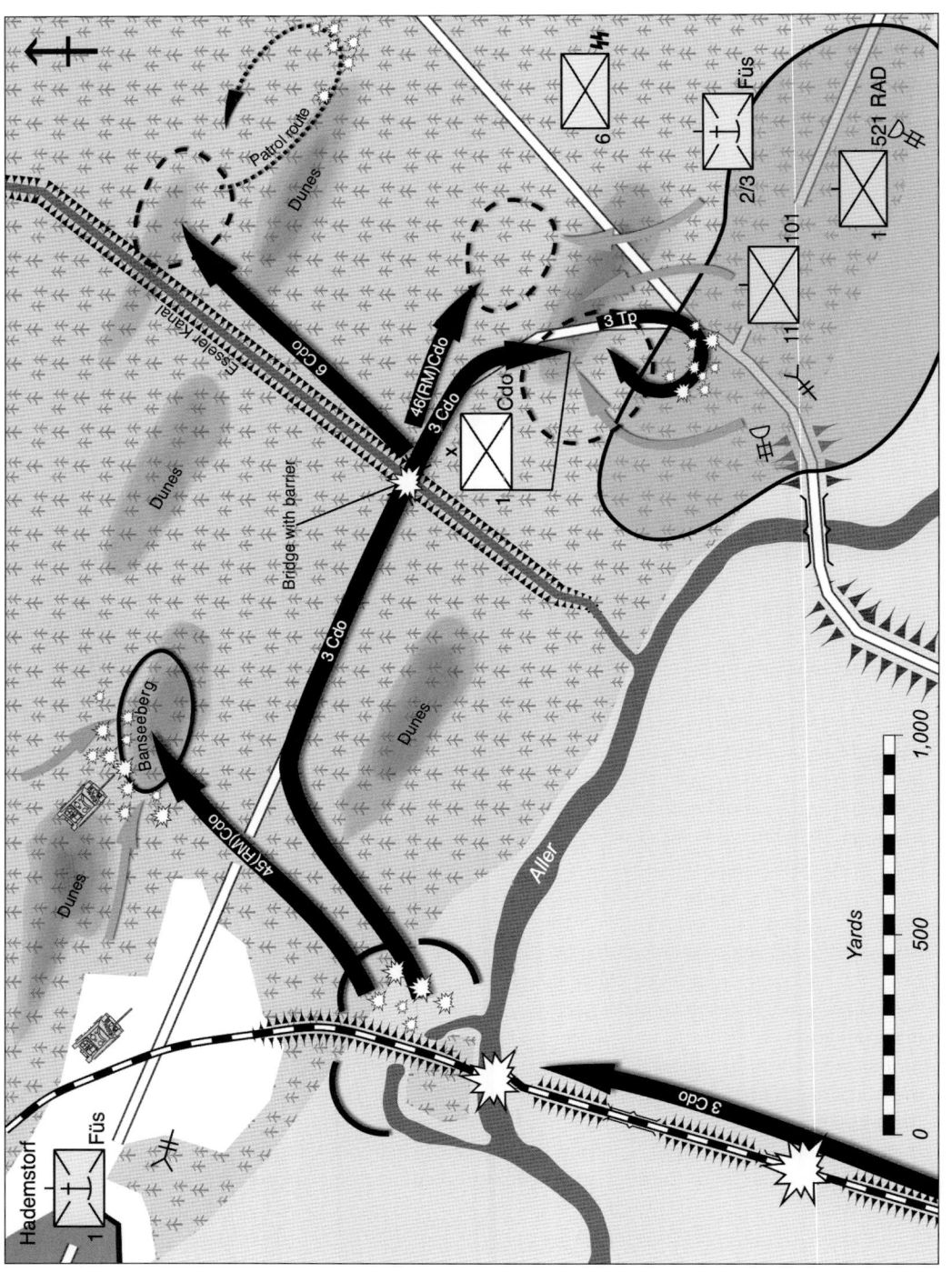

Map 39 1st Commando Brigade Crosses the Aller – 10–11 April 1945.

form of tourniquet to stop the bleeding. With my right hand I felt down my thigh to find the stump and slap on the field dressing only I felt my knee, which seemed OK but rather wet, then my shin, then my ankle, then my boot, then I wriggled my toes and rather shamefully got up and ran to find where 3 Cdo had got to. We were in a thinnish wood and as the wood seemed fairly full of Germans there was a lot of shooting going on and grenades going off. 3 Cdo had failed to get as far as the road bridge, which was about 400–500 yards ahead and were digging to get some form of protection or crouching behind trees.

Colin Rae was later awarded an immediate Military Cross for his courage storming the road-block and his citation records that he killed two Germans, wounded three and captured eight. While he was checking his wound, proving only to be a gash, 3 Troop rushed on to try to reach the road bridge over the Aller but began to meet increasingly stiff resistance and was forced to retire. By 0615 hours the troop had returned to join the remainder of 3 Cdo, by now dug-in in the forest to the south-east of the bridge over the Esseler Kanal.

Despite the successful lodgement on the right bank, Brigadier Mills-Roberts urgently needed to get the remainder of the brigade across the Aller in order to defend the bridgehead against the inevitable counter-attacks. To speed things up, he placed himself at the railway bridge where he was able to coax the men to go even faster. Signaller Morrish, who was a member of an OP party from 452 Battery 1st Mountain Regiment, describes the brigade commander's direct approach to command:[12]

> Brigadier Mills-Roberts was, as usual, right at the front of the column: 'Don't just stand there looking at it, go and get a bloody ladder!' we heard him shout. 'But where shall we find a ladder, Sir?' 'Nearest haystack!' I peered around in the half-light and, sure enough, there was a haystack visible across the field beside the track. The bridge had by now been blown in half so that one side was much higher than the other, but each section was intact. Some commandos returned with one or two ladders that were then securely lashed to each half of the bridge, and we proceeded to climb down. I was not looking forward to my turn; it looked a long way down, the load on my back was heavy and unwieldy, and I could see and hear the river rushing along some way below us. A commando NCO was hustling everyone along in order to get going as quickly as possible, but they always looked after us very well; he helped me onto the ladder and shouted to a chap below, 'Here's one of the gunners, give him a hand as he comes down!'

While 3 Cdo was in action in the forest, the next commando, 45 (RM) Cdo, had reached the railway bridge and begun crossing. David Ward describes the final stages of its move:[13]

> We moved off after dark along the railway line until the enemy woke up and started firing machine-guns on fixed lines down the railway. They seemed to have no shortage of ammunition and much of it tracer. We then changed to the bottom of the embankment and had to get up onto the railway every time we came to a ditch. This was not a popular move but would have been even less popular if we had swum and toggle-roped across these ditches. Somebody must have taken out these machine-guns as the last 300 yards to the bridge was very quiet. We crossed over and moved into the wood, stopping when about 100 yards from

---

12 Tudor, *Hoofprints in the Clouds – Jeep Tracks in the Mud*, p.227
13 Ward, 'My Time with 45 RM Commando'.

the bridge. Still all very quiet except for occasional Germans trying to get downstream. These were disposed of.

Once across, 45 (RM) Cdo left a troop to guard the railway bridge then pushed on into the forest to an area of higher ground known as the Banseeberg where it started to dig-in. By 0515 hours its hastily-dug defensive position was complete and the first prisoners interrogated, revealing the presence of companies of marines plus elements of a 'panzer-jäger regiment' (these would have been soldiers from Heeres-Panzerjäger-Abteilung 661). During the early hours of 11 April, 6 Cdo and 46 (RM) Cdo followed across the railway bridge without incident and began moving to their bridgehead positions. 6 Cdo made its way to the bridge over the Esseler Kanal, now held by 3 Cdo, and following the line of its channel infiltrated to the north-east through the forest eventually arriving at a clearing where the troops dug-in in all-round defence. Ominously, they could hear tracked vehicles moving in the forest beyond their view and the crack of direct fire heavy weapons firing from the area of the bridge. By 0530 hours 46 (RM) Cdo had also crossed the Esseler Kanal and was digging-in in the forest 200 yards beyond its bridge. Although by dawn the whole brigade was on the Aller's right bank, 45 (RM) Cdo was dangerously isolated from the rest of the brigade, now all on the far bank of the Esseler Kanal, and at this testing stage of the operation and in the half-light the Germans started to probe the commandos' positions with aggressive patrols. Brigadier Mills-Roberts and his brigade headquarters were as vulnerable as his commandos:[14]

> Suddenly a German appeared on our left. Donald [Hopson (Brigade Major)] was 10 yards in front and shouted, 'Shoot that man, someone. Don't let him get away with it.' I had the safety catch off my Garand rifle and let him have it. Shooting at night is a chancy business – but I hit him. A yell, a sob and a moan and no more. 'That was a bloody lucky shot,' said Donald. 'Who was it?' He did not know that I had returned to brigade HQ. 'The brigadier!', replied Ted Ruston.

Confusion was not, however, just affecting the commandos as the Germans were also suffering from lack of information, as evidenced by a half-track clattering up to the recently-captured bridge over the Esseler Kanal, resulting in the swift capture of the vehicle and seven marines.

At 0630 hours 6 Cdo sent a patrol with a PIAT to engage any worthwhile targets presenting themselves on the Ostenholz road, the future divisional axis for the breakout and some 1,000 yards to the east. Although the patrol commanded by Lieutenant Miller made progress towards the road, as it did so it came under increasingly heavy small-arms' fire, eventually making it impossible to get within range for a PIAT shoot. Having captured a marine from 2./Füs Kompanie and with Miller wounded, the patrol withdrew to their commando's position.

At 0730 hours, in compliance with the division's orders, C Squadron 15/19 Hussars with B Company 1 Cheshire moved off east from Schwarmstedt to take up a position to the north of Marklendorf from where the tanks could engage targets across the Aller and harass any attack coming in from the east against 1st Commando Brigade. Unfortunately, this position was over two miles to the east of the road bridge, well out of sight, and this will soon have bearing on a tragic incident involving Comets of 3 RTR.

---

14   Mills-Roberts, *Clash by Night*, p.186. Major Ted Ruston was 1st Mountain Regiment's liaison officer with HQ 1st Commando Brigade for the operation.

The German counter-attacks

As the brigade had not succeeded in capturing the road bridge as intended, by 0800 hours planning was in progress to launch 46 (RM) Cdo on a full-scale attack on the bridge. However, the commando brigade had no understanding of the strength of the enemy and at this vulnerable stage the Germans began to mount aggressive counter-attacks, supported by the two Panzer IV/70 tank-destroyers, half-tracks and armoured cars, which initially fell on 3 Cdo and brigade headquarters. These attacks would rage for the next two and a half hours, preventing any other action other than the commandos fighting for their lives. Brigadier Mills-Roberts vividly describes an attack on his headquarters:[15]

> Through the trees in front of us there was movement – skilled movement; German infantry were working forward in short, sharp rushes and despite the heavy rifle and Bren fire from 3 Cdo they were still coming on.
>
> We in brigade HQ now shot it out alongside 3 Cdo. Corporal Smith and I shared a weapon pit. Just to the right of us was Ted Ruston, the gunner from 1st Mountain Regiment with his two signallers. On our other side were Donald Hopson and Corporal Creed, his batman. Just behind us were our own brigade signallers – our wireless link was a vital one in this place. Joe Lawrence (Brigade Intelligence Officer) and Max Harper-Gow (DAA&QMG) were to our right front.
>
> Behind us the ground sloped gently away, and there was a space clear of trees. In the wood behind were the Germans and some of them had climbed into the trees and begun sniping. One section of 3 Cdo, about 15 yards to our left, spotted one of the snipers and let fly at him with a Bren gun; we watched him slowly topple out of the tree. The section just beyond was having a rotten time. The sandy bank in front had caved in with the constant hammering of the German light machine-guns. Among the wounded was one of their officers; he had been shot in the face and blinded and was in great pain.

This officer was Captain Alan Milne. Milne never regained his sight but later overcame this adversity to become a professor and distinguished political philosopher. Another loss during the counter-attacks was James Griffith. Oblivious to the fire and despite the brigade commander telling him to get in a weapon pit, he was shot in the back and died instantly. Brigadier Mills-Roberts realised that fire support from 1st Mountain Regiment was the only way to prevent the counter-attacks over-running his headquarters and 3 Cdo, but owing to the proximity of the enemy and the urgency of the situation this would demand high levels of skill from FOOs, GPOs and the guns. 1st Mountain Regiment had prepared thoroughly to support the commandos and 200 rounds were available for each gun, but only the most accurate fire would suffice and communications had to work. Signaller Morrish again:[16]

> My name was called out and I had to leap out of my trench and take over the set beside Major Fairclough (BC 452 Battery), relieving the operator who had been on duty for a long time. I think the set must have come slightly off net in the course of the night and it took a little time before I could get in touch with the guns. It was with enormous relief that I did eventually get through and heard my call for: 'Mike Target! Mike Target! Mike Target!' repeated.[17] All hell

---

15   Mills-Roberts, *Clash by Night*, p.189.
16   Tudor, *Hoofprints in the Clouds – Jeep Tracks in the Mud*, p.227.
17   A 'Mike' target was a regimental fire mission requiring fire from all twenty-four guns.

broke loose as what Brigadier Mills-Roberts describes as 'gunnery par excellence' took place. We heard the screaming and crunching of the shells and the sound of branches being ripped from the trees, all sounding uncomfortably close. It was very impressive to see how accurate the gunfire had been. There was not a tree unscathed in an area not much more than 50 yards from our trenches, but not one shell had overshot the mark.

The pressure to deliver accurate fire was not only on those calling for it but also on those delivering it from the gun positions. Geoffrey Tudor describes the atmosphere at the guns:[18]

> Everyone was in high spirits, but attentive, watchful, knowing how much depended on them. The greatest sin a gunner can commit is to drop a round short among his own infantry – and here the Germans were within 100 yards of our men – then as close as 70. All knew that the fighting was at desperately close quarters, that their gunfire must be accurate, and that it might well prove decisive. For the best part of three hours the guns were never out of action – men were sent off by turn to eat and rest. Target succeeded target as the German sailors attacked from various directions in search of a chink in the commando defences.

For those near the receiving end of 1st Mountain Regiment's support, it was decidedly unnerving. Colin Rae describes the situation:[19]

> It was now daylight, and the enemy were counter-attacking strongly with some climbing trees to snipe at us. No. 6 Troop were having the worst of it. We had by then taken a number of prisoners, all very young, and they were a marine cadet battalion [sic] and very frightened at what was going to happen to them. Their NCOs said that all prisoners would be shot, as had happened in Russia. The order came to keep our heads down, as the brigadier had asked the 1st Mountain Regiment FOO to put down a box barrage with their 3.7-in howitzers 200 yards all around us. It was no joke having shells exploding within a hundred yards or so.

Despite the effective artillery fire, it did not deter the German counter-attacks and Brigadier Mills-Roberts recognised that to stop the Germans over-running his headquarters he had to take a significant risk:[20]

> Somehow the stalemate had got to be dealt with as soon as possible. I got onto Ted Ruston again. 'I want a concentration here,' I shouted pointing to the fringe of the trees only 70 yards away. Ted shouted back: 'It's literally on us, Sir. I couldn't guarantee it.' 'Go ahead, Ted,' I said. 'I'll take the chance.' Though the 1st Mountain Regiment were splendid gunners there was a very real risk of us getting part of the next concentration ourselves. But we were dug in and the Germans were not, and the risk simply had to be taken.
> 'I've a medium regiment on call too Sir.' He grinned. A 5.5-in shell is a big one. 'Lay that on as well, a bit further back,' I said, 'and clout the German reserves on the far side of the wood by the river.' 'I only hope their barrels aren't too smooth,' he said. These medium guns had fought their way across Europe and the rifling was not what it had been and consequently caused some inaccuracy.

---

18   Tudor, *Hoofprints in the Clouds – Jeep Tracks in the Mud*, p.227.
19   Rae, 'Playing at Soldiers, 1939–1946'.
20   Mills-Roberts, *Clash by Night*, p.191.

'Shot!' yelled Ted. And we all ducked. I was about to rise from my pit when a belated medium shell landed five foot in front of us. It literally knocked us back into the weapon pits and put the wireless temporarily out of commission. There was however havoc on the other side of the clearing. The enemy pulled back.

The FOOs played a vital role and at one point in the battle Captain Cohen saw the marines trying to bring into action a 7.5cm infantry gun. When he called for the target to be engaged by a single gun from his own troop, he stressed it was a 'damned close target.' The gun and its detachment were destroyed. It was during the series of counter-attacks, which lasted until 1245 hours, that Korvettenkapitän Gördes was hit by a shell splinter and later found dead by 6 Cdo. Gördes had been commanding from a SdKfz 251 half-track and had refused to take cover during periods of shell-fire as in true naval tradition he wanted his men to see him commanding from the 'bridge'. With Gördes dead, the spirit went out of the counter-attacks and for a time resistance reduced to sporadic sniping while the surviving marines withdrew to the north and to the east either side of the Ostenholz road to lick their wounds and reorganise in the forest. They had suffered sorely and the 1st Commando Brigade diary records 300 enemy dead being counted in the woods and 100 prisoners captured.[21]

Korvettenkapitän Josef Gördes' grave in Essel's *Soldatenfriedhof*. The helmet was found in place when the photograph was taken in 1992. (Author)

The counter-attacks fell not only on the three commandos holding the east side of the Esseler Kanal but also on 45 (RM) Cdo in its exposed position on the brigade's left flank, starting at 1040 hours with the Panzer IV/70 tank-destroyers firing 20 rounds of HE at the commando. With no tanks or anti-tank guns yet in the bridgehead and PIATs the only anti-armour weapons available, the tank-destroyers were a significant threat. Fortunately for the commandos, they did not close with 45 (RM) Cdo's position as they were vulnerable in the close country and were instead used as stand-off, mobile artillery platforms. Possibly lack of fuel also restricted their use. Given the commando's exposed position, brigade headquarters wanted to move it to a new position to tighten the bridgehead but with the brigade staff fighting for their lives the order could not be issued until 1250 hours. Forty minutes later, as 45 (RM) Cdo was preparing to move, it was subjected to a counter-attack involving a tank-destroyer, infantry and a barrage of mortar rounds. Artillery support was, however, now available and 146th Medium brought down two fire missions on the enemy forcing their withdrawal and causing heavy casualties. The failure of this attack provided the commando with some respite and during the afternoon it was able to break-clean and head off through the forest to join the rest of the brigade on the east side of the Esseler Kanal. Once in its

---

21   TNA WO 218/73. 1st Commando Brigade GS.

new position just to the north of Alexanderplatz, the commando was welcomed by the enemy with a 50-round mortar barrage.

6 Cdo assaults the bridge

Turning the clock back to the early part of the morning when the German counter-attacks were at their height, Brigadier Mills-Roberts appreciated he needed to regain the initiative as soon as possible and get to the road bridge, which unknown to him was already blown. He therefore ordered 46 (RM) Cdo to mount a full-scale attack. The reply swiftly came back that they could not as A and Y Troops were heavily engaged by the enemy and if the commando moved it would open up the rear of both 3 Cdo and brigade headquarters to the counter-attacks. The brigadier therefore selected 6 Cdo in its defensive position to the north of the bridgehead and not in contact with the enemy. The commanding officer of 6 Cdo was Lieutenant Colonel Tony Lewis. Lewis was only 24 and very youthful-looking and his age had been the topic of a discussion between Brigadier Mills-Roberts and Montgomery a few months before:[22]

> 'You know,' he [Montgomery] said, 'he's rather on the young side.' I replied, 'Lewis is a first-class officer. He has twice commanded 6 Cdo for long periods in action. When this last vacancy occurred, I was determined to give him command and had some difficulty with my own general. If you're going to say anything, sir, I can see I'm going to lose him.' 'Shan't say a thing,' said Monty briskly. 'And how are your preparations for the battle of the Rhine going? That's the thing.'

At 0930 hours Tony Lewis got the order directly from the brigade commander to assault the bridge:[23]

> I had been listening to the command net and had gathered that the enemy was proving to be a very ferocious form of opposition. Eventually I received the order I expected from the brigade commander himself, whose radio procedure was non-existent, 'Tony – take the bridge! Out.' Although the Germans had blown the bridge there was no doubting the clarity or intent of this order, but where exactly 3 Cdo was in the thick pinewoods I did not know! I decided that they were not within 300 yards of the Aller's right bank and that the best course of action was therefore for me to rest my right flank on the river bank and to move towards the bridge with the unit at right angles to the river. I decided to use the bank of a steep drainage ditch, which was marked on the map as a canal, as a start line and to secure it immediately with 6 Troop.

Tony Lewis immediately ordered his commando to move south down the Esseler Kanal to the area of 3 Cdo's defensive position. While the move was in progress he sought information from brigade headquarters on the locations of the other commandos. However, owing to the confusion, this most basic information was not available and so in view of this and the failure of the earlier attacks on the bridge from the north he decided to attack due east, having moved as far as possible towards the river. But the plan to rest his right flank on the river depended on the amount of enemy opposition still existing on the Esseler Kanal. At 0955 hours he issued orders to his six troop commanders and the commando then set off southwards down the Esseler Kanal. The leading troop was soon

---

22   Mills-Roberts, *Clash by Night*, pp.154–155.
23   Letter to the author 1993.

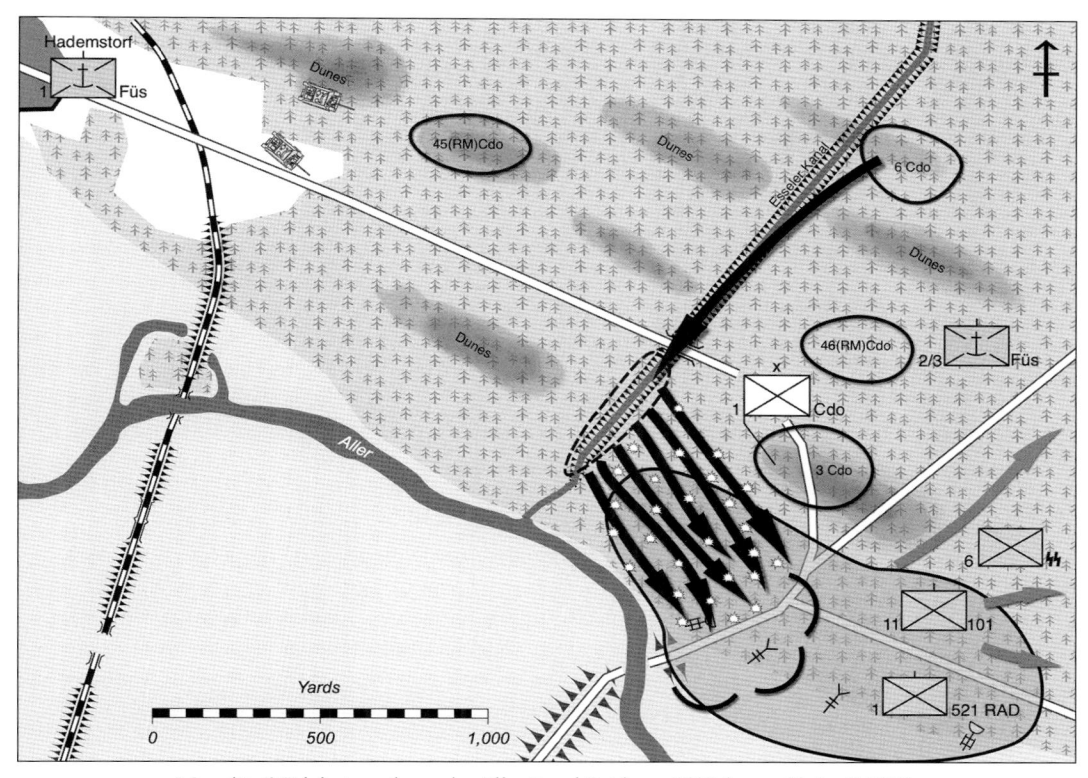

Map 40 6 Cdo's Assault on the Aller Road Bridge – 1030 hours 11 April 1945.

engaged by a strong party of marines and it was clear the commando would not be able to get as far as the river. It was now 1015 hours and with the commando halted but out of the line of fire in the depth of the substantial drainage channel, Tony Lewis decided that the best course of action was to charge the bridge directly from where he was, and as soon as possible. As a preliminary to the charge, the FOO, Captain Connolly, was tasked to neutralise the enemy on the commando's right flank near the river, with the subsequent 3.7-in fire proving effective. At the same time the Vickers of 5 Troop under Captain Emery were set up to support the charge from the right flank. Tony Lewis describes the events that followed:[24]

> We then moved swiftly, crossing a bridge over the ditch and ducking down behind the bank on the east side. As we settled down, girded our loins and fixed bayonets for the charge, 6 Troop commander returned from the direction of the river to say that he had been held up by a strong party of the enemy firing *Panzerfaust* at his forward section. I told him to leave a small party to occupy the enemy and to protect the Vickers teams. I then ordered the Vickers to start firing; when I heard their friendly chatter I said over the radio to the troops, 'OK, let's go!'

---

24 Letter to the author.

Four hundred and fifty men rose to the top of the bank shouting and hollering at the tops of their voices and our two horsey men – one a racehorse trainer[25] and the other a polo player – blew their hunting horns. Only I knew it was still 500 yards to the bridge! After about 100 yards we passed brigade HQ on our left. They all stood up and cheered and threw their berets in the air. We must have been an impressive sight, so many men on a narrow front and therefore in deep column, all with their bayonets flashing and shouting fit to burst.

About now the enemy woke up from the shock of seeing us bearing down on them through the wood. I was sad to see Sergeant Virgo, our intelligence sergeant, go down at this stage. On we went and I was beginning to feel the exhilaration similar to that I had experienced only once before when riding a motor-bike at 90mph; a sort of nirvana crept over me, which protected me from the fear of death.

The closer we got to the bridge the more intense became the enemy's fire. Some of the enemy machine-gun teams had a bad habit of firing at us until the last moment and then dropping their weapons and putting their hands in the air. Our soldiers cured them forever of this bad habit. After about the 300-yard mark, the enemy fire suddenly ceased, as if by order, and they broke and ran for the woods to the north. It was by now that we inflicted the highest number of casualties with men using the standing firing position as if at a hare shoot. The right flank wheeled on to the bridge's approach road while the left swept across the road to the forest on the opposite side.

We then dug in around the bridge and in the woods nearby. I had difficulty calling back the troops who had crossed the road as they were chasing a number of enemy, who were trying to get away. There was a momentary lull in the battle while those enemy who had not been concerned with the charge put in a series of small counter-attacks from the north, but each time we turned them back with casualties. It was during this phase that I decided to walk around our Bren positions in order to make sure that our men were taking on proper targets and not shooting up brigade HQ by mistake. I regretted this move as I realised that I might walk into our own fire from behind as well as the enemy's from the front. After about two hours the enemy withdrew. I was lucky with my plan, as I had not realised that 3 Cdo had cleared the area of the bridge over the drainage canal earlier that morning and that its bank would provide such a suitable and safe start line. Our record of casualties assessed that during the charge we killed some 55 and took 74 prisoners, of whom 30 were wounded, for a loss of nine dead and 26 wounded.

Some may consider killing the surrendering enemy machine-gunners a war crime. During the war signatories were bound by the Convention of 1929 that stated that soldiers were no longer belligerents if they clearly indicated an intention to surrender.[26] Although technically the surrendering Germans were therefore no longer belligerents and should have been made PoWs, the words of General Sir David Fraser are apposite:[27]

> The correct handling of prisoners depended not a little upon the circumstances of surrender. A British platoon might be fired upon by a German post and finally storm it. Fire – German fire – might be kept up against the attackers (bravely and effectively, causing casualties) until the last moment, and then the defenders would emerge, hands on high. In such circumstances

---

25 This was Captain Ryan Price, a renowned flat and National Hunt trainer in the 1950s and 1960s. He later admitted to being 'shit-scared blowing that horn.'
26 'Convention Relative to the Treatment of Prisoners of War, Geneva July 27, 1929', https://ihl-databases.icrc.org/customary-ihl/eng/docs/v1_rul_rule47 (accessed 9 May 2018).
27 General Sir David Fraser, *Wars and Shadows* (London: Allen Lane, 2002), p.227.

it is rare that quarter will be given. Blood is up, and if it were not men would not assault. Comrades have fallen. Surrender could have been earlier. The rest is imaginable.

It is a sad fact that among Allied soldiers, ruthlessness increased as the war's end neared. With the outcome so obvious, determined resistance by the Germans was strongly resented by Allied soldiers and the deaths of comrades generated a great deal of bitterness. This resentment, augmented by an unwillingness to take chances with surrendering Germans, resulted in prisoners being shot, as noted by Alan Moorehead, the war correspondent, who, in his account of this final period, recorded, 'At times the skirmishing grew so bitter prisoners were being shot.'[28] Even if they survived the act of surrendering, that most dangerous of moments, by this stage of the war there was little sympathy for Germans offering resistance to the last, particularly if they had caused casualties. Some may consider that the shooting of surrendering enemy gives credence to the massacre allegation mentioned in Chapter 5. However, that allegation purportedly described a calculated act of mass murder once action was over rather than killings in the heat of action. There is a world of difference.

By 1100 hours 6 Cdo had secured the approach to the bridge, captured the Pak 43 and found the two 10.5cm Flak from RAD Batterie 1./521 and the 10.5cm howitzer all knocked out from the airbursts directed by Captain Ap Evans, the FOO from 451 Battery supporting 46 (RM) Cdo. At 1400 hours 46 (RM) Cdo took over the bridge area from 6 Cdo, which moved to new positions in the forest to the bridge's west, and during the afternoon the previously hard-pressed 3 Cdo was able to reorganise, evacuate its wounded using one of the captured German half-tracks, replenish its ammunition and last, but by no means least, eat. During the course of the day it had lost Corporal Henderson killed, 22 wounded and six missing; of the missing, two were later found dead back at the railway bridge but three others were alive having joined 46 (RM) Cdo during the night's confusion.

B Squadron 3 RTR advance from Essel

While the commandos battled on the Aller's right bank, action was not yet over on the left and we will again step back a few hours to earlier in the morning of 11 April. At 0830 hours, 29th Armoured Brigade ordered 3 RTR Group to cross the bridge at Neustadt and advance north up the Leine's right bank in order to be in position for the breakout to Bergen-Belsen as soon as the bridge over the Aller at Essel was captured. The brigade also ordered 3 RTR to send a squadron ahead to contact the commandos in either Schwarmstedt or Essel; CO 3 RTR, Lieutenant Colonel Teddy Mitford, selected B Squadron, commanded by Major Bill Close, for this task.

At 0900 hours B Squadron's lead troop reached Essel but with no sign of the commandos the Comets cautiously continued on Landesstrasse 190 towards the road bridge. At this stage 3 RTR believed the bridge to be intact and its eastern end secured by commandos; it is not known why either was assumed and would soon lead to a tragic incident as Bill Close describes:[29]

> My leading troop commander was 2nd Lieutenant John Pearson who had only recently joined the battalion, aged 19 and with little battle experience. He had a very experienced troop sergeant, Sergeant Cranston, and another fairly new subaltern, Jeff Lomas, acting as his troop corporal. This was fairly common practice in RTR and was done specifically for young officers

---

28 Moorehead, *Eclipse*, p.215.
29 Major Bill Close, *A View from the Turret* (Tewkesbury: Dell & Bredon, 2002), pp.157–158.

to gain battle experience. Our approach to the river Aller was via the village of Essel and I gave instructions to Pearson to keep a sharp lookout for possible *Panzerfaust* men. In the event he reported only seeing a few dead Germans and he moved on rapidly towards the river. It was difficult tank country, a straight road leading to the river, the ground on either side of the road very marshy, making it impossible to deploy off the road.

I had moved my HQ tanks fairly close to Pearson's troop and, taking cover in a small stand of trees by the roadside, took stock of the position. Through my binoculars I thought I could see enemy movement in the woods across the river and accordingly warned Pearson to watch out and be prepared to engage anything that moved. 'Wilco out' was his response and he moved on towards the bridge. When about 100 yards short of it, he could see that it was blown, he duly reported that fact to me and that he thought the river was about 40 yards wide at that point.

I was somewhat concerned about the movement on the other side of the river as I knew 1st Commando Brigade had made an assault crossing over the river the night before and we were not quite sure of their whereabouts. I was in the process of reporting to the CO that the bridge over the river was blown when suddenly – Crash! Bang! – Pearson's and Cranston's tanks erupted into flames and I could see one or two crew members out but obviously wounded. Lieutenant Lomas in the third tank managed to get off the road, took cover in some bushes, and proceeded to engage the anti-tank gun which had knocked out Pearson and Cranston. Although his tank was hit twice he courageously carried on with the engagement and, eventually, with a direct hit on the enemy gun, knocked it out.

In the meantime I moved up close to the burning tanks and got out to go to the aid of the wounded crew. John Pearson and two of his crew, Shipley and Wyatt, his operator, were lying in the long grass beside the road, all badly burned about the hands and face. Trooper Rowe, another member of his crew, had also managed to get clear and was not badly hurt. The driver, Manning, [*sic* – he was the co-driver] was killed instantly. Sergeant Cranston and Lance Corporal Turnbull in the other tank were also killed instantly, with the remainder of the crew managing to get out with only minor wounds.

There was some small-arms' fire coming from across the river but not accurately enough to cause any problems and we were mostly concealed from view by the burning tanks. I immediately got on my radio for medical help and was told that Doc Whitehouse [RMO] was on his way. Johnny Pearson's first few days with the battalion had been quite eventful, two sharp engagements, but, in spite of his very serious burns, he was quite cheerful and without doubt was extremely thankful to be alive. He had also made every attempt to go to the aid of Cranston's crew. Shortly afterwards Doc Whitehouse arrived with his two medical half-tracks and the wounded were evacuated.

Lieutenant John Langdon recalls the incident:[30]

A message then came over the air from the CO to Bill Close ordering him to send his leading troop ahead to contact 'our new friends and to tell them that the battalion would be arriving shortly.' It would certainly appear that at this time the colonel was under the impression that the bridge was intact and that the commandos were on the ground at its eastern end. Bill called 2nd Lieutenant John Pearson…to come to his tank. John arrived within a minute and was ordered to advance with his troop via Schwarmstedt and Essel and cross the river by the road bridge, RV with the commandos on the far side and pass on the colonel's message. John

---

30   Langdon, *The Sharp End*, p.146.

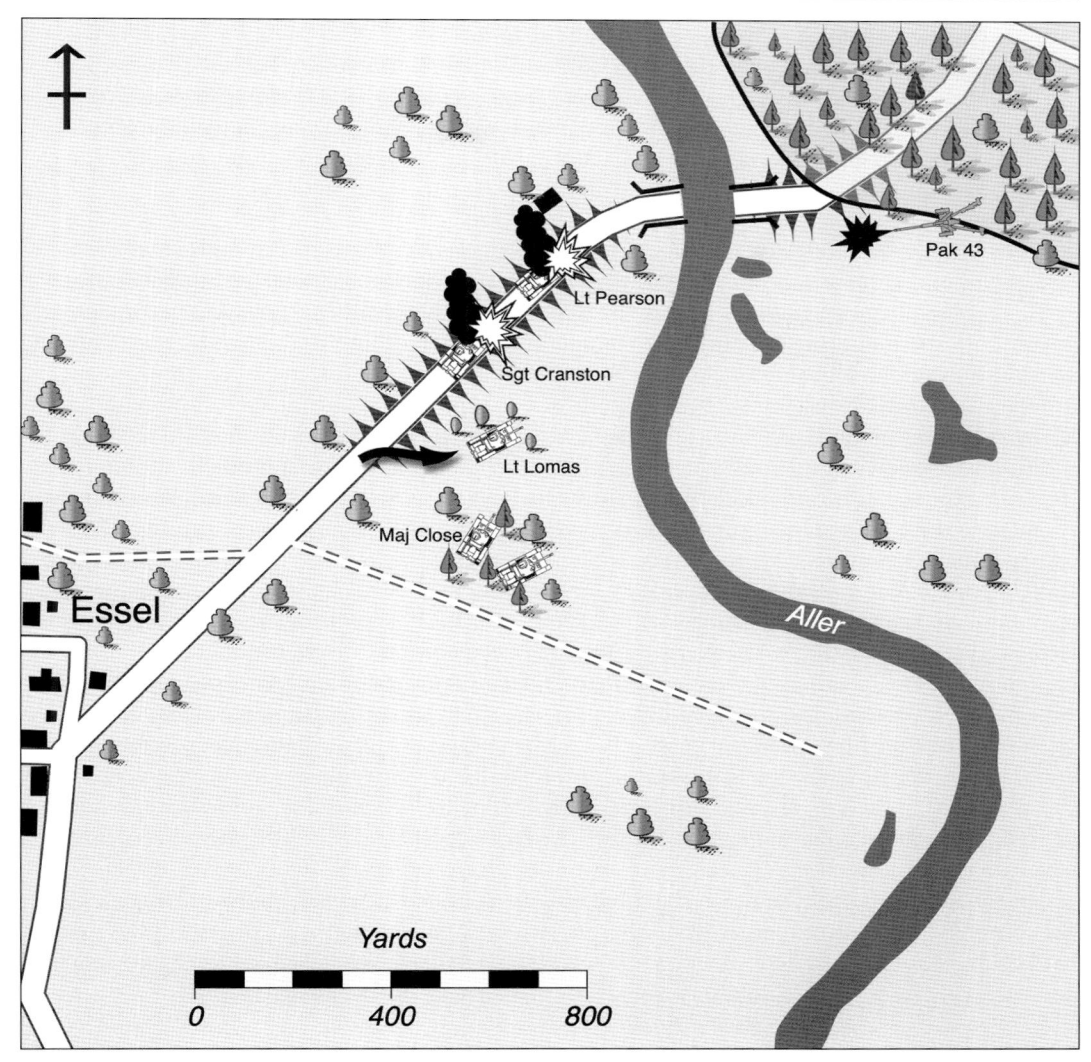

Map 41 B Squadron 3 RTR – 0925 hours 11 April 1945.

was also warned of the possibility of Essel being lightly held by the enemy. He then returned to his troop where he quickly briefed his troop sergeant, Sergeant Cranston, and his third tank commander, who that day was 2nd Lieutenant Jeff Lomas. With himself leading, the troop moved off slightly before 0900; there were some enemy dead in Schwarmstedt but no opposition and at about 0920 Essel was reached and passed, again without opposition.

On leaving Essel, a track from the left joined the road, the bridge was just coming into view so John halted in order that he could take a good look through his binoculars. He estimated that his position was then 600 yards from the bridge, from what he could see it appeared to be damaged at the far end. This was a considerable surprise and, in order to get a better view, he moved forward and led on to the approach to the bridge, crossing very open country to do so. Halting about 150 yards short of it, his worst fears were realised for the bridge had certainly been blown. He immediately passed his report to Bill stating that there was a gap of some 40 yards at the far end and that the roadway had dropped into the river. Almost at once his own and Sergeant Cranston's tank were hit by AP fire from a SP [*sic*] situated on the far side of the river and both tanks were knocked out. Jeff Lomas' tank was slightly to the rear of the other two, off the road on the right, observing across the river. As the SP fired Jeff's gunner saw through his gun sight the gun flash when the shots were fired, he quickly got onto the target, knocking it out first shot. We heard later that the SP was an 88mm and one of four [*sic*]. The gunner's quick action resulted in the enemy abandoning their remaining pieces.

As John Langdon was in a different squadron he did not witness these events, however the account has a first-hand quality so probably results from a conversation he had later with John Pearson.

The survey of tank casualties records a single 8.8cm round hitting John Pearson's Comet,[31] penetrating the mounting for the hull machine-gun then travelling back into the turret causing some ammunition, probably in the bins around the sides of the turret basket, to explode. The unfortunate co-driver was on the direct path of the projectile. Sergeant Cranston's Comet was hit by two 8.8cm rounds. The first penetrated across the front of the turret, then at the 11 o'clock position, just below the operator's hatch before exiting the turret's left-hand side in approximately the same position; this round killed Sergeant Cranston and Lance Corporal Turnbull. The second round tore the hull machine-gun from its mounting before passing obliquely through the front compartment; fortunately for the driver and co-driver they had already baled out.[32] Although 3 RTR reported that a SP gun firing from near the bridge on the Aller's right bank had attacked the tanks, no tank-destroyers armed with 8.8cm guns (such as *Elefant*, *Nashorn* or *Jagdpanther*) were on the Aller and the two Panzer IV/70 in the Hademstorf area were not only out of range but carried 7.5cm guns. Although there were three Tigers in the area, on the morning of 11 April they were still at Ostenholz and therefore not yet playing a part in the battle. The 8.8cm penetrations could therefore only have been made by a Pak 43 belonging to Heeres-Panzerjäger-Abteilung 661, and with all the penetrations being to the tanks' fronts, the gun must have been positioned on the forest's edge sited to fire straight down Landesstrasse 190. Anti-tank gunners normally seek defilade positions in order to hit tanks on their weaker side armour, but the brute power of the Pak 43 made this unnecessary.

The squadron felt badly let down that they had not been told that the bridge was blown and that the commandos had yet to secure its eastern end. This was later exacerbated by their belief that the road bridge was blown at 0200 hours, some seven and a half hours before the loss of the two tanks and their comrades. John Langdon wrote:[33]

> The whole of this unfortunate incident could have been avoided if the battalion had been passed the necessary information regarding the blowing of the bridge. We were certainly under the impression that the bridge was undamaged and that on crossing we would find members of the commando brigade. There was no doubt that there must have been a serious breakdown in communications somewhere along the line between the division and the commando brigade.

It is worth examining John Langdon's grievance to see where the truth may lie. First the orders and passage of information. At 0830 hours the 3 RTR war diary records 29th Armoured Brigade ordering the battalion to send a squadron ahead to contact the commandos in either Essel or

---

31   TNA WO 205/1165, 3 RTR, Serial D.20, Wright and Harkness, *A Survey of Casualties Amongst Armoured Units in North-West Europe*.
32   TNA WO 205/1165, 3 RTR, Serial D.16, Wright and Harkness, *A Survey of Casualties Amongst Armoured Units in North-West Europe*.
33   Langdon, *The Sharp End*, p.147.

Schwarmstedt. This strongly suggests that the armoured brigade was unaware that there were no commandos in either village and that the complete commando brigade had for some hours been in close and fierce contact with the enemy on the Aller's right bank. The passage of information at formation level would therefore seem to have been significantly awry. The brigade order makes no mention of a requirement to advance beyond Essel and it is not known why 3 RTR thought this necessary. Brigadier Mills-Roberts believed movement towards the bridge would trigger its demolition, and 2 FF Yeo Group had the day before been ordered not to exploit beyond Essel. Having found no commandos at Essel, 3 RTR should have sought clarification from 29th Armoured before advancing beyond the village. It therefore appears that Lieutenant Colonel Mitford had a false understanding of the situation; had he been aware of the true state of affairs he would have been far more circumspect.

Secondly, the timings for the bridge's demolition. An 11th Armoured Division G Branch log entry records the road bridge being blown at 0200 hours, and this would seem to be the source of John Langdon's reasonable censure. However, there are strong indications that the bridge was blown much later than this and that the 11th Armoured entry is the wrong timing for the wrong bridge. So when was the road bridge blown? The G Branch log entry is the only one recording, supposedly, the road bridge's demolition and neither HQ 1st Commando Brigade nor any of the four commandos mention in their war diaries hearing the demolition. The only reference to a demolition is a HQ 1st Commando Brigade entry recording 3 Cdo reporting the *railway* bridge blown at 2200 hours. Assuming this information was passed to division, it is possible that when later typing up the log a G Branch watchkeeper confused the railway bridge with the road bridge and 2200 hours with 0200 hours. War diaries are far from perfect records as they were produced by tired men with the information they had to hand. 3 Cdo believed the road bridge was still intact when 3 Troop tried to seize it at 0530 hours and during the commando's dawn attack Colin Rae remembers hearing a large explosion, which he assumed was the road bridge being blown. A German source suggests that it was blown at 0900 hours,[34] and Tony Lewis in his account of 6 Cdo's assault on the bridge states that he knew the bridge was blown when he received his order from the brigade commander at about 0930 hours. It was definitively down when, following the B Squadron incident, 3 RTR reported it destroyed at 0930 hours. Ten minutes later 11th Armoured Division asked 29th Armoured Brigade to get 3 RTR to confirm the report as they doubted that the bridge was blown, contradicting the division's own log entry recording the bridge blown at 0200 hours. The reason for the division's doubt is not known but perhaps it was aware that Brigadier Mills-Roberts had just ordered 6 Cdo to capture the bridge so assumed that it still stood. Although there is uncertainty around the timing of the bridge's demolition, the evidence suggests that it was blown between 0600–0900 hours on 11 April.

To conclude, the crux of the incident involving John Pearson's troop stems from the commando brigade failing to have the road bridge under observation from the left bank. Given the road bridge's importance this seems strange. This failure was compounded by poor passage of information, which led to Lieutenant Colonel Mitford misunderstanding the whereabouts of the commandos and his extrapolation of the brigade's orders. Had these aspects not gone amiss, John Pearson and his troop would not have advanced into the sights of the Pak 43 – a tragic incident among so many.

After the action, B Squadron spent the remainder of the day keeping the area of the bridge under observation while the rest of 3 RTR leaguered in Schwarmstedt and here Sergeant Grant, a cameraman with No. 5 Army Film Photographic Unit, filmed the crews maintaining their Comets. One of the clips shows a crew member on radio watch sitting on his turret and writing down what a 1945 cinema audience would have assumed was operational radio traffic. Freezing a frame shows

---

34 Saft, *Krieg in der Heimat*, p.145.

he is in fact finishing a letter home to his wife or girlfriend and he seems to have wanted to get her a photo of himself, as this is what he touchingly wrote:[35]

> …so anyhow it is all I have time
> for now so cheerio.
> yours forever
> all my love
> Peter
> PS There is a guy here taking
> my photo as I am writing
> to you so you may get one yet.
> Peter

Back in the bridgehead, as the bulk of the fighting had so far been in the centre and on the right flank, 45 (RM) Cdo on the left was having a relatively quiet time. David Ward describes this period:[36]

> The dawn quiet was broken by the noise of 6 Cdo doing their bayonet charge – bangs, hollers, hunting horn – just like a Rangers and Celtic match – but nothing came our way. Shortly afterwards we were moved across the road and deeper into the wood. We moved round the wood throughout the day and I vividly remember digging five slit trenches. At no time did we ever have a field of fire of more than 20 yards. Other sections were more involved judging by the noise of intermittent firing but never an enemy did we see that day. Just before dusk Tommy Unthank and I ate our evening meal. This was one small tin of compo rice pudding between the pair of us. As Tommy poured the pudding into a mess tin he was hit in the ribs by a spent bullet and dropped the duff! We carefully spooned off most of the sand and ate the resultant mixture. Not bad at all.

The forest's capacity to absorb infantry meant that more were urgently needed so 4 KSLI, in an assembly area near Essel, was assigned to the commando brigade and from 1830 to 2000 hours the commandos ferried the battalion across the Aller on rafts improvised by the engineers. Once on the right bank 4 KSLI occupied a tight area next to the commandos and here the battalion dug-in to spend an uncomfortable night under occasional shelling. But the need for reinforcement did not end there as tanks, vehicles and supplies were also urgently needed to support the lightly armed infantry in the bridgehead. The provision of bridging and rafting was therefore of the utmost importance. During the evening 257 Field Company moved up to the area of the road bridge and began constructing a 150-foot TD Bailey bridge,[37] and at 2100 hours 2 Troop 612 Field Squadron started building a Class 40 raft. With the noise of tracked vehicles audible to the north of the bridgehead the ferrying of tanks could not come too soon.

About 2 miles east of the Essel bridgehead, 1 Cheshire had meanwhile made good progress. 2 Platoon from A Company found intact footbridges over the sluice and lock gates to the south of Engehausen, enabling the platoon to cross the Aller, and by 2100 hours the battalion, less its vehicles and heavy equipment, was on the right bank with a secure bridgehead around the

---

35   IWM A70/300.
36   Ward, 'My Time with 45 RM Commando'.
37   TNA WO 171/5527, 257 Field Company RE war diary. 'TD' stood for 'triple truss, double storey' and comprised three trusses alongside each other in two storeys.

village, which straddled Landesstrasse 180, the road to Winsen. Also on this day Oberst Graf von Bassewitz-Levetzow, the newly-arrived replacement commander of 2. Marine-Infanterie-Division and now transferred to the navy in the rank Kapitän zur See, issued Divisional Operation Order No. 6 ordering,[38] inter alia, SS-A.u.E.Btl.12 'HJ' to hold itself in readiness to assist the *Füsilier* battalion, either via Hademstorf or Hodenhagen according to the developing situation; the youthful *SS* troopers will soon play a major role in the final phases of the battle of the Essel bridgehead.

Thursday 12 April

Battles in the forest

Thursday 12 April dawned a fine day.[39] Although the previous night was relatively quiet this did not indicate an absence of activity, and the most significant from the German point of view was the establishment of a blocking force around 1st Commando Brigade's bridgehead. The principal troops for this were provided by three SS-A.u.E.Btl.12 'HJ' companies, which, having recuperated in the forest between Eickeloh and Hademstorf, then infiltrated through the forests during the night 11/12 April to form an arc stretching from Hademstorf to the Ostenholz road: 5. SS-Kompanie occupied a position on the right near Hademstorf, 1. SS-Kompanie occupied the area between 5. SS-Kompanie and the Esseler Kanal, and 2. SS-Kompanie the area from the Esseler Kanal to the Ostenholz road. 6. SS-Kompanie's situation is not known, however it is probable that after the battles in the Schwarmstedt area on the Leine's right bank it was so severely depleted it was broken up and its manpower redistributed.

To complete the arc to the Aller, 1./Füs. Kompanie infiltrated from Hademstorf to the railway embankment in the forest, plugging the gap between 5. SS-Kompanie and the river, while the left flank from the Ostenholz road to Landesstrasse 180 was held by remnants from Marine-Füsilier-Bataillon 2, RAD Batterie 1./521, 11./101 Festungs-Pak-Abteilung and Heeres-Panzerjäger-Abteilung 661, all fighting as infantry since the failed counter-attacks of 11 April. The concealment offered by the forest would to some extent compensate for the Germans' numerical weakness and wherever possible they dug-in on the sand dunes to take advantage of the improved observation and fields of fire.

Additional to the forces sealing the bridgehead, infantry from further afield were also moving to reinforce the effort at Essel. Marines of Marine-Feldersatz-Bataillon 2, holding the Hodenhagen area downstream from Marine-Füsilier-Bataillon 2 and not yet in contact with the enemy, were ordered to move to reinforce their comrades in the vicinity of Hademstorf, and Bataillon Lotze from Grosan's Kampfgruppe Kahle was now at Ostenholz and in position to counter-attack the bridgehead from the north-east down the Ostenholz road. Although Korvettenkapitän Otto Kopp had taken over command of the *Füsilier* battalion after Gördes' death, it is likely that Oberst Grosan, as the senior and by far the most experienced officer present, now commanded the German effort to contain the bridgehead.

During the night the British heard the noise of German armour but naturally were unaware that the two tank-destroyers were being reinforced by three Tigers from Gruppe Grosan. The principal

---

38 TNA WO 171/4277. Special Supplement to 53rd Welsh Division INTSUM No. 231, 21 April 1945.
39 It was a particularly fine day for my father Lieutenant David Russell, erstwhile commander of 7 Platoon, C Company, 2nd Battalion The Parachute Regiment. On 12 April, four days after his 22nd birthday, soldiers of the US 30th Infantry Division liberated him from Oflag 79 at Brunswick, where he had been incarcerated since his capture at Arnhem some seven months previously.

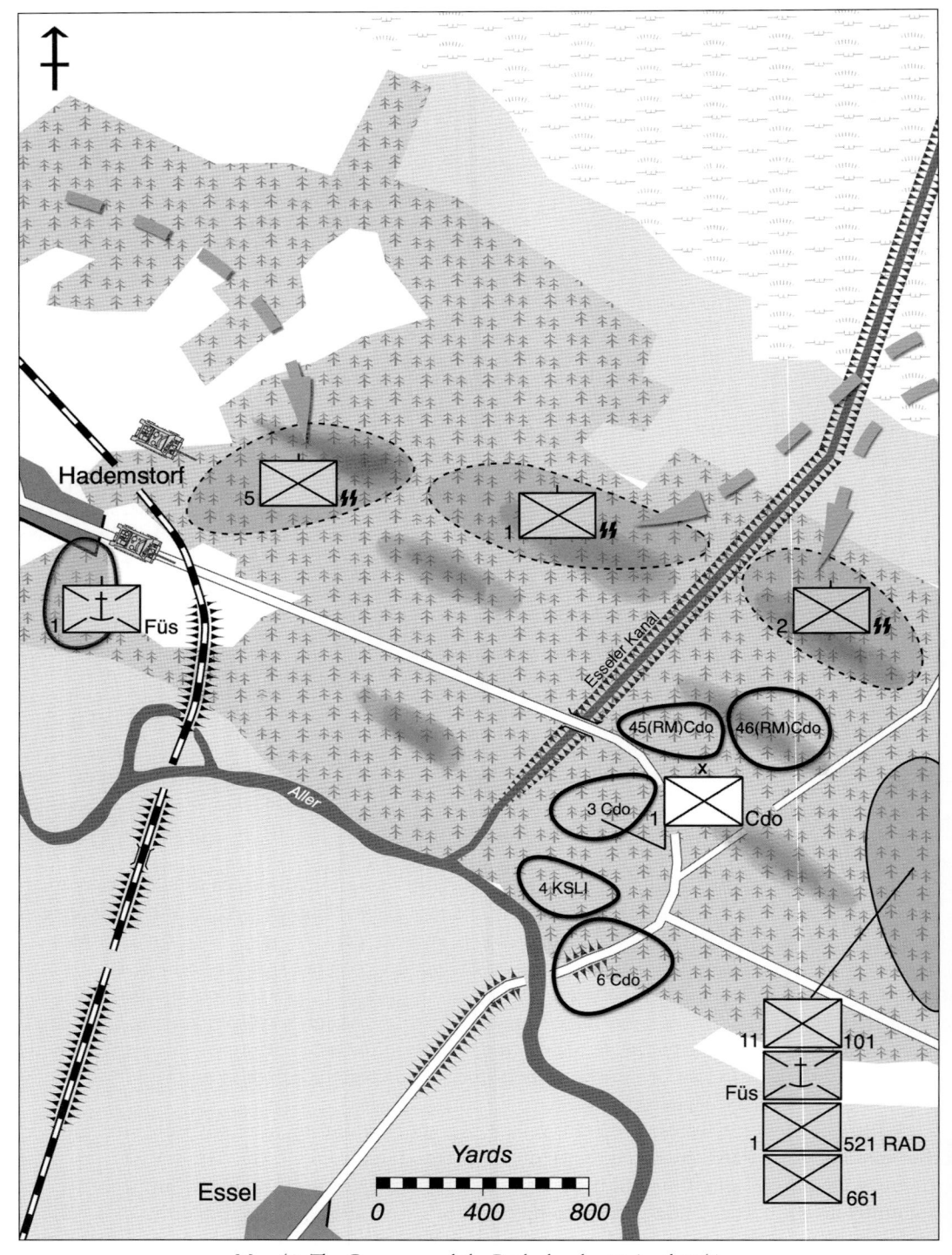

Map 42 The Germans seal the Bridgehead – 12 April 1945.

Tiger was callsign F01. It will be recalled that this tank received damage to its mantlet during Oberleutnant Fehrmann's counter-attack against 12 Devon on 6 April and under the command of Unteroffizier Franzen had returned to Fallingbostel for repair. Four days later, repair complete and still commanded by Franzen, F01 joined Gruppe Grosan. The second Tiger was possibly the tank that broke down with gearbox problems at Rethem during Kampfgruppe Schulze's move to the Weser on 3 April. As there is no mention of a Tiger by the British during the battle for Rethem, even one that was static, it seems likely that the broken-down Tiger was recovered to Fallingbostel, repaired then made available to join Gruppe Grosan. The third Tiger was probably one that became battleworthy after Kampfgruppe Schulze had departed for the Weser. All three Tigers had moved to Ostenholz to lie up five miles from the Essel battle and their crews spent the first half of 11 April preparing the tanks for action, including wiring fir boughs to the glacis plates, and waiting for orders to counter-attack the British bridgehead. The probable reason for the wait at Ostenholz was the need to get the SS-A.u.E.Btl.12 'HJ' companies – particularly 2. SS-Kompanie – into position as the tanks, even as well-protected as the Tiger, would be vulnerable in close country without protective infantry. In the early afternoon the period of waiting ended and the tanks were ordered to advance down the Ostenholz road towards the battle.

For the British the presence of enemy armour was already a particular concern and HQ 1st Commando Brigade had asked 11th Armoured Division for tank support at the earliest opportunity. By dawn it was also apparent that during the night significant numbers of Germans had infiltrated from the west to the area of the railway embankment and the forest to its north, so at 0630 hours brigade headquarters ordered 45 (RM) Cdo and 46 (RM) Cdo to mount a joint operation under the command of Lieutenant Colonel Gray, commanding officer 46 (RM) Cdo, to beat back through the forest and deal with this enemy. 45 (RM) Cdo would advance on the north side of Landesstrasse 190, the road to Walsrode, and clear the forest back to its old position on the Banseeberg while 46 (RM) Cdo would clear between the road and the Aller. As a preliminary to the operation, B and C Companies 4 KSLI would relieve the commandos in their current positions.

At 0745 hours 45 (RM) Cdo on the north axis set off into the forest and initially found little sign of the enemy, but at 0900 hours, as the troops closed on the Banseeberg, they ran into Hitler Youth from 1. SS-Kompanie, who opened up with machine-guns, small-arms and *Panzerfaust*. David Ward describes this action, to be his last of the war:[40]

> A quiet night but the enemy seemed to be moving small groups into the wood in the area of the rail bridge. '45' was ordered to line up and do a wood-clearing operation. I had the honour of the left of the line just in from the road. Off we went until coming over a slight rise we saw a company position of the enemy about 100 yards ahead. Sad to say they fired first and I got hit. Tommy Unthank was behind me and got part of the same burst, which killed him. We then fired back everything at the enemy and did a smart move backwards in bounds. I followed. There were no words spoken. I was stripped of my watch, compass and pistol and smartly removed to the RAP. Bandaged up and put on a stretcher then taken to the river. I was greeted by the QM, put in an ambulance and away.

The commandos pushed the Hitler Youth off the position but were immediately counter-attacked. At one stage the troop on the right flank was pinned down by very accurate machine-gun fire and a counter-attack by the Hitler Youth completely cut off this troop. The commando was placed under heavy pressure and the only reason the attacks did not over-run its position was the accuracy

---

40   Ward, 'My Time with 45 (RM) Commando'.

of the urgently called-for artillery support. As it was clear no progress could be made and the defensive perimeter needed tightening to fight-off further enemy attacks, at 1025 hours the two flanking troops were ordered to pull back towards the commando's main position and for the remainder of the day the commando was subjected to sporadic sniping and mortar fire, but thankfully no further counter-attacks. During their battle, in addition to Tommy Unthank, 45 (RM) Cdo lost seven others killed including C Troop commander, Captain Maurice Brockbank, and nine wounded, among them David Ward.

46 (RM) Cdo on the south axis had a similar experience. The commandos moved from their positions near the Esseler Kanal and with A, B and Y Troops leading advanced westwards through the forest, managing to get within 300 yards of the railway line before heavy fire from small-arms, machine-guns and *Panzerfaust* held them up. As it appeared progress could not be made without

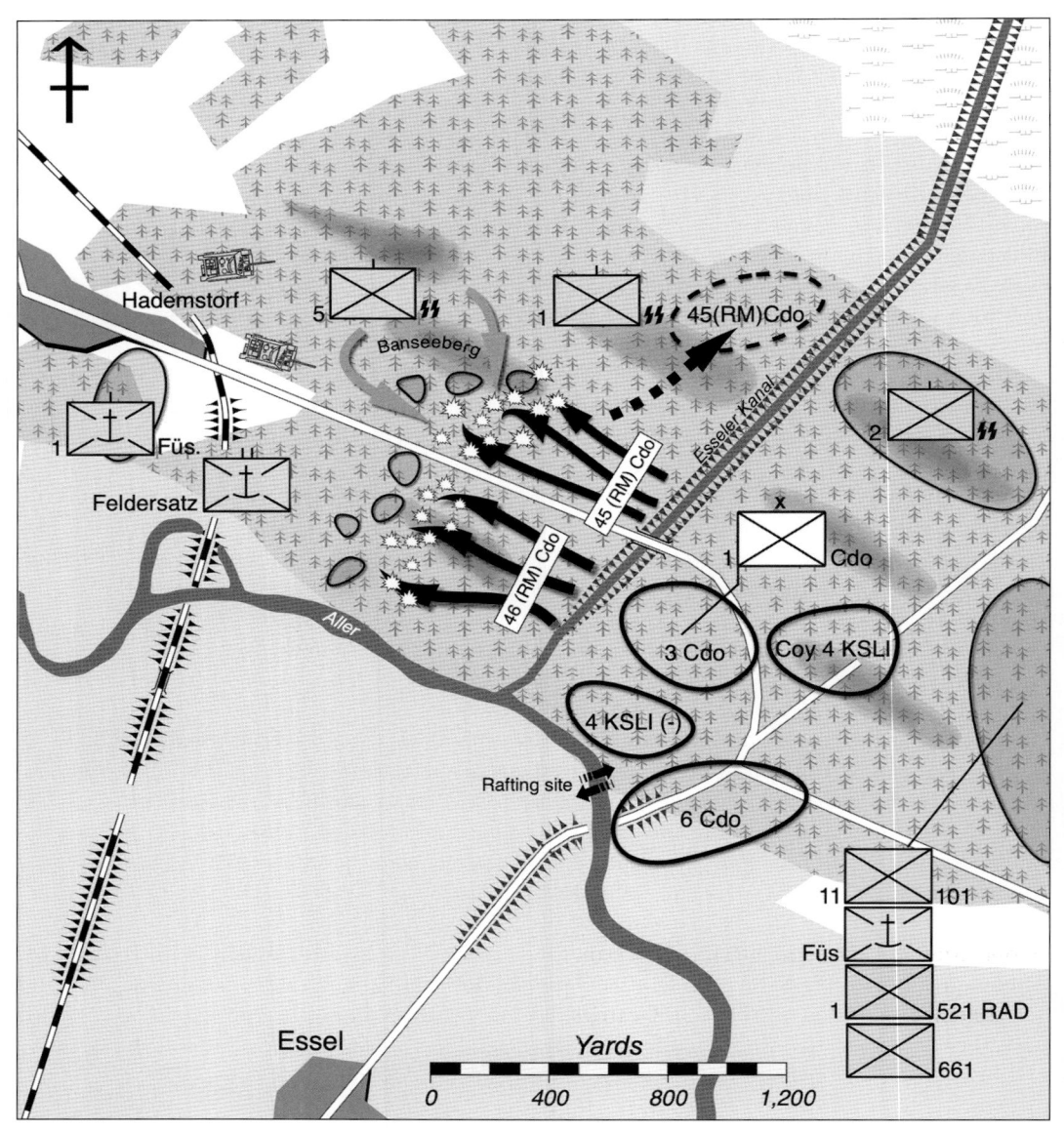

Map 43 45 and 46 (RM) Cdo Attacks – Morning 12 April 1945.

suffering heavy casualties, the advance halted and the FOOs from 1st Mountain Regiment brought down a number of fire missions on the German positions. Unfortunately, for the first time, some rounds fell on the commando's headquarters and among A and Y Troops, causing casualties. Air support was also called for and forward contact car 'Scalwag' ordered Squadron Leader Evan Mackie, in the area with seven Tempests from 80 Squadron, to shoot-up the north end of Eickeloh in an attempt to support the advance. As this target was three miles from the action in the forest, unsurprisingly the Tempest attack had no effect. By mid-morning 46 (RM) Cdo, with insufficient strength to overcome the enemy in the forest, sought authority from brigade headquarters to break-off the operation; this was given and the commando pulled back to the line of the Esseler Kanal where it dug-in on its west bank. The commando's losses for the day were Marine Cundall killed and nine others wounded. Five prisoners were taken and their interrogation revealed that the positions east of Hademstorf had been reinforced by a further marine battalion, with 11th Armoured Division's INTSUM for 14 April recording the presence of marines from Marine-Feldersatz-Bataillon 2. Although the *Feldersatz* battalion did not have the strength of a battalion and consisted, at most, of only a few hundred men, it fought both hard and successfully to prevent 46 (RM) Cdo from breaking through to Hademstorf. While the attacks by the two commandos did not achieve their aim of destroying the enemy on the bridgehead's left flank, the absence of enemy counter-attacks in the afternoon indicates that the Germans were significantly weakened by the attacks, with 1. and 5. SS-Kompanien suffering in particular, and there was now a large gap in the defensive arc between these companies and 2. SS-Kompanie on the Ostenholz road. The enemy's weakness was, however, as yet unknown to HQ 1st Commando Brigade.

With their comrades in 45 and 46 (RM) Cdo recovering, some members of 3 Cdo had a fortunate escape during the early afternoon, illustrating the confusion of fighting in the forest. At 1400 hours Troop Sergeant Major (TSM) Macnaughton, Lance Sergeant Hill and Trooper McPhilbin went forward to a house in front of their positions to make tea for the wounded as fires were not possible in the defensive positions. They were waiting for the water to boil when an *SS-Unterscharführer* (sergeant) and two soldiers burst into the room. Surprised at seeing British troops inside they ran out, slamming the door. The commandos rushed upstairs to a bedroom but looking outside saw the house surrounded by a platoon of the enemy. The Germans shouted at them to leave the house, so they hid their weapons and surrendered. They were searched, left with their effects, and treated civilly. However, they were then taken to an officer, and things now took a turn for the worse as Macnaughton heard the officer order them to be taken away and shot; Macnaughton did not reveal that he had understood. They were escorted by a soldier deeper into the woods, who told them his company had suffered 70 casualties from a total of 110. A British artillery barrage now came to their rescue and they were able to persuade their scared escort to surrender and come with them to the British lines, keeping up appearances by leaving him with his weapon (although removing his ammunition). Despite seeing parties of enemy, by long detours they were able to avoid them and return safely with their prisoner to 3 Cdo's position.

Back in the area of the road bridge, at 0600 hours the Class 40 raft was completed and opened for traffic; one of the first vehicles to cross being a bulldozer from 147 Field Park Squadron, needed to recover vehicles bogging-in on the soft ground on the right bank. The raft was able to take up to two tanks at a time and 2 Troop now worked it flat out for the next 11 hours. During its time in operation the raft ferried to the right bank:

20 tanks	50 carriers
10 half-tracks	Nine 3t trucks
Fifty-two 15cwt trucks	62 Jeeps
7 scout cars	Two 6-pdr anti-tank guns

The raft transporting M16 half-tracks belonging to a self-propelled troop from 172 Battery 58th LAA Regiment. In the foreground, infantry from 4 KSLI are ferried in an assault boat. On the far bank a recovery bulldozer is evident.

Among the first vehicles to cross were the Comets of A Squadron 3 RTR, as John Langdon describes:[41]

> It was a slow business for, although the river was only 40 yards wide, there was only one raft; this however was able to take two tanks at a time. 1 Troop was in the lead and I duly set off on the first crossing. All went well, the enemy had withdrawn back into the woods, which consisted mainly of fir trees. The commando brigade, assisted by 4 KSLI, had made the bridgehead reasonably secure; luckily for us there was no enemy air activity. As soon as Corporal Brindle had joined Elstob and myself we took up defensive positions close to the perimeter covering the centre line leading out of the bridgehead. This road led through thick woods in a north-easterly direction towards the village of Ostenholz. The second troop over moved to the west side of the bridgehead where they contacted the commandos. By 1100 the squadron was complete on the east [right] bank, the sappers had got on well with the bridge but it would still be sometime before it was ready and the rest of the battalion could cross over and join us.

While A Squadron's Comets were being ferried, 6 Cdo held a burial service for those killed during the assault on the bridge. It was a moving but short affair as 30 minutes later the commando was ordered to link-up with 1 Cheshire at Engehausen and a strong patrol was dispatched at 1100 hours to contact the battalion. At 1430 hours 6 Cdo handed-over the immediate vicinity of the road bridge to 75th Anti-Tank Regiment and moved off to occupy an area mid-way between the bridge and Engehausen.

---

41 Langdon, *The Sharp End*, p.149.

The battle on the Ostenholz road

At 1300 hours the commanding officer of 4 KSLI, Lieutenant Colonel Max Robinson, decided to clear the forest and an area of dunes to the east of the Ostenholz road from where the enemy could threaten the engineering effort at the road bridge. An hour later the battalion went into action with A Company on the left and D Company, reinforced with a platoon from C Company, on the right. The companies were supported from the road by John Langdon's troop, which since the loss of the Comet at Husum was still operating with only three tanks. John Langdon, the troop commander, describes what took place:[42]

> Soon after 1100 my troop was required to clear the centre line with two companies of 4 KSLI, one on either side of the road. Our immediate objective was a stream called the Drebber, which flowed under the road a mile away. I was the lead tank with Corporal Brindle behind me and Sergeant Elstob in reserve.[43] The going was very slow, as the woods on both sides were thick. We had to remain on the road while the infantry worked through the trees and scrub. As they moved forward we did the same, firing our Besas at any suspicious ditch or bush. The infantry had a Wasp with them, which came in very handy to burn the Germans out of their foxholes; it was indeed a fearsome weapon. The enemy were in considerable numbers and, before we moved any distance, the infantry began taking prisoners.
>
> The day was now very warm and the inside of the tank like an oven. There was a lot of smoke caused by the flame-thrower setting alight the undergrowth as we moved along. This, with the fumes from our machine-guns, made conditions very sticky. Before reaching the Drebber we came to a large continuous clearing where all the trees had been felled, it was marked on our maps by a double broken red line. This we later found out was the projected site of a new *Autobahn*…We reached our objective without any casualties to ourselves and very few to the infantry. After a while we received orders to pull back about half a mile to a track which disappeared into the woods. We settled in with two [*sic*] tanks on either side of the road; myself on the right side slightly forward of Corporal Brindle on the left, with Sergeant Elstob in reserve covering another track to the right. After approximately half an hour in these positions, all being quiet, I gave permission for a brew, which Lance Corporal Bourne and Troopers Charlton, Rice and Enever started to get ready behind the tank while I remained in the turret.

While the 4 KSLI companies and John Langdon's troop were fighting their way through the forest, the three Tigers, with F01 leading, were moving down the Ostenholz road and by mid-afternoon had reached the battle area.[44] Leaving two of the Tigers in depth, Unteroffizier Franzen in F01 drove on to meet the Hitler Youth of 2. SS-Kompanie on the northern edge of the forest. Having been updated on the fighting, he then advanced over the Drebber stream and started to round a bend in the road some 400 yards further on to observe the next straight section of road.

---

42 Langdon, *The Sharp End*, pp.149–150.
43 Peter Elstob had a remarkable life, including being a crew member of a cruise liner, pilot, owner of the Arts Theatre Club, beauty mask manufacturer, novelist, balloonist, publisher, military historian and much more. His semi-autobiographical novel *Warriors for the Working Day* (London: Jonathan Cape, 1960) covers his wartime experiences, including this tank action. His obituary in the *Guardian* rightly identified that he was born in the wrong century and would have been more at home in the reign of Elizabeth 1.
44 It is believed that F01 bore the chassis number 250158. A Tiger with this number was one of a batch of six issued to Schießschule der Panzertruppen (Tank Gunnery School) Putlos in March 1943. *https://blog.tiger-tank.com/incombat/crouching-tiger-hidden-comet/* (accessed 15 March 2017).

A blurry shot taken in action of prisoners hurrying down the Ostenholz road. On the right of the photograph is a tree-covered dune, dominant features in the forest. (Peston)

Franzen's view down the Ostenholz road as he rounded the bend in Tiger F01. John Langdon's troop were either side of the road near where it runs out of sight. (Author)

As he knew there were enemy tanks in the immediate area he had already ordered his gunner, Karl Sprecht, to load armour-piercing shot.

In the forest to the south the men of the unsuspecting 4 KSLI were reorganising after the successful wood-clearance and evacuating the 50 prisoners they had taken. The Comet crews of 1 Troop were taking the opportunity to relax after the action and next to John Langdon's Comet the water was bubbling cheerfully on the No. 2 cooker as his men prepared to make mugs of tea…[45]

> Suddenly there was a great deal of noise around us caused by infantry carriers moving, as though the 'hounds of hell' were after them, back down the road past our position, then the terrifying sound of an AP shot which screamed past me. I shouted to the crew, who scrambled back into the tank, and to my horror saw through my binoculars an enemy Tiger tank moving slowly around a corner of the road about 300 yards away. I looked down into the turret and saw Lance Corporal Bourne, my wireless operator/loader, who realising what was happening was trying to replace the HE already loaded with an AP. After what seemed an age, in reality only a few seconds, he managed it. Looking through my glasses while directing Trooper Rice, my gunner, onto the Tiger, I saw its 88mm gun slowly traversing onto us. We fired, followed immediately by a second shot, I shouted down the intercom to Trooper Charlton, my driver, the order to reverse; head on as it was to us we could not hope to knock out the Tiger. We were out-gunned even at this close range, and unable to penetrate its frontal armour. If I wanted to save my tank and its crew this was the only thing to be done.
>
> Behind us were fir trees, fairly dense and approximately 40-foot tall and if we were unable to crash our way through we would be knocked out in a matter of seconds. We moved slowly backwards, the first tree went down and the next, only 10 more yards and we were in cover. The Tiger continued to fire, a scout car that had been left at the side of the road was blazing. Another vehicle was brewing up further down. I glanced across the road and saw Corporal Brindle also attempting to reverse into the wood. An AP round ricocheted into his offside track, smashing it completely. He did the only thing possible and ordered his crew to bale out. Immediately afterwards a second shot went through the front of his tank where Lance Corporal Loynes, his driver, and Trooper Webster, his co-driver, had been seconds before. A third shot tore into the turret and if Brindle and the turret crew of Trooper Boyes, wireless operator, and Trooper O'Brian, gunner, had remained none would have lived to tell the tale.
>
> We managed to ease further back into the wood from where we took up position covering the road, the Tiger meanwhile remained at the corner. I got on the air, made my report and had the dubious pleasure of hearing someone back at RHQ saying that reports of Tigers had come in before and were generally unfounded. I told him quickly what I thought of this and rang off! Soon afterwards the KSLI reported a second Tiger with infantry support, this report however was never substantiated. An infantry patrol was despatched but the enemy, no doubt considering they had done a good day's work, withdrew and our own infantry was able to regain some of the lost ground, which was as far as the projected *Autobahn*. On reflection, I can only think that the Tiger's power traverse was out of order as, luckily, the gun appeared to take a while to bear onto us. This could indicate that the gun and turret were being traversed manually by the gunner.
>
> Fortunately, all my troop was unscathed. I sent Brindle and his crew, who had taken cover in the woods, back to the echelon, their tank obviously being completely wrecked. We remained in position until last light when we were called into squadron leaguer near the river crossing; our infantry remained dug-in on the perimeter.

---

45 Langdon, *The Sharp End*, p.150.

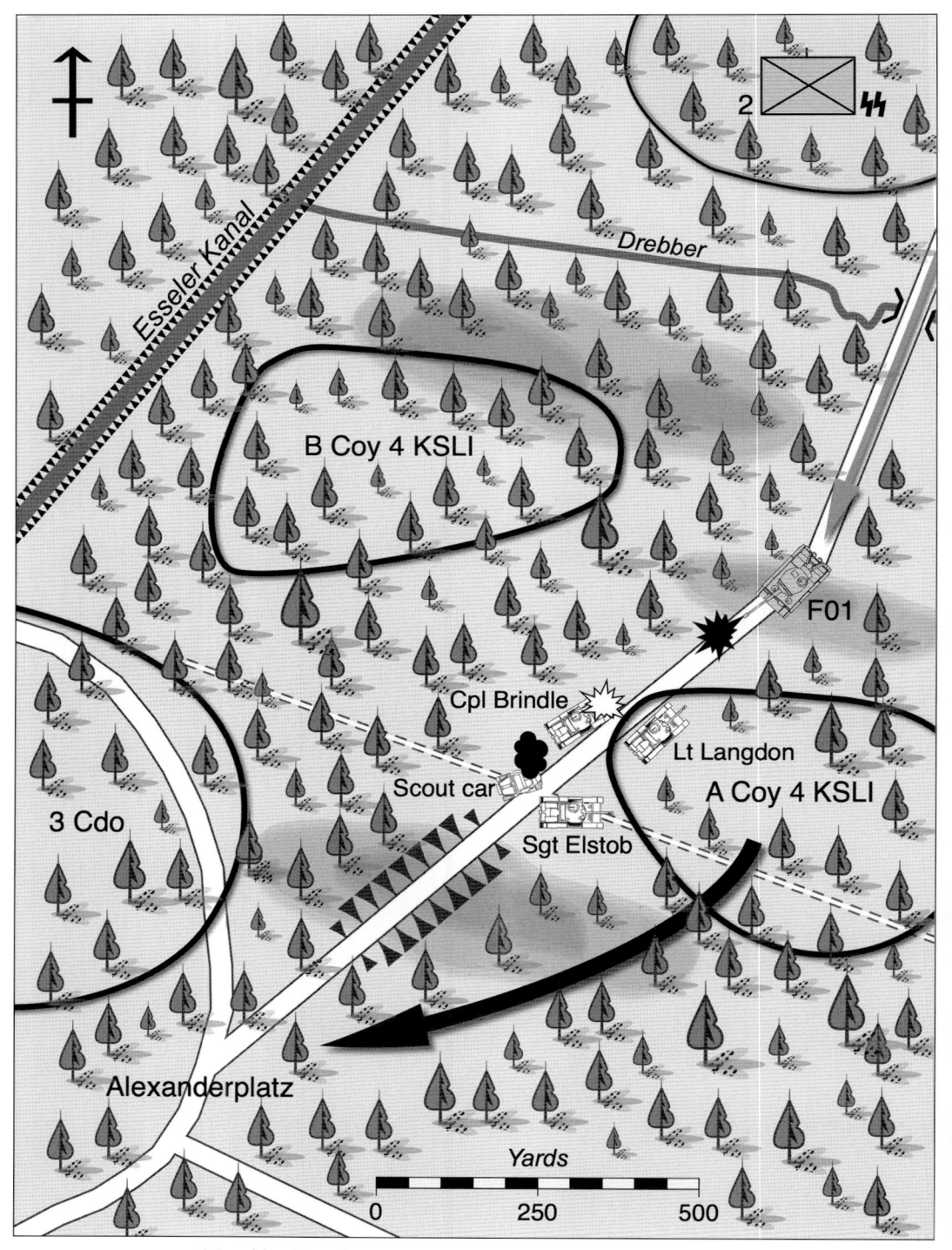

Map 44 1 Troop's Encounter with Tiger F01 – pm 12 April 1945.

John Langdon's observation about the power traverse indicates that F01 might not have been restored to full battleworthiness from the damage it received during the Fehrmann counter-attack six days previous. The turret traverse of a Tiger was powered by the engine via a transfer case, but the traverse was notoriously slow and was dependent on the engine revs. If the power system was inoperative, the turret could be hand-operated by a wheel, but this was even slower. Assuming there was a problem with the traverse system, it is odd that Franzen did not assist bringing the gun to bear by turning F01 on its tracks, by far the quickest method.

Having engaged 1 Troop, Franzen pulled back around the corner and reported that he had engaged Crocodile flame-throwing tanks, an understandable mistake as the German infantry withdrawing from 4 KSLI's attack would have told him about the presence of a flame-throwing vehicle (Wasp) and he would not have encountered a Comet before, further confusing him. Despite his success, Franzen did not advance further down the road as this would lose the protection of 2. SS-Kompanie, needed due to the proximity of the forest providing the enemy with ample opportunities to ambush him from the flanks. 4 KSLI's war diary records two Panthers being responsible for knocking out the Comet and the scout car. The survey of tank casualties recorded that Corporal Brindle's Comet WD No. 334921 had: a scoop from an armour-piercing round on the right driving sprocket; a jagged penetration at the junction of the glacis and lower front glacis plates roughly opposite the driver; and a penetration at the junction of the edge of the mantlet and the side of the turret. As the tank casualty survey recorded both penetrations having a diameter of 8.8cm,[46] only a Tiger could have fired these shots. The crew was indeed fortunate to have escaped unhurt. However, even with the immediate threat from the Tiger reduced for the time being, the threat to life and limb in the bridgehead was still very real, as John Langdon recounts:[47]

> While all this excitement was going on, Neil Kent had arrived back from leave to take over the squadron from Graham. Throughout the late afternoon and early evening spasmodic shelling of the bridge, which had now been completed by the sappers, and the adjacent area had been carried out by the German artillery. It so happened that, within five minutes of his arrival, Neil was caught in one of these bombardments and suffered a very unpleasant head wound, a small piece of shell splinter penetrating near an ear. Barry Whitehouse, who had been immediately called up, arranged his evacuation. All this happened before we got back to the squadron leaguer. We duly arrived and the troop, now only two tanks, Sergeant Elstob's and mine, were met and our position indicated by Squadron Sergeant Major Wood.

So 12 April came to a close with something of a stalemate. The commando brigade had achieved a relatively secure perimeter and to its east 1 Cheshire held Engehausen and had patrolled into the forests. The brigade had, however, failed to clear the Germans from the bridgehead's left flank and the presence of Tigers with supporting infantry was not only a threat to the bridgehead but also a serious challenge to further attempts to advance up the Ostenholz road, the division's intended axis. Although for the Germans the weakening of their forces around the bridgehead was a setback, they were still sufficiently strong to delay a breakout on the Ostenholz road.

Of more significance than the fighting in the Aller forests, 12 April saw the start of a chain of events that would lead to a discovery of such infamy that it would reverberate around the world. At first light, carrying a white flag, a German major and lieutenant from the *Sanitätsdienst*

---

46 TNA WO 205/1165, 3 RTR, Serial D.23, Wright and Harkness, *A Survey of Casualties Amongst Armoured Units in North-West Europe.*

47 Langdon, *The Sharp End*, p.150. Sergeant Elstob's Comet bore the name *Celerity* and its driver was Dennis Pannell, father of Dr Stephen Pannell mentioned in Acknowledgements.

(medical corps) crossed the lines to arrive at 1 Cheshire's headquarters at Engehausen. They brought news of a camp at Belsen suffering from an outbreak of typhus and advising that nobody should approach within three miles of the site. At 0900 hours two staff cars, both flying white flags, crossed the bridge at Winsen. The cars contained an Oberst Hanns Schmidt, the supply officer for the Hungarian armour training school at Bergen, and Oberstleutnant Bohnekamp, Grosan's deputy. The two emissaries were escorted to HQ 159th Brigade at Buchholz where they explained that they had been sent under instructions from Reichsführer-SS Himmler to negotiate, for humanitarian reasons, a neutral zone for a concentration camp at Belsen. They were blindfolded, taken to HQ 11th Armoured Division and then to HQ VIII Corps where they presented the Germans' terms for coping with the camp's 45,000 inmates, among whom typhus had broken out. In addition to the neutral zone, the Germans offered to leave the Winsen bridge intact. These terms were deemed unacceptable by the British so Brigadier Taylor-Balfour, Brigadier General Staff VIII Corps, crossed the lines and drove to HQ Armeegruppe Blumentritt, now occupying a former RAD camp at Wolterdingen to the north of Soltau, where he presented counter-proposals to Major Manthey, Blumentritt's chief of staff. It was now the turn of the Germans to reject proposals as they required them to withdraw some five miles north of a defined neutral zone, completely out-flanking their forces on the Aller. By 0100 hours on 13 April formal negotiations had broken down, but owing to the severity of the medical situation a gentleman's agreement was brokered and Taylor-Balfour went to Grosan's headquarters at Bergen where he signed a truce with Grosan, Oberst Harries (deputy commandant of the Bergen training area) and Schmidt. The two sides agreed, inter alia, a neutral zone around the camp and the British assumption of duties from the Hungarian guard force and their *SS* superiors, all to commence at 1200 hours 13 April. At this stage the true horror of the camp was unknown but would become immediately apparent when the first British units, possibly a Frankforce jeep patrol commanded by Lieutenant John Randall from A Squadron 1 SAS, arrived at the camp during the morning of 15 April. The patrol was closely followed at 1430 hours by 249 Battery 63rd Anti-Tank Regiment from VIII Corps Troops, which reported the appalling truth and became the first of many units engaged in the grisly and deeply traumatic process of relieving the camp.

8

'One of the Hardest Days':
The battles on the roads to Ostenholz and Winsen 13–14 April 1945

Securing the bridgehead's left flank

Friday 13 April dawned misty but it was going to be a fine day and at 0500 hours 257 Field Company completed the Bailey bridge at Essel, allowing the remaining tanks of 3 RTR to cross rapidly into the bridgehead. However, with the left flank still a concern and the enemy able to observe the Bailey bridge, at 0900 hours 46 (RM) Cdo was ordered to dispatch two patrols to discover enemy presence on the railway embankment as a preliminary to an attack to destroy the enemy in the Hademstorf area. Both reached the line without any interference, although activity was evident between the railway and Hademstorf, and a Pak 43 was identified on the village's edge. As the embankment had been reached with ease, the order was given for 46 (RM) Cdo to capture Hademstorf without delay. Also in the morning, Major Ian Beadle of 45 (RM) Cdo, accompanied by two marines, had courageously patrolled westwards through the forest to the commando's former position on the Banseeberg and found it clear of enemy. Although no enemy had been seen, brigade headquarters ordered 45 (RM) Cdo to mount a simultaneous assault on the Banseeberg area to protect 46 (RM) Cdo's right flank during its attack on Hademstorf and put maximum pressure on the enemy.

At 1040 hours 46 (RM) Cdo's assaulting troops moved to the edge of the forest and here orders were issued for a two-pronged attack: Y Troop on the left would secure the railway embankment before assaulting the southern part of Hademstorf; X Troop would follow Y Troop and pass through them if necessary; A Troop on the right would move through the edge of the forest north of the road and then enter the village; meanwhile B Troop would sweep through the forest on A Troop's right before entering the village from the north; Z Troop was in reserve. The commando would be supported by three Achilles tank-destroyers from H Troop, 119 Battery, 75th Anti-Tank Regiment, which would engage the Pak 43 identified on the edge of Hademstorf.

The five commando troops moved up through the forest to the start line and the Achilles positioned themselves on the edge of the forest in broken ground overlooking the railway line and Hademstorf's eastern edge. The attack began at 1400 hours with Y Troop advancing through the strip wood to secure the railway embankment, which it did without difficulty, but when advancing further and entering the small wood to the south of Hademstorf the commandos met considerable opposition from marines and Hitler Youth occupying well-concealed positions and armed with numerous automatic weapons. Almost immediately the troop commander, Captain Pierce, was killed, Lieutenant Burrows was shot and killed while administering morphine to a severely wounded marine, and Lieutenant Beardmore was wounded. TSM Davies took over command but

303

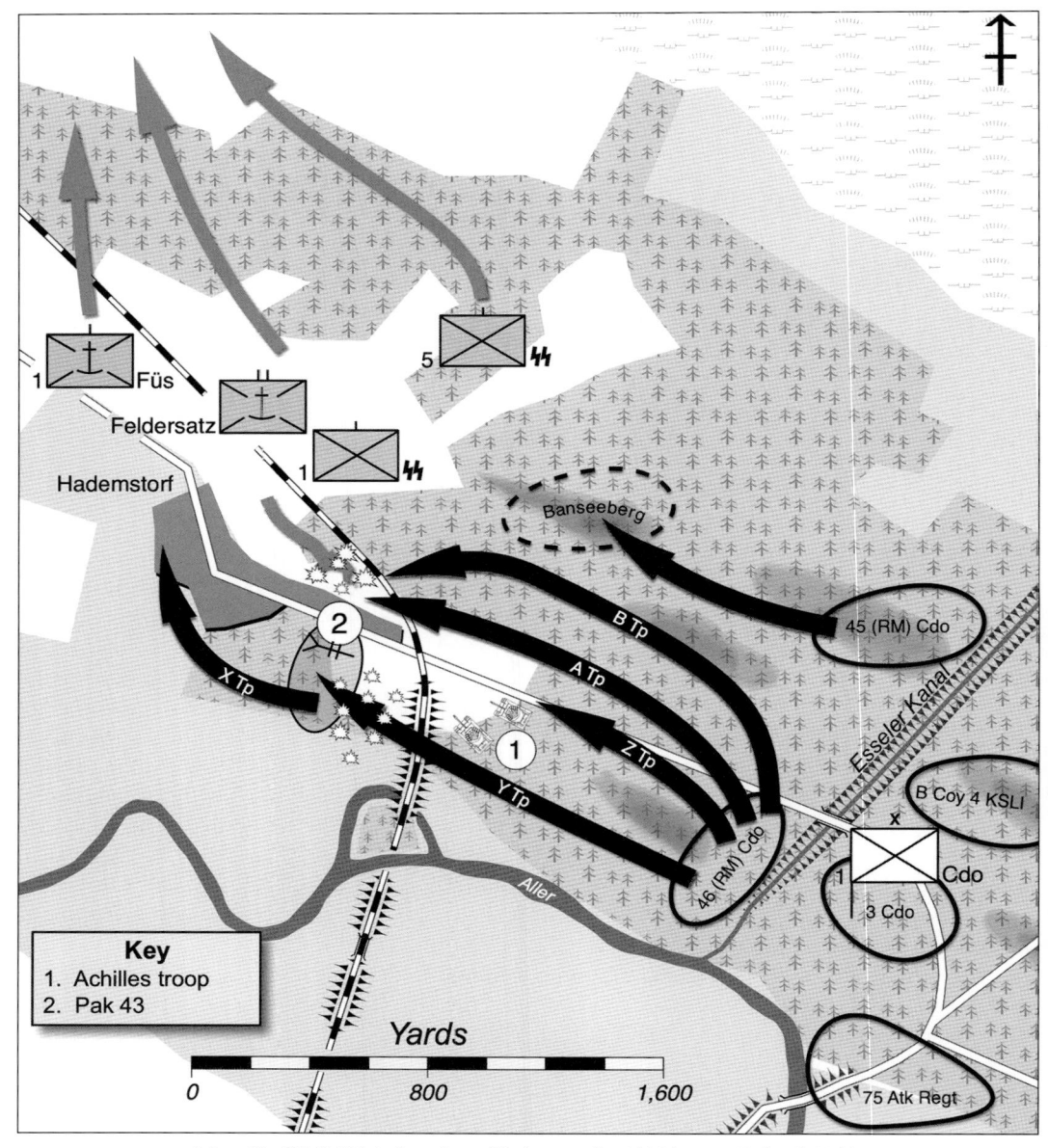

Map 45 (RM) Cdo's Attack on Hademstorf – 1400 hours 13 April 1945.

shortly after he also was killed, leaving Sergeant Cooper in command of the troop. Although the attack was faltering, Sergeant Cooper rallied the men and the troop slowly fought its way through the wood.[1] X Troop, commanded by Captain Easton, was pushed forward as planned but by the time it took over the enemy's resistance had been broken and the troop was able to reach the south-western part of the village. At this juncture, Hitler Youth from the remnants of 1. and 5.

---

1   Sergeant Cooper and TSM Mallorie of X Troop were both awarded the Military Medal for their parts in the Hademstorf action.

SS-Kompanien attempted to mount a counter-attack from the north-west but were immediately engaged by shellfire from 1st Mountain Regiment. An unnamed *SS-Unterscharführer* describes what befell the young men:[2]

> It was a nightmare! For the young boys it was the first shelling that they had experienced on open ground. They were running around in panic and in total confusion. The wounded lay crying out for their mothers. We were forced to withdraw quickly with the commando troops firing at us to add to our terrible casualties.

On the right flank, A and B Troops met much less-spirited resistance and by 1500 hours A Troop had occupied the houses in the area of the level-crossing and B Troop had cleared the village's northern edge supported by fire from A Troop, now on the main road. By 1700 hours Hademstorf was captured at a cost of two officers and three other ranks killed and eight wounded. The Pak 43 was found knocked out and 73 prisoners were taken from a variety of units including Marine-Füsilier-Bataillon 2, Heeres-Panzerjäger-Abteilung 661 (these would have included the crew of the Pak 43) and SS-A.u.E.Btl.12 'HJ'; 20 enemy dead were counted. The survivors escaped from Hademstorf and withdrew back through the forests to the east of Eickeloh then headed north towards Walsrode.

While 46 (RM) Cdo was attacking Hademstorf, 45 (RM) Cdo advanced on their right to the Banseeberg and by midday had secured the feature. The troops then spent the remainder of the day engaging infiltrating enemy groups with any weapon systems that could be brought to bear, including artillery, Vickers and small-arms. A 16-year-old member of 1. SS-Kompanie was captured and told his interrogator that his company had an original strength of about 130 and been equipped with eight MG 42, *Panzerfaust* and small-arms, but now had no officers. The company had set off from Hademstorf at 0730 hours that morning with the intention of attacking the bridgehead. He had, however, lost contact with his comrades when they were dispersed by accurate artillery fire and he was captured trying to make his way back to Hademstorf. From mid-afternoon onwards 45 (RM) Cdo recorded no activity in its sector.

The battle on the Ostenholz road

While activity on the bridgehead's left flank had largely died away, this was far from the case on the Ostenholz road where the main action of the day would occur. During the night 12/13 April, 29th Armoured Brigade took over responsibility from 1st Commando Brigade for the advance on the Ostenholz road and moved its headquarters to Essel. At 0750 hours 4 KSLI was ready to move off up the road when a report came in from A Company that there were three tanks in sight. One of the tanks was engaged at a range of 400 yards by two of the battalion's 6-pdr anti-tank guns and seven hits were claimed on it before one of the guns was hit by return fire and the detachment commander, Sergeant Muncaster, killed. Although the war diary makes no mention of type of tank, Major Thornburn's regimental account states one was a Tiger,[3] and seven 6-pdr strikes failing to knock-out a tank strongly supports this. At 0835 hours A Company reported its forward troops were under shell-fire and that a half-track and a second 6-pdr had been knocked out. Tank-stalking parties equipped with PIAT were sent forward to engage the tanks but met no success. John Langdon describes the events:[4]

---

2 Saft, *Krieg in der Heimat*, p.161.
3 Thornburn, 'After Antwerp – The Long Haul to Victory', p.110.
4 Langdon, *The Sharp End*, p.151.

We were up and about at 0500, for those with a superstitious nature the day and date, Friday the 13th, was duly noted. The whole crew had slept well despite the foreboding of spending another night in the pit. The enemy shelling of our leaguer area had ceased and, at first light, we were able to disperse taking up positions covering the road along which we had advanced the previous day. At 0600, there was the battalion net and, as soon as the light was suitable, we made preparations to advance again up the road, which was still the battalion's [3 RTR] and 4 KSLI's centre line. 3 Troop (Lieutenant Don Collie) was to lead followed by squadron HQ, then 2 Troop (Lieutenant Dennis Sullivan ['Sully']), 4 Troop (Lieutenant Mike Bullock), with my troop bringing up the rear.

At 0830, just as we were about to move off, to our dismay the Tiger re-appeared at the corner of the road and fired a few AP rounds. A troop-carrying vehicle, a 3 tonner, belonging to the 4 KSLI, who at the time were marrying up with us in preparation for the advance, was brewed up. It was sensibly decided to delay the start of the advance until the situation had changed. A heavy artillery concentration was quickly put down in the vicinity of the Tiger, which produced the desired effect of making the enemy retire; this enabled us to niggle slowly up the road.

Despite the presence of the Tigers, 4 KSLI also pushed cautiously up the Ostenholz road with B Company left and C Company right supported by the Comets of A Squadron 3 RTR. While the 4 KSLI Group was making slow progress, C Squadron 3 RTR, which had crossed the Aller that morning, went on a wide outflanking manoeuvre through the forest to the east of the Ostenholz road to see if it could attack the enemy from an unexpected direction. The squadron moved down Landesstrasse 180 to Engehausen where it swung north into the forest before heading west back towards the Ostenholz road. By 1025 hours it had worked its way along the forest tracks and the lead Comet, commanded by Sergeant Harding, was nearing the road. At 1030 hours, when Sergeant Harding's Comet was some 80 yards from the road and still among the pine trees, F01 suddenly rolled into view broadside on. As Sergeant Harding was expecting action against armour an AP round was already in the breech and his gunner immediately fired the round into the Tiger's flank, penetrating the engine compartment. F01's crew was lucky the strike was not a few inches to the left as it would have entered the Tiger's main fighting compartment. Fortune also favoured C Squadron. Had enemy infantry been in the woods through which the Comets had advanced, the tanks would have been easy targets for *Panzerfaust* ambush and it seems odd to have launched C Squadron into close country without the protection of accompanying infantry. Franzen was less fortunate and paid the price of advancing beyond the protective cover of 2. SS-Kompanie and other German infantry on the Ostenholz road.

It has been suggested that just before the shot slammed into F01's flank,[5] Franzen saw Sergeant Harding's Comet and shouted, 'Enemy tank. 10 o'clock!' As F01 and its main armament were pointing down the road, the expected target direction, the Tiger's slow turret traverse speed meant that there was no likelihood that the 8.8cm gun could be brought to bear in time to engage a flank threat. Even if the driver, Otto George, had thrown an immediate neutral turn to the left this was a race Franzen could never win. Tiger commanders and drivers were taught to angle their tanks to the threat in order to increase the thickness of the armour, but with the Comet ambushing them from a flank and at extreme short range this was impossible and F01 was doomed.

With fire breaking out, Franzen and his crew abandoned F01 and escaped on foot, eventually reaching Ostenholz. Here they were given a tractor and, picking up four other withdrawing soldiers, set off for Schneverdingen. On nearing Schneverdingen their luck ran out when the tractor drove over a mine and in the ensuing explosion F01's loader, Obergefreiter Heinrich Pfaffelhuber, and the four passengers were killed; Ernst Spahr, the radio operator, had both legs blown off; Franzen

---

5   Saft, *Krieg in Der Heimat*, p.162.

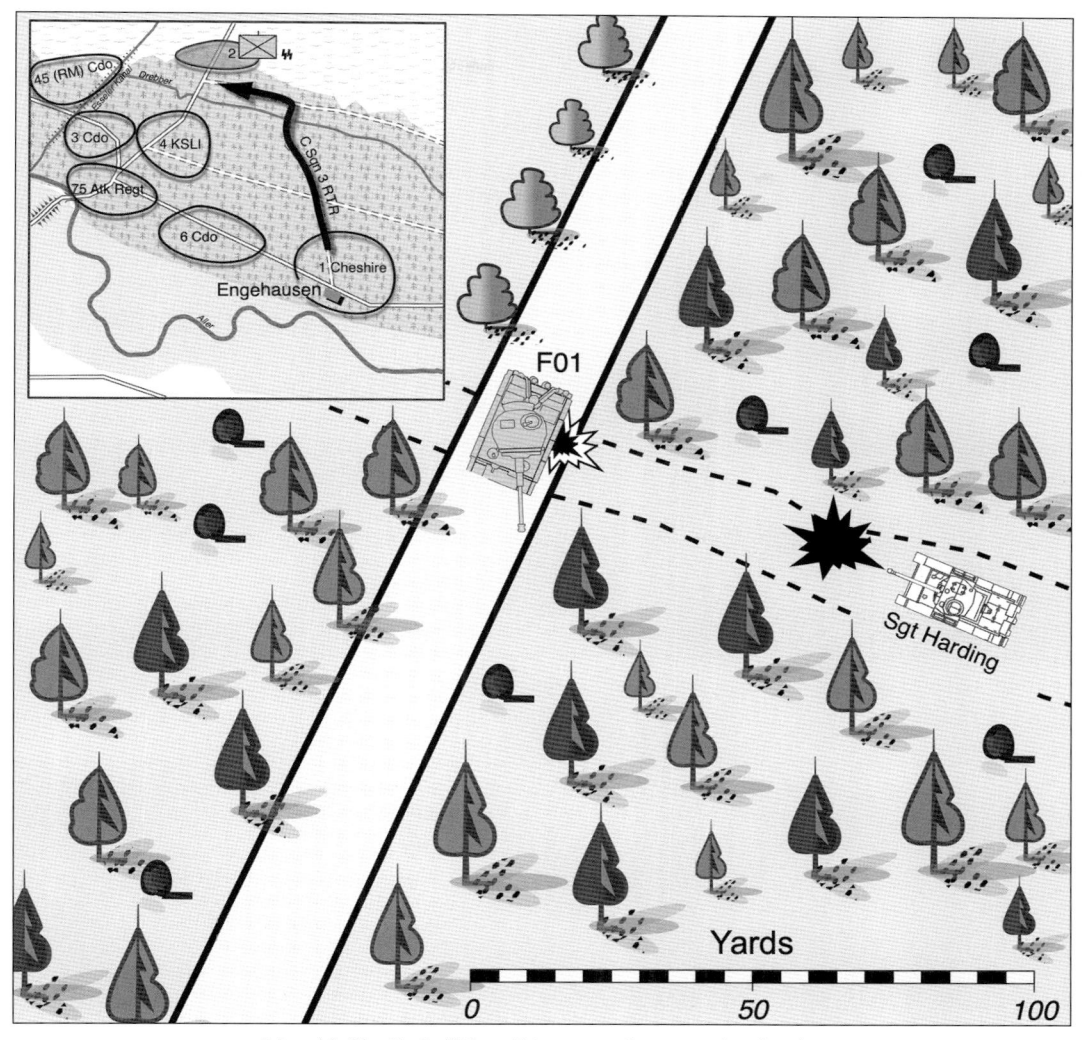

Map 46 The End of Tiger F01 – 1030 hours 13 April 1945.

lost an eye and lay comatose in the middle of the road with the dead; only Otto George and Karl Sprecht, the gunner, were unscathed but both were in deep shock. Franzen awoke on 6 May, the day after the cessation of hostilities in north-west Germany.

4 KSLI's war diary records that at 1100 hours 3 RTR reported knocking out a Tiger but added that this tank was already crippled by the battalion's anti-tank guns and was given the final *coup de grâce* by the tanks. With the fog of war, it is understandable that the battalion thought this was the case, but the gallant Sergeant Muncaster and his anti-tank gunners had hit a Tiger other than F01 as photographs of F01 taken after the battle show no multiple strike marks from 6-pdr shot on its frontal armour; two Tigers were therefore operating on the Ostenholz road during the morning of 13 April and we shall shortly meet this second tank. With F01 destroyed, John Langdon's two Comets were able to advance:[6]

---

6   Langdon, *The Sharp End*, pp.151–152.

F01 soon after its destruction. Smoke is still coming out of the commander's cupola and the soldiers of 3 RTR and 4 KSLI lean on the glacis plate, probably discussing the next stage of their battle up the Ostenholz road. A surrendering German soldier can be seen to the rear of F01. (Peston)

A toy-like Cromwell of HQ 29th Armoured Brigade bypasses the formidable bulk of F01 blocking the Ostenholz road. The state of the verge indicates that A Squadron 3 RTR had passed through by the time the photograph was taken. (Peston)

'ONE OF THE HARDEST DAYS' 309

The fire-damaged F01 after it was pushed off the Ostenholz road. The shot hole from Sergeant Harding's AP round is clearly visible above the sixth road wheel and the main armament is on full recoil after the round 'cooked off'. (The Tank Museum Ltd)

The menacing appearance of F01 belies its true, burnt-out state. An unfired *Panzerfaust* lies at the foot of the birch tree. (The Tank Museum Ltd)

The Ostenholz road and site of F01's destruction today. Sergeant Harding fired his shot from off the photograph to the right. (Author)

We were now able to move up the road, on rounding the bend we saw the Tiger with tanks of C Squadron close to it. The Tiger, on the road adjacent to the area partially cleared for the projected *Autobahn*, was brewing slowly. When we got level with it we were able to pull off the road and naturally had a good look at it. Suddenly its gun fired, caused no doubt by the heat from the fire in the turret. The round, an AP, narrowly missed some of our fellows who were nearby.

Further up the road the woods ended and there was open ground for at least a mile then more woods. The squadron was again ordered to take the lead and 2 Troop (Dennis Sullivan), who took over this role from 3 Troop (Don Collie), was attracting the attention of snipers. It was here that Sully's troop sergeant, Sergeant Probert, was hit in the head by a sniper's bullet. It killed him instantly. He was a popular member of the squadron, had proved to be an excellent troop sergeant, and was a cool and dependable tank commander in action. After a period of time the infantry, with help from 2 and 3 Troops, were able to clear the immediate neighbourhood of enemy.

At 1210 hours 4 KSLI reported two more tanks on the Ostenholz road further to the north. Air support was requested and Tempests from 80 Squadron launched an RP attack on the area, claiming the destruction of two self-propelled guns and a towed 8.8cm gun. The claim was not substantiated on the ground and the infantry saw the two tanks moving off into the forest to the west. B and C Companies 4 KSLI continued to meet stiff resistance in the forest from 2. SS-Kompanie, with the visibility very poor owing to burning undergrowth. 11th Armoured Division INTSUM for 13 April recorded that the strength of the *Waffen-SS* battalion was much reduced and that morale was correspondingly lower but that it still showed signs of coordinated action and leadership. Eventually 4 KSLI reached the forest's edge and gained a welcome view of open country ahead. The fighting in the forest had been exhausting and the infantry were near the end of their tether, as witnessed by Private Dave Dalton of B Company:[7]

> The enemy fire had been so well directed that we had no time to dig in. After two weeks of virtually non-stop campaigning both officers and men were dead tired. Some men were approaching exhaustion. One rifleman, Sam Lewis of B Company, took cover from the airbursts and in less than a minute had fallen fast asleep. A Comet tank starting up failed to wake him. Slowly rolling forward its nearside track went straight over Lewis's back. Having myself dug – and sometimes shared – as many as five shallow weapon slits in a single day with Sam earlier in the campaign I was saddened to see him end in this way. But, amazingly, out of a muddy depression deeper than most, the flattened but still stout-hearted rifleman began to rise to his feet. Swaying disjointedly, and with his head at an odd angle, he almost reached his full height before, unable to inhale properly, he staggered and fell. As the colonel's counter-fire plan bore fruit and the enemy fire slackened, Rifleman Lewis was taken to the RAP. He had shared the distinction with the colonel of being the only men still standing on the field!

The Germans too were exhausted, and the danger inherent in withdrawing northwards across the open area of marsh and moor worsened the situation for the young men of 2. SS-Kompanie. SS-Sturmscharführer Grabher-Meyer, *Der Spieß* of 2. SS-Kompanie, and eight soldiers escaped via ditches to a culvert under the *Autobahn*, becoming soaking wet and increasing their fatigue. Once in the clear they met SS-Unterscharführer Chales de Beaulieu and a group of men tasked to intercept those retreating and send them, at gunpoint if necessary, back to action. As Grabher-Meyer

---

7   Thornburn, 'After Antwerp – The Long Haul to Victory', p.111.

outranked Chales de Beaulieu he was able to avoid this outcome and reach the command post, where a confrontation then took place between SS-Obersturmführer Wilke on one side and Grabher-Meyer, SS-Obersturmführer Marsen and SS-Untersturmführer Fries on the other as to whether they should send troops out to look for weapons or get them to recover the wounded. The threesome successfully argued that as any further operations would be tantamount to murder, the wounded should be the first priority. Subsequently, using a SdKfz 251, every effort was made to evacuate the casualties to the *Reservelazarett* in Walsrode, but on arrival many were beyond medical attention.

The action at Half-way Wood

Although the divisional plan for 29th Armoured Brigade was still that it should advance to Ostenholz, and from there to Bergen, the road it would have to use to reach Ostenholz was narrow and far from ideal as it traversed the marsh and moor and there was no scope to deploy off it until reaching an area with firmer ground and blocks of woodland, a mile or so beyond the edge of the Essel forest. The brigade would therefore continue to advance on a single axis, led by 4 KSLI supported by the Comets of 3 RTR.

For this next phase, the lead changed to A Company left and D Company right and after a short pause the two companies set off, with the BC's Comet, the commanding officer's scout car and the intelligence officer's carrier moving on the Ostenholz road. To cover the advance, the Comets of A Squadron were in overwatch from the forest's edge and a smoke screen was fired to provide additional protection. As the riflemen moved slowly across the moor they came under small-arms' fire from a wood lying half-way between the forest and the Kröpke inn and held by remnants of 2. SS-Kompanie and infantry from Bataillon Lotze. This opposition required HE and Besa suppressive fire from the tanks to allow the infantry to make progress.

The moor today, with the much-improved drainage allowing cultivation. (Author)

'ONE OF THE HARDEST DAYS' 313

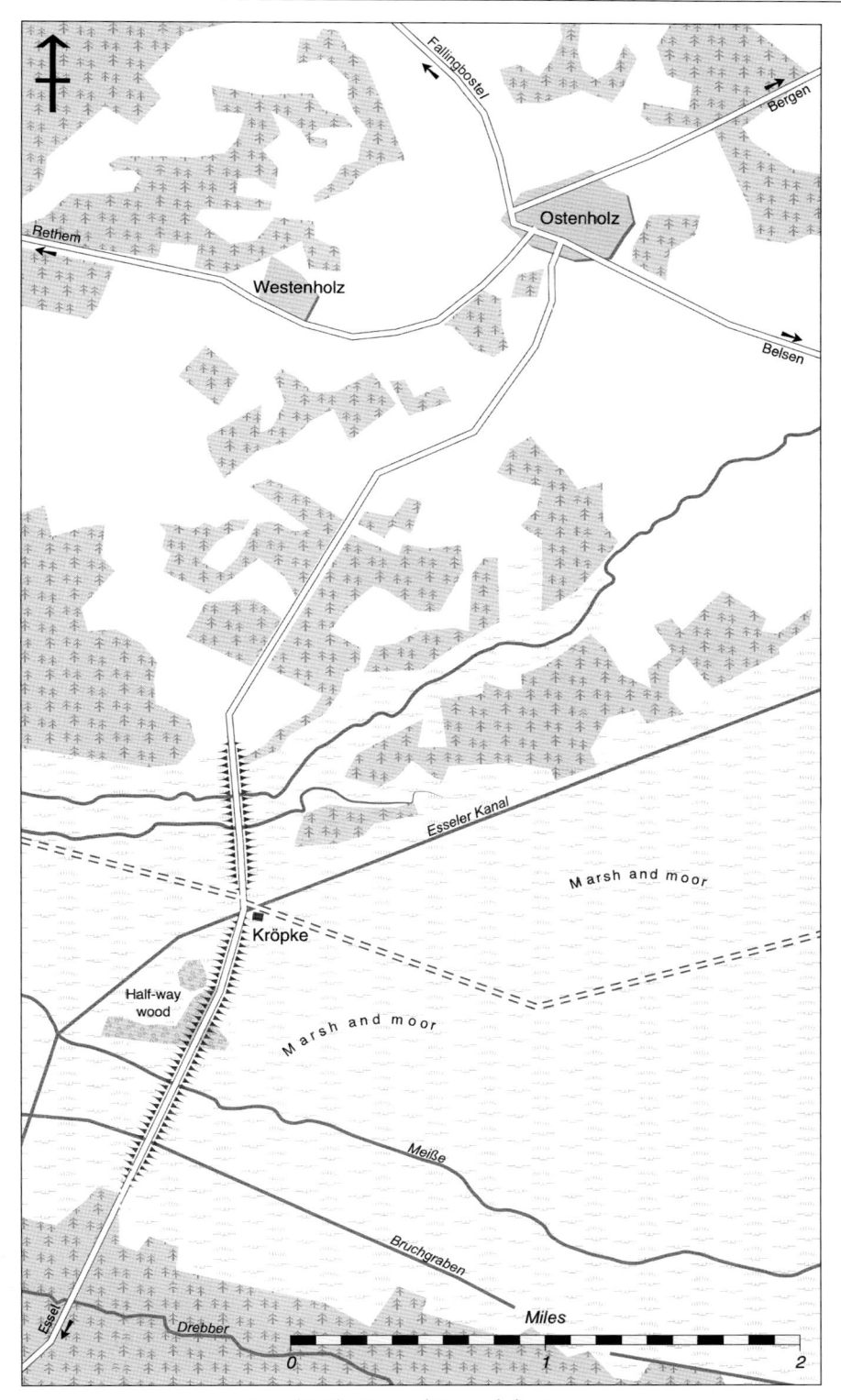

Map 47 The Ground Beyond the Forest.

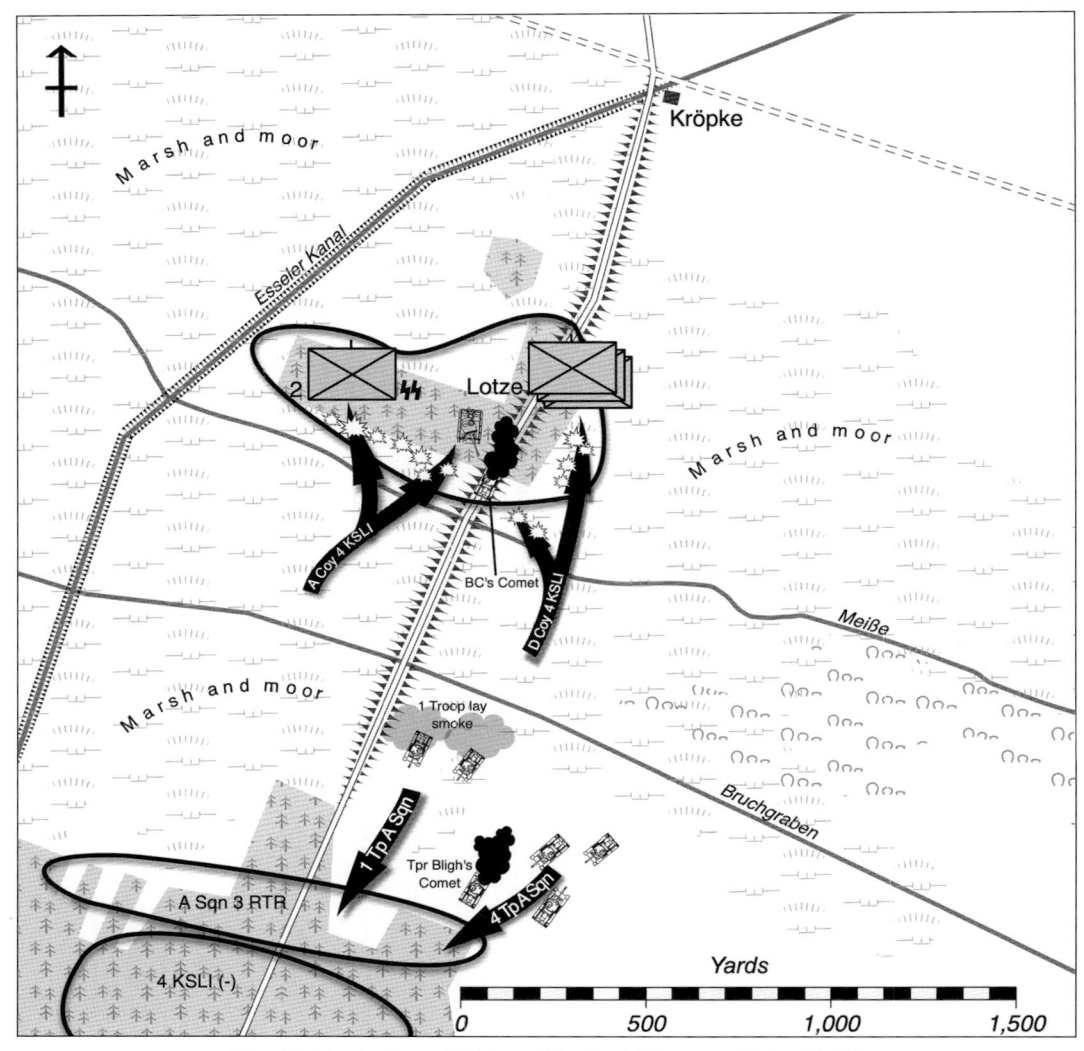

Map 48 The Action at Half-way Wood – 1400 hours 13 April 1945.

At 1400 hours, as A and D Companies closed on the wood, a Tiger suddenly emerged from the trees. The battery commander's Comet immediately reversed crushing Private Roberts (fortunately he survived) taking cover behind the tank against the intelligence officer's carrier. The Tiger proceeded to destroy the Comet at the very short range of 50 yards. Although the driver was seriously wounded, the crew, including Major George Smyth-Osbourne, BC H Battery 13 (HAC) RHA, survived. The Tiger then proceeded to destroy the carrier and the FOO's Comet. Both 4 KSLI companies were now pinned down, as was the commanding officer Lieutenant Colonel Robinson, who was caught in the thick of the action. Robinson shouted at Lieutenant Cunningham of A Company to bring forward a PIAT and attack the Tiger. Two hits were scored, convincing the crew to bail out. However, once on the ground the driver saw that the hits had caused only superficial damage so under cover of machine-gun fire he managed to climb back on board and reverse the vehicle to safety. The remainder of the crew rejoined the Tiger and immediately turned their attention to A Squadron, which by now had

'ONE OF THE HARDEST DAYS' 315

started to follow the infantry across the first stretch of open ground. John Langdon describes what happened:[8]

> Our next objective was the woods on our right, a mile up the road. It was considered the enemy had withdrawn to them and that they had at least one tank with them. Before moving a request was put in for Typhoons to *strafe* the front edge of the woods. They were soon circling overhead, then their dive onto the target and the release of their rockets. It was reported that they had claimed to have knocked out two 88mm anti-tank guns and one half-track.
>
> Immediately after this we were ordered to advance to the woods. 4 Troop (Mike Bulloch) was sent out to the right while I was closer to the road on his left. I was ordered to move up and take the lead. The ground was very open, flat, without a stitch of cover. I had only Sergeant Elstob with me. I pushed on with him about 40 yards to my rear, and as we passed 4 Troop was able to give Mike a quick wave. All went well until I reached a stream, where I halted to wait for the rest of the squadron to come up who, apart from 4 Troop, were well behind. I glanced over my shoulder and was surprised to see two of Mike's tanks withdrawing, the crew of another bailing out and Mike's tank reversing back to the woods from where we had started. At that moment I saw a man from Mike's tank clamber out of the turret, jump off the tank, which was still reversing, and run like hell back towards the wood. Although I hadn't heard a thing I knew that something serious must have happened. I gave the order to reverse and at the same time I called Mike up on the air but failed to get an answer. We only just moved in time as an AP shot landed where we had been seconds before, showering us with earth. I got my 2-in mortar going,[9] putting down all the smoke I could, this was taken up by Sergeant Elstob and, under quite a heavy screen, we were able to turn and withdraw back to the rest of the squadron, who had taken up positions at the edge of the wood. The gun, or guns, that had fired at us and 4 Troop must have been positioned in the woods ahead; I considered I had a lucky escape as I was well forward at the time.
>
> When I arrived back at the squadron at approximately 1415 I found things somewhat disorganised. It was confirmed that one of Mike's tanks had been knocked out and the driver, Trooper Bligh, killed. The shot had entered low front and he would have died instantly. The crew of Mike's tank had brought his tank back and then gone back on foot down the centre line to the echelon. Nobody knew what had happened to Mike, but it was thought he must have been killed. Scottie (Captain Graham Scott, commanding A Squadron) asked me to go over to Mike's tank, which had been left by its crew close to the road in front of the wood about 100 yards from where we were, to confirm Mike's death. I walked to the tank, climbed up on the engine deck, looked into the turret and saw Mike's body lying across the breach of the gun. An AP shot had grazed the cupola and taken his head off. I went back to Scottie with this grim and sad news, which naturally depressed us all. Fortunately, we did not have a lot of time to dwell on it as the infantry were preparing a two company attack to clear both sides of the centre line as far as the wood where the trouble had been coming from. This attack was to be supported by us, A Squadron, going out on both flanks to shoot them in and then to follow up as they reached their objective. The attack was due to commence at 1550.

Trooper Bligh's Comet was hit at a range of 1,200 yards. The AP round penetrated the lower front glacis plate at its extreme right corner before passing through the driving compartment. Bligh was

---

8 Langdon, *The Sharp End*, p.152.
9 The Comet had a 2-in mortar fitted in the turret roof; an early version of smoke discharger.

The entry hole of the 88mm AP round that hit Trooper Bligh's Comet. (TNA)

hit by the shot and in the blunt words of the survey 'disintegrated'.[10] Mercifully he would have known nothing about it.

As mentioned by John Langdon, B and C Companies 4 KSLI were now brought forward to deal with the enemy infantry in the wood. With this additional strength the battalion was able to clear the area, capturing some 40 enemy and finding a similar number of dead. Of the Tiger there was, however, no sign. While the two companies were mopping up the infantry of Bataillon Lotze, A Squadron moved across the open ground to support them; it was not easy, as John Langdon describes:[11]

> Don went out on the right and I went to the left. I now had three tanks in my troop as Sergeant Killeen had joined me. I was delighted to have him as, apart from being an original member of the troop from Bridlington and Aldershot days, he had done very well as a tank commander in Normandy and during the breakout in the *bocage*. I quickly put him in the picture about the forthcoming attack. 1 Troop were again on the right of the road, which for the most part was raised, presumably because of the boggy nature of the ground, on an embankment high enough to prevent us from seeing what was happening on the other side. On my right was 3 Troop (Don Collie). Squadron HQ were on the left of the road and, with them, was 2 Troop (Dennis Sullivan). 4 Troop had temporarily ceased to exist.
>
> The attack started on time. We got to our positions without trouble and found reasonable cover among thick scrub from where we were able to subject the front edge of the wood to

---

10 TNA WO 205/1165, 3 RTR, Serial D. 21, Wright and Harkness, *A Survey of Casualties Amongst Armoured Units in North-West Europe*.
11 Langdon, *The Sharp End*, pp.153–154.

a heavy concentration of fire, both HE and MG, which we continued during the infantry's advance. When they were close to the wood, we received orders to advance and follow them up to it. In front of us was a small stream [the Bruchgraben], which I managed to cross but after a short distance I noticed that my other two tanks were not following. They had both bellied while crossing the stream. The only action I could take was to push on and attempt to reach the cover of the wood. There was one more stream, the Meiße, to cross. Just as we were approaching it I realised to my dismay that we were gradually slowing down due to the boggy nature of the ground.

About 10 yards from the bank of the stream we were unable to make further progress. There we were right out in the open, well forward of the tanks of 4 Troop that had been knocked out earlier, without any support whatsoever. The one good thing was that the infantry appeared to have reached their objective, the front edge of the wood, but did not as yet have any tanks with them. A quick look behind confirmed my fear that 3 Troop would be in a similar condition, this proved to be the case. I reported my situation over the air, and as we were so exposed, decided it was best for us to get out of the tank and into a ditch about 20 yards distant. This we did taking with us one Besa machine-gun.

We had not been in the ditch long before C Squadron came down the road, they were above us as the road was still on the embankment. They were obviously being passed through in order that the infantry should have tanks with them. The time was then 1640. Just as the leading tank passed us there was a hell of an explosion showering us with dirt. A HE shell had landed in the ditch only a few yards away; it was amazing that we were not killed and the only reason I could think of for this was that the shell had buried itself in the soft ground before exploding. We did however have one casualty, Trooper Charlton, who had suffered a cut across his forehead. I gave the order to withdraw along the ditch, Charlton soon fell and had to be aided.

We arrived back at the first stream [the Bruchgraben] we had crossed, which at this point ran through a culvert under the road. Peering through the tunnel I could see some of the squadron at the far side. I thought it best to wade through the water as the road above was being sprayed by *Spandau* fire, also C Squadron who had come under heavy fire were withdrawing back along it. I jumped into the stream, got into the culvert, took a step forward and went up to my neck in water! It was a horrible feeling as I struggled back to the bank and, although the situation was serious, we could not help laughing at my plight as I was covered in thick slime with filthy water dripping from my clothing. Another HE close by decided me to risk the *Spandaus* and make a dash across the road to the other side. Everyone made it. On the other side of the embankment, an amazing sight met our eyes of the remaining tanks of the squadron, HQ and 2 Troop, all bogged down. The remainder of the battalion were in the woods behind us with C Squadron withdrawing along the embankment to join them, while the infantry appeared firm in the woods to our front.

I reported to Scotty who told me to remain with the squadron until it was dark enough for me to return to my tank. At 1830 it was ordered to go firm where we were and that recovery would not take place until the morning. With my depleted crew I returned to my tank as darkness fell. Trooper Enever, my co-driver and front gunner replaced Charlton as driver. I was very sorry to lose Charlton, a most dependable driver, who had been with me, on and off, since the reorganisation after GOODWOOD.[12]

---

12 Operation GOODWOOD took place in Normandy between 18–20 July 1944 and involved three British armoured divisions. Heavy tank losses occurred and whether it was a success or failure remains controversial.

> Despite the order that recovery would not take place until the morning, soon after we had reached my tank an ARV turned up and with its help managed to get my tank out. We reversed back but trying to climb the embankment onto the road got stuck again. My fault, I'm afraid as I thought it would climb the bank easily and didn't do a very thorough recce. It was decided to wait until the morning before further recovery was attempted. We were however level with squadron HQ and 2 Troop, though still on the other side of the embankment.
>
> By now it was pitch dark and the infantry started to pull back from the wood through my position, leaving us unprotected to the front. One section of infantry did, however, remain with us, as my tank was the furthest forward and therefore closest to the enemy. We spent an anxious and uncomfortable night anticipating the arrival of first light. Would the enemy attack and catch the whole squadron bogged down or would he withdraw?
>
> During the night we heard the sound of guns firing from behind the enemy's position, then the whine of shells overhead, their destination being RHQ at the front edge of the wood behind us where, at approximately 0430, twenty HE shells fell on their positions. Throughout the night we had been longing for a smoke, but we were too close to the enemy to take the risk of lighting up.

It is likely that the HE and machine-gun fire that engaged John Langdon and his crew came from the Tiger still dominating the Ostenholz road. Despite having captured the wood, 4 KSLI pulled back to the forest, where it concentrated for the night. Friday 13 April had been a tough day for the battalion and during the fighting 10 soldiers were killed, among them the commander of C Company, Major the Honourable Clegg-Hill, and 40 others were wounded including Major Ellis, commander of B Company for only five days, and Lieutenant Smith. The coming of dark did not bring respite and the battalion was on the receiving end of the desultory shelling described by John Langdon, with a tragic consequence recounted by Corporal Fred Ralph, a D Company signaller:[13]

> I was talking to one of the signallers in battalion HQ the next morning and he told me that Lance Corporal Wheeldon (CO's driver/operator) had been out in the CO's scout car quite late and on his return had decided not to dig himself in but had wrapped himself in a blanket and had crawled under a vehicle for protection. During the night only one shell had landed in the area and a piece of shrapnel had gone straight through Wheeldon's heart.

15/19 Hussars Group advance on the Winsen road

While 29th Armoured Brigade was making slow progress on the Ostenholz road, on Friday 13 April 15/19 Hussars Group from 159th Infantry Brigade prepared to advance eastwards on Landesstrasse 180, which followed the Aller's right bank to Winsen, the next bridging point. Grosan had recognised the threat posed by a British crossing of the Aller at Essel and had already deployed forces to Landesstrasse 180. The first infantry the British would encounter on the road were the men of Landesschützen-Abteilung 'Wietzendorf' and Volkssturm-Bataillon 'Lüneburg', both very low-grade units and Grosan would have known that they would offer little resistance. He reserved his better troops – men and marines from Marine-Füsilier-Bataillon 2 that had fought in the Essel battles – and his anti-tank firepower to establish a series of blocking positions in the forest through which the road to Winsen ran.

---

13   Thornburn, 'After Antwerp – The Long Haul to Victory', p.113.

'ONE OF THE HARDEST DAYS' 319

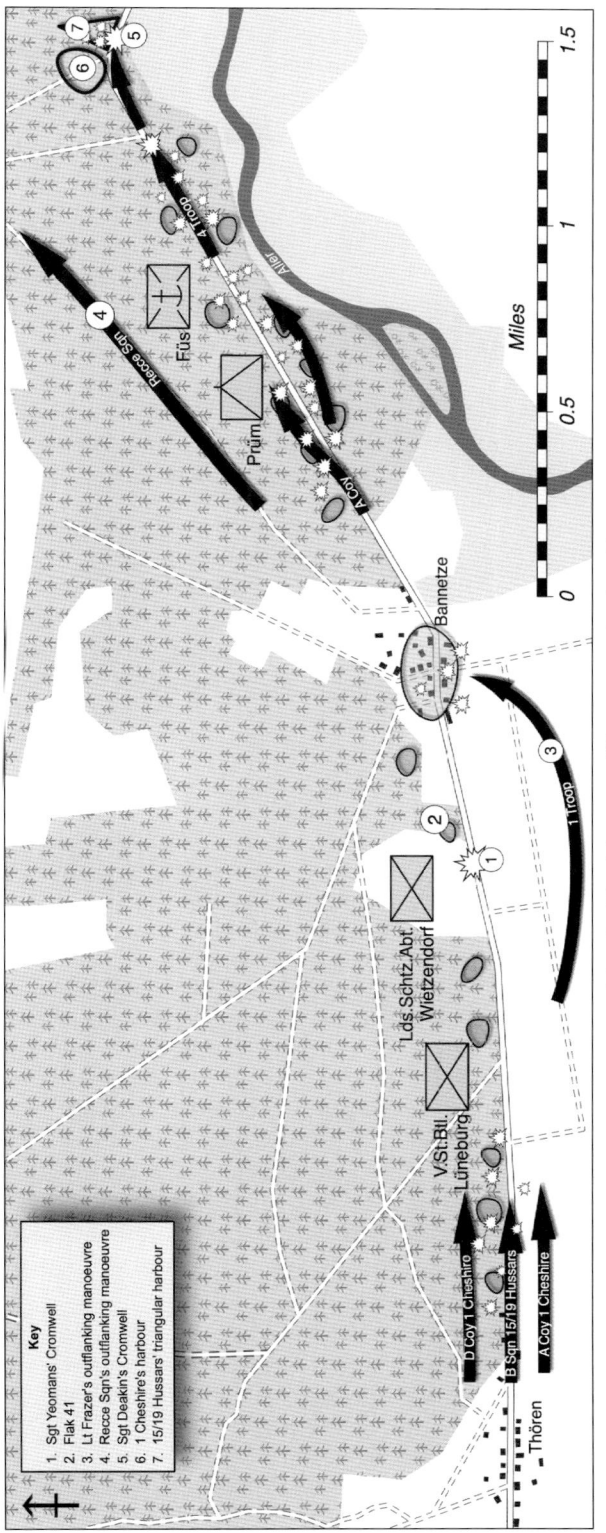

Map 49 The Advance to Winsen – 13 April 1945.

The road through the forest to Winsen. Photograph taken in 2015. (Author)

The blocking positions were based on the three 8.8cm Flak 41 manned by RAD gunners and the twelve 8cm Panzerwerferkanone (PWK) 8H63 crewed by anti-tank trainees from the Panzerjäger-Lehrgänge. The guns were sited to fire up the road or in partial defilade and each gun was protected by infantry equipped with *Panzerfaust* and automatic weapons. Also dispersed into the forest as ambush parties were Major Prüm's teams equipped with *Panzerfaust* and automatic weapons.

Beyond Gruppe Grosan was Kampfgruppe Totzeck, now responsible for defending Winsen from the Aller's right bank as the road bridge had been blown. Following their withdrawal to the right bank, he re-deployed his two infantry companies into the thick woods to the west of the town and his two batteries of 15cm Nebelwerfer 41 rocket projectors took up positions from which they could fire at targets to the west. Despite the poor quality of some of the German forces, their numerical strength, numerous anti-tank weapons and the thickness of the forest through which Landesstrasse 180 ran would soon make 15/19 Hussars Group's advance to Winsen no easy matter. Although the online video at Appendix A, Serial 13 is of fighting two days hence, it gives a flavour of the countryside in this area of Germany and of the fighting in its forests and villages.

The operation started with 1 Cheshire's vehicles and heavy equipment crossing the Essel Bailey bridge at 0930 hours, followed half an hour later by the tanks of 15/19 Hussars. The battalion and regiment then married up in Engehausen before starting the advance to Winsen, some six miles to the east. The first village, Thören, was captured with little difficulty and advancing either side of the road, A and D Companies, supported by the Cromwells of B Squadron, led the next phase, the advance to Bannetze. Although this initially proceeded steadily, opposition began to be encountered in the wood to the north of the road with the Germans, in well-concealed positions, holding their fire until the last moment. These positions were cleared by the Cheshire companies and the group gradually closed on Bannetze. However, when 500 yards from the village, the leading Cromwell, commanded by Sergeant Yeomans, was hit at a range of 100 yards by an 8.8cm round;

the round fortunately struck the outside of the hull-gunner's door causing little damage and no casualties. With the main road covered by an anti-tank gun, 1 Troop B Squadron, commanded by Lieutenant Frazer, was sent to the south of the village and here the better fields of fire allowed it to destroy a truck, a half-track and a Flak 41, the source of the 8.8cm round that struck Sergeant Yeomans' Cromwell. By 1530 hours the Cheshire companies had captured Bannetze, taken 90 prisoners, mainly *Volkssturm*, and either captured or found knocked-out an array of artillery ranging from 8.8cm to 2cm. While Bannetze was taken with relative ease, for the remainder of the advance 15/19 Hussars Group would encounter increasing opposition.

In the mid-afternoon the advance began again, with A Company and 4 Troop, commanded by Lieutenant The Earl of Harrington, setting off for the next objective, a pronounced bend in the road about a mile and a half further on. As soon as the lead Cromwell, commanded by Sergeant Deakin, rounded this bend it was hit by an 8.8cm round, wounding two of the crew. At the same time Corporal Sarginson saw a German armed with a *Panzerfaust* aiming at the tank in front of him. Although he traversed the turret onto the target, at the critical moment the Besa misfired. Quickly leaning down into the turret he fired the 75mm main armament, blowing the German to pieces. While the forces on the road slowly battled their way forward, Recce Squadron, supported by Comets of C Squadron, tried to outflank the opposition by moving through the forest to the north of the road, but the manoeuvre came to an end when a small bridge collapsed under the weight of a scout car. By now the thick woods and fading light made it difficult to locate the anti-tank gun that had hit Sergeant Deakin's tank so it was decided not to advance further and the regiment was ordered to harbour in a small triangular clearing north of the road. While the squadrons were moving into the clearing a salvo of *Nebelwerfer* rounds landed among them, wounding two troop leaders and four other men; the clearing was an obvious target for predicted fire and Totzeck's *Nebelwefer* batteries had evidently been alerted by the noise of the manoeuvring tanks. Fortunately, for the remainder of the night there was no further engagement of the harbour area. Lieutenant Colonel Kreyer, commanding 1 Cheshire, similarly decided that there was nothing to be gained from his companies trying to advance by night against determined opposition and he ordered the battalion to harbour close to the armoured regiment's location. By nightfall the 15/19 Hussars Group had managed to reach only a mile or so beyond Bannetze.

Saturday 14 April

Back on the Ostenholz road, the night 13/14 April was undisturbed for 4 KSLI and A Squadron, in marked contrast to a dramatic German account describing how Lotze's battalion pushed the British all the way back to the Drebber stream, where apparently only artillery fire stopped Lotze from continuing to the Bailey bridge over the Aller.[14] Lotze's supposed gallant attack reached the ears of Blumentritt, who recommended him for the Knight's Cross for his part in relieving the 'crisis on the Aller'; the war ended, however, before he could receive the award. Lotze's attack seems to have been an illusion as neither 3 RTR's nor 4 KSLI's war diaries make any mention of German attacks, far less being forced back into the forest through which they had recently fought. 8 Corps' INTSUM for 14 April records Bataillon Lotze as being badly trained and that its fighting value was much inferior to the Hitler Youth companies, making the attack even less likely. Despite the peace of the night, for John Langdon, isolated in the open ground on the Ostenholz road, 14 April dawned with considerable tension:[15]

---

14   Saft, *Krieg in der Heimat*, p.167.
15   Langdon, *The Sharp End*, pp.154–155.

Although still dark the battalion stood to at 0530; as dawn approached everyone was on edge. Suddenly, through the stillness, the sound we had been dreading, the high-pitched whirring of a Tiger's engine starting up. It roared into life somewhere in the wood to our front. Would it emerge from the wood and slowly trundle towards us? We waited, heard its gears and the movement of its tracks. Although immobile we were all in the tank, our gun covering the wood but against frontal assault it would have had very little effect. Was the Tiger coming towards us or moving away? After a few minutes the engine noise decreased, becoming fainter and fainter. We listened until we could hear it no more; the enemy had withdrawn.

Our relief at the enemy's withdrawal was profound. At 0600 the CO ordered C Squadron to send out two troops to cover the battalion's front and centre line while recovery of the bogged tanks took place. Throughout the morning all the battalion's ARVs under the control of Captain Adkins, commanding the regimental LAD, set about recovering the squadron's tanks, which were dragged out one at a time onto firm ground. By 1230 mine was the only one left but by 1300 hours I was on the road and on the way back to rejoin the rest of the battalion, who were still concentrated in the wood behind us. The recovery teams were fortunate to be unmolested by the enemy and must be congratulated for the manner they set about and achieved their task.

Naturally I was delighted to be back with the squadron, no move was expected for an hour or so, everyone was in good form as was always the case when one had come out of a sticky do, and this had certainly been one. I filled my canvas bucket with water, splashed it over my face, then the hard job of getting off three days' growth of beard. Finally, the best thing of all for morale: a hot meal and a brew provided by the crew.

...At 1630, the battalion moved out of the bridgehead to the area of Engehausen, a hamlet two miles along the road towards Winsen, a small town nine miles due east. Here we rejoined the rest of 29th Armoured Brigade who were already in the vicinity. We soon got ourselves comfortably settled in with our bivvies up. Some bottles of wine and a very welcome double rum ration were produced by Paddy Hehir [QM], which certainly went down well. At 2100, we were informed that no move was likely before 0900 in the morning.

The crews of A Squadron were fortunate that the commander of the Tiger had not attacked while their tanks were bogged down. Possibly he had exhausted his ammunition or, perhaps, he had had enough of the war and decided discretion was the better part of valour. During the day the *Luftwaffe* appeared over the Essel area and 172 Battery 58th LAA Regt reported a variety of enemy aircraft including a Fw 190, a Bf 109, an Ar 234 and two Me 262. Final, lone appearances were made at various times the next day by a Bf 109, a Fw 190 and a Ju 87.

Although by 14 April the Essel bridgehead was secure, it was far from evident to the British that the German effort to prevent their advance on the Ostenholz axis was spent and so the decision was taken to cease operations towards Ostenholz and concentrate instead on 159th Infantry Brigade's advance to Winsen, after which 29th Armoured Brigade would take the lead and swing north to Bergen-Belsen. The 15/19 Hussars Group had experienced a reasonably easy day's advance on 13 April and there was nothing to suggest that this would change. However, the second day's advance would involve 15/19 Hussars Group in intense fighting against the remaining forces of Gruppe Grosan and Kampfgruppe Totzeck and would prove the equal of anything its soldiers had experienced in the campaign to date.

Operations on the road to Winsen recommenced at 0200 hours with a patrol from C Company 1 Cheshire despatched to see if it could enter Winsen and discover the enemy's strength and locations. The patrol made little progress as it soon encountered a succession of enemy posts in the forest and attracted heavy fire from *Panzerfaust* and small-arms; the approach to Winsen was clearly strongly held.

'ONE OF THE HARDEST DAYS' 323

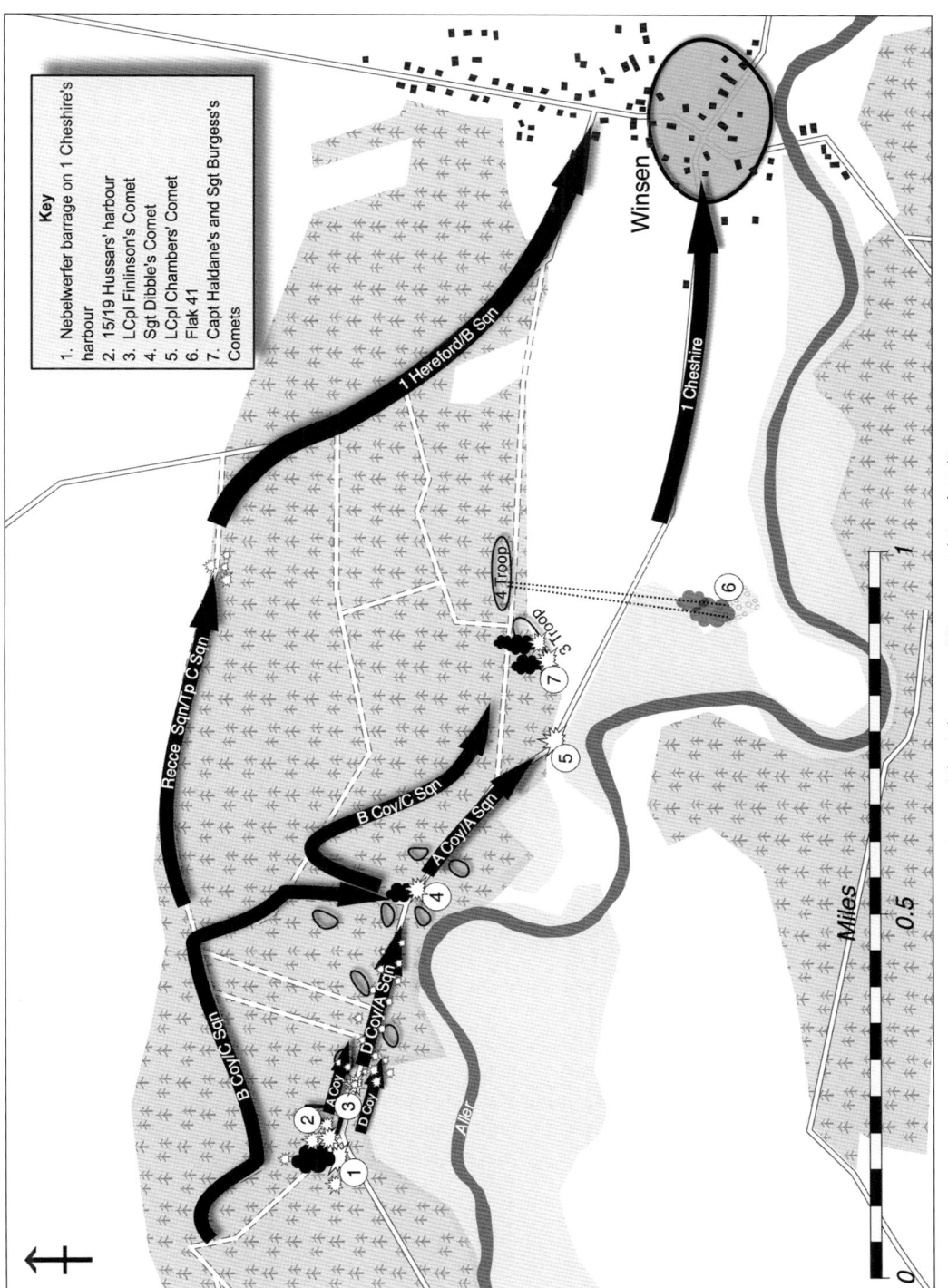

Map 50 The Advance to Winsen – 14 April 1945.

Before dawn, Lieutenant Colonel Kreyer ordered A Company to advance on the left of the road and D Company on the right. But at 0530 hours, shortly before H-hour, the Germans struck first and the area of battalion headquarters came under heavy fire from *Nebelwerfer*. A truck containing petrol and ammunition was hit and many casualties sustained, including Major Jack Cooke-Hurle, the battalion second-in-command, and Captain Hurley, the adjutant, who were both wounded. Despite the mayhem at the headquarters, the two companies set off and for a short distance all went well. But while moving through the forest some 350 yards beyond their start line the infantrymen came under a storm of fire from small-arms and *Panzerfaust* and the advance ground to a halt. Tank support was called for and 2 Troop A Squadron, commanded by Sergeant Burton, was ordered to move down the road to help D Company. Shortly after leaving the harbour area, the troop's leading Comet was hit several times by rounds from a PWK 8H63 firing straight down the road, and caught fire.[16] Despite the danger from exploding ammunition and enemy fire Lance-Corporal Finlinson, the commander of the burning Comet, and Trooper Tighe fought the fire and succeeded in extinguishing it. The tanks and infantry were now in close combat with the enemy in the forest and fierce and bitter fighting slowed the advance to a snail's pace. While Finlinson was fighting to save his tank, Sergeant Burton set off on foot to the south of the road in an attempt to find a route to bypass the enemy. Lance-Corporal Finlinson, with his tank saved, also set off on foot and reported that the PWK 8H63 had been abandoned as a result of fire brought down by the rest of 2 Troop and the road was clear. 2 Troop started to advance once more.

It was not long before the leading Comet was engaged by yet another anti-tank gun and there was renewed, heavy small-arms' fire which killed Corporal Stone, the tank's commander, and wounded Sergeant Burton in the head. Lance Corporal Finlinson gave first aid to the wounded and helped Burton to withdraw the troop to a position from which it could reorganise.[17] 3 Troop now took over the lead and for the rest of the day A Squadron slowly advanced with the Cheshires. In the forest the threat from anti-tank guns and *Panzerfaust*, coupled with the difficulty of knowing the location of friendly infantry, resulted in advances only being made after thorough reconnaissance on foot and close liaison between the commanders on the ground. The advance down the road therefore became extremely slow and deliberate.

While D Company supported by A Squadron battled their way on the road, C Squadron with C Company and the four Stuarts of Recce Troop were ordered to bypass the main road by using tracks to its north and work their way through the forest to take up a defilade position along its edge, from where they could bring fire to bear on the open country to the south. However, they found great difficulty in finding their way through the thick forest and turned south too soon, taking a track running southwards back to the road. This, as it turned out, worked in A Squadron and D Company's favour as the sudden appearance of tanks and infantry from an unexpected direction surprised the Germans and helped to ease the situation, enabling A Squadron and D Company to get forward at last and clear the road as far as C Squadron Group's new position. On 14 April the Cheshires lost 11 soldiers killed, with D Company suffering particularly badly losing its company commander, Captain Francis, two platoon commanders mortally wounded, and many others wounded; the CSM was now commanding what was left of the company. As a consequence, A Company was passed through the depleted D Company to take up the advance.

Meanwhile, Recce Squadron supported by the Comets of 4 Troop C Squadron went further to the north in order to investigate a track which ran along the forest's edge until it joined the

---

16   TNA WO 205/1165, 15/19 Hussars, Serial D.3, Wright and Harkness, *A Survey of Casualties Amongst Armoured Units in North-West Europe*.
17   For their parts in this action, Sergeant Burton was awarded the Distinguished Conduct Medal (the only one received by 15/19 Hussars during the campaign), Lance Corporal Finlinson the Military Medal and Trooper Tighe was Mentioned in Dispatches.

Winsen to Bergen road. Most of their move was uneventful until they met some opposition about 800 yards west of the road, which they shot up. While this was taking place, back on the main road A Squadron was advancing very slowly against continuing strong opposition and shortly after passing a bend the leading Comet of 3 Troop was hit twice by *Panzerfaust* rounds. One round produced a scoop on the gun mantlet while the second penetrated the turret near its roof, killing Trooper Hide the operator. Sergeant Dibble and Troopers Martin and Hayhoe bailed out unscathed but were all immediately killed by small-arms' fire; only the co-driver escaped death, although he too was wounded by small-arms' fire when outside the tank.[18] In spite of this, the squadron and A Company worked their way down the road until the group reached the edge of the forest. C Squadron and C Company had meanwhile moved from their position on the road and infiltrated down two tracks, which ran in a south-easterly direction, to reach the edge of the forest. Here most of the company, supported by 2 Troop, took up a position while Squadron HQ with 1 and 3 Troops and 1 Platoon C Company moved further to the east to try to find a defilade position covering Landesstrasse 180. However, the edge of the forest was not a healthy place to be as the trees extended further than shown on the map and to dominate the road and beyond the tanks were forced to move onto a forward slope.

While C Squadron was moving to find a defilade position, A Squadron and A Company continued to advance slowly down the road, with the tank crews dismounting to recce around the bends to try to identify enemy positions. The Germans' concealment was however excellent and when the leading tank turned the next bend in the road it was engaged by a well-camouflaged Flak 41, dug-in in low ground across the meadows to the south-east and close to a small wood near the Aller, with the first round hitting the top right-hand side of the driver's compartment. The tank commander, Lance-Corporal Chambers, managed to get his Comet off the road but when manoeuvering in the trees the tank was hit a further four times: on the left front bogie, on the right front mudguard and the top of the track, on the left track and through the exhaust cowls.[19] Very fortunately for Lance-Corporal Chambers and his crew, the tank was not knocked-out and, despite the risk, Chambers stayed with the tank and was able to report the location of the Flak 41; for his courage he would later be awarded the Military Medal.

Shortly afterwards, with C Squadron visible on the forward slope at the edge of the forest, the Flak 41 engaged a 3 Troop Comet commanded by Sergeant Burgess and the Comet of Captain Haldane, a FOO from 151st Field Regiment supporting 1 Cheshire, while they were static on the forest's southern edge. Three rounds hit Sgt Burgess's tank: the first penetrated through the visor plate into the driver's compartment, while the second and third rounds produced scoops on the turret, wounding the operator.[20] Captain Haldane's tank was then hit and quickly burst into flame. The crews of both Comets were lucky as only two men were wounded. Although getting another tank into a position to engage the Flak 41 without itself being engaged was impossible, with the gun sited in an area of dead undergrowth Lieutenant Egerton of 3 Troop recognised that the best way to eliminate it would be to burn or smoke-out the crew. From its position looking south across the Aller, 4 Troop was best-sited to engage and began to fire large quantities of Besa and Bren tracer into the area of the gun. Soon smoke was seen rising and shortly after the area was ablaze, resulting in the gun crew running for their lives as their stockpile of ammunition began to ignite.

---

18   TNA WO 205/1165, 15/19 Hussars, Serial D.9, Wright and Harkness, *A Survey of Casualties Amongst Armoured Units in North-West Europe*.
19   TNA WO 205/1165, 15/19 Hussars, Serial D.1, Wright and Harkness, *A Survey of Casualties Amongst Armoured Units in North-West Europe*.
20   TNA WO 205/1165, 15/19 Hussars, Serial D.4, Wright and Harkness, *A Survey of Casualties Amongst Armoured Units in North-West Europe*.

The Flak 41 crew's view to Lance Corporal Chambers' Comet as it emerged from the forest. Photograph taken in 2015. (Author)

It was now getting late in the afternoon and the brigade commander, recognising the toughness of the battle fought by the 15/19 Hussars Group, ordered the group to hold its positions so that an outflanking manoeuvre could be carried out by 1 Hereford. The plan involved 1 Hereford moving to the area on the Winsen to Bergen road held by the recce troop and 4 Troop C Squadron and then advancing down this road to attack Winsen from the rear. B Squadron was ordered to support the Herefords. After a long approach march through the forest, 1 Hereford subsequently advanced southwards astride the road to Winsen. Meeting little opposition, the village was captured and occupied by the Herefords and B Squadron before last light. Shortly after dark the Cheshires advanced into Winsen from the west, also nearly unopposed. Twenty-five prisoners from Kampfgruppe Totzeck were taken in Winsen but the bridge over the Aller was found demolished, blown on 13 April following the rejection of the Germans' proposals for Belsen. Totzeck, who wished to die a soldier's death, did so the next day when he was killed by artillery fire. B Squadron remained in Winsen for the night with the Herefords while the remainder of 15/19 Hussars withdrew to harbour in the area of Bannetze.

The battle through the forests to Winsen was very demanding, as summarised in the 15/19 Hussars' log entry for 14 April:[21]

> One of the hardest and most bitter day's fighting that the regiment had had during the whole campaign. The country was most unsuitable as movement down the centre line [axis] was almost entirely restricted to the roads, the woods on either side being extremely thick and the

---

21 TNA WO 171/4692, 15/19 Hussars war diary.

ground boggy in places. The enemy were most determined and had a number of 8.8cm Flak, which they were using in an anti-tank role, as well as other types of anti-tank guns in addition to their normal *Panzerfaust* and small-arms. They undoubtedly fought extremely well and with great determination in country well-suited for defence.

With the capture of Winsen, the Germans' defence of the Aller in VIII Corps' sector was over. Armeegruppe Blumentritt's left flank was turned and the way was clear for 11th Armoured to advance to Bergen-Belsen and beyond. A link to an online video of 23 Hussars and 8 RB in action in the forests north of Winsen, then moving rapidly past a German delegation at the entrance to Belsen concentration camp is at Appendix A, Serial 12.

Although the intended axis via Ostenholz was now abandoned, the Essel battle was not wasted effort as it had allowed 11th Armoured to roll up the remainder of the Aller Line from a flank and avoid what could have been a costly, opposed river-crossing mounted frontally against Gruppe Grosan and Kampfgruppe Totzeck. While the remainder of VIII Corps moved on toward the Elbe, 1st Commando Brigade stayed in the bridgehead to cover the dismantling of the Bailey bridge and, as as it had been in near-constant action since reaching the Weser on 6 April, the brigade was able to get some respite, relaxing and enjoying bonfires. On 16 April the dismantled Essel Bailey bridge departed on trucks for re-building at Winsen and the commandos moved off to the Elbe. Peace returned to the forest.

The battle on the right bank of the Aller had been tough for all participants. The Germans, heavily outnumbered, acquitted themselves well and deservedly earned the respect of the British. Although they delayed 11th Armoured Division for some five days, their resistance was of course futile and only resulted in pointless death and injury. Their gallantry can, nonetheless, be recognised. British accounts suggest 300 Germans died in the bridgehead but only a total of 160 lie buried in the Essel and Eickeloh cemeteries. Perhaps others still lie in graves now lost in the forest. A further 43 are buried in Winsen cemetery and 19 at Lohheide. The number of German wounded is unknown. 1st Commando Brigade and 15/19 Hussars both recorded that the fighting in the Essel forest was the most severe they had faced since the early days in Normandy. 1st Commando Brigade lost 20 dead and sixty-four wounded, while 29th Armoured lost some 39 dead and 91 wounded with 3 RTR losing six dead, five wounded and two Comets, 15/19 Hussars six dead, seven wounded and six Comets , 4 KSLI 13 dead and 50 wounded, and 1 Cheshire 14 dead and 31 wounded. It had been no easy victory and these casualties within three weeks of the war's end particularly tragic.

With VIII Corps now advancing beyond the Aller, we will go back three days to 11 April and return to XII Corps and 53rd Welsh Division in the Rethem area.

9

A Most Decisive Victory?: The Battle for Rethem 11–12 April 1945

1/5 Welch attacks on Rethem – Wednesday 11 April

Having failed to crack Rethem's defences in daylight, Brigadier Wilsey decided that 1/5 Welch should attack during the night 10/11 April. At 2300 hours he called the recently-promoted Lieutenant Colonel Bowker to brigade headquarters and ordered the battalion to attack before dawn on Wednesday 11 April. The attack would be supported by divisional artillery reinforced with two platoons of 4.2-in mortars from D Company 1 Manchester. The plan, if successful, would then involve 7 RWF and 1 E Lancs conducting an assault crossing of the Aller and securing a bridgehead for the division opposite Rethem.

In the early hours of Wednesday morning, Lieutenant Colonel Bowker gave his orders for a two-phase night attack with the first phase silent, meaning that the fire support would not automatically be used but, in order to achieve some surprise, left 'on call' until the enemy became aware of the attack. Lieutenant Colonel Bowker's plan was based on A and C Company attacking the town from the west. The companies would break-in and overcome the perimeter defence, allowing D Company to pass through to mop-up the opposition in the remainder of the town. Although it was essentially an identical plan to the one that had so signally failed the previous afternoon, it was assumed that the cover of darkness would give the attacking companies the advantage. But by now the men of 1/5 Welch were acutely feeling the strain of battle and over the last 48 hours had had very little sleep. Furthermore, casualties and lack of success had done little to bolster their resolve.

At 0345 hours the companies moved to their forming-up point for the attack, the area of the former '*Schweinebarth*' strongpoint, then infiltrated forward under cover of darkness to the Wölpe, the stream on the western edge of the town. Initially all went well; the stream was crossed on H-hour at 0445 hours and the attack achieved surprise with both companies reaching the town's perimeter. Their success was however short-lived and before they could break-in the marines became aware of the enemy and opened up with every weapon that could be brought to bear. In addition to fire from dug-in positions on the town's fringe, withering cross-fire was poured on the Welsh by the marines in '*Elfriede*' and the von der Kammer farm, with the two strongpoints becoming rocks around which the battle ebbed and flowed, with both sides well aware that these buildings were key to the defence. While the marines fought above ground, civilians were sheltering in the cellar of the von der Kammer farm; one of the civilians later described the frightening ordeal they experienced:[1]

---

1 Hans-Heinz Schulze, *Halb Rethem lag in Schutt und Asche*, (Walsroder Zeitung, 16 March 1985).

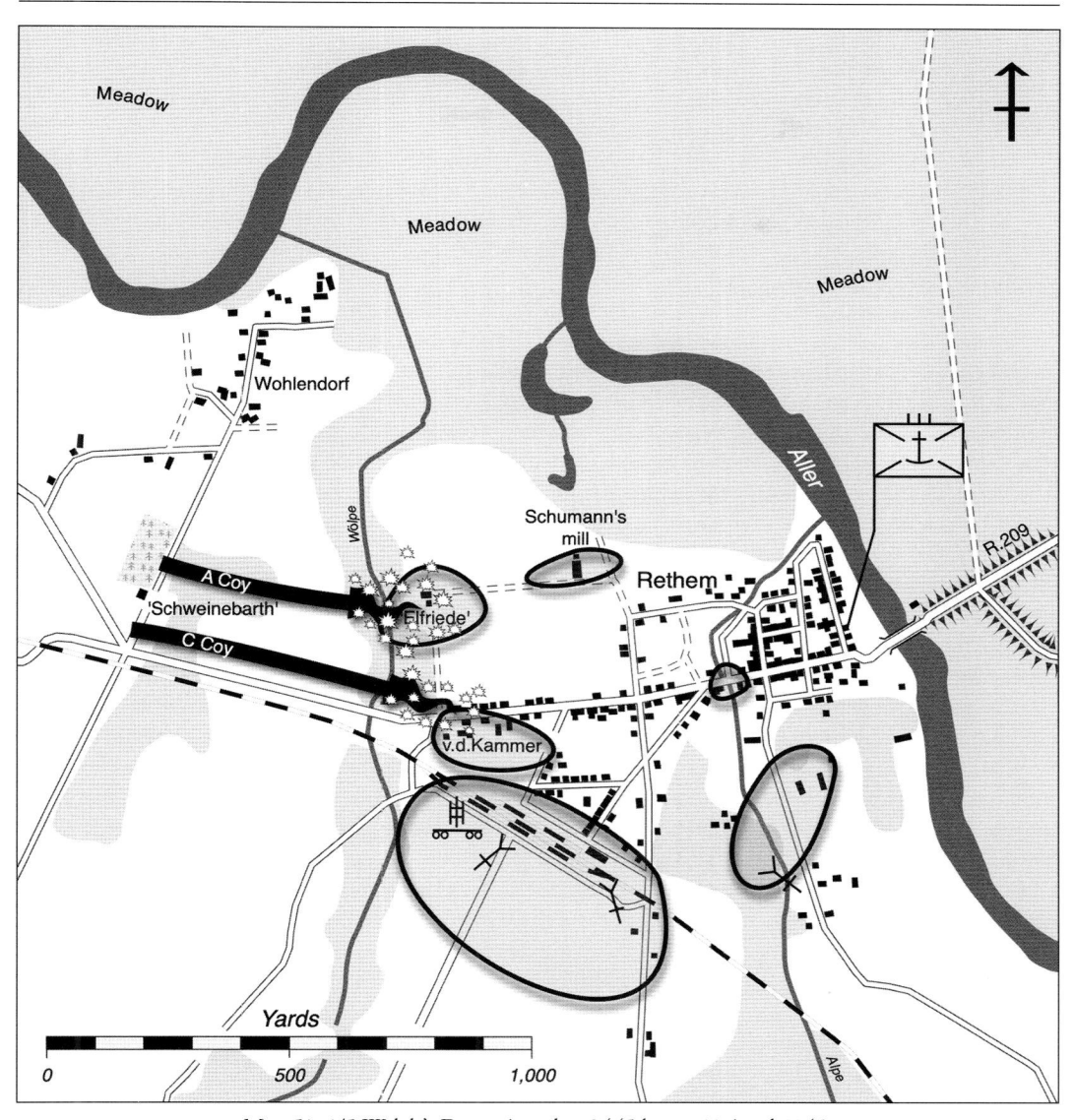

Map 51 1/5 Welch's Dawn Attack – 0445 hours 11 April 1945.

Over twenty civilians were huddled together in the cellar, which was only 3 metres by 3 metres. Our labourer – a French PoW – and a comrade from another farm arrived in the cellar and said, 'We have come to stay with you – we'll help when the tommies come'. This they later did. On Wednesday 11 April firing commenced onto our property and at 0500 hours the English [*sic*] attacked again. It came to hand-to-hand fighting, we could tell by the noise. Ownership of the house changed on several occasions. The house had been hit many times. Dust and dirt had made us unrecognisable and we could hardly identify each other. During a lull I crawled out and saw a mountain of bodies. The pig sty was being held by about 15 Englishmen and near the barn were several German soldiers. I heard the German sergeant say, 'Get the *Panzerfaust* here.' The English must have understood since they found a white flag and surrendered. We were subjected to German and English artillery fire. Only by some miracle was it that only the property was damaged. Later, when a cellar window barricaded with sandbags was ripped open by a shell burst we could see that the house was burning...we wanted to leave for Stöcken to my brother-in-law so the English, who had re-taken the ground floor let us go. At the next strongpoint the German soldiers prevented us going any further and told us we had to turn back as they were concerned we would betray their position. We had to return and hid under a dung-heap near the house. Here we were subjected to heavy small-arms' fire from Germans in Schumann Mill even though our house had been retaken by other German soldiers. One of our Frenchmen had been wounded in the meantime as he brought back some wounded.

Heavy fire forced us to leave our hide in the dung-heap and we crawled through the plough furrows to the Wölpe. The children gave us the most trouble. Even though we must have been recognised as civilians we were fired on by German soldiers. One of the women had a pram with her which was pierced by a bullet but luckily the baby was not hit. I dragged a child on top of a pillow behind me. At the Wölpe the women were so terrified that they stood in the cold water as they believed that they were safer there.

On the Friday we were able to move back to our house, bury the animals and tidy up. A little bit of joy was however left – a pig had given birth to 15 piglets.

Around the von der Kammer farm where these civilians were sheltering, bitter hand-to-hand fighting left seven members of C Company dead and many more wounded and captured. During a pause in the fighting the marines moved the enemy wounded to a neighbouring house for their protection and it was here that one of the soldiers who died was found to have on him 400,000 Reichsmarks from the Bocholt Sparkasse. The fortunate German finder soon ran out of luck as the cupboard where he hid the money went up in flames when the house later burnt to the ground.

While C Company was fighting to capture the von der Kammer farm, the men of A Company managed to get a foothold in the area of '*Elfriede*'. Their success did not last long as they were unable to eject the marines, fighting tooth and nail for this key point on Rethem's perimeter, and the strongpoint remained in German hands.

As the two companies had failed to break the town's outer defences and with the first glimmers of daylight evident, Lieutenant Colonel Bowker ordered the reserve company, D Company, to reinforce the attack in the hope that this would push the scales in the battalion's favour. The addition of D Company had, however, no effect and so he ordered all companies to pull back. The onset of daylight made their withdrawal far from easy and the men had a difficult time crossing back over the Wölpe while under small-arms' fire, and at 0630 hours smoke and HE barrages had to be fired by 83rd Field Regiment to try to assist the forward elements to break clean.[2] By 0740 hours the companies had eventually managed to escape the German fire and concentrate back in the area of '*Schweinebarth*', where the battalion took up defensive positions. The rifle companies were now so depleted that the decision was taken to reorganise, with the survivors of A Company distributed among the other three rifle companies.

The soldiers of 1/5 Welch were totally surprised by the strength of the resistance. Leslie George, who was a corporal in the anti-tank platoon, recalls his soldiers' reaction to combat and his part in steadying them:[3]

> I remember it was a total shock, especially for the younger intake, who had not until then encountered heavy action. As can no doubt be appreciated, some of the lads were used to

---

2   TNA WO 171/4827, 83rd Field Regiment RA war diary.
3   Letter to the author.

The Eystrup road after the battle, with the von der Kammer strongpoint among the buildings on the right of the photograph.

The burnt-out shell of '*Elfriede*' in a photograph taken after the capture of Rethem. The soldier is peering into a German trench, where at least four helmets and a stick grenade can be seen.

bloodshed and various setbacks and took things as they came. I myself was known as a 'bad bastard' as I was the first man in the battalion to gain an award (Distinguished Conduct Medal in Normandy). I was looked upon as mad and, thinking back, I did do some bloody stupid things but they had the desired effect of keeping the lads from panicking at times.

The casualties reported from the two companies were 20 wounded and 60 missing believed dead. The fate of 15 of the missing became the subject of a most unfortunate affair as a result of a statement made by Private Parry, the only soldier to return from the fight to capture *'Elfriede'*. Parry alleged a massacre had taken place at the hands of the *Waffen-SS*, and *The Times* newspaper reported the incident in its issue of 17 April:

BRITISH PRISONERS SHOT BY GERMANS

EYE-WITNESS ACCOUNT
From our Special Correspondent

OUTSIDE RETHEM, APRIL 11

The shooting of a number of British prisoners of war, probably about 15, after they had surrendered outside a house on the edge of this town this morning, was described to-day in a sworn statement by an eye-witness, Private Ivor Parry.

Private Parry has made and signed the following statement: 'On the morning of April 11 we were attacking the village called Rethem, we being members of a company of the…Regiment. We were slowly pushing our way into the village against heavy concentrations of shell-fire. The major who was leading the party made for a big house. When the party had occupied the house, the Germans opened up with a 20 mm gun, which is commonly used against aircraft, setting it on fire. Then they closed in on the house and entered it. They dragged our troops outside and set them up against the slowly burning wall and shot them with one of our Bren guns. I myself was 25 yards away and heard the screams of our men. Seeing what happened I shammed dead and when our 25-pounders laid a smoke-screen I took the opportunity of getting back to our own lines'.

Talking to correspondents afterwards, Private Parry said that the shooting took place between 5 and 6 o'clock this morning. In the half-light he was not able to distinguish how many of our men were brought out of the house, but he thought there were 15. One German held the gun and swept up and down the line, firing until they were dead. Parry managed not to betray any sign of life. It is not clear what German unit was responsible. The bulk of the resistance in this sector has come from a naval division, but there have also been reports of SS troops in the town.

Using the sworn testimony, the war artist Captain Bryan de Grineau subsequently drew a disturbing picture of the 'massacre', which was published in the *Illustrated London News* edition of 21 April 1945. News of the atrocity spread rapidly throughout 21st Army Group, generating widespread bitterness.

The 7th Armoured Division INTSUM for 13 April provided the following additional information:[4]

---

4   TNA WO 171/4171, G Branch 7th Armoured Division war diary.

Bryan de Grineau's drawing of the alleged massacre. (© Mary Evans Picture Library)

Nice Fellows When You Get To Know Them
Interrogation has revealed that the responsibility for the murder on 11 April of 15 PW from 53rd Welsh Division rests with 4 Company 12 SS Training Battalion.

TAILPIECE
Matrose BRAUNART, 8 Coy. 5 Marine Grenadier Regt
PW a smart and well-disciplined youth knew nothing about the murder of British PWs. It was impossible, he said, that such a thing could occur as no German was capable of such an unchivalrous act. Asked about the SS, he replied that they were normal German boys just like the Navy.

After the fall of Rethem an investigation into the massacre was immediately mounted and the civilian occupant of '*Elfriede*' describes his experience of the British investigation:[5]

> We were burying animals when a group of English officers came towards us. They searched the house and property. Suddenly one of them picked up a round, pointed to it and said in broken German, 'You comrade killed. Go away.' I had to submit to the anger of these men. The next day saw more high-ranking officers arrive and they too conducted a search. One of the officers who spoke perfect German accused me of shooting 15 English soldiers. I naturally denied this. Interrogations and interviews commenced but fortunately our Frenchman came forward and proved my innocence.

---

5   Hans-Heinz Schulze, *Halb Rethem lag in Schutt und Asche*.

The rumours of a massacre of prisoners not only further dented the Welsh's flagging morale but also led to some ugly scenes after Rethem fell, as Leslie George witnessed:[6]

> I came across a group of about three dozen German PoWs who were being searched by a warrant officer of the field security police. He was a cocky little so-and-so who had his lance corporals scattered around the immediate area. The PoWs had been some of the defenders of Rethem and quite a few had English cigarettes in their possession. The warrant officer had got to one of the PoWs who was about 40 years old and a bit portly. On finding a packet of 'Players' in his pocket, he threw them on the ground then told the German, using sign language, to pick them up. As he bent to pick them up he kicked him in the backside; as he straightened up he gave him a rabbit punch to make him bend down again. This treatment went on four or five times.
>
> By now, apart from his NCOs, my gun crew and myself, several other soldiers had gathered to the scene and I was becoming angry. I placed a magazine on my Sten gun, cocked it, pointed it at the warrant officer and said, 'If you touch that man once more, I will pull this trigger.' He ordered his NCOs to arrest me. My gun crew looked into my eyes, saw a sign that they now knew and told the NCOs not to go near me or the warrant officer would be a dead man. The warrant officer was by now screaming at his men, but when he looked into my eyes, as I told him to, he realised how close he was to death. I said quite quietly to him, 'I have been fighting bastards like you (meaning *SS* and *Nazis*) and unless you do your job properly, I shall treat you the same way as I would treat them, and if you take it out on the prisoners because of what I have just done to you, I shall find out and will trace you all over Europe and kill you. I have at least three dozen witnesses to what you were doing to that PoW.'
>
> My gun crew assured his NCOs that I meant every word I had said and that the best thing they could do was to treat the PoWs in accordance with the Geneva Conventions and to convince their warrant officer to do the same. Although I doubt if the Germans could speak English, they realised what I had done and I shall never forget the look in their eyes as they were loaded into the trucks, particularly 'fatso' who had been on the receiving end.

The massacre reported by Parry never took place and it was subsequently shown that the Germans had treated the wounded, evacuated them to the military hospital in Walsrode and had fully observed the Geneva Convention. A subsequent 7th Armoured Division INTSUM, dated 17 April, provided the truth behind the story:

TAILPIECE
Not So Atrocious After All

The tale of 15 PW alleged to have been murdered has now been discounted by the recapture of an officer from the party. The enemy formation involved was 2 MID and NOT 12 SS. They took our men prisoner and marched them away and apparently treated them quite correctly.

Several buildings in the neighbourhood were brewing, and some of these contained pigs and cows which were shot by the Germans with a Bren gun to put them out of their pain. The squeal of the animals no doubt accounted for the gruesome stories put forth. In actual fact therefore, the enemy seem not only to have behaved correctly but also to have trespassed on the prerogative of the Island Race – kindness to animals!

---

6   Letter to author.

Why Parry made the statement is not known. The most charitable reason would be that the poor light and his battle fatigue allowed his imagination to get the better of him; the least charitable is that he invented the story to distract attention from his less than gallant part in the fighting. Although the truth of the 'executions' was fairly quickly established, the true version of events would not spread at a similar speed to the false with the result that attitudes to prisoners hardened and it is likely that more prisoners than the ones evidenced by Leslie George were mistreated or, far more disturbingly, killed instead of taken prisoner. Parry's sworn statement was wholly reprehensible.

The 1/5 Welch war diary for 10 April (ie before battle was joined at Rethem) records the battalion's strength as 32 officers and 852 other ranks. By 12 April it had reduced to 26 and 696, a loss of six officers and 156 other ranks killed, wounded and missing during the fighting on 10 and 11 April. These were heavy losses for any period of the war but particularly so for this stage when the advance was largely unopposed. 10 and 11 April must have been hard days for 1/5 Welch and nobody in the battalion would have expected to meet resistance of this severity. Notwithstanding the casualties and missing, the lack of success in forcing the marines out of Rethem must have come as a bitter setback.

With Rethem proving to be a much tougher nut to crack than expected, divisional planning now concentrated on employing the other two brigades to unhinge the defence and plans based on two scenarios were drawn up for operations on 12 April. Plan A was based on a successful capture of Rethem by 160th Brigade. Once the town was secure, 7 RWF and 1 E Lancs from 158th Brigade would form a bridgehead over the Aller opposite Rethem, with 1/5 Welch remaining on the left bank as the reserve. Plan B was based on 160th Brigade failing to capture Rethem. In this scenario 158th Brigade would move north, assemble south-east of Westen, already held by 4 Welch, and then for 1 E Lancs to conduct an assault crossing of the Aller. With the battalion secure on the right bank, a Class 9 FBE would be built and 7 RWF and 1/5 Welch would follow across the Aller and expand the bridgehead to allow 71st Brigade to cross and advance in a south-easterly direction up the Aller's right bank to cut off the marines in Rethem, or force their withdrawal. Prior to 160th Brigade entering the town, medium bombers from No. 2 Group would reduce Rethem and with the assistance of flame-throwing Crocodiles, the infantry would mop-up anything that survived.

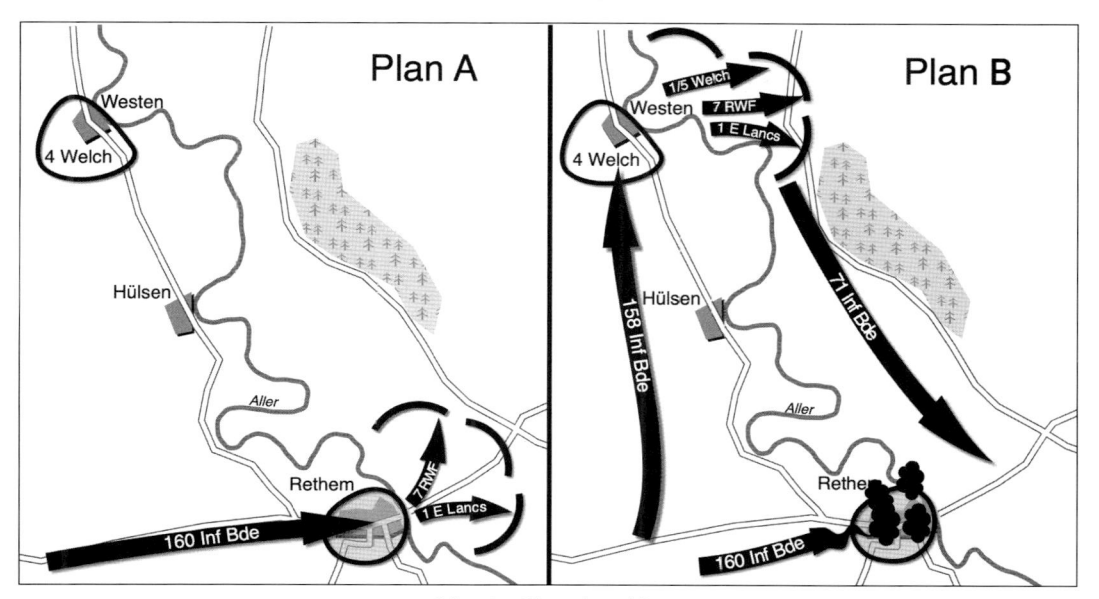

Map 52 Plans A and B.

With Rethem and a bridgehead on the right bank secure, work would begin on a Class 40 Bailey pontoon bridge to restore Reichsstrasse 209 and enable the corps to advance to Hamburg, led by 7th Armoured Division. In anticipation of this, 7th Armoured had been relieved from the approaches to Bremen by Major General 'Bolo' Whistler's 3rd Infantry Division and moved to a concentration area west of Nienburg.

To allow the prompt implementation of Plan B if the need arose, Brigadier Wilsey and Lieutenant Colonel Allen, commanding officer 1 E Lancs, visited the Westen area at mid-day on 11 April. Their recce revealed that although a bridgehead at Westen could sustain operations up to divisional level, it was unsuitable for a corps axis, thus confirming that Reichsstrasse 209 was essential for the corps to prosecute its advance to Hamburg and that there was no alternative to the bridging site at Rethem. The town had to be captured.

2 Mons attack on Rethem

During the early morning, responsibility for attacking Rethem shifted from 158th Brigade to 160th Brigade. At 0100 hours 160th Brigade warned 2 Mons that the battalion would be relieved in Nienburg by 4 RWF and that as soon as the handover had been completed it was to move to a concentration area at Anderten. By 0740 the battalion had reached Anderten and twenty minutes later the commanding officer, Lieutenant Colonel Frank Brooke, was called to the brigade headquarters where he was told his battalion would attack Rethem that afternoon. The brigade O Group followed at 0930 hours and Brooke was told that two squadrons of tanks from 5 RTR and full artillery and air support would be provided.[7] He gave his orders at mid-day. The plan had an H-hour of 1600 hours and involved a phased attack from the south-west on a two-company frontage: B Company right supported by a tank squadron; D Company left, similarly supported. The battle would open with a pre-H-hour attack by RP Typhoons, which would be followed by an artillery fire plan to cover the assault. The two attacking companies' mission was to capture the railway embankment and establish a breach in the town's outer defences. Once they had achieved this, C Company would pass through to clear the remainder of the town. It was subsequently decided that only one squadron of tanks would support the companies as there was insufficient manoeuvre space for two, and B Squadron was warned for the task. At 1445 hours the 2 Mons rifle companies began to move to the start line.

The omens for success were not promising and there were a series of significant difficulties facing 2 Mons. In short, the plan was hopelessly over-optimistic. First, none of the lessons of 1/5 Welch's bitter experience would seem to have been passed to 160th Brigade, and other than the addition of tanks and air support the British would be continuing to employ a single battalion, only this time it would be attacking on the most likely approach, and one that was not only lengthy but also one with excellent fields of fire for the enemy. Secondly, in his briefing that morning the brigade intelligence officer had estimated that the town was held by between 500 and 1,000 marines supported by 'railway guns'; even on the lower figure the combat ratio for the attacking companies was unfavourable and quite how a single company was expected to clear the town after the breach was made is unclear. Thirdly, although 2 Mons had received reinforcements from its sister battalion, 3 Mons, these were men who had suffered during the battle for Ibbenbüren and were now less than keen to put themselves in harm's way again so soon. Fourthly, B Squadron's troop leaders met the battalion's officers only shortly before H-hour and had little time to discuss tactics and how they would co-operate. Why this should have been the case is not known as there was

---

7 TNA WO 171/4711, 5 RTR war diary.

A MOST DECISIVE VICTORY? 337

time, admittedly short, during the latter part of the morning for liaison between the two arms; the result was that the squadron had misgivings about the attack from the outset. And there were other reasons for their misgivings. When 5 RTR was fragmented to support the various battalions of 53rd Welsh they lost the decisive leadership of their own commanding officer, Lieutenant Colonel Rea Leakey, the support of their divisional reconnaissance regiment, 11 Hussars, and the FOOs and fire support of 3 RHA. The positive effect on soldiers about to go into combat that they will be supported by known and trusted men and units should not be under-estimated and their absence did little to boost B Squadron's morale. One aspect, however, did prevent them feeling totally without confidence: they had an exceptional squadron leader in Major Dennis Cockbaine who, with his headquarters team, was unflappable and known to be very careful of the men under his command. Lastly, the attack would be without the fearsome support of Crocodiles. At 0910 hours

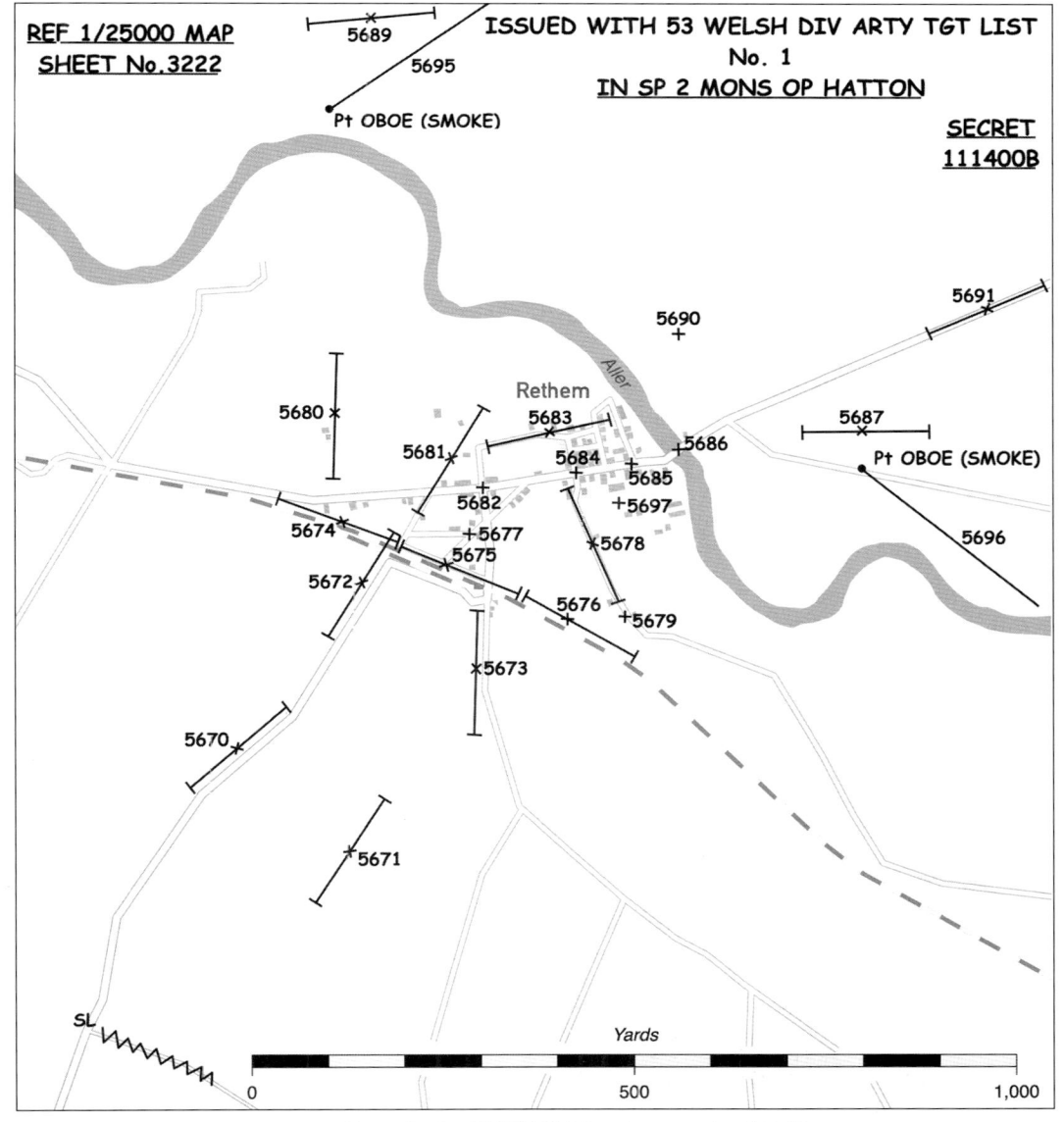

Map 53 Trace for Op HATTON fire plan – 11 April 1945.

on 11 April XII Corps belatedly recognised the requirement and ordered 52nd Lowland Division immediately to release half a squadron of eight Crocodiles to 53rd Division. The vehicles of B Squadron 7 RTR began their move at 1245 hours and for the next eight hours travelled 80 miles to reach Siedenburg, some 15 miles to the south-west of Hoya. Although an impressive move, for 2 Mons it was a day late.

The attack would be supported by a programmed artillery shoot provided by two field regiments and a medium regiment. Lieutenant Colonel Gore, commanding officer of 133rd Field Regiment, prepared the fire plan (see trace at Map 53) codenamed HATTON (the nickname for Rethem), which would be implemented by Major Richard Hughes, the BC of 497 Field Battery. For the first 10 minutes after H-hour, 83rd and 133rd Field Regiments would fire at the slow rate (two rounds per gun per minute) four linear concentrations on either flank of the attack's axis of advance (target numbers: 5670–5673). From H+10 to H+15 minutes 72nd Medium Regiment would join the plan and all three regiments would engage the line of the railway embankment (target numbers 5674–5676). After a five-minute pause, from H+20 to H+35 the two field regiments would fire two further linear concentrations (target numbers: 5687 and 5688 (not on Map 53)) and then re-engage the flanks of the assault (target numbers: 5670–5673) with concentrations fired at the normal rate (three rounds per gun per minute). The culmination, from H+35 to H+45, required all three regiments to re-engage the embankment (target numbers 5674–5676), with the medium regiment also allocated two targets in the embankment's depth (target numbers 5679 and 5697). At H+80 two smoke screens (target numbers 5695 and 5696) would be fired onto the right bank to mask any enemy OPs and interfere with his direct fire weapons. The fire plan was typical for the period being relatively complex, based on the assumption that the attack would proceed as planned and follow the rigid set of timings, and that the likely targets had been correctly identified. While the FOOs accompanying the assault were able to redirect fire in the event of unexpected targets, this required reliable communications, sadly lacking in 1945.

Prior to the attack, preliminary operations were needed to provide the battalion with a secure start line, which would be near Stöcken to Rethem's south-west. The previous night a patrol from C Company 6 RWF had reached the hamlet and reported that it was held by the enemy and

4.2-in mortar of D Company 1 Manchester firing in support of the attack on Stöcken.

that an 8.8cm Flak was present. As Stöcken dominated the approach to Rethem it would have to be cleared, so an attack was planned for the morning. At 0900 hours D Company, shot in by C Squadron 5 RTR and fire from medium and field artillery and 4.2-in mortars, assaulted Stöcken using the edge of a wood as an axis.

As the last 300 yards was dead flat and bereft of cover, smoke was used to protect the assaulting infantry, who were consequently able to reach the farmsteads with little difficulty. During the short fight most of the hamlet was burnt to the ground and the 8.8cm Flak from Batterie 2./604 and prisoners from I./5 Bataillon taken. With Stöcken captured C Company, supported by two troops of tanks from A Squadron 5 RTR, then exploited to Rethemer Moor, an area to the south of Rethem dotted with farmsteads, which they cleared by 1315 hours. The battalion then spent the remainder of the day consolidating its gains and taking a further 39 prisoners.

The opening action of 2 Mons' assault on Rethem was the attack by RP Typhoons, which preceded the artillery fire plan. Typhoon 1Bs of 137 Squadron took off at 1424 hours from the recently repaired B.106 strip at Twente in the eastern Netherlands and then married up with others from 182 Squadron.[8] At 1511 hours 25-pdrs fired red smoke shells at Rethem to mark the target and 14 minutes later the 24 Typhoons, commanded by Wing Commander George Webb,[9] were over the town. They were met by some fire not only from 2cm Flak but also from some of the 10.5cm Flak on the railway flats, whose crews managed to elevate their guns in time to meet the threat. The heavy aircraft peeled off and dived on the target area, the pilots firing their cannons to suppress the ground fire and launching their rockets as they neared the end of their dives. The raid was over in minutes and with rockets exhausted the Typhoons flew away to the west; by 1600 hours they had returned to Twente without loss. To the watching troops the attack appeared to have had customary devastating effect with the salvos of rockets throwing up clouds of smoke, dirt and rubble; many buildings seemed destroyed and numerous fires could be seen. 158th Brigade reported to division that the attack was a 'complete success' and that 'everything fell in the target area.'

Despite the apparent ferocity of the air attack, neither the marines' defensive positions nor the railway *Flak* in the sidings at Rethem station suffered and although HQ 53rd Division was pleased with the mission and described it as 'highly successful and accurate', photographs of the station area, and the railway *Flak* in particular, taken after the capture of the town show little apparent damage. How these large, obvious, static targets on 2 Mons' immediate objective escaped destruction seems at first sight odd. However, the effectiveness of RP attacks was usually wildly overestimated, as a report on Typhoon support in Normandy written by No. 2 Operational Research (OR) Section reveals. This joint Army–RAF report written in the autumn of 1944 found that 350 rockets involving 44 sorties would have to be fired at a gun position to obtain a 50 percent chance of a hit, and that RPs were at their most effective as a means of reducing enemy morale while raising our own.[10] For the troops about to assault Rethem, there was no realisation that the enemy was largely unaffected by the fury unleashed from above, but this was soon to become all too apparent.

While the Typhoon attack was in progress, the two companies and the tanks of B Squadron moved up to the start line and on H-hour at 1600 hours, 30 minutes after the Typhoon attack, artillery fire plan HATTON began; at the same time, the assault companies crossed the lane marking the start line and started the advance. As the approach to Rethem was so flat they were

---

8   TNA AIR 50/59, 137 Squadron RAF combat reports.
9   George Webb was an experienced recce pilot with a Distinguished Flying Cross and Bar but was relatively new to fighter-bombers. On 2 May he was shot down and killed by *Flak* while strafing a train near Gleschendorf in Schleswig-Holstein.
10 TNA WO 291/2357, Joint Report No. 3 – Rocket Firing Typhoons in Support of Military Operations.

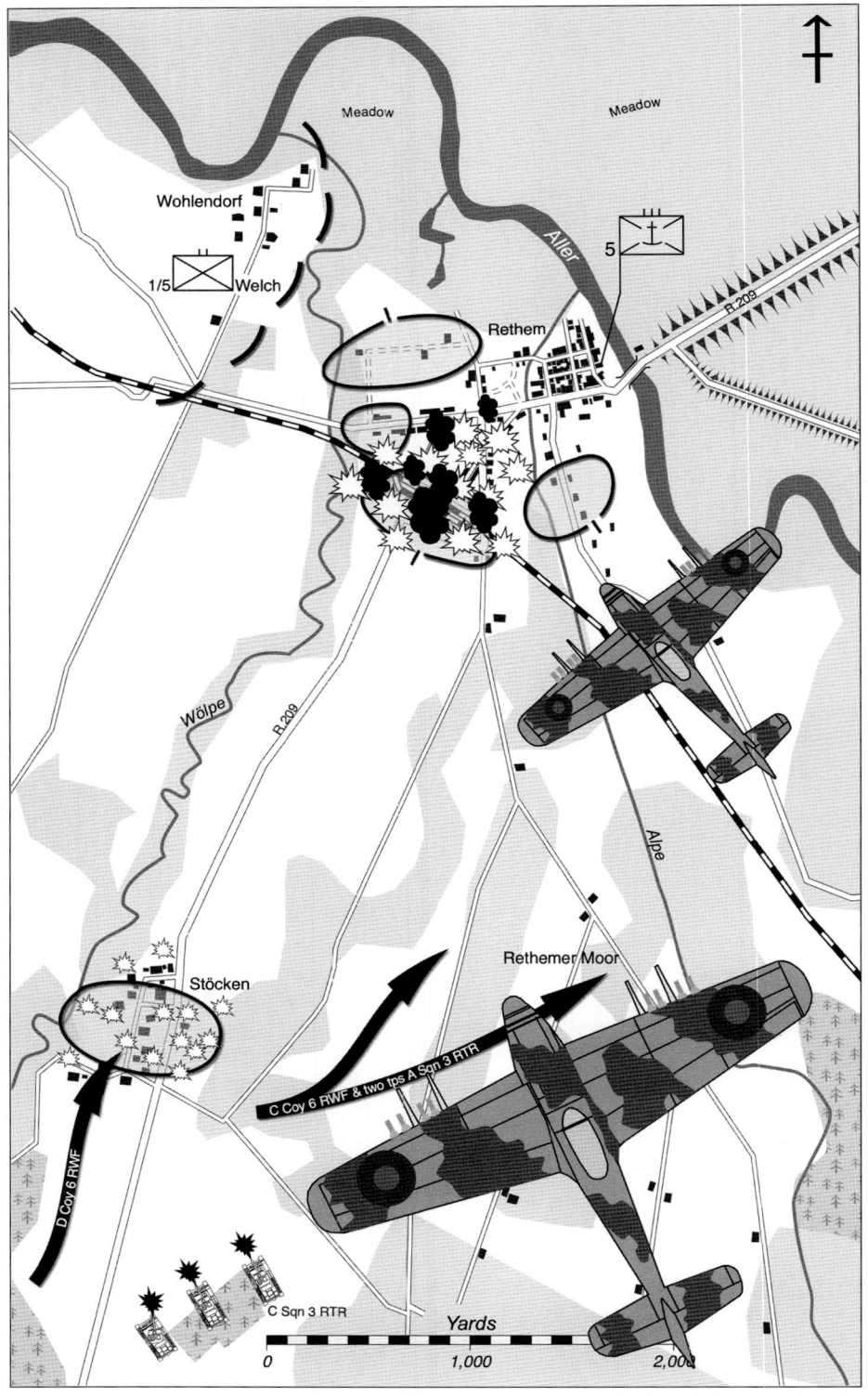

Map 54 Preliminary Operations – Rethem – 11 April 1945.

The 'huge arena' and the railway embankment viewed from the start line. Photograph taken in 1983. (Author)

soon in full view of the marines on the railway embankment. Edward Wilson, a troop leader in B Squadron, describes the ground:[11]

> The terrain was laid out more for a medieval than for a modern set-piece battle. The road we were on [the lane marking the start line] ran roughly north-west – south-east which meant it was approximately parallel to and about 1,500 yards from the railway embankment, which was so important a feature of landscape and so important a part of the battle for Rethem. The main part of the town lay on the far side of this embankment, the bridge and most of the houses being completely obscured by it. In front of the embankment, bounded by a straggling wood on the left and a substantial hedge on the right was an almost completely flat and open stretch of country. It was across this huge arena, 1,200 yards or so long and perhaps 600 yards wide and devoid of all cover that we had to advance. The most sinister feature of the embankment was the presence on it of the railway-mounted 10.5cm pieces of artillery.

Despite the openness, the advance was initially without incident. However, both companies and their accompanying tanks advanced cautiously, with the infantry following the tanks in single file and using whatever cover from view was available.

Although progress was being made, neither arm felt at ease: the close presence of the tanks made the infantry feel they would attract fire, whereas the tank crews manoeuvring at a walking pace felt vulnerable in their Cromwells and Fireflies, and the inability of either arm to communicate with the other added to the unease. By 1630 hours both companies reached report line 'Key' and line 'Dick' was similarly reached 15 minutes later. But on nearing line 'Smith', and still 450 yards short

---

11   Letter to the author.

Infantry of 2 Mons starting their advance towards Rethem. (Huett)

of their objectives, both companies came under heavy and accurate fire from machine-guns and light *Flak*, with the railway *Flak* and Pak 40 anti-tank guns engaging the tanks. From this point onwards the infantry and armoured attacks developed separately, particularly on the left axis, with inevitable results. Every time there was a burst of fire the infantry went to ground while the tanks, indifferent to small-arms' fire and as yet out of range of *Panzerfaust*, continued to advance unaware the infantry were no longer with them.

The gunner of 4 Troop leader's Cromwell was the aptly named Trooper Joe Cannon, who gained a close impression of the attack from his position in the turret:[12]

> We formed up just in front of the crossroads about a mile from Rethem and moved out towards the town. A short distance down the road the ground opened up to fields. On the right of the road were some allotments with sheds. Some Germans came out from there and were shot up. The troop leader's tank went to the right of the road, the other two Cromwells to the left with the Firefly on the edge of the road behind us. To our right were small heaps of hay in lines which had been cut, heaped and left to dry and here we spotted further Germans in the open, not dug in behind the hay. We took them out. By this time the forward infantry were trying to reach the railway embankment that ran in front of the town and were clearly in trouble. The enemy were dug-in in front of the embankment in holes with all the topsoil removed so that they were flush with the ground and hard to spot. The enemy were also behind the embankment and on the railway line were a hell of a lot of 88mm [*sic*] Flak guns all pointing down the line.

---

12 Letter to the author.

A MOST DECISIVE VICTORY? 343

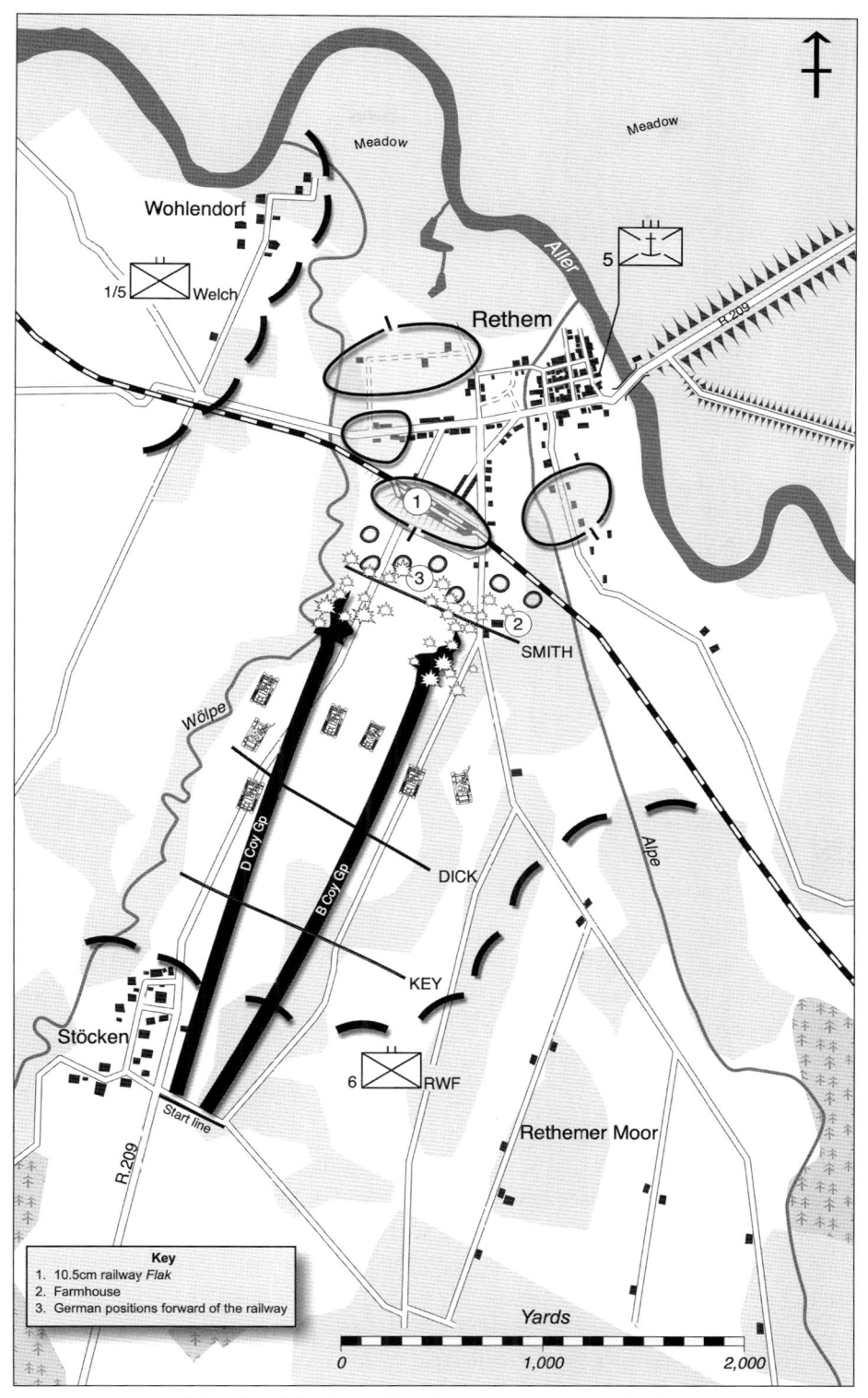

Map 55 2 Mons' Attack on Rethem – pm 11 April 1945.

The view from the German positions on the railway embankment of 2 Mons' approach. Panorama photograph taken in 1992. (Author)

On the right axis B Company initially made reasonable progress. The company had advanced in the order 11 Platoon, 5 Troop, company headquarters, then 10 and 12 Platoons. 11 Platoon's task was to seize a farmhouse and a group of farm buildings 300 yards short of the railway and establish a firm base for the assault by 10 and 12 Platoons, moving forward under cover of smoke if necessary, to establish themselves on the railway embankment. 11 Platoon was 90 yards away from the farm buildings when it came under effective fire but by moving in short dashes the whole company managed to gain the area of the buildings.[13] Supporting the attack were the Cromwells and Firefly of 5 Troop; the gunner of the troop's Firefly was Lance Corporal Harry Ireland:[14]

> What a field day of a shoot we had that day. There was a certain amount of hate at this time as we had been informed that Rethem was being held by fanatical marine troops from Hamburg and that they were shooting all prisoners captured the previous day.
> We took up position facing the railway line and set about engaging targets. The marines had brought up mobile 88mm [sic] guns mounted on railway flats and were firing HE at the infantry. For hours we engaged and appeared to knock out the guns but the determination vof the Germans amazed us. If it hadn't been such a life and death business you could say it was like being at a fair ground for as fast as I machine-gunned and HE'd the target up sprang another crew to take the place of the dead around the gun. However, after numerous attempts to crew the guns, we managed to knock them all out.

Although B Company had successfully reached its initial objective, the slightest movement outside the buildings brought a hail of fire from the marines on the embankment and casualties began to mount. A request was granted for smoke to screen the advance by 10 and 12 Platoons to the embankment and under its cover the platoons left the uncertain safety of the farm buildings, covered by fire from 11 Platoon's Brens. The smoke, however, proved ineffective and both platoons were forced back by the weight of enemy fire; casualties included one of the platoon commanders, Lieutenant Mackenzie, who was stunned by a shot through the helmet. Smoke was again called for and this time was much more effective, allowing the platoons to repeat their attack under its cover and they were soon engaging the marines in slit trenches in the field between the farm and the embankment. But this advantage quickly ended as once again the smoke drifted away leaving the platoons exposed and short of their objective. Although some of the enemy left their trenches, the majority fought bitterly and the two B Company platoons, silhouetted against the smoke, were fought to a standstill 40 yards short of the embankment, where yet more marines were dug-in.

---

13 In military terms 'effective fire' has a precise meaning: unless another form of manoeuvre is adopted casualties will be taken.
14 Letter to the author.

The only cover available were a few shell craters, but those who took cover in them were pinned down and any movement soon attracted bursts of fire from the marines. Bullets repeatedly hit the casualties and Lieutenant Mackenzie received five more wounds: two in an arm, and one each in the back, chest and face, but continued to encourage his men. Sergeant Williams, the acting CSM who had taken over Lieutenant Mackenzie's platoon when he was first hit, was killed and about a third of the platoon were casualties. Lieutenant Evans, the other platoon commander and now commanding both platoons, found a volunteer in Private Brock to take a message to company headquarters in the farm buildings telling them what had happened as they seemed unaware of events owing to the smoke and general confusion.

While B Company struggled to get forward to the embankment, D Company on the left was in similar difficulties. The armour and infantry attack was by now totally uncoordinated and the infantry, pinned down by small-arms' fire, were unable or unwilling to move up to support their tanks. As the armour was powerless to advance further without infantry support to clear the *Panzerfaust* firers, the tanks stood off and attempted to pick off enemy positions, as Joe Cannon describes:[15]

> At about 1,000 yards from the railway in front of Rethem, the Monmouths came under fire from weapon pits both on and in front of the embankment. We halted at 800 yards out and returned fire to enable the forward elements of the Monmouths to withdraw back to the main body. We engaged the enemy on the right of the road down by the railway line and took them out firing HE on delay. By this time all our infantry had moved to the left of the road and so we joined them, but were then asked to go back to the right. We went back and were firing on the embankment when we were hit by a heavy machine-gun, about a 20mm I think. We were really plastered and found later that he had nearly penetrated the turret. The troop leader spotted him just on the left of the road where it crossed the railway line and we finished him with a 75mm HE round. We then went back to the left of the road by what looked like a small electrical sub-station, which was 800 yards from the embankment.
>
> The troop leader had just said words to the effect, 'Thank God those guns are all pointing down the line' when one turned round and fired at us. He was bang on for line but short. At this all the Cromwells opened up with HE and AP and began to take out all the guns on the embankment. This went on for some time and we made sure they were out. By this time I was getting low on ammo and had to re-stock from under the turret floor and get Besa ammo from the lap gunner. We then concentrated on the enemy pits on the left of the road firing HE on delay for air bursts over the pits, watching for him to fire and then firing the machine-guns when he was exposed; we had fair success with this. Suddenly the troop leader spotted an anti-tank gun on the left of the road down by the level-crossing. The gun, a 7.5cm I think, was side-on so I aimed an AP round at the thick part of the barrel and put a hole right through it. Range was 800 yards; it was one of my best shots and I'm still proud of it! Sometime late in the afternoon a train engine to the right of the road and the signal box was getting up steam and I was told to destroy it. I fired a HE round into the cab and an AP through the boiler. I could hear our other troop firing at times but I never saw them as they were busy with their own bit of front. We were very short of ammo by now and we tried to conserve as much as possible but there were too many targets.

The difficult and confused situation is clear in 2 Mons' war diary entries. An entry at 1730 hours recorded that both companies were pinned down by small-arms' fire. An hour and a half later at

---

15   Letter to the author.

1900 hours, B Company is recorded as having two platoons on the embankment; 35 minutes later it is recorded as requesting a delay (what for is unknown) of 30 minutes to allow the situation to clarify; then at 2000 hours both company commanders return to the battalion's tactical headquarters to report a position of 'great difficulty' caused mainly by the open ground. The battalion attack had bogged down and Captain Eric Wilde, who was then in B Squadron headquarters, was clearly frustrated at the lack of headway:[16]

> While the tanks were advancing and dealing with two anti-tank guns, the infantry also advanced until they came some 400–500 yards short of the embankment. Then the enemy opened up with MG and rifle fire and the infantry went to ground – and that was virtually the end of the infantry attack. The enemy infantry were very well positioned. Some MG posts were on, or dug into, the embankment and these the tanks could observe and knock out. But the main enemy positions were sited in front of the embankment in flat fields. They were individual foxholes with no parapets to give away their locations. The excavated earth was scattered around so there was no indication of a foxhole until you were almost on top of it. The enemy infantry hid in these foxholes, popping up to fire their rifles, MGs and *Panzerfaust* and then dropping down again. It was extremely difficult for the tanks to deal with them. It was hard to identify the positions and difficult to get a HE round into them. Great care had to be taken of the *Panzerfaust*. We tried to get the infantry to close with the enemy but somehow nothing was achieved and everything petered out. The infantry never seemed to come up with the tanks. One troop of tanks actually managed to get onto the embankment but came under a shower of *Panzerfaust* – luckily badly aimed – and had to withdraw. After two hours' fighting the tanks had virtually run out of ammunition, the two leading troops had none left and they were relieved by two troops from C Squadron. The tanks continued to give maximum support and engaged every sign of enemy activity but the infantry were able to make no progress.

Trooper Denis Huett was a gunner in one of C Squadron's relieving Fireflies:[17]

> During the late afternoon my troop drove up the road towards Rethem. About halfway we stopped and the roofs of the houses, which ran across our front, were machine-gunned and set alight. As we got nearer to the level-crossing – it was getting dusk now – we stopped again. During this stop an English casualty was helped onto the back of our tank and laid down across the back. We also had two German prisoners, unwounded I believe, on the back. I always remember an incident at this point. As one of the prisoners bent down towards the wounded chap our radio operator, Mike Parker, gave him a sharp knock on his arm with his Sten gun apparently thinking the Jerry was going to harm the casualty. The Jerry looked up with a very hurt look as he was only bending down to take a cigarette out of the casualty's mouth as he couldn't do it himself and was about to get burnt. I felt a bit sorry for this Jerry as he was only doing something to help.

As it was clear to Lieutenant Colonel Brooke that the attack had failed, he ordered the companies to end the assault. To assist the break clean and withdrawal the artillery was asked for yet another smoke screen, to be thickened by fire from mortars and the tanks. Although there was an army-wide shortage of smoke rounds, as the need to avoid casualties had led to high usage, a screen was

---

16 Letter to the author.
17 Letter to the author.

fired 25 minutes later with the gunners using their last rounds to provide it. With radio communications broken down, immediately the smoke was laid B Company's carrier driven by Private Wild and commanded by Lance Corporal Dawson dashed forward conveying the order to 10 and 12 Platoons to pull back through 11 Platoon. Once the order was passed, the wounded were piled into the carrier for the return journey, while others were carried by their comrades. By this time much of the town was burning fiercely and the dark evening was lit by roaring flames, but despite the illumination Dawson and Wild volunteered to take the carrier forward a second time to collect survivors. Covering fire was given by the tanks and although the carrier was clearly visible they managed to drive within 35 yards of the enemy positions, where they dismounted and examined bodies for signs of life, bringing the living back to safety. Both these soldiers were awarded the Military Medal for their courage and Lieutenant MacKenzie was awarded the Distinguished Service Order for his gallantry during the battle. With the infantry fighting and dying in the fields in front of Rethem, the gunners of a battery from 72nd Medium Regiment also had their share of misery when a round exploded in the breech of a 5.5-in gun killing the No. 1, Sergeant Tomlinson, and wounding another gun number.

By 2100 hours the companies and tanks had withdrawn half a mile from the railway embankment and awaited a decision from higher levels as to what would happen next. The order for no further attacks was confirmed at 2200 hours by Major General Ross, who had been at HQ 160th Brigade throughout the 2 Mons attack, and the battalion was ordered to pull back and concentrate in the area of Stöcken and the start line. While it was clear to General Ross that the town could not be taken without more casualties, it was equally clear that a crossing site at Rethem had to be captured to open up the axis for 7th Armoured Division to exploit to Soltau and beyond. He therefore decided to implement his Plan B and directed that the town would not be re-attacked until dusk the following day, and then only if the town had been reduced by bombing and Crocodiles accompanied his infantry.

That night 2 Mons despatched a fighting patrol to discover whether any gaps existed in the enemy defences; the patrol reported back in the early hours of 12 April that the line of the railway was still strongly held and no gaps were evident. Edward Wilson describes the aftermath of the battle:[18]

> At twilight, when we got the orders from squadron HQ to pull back troop by troop, I looked around for our supporting infantry, only to find that they were no longer there. We met up with them again later because both tanks and infantry only pulled back overnight to the other side of the road from which we had started. Here we lay up for the night: ourselves snug in our tanks; the poor 2 Mons very much out in the open. We took pity on them, as we took pity on our own divisional infantry, by sharing the brew up which we quickly got going in the tanks. They came in relays for their brew and, during one relay's visit I had the only laugh of the day. While one of the platoon commanders and some of his men were with us our A echelon arrived with much needed replenishments. The platoon commander asked me who commanded the echelon: I replied it was the RSM. I then heard an awed, *sotto voce* comment from the ranks: 'Christ,' the voice said, 'you wouldn't find our fucker this close to the sharp end.'

Although he had repulsed all of 53rd Welsh's attempts to capture Rethem, Jordan had suffered serious losses of men, his ammunition was running low and he knew he would not be able to hold off the attacks for a third day. Aware that the British had reached Westen the day before and that

---

18 Letter to the author.

they would probably soon attempt a crossing there, Jordan ordered a withdrawal across the Aller that night to prevent his regiment being cut-off on the left bank. He was, however, faced with a problem as the afternoon's Typhoon attack had initiated a sympathetic detonation of the demolition charges on the Aller bridge and the ensuing explosion not only killed and wounded marines in the bridge's vicinity but also dropped it into the river, forcing him to rely on mustering civilian boats. During the night 11/12 April, while a weak rearguard provided cover, he and 100 of his marines crossed the Aller by boat. As soon as the bulk of his men reached the right bank the rearguard, commanded by an *Oberleutnant*, withdrew upstream from Rethem and crossed the Aller using the ferry at Eilte, scuttling it once across. As soon as they reached the right bank, Rethem's former defenders, now numbering some 200 men, withdrew to the cover of the woods between Nordkampen and Südkampen, about a mile in depth of the Aller, and here they regrouped and recovered from the ordeal of the past three days. The walking wounded that reached the right bank were evacuated to the military hospital in Walsrode, but those who were too serious were left behind in cellars where they were tended by the few townsfolk still remaining and by Hoffmeyer, Rethem's doctor. This 70-year-old provided first aid throughout the battle and his heroism was talked about in the town long after the war's end.

On 11 April fierce fighting was also taking place elsewhere on the Aller's left bank and 4 Welch in particular was encountering stiff opposition as it set about clearing the enemy from the Weser-Aller triangle. An especially bitter action was fought in Barnstedt, a river-side village similar to Westen, where the carrier platoon got into difficulties when it was encircled by 3./7 Kompanie. While attempting to relieve the platoon, a *Panzerfaust* knocked out a Cromwell from A Squadron 5 RTR commanded by Lieutenant Hargreaves and he and three crew members were wounded; two more tanks became badly bogged trying to move across country. The buildings the carrier platoon was occupying began to burn and it was only with the help of a second troop of tanks and a further platoon of infantry that the besieged men were extricated, leaving the village uncaptured, two carriers destroyed and three men dead.

Thursday 12 April

Other than the occasional round of harassing artillery landing in Rethem's smoking rubble, the night 11/12 April passed peacefully and, compared with the noise and confusion of the preceding days, 12 April dawned strangely quiet. Although no activity was evident and many of the fires had burnt themselves out, despite the eerie calm the British were still unaware that the marines had withdrawn and with Plan B in place they made no attempt to close with the town. But mercifully for Rethem and its inhabitants, the unpredictability of war now intervened on their side and as a direct consequence of a tank becoming bogged during 2 Mons' attack the town would be spared obliteration.

The tank, stuck in the fields short of the railway embankment, was Sergeant George Stimpson's Firefly from 10 Troop C Squadron 5 RTR. George Stimpson describes the events that unfolded:[19]

> When it got dark we were told to pull out (including the infantry) as a large bomber raid would be laid on. While doing this, the tank in my troop commanded by the corporal got bogged down. It was not possible to get it out without a lot of noise and light so we took the firing pins of the guns, locked the tank up and left it. Next morning after breakfast I asked if I could go back and recover the tank – this we were allowed to do. At this stage we were

---

19 Letter to the author.

four tanks on our own about 200 yards from the level-crossing. I had a talk with my other sergeant, Ted Lines – we had been together since early in the desert – and we agreed that there did not seem to be many enemy about so we did what we had done so many times before. We took the hull-gunners from a couple of tanks and we started to walk into the town, Ted with his man on one side of the road and me on the other. We soon reached the level-crossing with no trouble and were able to have a closer look at the dead soldiers lying in the field, there must have been a whole company of them and I don't think I have ever been so saddened as I was that morning. I called the tanks forward and we continued. Just around the corner we were met by a party of civilians with a white flag led by the *Bürgermeister*. He let it be known that the town was prepared to give in and I said that was OK provided all arms were laid down and the remaining troops formed up on the road. Failing this we would shoot the lot! At about 0930 hours all this was passed to our CO, Colonel Leakey, who came up quickly.

Fortuitously, Lieutenant Colonel Leakey had already come forward to talk to Major Crickmay, C Squadron leader; Rea Leakey takes up the story:[20]

When I arrived at his HQ I was told that he had gone forward to see if one of his tanks, which had been abandoned during the night, had been brewed up by the Germans. I went down the farm track he had taken and sure enough I came across this lone officer walking towards the main Rethem defensive line. He jumped onto the back of my small scout car and we continued on our way. It was the driver who called to our attention as to where we were. 'Blimey,' he said, 'What a lot of dead *Boche* about and look at them large railway guns.' We were passing through the outer defences which had been abandoned during the night. I called up the adjutant, Captain Dixon, on the radio and told him to order B and C Squadrons to move as fast as possible into Rethem. I also asked him to inform 53rd Welsh Division of the situation and suggest that the Monmouths might help us clear the town of the inevitable rearguard.

While his commanding officer was moving up, George Stimpson was taken to a large cellar beneath a public building:[21]

One of the Germans asked me to follow him to the basement of a large building where a hospital had been set up by some German nursing sisters. They explained to me that they urgently needed medical help and when I looked around the basement I estimated there was something like a hundred cases on the floor and at least half of them were British. I promised them all the help they needed and as soon as I got back to the troop I reported it to the squadron leader, who had by now joined us. Ted and I then continued to the river where we found the bridge blown and another anti-tank gun abandoned.

Their somewhat unconventional role in the final act of the battle for Rethem over, Ted Lines posed with George Stimpson and his crew on the abandoned Pak 40 near the barricade on the Alpe. Sitting on the gun shield at the rear of the group is George's hull-gunner, 'Coldsteel' Pearson, who had managed to shoot George in the leg in Normandy!

---

20 Letter to the author. David Leakey, one of Rea Leakey's two sons, was a lieutenant general in the British Army and subsequently Gentleman Usher of the Black Rod in the House of Lords 2010–2018.
21 Letter to the author.

Sergeant Stimpson (front, left) and Sergeant Lines (right) pose with crew members on a Pak 40 after the fall of Rethem. 'Coldsteel' Pearson is in the leather jerkin (centre, back). (Stimpson)

While Colonel Leakey was moving towards the centre of the town, Captain Dixon called him up on the radio:[22]

> He told us that divisional HQ had sent a message to say that 500 bombers were on their way to flatten Rethem and we were to get out immediately. This was one of several orders in my career I refused to obey! Thanks to Dixon's efforts the RAF were able to recall their aircraft – but only just. We were listening for them and did hear them. The town of Rethem owes Dixon a debt of gratitude.
> As the lead tanks approached the centre of the town an incident occurred which I shall never forget. I happened to be behind the leading troop of B Squadron. It was commanded by Lieutenant John Gwilliam, a large powerful Welshman. When his tank came up to a T-junction he rightly dismounted and poked his nose around the corner to see if there was an anti-tank gun covering the approach. A rifle shot whistled past his head and Gwilliam disappeared around the corner, reappearing moments later carrying a small German soldier, rather

---

22 Letter to the author.

View from the turret of a C Squadron 5 RTR Firefly as it entered Rethem. (Crickmay)

like a cat with a mouse. I asked Gwilliam if this was the soldier which had so nearly shot him and he replied that it was. 'Then why didn't you shoot him?' I asked, and back the answer came, 'Oh no colonel, he's much too small!' After the war Gwilliam went on to captain Wales at rugby.[23]

As Rethem's denouement was planned for the evening of 12 April and therefore still many hours off, the aircraft Leakey heard were presumably others. There is, however, no record in either 137 or 139 Wings' operational logs of raids in this area of Germany on 12 April so the story of the approaching bombers is colourful but doubtful.[24] At the same time as Colonel Leakey and C Squadron were entering Rethem from the south-west, 5 RTR's recce troop, operating from Rethemer Moor, had entered Hedern and then advanced north-west to the outskirts of Rethem.

Several poorly aimed *Panzerfaust* were fired at the leading Stuart, but the Germans were in no strength and by 0950 hours the recce troop was half-way into Rethem. 2 Mons was ordered into the town at 1120 hours and two hours later Rethem was finally secure. Members of C Squadron investigated the area of the railway embankment and found five knocked-out 10.5cm Flak on the railway flat-wagons, several 2cm Flak and many dead marines with their equipment scattered about. In this final phase of the battle, 120 prisoners were captured and 42 German dead counted in the town and on the southern outskirts. The road bridge was found lying in the Aller.

At 1415 hours A Company 2 Mons despatched a recce patrol across the Aller to check the condition of the next two bridges on Reichsstrasse 209 and report on the whereabouts of the enemy; the patrol had a busy time. Accompanied by sappers, it first visited a road culvert 150 yards from the river and found it thoroughly demolished and a 35-yard gap created. The patrol then moved further up the road to check a bridge crossing a small lake; this bridge was found intact. The last task was to check the bridge over an ox-bow lake at Rethemer Fähre; not only was this bridge found demolished but the patrol was also engaged with machine-gun fire from marines in

---

23 Gwilliam had an illustrious career with Wales, winning 23 caps, captaining it to two Grand Slam victories plus notable victories over Australia and New Zealand.
24 TNA AIR 26/198 and AIR 26/200. 137 and 139 Wings RAF combat reports.

German prisoners on the Eystrup road being marched away to the west. (Huett)

Captain Dixon (left) and Major Crickmay (right) of 5 RTR in the centre of Rethem immediately after its capture. German prisoners in the background. (Crickmay)

A MOST DECISIVE VICTORY? 353

C Squadron 5 RTR Cromwells in the centre of Rethem. The second tank is a Cromwell MkVI close support tank of squadron headquarters. As all the vehicles are pointing west, the photograph was probably taken when 5 RTR was about to pull out of Rethem. (Crickmay)

Two C Squadron 5 RTR Cromwells and a Stuart of Recce Troop in Mühlenstrasse in the centre of Rethem. (Crickmay)

Abandoned Pak 40 in the town centre with smoke from fires still billowing. (Huett)

Four of the 10.5cm Flak. The nearest gun has been stacked with sleepers in an attempt to protect the crew and has received a direct hit. Rethem station in the background. (© Crown Copyright, IWM negative number BU3569)

The 10.5cm Flak. (© Crown Copyright, IWM negative number BU3591)

Pak 40 in a hedge-line. Above the gun's muzzle brake, Denis Huett's Firefly can just be seen on the orchard's far side. (Huett)

the nearby woods and buildings. From this final position the patrol was able to see activity and possible defensive positions in the fields south of Gross Häuslingen, and on the return journey they were shot at from Kirchwahlingen. The patrol arrived back in Rethem at 1715 hours and its report made it clear to the divisional planners that because of the two route denials on Reichsstrasse 209, the road would not initially be available for the advance and a bypass would be needed. Regardless of this future challenge, bridging operations started at Rethem during the early evening of 12 April, with 2 Platoon 244 Field Company beginning to prepare the home bank for bridging; the platoon was joined at 2000 hours by 1 Platoon, provider of the bridging equipment, and two hours later by 3 Platoon.

At 1800 hours a rifle platoon from A Company 2 Mons established a defensive position on the right bank of the Aller to protect the construction of the bridge. This was a sound decision as a subsequent patrol, sent out in the small hours of the morning, was shot at entering the house overlooking the bridging site and in the ensuing fracas two enemy were killed and three members of the patrol wounded; a marine officer and six marines were captured. During the night the bridging site was shelled, but fortunately the accuracy was erratic, possibly due to the capture of the marines in the house, and no casualties or damage caused. The last entry in 2 Mons' war diary for 12 April concluded somewhat ruefully that the Germans had fought with great energy and spirit regardless of their heavy casualties and the fire support directed on them.

The battle of Rethem was costly for both sides: 53rd Welsh Division lost 251 men killed, wounded and missing,[25] with the majority coming from 1/5 Welch, while for 2. Marine-Infanterie-Division the battle resulted in the death of 73 soldiers, unknown numbers of wounded and 339 captured by the British.[26] Of the dead, the youngest was only 17 and the oldest 53; 11 were unidentified. Although Kapitän zur See Jordan's dogged defence was pointless and only served to delay the inevitable, his marines' courage is beyond dispute, as poignantly described by Eric Wilde:[27]

> When I inspected the area after it was all over, I was struck by the large number of infantry dead in their foxholes. They had almost all been hit in the head, showing that they had been hit as they stood in the hole engaging us. They could so easily have just crouched at the bottom and would have been safe from everything except air-burst. And they all seemed so young. I was myself a week from my twenty-third birthday but they seemed boys to me. I should think they must have been in the 16 to 18 age group. The war was hopelessly lost for them, but they fought so bravely. Even then, when one was pretty hardened to death and suffering, we all, I think, felt pity for such young lives being sacrificed.

For the civilians these were grim times. The face of Rethem in April 1945 was one of ruin, no power, little food, curfew and of course the dead and injured. The people were relieved to find the enemy humane as the injured were treated, the homeless cared for and medical supplies provided. Looting was minimal and support was later provided to rebuild Schumann's mill. Fifteen inhabitants died during the fighting and many more were wounded and injured. Perhaps the saddest of the deaths were the three children of the Bässmann family: Inge (9), Hilde (7) and Horst (5), who were killed by artillery fire on 11 April. The small town lay devastated: 65 houses were totally destroyed and a further 64 badly damaged. In the streets, houses, gardens and fields lay the debris of war: bodies, weapons, equipment and ammunition. Although the dead marines were swiftly

---

25 TNA WO 171/3873, HQ 21st Army Group 'A' SITREPs No. 306 and 307, 53rd Welsh Division battle casualties.
26 TNA WO 171/3873, PoW Supplement to HQ 21st Army Group 'A' SITREP No. 307, 53rd Welsh Division PoWs for 24 hours ended 1800 hours 11 April 1945.
27 Letter to the author.

The wrack of war. Pak 40 with dead anti-tank gunner from Marine-Panzerjäger-Abteilung 2, an unused *Panzerfaust* by his side.

collected by work parties of local men and buried in an orchard near the level-crossing where Reichsstrasse 209 entered the town, the battlefield remained a dangerous place and an unexploded munition claimed the life of a child nine days after the town's capture.

For 53rd Welsh Division the battle for Rethem was a most unpleasant surprise as it must have appeared that further coherent opposition was unlikely, an understandable impression gained from the virtually uncontested advance from Ibbenbüren to the Weser and the ease with which that river had been crossed. However, the Germans' resistance on the Aller should not have come as a surprise as intelligence regarding the presence of a fresh enemy division was contained in an Ultra decrypt of 6 April,[28] which clearly reveals the Heeresgruppe 'H' decision that the naval division would reinforce the defence of the Weser between Verden and Nienburg. The decrypt was given a ZZZ urgency rating by Bletchley Park (the ratings went from Z to ZZZZZ) and would thus have been sent promptly to the covert detachment from Ultra's Special Liaison Unit, co-located with HQ Second Army.[29] The decrypt's content, suitably doctored to protect Ultra, would then have been passed to Second Army's intelligence staff, who would in turn have forwarded it to 53rd Welsh Division. But there is nothing in the 53rd Welsh record to suggest that the division knew that it was about to face fresh troops and it can only be assumed that either the information did not reach the division or it did and its implications were ignored or down-played. The division's approach to the battle for Rethem would undoubtedly have been different had the information in Ultra decrypt BT 9591 been known.

The lack of intelligence besides, with the benefit of hindsight it is easy to see how the frontal attacks mounted by the two Welsh battalions were doomed to failure. Once the strength of the enemy opposition was recognised, the decision to mount a series of attacks from predictable

---

28 TNA DEFE 3/563, BT 9591, 6 April 1945.
29 Ronald Lewin, *Ultra Goes to War – The Secret Story*, (London: Hutchinson & Co Ltd, 1978), p.372.

A view of the destruction in Rethem taken from the remains of the demolished road bridge. The tower on the right is the St. Marien Kirche.

Bullet-riddled town sign and burnt-out house provide mute testament to the ferocity of the fighting in Rethem. (Huett)

directions has to be questioned and it is particularly surprising that neither brigade commander made more use of their other available infantry: to support 1/5 Welch, 1 E Lancs was waiting in a concentration area not far to the west at Hämelhausen, and to support 2 Mons, 6 RWF was conveniently close at Anderten. These battalions could have been used for deception, for mounting simultaneous attacks from additional directions or for adding greater weight to the main axis. At the very least their use would have complicated Jordan's defence and prevented him reinforcing threatened sectors with troops who were not under attack. Although 's-Hertogenbosch was much larger than Rethem, 53rd Welsh's successful use of multiple axes in its assault on the Dutch town the previous autumn should have provided useful lessons for assaulting Rethem. The divisional history glowingly describes the capture of 's-Hertogenbosch as '...the best example in modern times of a successful assault on a large town held by a resolute and skilful enemy',[30] but perhaps unsurprisingly it glosses over the division's failure to capture Rethem, a much smaller enemy-held town. Some accounts and histories attempt to justify the Germans' resistance on the presence in Rethem of *Waffen-SS* elements, asserting they were on the Aller not to take part in the battle but instead specifically tasked to ensure that the marines fought to the end.[31] There is, however, a total absence of evidence for the presence of *Waffen-SS* in Rethem and this is supported by the 53rd Welsh Division INTSUM of 11 April,[32] which stated that while there had been suspicions of SS troops in the town and that SS-A.u.E.Btl. 12 'HJ' had passed through Rethem some days prior to 11 April, they had then gone either in the direction of Celle or Verden. 1., 2. and 7. SS-Kompanien probably crossed the Aller at Rethem during their withdrawal from the Weser, with the first two companies then marching to the division's left flank to join Marine-Füsilier-Bataillon 2 while 7. SS-Kompanie withdrew to Walsrode. The INTSUM concluded that while the SS may not have been in Rethem in the flesh, they were certainly there in spirit, a backhanded compliment to the marines for their fighting spirit.

A German account of the battle describes the British using tactics based on irritation and is rightly critical of the failure to employ armour and infantry correctly, as well as the preference for mounting attacks over open ground.[33] The attack by 2 Mons shows nothing was learnt from 1/5 Welch's succession of failed attacks and the British persisted in using a single battalion, on an obvious approach over open ground and attempting to break-in where the defence was strongest. No efforts were made to probe or reconnoitre the defences to determine weak points. The lack of tank-infantry cooperation has been mentioned and it is significant that at no point in B Company 2 Mons' account is a tank referred to, despite having a troop under command; the tanks and the infantry fought separate battles, with the attack foundering as a consequence. The benefit of close teamwork between the two arms was by now fully accepted within 21st Army Group and it is odd that despite some time being available, there was little pre-H-hour coordination or discussions between B Squadron 5 RTR and the 2 Mons' companies. Lastly on the matter of armour, it was a distinct disadvantage for the 2 Mons attack not to have been supported by Crocodiles as these terrifying weapons were extremely effective against infantry and time and again had forced early surrender. Although XII Corps ordered the release of half a squadron of Crocodiles to 53rd Welsh, the order was made far too late for the tanks to make the long journey to join 2 Mons. Had it been

---

30   CN Barclay, *History of the 53rd (Welsh) Division* (London: William Clowes & Sons, 1956), p.87.
31   For instance, Patrick Delaforce in *Red Crown and Dragon* (Brighton: Tom Donovan Publishing, 1996) states on p.195 'it was clear that experienced SS were in Rethem to make sure the marines fought well...'; and Charles Whiting in *The Last Battle* (Marlborough: Crowood Press, 1989) on p.47 describes a totally fictitious assault with 'SS' men' firing from the hip, sweeping down Rethem's main street, setting fire to houses and causing 50 percent casualties to the Welsh.
32   TNA WO 171/4277, 53rd Welsh Division INTSUM No. 222 as at 2359 hours on 11 April.
33   Ulrich Saft, *Krieg in der Heimat*, p.116.

made a day earlier the tanks could have reached 2 Mons, with all the advantages that would have brought.

The interval between the Typhoon attack and H-hour dissipated the shock effect of the RPs and the length of 2 Mons' approach diminished the impact of the artillery fire plan, giving the Germans ample time to recover. There are also strong indications that the artillery fire plan failed to provide the desired effect. First there was the general point that the lethality of the 25-pdr HE shell was suspect and it was assessed that a shell needed to land within 4 feet of a slit trench to generate an effective shock wave on the occupants, and a direct hit to inflict casualties.[34] A far greater density of fire would therefore have been needed to suppress the enemy on the embankment. Secondly, there was a disconnect between the infantry's advance and the fire plan. The fire plan's timings assumed that at H+45 the companies would be 200 yards short of the railway embankment and starting the final assault. But at 1645 hours (H+45) the companies had just reached report line 'Dick', only halfway from the start line to the railway embankment and still more than 1,000 yards short of the embankment. Progress was therefore very slow and resulted in the relationship between the companies' advance and the artillery fire plan going seriously awry, with the result that the companies were unable to 'lean into' the artillery barrage and the enemy was clearly unsuppressed. There is no documentary evidence that the artillery programme was adjusted to meet the circumstances encountered at the embankment. Other than recording the start of HATTON at 1600 hours, there are only four 133rd Field Regiment log entries covering the period of the 2 Mons attack: three are Scale 5 shoots at DFs in the town fired between 1711 and 1728 hours, while the fourth at 1830 hours is a Scale 1 shoot to 'empty hot guns.' There are no entries calling for re-engagements of the embankment and the fields forward of it, perhaps indicating that the FOOs' communications failed.[35]

But there were other factors for the attack's failure beyond just failings in the coordination of arms and here the two quotes in Chapter 3 regarding the state of British infantry are germane. Despite the appearance of strength, the reality was that much of the infantry was both qualitatively and quantitatively exhausted and only capable of employing the simplest of tactics. Frontal assaults and plodding along with the tanks were probably all that the rifle companies of the two Welsh battalions could manage. Although not serving in 53rd Welsh Division, Captain Freddie Graham of 2nd Battalion The Argyll and Sutherland Highlanders describes the impact of manning on the infantry's tactics:[36]

> As a very young officer I became aware of the question of manpower as it affected the UK. After our first battles we got our LOBs as reinforcements. Then we got people from the Durham Light Infantry, Hampshires and others. Although we (the UK) didn't send many divisions to Normandy, within four months two were broken up to keep the remainder going. Infantry casualties were much heavier than expected. Some of our reinforcements were not even infantry. The number of people still serving who had landed with us in Normandy was quite small. So a combination of lack of trained leaders and trained manpower meant that simple tactics had to be employed. From this time on, attacks were like the infantry assaults of World War One. White tape was laid. People formed up and walked behind a barrage at a set pace; halted for three minutes; coloured smoke was fired indicating that you could go on, and so on. It was very undemanding, but anything more ambitious would have been beyond

---

34   Buckley, *Monty's Men*, p.117.
35   TNA WO 171/4845, 133rd Field Regiment RA war diary.
36   Julian Thompson, *Imperial War Museum Book of Victory in Europe. The North-West European Campaign 1944–1945* (London: Sidgwick & Jackson Ltd, 1994), pp.220–221.

us. The trained leaders were no longer there. That was the instrument with which we had to complete the campaign.

Although there were undoubtedly gallant acts by individuals, the attacks by 1/5 Welch and 2 Mons lacked determination. The stimulus to push home the assault was not there and it is probable that there were more casualties as a result. The loss of leaders in the preceding months, the low quality of reinforcements and the natural concern of every soldier not to become a casualty with the war's end so close were undoubtedly contributory factors.

General Dempsey addressed members of 53rd Division after the German surrender and said these words about the battle of Rethem:[37]

> Of the later battles you fought, one, to my mind, was outstanding – the crossing of the Aller at Rethem. You were then up against the best German troops on the whole front. You fought like tigers and by winning the battle as you did you opened the way for Second Army to get straight through to the Elbe and so to the Baltic. I have placed that last battle of yours very high; it was a most decisive victory...

Accepting that this was a time for congratulation and that the capture of Rethem indeed opened the way for XII Corps, Dempsey's words are overstated and arguably the victors of Rethem were Jordan's marines who repelled all attacks, achieved 48 hours' delay and were able to withdraw with the bridge blown. It was however a Pyrrhic victory for the regiment had suffered severe losses, and of course the delay achieved was irrelevant. The final words on the battle for this small German town belong to George Stimpson:[38]

> When I walked into Rethem with Sergeant Ted Lines I saw by far the largest number of dead and wounded British soldiers that I had ever seen. As a Regular soldier I was in a tank crew in C Squadron 5 RTR from the day the war started to the day it ended and I never left the regiment for a single day, so the significance of that scene is all the more terrible. I thought I had seen it all.
>
> Although it can never be compared with the larger battles of the war, a fair-sized battle involving heavy fighting took place but it never made the headlines; in fact it has hardly warranted a mention.

With Rethem at last captured, we will now follow XII Corps' operations on the Aller's right bank.

---

37 Delaforce, Patrick, *Red Crown and Dragon* (London: Tom Donovan Publishing Ltd, 1996), p.219.
38 Letter to the author.

10

Belt-fed Bazookas: 53rd Division across the Aller 11–14 April 1945

The quality of the German forces available to counter a crossing of the Aller's final reaches was now patchy, with the bulk of 2. Marine-Infanterie-Division's strength either to the south-east of Verden or to the south of Reichsstrasse 209 in depth of Rethem, resulting in the area in-between being weakly held. The force allocated to Verden's defence was known as Kampfgruppe Verden and was commanded by Kapitän zur See Neitzel, commander Marine-Grenadier-Regiment 7. The majority of Kampfgruppe Verden's strength was found from the two marine battalions of Neitzel's regiment and Artillerie-A.u.E. Regiment 22, an artillery training and replacement regiment from Division Nr.480. This regiment, also known as Regiment Schaffer after its commander, was supposedly the provider of Division Nr.480's artillery, but it would appear that as it had no guns it was deployed as infantry. The regiment was detached from the rest of the division, otherwise located in the area between Verden and Bremen, to join Neitzel's Kampfgruppe in the Verden area and consisted of two battalion-sized units: Abteilung 11 (Kampfgruppe Tebener) with three companies and Abteilung 22 (Kampgruppe Hornemann) with four. Additional forces for Neitzel came from a number of miscellaneous units: the remnants of Bataillon Kolotay, the Hungarian artillery training battalion that had performed so dismally at Westen two days previously; Bataillon Blinzler, a three-company battalion consisting of former members of the *Luftwaffe*; a *Flak Abteilung* with the name Hundertmark (perhaps after its commander); and a 120-strong tank-hunting company of Hitler Youth called Panzer-Löwe (Armoured Lion) 3. Kompanie. Neitzel's Kampfgruppe, with the equivalent of 28 infantry companies, was numerically strong and had the support of some forty 8.8cm and 2cm Flak, but despite this strength Neitzel would be hamstrung by the requirement to hold the bulk of his *Kampfgruppe* in the area of Verden, where its lack of mobility would prevent timely reaction if the British threatened to cross the Aller elsewhere.

By 11 April the British points of main effort at Rethem and Essel were clearly defined and Kapitän zur See von Bassewitz-Levetzow, commander of 2. Marine-Infanterie-Division, ordered a number of redeployments to counter the enemy attacks likely to follow at these points. In Divisional Operation Order No. 6 of 11 April he ordered Neitzel to assume responsibility for the right bank of the Aller sector as far south as Hülsen,[1] as well as the defence of the Verden area. For the former task a Kampfgruppe Aller would be created with two companies – Bergholz and Bormann – from Kampfgruppe Hornemann, Bataillon Kolotay, 13./7 Kompanie and a rifle platoon from Marine-Grenadier-Regiment 7, and half of 'Panzer-Löwe' 3. Kompanie. The divisional order required the regrouping for Kampfgruppe Aller to start at once and be completed by 0400 hours on 12

---

[1] TNA WO 171/4277, Special Supplement to 53rd Welsh Division INTSUM No. 231, 21 April 1945, p.3.

BELT-FED BAZOOKAS 363

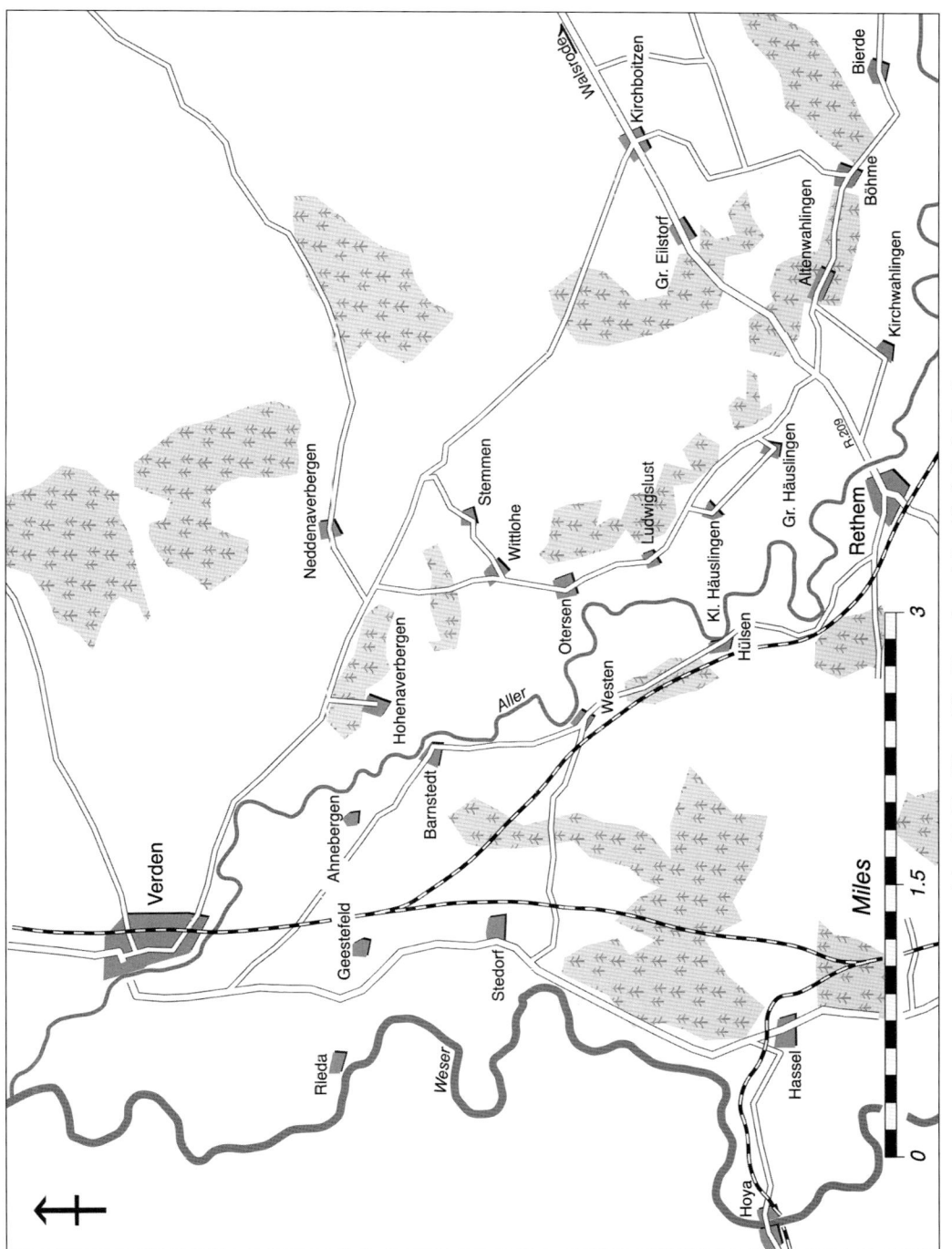

Map 56 The Weser-Aller Triangle and the Aller's Right Bank.

April. Hornemann was given written orders from Neitzel instructing him to defend the line of the Aller between Barnstedt and Hülsen so that 'any enemy crossing the river will be attacked and destroyed.'[2] As the Hungarians were already in place opposite Westen, Hornemann ordered them to 'hold the position at all costs.' This order was somewhat over-pitched as the Germans considered the Hungarians to be 'peasants' and knew they were low quality troops with suspect loyalty. In an attempt to thicken the defences opposite Westen, a platoon from Kampfgruppe Hornemann was deployed ahead of the main body to join the Hungarians. With the British already in Westen and a crossing in the area a strong possibility, it is curious why the Hungarians, who had fled earlier fighting, were not reinforced with more German troops.

158th Brigade across the Aller

On the evening of Wednesday 11 April Lieutenant Colonel Frisby, commanding officer 4 Welch, was ordered by Brigadier Wilsey to establish a small bridgehead that night on the right bank of the Aller in the Westen area with a view to a possible crossing in strength the next day. A platoon-sized force was duly despatched in assault boats, making its way with some difficulty as the Aller's swirling flood waters made navigating the cumbersome craft less than easy. The platoon commander reported the current was so powerful that a guide rope would be needed for future crossings as paddle-power alone was too hazardous. Once safely on the enemy-held bank the platoon pushed patrols forward and, meeting no opposition, the platoon commander reported all was clear. Armed with this encouraging information, Brigadier Wilsey ordered 1 E Lancs to be prepared to move from Hämelhausen to Westen and then cross the river during the remainder of the night. At 2215 hours General Ross confirmed the implementation of his Plan B and soon after 1 E Lancs received the order to start its night march to Westen. The night was pitch-black, the tracks inadequate and nearly invisible making the move across the open heath of the Hämelheide far from easy, but despite the challenges the battalion reached Westen by 0100 hours on Thursday 12 April and in good order.

British preparations for the river-crossing continued through the night. On arrival at Westen, the 1 E Lancs company commanders reported to battalion headquarters at 0130 hours and the details of the plan were confirmed. However, the night was so dark the companies had some difficulty in finding their appointed assembly areas and there was also some delay in assembling the assault boats so, to allow for this, H-hour, fixed for 0200 hours, was slipped by one hour. The crossing was not expected to be without some difficulty as the Aller at Westen was about 70 yards wide and the current strong. The rifle companies would cross in the order A, B, C then D with battalion headquarters crossing with A Company. It was planned for the initial assault to be on a narrow front and silent, at least for the first two companies. Support Company with rear battalion headquarters under the second-in-command, Major Griffin, would provide the defence of the crossing site and the administrative arrangements. A tight bridgehead would be secured and held for the remaining hours of darkness before the battalion advanced at first light to its objective, the village of Otersen.

The operation eventually got underway and the first boats from A Company were successfully launched and began to cross, carrying guide ropes to be fixed in position on the far bank. The strong current immediately created problems and when the boats were only a few yards from the bank they were rapidly swept downstream. The crews had great difficulty in handling their boats in the darkness and this generated noise, but eventually they succeeded in reaching the far bank undetected and only 100 yards from their intended landing point. A further long delay now

---

2   TNA WO 171/4277, Special Supplement to 53rd Welsh Division INTSUM No. 231, 21 April 1945, p.4.

ensued owing to difficulties establishing the ferry posts and guide ropes, and this took so long that the first streaks of dawn appeared on the horizon, causing the boat parties and the two platoons already across to look increasingly vulnerable. Fortunately for 1 E Lancs, there had thus far been no reaction from the enemy as the Hungarians had failed to establish OPs covering the river, and General Ross's decision to implement Plan B during the night 11/12 April had allowed the crossing to take place before the bulk of Kampfgruppe Aller arrived. Despite these two pieces of good fortune, events for the British soon took a distinct turn for the worse.

Thursday 12 April

Just after dawn, when B Company was crossing, the Hungarians, at last aware that something was afoot, started to engage the assault boat launching site on the left bank. They seemed unaware, however, that a full-scale crossing was underway and their initial weak reaction allowed A and B

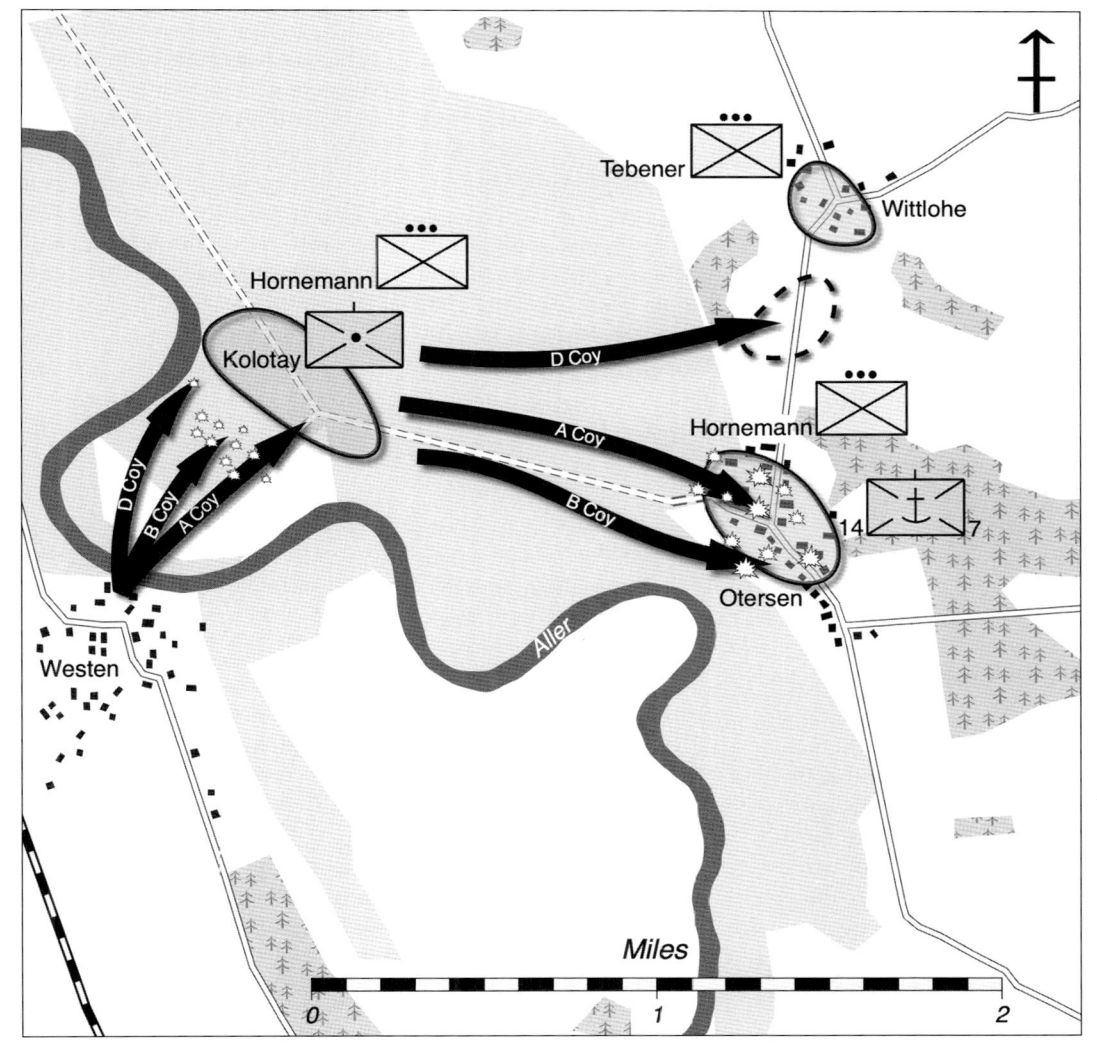

Map 57 1 E Lancs crosses the Aller – am 12 April 1945.

Companies and the advance battalion headquarters to tuck themselves into a small bridgehead on the right bank. But by the time C Company began to cross the action was hotting-up and Lieutenant Arthur Sutton, commanding 15 Platoon, describes the difficulties experienced by those crossing the river and those in the bridgehead:[3]

> Our turn came and I was in the leading boat of C Company. The men had loosened their belts and pack straps, had unslung their rifles and were kneeling in the boat. I took a firm hold on the guide rope and hung-on for dear life. The current was very strong. When we reached half-way we were fired on by rifles and machine-guns but the aim was high and the bullets cracked above us. Our luck held and we landed safely and took up position under the river bank. It was a very tight little bridgehead and now that the enemy was well-alerted, a very nasty spot to be in. Movement of any sort was impossible without drawing fire and we knew it was not going to be easy to get out of this muddy hole. First light was also coming fast, which added a further hazard and we deployed as best we could along the bank in support of A and B Companies.

The ground on the right bank was generally flat with open fields and hedgerows, but on the initial bridgehead's right flank there were slight undulations and therefore some cover allowing A Company to make progress. Fairly stiff opposition was met but the company, commanded by Major Whiteside, succeeded in getting forward along a path leading to a cross-tracks about 800 yards from the river; there, however, the platoons were pinned down by the fire and superior numbers of the Hungarians and although Whiteside tried several times to start a new attack, A Company could do little until B Company could come up on their left. But B Company, commanded by Major Storey, was held up by a series of mutually supporting machine-gun positions on their left flank and had lost an officer, Lieutenant Merrills, and the CSM, WO2 Potts. While A and B Companies were trying to advance, at 0700 hours D Company started to cross and now disaster struck. With the crossing site under continuous fire, Lieutenant Kershaw and two sections of 18 Platoon embarked on the first boat and began their perilous journey across the river. Arthur Sutton describes what happened:[4]

> D Company started to cross and it was then that I had a 'worm's eye' of a most tragic event. Suddenly the lead D Company boat lost contact with the guide rope and was swept past us in mid-stream. As some occupants stood up the boat capsized and in seconds the entire crew were in the water and went down at once. Only two soldiers managed to reach the bank on our side. I can only surmise that the party had not been prepared as we had been for such an event and had been dragged down by the weight of their equipment. This was most demoralising for us all, but we had our own worries.

Despite this tragedy, in which 13 drowned and four were never found, the remainder of D Company crossed safely. C Company then started to move forward behind A and B Companies and after a short time the Hungarians at the cross-tracks were sufficiently subdued to enable the two companies to advance east towards Otersen. C Company then took over and held the cross-tracks while D Company worked forward on the extreme left flank clearing away the enemy still holding out there. By 1200 hours, A and B Companies had fought their way forward to Otersen where their advance was halted by heavy fire from the village's defenders, artillery recruits from Kampfgruppe

---

3   Letter to the author.
4   Letter to the author.

The FBE at Westen.

Hornemann and marines from 14./7 Kompanie, who had reached the village during the night. Major Whiteside's A Company led the attack on Otersen, clearing it house by house to establish a firm base in the northern end. B Company then cleared to the southern exits and forced out the remaining defenders, who withdrew to the north leaving behind 29 dead comrades. While the remainder of 1 E Lancs consolidated in Otersen, D Company moved up the road leading from the northern exit of the village and placed itself in position half-way to Wittlohe. Pockets of enemy were still numerous and the commanding officer's scout car was shot up on this road, fortunately without any casualties.

While 1 E Lancs was consolidating the initial bridgehead, Brigadier Wilsey ordered the next battalion, 7 RWF, to cross the Aller. The battalion crossed without incident, passed through 1 E Lancs then during the early part of the morning made rapid progress by leap-frogging its companies through each other towards their objective, Wittlohe, experiencing only isolated fire on the way. With 1 E Lancs and 7 RWF expanding the bridgehead, the sappers of 555 Field Company began building 360 feet of Class 9 FBE bridge at Westen,[5] completing the bridge by 1230 hours; seven minutes later the first vehicle, a Wasp, crossed. A link to an online video, which includes an overflight of the Westen FBE, is at Appendix A, Serial 16.

The Germans, at last realising a full-scale crossing was in progress, began to move reinforcements to the area in an attempt to contain the expanding bridgehead. Kampfgruppe Tebener moved to seal the bridgehead's left flank while other reinforcements from Division Nr.480 began to move from further afield: Grenadier-A.u.E. Regiment 22 with two of its four battalions, 16 and 489; Grenadier-A.u.E. Regiment 269 with its battalions 47 and 65; and Pionier-A.u.E. Bataillon 34 were all ordered to move from their locations to the north-west of Bremen to a concentration area to the south of Rotenburg as a preliminary to deployment towards the Aller.

---

5   TNA WO 171/5570, 555 Field Company RE war diary.

The chaotic situation facing the Germans, even to the extent of knowing where their units were, is illustrated by the experiences of an artillery officer, Hauptmann Richard Lange. Lange had been the regimental adjutant of an artillery regiment on the East Front until badly wounded in June 1944. He was evacuated to hospital in Germany and was then sent to convalesce in Verden, his home town. As the fighting drew near he reported to Regiment Schaffer and on the morning of 12 April was ordered to take command of one of the batteries. Neither Lange nor the regimental headquarters knew where the battery was so he set off on foot towards the Aller to find it. He eventually reached Otersen only to see groups of British infantry where Hungarians should have been and narrowly avoided capture. Back-tracking, he found the battery in the southern part of Hohenaverbergen and thereafter fought with the gunners until captured a few days later when Verden fell.

During the early afternoon D Company 7 RWF assaulted Wittlohe, held by a platoon of recently-arrived recruits of Kampfgruppe Tebener occupying hastily-prepared defensive positions in the farms, houses and gardens. The company's brisk engagement was witnessed by Arthur Sutton:[6]

> A lot of sniping and noise, there were some casualties and the enemy were dashing about the village blazing away at everything. The place finally was cleared and when we later [on 13 April] made ourselves secure in the village, in the house I occupied I found a map of the Bremen area marked by the enemy with the German positions during the battle.

At 1430 hours 1/5 Welch, having earlier that morning been relieved by A and B Company 6 RWF from its positions to the west of Rethem and moved to Westen, began to cross the Aller to occupy positions in close defence of the Class 9 bridge and by 1830 hours had formed a defensive arc from west of Wittlohe to the Aller's bank. The battalion initially experienced some fire from isolated groups along the roads and tracks, but by mid-afternoon on 12 April organised opposition ceased and the Aller bridgehead was firmly established. Meanwhile the 7 RWF companies spent the remainder of the day expanding the bridgehead, but not without loss. In sending a platoon from D Company to investigate a road-block on the main road to the north of Wittlohe, two fusiliers were killed and three wounded when met by a volley of machine-gun and small-arms' fire.

During the afternoon B and C Squadrons 53rd Recce Regiment crossed the Class 9 bridge and began to push out into the wooded country beyond Otersen and Wittlohe. The task of the recce was to move up to the bridgehead line and then probe forward to discover the enemy's whereabouts. Crossing the bridge was not easy for the recce troops as Norman Mitchell, gunner/radio operator in 3 Troop commander's armoured car, describes:[7]

> As I recall there was considerable delay prior to C Squadron being able to cross the Class 9 bridge at Westen due to the difficulty of the bridging operation. It was only a pontoon type bridge and only one vehicle at a time was allowed to cross. The heavy armoured cars had to proceed extremely carefully and with only the driver on board. The assault troop, with its International half-tracks, was left behind as the vehicles were too heavy to cross the bridge.

---

6   Letter to the author. Arthur's widow kindly gave me the 1:100,000 map, which shows in red the British bridgehead line on the right bank.

7   PM Cowburn, *Welsh Spearhead, A History of the 53rd Reconnaissance Regiment 1940–1946* (Solingen Ohligs: Wilhelm Müller jr, 1946).

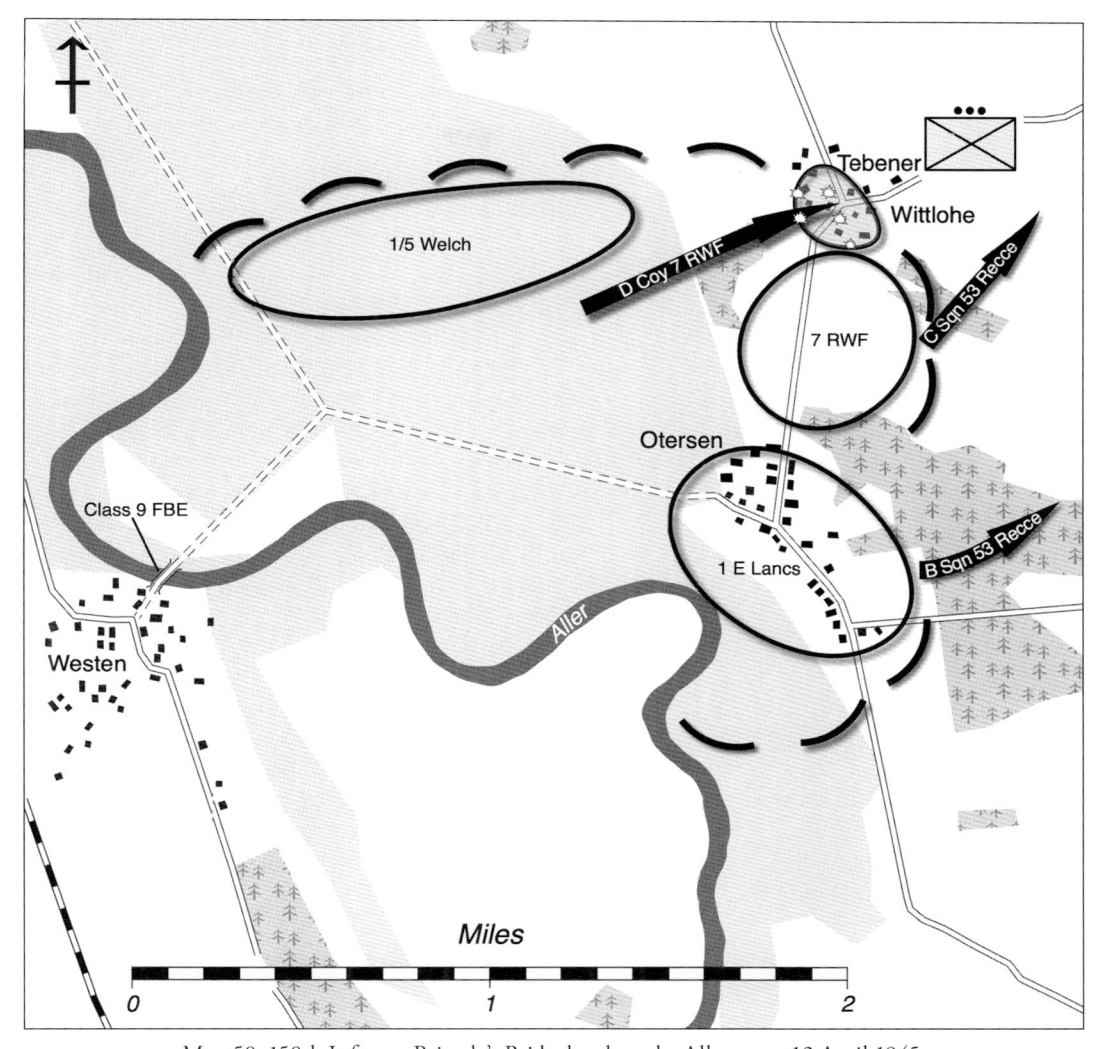

Map 58 158th Infantry Brigade's Bridgehead on the Aller – pm 12 April 1945.

By nightfall they had reached the outer edges of both Otersen and Wittlohe but as nothing more could be observed and with high risk of ambush by enemy patrols in the wooded country, the squadrons went firm for the remainder of the night.

For 158th Brigade, operations on 12 April closed with the bridgehead successfully secured and 331 prisoners taken, mainly well-armed Hungarians, who strongly protested that they always shot high to indicate their distaste for conscription into the German army. Despite their protestations, nine soldiers of 1 E Lancs were killed and 26 wounded by small-arms' fire during the course of the day. The last word on the Hungarian soldiers goes to the author of a XII Corps' log entry, who scathingly noted 'these gunners in theory appear to have been pioneers in fact, a not inappropriate fate for the representatives of a kingless kingdom until recently ruled by a fleetless admiral.[8] These

---

8   TNA WO 171/4055, GS Branch XII Corps war diary. The 'fleetless admiral' was Admiral Horthy. Following his October 1944 proclamation of an armistice with the Allies, the Germans replaced him with Szalasi, the

words notwithstanding, 158th Brigade was fortunate the crossing was achieved while Kamfgruppe Aller was still arriving. Even though the majority of the troops in the area were Hungarian, had there been time to organise counter-attacks then even these poorly-motivated troops could have made the Westen crossing a far tougher proposition.

71st Brigade advance up the Aller's right bank

While 158th Brigade fought to secure the bridgehead, Brigadier Elrington's 71st Brigade was moving to Westen to execute the second phase of the divisional plan: the advance up the right bank of the Aller. While 158th and 160th Brigades on 10 and 11 April were in action at Rethem and the area between the Weser and the Aller, 71st Brigade had been held uncommitted west of the Weser ready to exploit once an Aller crossing had been won. On 12 April divisional headquarters ordered the brigade to cross the Weser at Hoya, and by 1215 hours the lead elements were across and moving to a concentration area near Westen. During the late afternoon the brigade, led by A Squadron 53rd Recce Regiment, crossed the Class 9 at Westen in the order: 1 Oxf Bucks LI, 1 HLI and 4 RWF. The brigade plan was then to advance on a two-battalion frontage in a south-easterly direction following the line of Landesstrasse 159, with 1 Oxf Bucks LI on the left and 1 HLI on the right. Once 1 Oxf Bucks LI had captured Gross Häuslingen and 1 HLI Klein Häuslingen,[9] 4 RWF would pass through to capture Altenwahlingen and secure the area of the Aller's right bank in depth of Rethem to provide greater security for the bridging operation. To achieve this, the brigade would have to defeat Marine-Grenadier-Regiment 6.

Although 2. Marine-Infanterie-Division's concept for the battle on the Aller's right bank is unknown, the probable intention can be deduced. As Marine-Grenadier-Regiment 6's responsibility on initial deployment was to cover the Aller south of Reichsstrasse 209 between Altenwahlingen and Eilte, a frontage of some four miles, it can be assumed that there was an intention for Marine-Grenadier-Regiment 5, once it had withdrawn from Rethem, to hold a similar frontage north of Reichsstrasse 209 on the right of its sister regiment. The battle of Rethem had, however, so severely degraded Marine-Grenadier-Regiment 5 that Marine-Grenadier-Regiment 6 would now have to cover both regiments' frontages largely on its own. Divisional Operation Order No. 6 ordered the regiment to concentrate and hold itself in readiness in the area between the Häuslingens and Altenwahlingen and destroy any enemy forces attempting to advance on Reichsstrasse 209.[10] Accordingly, I./6 Bataillon, commanded by Korvettenkapitän Melzer, was given responsibility for the twin villages of Gross and Klein Häuslingen and II./6 Bataillon, commanded by Korvettenkapitän Meincke, had responsibility for Altenwahlingen. Melzer's marines were deployed with 1./6 Kompanie at Ludwigslust, 2./6 Kompanie at Klein Häuslingen, 3./6 Kompanie in the area of the cross-roads to the west of Altenwahlingen and 4./6 Kompanie in Gross Häuslingen. During the early hours of 12 April, the weary marines of Marine-Grenadier-Regiment 5 pulled back through 3./6 Kompanie to regroup in the nearby woods. Their battle-worn appearance would not have boosted morale and, with British forces known to be across the river, their comrades in Marine-Grenadier-Regiment 6 braced themselves for their part in the next, and probably final, phase of the battle of the Aller Line.

Led by A Squadron 53rd Recce Regiment, 71st Brigade's advance initially went well and no opposition was met until the recce troops hit positions near Ludwigslust held by marines from

---

leader of the ultra-nationalist 'Arrow Cross' movement.
9   TNA WO 171/5253, 1 Oxf Bucks LI war diary.
10   TNA WO 171/4277, Special Supplement to 53rd Welsh Division INTSUM No. 231, 21 April 1945, p.3.

BELT-FED BAZOOKAS 371

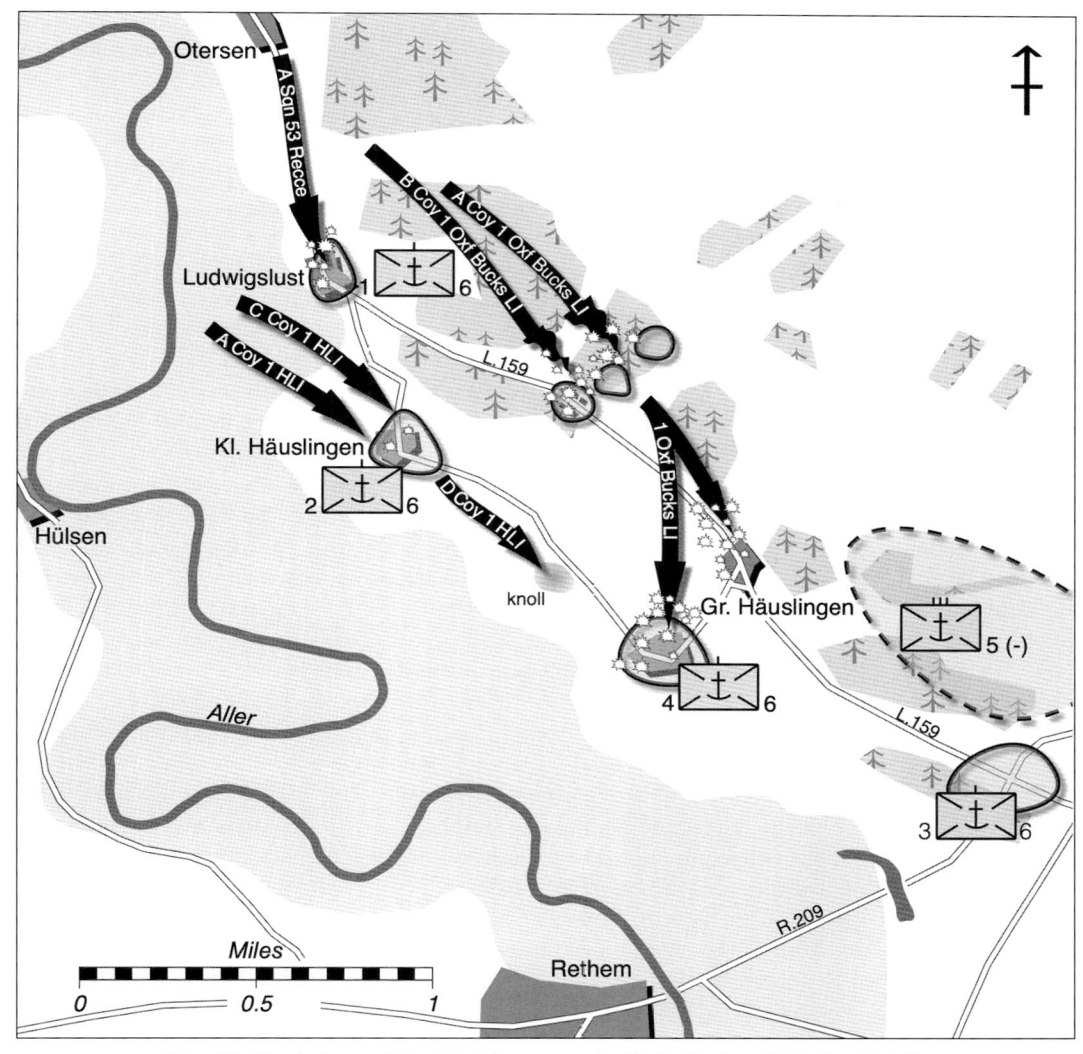

Map 59 71st Infantry Brigade's Advance on the Right Bank – 12/13 April 1945.

1./6 Kompanie heavily armed with *Panzerfaust*, and a short but vicious skirmish to eliminate these men ensued. While this action to clear the Landesstrasse 159 axis was in progress, 1 Oxf Bucks LI, commanded by Lieutenant Colonel Henry Howard,[11] bypassed Ludwigslust and with A and B Companies in the lead made good progress until they came under intense if inaccurate machine-gun fire from marines in the houses and woods about a mile short of Gross Häuslingen. It proved difficult to locate the enemy positions in the broken scrub and for a time the situation was confused. A Company attempted to outflank the opposition by manoeuvring to the left but this also met resistance and the battalion's advance came to a halt, with the two companies vulnerably strung out along narrow sandy tracks surrounded by thick pinewoods. With little knowledge

---

11 Henry Howard had an outstanding wartime career with awards of the Military Cross and Bar and Distinguished Service Order.

of the enemy's whereabouts and visibility vanishing fast with the onset of dusk, the battalion's position was precarious so Lieutenant Colonel Howard decided the companies should hold firm where they stood and await the arrival of 1 HLI to provide some flank security to their right.

While 1 Oxf Bucks LI was experiencing problems on the left axis, 1 HLI on the right initially had no such difficulties.[12] The battalion, commanded by Lieutenant Colonel Kindersley, had crossed the Westen bridge during the early evening and at 1830 hours started to advance towards its objective, Klein Häuslingen. Although opposition was encountered near Ludwigslust, the companies went forward largely unopposed. The commanding officer's plan to capture Klein Häuslingen and a prominent knoll to its south-east was to attack with two companies up: A Company right, C Company left, with D Company passing through to capture the knoll; B Company would meanwhile clear the road. Against negligible opposition the companies captured both village and knoll, and all objectives were secured by 2330 hours.

Fortunately for 71st Brigade's battalions, the ground on the right bank was flat, exposed and ideal for Vickers' fire missions and throughout the advance they received invaluable support from the guns of 1 Manchester.[13] Instead of allocating the machine-gun companies to the brigades, Major General Ross placed the companies under the centralised control of their own commanding officer, Lieutenant Colonel Crozier, to provide coordinated support for 71st and 158th Brigades' operations. Because of 158th Brigade's exposed position in the bridgehead, he sent two of C Company's Vickers platoons across the Aller to support the brigade, however it was clear to Crozier that the best way to support 71st Brigade would be to site A and B Companies' guns on the left bank in the area between Westen and Hülsen and shoot across the front of the advancing battalions; D Company, with its four 4.2-in mortar platoons, would also be best-sited on the left bank. The plan worked well as marines withdrawing south-eastwards across the meadows were unable to identify the source of the fire, resulting in them continuing to move in the open and provide a perfect target for the machine-gunners.

While 1 Oxf Bucks LI fought to clear the Gross Häuslingen area, 1 HLI held the right flank in the area of Klein Häuslingen, spending the day mopping up the few remaining enemy and waiting for 4 RWF to pass through to capture Altenwahlingen, expected to occur at first light on 13 April.[14] 4 RWF, commanded by Lieutenant Colonel Hanmer, had been detached from the brigade on 11 April to takeover the task of securing Nienburg from 2 Mons but was relieved of this task by 6 HLI and had subsequently moved by truck to concentrate in the woods a mile or so from Westen. Although a lone Fw 190, from either NSGr. 20 or III./KG 200, dropped a bomb in the area of battalion headquarters, the remainder of 12 April passed uneventfully for the battalion and at 2320 hours it began to cross the Aller, preparatory to following the brigade's other two battalions on the Aller's right bank. Once across, the first mile was covered fairly rapidly but the advance was then delayed owing to the problems 1 Oxf Bucks LI was having clearing the marines of I./6 Bataillon straddling the axis at Gross Häuslingen.

With 2. Marine-Infanterie-Division fighting desperately to hold the Aller Line, the bizarre world of the *Führer* conferences carried on, unruffled by real events. On 12 April Admiral Wagner, Dönitz's representative at the conference, received a report from Reichsleiter Bormann concerning alleged insubordination by members of the division when they were in Itzehoe.[15] The *Landrat* (town council) of Itzehoe had made the unspecified complaint. The matter had evidently been investigated already as Wagner was able to reply that the report was invalid and that Dönitz

---

12 TNA WO 171/5202, 1 HLI war diary.
13 The 1 Manchester war diary for April 1945 is missing from TNA Kew. However, when I started my research in 1982 it was present so the narrative includes information now lost to future research.
14 TNA WO 171/5281, 4 RWF war diary.
15 Jak Showell (ed.), *Führer Conferences on Naval Affairs*, p.483.

Vickers machine-gunners of 1 Manchester engaging targets on the right bank. Sticking upright in the field forward left of the gun is a zero post, used to align the gun when firing in the indirect role. A watering can has been appropriated to fill the gun's condenser can.

wished Bormann to take steps against its originator. With the Third *Reich* in its death throes and its soldiers dying in their tens of thousands in futile battles, discussion of trivia and petty point-scoring between the leaders continued unabated.

Friday 13 April

Clearing the Weser-Aller triangle

Despite progress on the Aller's right bank, fighting was still continuing in the Weser-Aller triangle. It will be recalled that 4 Welch had been tasked to clear this area, occupied by marines from Marine-Grenadier-Regiment 7, but the battalion's efforts to advance further up the left bank from Westen and Stedorf, captured on the evening of 10 April, had met stubborn resistance from Kapitän zur See Neitzel's marines and we heard in the previous chapter how hard the 4 Welch carrier platoon and A Squadron 5 RTR had to fight to capture Barnstedt. By 13 April, A Company was in Ahnebergen, B Company in Rieda, C Company in Barnstedt and D Company in Geestefeld (see Map 56).

The marines now attempted to seize the initiative by launching a series of small but violent counter-attacks on these villages, a manoeuvre that was also designed to cover the withdrawal to Verden of other marines still on the left bank. A captured set of Neitzel's orders have an air of desperation, not to mention an unusual mission:[16]

---

16 TNA WO 171/4277, Special Supplement to 53rd Welsh Division INTSUM No. 231, 21 April 1945, p.5.

Regrouping of the defences of Verden and the Aller sector

From now on and all through the night the enemy will be attacked in his positions by small assault forces (20–30 men). During the night 12–13 April the following attacks will be carried out:

1. By assault troops of II./7 Bataillon on Stedorf.
2. By assault troops of Kompanie Klemm on Barnstedt.
3. By assault troops of Bataillon Hornemann [Abteilung 22] on Wittlohe.

The object is to deprive the English of the pleasure of sleeping at night with honourless German women and to ensure that they live in a constant state of danger and uncertainty in the villages they have occupied. No assault troops without anti-tank weapons! Vehicles, guns etc are to be blown sky-high! Anything that is found belonging to the enemy must be destroyed. Weapons: MG 42, StG 44, MP 40, *Panzerfaust* and grenades. All packs will be left behind. Be as manoeuvrable and silent as possible. H-hour approximately 0230 hours.

In the event, Stedorf would be spared as the marines of II./7 Bataillon attacked Geestefeld instead. This village, situated about a mile to the north of Stedorf, was attacked either as a consequence of the fog of war or as the objective of a counter-attack. The following account by Major 'Zonk' Lewis, commanding D Company 4 Welch, illustrates the ferocity of a small but bitter action against Neitzel's troops:[17]

> On 12 April I was ordered to capture the village of Geestefeld with my company, supported by a troop of tanks. After the enemy had lost only a dozen killed they made a hasty retreat. We dug all-round defensive positions and prepared to hold it for the night. We were now some miles in front of the remainder of the battalion and the section and platoon positions could only be tied up with fire owing to the limited number of men available. Our strength was becoming slowly depleted.
>
> All went well until about midnight when a runner came into my HQ with the rather shattering news that a number of the enemy had penetrated our position unseen. Half the company were on duty at the time while the other half rested in the house. The enemy had entered the houses after overpowering the sentries and had awakened the occupants with the order to put up their hands. With their weapons removed my men had no option. The situation was serious. By this time company HQ was covered by *Spandaus* and any move brought a burst of fire. Before any action could be taken there was a series of loud bangs as the enemy started shooting up the transport and company HQ with *Panzerfaust*. The explosions in company HQ were deafening and the whole building was shaking and burst into flames as the assault continued. I gave instructions for company HQ to make a dash for it across the open stretch to a building 100 yards away from where we could organise one platoon not involved and attempt to restore the situation. Just at that moment the reserve ammo went up with a roar and the building started to collapse around us. We could not stay a second longer, so through the hole where a window had been we dashed to our new positions. By the light of the flames I saw my sergeant major dash past. He turned his head and shouted: 'And I was going on leave tomorrow, Sir!'.

---

17   Major General CEN Lomax, *The History of the Welch Regiment, 1919–1951* (Cardiff: Western Mail & Echo Ltd, 1952), pp.248–250.

The situation was now getting very involved and it was difficult to tell which were enemy and which were our own men. A general free-for-all started and the enemy found themselves being attacked by unarmed men with flying fists and feet. There is no etiquette in war. It was a display of guts and courage. Simultaneously, all those who had been taken prisoner turned upon their armed captives. One private soldier, shot through the lung in getting away, turned round and re-entered the house and set upon the enemy again, paying with his life. Before long the enemy dead included their two officers, neither of whom had a bullet wound on them, and all the enemy were learning by experience what the British soldier can do with his fists and hands. Unarmed combat instruction had not been in vain. Before long the enemy melted away leaving their dead and undoubtedly bearing many reminders of the fight. They had failed to take a single prisoner. I will not belittle them, however. They were German marines and had fought with real guts.

At first light the carrier platoon arrived to give us assistance but by that time the fight was over and we had reorganised ourselves. Not a brick of my former HQ remained standing. All the transport and equipment was destroyed with the exception of the three tanks and they were only saved by beating out the flames at great risk during the fighting. The stretcher bearers had a busy time binding up the injured fists. I found myself left with only that in which I stood up. A later claim from the army realised nearly a tenth of the value of personal kit that I had lost. It was equivalent to my having fought for some months with no pay at all. An expensive night's fighting! As far as we could ascertain, two enemy patrols each about 20 strong had slipped through our defences in the dark from two different directions.

Although not mentioned in Major Lewis's account of the prisoners turning on their captors, the lead role in the incident was played by members of 2 Troop A Squadron 5 RTR. Two crews of 2 Troop and members of D Company were resting up in a house after the village's capture when marines burst in. The first German through the door was a burly marine brandishing a MP 40, followed by the remainder of his patrol who rapidly rounded up the 15 British soldiers and began to disarm them. During the patting-down process, the thickness of the leather jacket worn by Lieutenant Louis Jones, the troop commander, prevented the German frisking him from noticing the Walther P38 pistol he kept inside his battledress. Once satisfied that the British were disarmed, the marines began to move their prisoners out of the house, and despite having a pistol held to his back by the marine officer commanding the German patrol, Louis Jones suddenly swung around and with the help of a NCO threw the officer to the ground and managed to shoot him with the Walther. The marines opened fire and hand-to-hand fighting ensued. In the confines of the building the tank crews and D Company soldiers were able to overcome the Germans, who now leaderless, retreated leaving behind two dead and three wounded. Louis Jones not only prevented the men in the house from being taken prisoner but the ferocity of the action checked other marines from attacking D Company's headquarters and convinced them to withdraw from Geestefeld. For his bravery and initiative Louis Jones was awarded an immediate Military Cross.

71st Brigade battle on the right bank

We had left 1 Oxf Bucks LI on the right bank trying to clear the enemy from the brigade axis at Gross Häuslingen so that 4 RWF could move through to attack Altenwahlingen and complete 71st Brigade's operation to secure the area opposite Rethem. During the evening the battalion's companies finally began to overcome the opposition from I./6 Bataillon at Gross Häuslingen and by midnight were once more able to start moving forward. In the early hours of 13 April, A Company attempted to capture a small wood lying to the east of Landesstrasse 159. This attack was unsuccessful against the marines of 4./6 Kompanie and so the company outflanked the wood to its left and established itself in another small wood to the south-east. C Company meanwhile had secured the area of the triangle of roads between Landesstrasse 159 and Gross Häuslingen allowing D Company to pass through and, by 0045 hours, capture the village unopposed. B Company completed the final manoeuvre of this phase by moving up through C Company to secure the houses straggling along Landesstrasse 159. This resulted in some small-arms' fire from the marines holding the houses, but they were quickly subdued by an artillery concentration fired by 72nd Medium Regiment and during the rest of the night there were no signs of enemy activity, allowing the companies to consolidate in the positions they had gained.

The relative peace of the night ended as dawn broke. Although it was thought the enemy were cleared from the area, small pockets of marines were in fact scattered throughout B and C Companies' positions and a strongpoint of platoon strength was discovered near C Company's headquarters in the centre of the triangle of roads. 4 RWF, expected to capture Altenwahlingen by first light, was once again held up by the confused fighting in the Gross Häuslingen area and

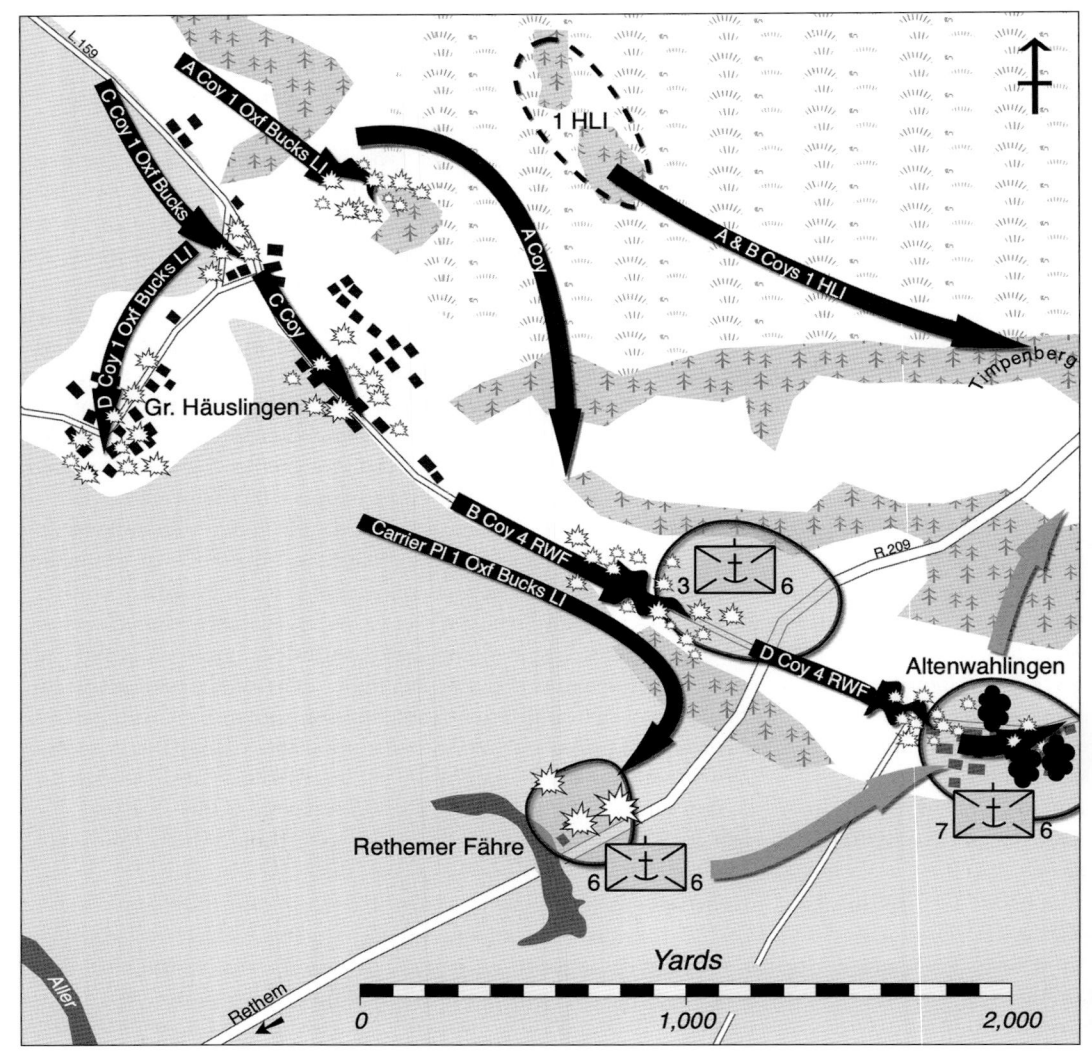

Map 60 71st Infantry Brigade – pm 13 April 1945.

confusion reigned for much of the day with both battalions attempting to clear the opposition. At 0730 hours the leading 4 RWF companies were ordered to push on towards their start line, the cross-roads 700 yards to the west of Altenwahlingen, but to do this B Company, with C Company following behind, had to mount an attack to force its way forward. The area of the cross-roads was held by 3./6 Kompanie and as soon as the two companies came within range, the marines opened up with intense machine-gun fire and the attack ground to a halt. With casualties mounting, and despite some of the battalion's carriers moving forward to provide a measure of protected fire support, the soldiers of B Company were pinned down by fire from both flanks. The problems faced by 4 RWF were exacerbated by a split developing between the lead and rear companies, still back in the wood in the area of Gross Häuslingen and caught up in renewed fighting in that area. The attack to clear 3./6 Kompanie from the area of the cross-roads lost momentum and the ensuing delay forced an indefinite postponement of the assault on Altenwahlingen. However, to ensure the marines from II./6 Bataillon in Altenwahlingen had no respite, during the morning the village was subjected to harassing fire. At 0900 hours it was engaged with sixty 4.2-in mortar rounds fired by 13 and 15 Platoons 1 Manchester followed by a shoot by the Vickers of B Company, and in the early afternoon Typhoons from 184 Squadron attacked with RPs.

While the battalions of 71st Brigade battled to clear the right bank, the sappers of 244 Field Company reinforced by two platoons from 555 Field Company were engaged in bridge-building at Rethem. By 1430 hours all the equipment necessary had been off-loaded from trucks and two rafts and 60 feet of a 110-foot Class 40 Bailey pontoon bridge began to be constructed. Progress soon came to a halt, however, as the site was subjected to well-directed artillery and mortar fire whenever the sappers started work, eventually forcing bridging operations to stop altogether. Further delay was caused when shell-fire sank one of the rafts and headway was only made after four flights of Typhoons were called in to attack the area from which the fire was thought to originate.

During the remainder of the day B and C Companies 1 Oxf Bucks LI, supported by S Company, fought hard to mop-up the marines in the houses and woods in the Gross Häuslingen area. This became an expensive business and the battalion lost Captain Hawley, killed with his driver when their carrier was hit by a *Panzerfaust*, and Major de Warrenne Warren, 2nd Lieutenant Norris and Lieutenant Hedges all wounded. Nine other soldiers of the battalion also died on this day. As so little progress was being made on the main axis, 1 HLI was ordered to concentrate in the woods to the north-east of Gross Häuslingen and be prepared to bypass 4 RWF, if the battalion was still unable to make headway, and attack Altenwahlingen from the north. By evening the situation gradually began to improve as 1 Oxf Bucks LI's hard work allowed the two rear 4 RWF companies to begin a contested but slow move forward to join the lead companies trying to clear the cross-roads. In an attempt to outflank the opposition on Landesstrasse 159, the carrier platoon and two sections from C Company 1 Ox Bucks LI moved through the woods on B Company 4 RWF's right with the intention of capturing the bridge and house at Rethemer Fähre, about 700 yards to the south-west of the cross-roads. This move met heavy opposition from marines of 6./6 Kompanie, commanded by Oberleutnant zur See Fuchs, the first marines from II./6 Bataillon encountered by the British. Following an artillery bombardment, Fuchs's company was eventually forced from the area and the remainder of C Company moved up to secure the objective. The nearby bridge carrying Reichsstrasse 209 over the ox-bow lake was found thoroughly demolished, as previously reported by the patrol from 2 Mons.

At 2000 hours B Company, now commanded by Captain Baxter in place of the wounded de Warrenne Warren, cleared the last marines that had resisted A Company during the previous night from the small wood to the east of Gross Häuslingen. The battalion's positions were finally secure and at 2035 hours it was able to report to 71st Brigade that 4 RWF was closing on the area of the cross-roads. By 2200 hours the Welsh had three companies digging-in at the cross-roads and one, D Company, had managed to enter the western edge of Altenwahlingen, although it was checked by vigorous small-arms' fire. Meanwhile, C Company 4 RWF was ordered to send a patrol to Kirchwahlingen to check whether the enemy was still holding this hamlet, situated on the only bypass route for Reichsstrasse 209.

The marines now readied themselves for the next phase of the British operation on the right bank, the assault on Altenwahlingen. 6./6 Kompanie, previously to the west of the village, had withdrawn in reasonable order when the cross-roads and Rethemer Fähre fell and now joined Oberleutnant zur See Marhenke's 7./6 Kompanie in its previously-prepared defensive positions in Altenwahlingen. The battle for the village began at 2245 hours when D Company 4 RWF pushed into the first buildings from its foothold near the western edge and systematically began to clear the houses and farms, making maximum use of flame from its Wasps. The two marine companies offered spirited resistance but were gradually forced out of the village as the buildings burnt down around them. By 2315 hours D Company seemed to have captured Altenwahlingen but, terrier-like, the marines refused to release their grip and clung on to the eastern end by the cemetery. A last desperate counter-attack launched by 7./6 Kompanie and Oberleutnant zur See Müller's 8./6 Kompanie from Böhme was halted and the marine companies withdrew to the woods to the north and east. By the end of the battle, half the village had been burnt to the ground and two officers and 34 marines lay dead; a heavy price for the futile defence of one small village.

It will be recalled that 1 HLI was ordered to be prepared to attack Altenwahlingen from the north if 4 RWF was unable to make progress towards the village. Even though Altenwahlingen was now captured, the first part of this plan was put into effect as it was felt that a measure of flank protection from the north was necessary, and so it soon proved. At 2230 hours A and B Companies 1 HLI were ordered to advance from the battalion concentration area and secure the forested sand dunes astride Reichsstrasse 209 in the area known as Timpenberg. Their advance is described by Captain Ramsay, second-in-command of A Company:[18]

> Earlier during the night, as the company had encountered no opposition we established a position in a large farm. One youthful German marine was taken prisoner, giving us an idea whom we were up against and as events showed they were brave and reckless fighters but had not much idea of the tactical situation. On Friday 13th, a day which must have given the superstitious cause to think, A and B Companies were to move across country and establish positions astride the main road leading forward from the area where the bridge was being built, into enemy country. Darkness fell just as the two companies set off, B Company leading, to make their way by rather indefinite tracks to the area ordered. F echelon transport was taken. The ground was low-lying in parts and intersected by deep drains. Eventually, spurred by a longer halt than usual, A Company commander went forward and found that progress was barred by a deep ditch, crossed only by a plank. Obviously the transport could not go on and so the two Jeeps and two carriers were left there and told to await further orders. They eventually made their way back to battalion HQ through enemy-held ground. The marching personnel then carried on and after a slight brush with an enemy patrol, reached the approximate area of the objective.

---

18 Lewis Balfour Oatts, *Proud Heritage – The Story of the Highland Light Infantry, Vol 4, 1919–1959* (London: Thomas Nelson & Sons Ltd, 1963), p.203.

The Westen bridgehead expands

Back on the left flank of the divisional bridgehead, 158th Brigade made slow progress expanding the perimeter against pockets of German resistance in the woods and heathland and much of the day was spent mopping-up. At 1600 hours orders were held at brigade headquarters at Otersen and instructions given for the brigade's next phase: 7 RWF was ordered to clear the road to Verden (the divisional axis) and capture Hohenaverbergen; 1 E Lancs, by now relieved by 1/5 Welch in Otersen, would move to concentrate in Wittlohe prior to advancing to capture Neddenaverbergen; once the two battalions had secured their objectives 1/5 Welch would complete the operation with an advance to capture Armsen. 53rd Recce Regiment was tasked to expand the bridgehead in an easterly direction and capture Stemmen. Norman Mitchell takes up the recce's story:[19]

> 3 Troop, an armoured car troop commanded by Lieutenant Frank Long, proceeded to the village of Wittlohe, which had been captured by a company of the East Lancs. They were in the process of digging-in a defensive position around the outskirts and having exchanged the usual pleasantries with their forward outpost ('Good luck recce – rather you than us!') we proceeded down the road towards Stemmen with the scout car leading the heavy armoured car in the standard first contact procedure. On reaching the farm where we later harboured for the night, Lieutenant Long called up the support troop in their carriers to check whether the farm was occupied by Germans. They reported it clear. In view of the nature of the terrain, hedgerows and heathland scrub, it was decided that the best way to approach and clear Stemmen was for the armoured cars to proceed down the road, with 6 Troop on foot clearing the hedges of any Germans who might be lurking with bazookas. From movement observed from the cars, it was obvious that Stemmen had a well-planned defensive ring of slit trenches, which on our approach were being reinforced by marines. At this point the leading scout car came under small-arms' and machine-gun fire and I heard Corporal Lilley shout to his carrier section to take cover. There then developed a heated exchange between his section and the Germans, with my armoured car firing HE into the row of houses, which was obviously the local HQ. At this stage dusk was falling and the squadron leader ordered a withdrawal to the farmyard, which we had passed earlier. Major Goldsmid then set up an all-round defensive ring around the farm building and within the farmyard.

Back on the Aller's left bank 160th Brigade had a relatively quiet day. The brigade plan in-being the night before had intended 2 Mons to cross the Aller in boats at first light and then take over the area between Altenwahlingen and Kirchwahlingen; 6 RWF would cross later via Rethem's Class 40 bridge as soon as it was completed and take over the area of the two Häuslingen villages. The execution of this plan was however delayed by the Germans' tenacity on the right bank and as a consequence 160th Brigade had remained in its concentration area on the left. At 1300 hours Lieutenant Colonel Brooke of 2 Mons was warned that his battalion would not now cross the Aller at Rethem but was to be prepared to move to Westen to take over defence of the FBE bridge site. He visited HQ 158th Brigade later that afternoon and was ordered to relieve, by 0700 hours on 14 April, the two companies of 1/5 Welch and one company of 1 E Lancs at the bridge.

6 RWF also received orders, but these were of a very different nature and concerned its part in operations on the right bank once the Rethem bridge was open. The battalion would come under command of 4th Armoured Brigade and advance from Rethem as an integral part of an armoured manoeuvre. To enable the infantry battalion to operate with the tanks, the brigade had been

---

19 Cowburn, *Welsh Spearhead, A History of the 53rd Reconnaissance Regiment 1940–1946*, Annex C.

allocated the Kangaroos of F Squadron 49 APC Regiment.[20] At 2000 hours the Kangaroos arrived in the concentration area near Stöcken and married up with the battalion. Despite the lateness of the day, the battalion immediately began rehearsing climbing in and out of their new steeds and learning about their tactical handling. For the Welsh infantrymen this was a totally new way of waging warfare and they spent most of the rest of the night discussing with the officers and men who crewed the vehicles how they would fight together over the coming days.

4 Welch, meanwhile, by way of a series of company attacks, finally overcame the opposition from the remaining German-held villages in the northern part of the Weser-Aller triangle. By evening C Company was in Barnstedt; A Company in Ahnebergen; D Company in Stedebergen and B Company in Rieda. B Company subsequently established an OP on the left bank of the Aller opposite Verden and virtually all Germans were now killed, captured or driven from the triangle and, in this area at least, organised resistance was at an end.

Night 13/14 April

The German counter-attacks

Any thoughts the men of 71st and 158th Brigades may have had that they had finished off the threat on the Aller's right bank were misplaced as the marines planned decisive counter-attacks for the night 13/14 April, with the intention of destroying the bridgehead opposite Westen, driving a wedge between the two brigades on the right bank, before cutting off and destroying 71st Brigade in the south. Notwithstanding its losses from the battle for Altenwahlingen the previous day, the Germans had sufficient forces in the shape of Korvettenkapitän Meincke's II./6 Bataillon to attack the bridgehead's right flank. However, equivalent strength was not immediately on hand for attacking the left flank, so both battalions of Marine-Grenadier-Regiment 7 were moved south to supplement Kampfgruppe Tebener for its attack on the British bridgehead. Also, additional troops in the form of Hauptmann Kessel's Pi.ROB.Btl.Nienburg were moved from their position in reserve at Kirchboitzen to a concentration area in woods near Stemmen, where they were held pending the attack. For the forthcoming operation Kessel's battalion was divided between Marine-Grenadier-Regiment 5 and 7, as detailed in a captured set of Kessel's orders giving the concept of operations for the attack:[21]

> **Battalion Operation Order for Tonight's Attack**
>
> Kampfgruppe Neitzel and Kampfgruppe Jordan are eliminating the Otersen bridgehead by a night attack. Pi.ROB.Btl.Nienburg less 3. Kompanie are under command Kampfgruppe Neitzel; 3. Kompanie under command Kampfgruppe Jordan. H-hour 2245 hours. Kampfgruppe Neitzel is attacking Wittlohe and Otersen with two battalions and will capture the two villages. Left battalion in contact with 1. Kompanie Kampfgruppe Tebener and pivoting on the latter will by-pass Wittlohe to the east and capture Otersen. This attack will take place when it is considered that the enemy has been sufficiently weakened by the attacks of Kampfgruppe Neitzel but in any event not later than 2200 hours.
>
> (Signed) KESSEL Hauptmann

---

20 TNA WO 171/4722, 49 APC Regiment war diary.
21 TNA WO 171/4277, Special Supplement to 53rd Welsh Division INTSUM No. 231, 21 April 1945, p.5.

BELT-FED BAZOOKAS 381

The situation for the British forces on the Aller's right bank before the counter-attacks struck was as follows: on the left flank in 158th Brigade's area 7 RWF was slowly advancing north to capture Hohenaverbergen, 1 E Lancs was in a concentration area at Wittlohe preparing to advance to Neddenaverbergen and 1/5 Welch was in the area of Otersen. On the bridgehead's right flank in 71st Brigade's area 1 Oxf Bucks LI's companies were holding the Gross Häuslingen area and tasked to keep open the brigade axis; 4 RWF's A and D Companies were in Altenwahlingen while B and C Companies held the area of the cross-roads to its west; 1 HLI was spread out with A and B Companies forward on 4 RWF's left flank consolidating in the forested area of Timpenberg, C and D Companies were moving from the Häuslingens to join them, while S Company was in Ludwigslust. 53rd Recce Regiment was reinforcing the two brigades, with C Squadron supporting 158th Brigade and located in the Wittlohe area, B Squadron covering Otersen, where RHQ and the Support Group were located, and A Squadron detached to 71st Brigade and on Landesstrasse 159 north of the Häuslingens.

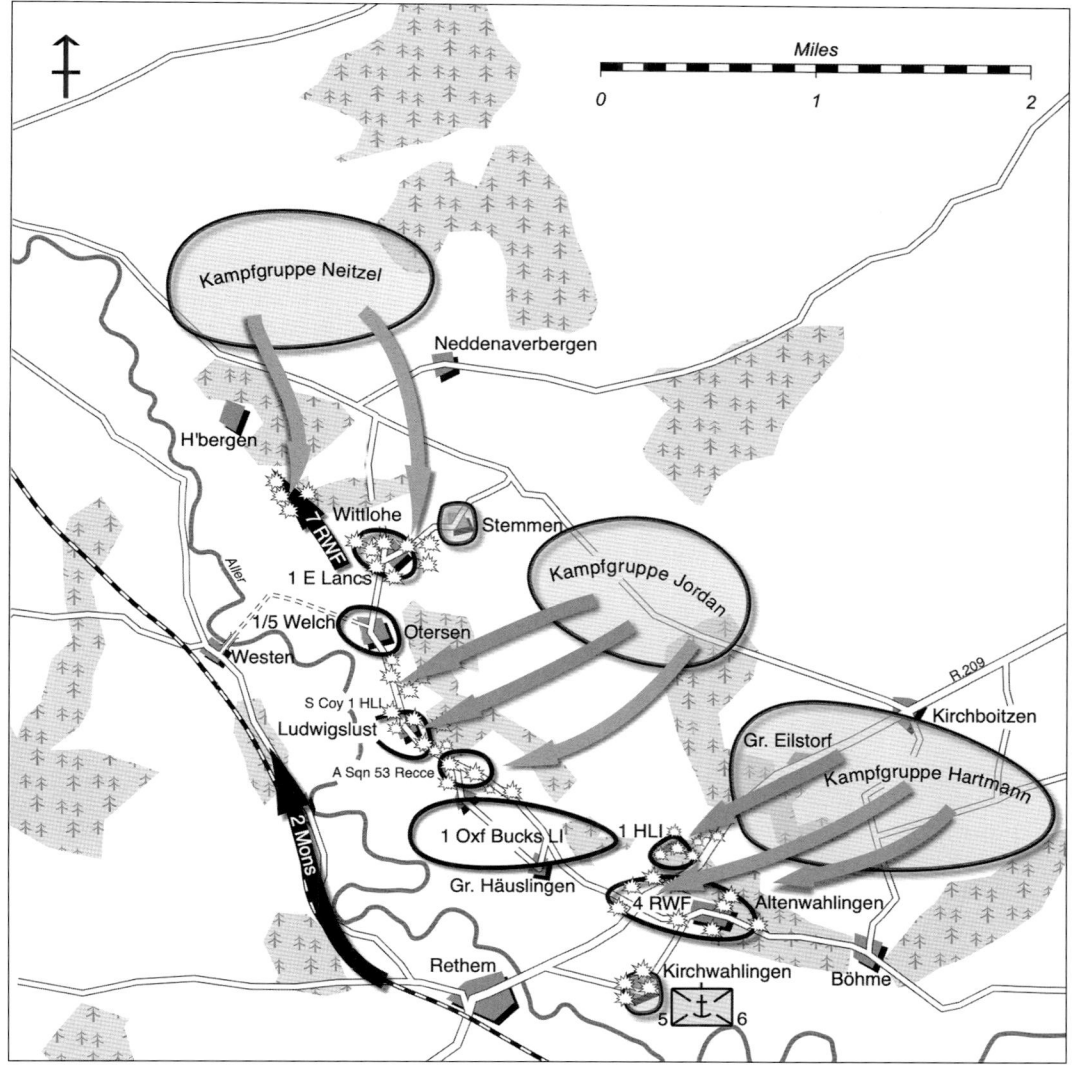

Map 61 The German Counter-Attacks – 13/14 April 1945.

At about 2300 hours the counter-attacks started on the left flank with fairly heavy artillery concentrations, including airbursts, falling on the British-held areas. The shelling was followed by infantry attacks on 7 RWF. As the night was pitch-black, the situation rapidly became extremely confused, resulting in D Company 7 RWF being overrun, C Company being encircled but not dislodged from holding the area of higher ground it had captured earlier that night, and the Germans infiltrating the woods where the battalion had its headquarters. For 7 RWF, bitter, close-quarter fighting ensued throughout the night. The recce regiment was also vigorously attacked and the associated confusion is clear from this account involving C Squadron:[22]

> The day [13 April] passed with patrols and a realisation that if the enemy was still lurking in the thick pinewoods frequently interspersed with sandy tracks, he would probably be very difficult to locate and push back completely. Towards evening C Squadron found that the village of Stemmen in their area was ringed with trenches and that these trenches were filled with an enemy who did not intend evacuating them without a fight. But at that moment it was necessary to prevent infiltration to the Westen bridge rather than to push ahead, so the squadron withdrew to a group of farm buildings round a central courtyard about a mile and half away and harboured for the night.
>
> At 2300 hours the squadron stood-to for an hour on information given by the night patrols who reported the sound of movement. At 2345 hours the first of four attacks began. This was from the north and was accompanied by a fusillade of small-arms' fire and bazooka bombs, one of which penetrated squadron HQ, shook-up the operators and destroyed the wireless link to regiment. Soon the buildings began to burn, and with this back-cloth of crimson and gold the scene began to resemble some medieval impression of hell. Burning buildings, persistent enemy, and vehicles and stores in increasing danger of destruction presented three simultaneous problems; the troops being concerned with the safety of themselves and their belongings as well as with the dispatch of the enemy. But the enemy was beaten-off and the harbour area had not been entered. There was a short time to breathe.
>
> At 0415 hours the enemy attacked from the rear in much the same strength as before but were repulsed by 6 Troop on its own, though the glare from the still burning buildings silhouetted, for the benefit of the enemy, the remainder of the squadron, which had been drawn in nearer to the central courtyard. At 0300 hours on 14 April came a third attack, this time from the west, the most persistent and dangerous of all coming immediately on the heels of the second.
>
> These two attacks were believed to have been made by two companies of marines, who had been fighting unsuccessfully with 1 E Lancs on our left for the possession of Wittlohe and had been attracted to Stemmen by the hope of a less bloody victory. This time they penetrated the perimeter of the farm defences and fought for a short time in the courtyard, even forming a small ammunition dump there. Major Goldsmid, although badly wounded in the face, arms and legs, disregarded his personal troubles and organised the defence with the Humbers firing all they had outwards over the heads of the carrier crews who manned the perimeter slit trenches. Burning vehicles cast an eerie light over the scene, but fortunately the enemy was not able to reinforce his original success, a fact which he seemed to take gradually and reluctantly to heart, for he withdrew at length, urged on his way by redoubled intensity of fire from every gun the squadron could bring to bear.

---

22 Cowburn, *Welsh Spearhead*, pp.123–126.

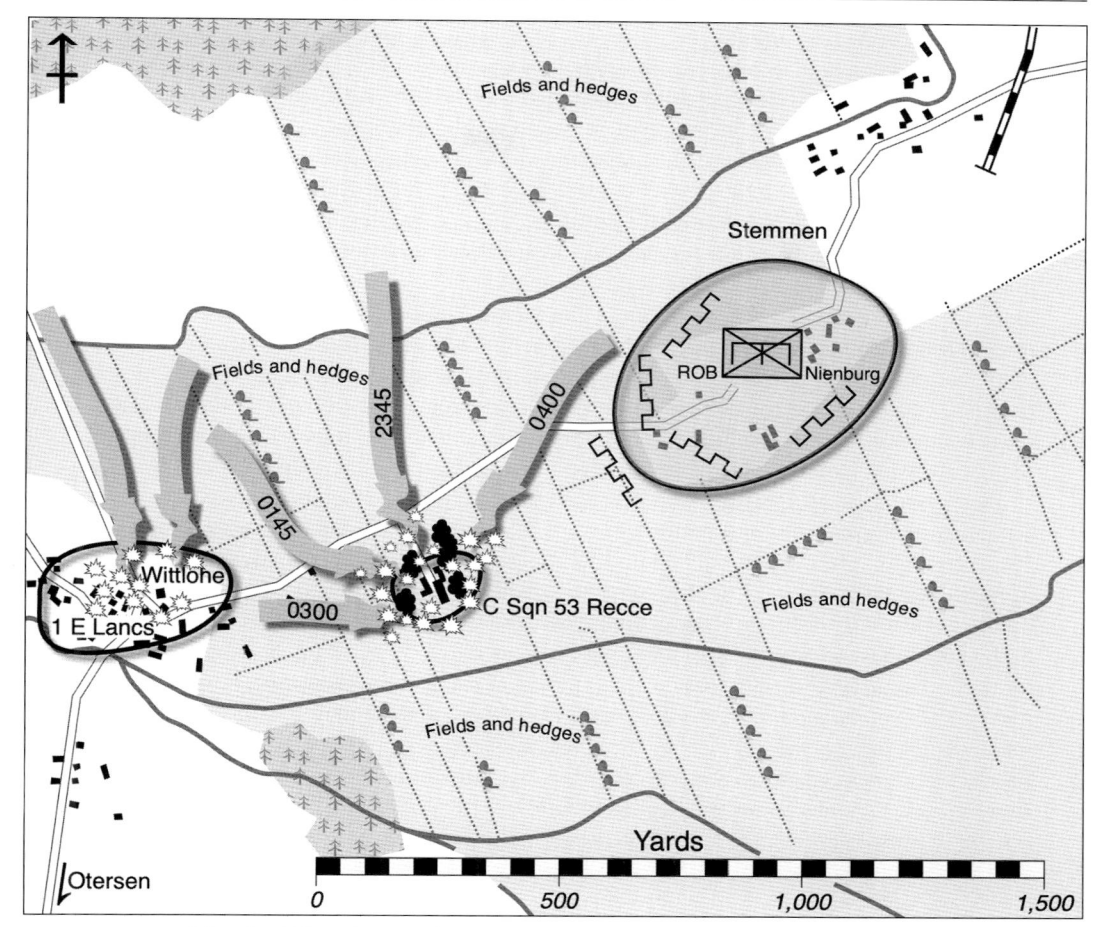

Map 62 C Squadron 53rd Recce Regiment under attack – 13/14 April 1945.

The fourth attack at 0400 hours was less bitter and might be likened to a Parthian shot to cover withdrawal.[23] Towards dawn, reinforcements from B Squadron arrived, necessarily prevented till then from any active form of assistance by C Squadron's all-round fire. When all was over, Major Goldsmid reported to RHQ to say that everything was in order, that only one man had been killed but a dozen had been wounded, that a good many vehicles and stores could no longer be considered serviceable parts of his squadron G1098[24] and finally that he would go to hospital to be patched up.

Corporal Henderson of 5 Troop C Squadron gives a vivid impression of the fighting:[25]

---

23 A tactic used by Parthian archers mounted on light horses, who would turn their bodies back to shoot at a pursuing enemy while retreating at full gallop.
24 G1098 is the table of stores held by a sub-unit (ie company or squadron) and includes objects such as spades and axes as well as serial numbered and controlled items such as compasses, watches and binoculars. Vehicles were not included in G1098.
25 Cowburn, *Welsh Spearhead*, pp.127–128.

We were bedded down nicely when at about 11 o'clock we were awakened by fighting and shouting in the village to our rear [Wittlohe]. No one knew what was happening until we were informed that a strong party of enemy had attacked the infantry [1 E Lancs] behind us and was holding half the village. Not so good we thought. Then it was our turn! Whoof, Bang, Crash! They were upon us having crept up to the copse from the village [Stemmen] in front of us. Bazookas, stick grenades, a lot of shouting and general confusion, all came at once. They infiltrated into our forward positions and two or three even reached the edge of the farmyard, but the Besas got to work and we eventually drove them back. I had foolishly not made a trench and in all this I was sweating blue bricks, hacking away roots with my blunt shovel in a foot-deep trench. In the end I gave it up and lay down flat with my nose just sticking over the top. Luckily nothing came my way as during this time I was getting all the ammunition and grenades I could, grenades being my favourite weapon because Jerry does not know which direction they come from and cannot therefore retaliate so accurately. I was between the road and a ditch, which had 11 inches of mud in it. I firmly believed that the enemy would come next time up this ditch so I found myself a new position and waited.

They came in from the right and managed to set the farm-house on fire, which had its advantages for both sides, but mainly for us as it lit up the surrounding ground better than any Verey light. There seemed to be hundreds of them by the row they made. The Besas were firing endless belts and Jerry seemed to be firing belt-fed bazookas back. The blast from those bazookas knocked all the wind out of your body, and I was 50 yards away on the opposite side of the farm-house I felt very sorry for anyone in that vicinity, and didn't hold out much hope for them. But somehow they stuck to their guns…A small party then tried to come in from the rear. They must have been absolute fanatics for they came straight for the farm buildings over a completely flat field, shouting in English to us, 'Hands up! The war is finished for you.' But you can guess what answer they got. The last attempt came from the left where there was even more shouting and scores of silhouettes, but I think Jerry was a bit shaken by this time as he was definitely not so bold. Nevertheless there was plenty of noise and danger. In the morning we were warmly congratulated by the CO and the divisional commander, for during the night chaos had reigned in the bridgehead, which had not been reinforced with armour owing to the need for bridging, and the division had been attacked by six battalions of marines with the object of blowing the bridge, and they had very nearly succeeded. I was in the only position that was not attacked and did not fire a shot so I can personally take no credit for the squadron's success; but I can always say I was there.

C Squadron, in their Alamo-like farmhouse, had the misfortune to be on the route taken by the left battalion of Kampfgruppe Neitzel, which was bypassing Wittlohe to the east on its way to attack Otersen when it encountered the recce troops in the farmhouse complex. The attacks from the north and west were conducted by marines of Neitzel's other battalion, while the last attack was probably mounted by the engineer officer candidates of Pi.ROB.Btl.Nienburg sallying forth from their positions in Stemmen. During the night the Germans also attacked A Squadron and cut the road between them and regimental headquarters in Otersen, but Lieutenant Ferguson dealt with this successfully with his troop the next morning on his way back to A Echelon for UK leave.

Owing to the ferocity of the German attack and the threat to the FBE at Westen, at 0300 hours 2 Mons, defending the bridging operation at Rethem, was warned to move as soon as possible to take over the defence of the Westen bridge. The battalion began its move at 0430 hours and was in position by 0700 hours, having left one company behind to guard the bridging effort at Rethem. As mentioned in Corporal Henderson's account, the Germans also attacked 1 E Lancs in Wittlohe. The battalion was attacked by three companies of Kampfgruppe Hornemann and marines from 13./7 Kompanie that had bypassed the two 7 RWF companies on the higher ground north of Wittlohe. The main brunt of the attack, which came in with determination, fell on B Company's area at the village cross-roads. About one company infiltrated the village where there was a vigorous battle in pitch-darkness with friend and foe alike indistinguishable. The Germans occupied a barn opposite B Company's position where they were engaged by PIATs and grenades; two were killed and four others captured. At one point in the battle Sergeant Oram produced additional light by throwing a No. 77 white phosphorous grenade into a nearby barn unaware that it was full of hay and B Company's cooks. The barn burnt well and as described in the regimental history: 'the cooks provided a shining example of a smart turnout!' The German attack on Wittlohe was eventually beaten-off and order restored.

The German counter-attacks were however by no means spent and in the early hours of 14 April attacks were launched by marines on the southern part of the bridgehead in 71st Brigade's area. In a determined attempt to eradicate the bridgehead opposite Rethem, the remainder of both battalions of Kapitän zur See Hartmann's Marine-Grenadier-Regiment 6 (Kampfgruppe Hartmann) and remnants of Marine-Grenadier-Regiment 5 (Kampfgruppe Jordan) were launched into battle. The ensuing fighting was far more ferocious than in the northern part of the bridgehead and a battle raged between Altenwahlingen and Otersen for three hours, with 4 RWF and 1 HLI bearing the brunt of the attacks.

Korvettenkapitän Meincke's II./6 Bataillon, notwithstanding its losses from the battle for Altenwahlingen the previous day, now threw its entire remaining strength against the tired and vulnerable companies of 4 RWF and 1 HLI. A Company 4 RWF was heavily attacked by 7./6 and 8./6 Kompanien near Altenwahlingen and was forced to give ground. Also attacked in strength were C and D Companies 1 HLI, just passing battalion headquarters in their move forward to support A and B Companies. These latter two companies had already had a difficult night attempting to secure the Timpenberg feature against stiff opposition and were badly in need of reinforcement. Captain Ramsay, second-in-command of A Company, takes up the story:[26]

> Major Hemelryk,[27] OC B Company, went forward to recce his company's position, which would be on the right of the main road. He took a platoon with him to place in position. The platoon having been placed on the ground, Major Hemelryk was making his way back when he was fired on by an enemy patrol and badly wounded. He was carried back to the position where the two company O Groups were waiting at the junction of a track and the main road. Major Greenaway, OC A Company, and Captain Pender, who had taken over B Company, decided to get the platoons in position as soon as possible.
>
> At this moment a long line of men was seen marching towards us in single file down the main road. Somehow one never thinks of the enemy approaching in this manner but it has to be remembered that they knew little of the tactical situation. A challenge was replied to by a smart burst of carbine fire and for the next few minutes all hell burst loose. The enemy got down in the ditch and started lobbing over grenades. In reply A Company had three Brens spraying the road while the remainder of the two companies were sorted out and reorganised in a defensive position in a copse about 300 yards to the rear. Several of our wounded, including Major Hemelryk, had to be left for the moment and Private Blythe, a B Company stretcher-bearer, gallantly stayed with them. For the next half-hour or so our men were trickling back to the defensive position and just as things were quietening down a voice was heard

---

26 Oatts, *Proud Heritage*, p.204.
27 Joseph Hemelryk was a CANLOAN officer. He was awarded a posthumous Military Cross on 21 June 1945. An account of his military career can be read at https://www.dyserth.com/Henfryn%20-%20Major%20 Joseph%20Hemelryk%20MC.pdf.

shouting, '1 HLI here.' It was Private Blythe, who had been taken prisoner, accompanied by a German officer. He came with an offer from the German commander to allow us to bring in our wounded. After permission had been obtained from battalion HQ by wireless, Lieutenant Heywood went forward to meet him and after a conversation in broken English and German arranged for the evacuation of 10 wounded personnel including Major Hemelryk. All the stretcher-bearers returned safely with the exception of Private Blythe who was compelled to stay with the enemy to look after their wounded. We heard that he was afterwards released by a subsequent attack and was in due course awarded the Military Medal for his bravery.

This attack was mounted by 6./6 Kompanie. Although its marines were relatively fresh, the complexity of mounting an effective night attack was beyond them and they had no clear idea of the whereabouts of the British. The presence of C and D Companies was most fortunate not only for battalion headquarters but also for Brigadier Elrington, who was visiting 1 HLI's battalion headquarters and had arrived there soon after 0500 hours. Without them the headquarters would have been over-run and the brigade commander captured or killed. S Company 1 HLI was also attacked in its depth position near Ludwigslust, a novel experience for a support company, as an unknown company author recounts:[28]

> Excepting of course for the carrier platoon, the company, or only a small part of it, had never come into actual contact with the enemy. The first time this happened was late in the campaign just after we crossed the river Aller. On the night after the battalion had crossed the river it was again ordered to push on, in this case to assist 4 RWF if necessary. At this time it was quite on the cards that it would not be necessary and everyone was cheerful at the O Group that evening. Especially so was S Company commander because he had been ordered to stay *in situ*, less the mortar platoon, and if necessary bring the carriers and anti-tanks up to the battalion HQ at first light. The '*situ*' consisted of a largish house, with barn and cowshed attached, lying alongside the axis of advance, which ran parallel to the river. One section of the anti-tank platoon occupied the house along with the company HQ and the pioneers. The remainder of the anti-tank platoon and one section of carriers occupied a farm cottage about 200 yards away. After the remainder of the battalion had left, everything was quiet and peaceful with the only fly in the ointment being the wooded and unprotected left flank. That night it was definitely a case of 'kip down' and in all cases trousers and boots came off. At about 0400 hours the anti-tank platoon commander went forward to battalion HQ and later sent back a dispatch rider to bring up the platoon. Once awake, they started to pack blankets and load carriers. As suddenly as a flash of lightning, *Spandaus* and other automatics opened up from the blue and grenades from discharge cups smashed against company HQ's house. The two sections of anti-tanks and the carriers were taken completely by surprise. They were herded into a room by very trigger-happy marines, forced to drop their slacks and were searched and stripped of watches, pens etc (poetic justice!).
>
> Inside the other house confusion would be a very weak word to describe the scene. Half-dressed, everyone was stampeding in a dazed kind of way. By a great deal of shouting order was gained and all possible entrances to the house covered. At first a lot of indiscriminate firing went on from both sides. In the house we had only two Bren guns and the usual ratio of rifles and Stens, but so great was the volume of fire poured out that the enemy seemed to grow quiet, while we wasted ammunition to such an extent that it was in great danger of running-out altogether. It was half light by now and we could see shadowy shapes as they worked their

---

28 Oatts, *Proud Heritage*, p.205.

way nearer and nearer to the house. As our firing slackened owing to shortage of ammunition, theirs increased from cleverly concealed machine-guns. Showing excellent fieldcraft, the marines got right into the vicinity of the house and even into some of the out-buildings. They used grenades with great skill and rendered the two rooms on the top floor a shambles and caused several casualties. In return some very fine shooting by cooks, pioneers and others took a heavy toll on the enemy. Even though the road had been cut, vehicles not aware of this were starting to come down and an ambulance managed to make the yard in safety. As well as the ambulance, a company jeep, seeing the position, volunteered to go back to contact an armoured car of the recce to help out. Without waiting for an answer he ran to his jeep and managed to run the gauntlet to safety.

Things were now reaching a climax. Ammo was at a minimum and the marines had closed in and were causing more casualties. Perhaps worst of all they had managed to set fire to the straw loft of the cowshed. This meant it was only a matter of time before the whole house too caught fire. The result would be a foregone conclusion for, being in the position that we were, the marines could have either killed or captured us at will. As it was everything was all right. At the critical moment the armoured car, summoned by the jeep driver, arrived and its Besa soon put paid to the marines. We just had time to make a very hurried exit before the fire really took hold. Placed beside others, this was probably a minor incident indeed, but it is certainly one that will live in our memories forever.

While S Company fought off the marines' attack, A and B Companies spent the rest of the night in a bleak and exposed position. Captain Ramsay describes their situation cut off from the remainder of the brigade:[29]

Although no further attack was made by the enemy on our defensive position, as soon as first light came up extremely accurate sniping started. About this time I went to see how Major Hemelryk was getting on and found to my sorrow that the gallant commander of B Company had died a few minutes earlier. The cold and damp of the early morning proved very trying for the wounded and it was impossible to evacuate them as no transport had managed to get through and we were still more or less surrounded. We asked battalion HQ if carriers or stretcher-bearers could be sent up but the reply came back that they were being attacked themselves and that they could give no assistance in the meantime. A short while later, looking to our right front we could see bedraggled members of the German marine battalion making their way back towards the enemy's area. They were the remnants of the forces, which had counter-attacked other units of 71st Brigade. Though they were too far away for good results to be obtained, we sped them on their way with Bren fire. As soon as it was possible, a patrol was sent out to recce forward to our original objective, and as it reported all clear the companies then moved up and occupied positions astride the road. One platoon from A Company was left to watch the left flank and reply to the sniper fire. It was well on in the afternoon before carriers arrived up the main road and we got the wounded sent back and our breakfast sent up.

With marines from Kampfgruppe Hartmann fighting 1 HLI in a confused battle in the woods, other marines from I./6 Bataillon attacked B and C Companies 4 RWF at the Altenwahlingen cross-roads and pressing them hard managed to cut the main road. A Company was heavily counter-attacked in Altenwahlingen itself and A Squadron 53rd Recce Regiment moved to help

---

29   Oatts, *Proud Heritage*, pp.206–207.

prevent the companies from being overwhelmed. The confused fighting made the situation very difficult and the marines infiltrated within 200 yards of HQ 71st Brigade, cutting communications to the battalions. At 0500 hours the 81st Field Regiment BCs with the battalions reported their areas infiltrated and that they were surrounded by large numbers of enemy.[30] The situation was perilous but the coming of first light now came to the rescue of the beleaguered British battalions and the marines, caught in the open, became what 81st Field Regiment's war diary described as a 'gunners' dream.' Soon on the receiving end of intense artillery concentrations, the marines suffered severe losses and large groups began to surrender. The last attacks were eventually beaten off with the help of B and D Companies 1 Oxf Bucks LI and by 0900 hours the German counter-attacks were spent. Although during the attacks the three infantry battalion headquarters were in close proximity to each other, and the task of coordinating fire accordingly easier, it is of note that during the early morning of 14 April 81st Field Regiment recorded more radio traffic and delivered more fire than at any other time in the campaign. During the course of this bitter fighting approximately 130 marines were killed and 79 wounded. The German dead included Korvettenkapitän Melzer, commanding officer of I./6 Bataillon, and Oberleutnant zur See Peters and Oberleutnant Mahler, the commanders of 1./6 and 2./6 Kompanien. A further 163 marines, including Kapitänleutnant Thoren, the commanding officer of I./5 Bataillon, were taken prisoner. The British suffered as well: 1 Oxf Bucks LI lost 11 dead, 1 HLI lost 15 and 4 RWF lost five; many more were wounded.

Despite the courage of the marines, the failure of the counter-attacks to eliminate the bridgehead led to the fragmentation of the German defence of the right bank. 2. Marine-Infanterie-Division's capacity to prevent the bridgehead from expanding was now spent and the effort of their attacks had exhausted the marines. The surviving elements of Marine-Grenadier-Regiment 5, I./6 Bataillon, Marine-Pionier-Bataillon 2 and Pi.ROB.Btl.Nienburg now withdrew to the forests and villages to the north, while Marine-Grenadier-Regiment 7 pulled back to defend the approaches to Verden. Only II./6 Bataillon could in any sense be considered battleworthy and its marines, supported by RAD Batterie 2./604 and Batterie 4./117, now fighting as infantry, prepared to counter the inevitable British advance up Reichsstrasse 209. II./6 Bataillon had pulled back to recover and regroup in the forests to the north and east of Altenwahlingen where it had further opportunity to exact delay and casualties on the British, who would soon have to advance through the close country. The marines, equipped with *Panzerfaust* and automatic weapons, organised themselves into tank-hunting teams, prepared ambush positions on Reichsstrasse 209 and the rides through the forest, and hurriedly constructed road-blocks by felling oaks that lined the road and established positions in depth at Gross Eilstorf and Kirchboitzen. Gross Eilstorf was occupied by marines from Marine-Grenadier-Regiment 5, fallen back on the village after the failure of their counter-attack on the Gross Häuslingen area the previous day, while Kirchboitzen was largely occupied by marines from I./6 Bataillon. The horse-drawn batteries of 10.5cm howitzers of Marine-Artillerie-Regiment 2 had at last arrived and had occupied gun positions to the north of Kirchboitzen. Although their arrival now provides much needed indirect fire support, it will be short-lived.

The night battles fought during the early hours of 14 April were not, however, confined to repelling German counter-attacks. Shortly after midnight 4 RWF's carrier platoon had passed through the cross-roads to the west of Altenwahlingen held by B and C Companies and then moved south to investigate Kirchwahlingen. This hamlet was held by 5./6 Kompanie, the last company of Korvettenkapitän Meincke's II./6 Bataillon still holding its original positions on the Aller's right bank. Commanded by Oberleutnant zur See Herbst, it would seem that after the fall

---

30 TNA WO 171/4826, 81st Field Regiment RA war diary.

of Altenwahlingen the company did not withdraw with the rest of the battalion. Although Herbst and his marines would have heard resistance come to an end to their north, which would have made an eastwards night-withdrawal to Böhme their only option, he knew that the demolitions on Reichsstrasse 209 would sooner or later force the British to come to Kirchwahlingen. On 13 April he ordered the inhabitants to leave but few did so and the mayor, Winkelmann, begged him not to defend Kirchwahlingen as it had no value; Herbst refused this plea stating it was his duty to stay and fight. When 4 RWF's carrier platoon neared the hamlet it was therefore met with heavy small-arms' fire and the Welsh were forced to dismount rapidly to begin a lengthy and bitter action involving hand-to-hand fighting to clear the houses and farms. The fighting went on for the remainder of the night and on into the next morning.

Meanwhile, the occupants of the *Führerbunker* in Berlin remained splendidly detached from the grim realities at the front and during the conference held on 14 April Dönitz enthused over 2. Marine-Infanterie-Division's apparent good shape, providing detailed statistics on its alleged strength.[31] His timing was, however, poor as 14 April was not only the day that XII Corps would start to break out of the Rethem bridgehead and begin its final advance to the Elbe but it was also the day that the marine division ceased to exist as a coherent organisation, as we will now hear.

---

31   Jak Showell (ed.), *Führer Conferences on Naval Affairs*, p.483.

11

Through the Crust: The Collapse of the Aller Line and XII Corps' Breakout 14–17 April

By mid-April the three corps of Second Army were poised to play their parts in the final act of the war in north-west Europe. On the right flank VIII Corps was continuing to advance strongly towards the Elbe: 15th Scottish Division had captured Celle and was closing on Uelzen against negligible opposition, 11th Armoured was breaking clear of the Essel bridgehead, while 6th Airborne in reserve was moving up behind 15th Scottish and mopping-up bypassed enemy pockets. On the left flank XXX Corps was fighting hard to secure the approaches to Bremen, while in the centre XII Corps, with the battle for the Aller bridgehead successfully concluded, prepared to take up the eastward advance once more. Speed remained vital, not only to prevent the Soviets investing Denmark but Eisenhower had also identified Norway as an area where prolonged resistance was likely and that if operations were needed there, they would need to be concluded before winter set in.[1] Furthermore, even with Germany defeated, he feared U-boat warfare could continue to be prosecuted from Norway and so it was imperative that the country was promptly liberated. He therefore directed Denmark to be taken as early as possible to serve as a mounting base for an attack on Norway via Sweden, the only viable approach. A thrust to Lübeck and Kiel was an essential preliminary to this strategy, and the port of Hamburg needed to be quickly captured to support operations in Scandinavia. Montgomery was left in no doubt that his advance must press on with maximum speed and he in turn impressed this on Dempsey. Dempsey's plan to reflect this imperative involved VIII Corps winning a bridgehead over the Elbe to provide XII Corps with a secure right flank for mounting an operation to capture Hamburg from an easterly direction.

On 14 April General Ritchie issued orders for the next phase of XII Corps' operations on the Aller's right bank. This would start with 53rd Division and 4th Armoured Brigade making the initial breakout before heading north-west to roll up the remainder of the Aller Line and capture Verden, a critical bridging site for XXX Corps' future attack on Bremen. 7th Armoured Division, concentrated in the Nienburg area, would be released as soon as possible to spearhead XII Corps' eastward advance on the axis Walsrode, Soltau and thereafter Hamburg. 52nd Lowland Division, presently clearing the corps' left flank, was warned it would join XXX Corps for the battle to reduce Bremen and its place in XII Corps would be taken by the Guards Armoured Division as there was no requirement for its armour in the battle for Bremen. Guards Armoured would be tasked to cross the Aller in the wake of 7th Armoured and then advance in a northerly direction to seize successively the towns of Visselhövede, Rotenburg, Zeven, Bremervörde and Stade. In

---

1 Dwight D Eisenhower, *Crusade in Europe*, p.453.

accomplishing this, the *Autobahn* linking Bremen and Hamburg would be cut and the higher ground between the two cities dominated.

The plan for 53rd Welsh's capture of Verden involved its three brigades advancing down the right bank of the Aller clearing the remaining forces of the Aller Line as they did so. The brigades would leap-frog past each other supported in turn by an armoured regiment and C Squadron 7 RTR's Crocodiles. 4th Armoured Brigade, under command of the division, would meanwhile cross the Class 40 bridge at Rethem as soon as it was completed, relieve 71st Brigade and then advance as fast as possible up Reichsstrasse 209 to Walsrode, where it would swing north-west in a manoeuvre to outflank Verden from the north.[2] Major General Ross ordered a regrouping to provide 4th Armoured with more infantry and in so doing release an armoured regiment to support the division's infantry brigades; consequently 3/4 CLY was allocated to come under divisional control and in exchange 4th Armoured gained, as we heard in the last chapter, 6 RWF mounted in Kangaroo APCs.

Saturday 14 April

Operations on Rethem bridgehead's right flank

The Rethem bridge neared completion during the late morning of 14 April and 71st Brigade redeployed in expectation of 4th Armoured Brigade's advance: 4 RWF swung round so that all four rifle companies in the Altenwahlingen area faced east and 1 HLI's rear companies were held back in preparation for the division's northward advance. Brigadier Mike Carver, commanding 4th Armoured, formed two regimental groups for his brigade's advance: 44 RTR[3] with 2 KRRC (44 RTR Group) and the Scots Greys[4] with 6 RWF (Scots Greys Group); the brigade's organisation therefore mirrored the regimental groups we followed in 11th Armoured Division. As soon as the Rethem bridge was completed, 44 RTR Group would cross followed by the Crocodiles of C Squadron 7 RTR, 3/4 CLY,[5] and two Archer anti-tank batteries required to support 158th Brigade in the north but too heavy to use the Class 9 FBE at Westen. 4th Armoured was expected to be clear of Rethem bridge by last light 14 April, by which time 7th Armoured Division would be ready to start crossing. To relieve 4 RWF in the Altenwahlingen area and free the battalion to take part in the advance to Verden, 2 Devon from 7th Armoured Division moved forward into the bridgehead to come under command of 4th Armoured.[6]

On 13 April, 4th Armoured moved to a concentration area near Hohenholz to await the completion of the Bailey pontoon bridge at Rethem, frequently delayed by shelling and mortaring. At 1200 hours on 14 April the bridge was finally ready and the carrier platoon of 2 KRRC, acting as a recce force, crossed and immediately turned off the main road and advanced east down the road leading to Kirchwahlingen.[7] Owing to the demolition of the bridge carrying Reichsstrasse 209 over the ox-bow lake at Rethemer Fähre, this minor road had to be used as a bypass route, but it was far from satisfactory as the brigade advance would be restricted to a narrow, raised road with the ground on either side boggy and unable to support armour.

---

2   TNA WO 171/4314, 4th Armoured Brigade war diary.
3   TNA WO 171/4715, 44 RTR war diary.
4   TNA WO 171/4683, Scots Greys war diary.
5   TNA WO 171/4697, 3/4 CLY war diary.
6   TNA WO 171/5171, 2 Devon war diary.
7   TNA WO 171/5212, 2 KRRC war diary.

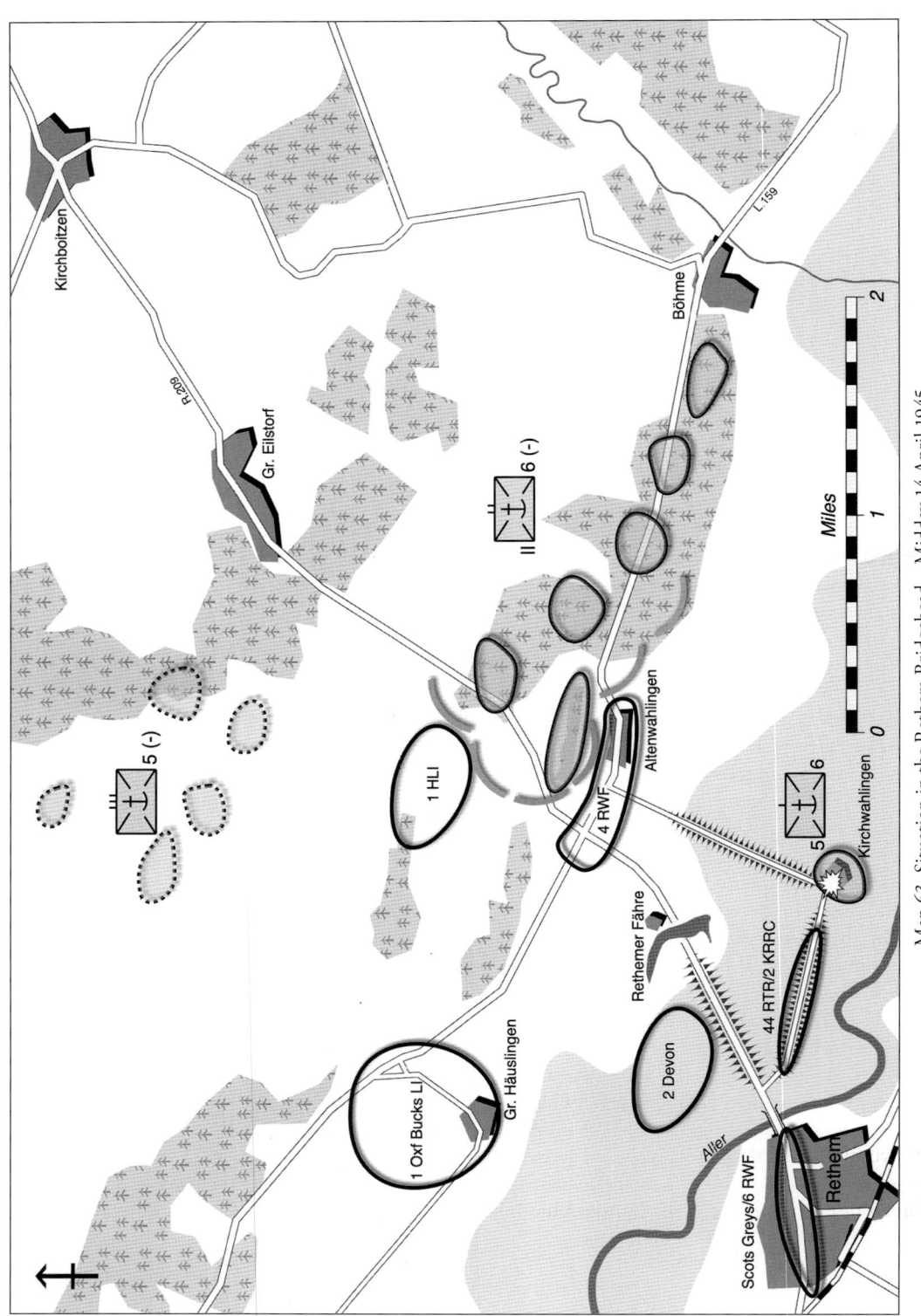

Map 63 Situation in the Rethem Bridgehead – Midday 14 April 1945.

The road to Kirchwahlingen on the Aller's right bank. The road crosses the middle of the photograph, with the hamlet and its church tower visible in the trees right of centre. Photograph taken in 2015. (Author)

Inevitably this would result in congestion, vulnerability and delay just when speed was required. A few minutes after the carriers had crossed, the Rethem bridge came under artillery fire again; fortunately, no damage was caused but it shook the high-ranking observers, among them the corps commander, gathered to watch the crossing. Despite this near disaster, the war diarist of 244 Field Company proudly recorded that the bridge was built under trying conditions, it was one of the best they had built and that they had deserved the corps commander's praise.[8]

For its advance, 44 RTR Group had formed three squadron/company groups. A Squadron and C Company was the first to cross the bridge and, with the tanks leading, the group slowly moved up the bypass route towards Kirchwahlingen. By 1330 hours it had reached 2 KRRC's carrier platoon, halted short of the hamlet as 4 RWF's carrier platoon was still fighting in the hamlet. A Squadron commander eventually managed to get the 4 RWF carrier platoon to disengage and then advanced his tanks towards the buildings. The marines were not unnerved by the appearance of the Shermans and fired, unsuccessfully, at the lead tanks with their remaining *Panzerfaust*. When these were exhausted they shot at the tanks with their rifles in a futile attempt to destroy the optics. Close-quarter fighting among the buildings was not however a healthy environment for armour, and as 2 KRRC's Wasps offered a more efficient way of dealing with the marines the flame-throwing carriers were called forward. Although they immediately proceeded to burn down three of the farm complexes they soon exhausted their fuel, sparing Kirchwahlingen complete destruction. Oberleutnant zur See Herbst was killed fighting from the mayor's garden and his deputy, Leutnant zur See Markert, took over the one-sided battle. The marines were eventually forced out of the back of the hamlet but continued to fight tenaciously from ditches and hedges

---

8   TNA WO 171/5520, 244 Field Company RE war diary.

Bailey pontoon bridge at Rethem with the demolished road bridge lying in the Aller next to it.

as they withdrew across the meadows towards Böhme. Markert was severely wounded during the withdrawal, dying of his wounds the next day.

While A Squadron Group was engaged in Kirchwahlingen, B Squadron Group bypassed the fighting and advanced directly to Altenwahligen, where it linked up with 4 RWF and relieved the Welsh from the task of securing the village. The remainder of 44 RTR Group followed. Support Company 2 KRRC, reinforced with a section of carriers, took over mopping-up Kirchwahlingen from A Squadron Group, freeing the squadron to follow B Squadron Group. Once it reached Altenwahlingen, A Squadron Group struck off towards the forest to the north of the village. However, as the tanks and half-tracks neared the edge of the forest they were halted by intense machine-gun and *Panzerfaust* fire from marines of II./6 Bataillon holding positions further back in the trees. Despite the dangerous situation, the tanks were cautious of returning fire as they were not in touch with A and B Companies 1 HLI, thought to be (and were) in the general area. These events are described by Major Roland Gibbs, commanding C Company 2 KRRC:[9]

> C Company 2nd/60th Rifles[10] was to advance on Gross Eilstorf but on a centre line east of the main Rethem–Gross Eilstorf road [Reichsstrasse 209]. With A Squadron we debouched from Altenwahlingen in the early afternoon. We had hardly put our noses outside when firing broke out from the edge of the woods just north of the road to Böhme. I led with a motor platoon on its feet supported by a troop of A Squadron with the rest of the company immediately to the rear. The country, being wooded, was an infantry task to clear. The leading platoon got into the edge of the wood, supported by the machine-gun fire of the tanks. I don't think they had many casualties. But the enemy were fighting with no thought of surrender – indeed they were well dug-in and camouflaged, difficult to locate and their positions were in depth back into the wood. The empty half-tracks and company HQ endured an extraordinary

---

9   Major Gibbs had fought with 2 KRRC in north Africa, Italy and north-west Europe since Normandy. In 1976 he became Chief of the General Staff and in 1979 was promoted field marshal on retirement.
10 2 KRRC was frequently referred to as '60th Rifles' harking back to its original title.

barrage which was difficult to recognise. It was solid shot from anti-tank guns cocked up to clear the trees. They hit one half-track. The tank machine-guns were clearly not having much impact and I was starting to plan a coordinated attack with the rest of the company when to my surprise one of my two Wasps (which were very slow and often broke down because of their excessive weight) hove in sight. So I thought, 'We will just try this on them first.' The little carrier heaved itself towards the wood, covered by the platoon and tanks. It stopped 25 yards from the edge and let off a squirt of liquid, which happily ignited. There were immediate shrieks from the enemy. With a few more squirts the nearest enemy got up and surrendered followed by the rest. I cannot say how many PoW we evacuated. Quite a lot. The dead we left for the villagers to bury. Having secured our open flank, we turned north-east to continue our advance. We had broken through the crust.[11]

At company level there probably were grounds for feeling confident, but the confused situation in the forest north of Altenwahlingen could not be quickly resolved and Brigadier Carver was increasingly frustrated that his brigade's advance was not making quicker progress. He was however unable to reinforce the advance with the Scots Greys Group, his second regimental group, as the armour moving to join 158th Brigade was also packed into the small bridgehead and the boggy meadows prevented any move to bypass the congestion. Between the Rethem bridge and Altenwahlingen the only place where vehicles could get off the road was at Kirchwahlingen, but as this area was in full view of the enemy-held ground to the north and under sporadic shelling it was far from desirable to have any more congestion on the single-lane road than was absolutely necessary. In an attempt to relieve the situation, a patrol from 3/4 CLY's recce troop was sent up a track leading direct from the bridge to Gross Häuslingen to see whether it could be used. Although the patrol reported very boggy conditions, it was decided to push a squadron of Cromwells up this track; the tanks eventually reached Gross Häuslingen but thereafter the route was impassable.

At 1715 hours 44 RTR's B Squadron Group, in the area of the cross-roads to the west of Altenwahlingen, was ordered to advance up Reichsstrasse 209 to try to ease the pressure on A Squadron Group stuck on the forest's edge; C Squadron and A Company followed in reserve. The marines from II./6 Bataillon were not however prepared to let the British seize the initiative and they slowed this advance to a crawl as well, refusing to be shifted despite the use of Typhoons from 184 Squadron,[12] indirect fire, machine-guns and flame-throwers, and by 2100 hours B Squadron Group's attempts to make further progress had come to nothing against endless *Panzerfaust* firers re-infiltrating through the thick woods. While B Squadron Group was trying to inch its way forward, C Squadron Group was ordered to concentrate with 1 HLI in the area of Timpenberg and provide mutual support in the event of enemy night attacks. By the early evening A Squadron Group began to have more success on its axis, gradually working its way forward against the marines in the forest and, as night fell, managed to get a troop and a platoon beyond the trees and established in a school-house some 300 yards from the centre of Gross Eilstorf.

While 44 RTR Group was fighting on the Aller's right bank, on the left the Scots Greys Group prepared for its advance. 6 RWF, now in their Kangaroos, moved forward from Stöcken during the morning and formed up along Lange Strasse, Rethem's high street, to await the arrival of the Scots Greys and then the order to move to the right bank. The Shermans arrived during the early afternoon and the group married up, but owing to the resistance on the right bank the long column of armour did not start to cross the Class 40 bridge until 1845 hours.

---

11   Letter to the author.
12   TNA AIR 50/76, 184 Squadron RAF combat reports.

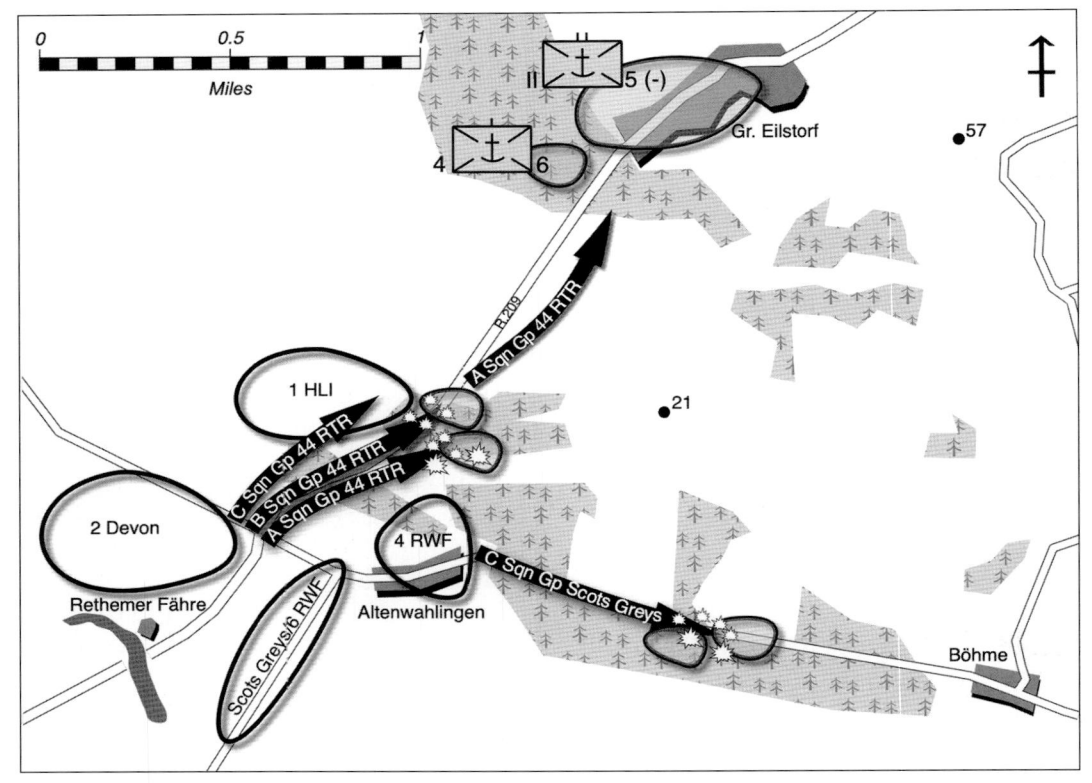

Map 64 4th Armoured Brigade – pm 14 April 1945.

A 4th Armoured Brigade Sherman crosses the Bailey pontoon at Rethem. The house on the left was where the 2 Mons patrol found the marine OP on 12 April.

Shermans of the Scots Greys and Kangaroo APCs carrying 6 RWF wait to cross the Rethem pontoon bridge. (© Crown Copyright, IWM negative number BU3648)

The cars of today replace the Shermans and Kangaroos of 1945. (Author)

With 44 RTR Group making slow progress on Reichsstrasse 209, considerable congestion in Altenwahlingen and a jam in Kirchwahlingen from vehicles destined for 158th Brigade, Brigadier Carver decided to bypass the area of delay by manoeuvring further to the east. Accordingly, the Scots Greys Group was ordered to try and find a route from Kirchwahlingen to the road and track junction mid-way between Altenwahlingen and Böhme. However, because of the ever-present boggy ground, no route was found and C Squadron Group in the lead had to move back to Altenwahlingen, eventually reaching it by 1800 hours. The group then started to clear Landesstrasse 159 to Böhme, but progress on this road was slow owing to trees felled across the carriageway, desultory artillery fire and parties of marines from II./6 Bataillon fighting from the flanking woods. Typhoon support from No. 175 Squadron struck Böhme,[13] as most of the artillery fire seemed to be coming from this area, but this did not have the desired effect and it was clear that little could be achieved in this direction. Despite the lack of progress, 61 prisoners from 4./6 and 5./6 Kompanien were captured during the course of the day, further reducing the marines' capacity to hold back the British.

With delay facing him in every direction, Brigadier Carver decided to seize the initiative by pushing the Scots Greys Group straight to Kirchboitzen, the next village on Reichsstrasse 209 after Gross Eilstorf. He decided that the tanks and infantry in their Kangaroos would employ a high risk, night advance through the forest north-east of Altenwahlingen, which, if successful, would get the group to the open country from where an attack on Kirchboitzen could be launched from the south-west. This was the same forest from which so much opposition had already been encountered and to tackle such an obstacle in the conventional way with infantry would have been slow and potentially costly, so Brigadier Carver decided to force the passage, a course not without significant risk as any destroyed or broken-down vehicles would block the forest track. To maximise the shock effect of the armour, the group would advance with alternating Shermans and Kangaroos, each vehicle training its machine-guns to left or right along the flanks of the vehicle in front, and orders were given to shoot their way forward whether or not any enemy showed themselves. The advance would start in the early hours of 15 April and the brigade would receive assistance from artificial moonlight provided by two searchlights from C Troop 344 Searchlight Battery. The high risk of a night manoeuvre through enemy-held woods had to be accepted as there had already been too much delay and speed was of the essence.

At 2100 hours Brigadier Carver held his orders in Altenwahlingen and gave the following tasks to the two regimental groups, for execution that night:[14]

> 1. Scots Greys and 6 RWF to move to Point 57 east of Gross Eilstorf via Point 21 but not to make any attempt to clear the woods through which they pass. As soon as possible on 15 April the group would attack and clear Kirchboitzen.
>
> 2. 44 RTR and 2 KRRC to patrol into Gross Eilstorf. If the village was clear, they would concentrate there and prepare to pass through the Scots Greys Group on the capture of Kirchboitzen. If it was held, they were to attack and clear it at first light on 15 April.

While during the earlier part of the night the Scots Greys Group prepared for its unconventional advance, A and B companies 2 KRRC mounted the patrols to probe the defences of Gross Eilstorf. These met a vigorous reaction and it was clear that a quick, night attack by the battalion would

---

13   TNA AIR 50/72, 175 Squadron RAF combat reports.
14   4th Armoured Brigade – Operations East of the River Aller, 14–19 April 1945 (Unpublished), pp.5–6.

probably not succeed. An amusing but potentially lethal incident happened during one of the patrols, as recounted by Major Gibbs:[15]

> I sent out a recce patrol later in the night because the enemy could well have slipped away. Lieutenant Bobby Morrison commanded it. On the outskirts of the village he saw a German sentry. Ambitiously he thought he could capture him. He crept up behind him, put his revolver in his back and said, 'Hands up!'. The German turned and grabbed Bobby's revolver. Bobby fired all six rounds and missed with the lot! Unarmed, he felt discretion the better part of valour and broke away before the German could use his rifle!

158th Brigade advances north

With 4th Armoured Brigade preparing to breakout of the southern part of the bridgehead, we will now return to 53rd Welsh's infantry brigades about to start their northward advance to clear the remaining vestiges of the Aller Line. The original plan envisaged a simultaneous advance by all three brigades but owing to the continuing threat to the Westen bridgehead and the confused nature of the fighting in the area of Altenwahlingen, it was not possible to extract 71st Brigade and the two battalions of 160th Brigade (the third, 6 RWF, was now with 4th Armoured) were as yet unavailable. The main contribution had therefore to be initially provided by 158th Brigade, with 160th Brigade joining the advance once 4 Welch had completed its operations on the Aller's left bank and 2 Mons was relieved from guarding the bridge at Westen. 158th Brigade's advance would involve it in a series of village and wood-clearing operations, some unopposed others pitted against determined opposition from men still prepared to fight to the last.

The first German forces to face the advance belonged to Neitzel's depleted Kampfgruppe Verden. Although his two marine battalions were still effective, Bataillon Kolotay had been destroyed and Schaffer's two *Kampfgruppen*, Hornemann and Tebener, had both been badly mauled during the counter-attacks and were in disarray following the night attacks on the northern part of the bridgehead. Further north in the Kirchlinteln area and in depth of the two *Kampfgruppen* were marines from I./7 Bataillon, and deployed forward to Armsen was the 100-strong 4./7 Kompanie holding the high ground and bolstering the shaky defence; the remainder of the regiment remained in the vicinity of Verden. Some horse-drawn 10.5cm guns from Marine-Artillerie-Regiment 2 were now available and a number of 8.8cm Flak were in Verden. For the Germans about to face the final phase of the battle of the Aller Line the prospects were bleak; nonetheless the opposition they were to offer in hopeless circumstances was a credit to their resolve.

158th Brigade's advance would take place on three axes: 7 RWF was on the left axis next to the Aller, 1/5 Welch was in the centre, and 1 E Lancs on the right. 7 RWF was responsible for clearing Landesstrasse 160, the divisional axis, and the battalion's advance began in the early afternoon from the positions it held on the left flank of the Westen bridgehead. The companies advanced progressively through each other, initially meeting only isolated pockets of resistance from Kampfgruppe Hornemann as they did so. Opposition then began to stiffen and Lieutenant Colonel Tyler asked brigade for tank support; this was granted, although due to the continuing congestion in the Rethem bridgehead it would be some time before the tanks could reach him. At 1730 hours B Company reported a well-constructed road-block to the south-east of its objective, Hohenaverbergen. While the pioneer platoon checked the obstacle, Colonel Tyler deployed forward the other companies to be ready for the attack and at 1830 hours Crocodiles of C Squadron 7 RTR

---

15   Letter to the author.

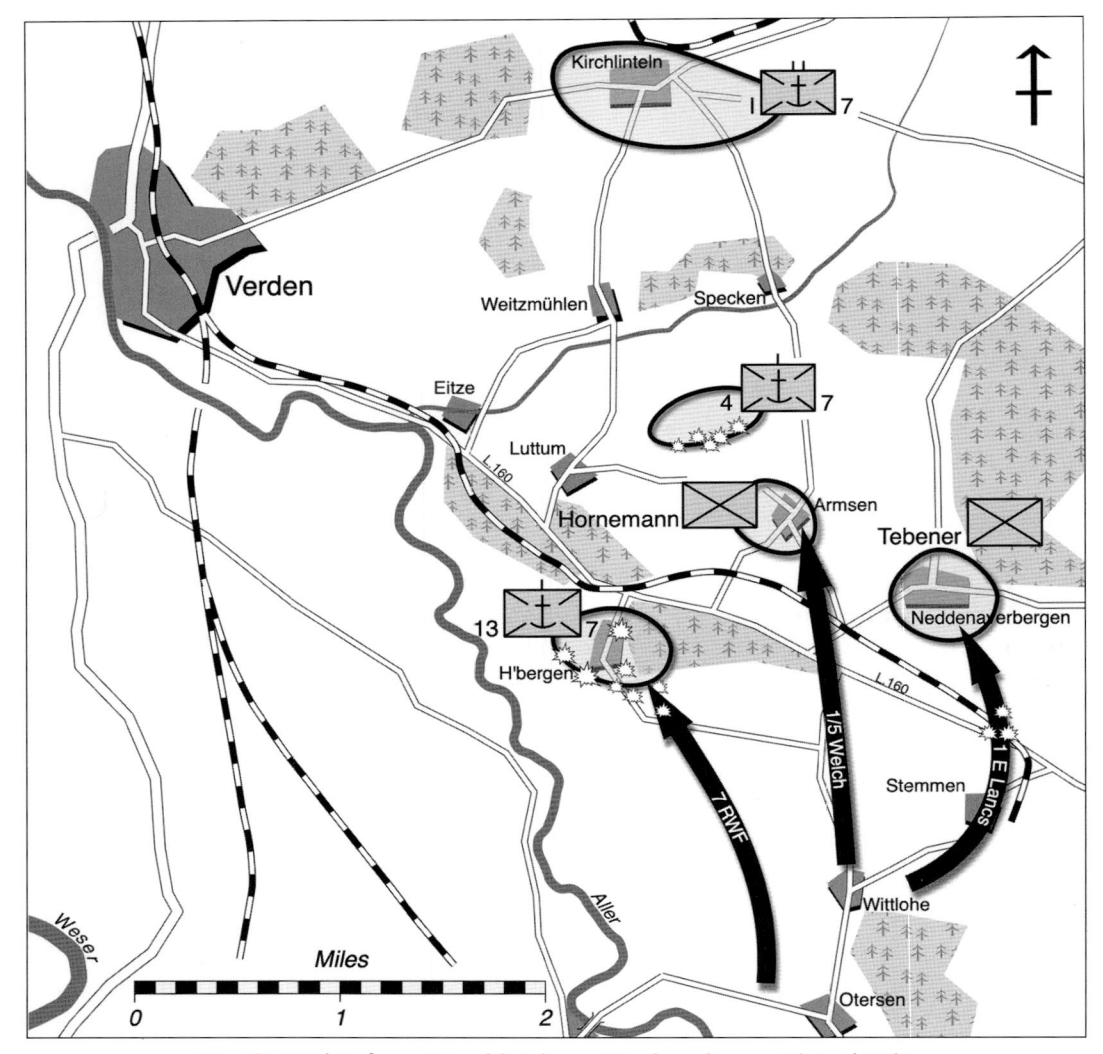

Map 65 158th Infantry Brigade's Advance Northwards – pm 14 April 1945.

eventually arrived.[16] However, before the orders for the attack could be completed the Germans launched a counter-attack against B and D Companies in the area of the road-block and both companies were forced to give ground. Colonel Tyler now decided to attack the village using A and C Companies advancing from the south-west. At 1950 hours the companies crossed the start line and by 2030 hours had reached the village's outskirts. Defending Hohenavervbergen was 13./7 Kompanie, commanded by Oberleutnant Gallhof, reinforced with a platoon of artillery recruits and some *Luftwaffe* personnel. Although they resisted fiercely with the usual fire from machine-guns, rifles and *Panzerfaust*, they were gradually forced out of the village as it burnt down around them. Gallhof managed to withdraw north with a number of survivors but 41 marines and others were killed in the action and now lie buried in the village cemetery. By 2130 hours resistance had

---

16   TNA WO 171/4712, 7 RTR war diary.

ceased and 7 RWF, after a short pause, prepared to push on. Throughout the day the battalion was supported by the Vickers and mortars of A and D Companies 1 Manchester, once again the guns causing many casualties to Germans caught in the open.

At 1400 hours Brigadier Wilsey ordered 1/5 Welch to advance on the centre axis and capture Armsen,[17] some two miles north of the battalion's concentration area, and then push on to cut the Verden to Kirchlinteln road. During the counter-attacks of the night 13/14 April, the battalion had been guarding the Westen bridge but was relieved early in the morning of 14 April by 2 Mons from 160th Brigade in order to release it to help defend the bridgehead and be ready for the brigade's subsequent northwards advance. 1/5 Welch subsequently moved to relieve 1 E Lancs in the Wittlohe area and married-up with a squadron of Shermans from 3/4 CLY and half a squadron of Crocodiles. Lieutenant Colonel Bowker ordered C Company, supported by B Squadron, to capture Armsen and then for D Company to pass through to capture the high ground to the north-west of the village; B Company would then advance to capture Weitzmühlen. Once the village was secure, C Company, still with the armour, would clear Luttum and Eitze to the west leaving D Company to advance and cut the road. At 1700 hours Colonel Bowker was told that he would now have all of 3/4 CLY in support but no Crocodiles. By the time the armour arrived the light was fading so he ordered his companies to move mounted on the decks of the tanks to make best speed. At 1830 hours the advance began and although an A Squadron Firefly was destroyed during a halt and its driver killed when it was hit on the gun mantlet by an 8.8cm HE round, Armsen was reached without difficulty and by 2000 hours captured with little resistance from the artillery recruits of Kampfgruppe Hornemann. However, when D Company attempted to capture the high ground to the north it ran into trouble and the Welsh were beaten off by heavy fire from 4./7 Kompanie dug-in on the ridge and in the wood backing it. As the battalion had met determined opposition, Colonel Bowker decided to halt the advance until daylight to allow more information to be gathered on the enemy's positions.

On the right axis 1 E Lancs faced less resolute resistance. Once relieved by 1/5 Welch in the morning, the battalion advanced steadily towards its objective, Neddenaverbergen, held by artillery recruits from Kampfgruppe Tebener. The advance started quietly enough and Stemmen was cleared with only a few pockets of resistance. With the village taken, D Company's next objective was the level crossing to its north, but just as the lead section reached this point the company was warned that it had been mistaken for Germans and was the target for an incoming medium artillery concentration. Fortunately, the company radio net had worked and the platoons had time to take immediate cover in the cellars of nearby houses and avoid the storm of steel falling on the area moments later. Apparently other troops advancing on the right flank had mistaken D Company for a counter-attack force and had called for fire. Although enemy shelling during the morning caused some casualties, the fire was inaccurate and the advance continued unhindered. By early afternoon the battalion was close to its objective and H-hour for the attack on Neddenaverbergen was set for 1500 hours. After a short artillery bombardment, B Company entered the village and cleared to the western end; A Company then passed through to clear to the eastern. Some machine-gun fire caused three casualties, but Neddenaverbergen was taken with little opposition and 73 men from Kampfgruppe Tebener captured in the process. 1 E Lancs then consolidated for the remainder of the day in the area of the village and commanders were briefed on the brigade

---

17 It has been suggested (TD Dungan, *V-2 – A Combat History of the First Ballistic Missile* (Yardley: Westholme Publishing, 2005, p.196) that V-2 rockets were fired from the Armsen area in early March 1945 by the Lehr- und Versuchsabteilung z.V. (formerly Batterie 444) as part of tests to improve the V-2's accuracy by the use of a guidance beam (*Leitstrahl Technik*). The development organisation was apparently known as Entwicklungskommando Rethem. By the time 1/5 Welch arrived in the area the rocket troops had withdrawn to Schleswig-Holstein.

plan for the attack on Verden, which would start with 1/5 Welch occupying Weitzmühlen then, with 1 E Lancs on the right and 1/5 Welch on the left, the brigade would conduct a night advance to secure the main road in order to cut off the Verden garrison from the east before launching the assault on the town. The key to a successful attack was considered to be control of the Verden to Kirchlinteln road and a wooded area to the west of Kirchlinteln.

During the afternoon a lone Ar 234, probably belonging to KG 76, overflew the bridgehead and was engaged by H Troop 25th LAA Regiment; no hits were scored on the fast-moving aircraft. The Ar 234 was quite possibly the same aircraft which had earlier overflown the Essel bridgehead and been engaged, equally unsuccessfully, by 172 Battery.

Sunday 15 April

4th Armoured Brigade advances

When last mentioned, the Scots Greys Group was poised to start its night advance into the forest north of Altenwahlingen, with the village now held by 2 Devon. Led by C Squadron group, the advance began at 0100 hours with guns blazing to the front and flanks and in a very short time the dry undergrowth had caught fire, resulting in the column driving down the sandy track between walls of flame choked by smoke. On reaching the first bound the squadron group took up all-round defence and signalled to the next group to pass through. The immediate effect of the inferno was to force the Germans to withdraw quickly and the passing of squadron group through squadron group continued until, by daybreak, the regimental group's 150 tracked vehicles reached a saucer-shaped dip at the foot of the higher ground dominated by Kirchboitzen. Here hull- and turret-down positions were adopted and those present remember an eerie feeling from not only knowing they had passed right through the German lines but also from being able to see behind them, and only 600 yards away, 44 RTR Group battling for Gross Eilstorf.

Gross Eilstorf was held by marines from the depleted II./5 Bataillon, Rethem's defenders, and to its south-west Oberleutnant zur See Shrickel's 4./6 Kompanie, dug-in on the fringes of the beech woods through which Reichsstrasse 209 passed as it climbed the gentle escarpment to the village. This company had become detached from its parent battalion now in Kirchboitzen and Altenboitzen after the failure of the counter-attacks. At 0600 hours 2 KRRC assaulted Gross Eilstorf with B Company left, A Company right supported respectively by B and A Squadrons 44 RTR. Although B Company initially made progress, B Squadron was held up by road blocks of felled trees and it took until 0735 hours to clear these obstacles. Better progress was made on the right where A Company closed up to the village without difficulty; the ensuing attack, with a tragic incident, is described by the company commander, Major Gosse:[18]

> The first phase of the attack went quite well and 4 Platoon under Lieutenant Humphreys reached its objective, which was a bit of high ground overlooking the first half of the village. One prisoner was taken. The attack then went in with 2 Platoon advancing on the left of the road and 3 Platoon on the right. 2 Platoon soon ran into trouble and Rifleman Downing was killed and Lance Corporals Timson and Hewson and Rifleman Deaves all injured. Lance Corporal Timson later died of his wounds. All these men were experienced and could be ill-spared. 3 Platoon got on well on the right but were very unlucky as the tanks supporting them thought that they were enemy, opened up and killed one corporal and wounded a

---

18   TNA WO 171/5212, 2 KRRC war diary.

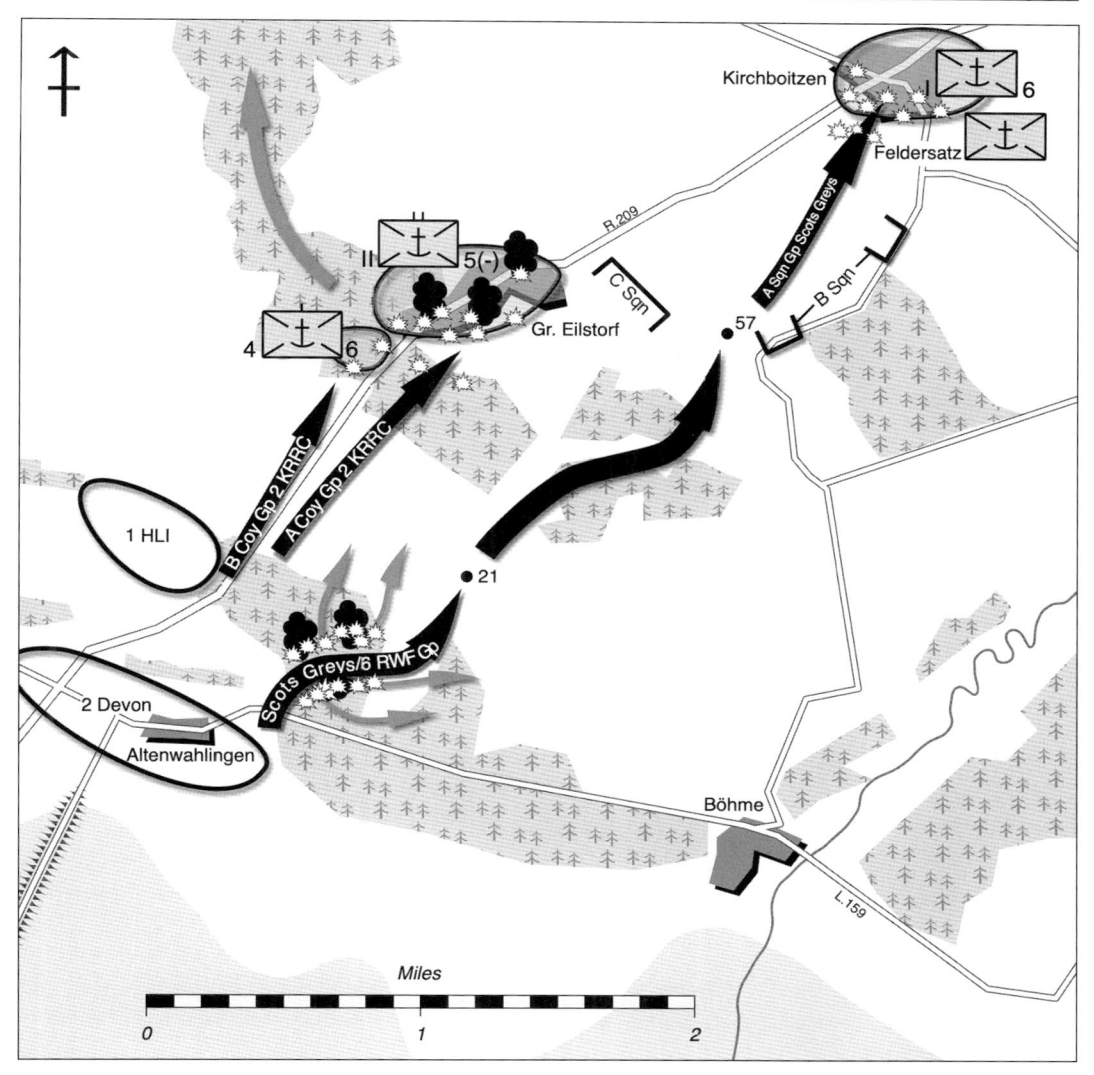

Map 66 4th Armoured Brigade's Attacks on Gr. Eilstorf and Kirchboitzen – 15 April 1945.

rifleman.[19] The carrier platoon was meanwhile giving wonderful support and the Germans, though fighting very hard, were obliterated. Rifleman Matthews of 3 Platoon lost his platoon and cleared a large farm single-handed with a German dog as his companion! 4 Platoon then pushed through and cleared the rest of the village which was by then under accurate shell-fire. Altogether 40 enemy were accounted for in a short but bitter struggle.

While A Company and A Squadron assaulted from the south, B Company and B Squadron moved up from the west and cleared the northern part of Gross Eilstorf. Watching the assault was a young member of 4./6 Kompanie, Helmut Krieg:[20]

---

19 This was probably Corporal Sydney Nash, killed on this day and now lying in CWGC cemetery Becklingen.
20 Saft, *Krieg in Der Heimat*, p.264.

> Suddenly the artillery fire we had been subjected to lifted and we saw the attackers coming towards us. No infantry were to be seen but just tanks – tanks in long lines. They rolled down the road slowly, shooting into the woods as they came. We waited for the tanks to turn off the road and roll over us but we were to be surprised. The tanks did not turn left in our direction but went to the right. A great weight was lifted from me.

Krieg and his comrades were not to know however that the assault was intended to bypass their position and later they were mopped-up complete. When B Squadron Group broke into the western part of Gross Eilstorf, it experienced difficulty with burning houses and sniping and it was not until 1055 hours that brigade headquarters was informed that the village was clear and the road passable. The marines put up staunch resistance and the 2 KRRC war diary describes them as 'very good, very tough and always offensive and coming back for more.' One German officer and 94 marines were captured in the fight for Gross Eilstorf, those that avoided capture withdrew through the forest to Gross Eilstorf's north and we will soon encounter these men. On the south-eastern edge of the village an oak tree still bears the scars of battle and at the base of this tree a *Leutnant* and a *Fähnrich* were buried in a temporary grave. A female villager tells the following story:[21]

> For some days a battle had been raging to our west in Rethem where the Allies were trying to cross the Aller. Early in the morning of 15 April young German soldiers began coming through the village from the south-east [Altenwahlingen]. They were in a terrible state, one had a very damaged helmet. The shed opposite us was destroyed by fire. The mare, which had foaled five days before, was killed. Several houses in the village were destroyed, including one which was used as a temporary hospital. I and several of the women buried the young officers next to the oak tree. We covered their faces with a vinegar-soaked cloth so that they could be identified at a later date.

While 44 RTR Group was attacking Gross Eilstorf, the Scots Greys Group, concentrated in the saucer-shaped dip, prepared for its forthcoming attack on Kirchboitzen. The plan involved A Squadron with two companies of 6 RWF in Kangaroos assaulting from the south; C Squadron would provide fire support from hull-down positions from the south-west and B Squadron was split to cover the other squadrons' rear flanks as the country was open and not positively clear of enemy. H-hour was set for 0800 hours. Kirchboitzen was held by marines from I./6 Bataillon and some from Marine-Feldersatz-Bataillon 2, withdrawn to their position on the Aller near Bierde to avoid being cut off by the expanding British bridgeheads at Rethem and Essel. Over the preceding days Kirchboitzen had been rocketed by Typhoons on a number of occasions and destruction of houses and deaths of inhabitants had already occurred.

The attack began at 0815 hours with an artillery fire plan fired by 4 RHA.[22] Despite the accuracy of the shelling, while closing on the village the attacking tanks and infantry in their Kangaroos were met with intense small-arms' fire accompanied by heavy shelling and mortaring, indicating that the guns of 2. Marine-Artillerie-Regiment 2 had eventually reached the front after their long horse-drawn move from Schleswig-Holstein. Possibly due to inexperience, the Welsh infantry dismounted when still 200 yards from the houses and were quickly pinned down, resulting in the leading tank troop, 1 Troop commanded by Lieutenant Andrews, closing on the village without any infantry support. Despite this the troop, accompanied by the squadron second-in-command Captain Lewis in his tank, pressed on. Various mishaps then overtook 1 Troop's tanks resulting in

---

21   Saft, *Krieg in Der Heimat*, p.265.
22   TNA WO 171/5081, 4 RHA war diary.

only Lieutenant Andrews' and Captain Lewis's tanks entering the village. On reaching the church, Lieutenant Andrews was greeted by a salvo of six *Panzerfaust* fired from 30 yards away; five missed but the sixth, fired by an inhabitant of the village, struck the ground by the track at the rear of the tank temporarily immobilising it. At this point the co-axial Besa jammed and the gunner had to resort to firing HE rounds from the main armament at targets as they appeared. Fortunately, the remainder of 1 Troop soon joined these two leading tanks and with the armour dominating the village's western perimeter the infantry were able to advance and clear the village building by building; by mid-morning the battle for Kirchboitzen was over.

Sixty-seven prisoners were taken and 47 marines were killed defending Gross Eilstorf and Kirchboitzen. Those marines managing to avoid death or capture in Kirchboitzen retreated northwards to take up positions in Vethem and Südkampen. While the Scots Greys and 6 RWF regrouped after the successful attack, a patrol of the Scots Greys' recce troop pressed on up Reichsstrasse 209 beyond Kirchboitzen to report on the state of the road. It soon reported back that the road was cratered where it crossed the Jordanbach stream and no deviation was possible. A patrol was also dispatched to Altenboitzen, to the south of Reichsstrasse 209, as the village had earlier been thought to contain enemy; the patrol reported it to be clear.

By this time the lead elements of 22nd Armoured Brigade were across the Rethem bridge and straining at the leash to take over the advance.[23] XII Corps therefore decided that 4th Armoured should not continue to Walsrode but turn north to help 53rd Division clear Verden and Rotenburg, and in so doing free Reichsstrasse 209 for 7th Armoured's use. However, once again traffic congestion in the restricted area of the Rethem bridgehead now became a problem, delaying a sensible change of plan. While unwelcome at higher levels, for 4th Armoured there were sound reasons favouring some delay, despite Brigadier Carver being anxious to get the tail of his brigade clear of Gross Eilstorf as soon as possible. It was not yet safe to move the Sextons of 4 RHA beyond the village, and before 4th Armoured could take up its new northward advance he needed to pass 1 RTR, from 22nd Armoured, through Gross Eilstorf to Kirchboitzen to relieve the Scots Greys and 6 RWF. Furthermore, there were also pressing administrative reasons for some delay as 6 RWF had not had a meal since the previous afternoon, ammunition needed replenishing and the two regimental groups had to regroup. Despite the pressure from on high and 22nd Armoured's frustration, for the time being 4th Armoured remained in situ and, with his brigade pausing, Brigadier Carver completed planning for the next phase.[24] He decided to advance on two regimental axes: on the left 44 RTR Group directed on Südkampen, Nordkampen and Hamwiede; and on the right Scots Greys Group with Vethem and Idsingen as its objectives. Although the right axis with fewer villages and woods offered the best opportunity for rapid progress, it was still essential to clear the left axis as the brigade needed it for its logistic tail.

Awaiting the two regimental groups were marines and engineer potential officers of Pi.ROB.Btl. Nienburg, who had retreated to the area after the fighting on the Aller and at Gross Eilstorf and Kirchboitzen and had regrouped to defend the villages. Although these much-weakened forces were all that was available to prevent the British advance, they made every effort to improve their circumstances by creating strongpoints in the villages, blowing bridges and felling trees across the roads. Captured orders written by Hauptmann Kessel admit the failure of the counter-attacks but reveal that the defence was still organised and with a continuing determination to fight:[25]

---

23 TNA WO 171/4340, 22nd Armoured Brigade war diary.
24 4th Armoured Brigade, Operations East of the River Aller, 14–19 April 1945 (unpublished). This after action review provides the majority of the source material for the narrative's description of the brigade's activity.
25 TNA WO 171/4277, Special Supplement to 53rd Welsh Division INTSUM No. 231, 21 April 1945, p.6.

Battalion Orders for the Defence of the Sector Waterloo (inclusive) to Südkampen (exclusive)

The enemy has repelled last night's attack and is now attacking from the Verden road towards Stemmen. 2. Marine-Infanterie-Division is now holding the general line Armsen–Waterloo–Südkampen–Gross Eilstorf. Pi.ROB.Btl.Nienburg (all three companies) is now under the command of Marine-Grenadier-Regiment 7 – right boundary Waterloo (inclusive), left boundary Südkampen (exclusive). Battalion HQ Nordkampen. Outposts and standing patrols are to be pushed out to the south. 1. Kompanie (on right) will maintain contact with Marine-Grenadier-Regiment 7.

Signed: Kessel, Hauptmann

Südkampen was held by the headquarters of II./5 Bataillon and 40 remaining marines of 7./5 Kompanie, Vethem was held by marines from Jordan's regimental headquarters and 3./5 and 5./5 Kompanien, while Nordkampen was held by the engineer potential officers of Pi.ROB.Btl. Nienburg. Also in the area were batteries of 10.5cm field guns of Marine-Artillerie-Regiment 2; these guns will soon meet British armour, with predictable consequences. The defenders of Südkampen also had three Renault FT-17 light tanks. These ancient French tanks of 1917 vintage were mentioned in an Ultra decrypt of 13 April,[26] which recorded that on 5 and 6 April Renault and 'Wolff' tanks were ordered to come under command of 8. Flak-Division and report to Flak-Regiment 122(E) at Walsrode; they were presumably then dispatched to the Aller. The Renaults possibly came from nearby Rotenburg airfield, where they would have been used for base security, but the 'Wolff' tanks are something of an enigma. As the Wolff munitions plant was nearby at Bomlitz near Walsrode it is possible that in some way the decrypt confused the plant with a type of tank. Alternatively, as Harland and Wolff manufactured Matildas, Churchills and Centaurs perhaps it was the nickname for captured British tanks. The decrypt states that the 'Wolffs' were a mystery to MI 14 (the intelligence agency of the War Office specialising in intelligence about Germany), and are likely to remain so.

4th Armoured's advance resumed at mid-day and the Scots Greys Group soon discovered Vethem defended. In trying to outflank it the Stuarts of the recce troop were engaged by five 10.5cm howitzers belonging to a battery of Marine-Artillerie-Regiment 2 firing from the wood line to the north-east of the village. Operations by the group were also hindered by the ridge to the north-west of Vethem, which overlooked the area and was topped by the Nordkampen windmill. Attempts to find a route through the wooded slope south of the road were finally successful but took time, and it now also became apparent that the bridge over the Vethbach stream to Vethem's south was blown and all other approaches to the village were difficult. Furthermore, the area of the Vethbach was boggy, effectively protecting the village on all sides less the west, and the approaches from the south and east were open and overlooked by both the village and the Nordkampen ridge. It was clear that Vethem might not be easy to capture, requiring at least two of 6 RWF's companies, and the ridge with its windmill would also have to be taken as it dominated the axes of both regimental groups.

Unfortunately for the German artillerymen, as soon as they opened fire on the Stuarts their five guns were spotted by the Scots Greys' commanding officer, Lieutenant Colonel 'Duggie' Stewart, and he ordered B Squadron to mount an immediate attack on them. In something of the spirit of the Light Brigade the tanks charged the guns knocking them out at point-blank range. From its position on the fringe of the wood, B Squadron was then able to provide overwatch while

---

26 TNA DEFE 3/566, KO 316.

THROUGH THE CRUST 407

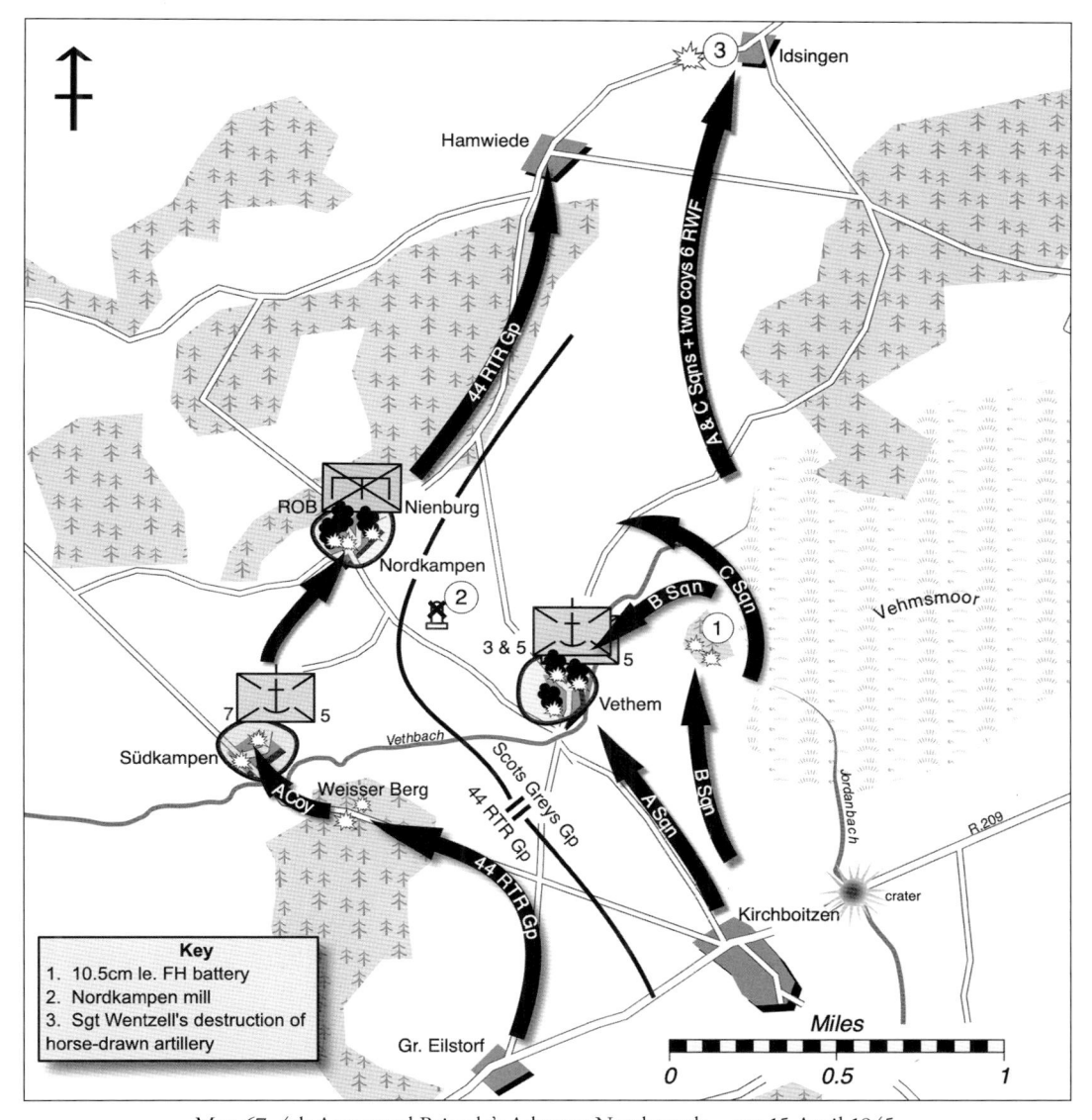

Map 67 4th Armoured Brigade's Advance Northwards – pm 15 April 1945.

C Squadron pushed around to the north-east to isolate Vethem. A Squadron, given the task of attacking the village from the south with two companies of 6 RWF and supported by the other two squadrons, only managed a short distance before it was held up by the Vethbach and the poor going, and so B Squadron was ordered to attack from the east as it was already across the stream. As it entered the village, stubborn resistance was immediately encountered from all forms of small-arms and ever-present *Panzerfaust*. Although the marines suffered many casualties, the British did not escape unscathed; Lieutenant Briggs, troop leader of 2 Troop, was killed by a shot fired from an upstairs window and 6 RWF suffered five killed and 20 wounded.

At the same time as the Scots Greys Group was involved in Vethem, 44 RTR Group was moving north from Gross Eilstorf, with Südkampen as its objective. Although the road to Südkampen avoided the bulk of the forest stretching north from Gross Eilstorf, it passed through the forest's hillocky, northern part in the area known as the Weisser Berg and as soon as the armour entered this area it was engaged by machine-guns and *Panzerfaust* fired by ambush parties among the trees. Despite sustaining some casualties 44 RTR Group was able to brush this resistance aside and reach the outskirts of Südkampen. A Company 2 KRRC was directed to take the village and Major Gosse ordered 3 Platoon to make the initial attack. The platoon found the main bridge over the stream on the village's southern edge blown and a 30-foot scissors bridge (mounted on a Valentine tank chassis) was called up from brigade to span the gap. With 3 Platoon committed on the southern approach, 2 Platoon and the carrier platoon made their way round the right flank, entered the village and by last light had quickly cleared the remaining opposition, in the process capturing many prisoners and the three Renault FT-17 light tanks.

With 44 RTR Group busy clearing Südkampen and Vethem still contested, Brigadier Carver ordered Lieutenant Colonel Stewart to leave the Scots Greys' A and B Squadrons and the two companies of 6 RWF to complete the clearance of Vethem and with C Squadron and the other two 6 RWF companies advance to Idsingen. This move was completed practically unopposed, passing on the way the 10.5cm howitzers knocked out earlier by B Squadron. As Idsingen was well in depth of the fighting in Südkampen, on arrival the tanks and infantry were positioned at each of the village's entrances as it was anticipated that the Germans might enter unaware that it had been captured and now held by two companies of enemy infantry and a squadron of tanks. At about 2100 hours this theory proved correct when numbers of Germans entered from the west and in the ensuing skirmish 40 were captured. Worse was to befall the Germans when, during the small hours of the morning of 16 April, soldiers on foot and horse-drawn 10.5cm howitzers of Marine-Artillerie-Regiment 2 approached Idsingen from the west. As they neared they were engaged by Sergeant Wentzell's troop, which opened fire at a range of 80 yards. When the target area was revealed at first light it was discovered that the troop had killed 20 Germans and destroyed three horse-drawn 10.5cm howitzers, with the horses still in harness.

Despite the success in reaching Idsingen, Vethem was still not cleared owing to a stubborn stronghold held by marines in the centre of the village. Even after houses were cleared, groups of marines kept on reappearing; a typically courageous performance. The whole village was by now ablaze and as the two 6 RWF companies engaged in clearing it were somewhat disorganised and weary, the decision was taken to pull back and destroy the village with concentrated 75mm and 17-pdr HE gunfire; Vethem was subsequently hammered into submission and taken at 2300 hours with no further opposition. It was, however, difficult to reorganise in the village as farm animals, maddened by the fire and shelling, were stampeding in all directions, terrified civilians were attempting to rescue their remaining belongings and the ground was hot under foot; only three houses were not burnt to the ground.

As the tactic of reducing villages with HE saved time and casualties, 44 RTR Group decided to treat its next objective, Nordkampen, in similar fashion. A call to the defenders to surrender was made by a psychological warfare team with a loudspeaker and a small demonstration was laid on, demolishing a house. As this brought out only the *Bürgermeister*, A Squadron slowly entered the village. The tanks were greeted with a hail of fire so the village was raised to the ground and occupied without further trouble. We will now leave 4th Armoured Brigade while it continues its northwards advance and follow 7th Armoured Division.

7th Armoured Division breakout

Major General Lyne's plan for 7th Armoured's advance involved 22nd Armoured Brigade leading with Lüneburg as its objective; 131st and 155th Infantry Brigades would follow the armour and mop-up bypassed enemy and secure the flanks. At Brigadier Wingfield's subsequent orders held

Cromwells moving through the smoking ruins of Vethem.

during the morning of 14 April he described his concept, which involved an advance on two axes with a regimental group on each: on the left on Red route the 1 RTR Group comprising the tank regiment with a motor company from 1 RB in half-tracks and a battery of 25-pdr Sextons from 5 RHA; and on the right on Yellow route the 8 Hussars Group, mirroring 1 RTR Group's organisation; in reserve would be 5 RTR, 1/5 Queens mounted in Kangaroos and 1 RB less the two motor companies. He concluded his orders by placing the brigade at one hour's notice to cross the Rethem bridge. The next day, with pressure mounting from the corps commander to get the armoured division underway, it was decided to launch the 8 Hussars Group on Yellow route before 4th Armoured was clear of Reichsstrasse 209. Although fighting was still ongoing in Kirchboitzen, this was achievable if the 8 Hussars Group deviated well to the south and only rejoined Reichsstrasse 209 near Walsrode, the next town on the road after Rethem. Brigadier Wingfield ordered the group to advance and at 0800 hours on 15 April the long column of vehicles began to move off.

With the Aller Line in an advanced state of collapse, there were very few German forces available to block 22nd Armoured. The remaining battle-worthy elements of 2. Marine-Infanterie-Division were falling back to the north and north-east leaving Reichsstrasse 209 largely undefended. Some marines from I./6 Bataillon had reached Walsrode, and as they retreated from Kirchboitzen an Organization Todt team blew the demolition charge in the culvert carrying the Jordanbach stream under Reichsstrasse 209, producing a sizeable crater and most effectively denying the road. This was the crater previously reported by the Scots Greys recce troop. The only forces capable of offering any resistance on Reichsstrasse 209 between Kirchboitzen and Walsrode were the former gunners of Flak batteries 4./117 and 4./162. These men had lost most of their guns and were now swept up as infantry with members of RAD Flak-Abteilung 366, to form an *ad hoc* rifle company of two platoons known as 5./366 Kompanie and commanded by a Hauptmann Tesch. 5./366 Kompanie occupied hastily-developed positions with a platoon either side of Reichsstrasse 209 in the area between Sindorf and Schneeheide. The company was supported by two 8.8cm Flak and two 2cm Flak belonging to RAD Batterie 2./604, which had withdrawn from the Timpenberg area before it was taken by 1 HLI.

410 THEIRS THE STRIFE

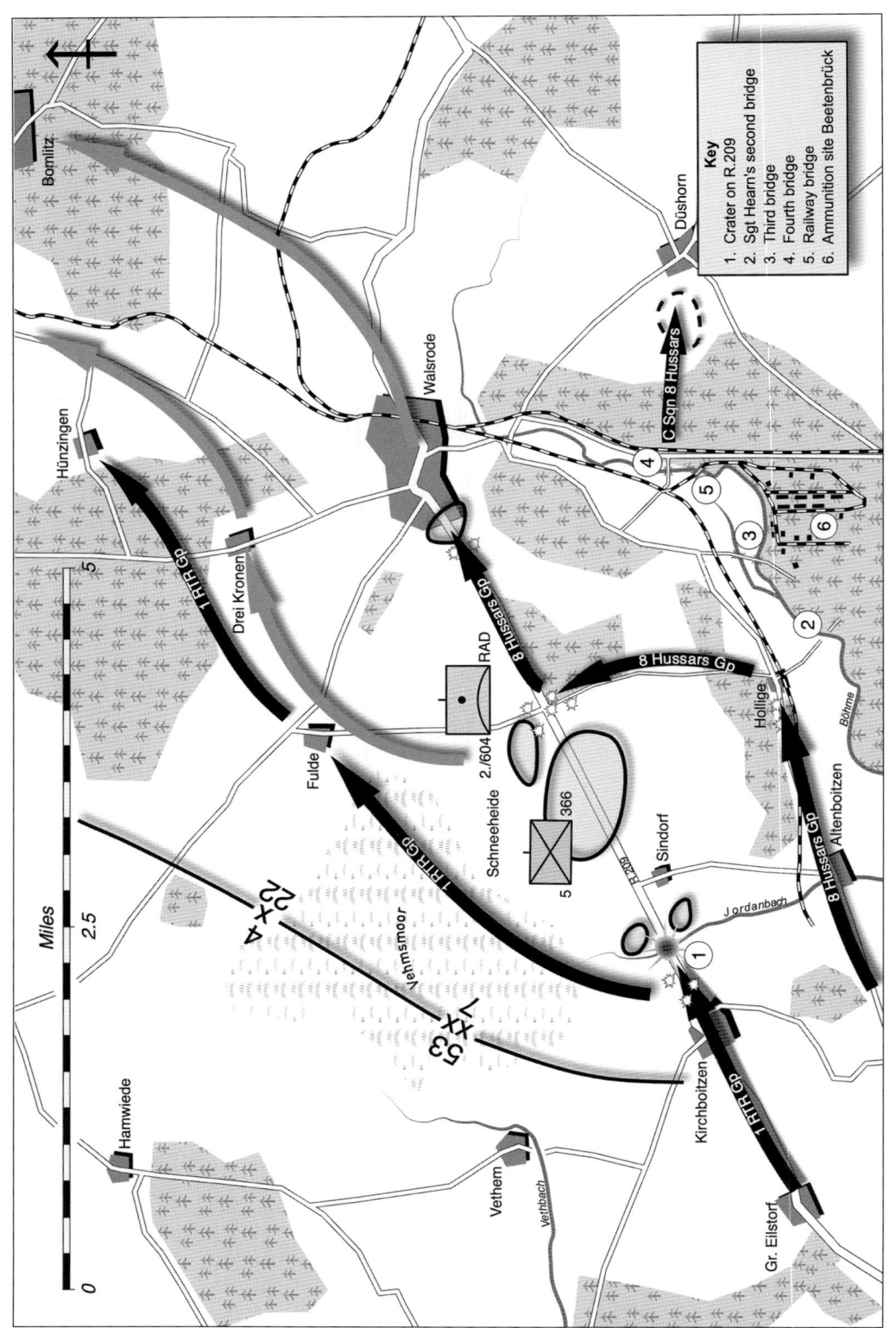

Map 68 22nd Armoured Brigade's Advance to Walsrode – 15 April 1945.

8 Hussars with A Company 1 RB and K Battery 5 RHA crossed the Rethem Bailey bridge and then deviated to the south to bypass Kirchboitzen.[27] The group made good progress on the sandy tracks and by 1130 hours had reached Altenboitzen. The atmosphere of the day is evident from the diary entries of Edward Ardizzone, the famous artist and illustrator, who was attached to the regiment as an official war artist:[28]

> A very cold, grey morning – busy packing-up as we hope to leave. Leave about 0930 (a long procession, one squadron in front of us and other squadrons behind us) before we halt in a stretch of ploughed land. Then across a Bailey bridge [Rethem] and by devious ways with many halts, through wooded country. Sounds of battle in the forest to our left. Column of B carriers and Kangaroos cross our path. The forest thick pine. In the open places and along the dirt roads many aspen in first leaf…
>
> Pass through two half-timbered and brick forest villages. In the second one [Hollige] a man fired a *Panzerfaust* at our tank from behind the corner of a barn, about 20 paces away. Thank God he missed. Go cautiously forward after this, scanning every nook and corner. Relief when we get out of the village into open country…

By early afternoon B Squadron, leading the advance, was well beyond Kirchboitzen and able to head north to join Reichsstrasse 209. As the tanks neared the road they were engaged by the *Flak* at the Schneeheide position and small-arms' fire from 5./366 Kompanie. The war diarist of batteries 4./117 and 4./162 describes these events:[29]

> 15.4.45…At mid-day the tanks advanced against the positions. The tanks crossed the main road advancing towards the first group's positions and those of RAD 2./604. The company commander located on the Schneeheide came under fire from two tanks and machine-gun and artillery fire. The second group came under heavy, machine-gun fire and had to vacate their positions. Part of the first group was over-run by tanks. With the exception of one soldier, no news about the fate of those men is known. The remainder of the first group was able to withdraw via Fulde to Drei Kronen.
>
> Killed: Leutnant Bornhofen from a splinter wound to the head.
>
> Missing: Wachtmeister Passek, Stabsgefreiter Kruse, Obergefreiter Koch, Gravenits, Strack, Effer and Gefreiter Wieprecht.[30]
>
> Wachtmeister Passek managed to fire a last *Panzerfaust* towards an attacking Sherman. Obergefreiter Bartl from the second group fired a *Panzerfaust* at a tank driving up the main road and destroyed it.[31]
>
> Missing: Flak-v. Schroers deserted through fear at the start of the attack.
>
> The soldiers of the second group were reformed on Reichsstrasse 209 by the company commander and repositioned with the 8.8cm Flak near the road intersection at the Schneede farm. After a further advance of the tanks, these soldiers helped evacuate two 2cm guns and one 8.8cm gun from falling into enemy hands. As Walsrode came under fire during the same afternoon all units were withdrawn to Jarlingen and after a short rest withdrew further to Bommelsen.

---

27 TNA WO 171/4688, 8 Hussars war diary.
28 Edward Ardizzone, *Diary of a War Artist* (London: The Bodley Head. Reproduced by permission of The Random House Group Ltd © 1974), p.196.
29 *Gefechtsbericht der 4./117 und 4./162*, 4 May 1945.
30 *Wachtmeister* was a rank used in the *Flak* arm and equivalent to *Feldwebel* (sergeant).
31 Neither the regimental war diary nor the survey of tank casualties record an 8 Hussars tank destroyed by *Panzerfaust* on 15 April.

It is not surprising that Schroers fled the fighting. As a 17-year-old *Flak-v. Soldat* he would have had no military training whatsoever and he very wisely removed himself from the action. Hopefully he was not later found and executed.

Despite their best efforts, the German defenders at Schneeheide were no match for the British armour and motorised infantry, which quickly cleared the area knocking out three 2cm guns, and by 1550 hours 8 Hussars Group had established itself astride Reichsstrasse 209 on the high ground overlooking Walsrode. Ardizzone gives his impressions of the advance:[32]

> A long halt on a road with silver birch and in open country. Sounds of battle forward and to our left. A big fire ahead too. Some prisoners came back riding on the bonnet of an armoured car. All the time voices on the wireless giving battle positions. Forward onto the main road, past burning cottages and one dead German soldier by the roadside, then up to the high ground overlooking Walsrode. A big fire in the village and one in a farmhouse to the right of us. Dotted about around us are more tanks, half-tracks and a little group of prisoners. Enemy planes overhead and sound of Bren and shellfire…

With the main body of 8 Hussars Group on Reichsstrasse 209, the recce troop was sent south-east with the dual task of providing a measure of flank protection while assessing the state of four bridges over the river Böhme in case an alternative route to the main axis was needed. This however was a task not without risk as the recce cars were soon engaged by small bands of Germans lurking in the woods and farms; opposition that was dealt with by return fire from the Stuarts' 37mm guns and Besa machine-guns. Civilians questioned by members of the troop informed them that all four bridges were blown. Sergeant Hearn soon discovered that the civilians were correct in respect of the first and second bridges. Sergeant Spencer was checking the third when he got into a potentially dangerous situation. The road leading to the bridge over the Böhme first crossed a small stream via a rickety wooden structure, which collapsed as soon as his vehicle reached the far bank. Then moving on a few hundred yards, he found the bridge over the Böhme blown, so faced a blown bridge to his front, a collapsed one to his rear and nothing but marshes either side of the road; he was a sitting duck. Fortunately, close at hand were some telegraph poles and sleepers lying alongside the nearby railway track. The section's Stuart pushed down the telegraph poles and using these with the sleepers the section rebuilt the collapsed bridge and Sergeant Spencer was able to make his escape; he was fortunate to have been left unmolested for the two hours it took to rebuild the bridge.

While Sergeant Spencer was honing his skills as a sapper, Sergeant Hearn discovered the fourth bridge to be a fairly substantial and intact wooden structure and, in the event of it being unable to take the weight of a Cromwell, less than 70 yards away stood a massive stone and concrete railway bridge, which carried a spur line to the Beetenbrück ammunition storage site hidden in the nearby forest. Sergeant Hearn's section gingerly crossed the wooden bridge and his lead Stuart, breasting a small wooded rise on the far side, narrowly missed a crowded German staff car driving flat out along the broad concrete road and making its escape to Walsrode. Some sappers were sent to pass professional judgement on the wooden bridge and as they thought it might take a Cromwell, the troop leader of the leading troop of C Squadron, by now on the scene, was selected as the guinea pig. The recce troop watched mesmerised as the timbers creaked and sagged while the Cromwell slowly, and successfully, crossed. The remainder of the squadron then followed and with the recce troop pushed on up the other side.

---

32 Edward Ardizzone, *Diary of a War Artist*, p.196.

Back on Reichsstrasse 209, B Squadron and A Company 1 RB were located on the high ground to the west of Walsrode waiting for the remainder of 22nd Armoured to close up before pressing on into the town. Ardizzone describes the scene:[33]

> 7 pm: Still on the high ground above Walsrode. We seemed to be ringed by fires, some very distant, some nearer. Also distant explosions as bridges are blown by the enemy – some shelling too. The evening sun lighting the scene and the great columns and mushrooms of smoke. Forward again about 7.30 pm. Have the misfortune to misplace a track in a ploughed field near a monolith.[34] Get the tank to the road. Repairs seem almost hopeless. We are visited by an insolent *Nazi* boy. Getting dark and nervous of being a lone tank crew after dark. Tank mended at last, very late – but we had the company of endless convoys of tanks, Kangaroos and lorries. Find Tac HQ after a devious route through the outskirts of the town. A great fire in a factory lit us part of the way. Arrive at 1 am very tired and dirty. Stumble off my tank and hurt my leg horribly. Go to bed on the floor of a dirty kitchen.

Although a reasonably-sized town, Walsrode was largely undefended. However, its south-west entrance was heavily cratered and held by a company of marines, probably from Marine-Grenadier-Regiment 6, and some Hitler Youth from 3. SS-Kompanie. B Squadron group soon disposed of this opposition and those who escaped capture withdrew northwards to Bomlitz. By 2200 hours Walsrode had been occupied by 1/5 Queens and found to be over-flowing with civilians.[35] In addition, the town was serving as a casualty evacuation centre and its three hospitals were full of wounded, among them eight British soldiers from the battle of Rethem. Today in Walsrode's cemetery lie 106 German soldiers, the majority casualties from the fighting on the Aller and among them Vizeadmiral Ernst Scheurlen. With Walsrode captured, 8 Hussars Group leaguered for the night on the high ground to the west of the town, but the recce troop and C Squadron leaguered to the south of Reichsstrasse 209 as they had not managed to get through Düshorn to rejoin the regiment. Their leaguer was in a field of roots, the largest patch of open ground they could find, with the vehicles massed in a tight bunch in the middle. Although the troops had not eaten since their early breakfast that morning, they dared not light any kind of fire and risk revealing their position.

Owing to the delay in 4th Armoured Brigade moving north of Reichsstrasse 209, the other 22nd Armoured Brigade group, 1 RTR, only began to move at 0930 hours and did not cross the Rethem bridge until 1200 hours. The group then slowly moved up Reichstrasse 209 and by mid-day had reached Kirchboitzen. Here 1 RTR dropped off A Squadron to relieve the Scots Greys and then moved on to catch up with 8 Hussars advancing on the right axis. By 1500 hours the lead squadron had reached the demolished culvert of the Jordanbach stream but was then held up not only by the demolition but also by numbers of Germans covering the crater and firing *Panzerfaust*. This stream's name brought a wry smile to members of the division as the Class 40 Bailey pontoon built by 7th Armoured Divisional engineers over the Weser at Nienburg was confidently given the name 'Jordan Bridge' as there appeared to be only one more river – the Elbe – to cross. The first water obstacle the division encountered on the resumption of its advance was the Jordanbach!

1 RTR's squadrons remained in the area of the demolition until mid-afternoon awaiting engineer assistance. At 1630 hours the commanding officer, Lieutenant Colonel Hobart, was told to wait no longer and advance north-east to Fulde as this more northerly direction matched the new

---

33 Edward Ardizzone, *Diary of a War Artist*, p.196.
34 This is the Bismarkturm, a massive, baleful stone monument erected in 1910 in Bismark's honour.
35 TNA WO 171/5275, 1/5 Queens war diary.

divisional axis allocated to Major General Lyne. 7th Armoured was now not to capture Lüneburg but instead head towards the bridges over the Elbe at Harburg, lying to the immediate south of Hamburg. This required a marked swing to the north and Soltau became the division's new objective. 1 RTR Group accordingly struck off across the heath and meeting only sporadic opposition from groups of marines from Marine-Grenadier-Regiment 5 and some Hitler Youth from SS-A.u.E.Btl. 12 'HJ', had cleared Fulde and Hünzingen by 1900 hours. At Appendix A Serial 18 is film of captured members of SS-A.u.E.Btl. 12 'HJ' being interrogated. During its advance the following day the group swept past Bomlitz. Shortly before the British arrived, Untersturmführer Fries formed up his 40 remaining soldiers of 3. SS-Kompanie in a factory yard of Bomlitz's heavily-camouflaged Waldhof explosives' production complex, made a short speech and then ordered all those under 18 to step forward: 12 moved. These soldiers then had their *Soldbücher* stamped 'Dismissed, Bomlitz, 16 April 1945' and were ordered to go home, which, after some protest, they did. The remainder would fight on.

4 KOSB clear the Gross Eilstorf woods

While 22nd Armoured pushed slowly forward, 155th Brigade waited on the Aller's left bank to follow in its wake. The brigade's task was to mop up any stragglers in the villages of Böhme, Gross Eilstorf and Altenboitzen and in the forests bypassed by 4th and 22nd Armoured Brigades, with its battalions directed on these tasks: 7/9 R Scots to clear Böhme, 6 HLI to clear Altenboitzen and 4 KOSB to clear Gross Eilstorf.[36] At 1430 hours, after a frustrating morning spent waiting at immediate notice, the brigade eventually began to move. Lieutenant Peter White, commanding 10 Platoon B Company 4 KOSB, describes Rethem as they were trucked forward from the concentration area:[37]

> …over a thickly mortared field a complete trainload of 88mm [sic] guns was drawn up along a railway embankment…some of the guns appeared intact. The town of Rethem itself was in a really awful mess from bombing. Hardly a building was standing with four walls. Miserable, dazed civilians dejectedly turned over the rubble of their homes, beachcomber fashion, as they hunted for any surviving valuables and clothes. They took no notice of our heavy military traffic winding bumpily past. At times the pattern of the streets had been so obliterated by craters and explosives that the engineers had bulldozed new roads straight through the powdered brick, glass, wood and mess.
>
> This trail led us to the banks of the Aller, where, besides the remains of Rethem church, we ran onto and swayed creaking over the new pontoon bridge which had been floated over the Aller beside a wrecked road bridge.

With dusk falling, B Company reached two road junctions on Reichsstrasse 209 between Altenwahlingen and Gross Eilstorf, its destination, and had begun digging-in when it received a message that Germans had been seen in the forest to the north of the main road and the company was to investigate. These were marines from II./5 Bataillon and I./6 Bataillon, withdrawing north into the forest following the fall of Gross Eilstorf and by-passed during 44 RTR Group's northward advance to Südkampen that afternoon. B Company stopped digging-in and moved up Reichsstrasse 209 towards Gross Eilstorf. It was a cold night matched by an inner coldness and tension, which Peter White felt as the company left the road and headed up a sandy track. They

---

36   TNA WO 171/5215, 4 KOSB war diary.
37   Peter White, *With the Jocks* (Stroud: Sutton Publishing, 2001. By kind permission The History Press), p.325.

THROUGH THE CRUST 415

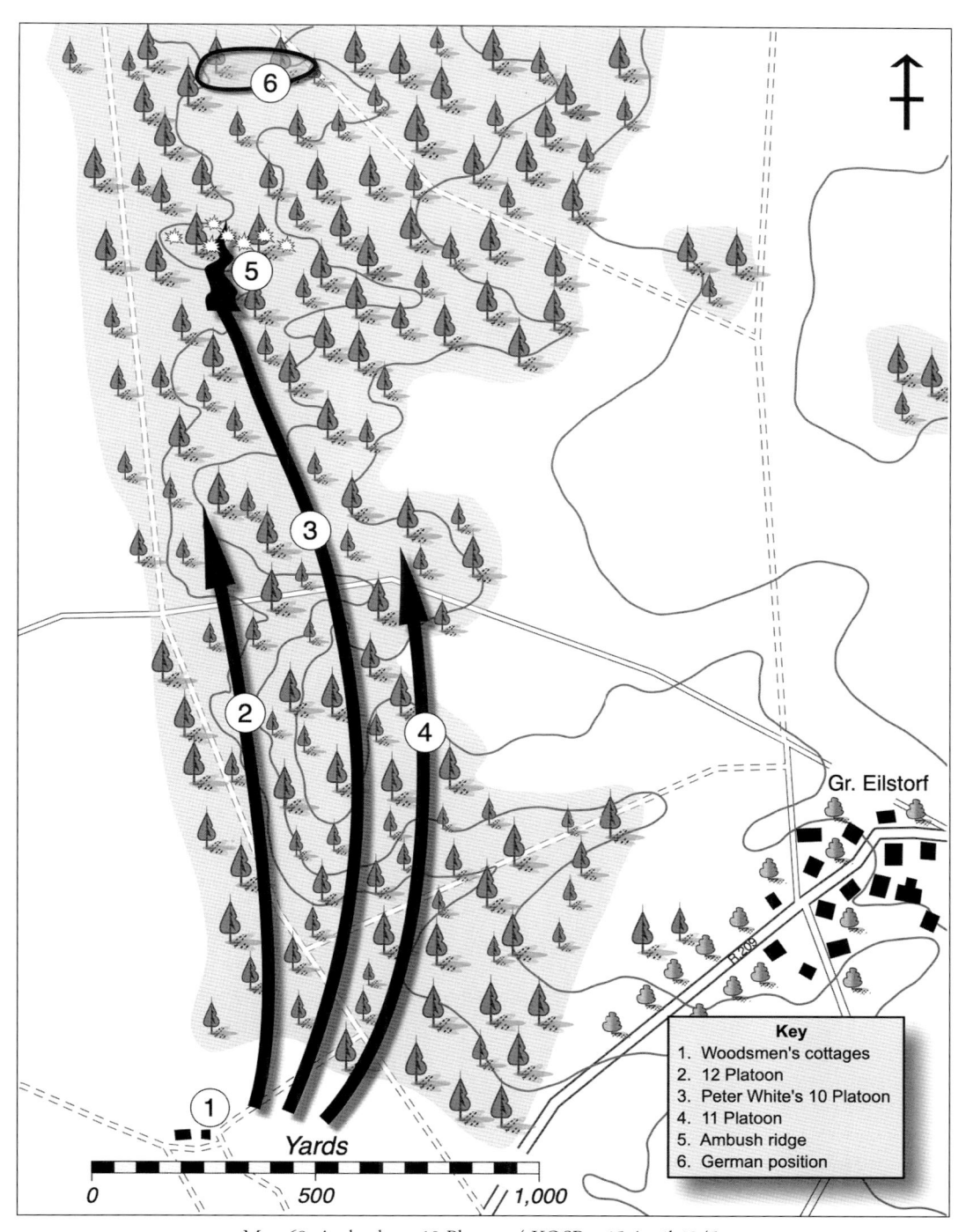

Key
1. Woodsmen's cottages
2. 12 Platoon
3. Peter White's 10 Platoon
4. 11 Platoon
5. Ambush ridge
6. German position

Map 69 Ambush on 10 Platoon 4 KOSB – 15 April 1945.

passed a couple of forestry workers' cottages then spread out to present as small a target as possible to any enemy hiding in the nearby sombre pine forests.

The forest the company was ordered to clear follows the line of a north-west–south-east oriented escarpment that gradually climbs from the Aller's valley to more open, higher ground to the east and features a series of gentle spurs and re-entrants, like the teeth of a saw. After receiving their orders, with 12 Platoon left rear and 11 Platoon right rear, Peter White and 10 Platoon led the company's advance and began to ascend and descend the spurs:[38]

> The Jocks were treading warily and not too keenly with rifles at the port across their bodies, hunched to a stoop to compress themselves into as small a target as possible. There were only eleven of us in the first wave as we were not yet up to full strength. If and when we met the enemy, I realised with a tense dryness in my throat, the advantage lay entirely with him in choice of ground – concealment as against our open movement – and surprise. We would only know we had located him when some or all of us forward were suddenly fired on, perhaps from point-blank range. I wondered if all the Jocks realised this…Now we were among the trees. It was far darker under the canopy of the pines than I had expected. The pine-incensed, cathedral half-light and columns of the tall tree trunks receded into the gloom as far as the eye could penetrate with here and there a tangle of dimly seen undergrowth. The woods seemed pregnant with an eerie oppressive silence but for the crunch and slither of our boots in the pine-needle carpet and sand underfoot. High above a slight breeze whispered in soft waves of sound, combing through the swaying pine-tops with the sigh of distant surf and cold eddies penetrated the murk beneath to waft the clean scent of pine resin freshly to tense nostrils.
>
> Every now and then a section commander's voice cut the silence to join my own in keeping the Jocks from bunching, in line and maintaining direction. There unfortunately seemed an almost constant need for these vocal corrections to control the chaps in the leading line to my extreme right and left.

10 Platoon moved on through the forest with the light getting fainter and fainter. It began heading up to another crest line and could see the ground opening up into some form of sand quarry. Peter White was with the left forward section slightly ahead of the rest of the line:[39]

> As we crossed the crest in line together, some very loud whiplash cracks of rifle bullets slashed the silence and the echo carried away into the surrounding woods. Corporal Parry fell like a log, shot through the head. Private Byles pitched forward grasping his stomach and lay perfectly still in a grotesque posture. About a fifth of a second passed before the implications had sunk in and the (other) three of us still carrying forward on our feet dropped to cover as several more shots cut past us, one with a twanging, ear-searing whine as it cut up a spurt in the sand just ahead of me and to the left. There was no sign at all of any visible enemy ahead but I fired off a couple of rounds forward at random as I painfully crawled back off the skyline. The tall Jock was groaning indicating the second volley had got him too.

With the assistance of the platoon's 2-in mortar firing HE, 10 Platoon was able to extract itself and pull back with the rest of B Company to Reichsstrasse 209. Once the company had regrouped and drawn breath, orders were given for an early morning attack on the enemy position in the forest, supported by artillery and tanks.

---

38 Peter White, *With the Jocks*, pp.328–329.
39 Peter White, *With the Jocks*, p.331.

Peter White and his lead section were advancing down the slope towards the camera when the ambush was sprung. Photograph taken in 2015. (Author)

In the early dawn of the next day (16 April) B Company moved to a forming-up point and then listened to the barrage of 25-pdr and 5.5-in guns pounding the area of the ambush. A troop of Cromwells from 5 Innis DG started up and headed off up the long sandy track at the foot of the escarpment and paralleling it; once the tanks started firing this was the sign for the infantry to advance:[40]

> The volume of fire was extraordinarily heavy and sustained. The barrel of my own rifle was soon beginning to ooze grease through the wood stock joints as it grew really hot and the bandolier round my shoulder grew lighter. It was really comforting to listen to the incredible racket of shelling, tanks firing, automatics and rifles and to feel the repeated vicious kicking of the rifle in one's own hands. How different to our previous gloomy stalk through the trees. Several times a sudden heavy explosion and tumbling blackness of smoke 50 to 100 yards ahead, followed by a crashing tree or two, marked the odd tank shell which had come far too far to the rear.
>
> The trunks of the trees were increasingly chipped white, gashed and drilled by the solid hail of bullets. We were approaching the dip before the fatal hill, still nothing had fired back at us. I was again up with the line of the forward two sections reinforced with the Bren guns of the third section and of platoon HQ. Looking back, it was reassuring to see the movement of 11 and 12 Platoons and company HQ following us up…
>
> Tension grew to its height as we started to climb the crest. I felt queerly alive as though living at twice normal speed. I could see the shapes of the tanks now ploughing along at the border of the wood. The racket of their shells crashing through the wood must, I reflected, be most depressing to any enemy, quite apart from the now intensifying stream of bullets from my chaps. The artillery had stopped…the next few steps would bring our heads out above the skyline and in view of the enemy. Sweat was running from under my tin hat and down my cheeks and nose. Subconsciously I tasted the salt of it as I bit my dry lips and swallowed. The next second or two would tell. Our firing was lifting spurts of yellow sand every now and then off the crest of the hill a few feet ahead.

---

40 Peter White, *With the Jocks*, pp.335–336.

Once over the spur's crest 10 Platoon swept down into the re-entrant on the far side. No enemy fire came its way as the Germans had left their positions and pulled back after the artillery lifted, but were then caught by the hail of machine-gun fire from the tanks. Fifteen dead Germans were counted but Peter White recounted how he felt no sense of achievement that the men who had killed Byles and Parry were now themselves dead and instead he felt a sense of depression and shame at man's inhumanity to man.

Although 10 Platoon's and B Company 4 KOSB's action in the woods was by any yardstick minor, Peter White's poignant and detailed description illustrates the courage needed to prosecute the war in its final days. With the wood cleared, B Company returned to Reichsstrasse 209, mounted its trucks and at Kirchboitzen met up with the remainder of the battalion, which had suffered no casualties.

158th Brigade northward advance

Following the solid progress it had made the previous day, on 15 April 158th Brigade continued its advance northwards. On the left flank 7 RWF resumed operations shortly after midnight and 30 minutes later C Company reported a road-block. As the accompanying tanks of 3/4 CLY had unsuccessfully tried to knock it down, sapper assistance was sought from brigade and by 0100 hours the block was clear, allowing the company to reach its objective, the road and railway crossing north of Hohenaverbergen. Rather than advancing further, the battalion spent the remainder of 15 April consolidating, although a patrol was sent to investigate Luttum, the next village.

1/5 Welch on the centre axis had a busier time. At 0815 hours D Company, with the Shermans of A Squadron 3/4 CLY, mounted an attack against 4./7 Kompanie on the ridge where they had been stopped the night before. But the attack was beaten-off and at 1300 hours another attempt had to be mounted. This attack was successful, probably due to the presence of eight Crocodiles accompanying the tanks and convincing the marines that further resistance was not in their interest. With the ridge clear, D Company and the tanks swung west and captured the area of the cross-tracks to the north-east of Luttum and at 1405 hours Lieutenant Colonel Bowker was visited by Brigadier Wilsey, who ordered him to press on and capture Weitzmühlen. The Weitzmühlen area was held by marines of II./7 Bataillon and the village itself weakly-held by artillery recruits from Kampfgruppe Hornemann, following their ejection from the villages to the south. Lieutenant Colonel Bowker planned a two-phase attack with B and C Companies attacking alongside each other. Following a short and uneventful advance the village was attacked and, by 1900 hours, cleared.

1 E Lancs on the right axis moved to a concentration area during the early part of the morning and here Lieutenant Colonel Allen gave orders for a northward advance to the main road at Kirchlinteln. Once reached, 160th Brigade would seize the high ground east of Kirchlinteln as a preliminary to the assault on Verden. The battalion began the advance at 1600 hours and while B Company moved down an exposed slope just north of Armsen it was shelled by 8.8cm Flak and took a few casualties. No infantry opposition was met, however, until the advance was two miles north of the village where the companies met outposts holding the line of the stream near Specken, which formed an obstacle to armour. D Company successfully crossed the only bridge in the area and drove the Germans back to what appeared to be their main defensive position. The armour then attempted to follow but when the lead tank from B Squadron 3/4 CLY crossed the bridge it collapsed and the tank was tipped upside down, drowning Trooper Green. This was a bad day for the squadron as that morning it had been caught in an artillery barrage, leaving the squadron leader, Major Phelps, and six other tank commanders wounded and one trooper dead. To try to resolve the problem of the stream where the tank was stuck, a bulldozer was sent for but it was late

THROUGH THE CRUST 419

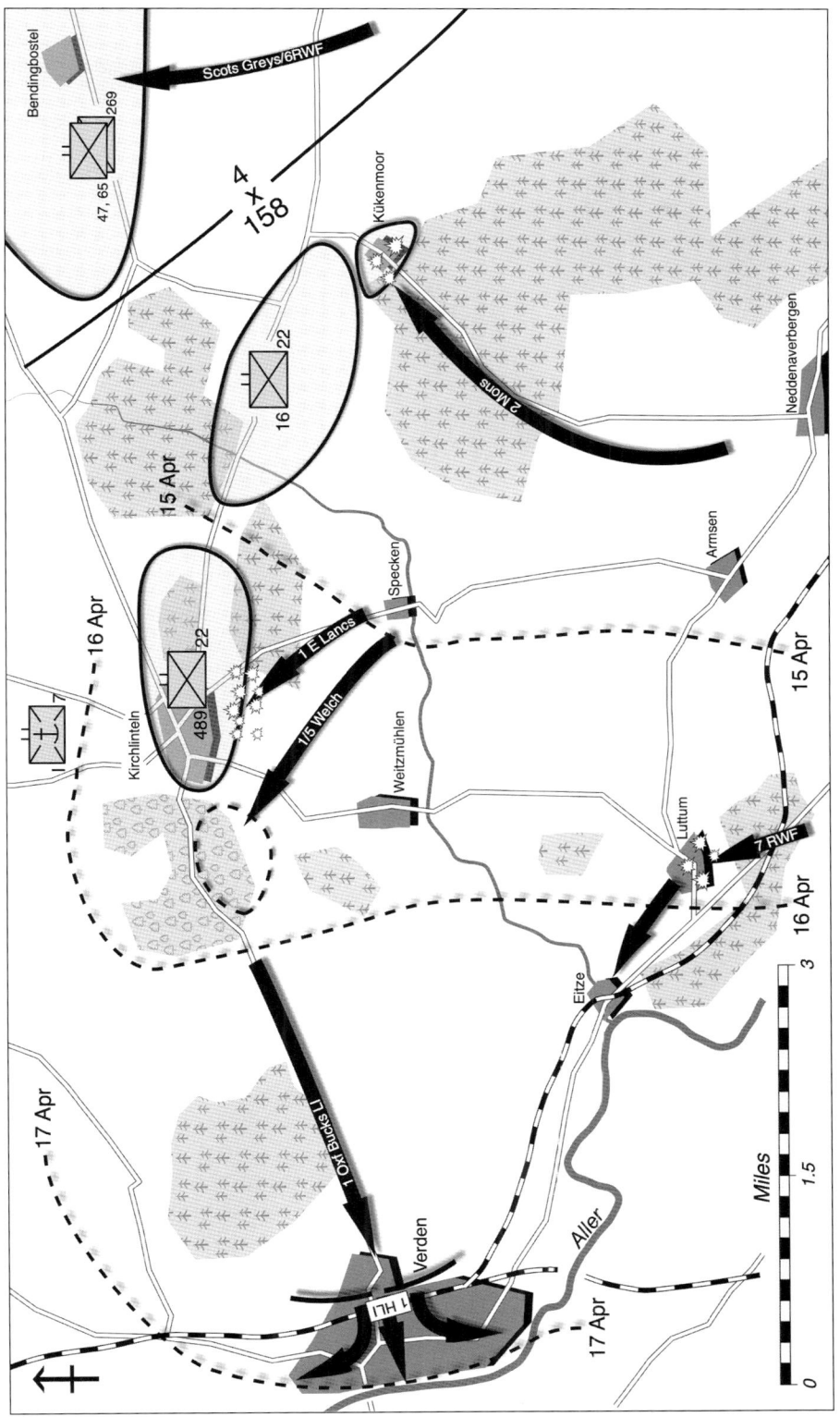

Map 70 158th and 71st Infantry Brigades and the Capture of Verden – 15–17 April 1945.

before an alternative route was made and well after midnight before the battalion's vehicles and the tanks began to advance again. C Company had in the meantime moved around the right flank to ease the pressure on D Company, the leading company, and the battalion spent the rest of the night consolidating in the area of Specken.

160th Brigade joined the divisional advance on 15 April but only on a single, battalion axis as 6 RWF was operating with the Scots Greys and 4 Welch had yet to be replaced on the left bank by 4 RWF from 71st Brigade. At 1430 hours 2 Mons began this advance on the right of 1 E Lancs and directed on Kükenmoor. Good progress was made and by 2100 hours the battalion had captured the hamlet and taken 52 prisoners. The divisional plan was now for 158th Brigade to capture Kirchlinteln and then, if fresh enough, to swing south-west to Verden. Failing this, 71st Brigade would pass through 158th Brigade and capture the town while 4th Armoured covered the manoeuvre from the right flank.

During the night 15/16 April Schaffer's artillery recruits were joined by the remainder of Division Nr.480, now deployed to the Aller Line from its concentration area north of Verden. In addition to Schaffer's Artillerie-A.u.E. Regiment 22, the main components of the division were Grenadier-A.u.E. Regiment 22, Grenadier-A.u.E. Regiment 269, Pionier-A.u.E. Bataillon 22 and Pionier-A.u.E. Bataillon 34. The division was supported by various *ad hoc* mortar, *Nebelwerfer* and signals units. Grenadier-A.u.E. Regiment 22 occupied the area between Kirchlinteln and Kükenmoor with its Grenadier-Ausbildungs-Bataillon 16 on the left and Grenadier-Ausbildungs-Bataillon 489 on the right, thus allowing I./7 Bataillon to pull back to the north of Kirchlinteln. Grenadier-A.u.E. Regiment 269 assumed responsibility for the area of Bendingbostel with its two training battalions 47 and 65. The regiments were allocated artillery support from Artillerie-Ersatz-Abteilung 58 and the fifth *Abteilung* from Volks-Artillerie-Korps 402. The types of guns equipping Artillerie-Ersatz-Abteilung 58 are not known but Volks-Artillerie-Korps 402 had a mix of 7.5cm FK 18 field guns, 10.5cm le. FH field howitzers and former Soviet 15.2cm 433 (r) heavy field howitzers. An Ultra decrypt of a SITREP from an unnamed naval authority stated that the *Artillerie-Korps* unit arrived in the naval division's area with 90 rounds of ammunition, not a quantity to have much impact on the inexorable flow of events.[41]

The *Luftwaffe* attack on Rethem bridge

On 7 April an Ultra Air Digest produced by the air staff at SHAEF logged I./KG 66[42] on 5 April requesting information on the whereabouts of the front line in north-west Germany, the Ruhr and Central Germany in order to carry out operations from its current base at Dedelstorf. The accompanying comment in the digest predicted that I./KG 66, as a night pathfinder unit, might be intending night bombing attacks against Allied bridges and crossing points over the Ems, Weser or Dortmund-Ems Canal. The author of the comment was prescient, although the target would be the Bailey pontoon bridge over the Aller at Rethem as this was closer to the *Luftwaffe's* remaining bases and of greater tactical importance owing to its proximity to the front line.

The attack was planned and coordinated by 14. Flieger-Division, with two waves of aircraft taking-off on the night 15 April to attack the bridge and bridgehead area. The first wave consisted of eight Fw 190 F-8 fighter-bombers from III./ KG 200, which took off from Lübeck-Blankensee at approximately 2000 hours, while the second wave consisted of a mixed force of Ju 88S and Ju 188 bombers and Ju 88G night-fighters, all from I./ KG66, which progressively took off from

---

41 TNA DEFE 3/567, KO 593, 17 April 1945.
42 TNA DEFE 3, Ultra Air Digest No. 237, 24 hours ending 1200 7 April.

Tutow between 2005 and 2026 hours.[43] The two waves headed off towards the Aller and at 2030 hours the Fw 190 F-8 attacked. The bombers followed, with the first act being the dropping of LC50 parachute flares to illuminate the target.

Unfortunately for the aircrew, the importance of the bridge to the British resulted in the Rethem area containing a high density of anti-aircraft guns and in position were the batteries of 25th LAA Regiment. H Troop with six 40mm Bofors and 41 Battery of 15th LAA Regiment, with its recently-issued M16 half-tracks with quadruple .50-in guns,[44] were in point defence of the bridge. As the aircraft swept into the attack the batteries crashed into action and all guns began to engage, with the wall of fire that rose to meet the aircraft preventing low-level runs and a resultant loss of bombing accuracy. Nonetheless, a number of SC250 cluster bombs landed close enough to the Class 40 bridge to damage the central section and subsequently force its closure, and others landed in the town causing destruction and fatalities among British soldiers and German civilians alike. Those on the ground were also subjected to strafing from the 20mm cannon of the Ju 88G night-fighters. The raid was an unpleasant experience for those on the receiving end and among them was Lance Bombardier John Mercer, a member of the Counter-Mortar Officer's staff in HQ 7th Armoured Division, who describes the attack:[45]

> As dusk fell the *Luftwaffe* came over and bombed and strafed our positions. This was the first time we had met German bombers since the night at Demouville [in Normandy], though we had seen some German jet fighters in the sky flying incredibly fast…On the British side there was a notable reluctance to engage the enemy too closely as the end of the war seemed imminent and no one wanted to die within a few days of victory and peace. Fortunately there was a steadily reducing need to go into a pitched battle. But at Rethem there was strong resistance and some necessary fighting and the *Luftwaffe* assault was both unexpected and extremely unpleasant. I was more scared at Rethem under air attack than I had been at any previous stage of the campaign…Rethem seemed to be the last vicious throw of a defeated enemy as we took cover in a meadow beneath the half-track. The Heinkels [*sic*] rumbled overhead on their bombing run and we wondered where the RAF was. Maybe I had run out of endurance, maybe the war experience banked in my mind was becoming overdrawn.

257 Battery 65th Anti-Tank Regiment had the misfortune to be passing through the town at the time of the attack and suffered three killed and four seriously wounded.[46] In addition, it lost four trucks including the battery sergeant major's truck and the towed, battery charging plant. Austers of A Flight 653 (AOP) Squadron suffered damage when a bomb landed in the field serving as the landing strip and showered the flimsy aircraft with earth and stones, tearing their fragile flight surfaces. Three civilians also died in the raid and more houses in Lange Strasse were destroyed.

After the aircraft flew away into the night there was feverish activity to extinguish the burning trucks and houses to prevent them acting as beacons for follow-on attacks; fortunately, none were forthcoming. Seventeen of the Class 40's pontoons were holed and the sappers worked through the night and into the next day to make the bridge negotiable; by 1000 hours on 16 April they had managed to repair it sufficiently to accept Class 24 loads, and it finally regained Class 40 at 1600 hours. The anti-aircraft batteries had some success, with the .50 calibre guns of 41 Battery shooting down a Ju 88 and damaging a Fw 190 and the Bofors of 42 Battery registering hits on another

---

43 Information provided by Marcel van Heijkop.
44 TNA WO 171/4936, 15th LAA Regiment RA war diary.
45 John Mercer, *Mike Target* (Lewes: The Book Guild, 1990), p.116.
46 TNA WO 171/4774, 65th Anti-Tank Regiment RA war diary.

Ju 88 and a Fw 190. A 14. Flieger-Division report on the attack decrypted in an Ultra message,[47] revealed that a mixed force of 53 Me 109, 47 Fw 190 and 12 Ar 234 attacked enemy transport, advancing columns and Rethem bridge with bombs and aircraft armament; eight aircraft were missing. The numbers of participating aircraft look suspiciously high, perhaps to avoid unwelcome criticism from higher headquarters, and oddly the report makes no mention of the participation by the Ju 88 of KG 66.

Monday 16 April

Operations by 158th Infantry and 4th Armoured Brigades

The night 15/16 April and the next day were spent by the British preparing for the final advance to Verden (see Map 70). 158th Brigade concentrated its activity at Specken on 1 E Lancs' axis, with 555 Field Company working on the weak bridge as the intention was for it to be crossed by the supporting arms of both 1 E Lancs and 1/5 Welch. Even when the bridge was open, it remained very weak and as a consequence the advance north from Specken by both battalions was significantly delayed. However, by mid-afternoon 1/5 Welch had reached its objective, the spur to the south-west of Kirchlinteln and here they dug-in to protect the division's right flank.

At much the same time, 1 E Lancs neared the dominating spur to Kirchlinteln's south-east and was directed to capture the town, which was held by Grenadier-Ausbildungs-Bataillon 489. Prior to the start of the day's advance it was believed that Kirchlinteln formed part of an undefended hospital area and would not therefore be attacked. However, during the morning enemy soldiers were seen digging in on the spur and it was clear the Germans had realised its tactical importance and were hastily preparing to defend this area of key terrain. Brigadier Elrington therefore ordered the battalion to attack immediately and at mid-day, after an artillery fire plan, A Company followed by B Company advanced, with both companies supported by Shermans from B Squadron 3/4 CLY and Crocodiles. Their advance had to deal with opposition from machine-gun teams covering the tracks leading through woods and, as each team had to be separately eliminated, the whole morning was taken up slowly pressing onwards to reach the forward edge of the woods about 800 yards short of Kirchlinteln.

When the attacking infantry reached the spur, German resistance increased and A Company was heavily engaged on its way up to the town, losing its company commander, Major Whiteside, and two platoon commanders all wounded. During the course of the fighting a 3/4 CLY Sherman Firefly commanded by 2nd Lieutenant Rhodes was knocked out. The tank had got ahead of its protective infantry and had just fired machine-gun and HE into a slit trench and thought it safe to proceed when a *Panzerfaust* was fired at it from another trench. From a range of six yards the warhead hit the stationary tank on the turret roof in front of the gunner and the molten jet instantly killed him and Rhodes; the driver was unhurt but severely wounded by shell fire after baling out, and the operator was wounded. Owing to the resistance, B Company had to be passed through earlier than intended, but with assistance from the Crocodiles was able to capture the spur. Lieutenant Colonel Allen then combined A and B Companies for the assault on the village itself. Both companies fought hard to clear the Germans from the houses and farms, especially around the area of the village's cross-roads, but by early evening the battle was over and 36 German soldiers buried in the cemetery are testimony to the strength of the resistance. With Kirchlinteln captured, D Company moved up to join the two assault companies while C Company provided

---

47   TNA DEFE 3/567, KO 587, 17 April 1945.

right flank protection and sent out carrier recce patrols. Sixty-five prisoners from Grenadier-A.u.E. Regiment 22 were taken and one 8.8cm gun captured on the southern edge of the village. 1 E Lancs' history records many of the prisoners were wearing *Luftwaffe* uniforms and that they told their interrogators they were rushed into the breach in the Aller Line so fast they did not know where they were or in what sort of division they were fighting. 1 E Lancs' casualties were four killed and 20 wounded or missing. During the afternoon it was decided that 158th Brigade would not be sufficiently fresh to mount the attack on Verden and so 71st Brigade was warned to take on the task. The brigade therefore moved up during the rest of the day to concentrate in the Weitzmühlen area to be positioned for an attack on the town in the early hours of 17 April. The axis would be from the east down the main road from Kirchlinteln.

While 1/5 Welch and 1 E Lancs were involved in the Kirchlinteln area, 7 RWF on the left axis was advancing steadily towards Verden. The patrol sent to investigate Luttum reported the village held and at 0945 hours Lieutenant Colonel Tyler was ordered to occupy it, but only after RP Typhoons had softened it up prior to the assault. The Typhoons, always a popular sight for the infantry, attacked at 1230 hours and the battalion supported by C Squadron 3/4 CLY then assaulted Luttum. Perhaps unsurprisingly knowing the inaccuracy of RPs, the Shermans encountered stiff opposition and the leading tank was hit by a *Panzerfaust* on its mantlet, fortunately the area of thickest armour and the tank survived. The forward troop provided covering fire and smoke, killing many of the enemy and allowing 7 RWF to capture the village and take 20 prisoners in the process. The companies then took up defensive positions to consolidate their gains and the pattern of the previous day was repeated with a recce patrol dispatched to investigate the next village, Eitze.

Further to the east 4th Armoured Brigade's two regimental groups pressed on northwards (see Map 67). On the Scots Greys Group's axis the squadrons and companies that had been involved in Vethem closed up to Idsingen during the morning of 16 April and the advance started off towards the next objective, Bendingbostel. It reached half a mile beyond Idsingen only to find the bridge blown over the Lehrde stream, so a Churchill scissors bridgelayer was called forward to lay its bridge and the RE platoon commander was ordered to assess whether the demolished bridge could be repaired. Although the scissors bridge was laid, the ground was boggy on both sides of the bridge and progress of the armoured vehicles soon began to slow. The RE platoon commander reported that the demolished bridge could be crossed but that it would take seven hours and involve 50 feet of Bailey bridging. Not one to have any truck with those he believed to be lacking drive, the RE officer's report resulted in Brigadier Carver soon appearing at the bridge site. The brigade after action review describes what eventuated:[48]

> The brigade commander went and inspected the bridge himself: he suggested to the RE platoon commander that by sending a tankdozer over the scissors, grading down the far side of the bridge approach and building a causeway of tree trunks over the collapsed single span bridge, the tree trunks being on the spot in the form of a road block, an improvised bridge could be made. The RE officer agreed it might work, but doubted if it would take tanks: the brigade commander told him to get on with it. A tank-bulldozer was sent up from Tac Brigade HQ and crossed the scissors bridge. Tanks and later the winch on the front of a half-track were used to haul the tree trunks into position. Meanwhile the state of the ground round the scissors was getting very bad and several tanks had bogged on the far side…By 1430 hours the improvised bridge was complete and showed no signs of strain under the first tank. It was ready just in time as passage over the scissors was no longer possible.

---

48   4th Armoured Brigade, Operations East of the River Aller, 14–19 April 1945 (Unpublished), pp.11–12.

The future relationship between Brigadier Carver and the hapless RE officer is not known. With the bridge trafficable, the advance made good progress and by 1930 hours Bendingbostel was captured. Forty-two members of Bataillon 65 of Grenadier-A.u.E. Regiment 269 lie buried in the town's cemetery.

On 16 April, 44 RTR Group made rapid progress and by 0845 hours it had captured Hamwiede without opposition and advanced towards Sieverdingen, but in so doing came under fire from 8.8cm Flak sited on the southern edge of Stellichte. It was clear that the capture of Stellichte would require a major operation so the group was ordered by the brigade commander to concentrate in the Idsingen area. Here we will leave 4th Armoured and its northwards advance, which would continue for three more days. The brigade did not reach Rotenburg, its objective, as it was decided it would move to the north of Verden and support 52nd Lowland Division for the assault on Bremen. 19 April would therefore mark the end of its operations on the Aller's right bank. During the 6-day period the brigade had mopped up numerous groups of withdrawing marines and cut a swathe through the gun areas of Marine-Artillerie-Regiment 2 and Abteilung V from Volks-Artillerie-Korps 402, destroying or capturing a total of twenty-five 10.5cm guns and 16 other assorted guns ranging in calibre from 3.7cm to 15.2cm. In addition, it had captured some 1,945 prisoners and estimated it had killed some 165. This was at a cost of 15 dead, 62 wounded and four Shermans knocked out. Although this balance was hugely in favour of 4th Armoured Brigade, the losses in men were tragic given their proximity to the war's end. In his memoirs Michael Carver recorded his satisfaction with the operation and his thoughts on the future organisation of an armoured brigade:[49]

> It had been a most successful battle, a model of its kind, in which we had been able to combine mobility and firepower more effectively that at any other time since we had crossed the Somme. It convinced me that the organisation of the brigade into two battle groups, each of an armoured regiment and a mobile infantry battalion, was the best one for an armoured brigade, certainly for the majority of operations.

The capture of Fallingbostel and the relief of Stalag XIB and Stalag 357

At daylight on 16 April, 22nd Armoured Brigade began to advance once again with 8 Hussars Group on the main axis and 1 RTR Group further to the north on the subsidiary. Intelligence reports suggested 8 Hussars could expect to encounter opposition from 7. SS-Kompanie defending the line of Reichsstrasse 209 between Walsrode and Fallingbostel, the next town. Numerous roadblocks of felled and booby-trapped trees, mines on the verges and blown culverts and bridges were also to be expected. Despite the dangers, it would prove a momentous day for it saw the liberation of two large PoW camps near Fallingbostel: Stalag XIB and Stalag 357.

Stalag XIB had its origins in 1935 as hutted accommodation for workers constructing the barracks at Fallingbostel-Örbke, later to become the Westlager of the newly-formed Bergen training area. In 1939 a perimeter fence was built around the huts and the camp thus created was designated Stalag XIB and initially used to accommodate Polish PoWs.

From May 1940 onwards the population of the camp increased significantly as it took in prisoners from every Allied nation. In 1941, with the influx of vast numbers of Soviet PoWs, a second

---

49   Michael Carver, *Out of Step: The Memoirs of Field Marshal Lord Carver* (London: Hutchinson, 1989), p.216.

Stalag XIB – *Appelplatz* with the camp's main administration building in the background.

camp was created; this was originally named Stalag 321 but later changed to Stalag XID.[50] The word 'camp' is however a complete misnomer as the Soviet prisoners were held in a fenced-off field and left to fend for themselves in the open and, with no shelter whatsoever, lived in holes dug in the field. Thousands died of typhus. Some huts were later built but the camp was dissolved in July 1942 and the remaining Soviet prisoners transferred to a compound adjacent to Stalag XIB. To escape the Soviet advances, in September 1944 the largely British and Commonwealth prisoners held in Stalag 357 at Thorn in Poland were transferred to Stalag XID, by now a hutted camp and renumbered '357'. The populations of both Stalag XIB and 357 were further added to in early 1945 by prisoners from other camps in the east, who marched hundreds of miles to them through appalling weather conditions. By early 1945 both camps were in deplorable condition with chronic over-crowding, malnutrition, disease, and extreme shortages of food and medical supplies. Mercifully for the prisoners, this situation was about to end.

The 8 Hussars' history describes the opening of the day:

> It was a 5 o'clock in the morning start, in the dark and the cold, and a hurried breakfast of a fried egg between two pieces of bread [universally known in the army as an 'egg banjo'] and a mug of tea beside the tanks. Some were parked near a small garden in which were two cherry trees in blossom, and through the branches could be seen the other tanks in the meadow below, their brew fires flickering in the half light. It was an oddly beautiful scene, and a fine dawn which promised an even finer day. B Squadron with a motor platoon of 1

---

50 Stalag XIA was at Altengrabow, 56 miles south-west of Berlin. Stalag XIC was at Bergen-Belsen and had the same origin as XIB. It was converted to the infamous concentration camp in 1943.

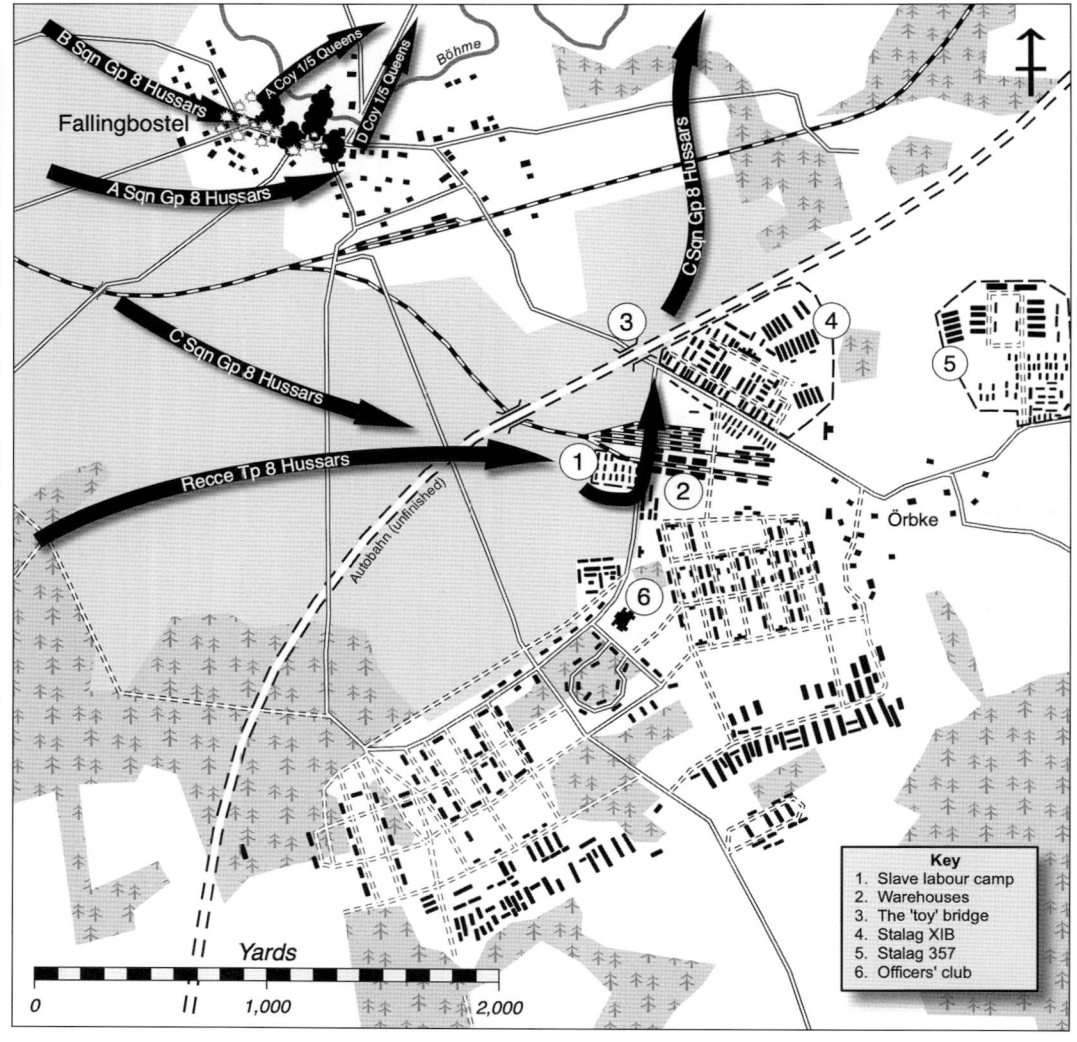

Map 71 The Relief of Stalags XIB and 357 – 17 April 1945.

RB in half-tracks under command were ordered to move east to Fallingbostel.[51] C Squadron likewise were ordered to advance from its night leaguer among the turnips through Düshorn to Fallingbostel. A Squadron with a section of carriers were to cross the river Böhme and establish themselves on the higher ground to the north of Fallingbostel. Recce Troop, which had spent the night with C Squadron, were ordered to find the two PoW camps which were thought to lie somewhere to the east of the town. The map showed a large expanse of ground covered with regularly grouped blocks of buildings, any of which might have been the camps. It also showed part of an *Autobahn*, which with the mental picture it gave of broad concrete roadways, fly-overs and bridges was likely to prove an unmistakable landmark.[52]

---

51 TNA WO 171/5255, 1 RB war diary.
52 Olivia Fitzroy, *Men of Valour, History of the 8th King's Royal Irish Hussars* (Liverpool: Tinling & Co, 1961), p.214.

C Squadron Group set off and reached the railway bridge to the south-west of the town without incident. But the B Squadron Group was held up by infantry when it arrived at the town's western edge, and A Squadron reported the bridge over the Böhme blown and that its tanks were unable to cross anywhere else. By 1100 hours it was apparent the town's clearance would need more than one motor company and at 1250 hours 1/5 Queens, commanded by Lieutenant Colonel Freeland, began to move in its Kangaroos along Reichsstrasse 209 towards Fallingbostel, having been relieved in Walsrode by 2 Devon. As the battalion closed on the town it received a report that the German defenders had, with a few exceptions, withdrawn and a deliberate attack was no longer necessary. When, however, the lead troops reached the end of the main street, by now well-alight from the fighting involving A Company 1 RB, they could see the blown bridge over the Böhme. A new plan was therefore made involving A Company wading the river to the north-west, supported by B Squadron, in an attempt to cut-off any remaining defenders. D Company meanwhile would get across the remains of the demolished bridge and work forward through the town on the right bank to join A Company. Fire support would be provided by A Squadron from the higher ground to the town's south. All went to plan and by mid-afternoon the town was captured and with A Company 1 RB now under command, 1/5 Queens held positions in the town and spent the rest of the afternoon mopping up some stay-behind parties of Hitler Youth. To minimise the risk of own casualties, fire from the 25-pdrs of 5 RHA was liberally used.[53] A link to an online video showing captured members of SS-A.u.E. Btl.12 'HJ', probably from 7. SS-Kompanie, is at Appendix A, Serial 18.

While these events were taking place, 8 Hussars' recce troop, commanded by Captain Pierson, was the first British force to reach the PoW camps; he tells the moving story:[54]

> Nosing its way cautiously along sandy tracks that skirted or went through the many pine-woods that were the main feature of this country, the leading section of Honeys started off slowly. Though there was no sign of the enemy, similar woods had produced quite a few the day before, the leading tank occasionally raked the edges of the trees and suspicious hollows and clumps of grass to discourage any *Panzerfaust* expert that might be waiting hopefully for us to get within range of his very useful weapon. The afternoon before, when he had been missed three times, Lieutenant Anstey, the leading troop commander, confessed to feeling like a goalkeeper in a football match, but this particular sunny morning there was, much to our relief, no sign of them. A wide clearing confronted us, obviously man-made, cut at right angles through the woods, its sandy surface covered with tufts of grass, stretching dead straight to the right as far as the eye could see, and to the left turning out of sight through two small mountains of earth. This must be the *Autobahn*, though scarcely what we had expected; the maps had given no hint of this rudimentary stage in its construction.
>
> We turned left, came to the large heaps of earth and halted while the leading commander, Corporal Spencer, dismounted to have a look at what lay around them out of sight. No more woods, but a flat open expanse of grass bounded, some 1,000 yards away, by a long, uneven line of low buildings, out of which, further to our left, rose what looked like half a dozen tall warehouses.
>
> Binoculars showed a main mass of low buildings lying behind a high wire fence and people; at first, we saw one or two moving about then made out a group of a dozen, and finally realised that the thickening of the bottom half of the fence was in fact a solid mass of them. At this moment the leading tanks of C Squadron, approaching on a different route, came up behind us, and without waiting to see any more we jumped into our tanks and shot out into

---

53 TNA WO 171/5082, 5 RHA war diary.
54 Olivia Fitzroy, *Men of Valour*, pp.214–217.

'…what looked like half a dozen tall warehouses.' Photograph taken in 1982. (Author)

the open. In high spirits we crossed the grass as quickly as the ground would allow, but as the distance between us grew less we noticed that the predominant colour of the mass that was now streaming out of the gates towards us was grey, dark grey. And at the same moment we saw a French flag – or was it Dutch – which in our excitement we had not noticed before, fluttering behind the main gate. Our hopes sank; these were not British prisoners, but another of the camps full of all nationalities of Europe that we had come across so many times before. Perhaps there were some British among them, then again perhaps there was no British camp at all, and the Germans had moved XIB as they had moved so many others out of the way of the armies advancing from east to west.

The leading tank came to a stop as the first of the breathless shouting stream of humanity surrounded it, and Corporal Spencer, still clinging to a faint hope, bent down and yelled, 'English soldaten?'. He repeated himself in a moment's hush, and then a hundred hands pointed to his left, and the clamour of the excited crowd broke out with increased intensity. As he looked round for someone out of whom he could get some sense it seemed that every nation was represented, women as well as men, the majority in civilian clothes, with but two things in common, they were all happy and all indescribably dirty. Noticing one persistent man who seemed to have a smattering of English he hauled him up onto the tank and asked which way. The fellow pointed and as the tank moved slowly forward the crowd melted away in front. He glanced over his shoulder and noticed that he was still leading, the Cromwells of C Squadron were as uncertain as he had been as to the route but were now following hot on his heels. It was going to be a close thing as to who reached the camp first.

Parallel to the fence, which we had now reached, ran a concrete road and turning left on this, to the accompaniment of cheers from the waving smiling crowd of prisoners and DPs [displaced persons] that thronged its entire length, he soon passed the tall warehouses that had first been noticed in the distance. The fellow in the turret pointed excitedly forward, but Corporal Spencer could see nothing except a road, tree-lined on both sides, that met ours at right angles. We halted at the junction; to our left the road went under a stone bridge built to carry the *Autobahn*, but with no *Autobahn* to carry looking comically like a piece of a child's set of toy bricks.

A quick glance to the right revealed nothing more than an empty road. But the guide was tugging at Spencer's sleeve and jabbering away – and following with our eyes the direction of his pointing arm we saw across the road through a gap between two trees a khaki-clad figure wearing a maroon-coloured beret, clinging to a wire fence beyond and jumping up and down, obviously shouting his head off, though not a word reached us over the noise of the engines and earphones. And then all the way down to the right we could see between the tree trunks more figures racing along the wire. We'd got there, and before the Cromwells, which came up behind just as we moved off down the road giving the glad news over the air. Three or 400 yards down the road was the main gate to the camp and as we approached the sound of welcome from the crowd that lined the wire and covered the roofs of the camp buildings grew to a roar that penetrated our earphones above the noise of our engines. Inside the main gates was an open space packed with British prisoners and, beyond, was another wire fence and what looked like an inner enclosure black with figures. This was Stalag XIB.

Quite staggering was the contrast between this scene and that which we had seen at other camps containing prisoners of the Allied nations. Despite the enthusiasm of the men inside you could see at a glance there was order and discipline. The remarkable RSM John Lord, Grenadier Guards, of the 1st Airborne Division had already taken charge and was busily engaged in his office giving peacetime orders to his orderly warrant officers.[55] Camp MPs, each with a red armband, policed the gates, and as the crowd came out to meet us there was no ugly rush but a steady stream wearing the headgear of what looked like every unit in the Army. The airborne beret predominated – men of D-Day, Arnhem, even the Rhine crossing who had only been inside for a few weeks – but you could pick out the hats, caps, berets and bonnets of a score of others. And under each one was such a look of happiness and thankfulness that made us as happy to be the cause of it. It was a quiet crowd that thronged around us; they had had their cheer, and now when the moment came for words, few words came. Mostly they were too moved to speak, men who could only grin broadly and clasp your hand as the tears ran down their cheeks. You couldn't speak yourself, only shake as many as possible of the hands that stretched towards you, and grin back, trying to take it all in, and marvel. For these men didn't look like prisoners; their battledress was pressed and clean, here and there web belts and gaiters were scrubbed white and the brasses gleaming, they might have been off duty in a town at home instead of just walking out of prison wire behind which they had been for anything from five weeks to five years.

Memories of that scene leaves a picture of a healthy and, if not overfed, certainly not starving crowd; of apologetic requests for cigarettes and one man turning green with his first puff, having given up the habit for his three years inside; of the creases in the tartan trews and the shining buttons on the jacket of a CSM in the 51st Highland Division, who admitted having marched three or 400 miles from East Prussia and who didn't look as if he had been more than three or 400 yards from his own front door; of the camp MO indignantly denying any cases of typhus; of the German commandant and a few of the camp guards standing apart in a small group watching unmoved the reversal of his role, and handing over his automatic with an offer to show us over the nearby storehouses; scraps of conversation, 'I've been waiting five years for this day' – 'Three days ago we expected you,' and in contrast, 'You've come too soon, my jacket's still wet', this from one who had washed his battledress specially for the occasion; and from one as impressed by our appearance (we hadn't washed or shaved for nearly 48 hours) as we were by theirs, 'You look like real soldiers'. There were several requests to see a

---

55 Prior to his capture, John Lord was RSM 3 Para. In 1948 he became the first Academy Sergeant Major of the Royal Military Academy Sandhurst.

jeep, which we could not unfortunately produce at the moment; much signing of autographs on both sides and nearly always the first question, 'What's your mob?' and finding several members of the regiment in the camp, taken at Sidi Rezegh in 1941; and finally, on asking news of their erstwhile captors, being told that they were not long gone and were carrying *Panzerfaust*. This was more serious, with all these fellows about, and on asking the police to clear the road we got the most startling proof of the state of the camp discipline. For at a word from a tall figure wearing the airborne beret, RSM Lord, the camp MPs went round and in a very few moments and without a murmur these scores of men, some of whom were tasting freedom for the first time in more than five years, made their way back behind the same barbed wire and netting that to them must have been the symbol of all that was hateful and depressing in this life.

We left as the vanguard of visitors, the VIPs and not so VIPs, the press and the frankly-curious, all wishing to get a first-hand glimpse of the first large, predominantly British camp to find itself in the path of the British Liberation Army. And we left taking with us an impression that will never fade of men whose courage and hope had been kept alive through long years of boredom and privation by their faith in their comrades and their country; and whose behaviour was an example of the highest traditions of the army to which they belonged. And that might have been the end of our part in the proceedings of what was for all of us a great occasion. But later that day we happened to pass that way again when things were more normal; erstwhile prisoners were strolling about in groups or sitting in the sun enjoying a smoke and waving contentedly at the passing traffic. But all was not quite normal, for as we came up to the main gates where we had received such a reception a few hours earlier, we saw a troop of armoured cars obliging some movie cameramen by driving slowly past a group of wildly waving and shouting ex-prisoners; and, for a brief moment, as we beheld the scene as spectators and not actors, we felt again all the emotions of that most memorable day.

The remarkable John Lord, who had maintained morale and discipline among the prisoners through his strength of character and example, describes the camp's relief:[56]

Early on 16th April, news was received that the British Army was just along the road. I went to the front gate where everything was ready. Our sentries were there and all the nations in their own compounds under control. Along the road came a Honey tank, I shall never forget this arriving at the front gate and others coming along behind. The barbed wire was thronged with men. The first figure out of the tank was a corporal of the 8th Hussars and spotting me at the gate, he came and stood to attention to report. It was a wonderful moment and I shall never forget it. There was only one privilege which I reserved for myself and this was the moment: I took it upon myself to lower the swastika of the Third *Reich* and in its place hoisted up our own home-made Union Jack, which had been placed on the coffins at so many funerals. As I raised it and looked up the flagstaff I can hardly describe my feelings, I felt thankfulness and relief and in company with everyone I inwardly gave thanks to God for this moment.

But at the other camp, Stalag 357, it was a different atmosphere, as Captain Pierson recalls:[57]

---

56   Richard Alford, *To Revel in God's Sunshine, The Story of RSM JC Lord, MVO, MBE* (Kendal: Westmoreland Gazette, 1981), p.70.
57   Olivia Fitzroy, *Men of Valour*, pp.217–218.

Outside Stalag XIB's wire, newly-liberated prisoners enjoy their freedom.

Here we were the first troops to arrive and when we halted in the wire approach to the camp we were surrounded by a great crowd of men almost hysterical with joy. They nearly overwhelmed us, climbing over our cars, patting us on the back, shaking hands, bombarding us with questions, shouting, laughing, some even crying.

Here, unlike the other camp, was none of that air of discipline and smartness. The clothes most of the men wore were nondescript. Many wore gym-shoes and few had either hats or caps.

I am not for a moment suggesting that morale and discipline had gone, far from it. But these men, unlike the others, had been prisoners for a long time, some for as much as four or five years, and even their faces showed it. It was a very moving and wonderful experience. As I have said some men were crying and I do not think we ourselves were far from tears; but perhaps the saddest and most moving sight of all was when, after disentangling ourselves from the crowd and having been given a parting cheer as we drove away, we looked back and saw so many hundreds still clinging to the wire as if by habit, a habit caused by long imprisonment. They could not realise that they were free.

The total freed from the two camps was some 10,000 British and American prisoners, and 12,000 Allied nationals. After liberation, as was often the case, there were ugly incidents when freed forced labourers and Soviet prisoners began to pillage the surrounding countryside and exact revenge. A number of barrack blocks were burnt down and the Fallingbostel officers' club destroyed. John Lord contained these incidents by deploying patrols and providing guards for the farms; many local people owed their lives to his action and nine days later the last groups of former prisoners left the camps forever. Links to online videos of scenes following the relief of Stalags XIB and 357 are at Appendix A, Serials 14 and 17.

While elements were involved in Fallingbostel, the remainder of 8 Hussars Group advanced to the area of Dorfmark, four miles to the north-east of Fallingbostel. 1 RTR Group also made good progress on 16 April and by the evening had advanced to within two miles of Soltau, which it reported strongly held by infantry and 8.8cm guns. 131st Infantry Brigade,[58] in reserve throughout the advance from the Aller, remained in Walsrode while 155th Brigade spent the day mopping up isolated pockets of resistance before concentrating in the Walsrode area for the night.[59] The next day would however be busy for the brigade as it had orders to clear the divisional axis between Fallingbostel and Soltau, which it would then capture, allowing 22nd Armoured to bypass the town. On 16 April, 2. Marine-Infanterie-Division received its first and only mention in a *Wehrmachtbericht*, which proudly announced to the world that the division had prevented an enemy breakthrough on the lower Aller.[60] As this day marked the end of the division's gallant attempt to hold the Aller Line, the report is not exactly free of irony.

Tuesday 17 April

The capture of Verden

The Aller Line's finale took place on 17 April with Verden's capture (see Map 70). The town had suffered its first significant damage some 10 days previous when German engineers blew up the road and rail bridges over the Aller causing extensive blast damage, particularly to the town's Lutheran cathedral. Although the civic authorities had gingerly made a proposal for Verden to be declared an open city, this was rejected out-of-hand by the authorities in Lüneburg and Hamburg. In the Germany of 1945, where civilians could be executed for any sign of wavering, it took a brave man to suggest such a proposal and an even braver one to authorise it. This was particularly so in light of an OKW order signed by Keitel, Bormann and Himmler on 12 April, which ordered all towns to be defended to the last and that an assigned commander was personally responsible for each town's defence,[61] with the death sentence to be used for any failings. On 14 April wall posters were pasted up in Verden warning looters would be shot and there was widespread fear among the inhabitants that the town was about to become a battleground. At 1800 hours the same day, Verden was bombed. The target was probably the *Flak* battery on the Burgberg on the southern edge of the town but many bombs fell within the town causing serious damage and killing 31 civilians. The inhabitants' worst fears for their and their town's future would not however be realised as Kapitän zur See Neitzel had no intention of defending Verden. His forces had already made their last stand during the fighting on the approaches to the town and his troops were dispersed and too depleted to take on its defence. In the early hours of 17 April, Neitzel's marines withdrew from Verden telling the inhabitants that the town was lost and that the war would soon be over for them. Neitzel's regiment was not however out of battle for long. Having withdrawn from the Verden area it marched some eight miles to the east to Jeddingen and Visselhövede where it joined other units of the division, and here in two days' time we will meet it again.

While the marines were withdrawing, 71st Brigade, unaware of the German situation, was preparing to attack the town. 1 Oxf Bucks LI and 1 HLI moved from the Weitzmühlen area to the start line secured by A Company 1 Oxf Bucks LI; all indications pointed to a hard fight ahead and there was nothing to suggest Verden would not be heavily defended. The brigade plan had two phases: 1 Oxf Bucks LI would attack first to clear the approaches to the town and break in; 1 HLI

---

58   TNA WO 171/4393, 131st Infantry Brigade war diary.
59   TNA WO 171/4414, 155th Infantry Brigade war diary.
60   Wegmann (ed.), *"Das Oberkommando der Wehrmacht gibt bekannt…"*, p.539.
61   Ian Kershaw, *The End*, p.323.

would then pass through to clear the remainder of the town. At 0130 hours C Company 1 Oxf Bucks LI, accompanied by half a squadron of Crocodiles and moving behind a series of artillery concentrations, headed down the main road from Kirchlinteln to seize the string of houses on the town's outskirts. This was successfully accomplished against negligible opposition and the German soldiers dug-in among the houses surrendered at the first opportunity. D Company then passed through and occupied a small housing estate. A Company followed and captured the cemetery area against some opposition from two machine-guns; the first was silenced by the fire of the company and the second was flamed by a Crocodile. During its part in the attack, 1 Oxf Bucks LI captured 112 prisoners and killed one – clear indication of the Germans' collapsing morale.

With the approaches to the town secured, at 0530 hours 1 HLI moved through 1 Oxf Bucks LI and began to enter the main part of the town. By 0830 hours C and D Companies had reached their objectives and had pushed patrols forward to check the defences within the town. These patrols reported no evidence of opposition so A and B Companies advanced and cleared the remainder of the town capturing an ordnance dump, a field hospital and eight 10.5cm Flak. Five soldiers of 1 HLI were killed and 16 wounded during the clearance operation. Despite the Germans' frequent declarations to fight to the last man, much to the relief of its inhabitants Verden was essentially handed over as an open city. The *Wehrmachtbericht* for 18 April announced, however, that the town was lost only after many hours of heavy fighting. Following the town's capture, 53rd Division remained in the area for a number of days mopping up the country to the east. XII Corps' focus now swung to operations by Guards Armoured and 7th Armoured Divisions.

The final event on the Aller, a further *Luftwaffe* raid against the Rethem bridge, took place on the afternoon of 18 April. The raid began with a weather reconnaissance flight flown during the early afternoon, followed by a low-level attack by seven Ar 234 from III./KG 76. Although in an attempt to gain accuracy the jet bombers flew at only 1,200 feet, their bombs missed the Bailey pontoon bridge and little damage was caused. One bomb, however, hit the post office killing the wife of Müller, the postmaster, and her sister. There were no British casualties and one aircraft was shot down. With the raid over and the aircraft disappearing over the eastern horizon the German defence of the Aller passed into history.

12

Die Stunde Null: 15 April–8 May

For the men of Second Army the last two weeks of the war were characterised by a mix of inactivity and sudden violent action, anguish and elation. The desire to avoid death or injury was by now intense and commanders did all in their power to limit casualties, even if this was at the expense of the German civilian population and their villages and towns. Although the job had to be finished, the fighting troops were not helped by uncertainty and rumour, which, as Alastair Borthwick describes, sapped morale:[1]

> In the wars of the past, envoys seeking peace had carried out their missions in silence, leaving the ordinary soldier to carry on with the fighting undisturbed by the knowledge that some day soon the fighting was going to stop. In this war we had no such luck. The papers were full of rumours. Statesmen made cryptic announcements. Hitler was variously reported to be dead, alive, mad, and dying of a cerebral haemorrhage. Himmler had surrendered to us, but not to the Russians. Himmler had surrendered to everybody. Himmler had not surrendered at all. The war would end in a day, a week, a month. This was no doubt extremely entertaining to non-combatants in Britain and must have given intense pleasure to the circulation managers of newspapers, but it did the poor bloody infantry no good at all…the only time for the end of the war that interested us was before H-hour. People who had fought in twenty actions, seeing their friends drop one by one, began to think that once more would be once too often; and there was no-one to blame them. Not a man went in at Bremervörde [on 2 May] without a sense of grievance. We did not object to fighting: we knew that had to be done. But we were bitter at the people who made it difficult for us with too much talk.

Most would have shared Borthwick's viewpoint.

The endgame for Second Army was no walkover and Dempsey would face a number of significant operational challenges during the last three weeks. For this final phase of the campaign, he was tasked by HQ 21st Army Group to capture Bremen and the whole of the Cuxhaven peninsula, take Hamburg, position a corps of four divisions across the Elbe to hold a line from Darchau to Wismar on the Baltic coast, and secure Schleswig-Holstein. To achieve this, three major operations were necessary, all requiring more or less simultaneous troop movements and administrative planning. Hindsight also makes us forget that nobody knew the end was so close and that in addition to possible formidable defences at Hamburg and Bremen, the British believed they could still face 400,000 German troops in Denmark and Norway, as well as resistance in Germany from fanatics of the *Werwolf* guerrilla organisation.

---

1 Alastair Borthwick, *Battalion* (London: Bâton Wicks Publications, 1994), p.253. Borthwick was a captain in 5th Battalion The Seaforth Highlanders, a battalion in 51st Highland Division, XXX Corps.

For the Germans catastrophe neared and in north-west Germany the final weeks were dominated by continual retreat, a few desperate rearguard actions and surrender. Though formal structures were breaking down, the Germans' remarkable capacity for creating improvised groupings from any troops available allowed them to resist to the last, but at increasingly small scales and random times and places. With a high probability the Allied advances would soon split the *Reich* into northern and southern parts, on 15 April Hitler issued a provisional *Führer* order allocating responsibility to Dönitz for civilian authority for the northern part and to Kesselring for the southern, although responsibility for military command would only transfer if Hitler deployed to one or other of the parts or he became isolated in Berlin.[2] On 18 April the last recorded *Führer* conference on naval affairs took place.[3] Dönitz informed the conference that he had received a request from Generalfeldmarschall Busch for two *Marine-Alarm* (emergency-raised) regiments at Kiel to reinforce 2. Marine-Infanterie-Division. He then told the meeting he could not meet the request as the marines' supply of Dutch rifles was inadequate, they had little ammunition and they were needed for local security in Kiel as it was overcrowded with foreign workers; a neat summation of the state of the *Wehrmacht* and Germany in late April 1945. He chose not to mention that the marine division was in the last throes of its short existence.

15–28 April

XII Corps

Although of the three British corps XII Corps probably had the least demanding final weeks, it would be responsible for the demise of 2. Marine-Infanterie-Division. The division's denouement began on 17 April with Guards Armoured Division's advance from Walsrode to Visselhövede and over the next two days it was in the Visselhövede area that against the Guards the remnants of 2. Marine-Infanterie-Division fought their final act of resistance.[4]

By 17 April the marine division, now under the command of Korps Ems, had pivoted anti-clockwise by 90 degrees and was now facing south along the line of Landesstrasse 171 between Jeddingen and Neunkirchen, a frontage of some nine miles, with Visselhövede the point of main effort. On the right marines from Marine-Grenadier-Regiment 7 were holding Jeddingen. Visselhövede in the centre was held by the residue of Marine-Grenadier-Regiment 5, still commanded by Kapitän zur See Jordan, reinforced with marines from 2. Kompanie of Marine-Feldersatz-Bataillon 2 holding outpost positions forward of Visselhövede in Kettenburg and Wehsen. Kapitän zur See Hartmann and Marine-Grenadier-Regiment 6's remaining marines were on the left in the Neunkirchen area with the vestiges of Marine-Füsilier-Bataillon 2 in outpost positions holding the villages of Ottingen and Riepholm. With their strength severely depleted, artillery eradicated, command fractured, ammunition low and exhaustion widespread, the marines' capacity to offer resistance was nearly spent. Their spirit and courage, however, remained undiminished.

The battle for Visselhövede opened during the morning of 18 April. Advancing north from the Walsrode area and with Visselhövede as its objective, 32nd Guards Brigade initially met little resistance.[5] Other than mopping up a few isolated pockets and taking some prisoners, the Scots-Welsh Group had a clear run until it reached Kettenburg,[6] where it met the marines from 2. Kompanie

---

2   Kesselring, *Memoirs*, p.268.
3   Showell, *Führer Conferences on Naval Affairs*, p.486.
4   TNA WO 171/4104, Guards Armoured Division war diary.
5   TNA WO 171/4357, 32nd Guards Brigade war diary.
6   TNA WO 171/5149 and WO171/5152, 2 Scots Gds and 2 Welsh Gds war diaries.

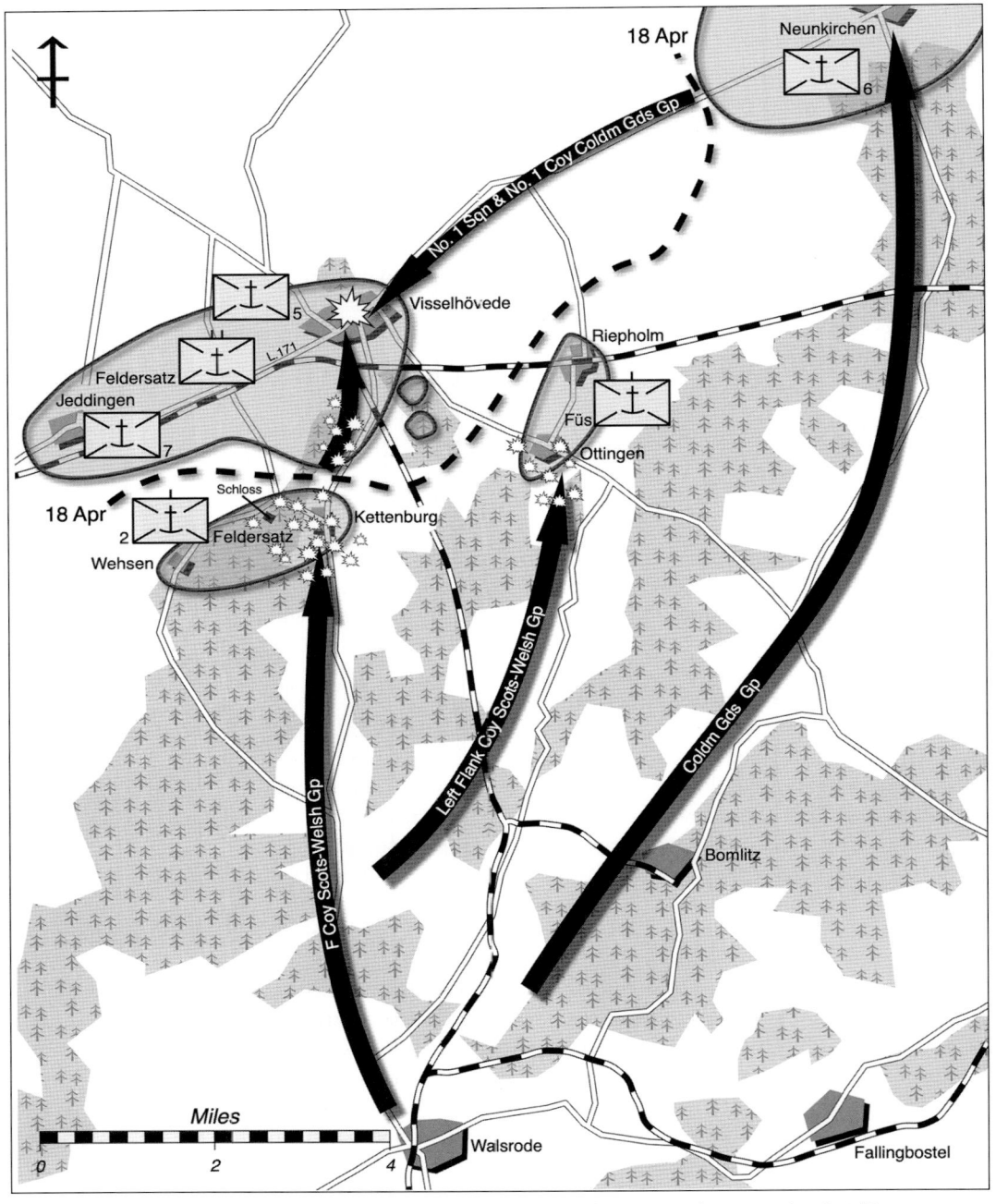

Map 72 Visselhövede – 2. Marine-Infanterie-Division's Last Stand – 18–19 April 1945.

Marine-Feldersatz-Bataillon 2 in positions dominating the southern approach to Visselhövede. Left Flank Company 2 Scots Gds successfully bypassed the village by moving to the east but this move then ran into marines from Marine-Füsilier-Bataillon 2 in Ottingen, who did not give in lightly, as this extract from a 32nd Guards Brigade INTSUM describes:[7]

> These men were raw and untrained, but from all accounts they fought extremely bravely. They were well-equipped with bazookas – according to PoWs they had 12 per company – and, to cite one instance, some of them at Ottingen tried to stalk some of our tanks that were some 500 yards from the nearest thick cover. Their attack resulted in annihilation, as was only to be expected, but their courage must be admitted, and their aggressive tactics certainly had the effect of holding us up in no uncertain manner.

During the attack on Ottingen a Cromwell of 3 Squadron Welsh Guards was struck on the turret by an HE projectile when stationary.[8] The crew baled out successfully but outside the tank Sergeant Williams, the commander was killed, and the co-driver wounded. The tank received only minor damage and was rapidly repaired by the battalion's LAD.

Meanwhile F Company 2 Scots Gds was fighting an extremely bitter action to clear the marines of 2. Kompanie from Kettenburg, which the regimental history described as one of resistance to the death, and it took until 1900 hours before the hamlet was clear. Twenty-five marines were killed in the defence of Kettenburg and its nearby manor house, *Schloss* Kettenburg. With the hamlet now in the Guards' hands, the Scots-Welsh Group began an attack on Visselhövede from the south. However, they encountered heavy fire from the woods dominating the approaches to the town and with darkness falling and communications difficult, the attack was called off and the group spent the night in a tight defence of the Kettenburg area. While the Scots-Welsh Group were involved to the south of Visselhövede, the Coldstream Group bypassed to the east and advanced on Neunkirchen.[9] Here marines of Marine-Grenadier-Regiment 6 attempted to block the advance but were soon overcome by No. 3 Company and No. 3 Squadron and the village fell without difficulty with 60 prisoners taken in its area.

Early in the morning of 19 April, No. 1 Squadron and No. 1 Company from the Coldstream Group conducted a reconnaissance in force from the north-east into the northern outskirts of Visselhövede. This manoeuvre avoided the marines covering the southern approaches, encountered only light opposition and by 1200 hours the northern half of the town was secure. While the Coldstream Group moved in from the north, the Scots-Welsh Group advanced from the south and west. During its approach from the west, Right Flank Company, carried on the decks of the Welsh Guards' Cromwells, came under heavy fire from the woods. Although it managed to bypass this opposition and press on towards the town, to ensure no more opposition from this area, F Company was ordered to clear the troublesome enemy; this took the remainder of the morning. Supported by the Cromwells, G and Right Flank Company meanwhile broke through the perimeter defence along the railway embankment on the town's southern edge and against determined opposition from the marines fought their way into the town. By 1100 hours the southern half of the town was secure and the Scots-Welsh established their headquarters in a hotel on the main street and relieved the Coldstream Group in the northern part of the town. Two Cromwells were

---

7 TNA WO 171/4357, 32nd Guards Brigade INTSUM up to 2000 hours 19 April 1945.
8 TNA WO 205/1165, 2 Welsh Gds, Serial C.22, Wright and Harkness, *A Survey of Casualties Amongst Armoured Units in North-West Europe.*
9 TNA WO 171/5141 and WO 171/5143, 1 Coldm Gds and 5 Coldm Gds war diaries.

positioned outside the headquarters and peace reigned, allowing the Guards to reorganise and rest after the fight.

The marines had not, however, given up and although they had withdrawn northwards from the town they had pulled back only a short distance to a thick wood and here they regrouped. Under the command of Kapitän zur See Jordan, marines from the *Feldersatz* battalion and I./7 Bataillon worked their way undetected back into the town using the cover provided by garden hedgerows and attacked without warning. The centre of the town was soon engulfed in hand-to-hand fighting during which a Cromwell Mk IV was struck on the turret by a *Panzerfaust* fired at very close range. The turret began to burn immediately and the turret crew, all wounded, baled out; the operator subsequently died of wounds and the tank completely burnt out.[10] Two mortar carriers were also destroyed, a platoon from G Company was surrounded and the members of the headquarters in the hotel had to fight off the enemy with their pistols. Confusion reigned for two hours with radio communications lost and movement between the houses impossible owing to the torrent of small-arms' fire. Help eventually came from a tank commanded by Captain The Hon Mildmay from 3 Squadron, which managed to make its way back into the town, blazing away with its Besa as it did so. This tank and its commander both had lucky escapes when a *Panzerfaust* exploded against a wall beside it and Captain Mildmay had an earpiece of his radio headset shot off. It was only from this tank's presence, and a troop from 1 Squadron later joining the fray, that the Guards gradually began to repulse the marines, though most of the tanks ran out of Besa ammunition and had to resort to firing their main armament at individual Germans. By the evening of 19 April the town was firmly in British hands and 12 officers and 282 marines captured; ninety-six members of Marine-Grenadier-Regiments 5 and 7 were killed in the fighting at Visselhövede and today lie buried in the town's and Jeddingen's war cemeteries. Among the prisoners was Kapitän zur See Jordan and five of his regimental staff, captured in a house only two away from the Scots-Welsh headquarters in the hotel. Jordan would not survive the war. The Scots Guards' history records that the next day a sentry shot him dead when he tried to escape in plain clothes from the brigade PoW cage. Perhaps a predictable end for a man who had fought unceasingly since the opening shots at Rethem some nine days previous.

19 April at Visselhövede was a very hard day for the Guards, with the regimental history of 2 Scots Gds recording the fighting in and around the town as among the toughest the battalion had experienced, with 13 of their own killed. Clearly reflecting the division's respect for the opposition, the author of the Guards Armoured INTSUM made the following entry for 19 April:[11]

> There is no doubt that these sailors fight like fury, and this afternoon's battle in Visselhövede was a tough one at close quarters…The manner in which the marines that are still organised in properly controlled units have fought us during the last two days shows clearly enough that the Germans will remain formidable enemies as long as there are troops to lead and officers to lead them. This will hold good no matter how hopeless the situation may be, as few operations could have been more senseless and more costly in the sacrifice of soldiers than today's counter-attack.

The Guards Armoured history subsequently added detail to the war diary entry with this impression of the marines:[12]

---

10   TNA WO 205/1165, 2 Welsh Gds, Serial C.1, Wright and Harkness, *A Survey of Casualties Amongst Armoured Units in North-West Europe.*
11   TNA WO 171/4104, Guards Armoured Division war diary.
12   The Earl of Rosse, Captain; Hill, Colonel ER, *The Story of the Guards Armoured Division* (London: Geoffrey Bles, 1956), p.258.

They were nearly all ex-sailors, many of them until lately members of submarine crews. They had had little time for military training and therefore lacked the fighting skill of the paratroops, but their discipline and bravery were exemplary. They were all equipped with bazookas, which they used in particularly daring fashion; their tactics often involved them necessarily in annihilation but their aggressive spirit certainly delayed our progress most effectively.

The fall of Visselhövede and Jordan's death marked the finale to 2. Marine-Infanterie-Division's short but bloody part in the war, with the marines' spirited counter-attack on the town a fitting climax to their courage and commitment. After Visselhövede the surviving elements of the division were pushed away to the north to the Rotenburg area where they ceased to play any further part of significance. The last reference for an action against 2. Marine-Infanterie-Division is for 20 April when a squadron-company group from the Irish Guards Group intercepted a convoy of trucks from Marine-Versorgungs-Regiment 200 heading from Rotenburg to Elsdorf to set up an administration area in Elsdorf.[13] The convoy was wholly unaware of the presence of the Irish and as it neared Elsdorf fire was opened on it, destroying eight vehicles. Sixty prisoners were taken and an unknown number of marines killed and wounded. The same day a German situation map records the locations of only II./7 Bataillon and Marine-Feldersatz-Bataillon 2, and the strength return for 21 April at Figure 25 starkly shows the losses the division had sustained;[14] it probably does not include the losses from the actions in the Visselhövede and Neunkirchen areas:

Unit	Officers	Men
2. Marine-Infanterie-Division Stab (HQ)	12	65
Marine-Grenadier-Regiment 5	1	100
Marine-Grenadier-Regiment 6	18	365
Marine-Grenadier-Regiment 7	20	410
Marine-Füsilier-Bataillon 2	3	80
Marine-Artillerie-Regiment 2	9	270
Marine-Panzerjäger-Abteilung 2	4	80
Marine-Pionier-Bataillon 2	3	65
Marine-Feldersatz-Bataillon 2	10	300
Total	80	1,735

Figure 25 2. Marine-Infanterie-Division strength return – 21 April 1945.

Although 2. Marine-Infanterie-Division was fast approaching combat ineffectiveness, the division had done all that could have been expected of it and had fought courageously to the last. Its remaining marines ended the war in the Cuxhaven pocket, although some made it back over the Elbe to Schleswig-Holstein where, with the thousands of other German soldiers bottled-up in the peninsula, they later surrendered. A measure of its reduced status is revealed in a XII Corps INTSUM published 12 days after the war's end, which shows the division, along with Panzer-Ausbildungs-Verband 'Grossdeutschland' and Volks-Artillerie-Korps 402, under the command of II. Flak-Korps, previously the provider of air defence for Heeresgruppe Weichsel on the East Front.[15]

---

13 TNA WO 171/5147 and WO 171/5148, 2 Irish Gds and 3 Irish Gds war diaries.
14 *Tagesstärke der dem Korps Ems Unterstellten Truppen, Stand 21.4.1945.*
15 TNA WO 171/4055, Appendix A to XII Corps Int Notes No. 3, 20 May 1945, Orbat Korps Witthöft.

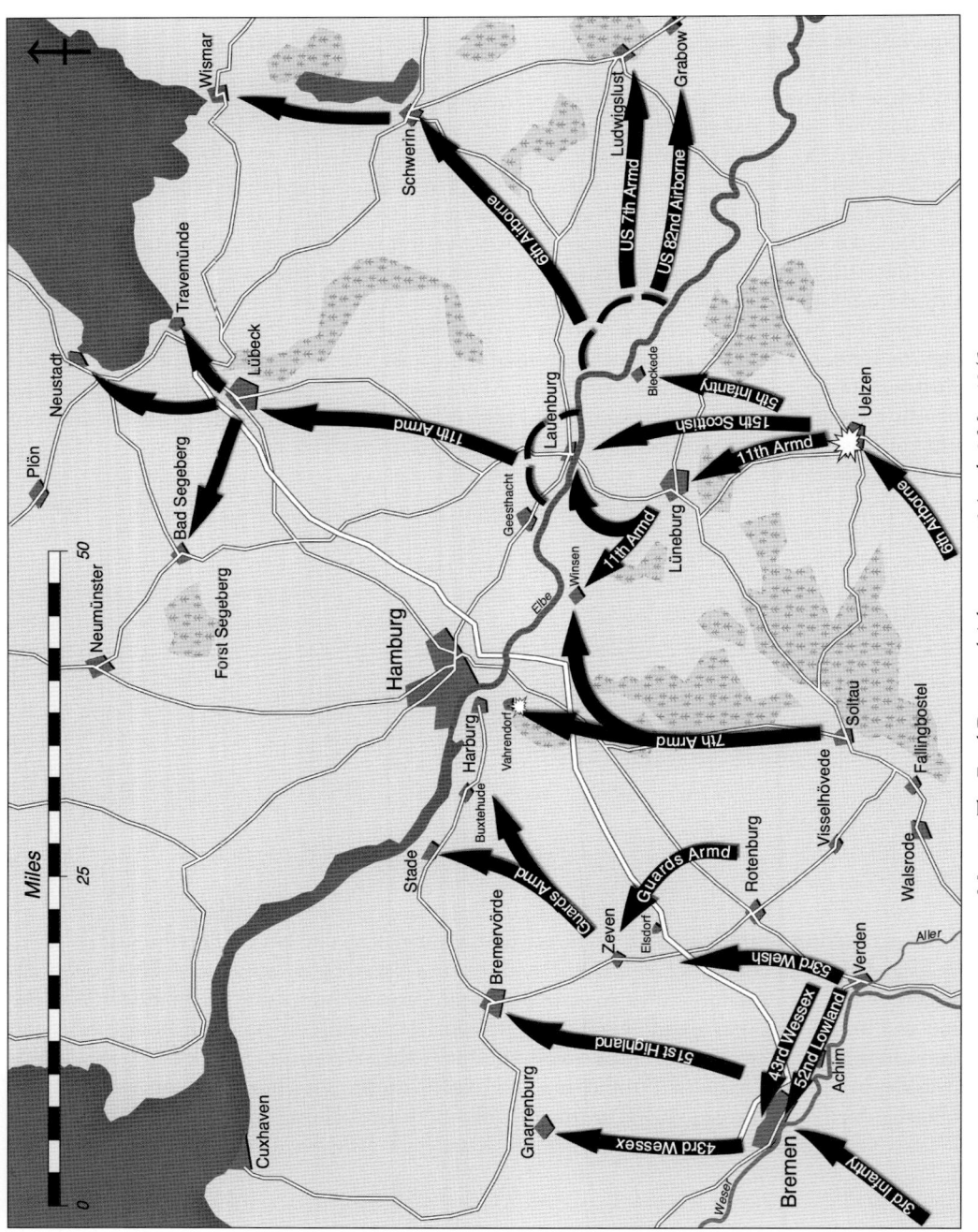

Map 73 The Final Divisional Advances – 15 April–3 May 1945.

With Visselhövede captured, Guards Armoured Division advanced north-west towards Rotenburg and Zeven, captured on 22 and 24 April respectively. During the advance to Zeven Guardsman Eddie Charlton of 2 (Armoured) Irish Gds posthumously won the last VC of the European war when on 21 April he single-handedly held up a German counter-attack near the village of Wistedt. Once Zeven was cleared, Guards Armoured returned to XXX Corps on 29 April and will play no further part in this account.

While the Guards were involved at Visselhövede, 7th Armoured continued its advance on Hamburg, with Soltau the next major town on its axis after Fallingbostel. Although defended by approximately a battalion consisting of *Volkssturm*, marines, some youths from SS-A.u.E.Btl. 12 'HJ' and the staff of the town's cavalry riding school, the town was rapidly cleared by 7/9 Scots of 155th Brigade reinforced by 5 Innis DG.[16] Meanwhile, 53rd Welsh cleared the right bank of the Weser, then the area to the east of Verden and the ground between Zeven and Rotenburg. The division detached 160th Brigade to 7th Armoured to help mop up a troublesome pocket formed by Gruppe Grosan, which had withdrawn to woods to the east of Soltau where it posed a threat to the tactical headquarters of Second Army and 21st Army Group. The brigade had to fight hard against the remains of the *Gruppe*, but by the evening of 22 April the gallant Grosan recognised that further resistance was futile so called his senior British prisoner to his headquarters at Suroide, handed him his pistol and announced that as his troops had run out of ammunition and he had no communications with Korps Ems he wished to surrender with his staff and dissolve his *Gruppe*. Two thousand prisoners were subsequently rounded-up and Gruppe Grosan was no more.

On 22 April 53rd Welsh was ordered to advance in a north-westerly direction to cut the Bremen-Hamburg *Autobahn* near Elsdorf; 71st Brigade and 53rd Recce Regiment would lead the infantry division's advance, to begin the next day. Progress was slow against substantial groups of Germans supported by artillery and it was while directing his brigade in these operations that tragedy overtook Brigadier Elrington, who was mortally wounded when his Jeep ran over a mine buried in a roadside verge. Mines laid in verges and powerful devices linking mines to aircraft bombs were used extensively in the closing days and many met tragic deaths from these devices. By 25 April his brigade had reached its objective and two days later 53rd Welsh cleared the German forces still resisting in the area between Zeven and Rotenburg. Soon after, with 158th Brigade allocated to 15th Scottish as part of VIII Corps' operation to cross the Elbe, the remainder of the division moved to the corps' right flank to relieve 11th Armoured and free the armour to take part in the breakout from the Elbe bridgehead.

Once Soltau was captured, 7th Armoured rapidly advanced towards its next objective, the bridges over the Elbe at Harburg. The division cut the *Autobahn* between Bremen and Hamburg on 19 April and the next day began to close with the defenders of Harburg, making contact as it did so with 11th Armoured Division at Winsen (not to be confused with Winsen/Aller). On 22 April, 22nd Armoured Brigade captured Buxtehude, complete with the headquarters of 2. Admiral Nordsee/Ostsee. 7th Armoured then reached the high, wooded area above Harburg but as the ground was unsuitable for armour the division was ordered to hold its positions and contain the Germans in the town. Once VIII Corps had crossed the Elbe and secured a bridgehead, the intention was for 7th Armoured to cross to the river's right bank and attack Hamburg from the east. The Germans in Harburg maintained an aggressive defence against the armoured division, reaching a peak on 26 April in the area of Vahrendorf, a village just to the west of the main road leading to Hamburg. Here a composite force consisting of members of 7. SS-Kompanie, commanded by SS-Untersturmführer Heinz Früh, with marines and soldiers from a variety of units and two StuG III from Fallschirm-Sturmgeschütz-Brigade 12 mounted a last, determined counter-attack against

---

16 TNA WO 171/4686, 5 Innis DG war diary.

1/5 Queens and 2 Devon. The battle for Vahrendorf started in the small hours of the morning and lasted all day; the attack was eventually repulsed and 45 German soldiers were killed and 83 taken prisoner. 2 Devon lost seven killed and seven wounded during the action. Propagated over the years by the village and elements of the political far right, a legend has developed suggesting most of the 45 were systematically shot after surrender. An impartial review of the legend considered a large-scale massacre unlikely as there was no collateral for the single eye-witness account and lack of conclusive evidence from post-mortems.[17] The post-mortems did reveal however that there were more shots (14) to the head, and head and body, than might be expected. It therefore seems possible that some prisoners were shot, perhaps as a consequence of emotions running high owing to British deaths during the battle, revenge for the Rethem 'massacre' of 11 April and reaction to Belsen.

VIII Corps

On VIII Corps' axis two major actions were fought in the final days. The first took place in the Uelzen area between 15–18 April against elements of Panzer-Division 'Clausewitz', an extemporised formation raised earlier the same month and commanded by Generalleutnant Unrein. On 11 April Unrein was ordered by OKW to move his forces from the Lauenburg area to concentrate to the north of Uelzen before advancing in a southerly direction to cut the US Ninth Army's supply lines. This was a supporting manoeuvre to an utterly unrealistic plan involving General der Panzertruppen Walter Wenck's 12. Armee, forming in the Harz, advancing west to break the encirclement of Model's Heeresgruppe 'B' in the Ruhr. The plan for 12. Armee was not only stillborn but also hopelessly out of touch with events as Heeresgruppe 'B' was on the verge of capitulation, an event that took place on 16 April with the surrender of 325,000 men. Regardless of these grand intentions, even with the name Clausewitz the division's manoeuvre was doomed and during a fierce, three-day meeting engagement in and around Uelzen it was largely destroyed by 15th Scottish, supported by brigades from 6th Airborne and 11th Armoured. Those elements of Panzer-Division 'Clausewitz' which managed to bypass Uelzen were then unable to cross the Mittelland Canal, as the bridges were either blown or captured, and were subsequently destroyed by Combat Command 'B' of the US 5th Armored Division. Uelzen was mopped up on 18 April and on the same day 11th Armoured captured an undefended Lüneburg.

On 19 April Lieutenant General Barker ordered 11th Armoured, 15th Scottish and the recently-joined 5th Infantry Division to advance to the Elbe and three days later the corps was firmly established on the left bank and preparing for Operation ENTERPRISE, the crossing of the river. However, an assault across such a wide obstacle was not something for hasty action and it took nine days to bring forward the necessary troops, particularly US XVIII Airborne Corps still in the Ruhr but allocated to reinforce Second Army, and bridging and engineer stores.

XXX Corps

While VIII and XII Corps were advancing to the Elbe, XXX Corps was investing Bremen,[18] by now largely a shell from years of bombing. The defence of Bremen and its locale was the

---

17 Markus Denkhaus, 'Vom Entstehen und Verschwinden einer politischen Sage', *www.kultur.uni-hamburg.de/volkskunde/Texte/Vokus/2002-2/denkhaus.html* (accessed 24 May 2019).
18 TNA WO 171/4079, GS Branch XXX Corps war diary.

responsibility of General der Infanterie Rasp's Korps Ems, the last surviving part of Armeegruppe Blumentritt and now including the remnants of 2. Marine-Infanterie-Division following its withdrawal from the Aller Line. Although some of Rasp's forces were capable of offering resistance, there was no likelihood of a successful defence of the city.

With the British assault on the city needing infantry in quantity, XXX Corps was reconfigured, losing Guards Armoured to XII Corps but gaining two additional divisions, 3rd Infantry and 52nd Lowland. To capture the city, Lieutenant General Horrocks devised a shrewd plan avoiding the obvious approach from the south-west and instead placing the main effort on the Weser's right bank with a two-division assault from the south-east: 52nd Lowland Division on the left axis and 43rd Wessex Division on the right. This assault would be supported from the south by 3rd Division crossing flooded land in Buffaloes and then clearing the built-up area of Bremen situated on the Weser's left bank, and a feint attack from the south-west by 51st Highland Division. On 19 April, 52nd Lowland crossed the Weser at Verden, using a Class 40 bridge completed the day before by the divisional engineers, and advanced up the right bank clearing the villages lying in its path, experiencing stiff resistance from pockets of infantry supported by a high density of *Flak* from 8. Flak-Division and it took the division four days to clear as far as Achim, which had to be secured before the division could begin its attack on the city. 43rd Wessex followed 52nd Lowland across the Verden bridge the same day and was complete on the right bank by 22 April. The division started its advance on 23 April and encountering only sporadic opposition from Division Nr.480, fought its way to a park where General Becker, Kampfkommandant Bremen, had his headquarters in a bunker. 52nd Lowland's main assault began on 24 April; two days later it had taken the city centre and the docks. Bremen could have fallen even quicker had movement not been slowed owing to debris in the streets from recent Allied bombing raids. 3rd Division's attack across the flooded area took the Germans by surprise and by 26 April the division had cleared the left bank. 51st Highland meanwhile mopped up units of Korps Ems in the villages to the south-west of Bremen and by 20 April had captured Delmenhorst. By 27 April all objectives were secure and General Becker captured.

29 April–3 May

Finale

The story is now nearly over. In northern Europe the German army was squeezed into three, fast-reducing pockets: 25. Armee was trapped in the northern Netherlands; a second pocket containing what was left of 1. Fallschirm-Armee and Armeegruppe Blumentritt stretched from Emden to the Elbe and into Schleswig-Holstein; and eastwards from the Elbe to just west of Stettin a third pocket contained what was left of Heeresgruppe Weichsel. The *Luftwaffe's* few remaining operational units were flying from a scattering of bases littered with abandoned and damaged aircraft. The pockets in north Germany and the formations they contained on 3 May 1945 are shown on Map 74.[19]

Although the end neared, the Germans' summary execution of deserters and waverers continued without let-up. A typical case was 17-year-old Matrose Kurt Albrecht. Albrecht joined the *Kriegsmarine* in August 1944, transferred to Marine-Grenadier-Regiment 5 on its formation and had fought with 8. Kompanie from Rethem onwards. He fled his unit by bicycle on 23 April in the Rotenburg area and was subsequently caught in civilian clothes masquerading as a farm

---

19 TNA WO 171/3959, Second Army GS Int.

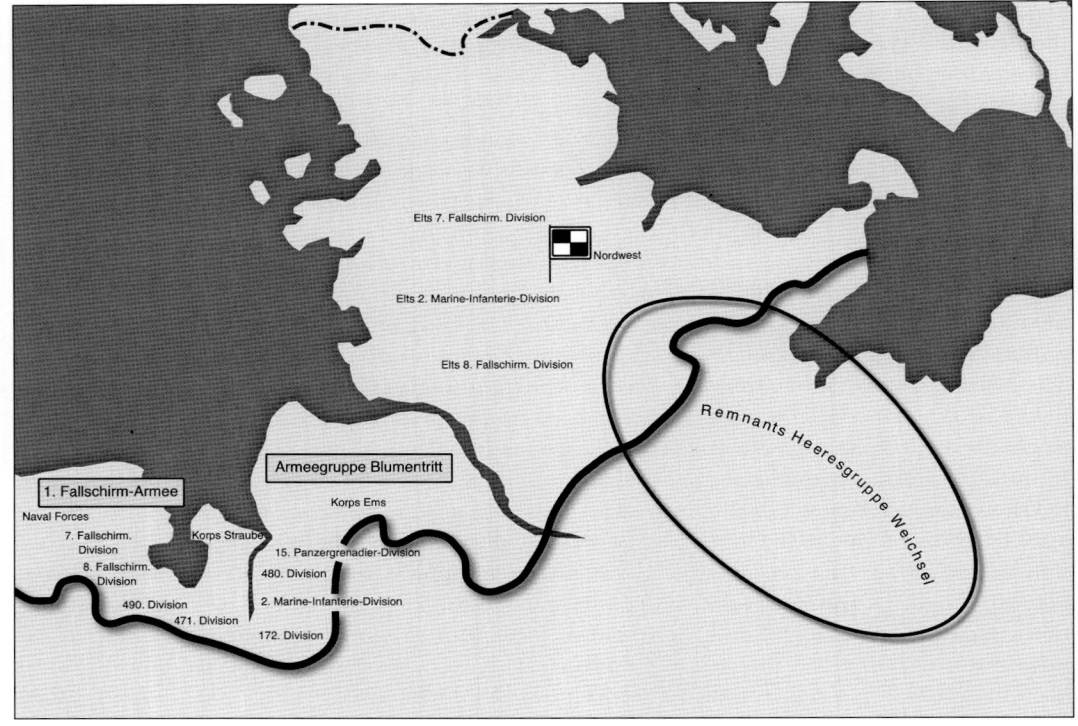

Map 74 Final Dispositions of 1. Fallschirm-Armee and Armeegruppe Blumentritt – 3 May 1945.

worker. His captors were probably *Kettenhunde* ('chain dogs'), the feared *Feldjäger* given their nickname from the metal gorgets hung on chains from their necks. On 28 April a three-man court comprising a judge and two officers from 2. Marine-Infanterie-Division tried Albrecht. The judge, Marine-Oberstabsrichter Dr. Kurt Göller, sentenced him to death for desertion from the field of battle and at 2024 hours the same day he was shot at Osterholz-Scharmbeck north of Bremen by a 10-man firing squad provided by Marine-Füsilier-Bataillon 2. He was buried without ceremony and his grave is now lost.[20] An even later case involved Leutnant Hermann Gern of JG 11 arrested by *Luftwaffe* military police on 3 May for attempting to steal a Me 108 at Leck airfield to fly home to southern Germany. He was tried, found guilty of desertion and executed by a firing squad of groundcrew on 7 May – two days after the cessation of hostilities in northern Germany.[21]

On 19 April Dönitz ordered his staff to evacuate 'Koralle' (HQ OKM) 20 miles north-east of Berlin and move to Plön, 50 miles to the north of Hamburg.[22] Dönitz stayed in Berlin for Hitler's birthday on 20 April and at their last meeting Hitler charged him with the defence of Germany's northern area and command of Heeresgruppe Weichsel on the East Front, OB Nordwest and all forces in Denmark and Norway.[23] He then instructed Dönitz to leave Berlin quickly to avoid becoming trapped.[24] The next day OKW evacuated its headquarters at Zossen south of Berlin and

---

20 Milan Spindler, '*Hinrichtung eines 17-jährigen Deserteurs*', https://blog.befreiung1945.de/hinrichtung-eines-17-jaehrigen-deserteurs/ (accessed 14 November 2018).
21 Donald Caldwell, *The JG26 War Diary, Volume Two 1943–1945* (London: Grub Street, 2007), p.476.
22 Peter Padfield, *Dönitz – The Last Führer*, p.399.
23 Kershaw, *Hitler. Nemesis, 1936–1945*, (London: Allen Lane, 2000), p.792.
24 Karel Margry, 'The Flensburg Government', After the Battle No.128, p.2.

on 22 April split in two: Führungsstab Nord moved to Neu-Roofen, north of Berlin, followed shortly after by a move to Dobbin-Linstow to the east of Schwerin; Führungsstab Süd moved straight to Berchtesgaden in Bavaria. Three days later Soviet and US forces met on the Elbe at Torgau and the *Reich* was split in two. On 30 April, with the Russians closing on the *Reich* Chancellery, Hitler dictated his political testament in which, inter alia, he appointed Dönitz as his successor as *Reichpräsident*. He then committed suicide in the squalor of his bunker. Following a confused series of telegrams from Reichsleiter Bormann, on 1 May Dönitz eventually recognised that Hitler was dead and that the office of *Reichpräsident* had transferred to him. Unaware of Göring's and Himmler's sudden and dramatic falls from grace, this came as a surprise. On 2 May OKW claimed, in typically mendacious terms, that 'at the head of the heroic defenders of the *Reich* capital the *Führer* has fallen.'[25]

At 0200 hours, on the day of Hitler's suicide, Operation ENTERPRISE began. Led by 15th Scottish and against light opposition VIII Corps rapidly secured the initial bridgehead over the Elbe and despite some delays caused by German artillery and attacks by the *Luftwaffe*, by the end of the day a Class 9 bridge was completed at Lauenburg and a Class 40 at Artlenburg. Operation VOLCANO, the breakout from the bridgehead, could now begin. On 1 May, 11th Armoured Division passed through 15th Scottish in the bridgehead and made rapid progress to the Baltic. 29th Armoured Brigade reached the coast at midnight on 2 May, having cleared Lübeck on the way, and on 3 May 5th Division relieved 11th Armoured at Lübeck, freeing the armour to advance north and occupy Travemünde, Bad Segeberg and Neustadt. The roads were filled with tens of thousands of German troops and countless civilians, offering no resistance and intent on moving west to cross the Elbe in advance of the Russians.

While VIII Corps was advancing northward, US XVIII Airborne Corps, comprising 82nd Airborne Division, 8th Infantry Division and 7th Armored Division, and reinforced with British 6th Airborne Division and 1st Commando Brigade, started to cross the Elbe shortly after midnight on 30 April and despite heavy and accurate shelling had by 2000 hours the next day built a Class 40 bridge at Bleckede. On 2 May the corps broke-out against light opposition. Ludwigslust and Schwerin were soon occupied by 82nd Airborne, and British 3rd Parachute Brigade reached the Baltic coast at Wismar at 1600 hours; five hours later it contacted the Soviet Army. The next day 82nd Airborne contacted the Soviets at Grabow. Relationships with the Russians were difficult from the start, as this story by Sergeant Fraser Edwards, 317 Airborne Field Security Section, describes:[26]

> Russians came into Wismar and saw us queue up for tins of hot food, cigarettes and chocolate every day while they lived off the land. Some even tried to pinch cigarettes and got beaten up. They were then forbidden to enter our sector – Rokossovsky did not want his troops to see how capitalist soldiers were fed. On 7 May a Russian officer stole Jack Kershaw's bike and rode off. I followed with Jack on the pillion out through no-man's land. We caught up with him at the Russian checkpoint. I could speak quite a bit of Russian but when I asked for the bike back he said, 'I am a Russian officer. I need this bike' whereupon the guards surrounded us with machine-guns aimed at us. I said to Jack, 'If we're not careful they will have two bikes and two corpses in the ditch.' I then said we were comrades etc etc and he could keep the bike as long as he needed it. We about turned and fled back to the safety of our own lines. We reported the theft and were congratulated on not causing an incident (our deaths!). They were

---

25 Kershaw, *The End*, p.346.
26 Graeme Deeley, *Worst Fears Confirmed. The History of the Intelligence Corps Airborne Units and the Intelligence Gathering and Security Measures Employed for British Airborne Operations* (Hough on the Hill: Barny Books, 2005), p.180.

desperate for Russian speakers but I did not want anything to do with them so I conveniently 'forgot' my Russian.

Deaths and injuries in these final days were the most tragic and, while there were many, one case will suffice for all. On 2 May, Major 'Pete' Jepson, the GSO2 (Intelligence) HQ 6th Airborne Division, annoyed at the lack of information being reported by 3rd Parachute Brigade, borrowed a motorcycle from a Military Police patrol and despite being warned that snipers were active, set off for Gadebusch, some 15 miles from Wismar; his body was later found by the lead troops lying next to the motorcycle. Pete Jepson lies today in CWGC cemetery Berlin 1939–1945.

While 6th Airborne headed for the Baltic, 15th Scottish were clearing the Elbe's right bank westward as far as Geesthacht, providing right bank security for XII Corps to construct a bridge. Although 71st Brigade subsequently crossed the bridge as a preliminary to the operation to attack Hamburg from the east, operations to attack the city developed no further as it became evident that negotiations were in train not only for the surrender of the city but also for the surrender of Armeegruppe Blumentritt and all German forces in north-west Germany. On XXX Corps' front the divisions spent the final days mopping-up pockets of resistance, with 51st Highland capturing Bremervörde on 2 May and Bremerhaven on 4 May, and 43rd Wessex capturing Gnarrenburg on 3 May. Meanwhile First Canadian Army had reached the North Sea coast in the northern Netherlands, bottling-up the residue of Heeresgruppe 'H' and was closing fast on the Emden-Wilhelmshaven area.

The fanatical Dönitz attempted to keep operations going to the last, demanding the fight continue against the British and Americans 'in so far as they hinder me in the prosecution of the fight against Bolshevism' and advising the *Wehrmacht* that 'the oath of loyalty which you gave to the *Führer* is now due from each one of you to me as the *Führer's* successor.'[27] But the *Wehrmacht*, released from its oath to Hitler by his death, was not prepared to transfer its allegiance to Dönitz and localised peace negotiations began to break out. The first capitulation had in fact taken place in Italy on 29 April, the day before Hitler's death, when SS-Obergruppenführer Karl Wolff agreed to the unconditional surrender of all German forces in Italy and to the cessation of hostilities on 2 May. On the same day opposition collapsed on the north-west Europe front. On 3 May Dempsey ordered the commanders of VIII, XII and US XVIII Airborne Corps to stand fast and announced that a delegation from Dönitz and Keitel had passed through HQ Second Army during the morning and was now at HQ 21st Army Group. The same day Hamburg was formally surrendered to Dempsey by its *Kampfkommandant*, General der Flakartillerie Wolz, and occupied by 7th Armoured. 53rd Welsh followed in the armoured division's wake to take over responsibility for the great but shattered city. A link to an online video of 7th Armoured's entry into Hamburg and the surrender of the city to Brigadier Spurling, commander of 131st Brigade, is at Appendix A, Serial 21.

The defeat of the nation and the *Wehrmacht* was absolute and it was not for nothing that the Germans used the term *'Die Stunde Null'* – the Hour Zero – to describe this period.[28] The link to an often-disturbing online video, which seeks to give a flavour of the period, is at Appendix A, Serial 22. Throughout northern Germany columns of dejected German troops, some still heavily-armed but others weaponless and leaderless, blocked the roads as they came to give themselves up. Lieutenant Brett-Smith of 11 Hussars describes a typical scene of the endgame:[29]

---

27 Padfield, *Dönitz – The Last Führer*, p.413.
28 The term is not uncontroversial and some still see it as a way for the Germans to wipe clean the slate and disassociate themselves with the *Nazi* period and the part the nation played in it.
29 Delaforce, *Churchill's Desert Rats in North-West Europe* (Barnsley: Pen & Sword, 2010), p.186.

DIE STUNDE NULL 447

A typical scene of the final days. A Ford 3000 series truck laden with surrendered German troops drives past Cromwells of 5 RTR pausing in a street. (Huett)

A picture with a dreamlike air. Under a large oak, two surrendered German officers wait with their bicycles and belongings, ignored by the crew of a Cromwell busy adjusting their tank's tracks. (Huett)

It was indeed a wonderful and an astonishing sight to see the end of the German army. We had known for long how disorganised they were and that all administration had broken down completely. Even so the sight that we now saw was more than we had expected. Infantry, air force, anti-tank gunners, navy, Hungarians, Rumanians, Austrians, non-combatants, labour corps, men of every conceivable age and unit jostled one another in complete disorder: staff cars full of officers, wagons full of soldiers, trucks towing other trucks (the record was eight cars pulled by one lorry). Motorcyclists, footsloggers, ambulances, even trains. Down every road the *Wehrmacht* marched in to give itself up, its pride broken, its endurance at an end.

But not all surrenders matched that description and some German units maintained their discipline and bearing to the last, as witnessed by David Fraser of 2nd (Armoured) Battalion Gren Gds:[30]

On the green was drawn up a company – about a hundred – of German soldiers. We were expected, and as we dismounted from our scout cars the German officer in command emerged from the church to meet us. He saluted. We saluted. He was immaculate. This was a medical company, and his second-in-command was, I think, an *Unteroffizier* [corporal]. There were no other commissioned officers. The company commander's black field boots were brilliantly polished, and his cap set at a jaunty angle. We gave him various instructions. He nodded and said he had only one request. There were two civilian nurses, two women, with the unit. He asked that they should be dealt with correctly. We gave our assurances.

The soldiers, towards whom we now moved with some curiosity, were also immaculate. Trouble with turnout had clearly been taken – these were men determined not to let themselves or the *Wehrmacht* down in the eyes of their enemies. Morale among soldiers manifests itself by small signs, and here it seemed pretty good – evidenced by the *Unteroffizier*, who, having received word from his superior, now approached them, called them to attention and gave out a few details. Drill was impeccable. He obviously cracked a joke and there was an answering roar of laughter – we were at some distance and it may well have been at our expense. These men were in good shape. They came from 7th Parachute Division, whose uniforms were a slightly different shade from the ordinary cloth of the army. Their discipline and spirits were manifestly high. We had met these parachute troops many times and always with respect. Like the *Waffen-SS* they constituted something of an elite.

Some *Luftwaffe* units also surrendered in style, as a German pilot based at Leck in Schleswig-Holstein recorded:[31]

6 May 1945. We lined up the aircraft ground equipment in parade order. The English were astonished at the imposing scene at the airfield: a view of more than a hundred aircraft, standing with a pride born of sadness. The newer types, the Me 262s and the He 162s, which had hardly begun operations, stood between the well-blooded Bf 109 and Fw 190s, victors in thousands of air battles; all of these were to be handed over to the enemy.

With the situation collapsing about them, the German hierarchy made last minute, frantic approaches to the Western Powers to buy time to allow as many soldiers and civilians as possible to reach the west, but these approaches were flatly turned down and even Dönitz realised the end had come and

---

30 Fraser, *Wars and Shadows*, p.255.
31 Dr Alfred Price, *The Last Year of the Luftwaffe, May 1944 to May 1945* (London: Arms & Armour Press, 1991), p.170.

began to prepare to sue for peace. A German delegation sent to Montgomery, led by Generaladmiral von Friedeburg, Dönitz's successor as OB OKM, and General Kinzel, chief of staff of Führungsstab Nord, agreed to surrender all forces in the Netherlands, the Friesian Islands, Schleswig-Holstein, Heligoland and Denmark and at 1820 hours on 4 May the Instrument of Surrender was signed at Montgomery's tactical headquarters on Lüneburg Heath. Shortly after midnight Montgomery sent out the message that all offensive operations in 21st Army Group's area were cancelled forthwith and that a cease-fire was effective from 0800 hours on 5 May. For the combatants in north-west Germany, who had fought to the bitter end, and for the civilians, peace had come at last.

Although some British units celebrated with huge bonfires, the bottle and firing off ammunition, for many the end was an anti-climax, to a large degree a reflection of collective emotional weariness and physical exhaustion:

> **Lieutenant Peter White, 4 KOSB**.[32] As the noise and the queries of the Jocks died down, I continued to stand at the door of the farm looking out into the night, listening to distant laughter and commotion. Could it be true? It must be. It was. Excited confirmation came from my own 38 set operator who had tuned in to get the BBC faintly! I quite suddenly felt tremendously tired. It was not just the tiredness due to our long, nervy patrol. It seemed to be the tiredness of all the sleep we had lost over the last few months, yet curiously more of the mind than the body. With it, however, came a paradoxical feeling of lightness as though a heavy weight were slipping off one's consciousness, a weight so long a part of life that at times it was almost impossible to imagine it had always been there…I had never pictured that the reception of this so long hoped for and magical news of the war's end would have been taken so quietly. Apart from the first boisterous announcement, no one had rushed about yelling the glad tidings.

> **Padre Iain Wilson, 1 KOSB**.[33] So this was the end. Partly because it had come so gradually and partly through sheer mental exhaustion, the news was received without emotion. There was little inducement to wild celebrations surrounded as we were by the defeated Germans between whom and ourselves lay the barrier of silence. We were neither elated with success, nor were we filled with emotions of hatred or revenge. We were simply thankful, far below consciousness that the destruction and slaughter had ended.

> **4 KSLI**.[34] It was an unexpectedly low key ending to 11 months of bitter and often dramatic fighting. Perhaps this was because the eventual German collapse was so total when it came. The predominant British emotion was one of thankfulness. After all the disasters and suffering of five years of war against as monstrous a tyranny as ever disgraced the human race, one felt a sober thankfulness at having survived. Next, perhaps, was a feeling of satisfaction and pride at having seen the job through to the bitter end.

> **Lieutenant Bill Bellamy, 8th Hussars**.[35] Although I believe many members of the regiment got together and celebrated VE night with a bonfire, showers of Verey lights and singing, we in recce troop didn't seem to react that way. We had a good meal, a few drinks and then separated into small groups of rather pensive men talking and wondering about the future.

---

32 White, *With the Jocks*, p.462.
33 Delaforce, *Monty's Ironsides* (Stroud: Allan Sutton Publishing Ltd), p.206.
34 Thornburn, 'After Antwerp – The Long Haul to Victory', p.125.
35 Bill Bellamy, *Troop Leader. A Tank Commander's Story* (Stroud: Sutton Publishing Ltd, 2007), p.204.

The surrender to Montgomery was not however the unconditional surrender of all German forces demanded by the Allies and three more days passed while the Germans played for time. Eisenhower's patience soon ran out and Jodl was told that unless he agreed to the Allies' terms he would seal the Allied line and German civilians and members of the *Wehrmacht* would be prevented, by force if necessary, from coming to the west. The game was up and at Reims at 0241 hours on 7 May Jodl, with Dönitz's authority, signed the act of surrender. All combat operations would cease at 2301 hours on 8 May. Generalfeldmarschall Keitel travelled to Berlin on 8 May and signed a similar document with Marshal Zhukov. Although the European war was officially over, fighting did not cease entirely and operations continued in isolated pockets for a few more days. One such began on 8 May and curiously featured the British employment of 8. Fallschirmjäger-Division against *Waffen-SS* elements in the Segeberg forest. An 11th Armoured Division signal warned divisional units of the operation and described the *Waffen-SS* as 'recalcitrant' and that tanks and self-propelled guns would be used against them.[36] Although it is unlikely that German fought German, what is known is that elements of the *Waffen-SS* in the forest were only prepared to surrender to their enemies, as Bill Close of 3 RTR describes:[37]

> To all intents and purposes the war was over and it seemed to most of the tank crews to be rather an anti-climax. There was some clearing up to be done and the German 8th Parachute Division, which had already surrendered, was rounding up odd isolated units. 3 RTR was told however that a strong force of *SS* troops was holed up in Forst Segeberg refusing to surrender other than to the British. A squadron of tanks was required to assist in rounding up the German unit. I drew the short straw and duly set off with my squadron and a company of 4 KSLI for the forest, not without some trepidation as we had enjoyed a considerable celebration party the night before and I was not feeling my best.
>
> There were however no difficulties. We found the *SS* unit to be a complete anti-tank battalion recently returned from the Russian front. They were drawn up in full array, officers in dress uniform, almost as if for inspection. Getting out of my tank I approached the senior officers standing in front of their troops. Immediately one of them stepped forward and in perfect English said, 'My colonel will only surrender his unit to a British officer of field rank!' I was able to assure him that I was of field rank, borne out by the 17 tanks of my squadron now surrounding his unit, and that I would be pleased to accept his colonel's sword and pistol. In convoy, we escorted the complete unit back to Bad Segeberg, with the colonel and his adjutant riding on the front of my tank.

While its armed forces surrendered, the Dönitz regime aped the business of government in increasingly bizarre circumstances, ensconced since 3 May in an enclave centred on the Marine-Schule at Mürwik near Flensburg. The regime lasted for two or so weeks until the Allies decided their policy towards Dönitz and his government, the result of which was the order issued on 22 May to Brigadier Churcher's 159th Brigade to clear the enclave.[38] The next day tanks of 15/19 Hussars and infantry from 1 Cheshire and 1 Hereford entered the enclave and forced the surrender of all military personnel, including Dönitz, Speer, Jodl and the cabinet. It was over.

* * *

---

36   TNA WO 171/4184, 11th Armoured Division signal 080001B.
37   Close, *A View from the Turret*, p.161.
38   Margry, 'The Flensburg Government', pp.12–13.

Although the fighting had ended, the Allies immediately faced immense challenges with Germany in chaos and ruins. There was no government, either central or regional, through which instructions could be issued, millions of civilians were homeless, there were countless thousands of liberated slave labourers, millions of PoWs and further millions of wounded, a non-functioning transport system, and industry and agriculture at a standstill. In the north, Montgomery, since 22 May Commander-in-Chief and Military Governor of the British zone of occupation, decided to treat the challenge as a military operation and identified the provision of food, work and homes as his priorities. On 10 September 1945 he issued his directive for the actions to be taken by the Army and the civilian Control Commission Germany to restore German politics and the economy, and from these small beginnings today's Germany slowly began to evolve.[39]

The two million German PoWs in the British zone were taken into custody in four reception areas, with the marines interned in the areas in the Cuxhaven Peninsula and in the Eiderstedt district in Schleswig-Holstein. The prisoners were not given PoW status under the Geneva Conventions but were referred to instead as 'surrendered enemy personnel' (SEP) as this allowed the British to search more easily for war criminals, use the existing German structures to dismantle the *Wehrmacht* and employ SEPs for clearing minefields and war material. The SEP were self-governed, controlled by *Feldjäger* and had considerable freedom of movement as there was no point in escaping since without discharge papers SEPs could not get food ration stamps, and residency and work permits. Uniforms, rank insignia and awards were allowed to be worn although the swastika was banned. Releases of *Volkssturm*, *Flakhelfer*, RAD members and the seriously wounded or ill took place almost immediately after the surrender, followed soon after by former agricultural and transport workers and miners. By January 1946 the vast majority of SEPs had been released, leaving only former members of the *Waffen-SS* (including the commanders of SS-A.u.E.Btl.12 'HJ'), paratroopers and *Gestapo*, who were transferred to camps in Belgium where they remained until progressively released from March 1946.

However, it was not just the management of Germany and the former *Wehrmacht* that Montgomery had to tackle as there was also the matter of the 800,000 troops of 21st Army Group and the military restructuring required for an army of occupation. BAOR was formed from the British Liberation Army on 25 August 1945, with its headquarters in the Hotel Königshof in Bad Oeynhausen near Minden, with the British zone divided between the four corps: I Corps to Nordrhein-Westphalia, VIII Corps to Schleswig-Holstein, XII Corps to Hamburg (though the corps was quickly reduced and disbanded) and XXX Corps to Niedersachsen.[40] The first six months after the war was characterised by massive movement of soldiers from place to place as the BAOR organisation settled. Soldiers changed role from war to peace-keeping overnight, and were used for military-type activities in securing the peace, such as control of refugee and civilian movement, search, and weapon and munitions handling and destruction. Simultaneously, thousands of drafted soldiers had to be demobbed and formations and units either decommissioned or returned to the UK, where a number prepared to deploy to the Far East and the war against the Japanese. Some of the moves back to the UK were expedited very quickly, for instance 6th Airborne Division was back in the Bulford area by the end of May, while other formations, required for the army of occupation, remained in Germany, generating considerable frustration for their soldiers, who understandably felt they had 'done their bit' and wanted to get home. For the soldiers who had fought to the end, the post-war years were far from easy and were marked by the personal strife of overcoming physical and mental injury, finding jobs and assimilating themselves back into civilian life.[41] But that is another story.

---

39 Christopher Knowles, *Winning the Peace, The British in Occupied Germany 1945–1948* (London: Bloomsbury Academic, 2017). Recommended reading on the Allied occupation and post-war history of Germany.
40 These states and their titles were created in 1946–1947.
41 Alan Allport, *Demobbed. Coming Home After World War Two* (London: Yale UniversityPress, 2010).

Epilogue

Though the ferocity was the equal of far better-known battles of the campaign and their proximity to the war's end gives them a unique and tragic character, the actions on the Weser and Aller have left few historical ripples and have largely faded from view. They were fought by a British Army at the zenith of its wartime development against an enemy at the nadir of his fighting power but often prepared to fight to the last. Although the outcome of the campaign was never in doubt, despite their overwhelming strength and military maturity, at times and places the British struggled to defeat their enemy. The Epilogue will therefore assess the British strengths and weaknesses before analysing the reasons why some German units fought to the bitter end and provided such a determined foe. So, first to the British strengths.

It was mentioned in the Preface that Second Army in 1945 was at its most potent but that the combat arms – particularly the infantry – were physically and mentally exhausted and extremely casualty conscious. While those latter aspects were apparent, and the battle for Rethem certainly provides evidence for them, the account shows that there was no general decline in the Army's capacity to wage war and in the narrative there are numerous instances of well-led units fighting with determination, for example: C Company 12 Devon's defence of Bierde against the Panther counter-attack, 11th Armoured Division's clashes during the advance to the Leine, 1st Commando Brigade's battle in the Essel forest, and 71st Infantry Brigade's action on the Aller's right bank against the counter-attacks. These and many others were fought by men only too aware that the war was nearly won, yet they fought with resolve and skill despite their fatigue. Regardless of the general exhaustion, the morale and motivation needed by the British held to the end.

British tactics, particularly those combining armour and infantry, had by 1945 come of age. The actions of 4th Armoured, 29th Armoured and 159th Infantry Brigade Groups clearly show that the two arms were able to fight effectively in concert, even when the infantry did not have protected mobility. When Kangaroos were available, the infantry's effectiveness significantly increased and 6 RWF's advance with 4th Armoured Brigade shows how far the employment of infantry had come in the 10 months since D-Day. The infantry's ability to operate closely with supporting armour negated to a large extent the threat from *Panzerfaust,* and British armour, while unsophisticated and, less the Comet, the same as that used in Normandy, was now fully suited to the operations for which it was designed: the breakout battle and advance. For these operations it was ideal, contradicting the criticism of those who deliver sweeping condemnation of British tanks. There was, furthermore, no shortage of innovation in British infantry and armour tactics and the artillery was not relied on simply to bludgeon assaults forward, as had been the case in previous months. 1st Commando Brigade's long, night infiltration to attack Leese from the rear, 6 Cdo's assault on the Essel road bridge, the Scots Greys Group's night move through the forest at Altenwahlingen and C Squadron 3 RTR's outflanking of the Ostenholz road leading to the destruction of Tiger F01 all demonstrate how the new class of commanders was prepared to innovate, take risks to seize the initiative and, as a result, save casualties.

The power of the British artillery was highlighted in Chapter 3 and by 1945 the efficiency of its survey and its command, control and communications had contributed to making it a fearsome weapon. However, over-reliance on artillery still tended to slow the tempo of set-piece operations and the ineffectiveness of its shells, particularly the 25-pdr, against dug-in infantry was by 1945 widely recognised; the same lack of effectiveness extended to RPs fired by Typhoons. Conversely, prior to D-Day it had been identified that German counter-attacks would be the targets against which the artillery could cause the most damage, and this was certainly borne-out in the account with the annihilation of Kampfgruppe Tischler's counter-attack at Leese and the savaging by 1st Mountain Regiment of the counter-attacks in the Essel forest.

Lastly, the Royal Engineers and their tactical bridging. The flexibility offered by the range of bridging and the speed with which bridges could be flung across the rivers was a battle-winning advantage and one which negated German demolitions, allowed defences to be outflanked and the advance's momentum maintained. The three bridges built over the Weser in the Petershagen area rapidly unhinged the river's defence, forcing the withdrawal of the SS-A.u.E.Btl.12 'HJ' companies at Leese and I./6 Marine-Grenadier-Regiment at Nienburg; the bridge at Westen enabled Rethem to be outflanked; the bridge at Helstorf allowed the marines in the Schwarmstedt area to be attacked from an unexpected direction; the Bailey sections built on the bridge piers at Hoya, Neustadt and Essel allowed the rapid build-up of combat power; and the Bailey raft at Essel allowed 1st Commando Brigade to be rapidly reinforced with armour. Thus bridging was a critical advantage for the British in their battles for the three rivers.

The British weaknesses evident in the account are almost all concentrated into the two days of the battle for Rethem. At Rethem, all that the army had learnt over the preceding months seems to have been forgotten and the infantry were pitched with insufficient strength into unsubtle frontal attacks against a prepared defence. Furthermore, the attacks were mounted from obvious directions and over open ground, and initially without armour support. Even when tanks were available, the necessity for the closest cooperation between infantry and the tanks, which had been accepted since Normandy, was overlooked. The ineffectiveness of 25-pdr HE shells against dug-in infantry and the inaccuracy of RPs was also disregarded, with the result that the enemy was not neutralised by the artillery fire plan. There are also strong indications that the fire plan and the 2 Mons' advance became disjointed, with inevitable results. Unsurprisingly, the war-weary infantry were less than keen to prosecute their attacks under these circumstances and as a consequence all the attacks failed. The shortage of experienced junior commanders was without doubt a key factor and, from a leadership point of view, there is distinct feeling that come Spring 1945 parts of the British Army were close to running on empty. Rethem was an aberration and perhaps that is why it gets little mention in history. Why did it happen? The under-lying reasons were over-confidence, poor tactical planning, excessive haste and the infantry's general exhausted state, which was intensified when the battalions experienced unexpected setbacks. The failure and ineptitude at Rethem was not, however, representative of 53rd Welsh Division and its defeat of the counter-attacks on the Aller's right bank and subsequent advance to Verden and beyond show that its men remained resolved and courageous to the end.

While the British Army in the earlier war years undoubtedly struggled, it was learning its trade and by 1945 was wholly different from the one that went to war in 1939, and significantly different from the one that stormed the Normandy beaches on 6 June 1944. The differences lay not just in its increased size and improved equipment, although both were important, but also in its professional development, a development that extended from the senior leadership, through the staffs and commanders to the soldiers themselves. David Fraser eloquently summarises the army's achievement:[1]

> The British Army did not always behave impeccably, whether in battle or out of it. It was sometimes ponderous, lacking in *élan*...But it came to know its business. And, without histrionics, it did it. Providence, the extraordinary course of events, and the mistakes of the enemy

---

[1] Fraser, *And We Shall Shock Them*, p.397.

provided time for the army to make good its mistakes, repair and restart the machine and drive to ultimate triumph. The men who composed the British Army of the Second World War learned their trade and became entirely professional. They came from an unmilitary and in some degree an anti-military generation. They were called to an army which had been neglected as to equipment, training, tactical doctrine and the provision of a cadre of sufficient officers and NCOs for expansion. They had never until 1939 been exposed to the beneficent effects of even a short period of national service. They suffered, in the early encounters, considerable blows to their confidence and their self-respect. They were, at the beginning, too often ineptly commanded and placed in situations where no soldier could win. They were, at the end, richly endowed with equipment, worthily led, confident, skilful and deservedly victorious. They had reached the same point, after many vicissitudes, as their fathers in November 1918.

Fraser's commanding words paint a far more accurate and perceptive picture of the army than that depicted by historians who have focussed on its supposed failures to create an image of a bungling organisation that only defeated a quick-witted and vigorous enemy through massive resources and attritional warfare. Their focus on the earlier battles of the campaign, when the army was learning its trade and coming to terms with new equipment and tactics, has not served the reputation of the British army and its commanders well. When the focus is shifted to the campaign fought in 1945 a very different picture can be painted. In short, the British Army comprehensively defeated its enemy by understanding how to fight a campaign rather than the close battle; by excellence of leadership and the development and application of up-to-date doctrine; by the employment of artillery and understanding the enemy's vulnerabilities to it; by the superiority of its logistics, including first rate medical support; and by engineering, in particular bridging. Arguably the strongest factor of all, however, was the motivation of the civilian-soldier to see the war through to the end to destroy a detestable regime.

Let us now turn to the Germans and an analysis of why so many kept fighting to the bitter end.

* * *

While there was never the remotest chance that Armeegruppe Blumentritt could block VIII and XII Corps' advances, against the odds its forces managed to delay them for a number of days. One can only respect the tenacity of the marines, Hitler Youth and others who fought hopelessly outnumbered, with minimal training, woeful lack of armour and heavy weapons, fractured command and control, dearth of combat supplies, and at a time when the air of defeat pervaded. Likewise, the *Luftwaffe* pilots, who prosecuted their low-level attacks with determination against an enemy with near air supremacy, and in the face of heavy ground fire. Despite the impending catastrophe, many Germans continued to fight with great courage and it was not without a grudging sense of respect that the British soldiers gave them nicknames such as 'Blue *SS*' and 'Steel-Eyed Boys'. This determination to resist resulted, however, in the Germans suffering needless deaths and destruction as their opponents saw their resistance in a very different light and reacted forcefully to seeing comrades pointlessly killed or maimed on the cusp of peace. The German Army excelled in close combat, flexibility and rapid manoeuvre, and in concert with their criticisms of the British Army some military historians have lauded the German soldier and his commanders for these and other perceived qualities.[2] While the German Army had strengths which the British Army did not, it

---

2 John Buckley argues this started with Liddell Hart but was continued by Chester Wilmot, Cornelius Ryan, Max Hastings, Carlo D'Este and others. *Monty's Men*, pp.8–13.

also needs to be remembered that throughout the war most of it relied on the horse, had at best inadequate logistic support, was brutalised and, especially in the war's last year, fighting under extreme compulsion.

By the spring of 1945 few Germans still believed in either victory or a negotiated end to the war and with the downfall of the *Reich* in sight it begs the question why elements of the *Wehrmacht* and *Waffen-SS* continued to resist so staunchly. The answers lie buried in a complex amalgam of the nation's character, the culture of the armed forces, the enduring influence of events at the end of the First World War and the malign effect of Hitler and National Socialism. Although the analysis that follows concentrates on the military aspects, it is course part of a wider question, namely how was Hitler's Germany able to last until May 1945? The answers to that question are beyond the scope of this account but are dissected in Ian Kershaw's seminal book 'The End', which concentrates on the societal rather than the purely military reasons why the Third *Reich* fought to the death. It is highly recommended.

In searching for answers to the more restricted military question, we need to understand the mentality of the German combatant of 1945, and in this we have been greatly assisted by the research undertaken by Professors Sönke Neitzel, a historian, and Harald Welzer, a social psychologist, into the conversations between German PoWs,[3, 4] secretly recorded in camps in Britain and the USA and providing insight, often disturbing, into the mentality and behaviour of the German fighting man. The central premise of Neitzel and Welzer's analysis is that we all act within frames of reference,[5] which provide the basis for our understanding situations, making judgements and determining the likely consequences of decisions we subsequently take. As frames of reference can vary profoundly over historical time and are heavily influenced by contemporary cultural factors, viewing the attitudes of 75 years ago through the lens of current standards and cultural norms inevitably leads to misconstruction and false impressions; socio-historical analyses therefore need to employ frames of reference relevant to the German combatant of 1945. Although Neitzel and Welzer identify that frames of reference lie within four orders, ranging in scale from the first's broad, socio-historical environment down to the fourth's psychology of the individual, their analysis concentrates on the second and third orders as these are more concrete and best suited to their source material. The second order concerns a definable historical and cultural period, in this case the lifespan of *Nazi* Germany, while the third comprises a specific series of socio-historical events within that lifespan, namely the war years.[6]

So it is to the second order – the Third *Reich* and the Nazification of Germany – that we initially turn. Although German society did not abruptly become Nazified when Hitler became Chancellor on 30 January 1933, in the six years before the outbreak of war and then during the war's first few years, the *Nazis* managed to establish a *Nazi* mentality in the populace, reinforced by propaganda, repressive laws, state violence and arbitrary imprisonment in the concentration camps. As a central aspect of the Nazification process was to militarise German society to the fullest extent possible, in the pre-war years the *Nazi* elite concentrated on readying the nation for war and inculcating its armed forces with the need to make unconditional sacrifices, including giving their lives for the *Volk* and state, and promoting as soldierly yardsticks the virtues of fighting courage, steely determination, drive and decisiveness.[7] Although militarisation was a central tenet

---

3   Sönke Neitzel and Harald Welzer, *Soldaten, On Fighting, Killing and Dying* (London: Simon & Schuster UK Ltd, 2012).
4   Sönke Neitzel, *Tapping Hitler's Generals, Transcripts of Secret Conversations* (Barnsley: Frontline Books, 2007).
5   Neitzel and Welzer, *Soldaten*, p.8.
6   Neitzel and Welzer, *Soldaten,* pp.9–10.
7   Neitzel and Welzer, *Soldaten,* p.36.

of National Socialism, its foundations had been laid many years before in the unification wars of 1864–1871 and then reinforced during the Second *Reich*. The *Nazis* and the military leadership took it, however, to a new level of intensity, leading to the armed forces and a range of paramilitary organisations becoming wholly accepted and integrated parts of the nation's social order; this was achieved by:[8]

> ...anchoring military values within the general populace, making the *Volk* fit for battle, and forming a unified and willing 'community of destiny.' Working together, these leaders succeeded in militarising German society to a high degree. *Nazi* party organisations like the Hitler Youth, the *SA* and the *SS*, along with initiatives like the *RAD* and the reintroduction of universal conscription in 1935, increased the fighting capacity of the German people to unprecedented levels. The German populace may not have celebrated the start of World War II in September 1939 with the same euphoria that they had World War I in 1914. In fact, the mood was largely sombre. But 17 million German men let themselves be drafted without protest into the *Wehrmacht* during the course of World War II. Without them Germany would not have been able to fight on until 1945. The success with which German society was militarised was less about getting all German men to support the war than about producing a framework within which they shared or at least did not question military value systems. This cannot be explained only with reference to the massive propaganda efforts of the *Nazi* and *Wehrmacht* leadership. On the contrary, the *Nazis* were able to build upon a radicalisation of the military sphere that had taken place in decades before the Third *Reich*.

The impact on the German fighting man was most intense in the years prior to 1941 as it was during this period that the *Nazis* had their greatest successes: at home in terms of economic recovery, however illusory, and at war with the early triumphs. These successes contributed significantly to the continuing Nazification effort, provided the setting for the *Wehrmacht's* attitudes to war, their enemies and victories and defeats, and resulted in its fighting men going to war believing in the state and their racial superiority.[9]

Although Nazification became less intense during the later war years, the failure of the 20 July 1944 plot roused the regime to make concerted effort to Nazify the officer corps. Younger officers, already subjected to *Nazi* 'education' prior to conscription and therefore more susceptible than their older brethren, had their obedience to the cause reinforced by this effort; attempts were also made to create a National Socialist soldier driven by fanaticism and willingness to die. Although some were undoubtedly influenced by the rhetoric, the ideal of the political warrior generally failed to gain traction, revealing that there were limits to the *Nazi* frame of reference and that despite Nazification and the militarisation of society, for the vast majority of German combatants their principal frames of reference were their immediate social environments and military values.

Social environments have profound influence on the way people behave, with the fundamental drivers for behaviour usually found in social ties and relationships. For the combat soldier (and to a lesser extent the airman and sailor) social ties are restricted to small but intense social groups all working with the same frames of reference and goals and to the same aim, which is survival. A team of soldiers forms the strongest of all social groupings and can be summarised in the word 'camaraderie', which is of course not unique to *Nazi* Germany and is widely accepted as being the

---

[8] Neitzel and Welzer, *Soldaten,* p.35. Text copyright © 2011 by Sönke Neitzel and Harald Welzer, translation copyright © 2012 by Alfred A Knopf, a division of Random House, Inc, reproduced by kind permission of Simon & Schuster UK Ltd.
[9] Neitzel and Welzer, *Soldaten,* pp.26–35.

principal wartime source of individual and small group orientation and motivation. In the final days of this lost war, the strength of camaraderie in certain combat units was such that as long as social cohesion remained intact and the soldiers felt they were reasonably led and equipped, they would fight far more fiercely than would be expected. The young soldiers of SS-A.u.E.Btl. 12 'HJ' clearly exhibited a strong sense of camaraderie and it is of note that Neitzel and Welzer single-out 2. Marine-Infanterie-Division as an exemplar of the power of camaraderie.[10]

The social ties were reinforced by military values. Germany's militaristic tradition mentioned earlier was bolstered by the emphasis that the nation, equalled only by Japan, placed on these values, in particular obedience, bravery and devotion to duty, all three strongly contributing to the soldier's overall frame of reference. Obedience was paramount and was embedded in the armed forces' soul, binding the organisations together. Refusing or even questioning orders was wholly unacceptable and seen as tantamount to undermining the foundations of the organisation. The oath of allegiance sworn personally to Hitler by all members of the armed forces reinforced obedience.[11] Senior officers in particular saw the oath as wholly binding, leading to unquestioning obedience to orders regardless of rationality or the hopelessness of the situation. Evidence of the oath's power over the *Wehrmacht* can be seen in the rapidity with which it was no longer regarded as binding once troops heard that Hitler was dead. Linked to obedience was a strong, if wholly warped, sense of honour, with many soldiers believing that keeping fighting was inextricably linked to military honour, while others felt that by fighting to the last the German people could lose the war honourably.

Bravery, the second element, although of relevance to all fighting men, was particularly significant for the infantry soldier. Unlike those who could count tanks destroyed, aircraft shot down or ships sunk, the infantry had no comparable metric and the only standard against which they were judged was their ability to fight on and complete missions under the most difficult circumstances. The abstract concept of bravery was however supported by a visible system of awards and distinctions for battle service, which played a significant role as incentives. The awards for bravery, principally the classes of the Iron Cross, were supplemented by a variety of distinctions, such as assault badges, close combat bars, and badges for the single-handed destruction of tanks. The *Kriegsmarine* and *Luftwaffe* had their own award systems with, for instance, badges in recognition of service in the High Seas fleet or completing various totals of bombing sorties. All these medals and badges, prominently worn on uniforms, had substantial impact in terms of social recognition and acted as further reinforcement of the military value system.

By the latter war years, the third element, devotion to duty, was interpreted as willingness to die for the *Reich*, reinforcing *Wehrmacht* Regulation No. 2: 'It is expected of every German soldier that he prefers to die with a rifle in his hand to being captured.'[12] By 1945, the elite no longer expected soldiers simply to fight until a battle had been decided, but to continue fanatically until they were killed. German soldiers were, however, generally not prepared to fight to the last bullet and would surrender if they saw that becoming a casualty was pointless. During 1945 fighting-on increasingly became an end in itself and many did so because there was no other option. While this was not a positive stimulus, it did not represent any form of impediment to the continuance of the war, as Richard Bessel describes:[13]

---

10   Neitzel and Welzer, *Soldaten,* pp.253–254.
11   'I swear by God this holy oath, that I will render to Adolf Hitler, *Führer* of the German *Reich* and people, Supreme Commander of the Armed Forces, unconditional obedience and that I am ready, as a brave soldier, to risk my life at any time for this oath.' US Memorial Holocaust Museum, *https://encyclopedia.ushmm.org/content/en/article/german-military-oaths* (accessed 3 July 2017).
12   Neitzel and Welzer, *Soldaten,* p.244.
13   Bessel, *Germany 1945,* p.42.

In the extreme conditions of early 1945, people's horizons became limited to day-to-day survival. The sense of comradeship, not wanting to let down one's fellow soldiers, and of sharing a common fate as their world came crashing down, assumed tremendous importance.

This intensely individualistic frame of reference can only be fully comprehended by men who have fought for their survival, as Guy Sajer illustrates:[14]

> We no longer fought for Hitler, or for National Socialism, or for the Third *Reich* – or even for our fiancées or mothers or families trapped in bomb-ravaged towns. We fought from simple fear, which was our motivating power…We fought for ourselves, so that we wouldn't die in holes filled with mud and snow.

* * *

Let us now turn to the third order, the war years, and specifically 1945. Unsurprisingly, the psyche of Hitler and the grip he maintained on Germany is pivotal. It was imposed to the last through the members of the *Nazi* ruling elite, who were in turn dependent on Hitler for the source of their authority. Hitler, largely driven by his conviction that the surrender of 1918 was the cause of all Germany's post-First World War ills, refused to countenance any other course of action than a fight to the end. He was not alone in holding this belief and many senior commanders, who had been junior officers in the First World War, held similar sentiments, believing that the failure to fight to the last in 1918 was an enduring dishonour that could not be repeated. Furthermore, as defeat loomed, Hitler believed it would be largely as a consequence of the German people and *Wehrmacht* being unworthy of him. Consequently, they should therefore die fighting in a *Götterdämmerung*, a monstrously perverted belief which he linked to Clausewitz's maxim that the destruction of a nation 'after a bloody and honourable struggle assures the people's rebirth. It is the seed of life, which one day will bring forth a new, securely-rooted tree.'[15] Unfortunately for the German people and their armed forces, Hitler was selective in his use of Clausewitz as he ignored another of Clausewitz's dictums, namely that 'Inability to carry on the struggle can, in practice, be replaced by two other grounds for making peace: the first is the improbability of victory; the second is its unacceptable cost.'[16] In short, as it was impossible for Hitler to consider capitulation, he shackled the nation to its grim destiny and any suggestions of withdrawal, or even worse surrender, were therefore equivalent to treason and attracted the full weight of state terror.

Thus fear is the next theme. Any real or suspected lack of resolve among the soldiery, and increasingly in 1945 the civilian population also, attracted swift and exceptionally harsh vengeance from flying courts martial, with capital punishment freely administered. The estimate that some 20,000 German soldiers were executed in the Second World War compared to 150 in the First is a horrifying testament to the brutality of a regime,[17] whose savagery towards its own increased as the operational situation declined. Indeed, the *Nazi* leadership seemed to revel in this violence as if equating it to battlefield success, with the aim being to take vengeance on assumed cowards while terrorising the rest into compliance. For the soldier caught away from the front line but with luck on his side, the likely consequence was to be rounded up and sent back into battle; for those less lucky, the consequence was prompt execution by hanging or firing squad, increasingly conducted

---

14 Sajer, *The Forgotten Soldier*, p.316.
15 Carl von Clausewitz, *On War* (Michael Howard/Peter Paret translation, Princeton University Press, 1976/84), p.97.
16 Clausewitz, *On War*, p.117.
17 Kershaw, *The End*, p.220.

without the niceties of even a dubious trial. In the minds of the soldiery it was therefore safer to keep fighting with one's comrades than to leave the front and risk arrest by the military police and *SS* squads patrolling in the rear. Mutiny was out of the question for reasons already mentioned, and the aftermath of the 20 July plot provided little room for doubt as to the price of failure.

Although on the East Front fear of becoming a prisoner of the Soviets was a major incentive to keep fighting, this was not so on the West Front where there was no particular fear of being taken prisoner by the British or Americans. However, excepting the capitulation of the Ruhr pocket and the surrenders of the final days, mass surrenders did not take place in the west. This may appear surprising given the German army's exhausted and demoralised state, normally the perfect breeding ground for mutiny, mass surrender or desertion. However, the worn-out state of the soldiery was such that it was unable to rebel and the intensity of the fighting, the turmoil of retreat and continual heavy losses made the planning of joint enterprise well-nigh impossible. Furthermore, the failure of the 20 July plot had led to a cull of the very officers who may have been able to steer the war in a different direction had the assassination attempt not been made. Desertion was therefore an individual and risky decision and for most there was no option but to fight on, breeding a fatalistic attitude. For the period of the account the Germans were of course fighting on their own soil and for some this would have motivated them to fight the harder, but for others this motivation was probably balanced by the demoralising impact of being the cause of death and destruction in the homeland. Unquantifiable, but one which permeated military and civilian life, was the submissive acceptance of one's lot as there were no alternatives to carrying on and struggling to survive. This acceptance played its part in allowing the military system, and thus the war, to continue.

Despite growing doubts about his military abilities and the obvious defeats being suffered, faith in the *Führer* and the cult that surrounded him lasted for a surprisingly long time. This faith was a result of the Nazification of society and the euphoria generated by the triumphs of the early war years, which transformed Hitler into a messianic figure in whom the German people held a quasi-religious belief.[18] Over the years the nation and its armed forces invested a vast amount of emotional capital in Hitler and for many doubting him would have been unthinkable. Even though the war was self-evidently going against them, large numbers of Germans therefore clung to Hitler as their sole saviour against disastrous defeat and even as hopes for final victory began to evaporate, faith in him remained. Many not only saw him as being separate from the *Nazi* elite but also blamed that elite for Germany's woes, believing its members to have duped or deliberately kept Hitler in the dark; as a result his status remained surprisingly intact even as the *Reich* collapsed. The junior ranks were generally unaware of his military inanity and many, in spite of everything, believed in his near-mystic aura of invincibility created in the years of success. Although by 1945 these believers were few, they fought on in the expectation that the *Führer* would, even at the last moment, pluck victory from the jaws of defeat. Additionally, Neitzel and Welzer suggest that many at the lower levels kept fighting as they would not have known that the war was lost, were unaware of the bigger picture and that in any case the issue of whether it was lost or not was largely irrelevant compared to the far more immediate demands of battle and survival.[19] It is worth noting however that it was not only German junior ranks who were unaware of the European war's imminent conclusion and even the Allies believed that major engagements were probable against German forces in Denmark and Norway and the supposed Alpine Redoubt.

Some Germans still believed the leadership's declarations that the western nations were on the brink of recognising the Soviet Union as the true enemy and that the alliance would soon

---

18 Neitzel and Welzer, *Soldaten*, p.210.
19 Neitzel and Welzer, *Soldaten*, p.317.

break-up; they therefore needed to keep fighting to buy time for this to happen.[20] Others thought, even more fancifully, that the Americans and British would advance to establish a front against the Soviet armies. Although the holders of these views correctly identified that the alliance would soon end, they failed to understand the Allies' overwhelming desire, above all other considerations, to crush the *Reich*. The *Nazi* hierarchy had also tried to capitalise on the Allies' demand for Germany's unconditional surrender, declaring that the response was a fight to the end. Though it played well for German propaganda and provided justification for continuing the war, there is no evidence that the demand motivated the German armed forces. In his memoirs, Kesselring mentions that the threat of unconditional surrender forced the Germans to fight on as long and as hard as possible in the hope that this would exhaust the Allies and make them more open to negotiation,[21] a hope that was of course far-fetched in the extreme and one that disregarded the Allied strength and German weakness.

By April 1945 one reason had, however, ceased to have relevance to continuing the fight: the need to gain time for the deployment and use of *Wunderwaffen* (wonder weapons). During 1944 and early 1945 the *Nazi* leadership had made much of this, but the V-1, V-2 and others had come and gone with little apparent impact on the enemy and even the *Nazi* hierarchy had stopped beating this particular propaganda drum. However, some diehards and fanatical believers in Hitler held faith that he would, at the last moment, produce either a weapon of mass destruction or a range of new weapons, which would wipe out Germany's enemies, and that they therefore had to keep fighting to buy him time for their deployment and use.[22] They would be disappointed.

Despite the patent grimness of the situation, the German generals were neither prepared to make independent judgements nor to take independent action. This perfectly suited those senior officers – particularly Keitel and Jodl – who were in Hitler's presence on a daily basis and who had long since, if ever, showed any courage to challenge him. Furthermore, the impact of 20 July 1944 on the leadership of the *Wehrmacht* resulted in only loyalists remaining and an organisation that was so eager to prove its loyalty that it never dared question the necessity of fighting on German territory, irrespective of the price its soldiers, the civilian population and the nation's infrastructure would have to pay. The senior generals, right up to the war's end, continued to issue hollow, bombastic statements in an attempt to fire their troops with vehemence and, far more importantly for their own survival, display their continuing loyalty to the *Führer*. These words of Busch's, issued within three weeks of the war's end, are typical of the genre:[23]

> Soldiers, Comrades!
> The time for long speeches and words is now over! The war gets ever more intense and we are now battling for the freedom of our land! A calm, sure heart is needed for victory! The *Führer's* will is clear: the very freedom of our German soil. The way ahead: fight to the end!
>   Your Commander-in-Chief, Busch, Generalfeldmarschall

Not surprisingly, statements like this had little or no effect on a German soldiery inured to the stream of cynical exhortations issued by its leaders.

The generals remained fiercely loyal to the end, but this loyalty was upwards to Hitler not downwards to their troops. They hid behind military honour to avoid taking difficult decisions about surrender, leading to the needless deaths of multitudes of their soldiers: in the four months of 1945

---

20   Kershaw, *The End*, pp.271–272.
21   Kesselring, *The Memoirs of Field Marshal Kesselring*, p.282.
22   Neitzel and Welzer, *Soldaten*, p.190.
23   Buchwald, *Endkampf*, p.55.

1.2 million German soldiers were killed, more than the years of 1942 and 1943 combined.[24] When soldiers did capitulate, this was never at the prompting of the highest levels of command and was usually instigated by junior officers or soldiers recognising the pointlessness of further action. Some generals believed that they should fight on to prevent mass surrenders creating another 'stab in the back' myth for use by future politicians or regimes,[25] and so required the German people to witness not only the total collapse of Germany but also to leave no doubt that blame for the collapse lay squarely with Hitler and National Socialism and not the army. Others, who believed in the 'stab in the back' myth, thought that the army should fight to the last to abrogate the dishonour of the failure of German arms in 1918 and the part played by soldiers in the German Revolution of November that year. It is of note that while they demanded of their men that they fight to the last, few generals followed their own sermonising and this summary by Neitzel encapsulates the part they played in prolonging the war:[26]

> Only very few generals were prepared to follow their troops to death…The picture we have of the highest generals in the closing weeks and months of the war is not a flattering one: to avoid falling victim to a flying court martial for the premature laying down of arms, or not obeying orders to hold out was for many generals the foremost consideration in their planning. They would rather sacrifice their men than endanger their own lives by disobeying orders from the *Führer*…'However highly we may esteem bravery and steadfastness in war, there is however a point beyond which holding-out in warfare can only be described as the madness of despair, and can therefore never be approved,' Clausewitz wrote in 'On War'. The German generals of World War II rejected the Prussian military theoretician in favour of Hitler.

As they were not prepared or able to challenge Hitler, senior German commanders generated a moral and operational justification for continuing the fight on the West Front. In his memoirs Kesselring describes how the strategy in the west up to 20 April was to prevent the western allies from advancing eastwards to split Germany in two and influence operations for the final battle against the Russians.[27] 12. Armee, forming in the Harz, was seen as a key part of the strategy as it was expected to check the Americans advancing either side of the Harz and to destroy their bridgeheads over the Elbe. In the event it was not used for either mission but was launched instead on a doomed, forlorn hope to rescue Hitler in Berlin, followed by a courageous but failed attempt to free 9. Armee from the Halbe pocket. After 20 April Kesselring's strategy in the west was to keep fighting in order to buy time for those in the east to battle their way back to surrender in the British and American zones. If the forces in the west stopped fighting and surrendered *en masse*, so his logic went, their comrades in the east would feel betrayed and abandoned and would fall wholesale into Russian captivity. This was, Kesselring believed, his 'absolute duty to prevent,'[28] but his duty resulted in the needless deaths of thousands of German and Allied soldiers.

Additional to the two frames of reference, which are necessarily abstract, were Albert Speer's wholly concrete achievements as Minister of Armaments and War Production. Despite the devastating Allied air attacks on German industry and infrastructure Speer, through his energy, talent for organisation and skill in influencing Hitler, was able to keep armament production at a relatively high intensity through to the autumn of 1944. Although production thereafter progressively collapsed, and by April 1945 had virtually ceased, were it not for Speer's efforts it is likely that

---

24 Neitzel, *Tapping Hitler's Generals*, p.49–50.
25 Neitzel, *Tapping Hitler's Generals*, p.47.
26 Neitzel, *Tapping Hitler's Generals*, p.50.
27 Kesselring, *The Memoirs of Field Marshal Kesselring*, p.278.
28 Kesselring, *The Memoirs of Field Marshal Kesselring*, p.279.

the German armed forces would have disintegrated well before May 1945. The men and units still willing and able to fight in April were therefore using the last bullets and bombs made available by Speer's determination to keep the nation's industry and transport networks functioning for as long as possible. His success in doing so directly contributed, however, to the toll of German soldiers killed during the first four months of 1945.

To conclude this part of the analysis, in the final paragraph of 'The End', Kershaw declares that the decisive reason why the Germans were able and willing to fight on was not so much lingering support for Hitler, the terror apparatus, the power of the leading *Nazis* (Bormann, Goebbels, Himmler and Speer) or the willingness of senior civil servants and the generals to continue doing their duty despite the war being obviously lost, but rather the survival of the *Führer* system, and it was this that allowed Hitler to take Germany to destruction.[29]

* * *

The analysis will now examine the reasons particular to the marines, the Hitler Youth of SS-A.u.E.Btl.12 'HJ' and the *Luftwaffe's* pilots. For the marines, the themes described above were augmented by a number of *Kriegsmarine*-specific aspects, foremost being the personality and motivations of Grossadmiral Karl Dönitz, their commander-in-chief. In his first directive to his staff, issued on assuming command of the *Kriegsmarine* on 30 January 1943, he stated:[30]

> Our life belongs to the State. Our honour lies in our duty-fulfilment and readiness for action. No one has the right to private life. The question for us is winning the war. We have to pursue this goal with fanatical devotion and the most ruthless determination to win.

The words – archetypically fascist in tone – set the tenor for Dönitz's command and were to be endlessly repeated by him. Despite his carefully fashioned post-war image of the strictly professional military officer aloof from politics, Dönitz was a committed, fanatical *Nazi* and one of Hitler's most fervent followers, determined to support him in his desire to fight to the end. His fanaticism is clearly evident in the first of a series of short situation reports he issued from 4 March 1945:[31]

> There is no need to explain to you that in our situation capitulation is suicide and means certain death; that capitulation will bring death, the quick or slower destruction, of millions of Germans, and that, in comparison with this, the blood toll even of the harshest fighting is small. Only if we stand and fight have we any chance at all of turning around our fate. If we voluntarily surrender, every possibility of this is at an end. Above all, our honour demands that we fight to the last. Our pride rebels against crawling before a people like the Russians or the sanctimony, arrogance and lack of culture of the Anglo-Saxons.

He gave unshakable loyalty to Hitler, boundless optimism regardless of the situation, and a bizarre conviction that Hitler was always correct, despite palpable evidence to the contrary. His besotted support for Hitler, and the extent to which he was prepared to shift blame onto OKW and lie to his own men about Hitler's abilities, is evident in this extract from an Ultra decrypt of a message

---

29 Kershaw, *The End*, p.400.
30 Padfield, *Dönitz – The Last Führer*, (London: Orion Publishing Co, 1993; © Peter Padfield), p.270.
31 Kershaw, *The End*, p.264.

sent by Dönitz on 5 March 1945 to all naval commanders-in-chief and commanding officers; how much is toadying and how much he believed, we will never know:[32]

> Let us trust blindly to the leadership of Adolf Hitler. Believe me, in my two years as Commander-in-Chief of the Navy I have seen over and over again that the *Führer* has always been right in his strategic and tactical ideas. Very often he stood alone in his ideas. Our war situation would be more favourable today if only our military executive authorities had believed him without reservation and had taken immediate action accordingly. Very often it was appreciated only weeks later that the *Führer* had been right once again, but by that time it was usually too late. Let us therefore fortify our troops by faith in our *Führer*.

With its ships and submarines either sunk or confined to port owing to lack of fuel, mandatory displays of high morale and faith in the *Führer* was about all that was left in the *Kriegsmarine's* magazines. Displays of loyalty were also the best way remaining for it to impress Hitler and gain recognition and influence within the state, and it was surprisingly effective in this respect with Hitler greatly admiring the *Kriegsmarine* for its alleged high morale and willingness to fight to the last. Hitler's belief in the *Kriegsmarine's* fight-to-the-last myth was such that on 26 March 1945 he ordered naval officers be placed in command of the remaining coastal fortresses in the west as he asserted that no ships were ever lost without fighting to the last man,[33] conveniently forgetting the 1939 scuttling of the heavy cruiser *Admiral Graf Spee* and the surrender of its crew. Driven on by Dönitz, the *Kriegsmarine* elevated fighting to the last, dying with honour and going down with the flag to almost cult status although, despite the clamour, there is no evidence that its sailors were any different to their comrades in the army or *Luftwaffe* in not wishing to die when all was lost.

Hitler and Dönitz had a symbiotic relationship: Dönitz fed Hitler a diet based on eternal optimism in the face of all difficulties and setbacks, unbending determination and the reassurance of a man who would follow him to the end, while Hitler provided Dönitz with an exemplar in whom he could believe as '…here was *the* man of iron will whose political and military genius had rescued Germany from internal chaos, Bolshevism and the hate-inspired diktats of the western powers.'[34] Hitler's admiration of Dönitz is clearly shown in his words recalled by Speer after the war:[35]

> There's a man whom I respect. The way he is knowledgeable on all matters! From the army and the air force I receive only vague information. It drives me to despair. With Dönitz I know where I am. He is a National Socialist through and through, and he also keeps the navy free of all bad influences. The navy will never surrender. He has implanted the National Socialist concept of honour in it. If the army generals had had that spirit, they would not have abandoned cities without a fight and pulled back front lines that I had strictly ordered them to hold…The grand admiral would come down with an iron fist if there were a trace of even the slightest defeatism. I regard him as my best man.

At the moment that 2. Marine-Infanterie-Division joined battle with the British, Dönitz issued a decree to the *Kriegsmarine* reminding them of his expectations for naval forces participating in

---

32 TNA DEFE 3/545, Part 2, pp.228–229.
33 Neitzel and Welzer, *Soldaten*, p.258.
34 Padfield, *Dönitz – The Last Führer*, p.268.
35 Albert Speer, *Spandau – The Secret Diaries* (London: Macmillan Publishing Co Inc, 1976), p.194.

land battles and demanding that all his commanders 'clearly and plainly tread the path of soldierly duty.' He then stated:[36]

> The honour of our flag on board is sacred to us. No one thinks of giving up his ship. Rather go down in honour. That is self-evident to all of us. Exactly so in a land battle. Should it come to the point of having to defend our naval positions, so according to the *Führer's* order, the place is to be defended to the end. It is then victory or death. The commander who lacks the spiritual strength for this and wants to weaken has the duty, according to the *Führer's* order, to question his troops and surrender command to a harder warrior.
>
> The navy will fight to the end. Some day its bearing in the severest crisis of the war will be judged by posterity. The same goes for each individual. Earlier deeds are wiped out if, in the decisive hour for which he is a soldier, he fails. Or does anyone believe that the enemy respects one who in cowardice capitulates? Certainly he welcomes him, but he will despise and treat him accordingly.

Contained in that statement are a number of revealing themes. References to the '*Führer's* order' reflect Dönitz's view that it was never a subordinate's place to question orders. Dönitz was not only utterly obedient but he also wholly accepted the *Führer* system where political will was imposed by a single leader through propaganda and violence,[37] and he had either lost the capacity to distinguish between truth and lies or suppressed it through fear of the consequences of stepping out of line.[38] Either way, in the *Führerbunker* he operated in an increasingly irrational world where for its inhabitants the capacity to suspend belief was an essential condition. The references to 'honour of the flag', 'go down in honour' and 'fight to the end' were recurrent themes for Dönitz and reflect a lingering,[39] deep-seated shame for the failure in 1918 of the *Kaiserliche Marine* (Imperial Navy) to engage the Royal Navy in a final, mass confrontation designed to uphold the navy's honour even if it ended in disaster. Not only did the *Kaiserliche Marine* fail to engage the Grand Fleet in this final battle but the order issued on 28 October 1918 to dispatch the fleet served as the trigger for the naval mutiny, which started in Wilhelmshaven but soon spread to Kiel and rapidly became a full-scale revolution sequentially leading to the collapse of Imperial Germany, the end of the war, the Versailles Treaty and subsequently the Weimar Republic;[40] outcomes all held in particular loathing by the *Nazis*. For many, the fleet's failure to put to sea was a stain on their honour, while the mutiny introduced deep-seated shame and it has been suggested that fear of a second mutiny was a prime motivator for Dönitz's enthusiasm to supply personnel for the ground forces as he had seen the effect of idleness on sailors.[41] The dishonour and shame of 1918 was therefore ingrained in Dönitz's and the *Kriegsmarine's* collective psyche, resulting in a determination to be loyal to the end. For Dönitz there could be no repetition of the mutiny and he sympathised with Hitler's views regarding the need to go down fighting. Interviewed in Allied captivity in the summer of 1945, he attempted to give an intellectual veneer to this perverted logic, 'The truth of Clausewitz, [is] that a rebirth can only arise one day from an honourable struggle and ending.'[42] That he viewed the war

---

36   Padfield, *Dönitz – The Last Führer*, p.397.
37   Kershaw, The End, p.351.
38   Padfield, *Dönitz – The Last Führer*, p.398.
39   Kershaw, The End, p.265.
40   Robert Gerwarth, *The Vanquished. Why the First World War Failed to End, 1917–1923* (London: Allen Lane, 2016), pp.62–63.
41   Padfield, *Dönitz – The Last Führer*, p.401.
42   Bessel, *Germany 1945: From War to Peace*, p.109.

as an honourable struggle confirms how closely wedded he was to the *Nazi* view of the war; those who endured its horror and misery would have seen matters differently.

During the final *Führer* conferences on naval affairs Dönitz's rigid, unwavering support is obvious and the minutes record his continuing promises of manpower, made in a manifestly calculated way to maintain favour. Most of the promises came to nothing but in late April, with his marine divisions already shattered and the fall of Berlin only days away, he had young, untrained naval personnel flown at great risk to fight in the city; an act nothing short of murder.[43] In short, Dönitz was a blinkered, ardent *Nazi*.

With a commander-in-chief holding and enforcing views such as these it is therefore not surprising that the marines offered fierce opposition. Their resistance at Rethem and the Essel bridgehead, their persistent counter-attacks, Korvettenkapitän Josef Gördes' conviction that he must remain 'on the bridge' despite the enemy shellfire, and the final stands at Kettenburg and Visselhövede are clear evidence of their determination to fight in accordance with Dönitz's demands. While their resistance was gallant, Dönitz shares responsibility with Hitler for the needless deaths of many thousands of his sailors, and these words of Peter Padfield bluntly sum up his liability:[44]

> Anyone as close to the *Führer* and his principal lieutenants for as long as Dönitz who remained unable or unwilling to distinguish between propaganda and closer approximations to the truth must by the same token have been unable to distinguish between loyalty and treason, honour and dishonour; this may have been his misfortune and it may be posterity's judgement, for it seems to accord with what he was doing – had been doing for some time; stripped of fine words, he was harnessing the natural idealism of his young men for a plainly lost cause and sending them out to die to please a tyrant whose egomania was so monstrous he was prepared to sacrifice an entire nation for himself – a precise inversion of what he was demanding from his people.

Beyond Dönitz and his personality there were two additional factors specific to the navy. The *Kriegsmarine* was bolstered by higher morale and optimism than the other branches of the *Wehrmacht* because Dönitz had nurtured his sailors with good welfare and, excepting the U-boat arm, its personnel had generally not been exposed to the same degree of continual danger as the *Luftwaffe* and land forces.[45] Morale remained high, ill-discipline rare and above all there was a strong sense of camaraderie, found from serving as crews with the officers sharing the dangers. Last, but far from least, was the part played by inter-Service rivalry. The 1b[46] of Divisions-Kommando 2. Marine-Infanterie-Division said to his captors after the capitulation: 'The marines have fought so well because they wanted to show the German Army what the Navy could do if tested!'[47] The rivalry aspect aside, perhaps this sentiment also reflects some discomfiture with the lack of activity and success of the *Kriegsmarine's* surface ships; a mirror-image therefore of 1918.

* * *

---

43 Padfield, *Dönitz – The Last Führer*, p.401.
44 Padfield, *Dönitz – The Last Führer*, p.398.
45 Kershaw, *The End*, p.265.
46 The 1b was a General Staff officer in the supply group of a division HQ responsible for all matters of supply including logistic movements, and the evacuation of casualties and prisoners.
47 TNA WO 171/4277, Special Supplement to 53rd Welsh Division INTSUM No. 231, 21 April 1945.

But what of the Hitler Youth of SS-A.u.E.Btl.12 'HJ' and the pilots of the *Luftwaffe*? In addition to the points made above, the young men of the *Waffen-SS* were subject to further influences, the most significant being the blast of *Nazi* indoctrination they had received during their short lives. From their first days in school, German children were imbued with the cult of Adolf Hitler and in the Hitler Youth instruction was deliberately aimed to produce race-conscious, obedient Germans willing to die for *Führer* and Fatherland. The *Nazis* used the Hitler Youth as a means to shape the beliefs, thinking and actions of German youth, with the principal intention being to integrate boys into the *Nazi* national community and prepare them for service as members of the *Wehrmacht* or *Waffen-SS*. During Hitler Youth training, German adolescents swore allegiance to Hitler and as future soldiers pledged to serve the nation and its leader. The young soldiers of SS-A.u.E.Btl.12 'HJ' had therefore been subjected to years of this indoctrination and it is therefore no surprise that most fought hard under the leadership of officers and NCOs not only similarly immersed in *Nazi* ideology but also with significant operational experience from the fronts. Despite the insufficiency of their military training, there was therefore never any doubt that the youths would fight with anything but resolve. However, it is easy to be swayed by *Nazi* propaganda, which delighted in portraying the *Waffen-SS* as an elite force whose members had no fear whatsoever of death. Evidence would suggest that although on occasions it did show greater preparedness to follow orders to the letter and fight to the death, its best divisions generally fought in much the same way as other elite forces of the *Wehrmacht*,[48] such as the panzer divisions and the paratroops, which put up fierce resistance when the conditions were right. SS-A.u.E.Btl.12 'HJ' followed this trend, fighting hard when the circumstances were in their favour but withdrawing when their positions were threatened. The youths were clearly respected for their fighting ability by the British soldiers of 11th Armoured Division and 1st Commando Brigade and the only evidence in the historical record of the youths cracking is on 13 April at Hademstorf, but this followed two days and nights of fighting on the Weser, a three-day withdrawal, often in contact, to the Aller, three days of bitter fighting in the Essel forest against the first-class soldiers of 1st Commando Brigade, and intense shelling. They remained a dangerous foe to the last.

Turning to the *Luftwaffe*, Göring's and the *Luftwaffe's* failure to defend the *Reich's* air space had drastically reduced its standing in the eyes of the nation, doing little for its sense of esteem. Yet despite the deep problems it faced, the *Luftwaffe's* pilots courageously flew to the war's end and actions such as the low-level, daylight attacks at Stolzenau, the mass volunteering for Schulungslehrgang Elbe and the night attacks on Rethem's pontoon bridge provide evidence of no general collapse in morale or offensive spirit. Although professionalism and desire to defend the homeland were probably the most significant factors in the Luftwaffe's motivation, both strongly reinforced by the close camaraderie of the *Staffel*, perhaps also a continuing thirst to avenge the Allied bombing campaign, particularly the 13–15 February 1945 raids on Dresden, had a part to play. Although describing an elite fighter unit, JG 26, these observations of Donald Caldwell's provide interesting insight into the morale and motivations of a *Luftwaffe* unit in 1945:[49]

> The performance of any combat unit can generally be related directly to its morale and leadership. But the morale of the *Geschwader* at this point in the war cannot be summarised in simple terms, nor can it be determined merely by interviewing the surviving pilots – each man's opinion is inevitably coloured by his own morale at the time. The morale of most of the enlisted pilots who survived the war was surprisingly high at this time – one former *Obergefreiter* claims to have believed in the *Endsieg* (final victory) until his own city,

---

48 Neitzel and Welzer, *Soldaten*, p.300.
49 Donald Caldwell, *JG 26 War Diary, Volume Two 1943–1945* (London: Grub Street, 2007), pp.425–426.

Hamburg, fell to the Allies in late April. The pilots were serving in the most glamorous and exciting of the combat arms, and were convinced of their own elite status, although some were too embarrassed to go home on leave during the last year of the war and face the glares of their bombed-out neighbours. The Second *Gruppe*…fostered the spirit and individuality of its pilots by reducing military discipline to a minimum. [The]…First *Gruppe*, on the other hand, observed all military courtesies with the greatest rigidity…and this technique seemed to work, as well. The morale in…the Third *Gruppe*, on the other hand, was very low, if the surviving enlisted pilots can be believed.

By 1945, none of the JG 26 *Staffelkapitäne* were professional officers. All had been promoted from the enlisted ranks, and few had had any form of officers' or formation leaders' training. They had not been promoted because of their abilities as leaders, and these abilities varied widely. Several surviving pilots divide the leaders into two categories: the majority, who tried conscientiously to fulfil the role of combat leader that had been thrust upon them, and the rest, who thought only of their own personal survival. There was a third category, containing those men who still hungered after personal glory and decorations.

To conclude, the reasons why significant numbers of Germans fought-on despite the nation's approaching disintegration are varied, but all have foundations laid decades before the *Reich* and the war. While from a military viewpoint one can respect the *Wehrmacht's* perseverance, its efforts only served to prolong the survival of a criminal regime responsible for inflicting death and misery on a massive, unprecedented scale. This must not be forgotten. Many lives could have been saved if senior officers and commanders had had the moral courage to decide that enough was enough and surrendered, probably after the Allies' crossing of the Rhine, and there was little or nothing that the regime could have done to prevent such a capitulation. The generals' failure to do so makes them uniquely responsible for the continuance of the war on the West Front and the needless deaths that occurred.

* * *

What of the area of the Weser and Aller today? Although the events described in this account took place 75 years ago, physically the area is little-changed from 1945 and it is not hard to imagine many of the events described in the account. Naturally the villages and towns have expanded and modernised, but the *Fachhallenhauser* can still be admired and the Germans have successfully preserved the character of the villages. Agriculture continues to dominate the local economy and the areas of sandy soils are particularly favourable for asparagus, a popular crop. Wind turbines and photo-voltaic arrays now abound and 4 RWF would in particular be amazed at the massive masts dominating the area of the cross-roads where they dug-in to the west of Altenwahlingen. Most low-lying land has been drained and the rivers have levees to prevent flooding. Extensive gravel extraction from the meadows beside the Weser, particularly to the south of Lahde and to the west of Leese, has created lakes where men once fought.

When I first visited Rethem in 1982 it was easy to visualise the attacks on the town and the 10.5cm railway *Flak* on the sidings. This is not so easy today: the railway is no more, commercial buildings occupy the area of the former sidings on the embankment and in the field forward of it, and tree lines and a deep drainage ditch now break up the 'huge arena' so accurately described by Edward Wilson. The station, still displaying the sign 'Rethem (Aller)' on an end wall, stands as a rather dilapidated, sad reminder of the busy Allertalbahn. Although some of the town's buildings show the evidence of April 1945, war damage is not often visible and the Germans have been skillful at repairing the marks made by bullet and splinter.

For many years weapons and equipment emerged from the countryside and in the early 1990s ploughing in the fields forward of Rethem's embankment produced a MG 42 and StG 44 in remarkably good condition.

Splinters, ammunition and empty cases frequently surface and recently a stout fence-post was identified as an 8cm mortar tube. Placed near Rethem's bridge in 1994, stands a large memorial stone carved with the *Kriegsmarine's* crossed anchors and with bronze letters commemorating not only the fallen of 2. Marine-Infanterie-Division but also the civilian victims and, in commendable spirit of reconciliation, the dead of 53rd Welsh Division.

The forest where Peter White's platoon was ambushed is largely unchanged; the accuracy of his description of the ground is uncanny and the wind still blows in the tree-tops like the 'sigh of distant surf.' The Essel forest is also largely unchanged, although there are now week-end chalets in the area where 3 Cdo and the brigade HQ fought-off the counter-attacks. The Esseler Kanal remains a major feature and close to the Alexanderplatz, unseen in the forest, is a war cemetery for the 114 Germans killed in the Essel battles; among the graves are those of Josef Gördes and the Schulungslehrgang Elbe pilot, Hans Nagel.

Naval badges and buttons are sometimes found in the woods and the location where Sergeant Harding knocked out F01 is easily identified. Hidden in other forests of the region are mossy roads and the concrete remains of the war industries that provided the *Reich* with its destructive

Splinter-damaged *façade* in Rethem. (Author)

MG 42 and StG 44 found on the battlefield. (Author)

Rethem's memorial stone. (Author)

Soldatenfriedhof Essel in the forest where 3 Cdo and HQ 1st Commando Brigade fought for their survival against the counter-attacks. (Author)

The last remaining section of the railway line leading through the forest to Kampfstoffabrik Leese. (Author)

resource. Many of the buildings of Kampfstoffabtik Leese can be seen and some still carry their camouflage of vegetation. Despite the sophistication of the camouflage, concealment of the industries in the forests was far from perfect. Their railway networks and connections to the main railway system were particularly obvious indicators so it is surprising that although the plants' locations were generally known to Allied intelligence, they were judged less important targets and seldom bombed. At Leese there is a very short section of railway track, which once linked the site to the main line, but of the destroyed V-2s and their transporters and railway wagons there is no sign.

You can visit the sites of Stalag XIB and 357. Much of Stalag XIB's site plays host to a housing estate but visible in the adjacent woods are concrete foundations and short sets of steps leading to the entrances of buildings long-since gone. Stalag 357's site is grassland with copses of birch and contains a cemetery dominated by a large concrete monument to the 30,000 Soviet soldiers believed buried there.

Steps in Stalag XIB. Photograph taken in 2015. (Author)

When we had an army in Germany I ran battlefield tours to areas of the fighting and introduced our soldiers to battles fought by their fathers, grandfathers and now great-grandfathers during the final days of the greatest conflict the world has had the misfortune to experience. Latterly members of the *Bundeswehr's* Panzerlehrbrigade 9 joined the tours and it was rewarding to tell them about a little-known part of their nation's history. On 16 April 2005, the 60th anniversary of the camps' relief, a memorial close to the former main entrance of Stalag XIB was unveiled. The memorial was built by 2 Close Support Battalion REME and commemorated those who were incarcerated in the two camps. Following the withdrawal of the army, the memorial has been transferred to the National Arboretum where it is now fittingly the memorial for the National Ex-Prisoner of War Association.

In the epilogue to 'No Triumphant Procession' I mentioned the reunions held by the old comrades of both sides. These take place no longer as age has taken its toll where bullet and bomb failed. In the 1990s I attended two reunions of the *Alte Kameraden* of 2. Marine-Infanterie-Division and joined them for lunch at the guesthouse at Rethemer Fähre. They were most welcoming and intrigued by my research. In 1995 I attended the 50th anniversary of the battle of Rethem, hosted by the *Stadt* and with George Stimpson as the principal guest. Peace and reconciliation were key themes of the various events and church services. It took many years for the Germans to make good the human losses of the war and owing to the appalling casualty toll they exacted on other nations and peoples, the Germans' own terrible losses are sometimes overlooked. It is estimated that some 6.5 million Germans lost their lives in the war and most families lost at least one member. The casualties suffered by the *Wehrmacht* were far in excess of those of the First World War, usually considered as holding grim pride of place, and the losses were especially felt by rural Germany, for instance Rethem lost 76 in the First World War and 120 in the Second, and Hülsen lost 35 in the First and 61 in the Second.

Many of the villages and towns mentioned in the account contain war cemeteries for the German soldiers and airmen killed in the local battles, and most also include a memorial stone to the countless thousands killed on the East Front but with no known grave. The majority of the British dead rest peacefully in the beautiful CWGC cemeteries at Hannover and Becklingen, south of Soltau.

CWGC cemetery Becklingen. (Author)

We will remember them.

Appendix A

Listed below, with summaries of their content, are online free-to-view videos, which support parts of the account with clips of contemporary film. Seeing the faces, gestures and movements of those involved in the events of April 1945 adds greatly to the narrative and provides a human dimension impossible to gain from the written word. The majority of the videos are provided by the IWM and mostly concern units of 6th Airborne and 11th Armoured Divisions. It should be noted, however, that the films reinforce the false impression mentioned in the Preface that the advance through Germany was an uncontested 'swan'; there is therefore little in them illustrating the toughness and misery of the final weeks' fighting. Included for completeness are references to IWM films relevant to the narrative but not yet uploaded.

Online IWM film

Serial	Link	IWM Title and Reference	Date of film (as given)	Summary/Comment
1	https://www.iwm.org.uk/collections/item/object/1060031908	RAF 2nd Tactical Air Force attack on German motor transport and locomotives. OPE 90	2 April 1945	At 12:36 to 12:58 is the downing by Sqn Ldr Mackichan of two Fw 190 F-8 from 10./KG200 on 6 April (see Chapter 4).
2	https://www.iwm.org.uk/collections/item/object/1060015029	Soldiers of 13th Battalion, 5th Parachute Brigade advance through occupied villages around Neustadt, Germany (Part 1) A70 293-1	7 April 1945	Advance to the Leine (connect to Chapter 5), although some action seems staged for the camera. Villages are Wiedensahl, Hagenburg and Steinhude. Achilles from 146 Battery 63rd Anti-Tank Regiment. Vickers, 30 calibre and Besa machine-guns in action. 25pdr guns from either 6th or 25th Field Regiments on the move.
3	https://www.iwm.org.uk/collections/item/object/1060015030	Soldiers of 13th Battalion, 5th Parachute Brigade advance through occupied villages around Neustadt, Germany (Part 2) A70 293-2	7 April 1945	More film of the advance to the Leine (connect to Chapter 5).
4	https://www.dailymotion.com/video/x6c326d	Fliegerhorst Wunstorf (Airfield B.116) Germany	8 April 1945	Film shot the day after the airfield's capture (connect to Chapter 5). Aircraft: Ju 87 D-5, Siebel Si 204 transport/trainer, Bf 109 and Fiesler Storch, Ju 88G night-fighters. Also shown: 25pdrs and quads of 6th Field Regiment RA and *Luftwaffe* bomb dumps.
5	https://www.iwm.org.uk/collections/item/object/1060015033	Soldiers of the King's Shropshire Light Infantry and Comet tanks of 29th Armoured Brigade advance north of Bad Rehburg, Germany. A70 293-4	8 April 1945	Action during 3 RTR and 4 KSLI's advance to the Rehburg area (connect to Chapter 5), possibly the start of action against 5. SS-Kompanie and the Stamm Kompanie SS-A.u.E. Btl.12 'HJ' in the woods north of Rehburg involving C Squadron 3 RTR and B Company 4 KSLI.
6	https://www.iwm.org.uk/collections/item/object/1060015039	Remains of a V1 'Flying Bomb' installation near Steyerberg, Germany. A70 293-13	9 April 1945	Film starts with surrendered German personnel marching south following the capture of Leese (on 8 April). Destroyed rolling stock and locomotive with V-1 on railway wagons at Steyerberg (connect to Chapters 2 and 5). Soldier looking (unwittingly) at a V-2 warhead ignition assembly and a V-2 combustion igniter. Shots of V-2 warhead drums, *Meillerwagen* transporter/launch trailer and *Betriebstoffanhanger* liquid oxygen bowser.
7	https://www.iwm.org.uk/collections/item/object/1060015040	Remains of a train carrying German 'V' weapons in woodland north of Leese, Germany. A70 293-14	9 April 1945	Comets either from C Squadron 23 Hussars on their way to support 1st Commando Brigade at Leese, or from 2 FF Yeo or 15/19 Hussars in the Rehburg area (connect to Chapter 5). V-2 on a goods wagon lagged with wickerwork cylinders normally used for protecting cased ammunition in transit.

Serial	Link	IWM Title and Reference	Date of film (as given)	Summary/Comment
8	https://www.iwm.org.uk/collections/item/object/1060015036	Soldiers of 1st Battalion The Herefordshire Regiment, supported by tanks of 2nd Fife and Forfar Yeomanry, capture a fuel installation at Loccum, Germany. A70 293-9	9 April 1945	Film of Loccum *Luftwaffe* fuel storage depot and 159th Infantry Brigade Group's advance towards the Leine (connect to Chapter 5 and Map 24). Drum marked 'Nebelsäure' contains chemical for injection into artificial fog generators for concealing targets from enemy bombers. Drum of methanol used in 50:50 mix with water for injection into fighter aircraft superchargers to boost climb rate and level speed. Shots of 2 FF Yeo Comets carrying infantry, line of Comets and Loyd carriers towing 6pdr anti-tank guns.
9	https://www.iwm.org.uk/collections/item/object/1060015221	Soldiers of 3rd Parachute Brigade, travelling in lorries, advance over Neustadt Bailey bridge at Scharrel, Germany. A70 293-11	10 April 1945	Confused IWM title. Initial shots are of Bailey bridge sections over demolished span of Neustadt bridge (see Map 23). Force of the demolition evident from shredded trees and damaged houses in background. Cap-badge shows men in trucks are 1 CAN Para. Monument on the left of frame now stands at the eastern end of the present bridge and carries a plaque in memory of the members of 7 Para killed at Neustadt. Film of brigade's advance on the Leine's right bank (connect to Chapter 5): marching paras from 8 or 9 Para, paras carried on Achilles from L Troop, 146 Battery, 63rd Anti-Tank Regiment.
10	https://www.iwm.org.uk/collections/item/object/1060015038	Remains of a V2 rocket installation in woodland near Leese, Germany. A70 293-12	10 April 1945	Remains not of a V-2 installation but Kampfstoffabrik Leese with demolished rockets and associated equipment on the spur line leading to it. The film shot two days after the site's capture (connect to Chapter 5).
11	https://www.iwm.org.uk/collections/item/object/1060015057	Units of 15th (Scottish) Division advance past an abandoned aerodrome at Celle and onward over the scissor bridge in the Sprakensehl Forest, Germany. A70 297-5	13 April 1945	Celle airfield mainly used by transport units and as refuelling/rearming base for *Luftwaffe* fighter units. Sprakensehl Forest lies halfway between Celle and Uelzen and on 15th Division's axis of advance. British transport in Celle. Aircraft: Gotha Go 145 trainer/night harassment, Bücker Bü 131 'Jungmann' trainer, Ju 87 D-5 of NSGr. 1 (Nord), remains of a Heinkel 111.

APPENDIX A 475

Serial	Link	IWM Title and Reference	Date of film (as given)	Summary/Comment
12	https://www.iwm.org.uk/collections/item/object/1060015093	Military camp where German and Hungarian soldiers have been taken ill with typhus in the Fallingbostel-Belsen area, Germany. A70 303-3	15 April 1945	First part: Comet tanks in area of burning forest and recent action. Shots probably of 23 Hussars and 8 RB. Second part: German and Hungarian group outside entrance to Belsen soon after its liberation (connect to Chapter 7). Among group: *Luftwaffe Flak* personnel and an *SS-Untersturmführer*. Group watches British armour moving rapidly on the road to Bergen. Armour went through the neutral area at top speed, unsure that the agreement with Germans would hold.
13	https://www.iwm.org.uk/collections/item/object/1060015091	Units of 159th Infantry Brigade in action during the advance from Winsen to Sülze, Germany. A70 303-1	15 April 1945	Although not in area of the account, film gives flavour of the countryside and the fighting in the forests and villages. Village in flames is possibly Muden. Here a squadron of 2 FF Yeo with two companies of 1 Hereford had major skirmish with German infantry, during which a Comet was knocked out and most of the village burnt down. Prisoners being escorted to the rear while crews of carriers dig-in. Carrier and crew from 2nd Independent Machine-Gun Company enjoy a brew and an 'egg banjo' while a Morris quad and 25pdr drives past.
14	https://www.iwm.org.uk/collections/item/object/1060015078	Scenes at Stalag 11B after its liberation by 22nd Armoured Brigade, Fallingbostel, Germany. A70 301-2	16 April 1945	Liberation of Stalag XIB (connect to Chapter 10). Film of former PoWs, surrendered German soldiers and British infantry, probably from 1/5 Queens.
15	https://www.iwm.org.uk/collections/item/object/1060015079	German train carrying V2 rockets after being wrecked in an RAF air strike near Nienburg, Germany. A70 301-3	16 April 1945	V-2 remains probably the trainload found at Landesbergen, between Leese and Nienburg, either destroyed by RAF or demolished by V-weapon personnel (connect to Chapter 5).
16	https://www.iwm.org.uk/collections/item/object/1060015080	Aerial views of the area around Verden, Germany. A70 301-4	16 April 1945	Film shot from an Auster. Verden not captured until 17 April so in German hands at the time the film was shot, which explains why the aircraft is at a healthy distance. Smoke in distance from 158th Infantry or 4th Armoured Brigades' actions. At film's end Auster flies down the Allertalbahn and does a low pass over the Class 9 FBE at Westen (connect to Chapters 9 and 10).
17	https://www.iwm.org.uk/collections/item/object/1060015077	Scenes at Stalag 357 after its liberation by 7th (Armoured) Division, Fallingbostel, Germany. A70 301-1	16 April 1945	Film shows depressing bleakness of a PoW camp (connect to Chapter 10). Blackboard showing nationalities and numbers of prisoners. A prisoner then crosses out Allied totals and writes in number of German PoW.

476 THEIRS THE STRIFE

Serial	Link	IWM Title and Reference	Date of film (as given)	Summary/Comment
18	https://www.iwm.org.uk/collections/item/object/1060015082	Captured German SS officer gives information to Lieutenant Cooke, Information Officer of 22nd Armoured Brigade, Fallingbostel, Germany. A70 301-6	16 April 1945	Members of SS-A.u.E. Btl.12 'HJ' being interrogated by Captain Cooke. (connect to Chapter 11). Cooke was the Intelligence Officer not 'Information Officer'.
19	https://www.iwm.org.uk/collections/item/object/1060015088	Liberated French PoW and capured German PoW, Bergen and Trauen, Germany. A70 302-5	16 April 1945	11th Armoured Division collecting point for Allied PoW. Column of army and *Luftwaffe* PoWs. M14 half-track taking a corner at speed in Bergen. Soldier wearing white armband probably Hungarian. Comet from unidentified 11th Armoured Division regiment travelling at speed across a field, a 61-minute barrier and liberated French PoWs.

Miscellaneous online film

Serial	Link	IWM Title and Reference	Date of film (as given)	Summary/Comment
20	https://www.youtube.com/watch?v=jg9onRuHBQk	Deutsche Wochenshau Nr.741	16 November 1944	Formation of Danzig Volkssturm battalion. At 01:58 KzS Hartmann talking to Gauleiter Forster then in front row of marchers.
21	https://www.youtube.com/watch?v=m6FQa2CcDqs	Last film from the Oder Front	February – April 1945	Film shows troops of 1.Marine-Infanterie-Division and supporting artillery and assault guns when in the Zehden bridgehead on the Oder front, February-April 1945. Gives impression of marines' uniforms, weapons and equipment.
22	https://www.youtube.com/watch?v=en3hkuc1QoM	British Pathe News	3 May 1945	Entry into Hamburg of 7th Armoured Division. Brig Spurling, Commander 131st Brigade, arriving at Hamburg town hall to take city's surrender. German officer is General Alwin Wolz, Kampfkommandant Hamburg and former commander 3.Flak-Division.
23	https://www.youtube.com/watch?v=lUeHyHnxuPw	Germany May 1945 – *Die Stunde Null.*		An often disturbing composition but one which seeks to give a flavour of 1945.
24		IWM A70 290	5 April 1945	Film shot at Stolzenau showing the demolished bridge; infantry crossing the Weser in assault boats; burning RE transport and damaged bridging; *Luftwaffe* aircraft flying overhead at height.
25		IWM A70 292-1	9 April 1945	Infantry waiting by a roadside; building the Bailey bridge over the Weser at Hoya; 53rd Welsh Division vehicles crossing the Hoya bridge.
26		IWM A70 291-2	7 April 1945	Slave labourers, infantry in action and burning village; Comets of 2 FF Yeo crossing the Class 40 Bailey pontoon at Petershagen; surrendered members of Panzerjagdverband 'Großer Kurfürst'; the tile factory and FBE; German prisoners of war in a temporary 'cage'; interior of an *Allgemeine-SS* headquarters after capture.

Serial	Link	IWM Title and Reference	Date of film (as given)	Summary/Comment
27		IWM A70 299-3	10 April 1945	Vehicles of 53rd Welsh Division on the move; burning oil tanks and railway locomotive near Hoya.
28		IWM A70 299-5	13 April 1945	Vickers of 1 Manchester in action at Rethem; railway *Flak* at Rethem.

Other existing IWM film but not yet online

Serial	Link	IWM Title and Reference	Date of film (as given)	Summary/Comment
29		IWM A70 300	14 April 1945	3 RTR maintaining their Comets at Schwarmstedt; Comets advancing by road; armour in a leaguer; oil production facilities near Steimbke; soldiers of 1 Cheshire resting in the forest near Engehausen.
30		IWM A70 300-2	14 April 1945	Activities in Thoren.
31		IWM A70 304-17	19 April 1945	German PoW at Walsrode.
32		IWM A70 307-1	22 April 1945	2nd (Armoured Recce) Battalion Welsh Gds in Rotenburg after its capture.

Bibliography

Published Books

Aggett, WJP, *The Bloody Eleventh* (Exeter: The Devonshire and Dorset Regiment, 1995).
Alford, Richard, *To Revel in God's Sunshine* (Kendal: Westmoreland Gazette, 1981).
Allen, Peter, *One More River* (London: JM Dent & Sons, 1980).
Anderson, Dudley, *Three Cheers for the Next Man to Die* (London: Robert Hale, 1983).
Anon., *The Story of the 23rd Hussars 1940–1946* (privately published, 1946).
Anon., *A History of 44 RTR in the War of 1939–1945* (Brighton: 44 RTR Association, 1965).
Anon., *'Taurus Pursuant': A History of the 11th Armoured Division* (BAOR, 1945).
Anon., *A Short History of the 6th Battalion the Royal Welch Fusiliers, North-West Europe, June 1944–May 1945* (Caernarfon: Gwenlyn Evans & Son, 1946).
Ardizzone, Edward, *Diary of a War Artist* (London: The Bodley Head, 1974).
Barclay, CN, *History of the 53rd (Welsh) Division* (London: William Clowes & Sons, 1956).
Barker, AJ, *German Infantry Weapons of World War 2* (London: Arms and Armour Press, 1969).
Barnett, C (ed.), *Hitler's Generals* (London: Weidenfeld & Nicolson, 1989).
Bell, Noel, *From the Beaches to the Baltic, The Story of G Company, 8th Battalion the Rifle Brigade, During the Campaign in North-West Europe*, (Aldershot: Gale & Polden, 1947).
Bellamy, Bill, *Troop Leader. A Tank Commander's Story* (Stroud: Sutton Publishing Ltd, 2007).
Bender, RJ and Taylor, HP, *Uniforms, Organization and History of the Waffen-SS, Volume 3* (San Jose: R James Bender Publishing, 1986).
Bessel, Richard, *Germany 1945 – From War to Peace* (London: Simon & Schuster, 2009).
Bidwell, Shelford, *Gunners at War* (London: Arms & Armour, 1970).
Boiten and Bowman, *Battles with the Luftwaffe* (London: HarperCollins, 2001).
Bolland, AD, *'Team Spirit': Administration of 53rd Welsh Division During 'Operation Overlord' June 44–May 45* (Düsseldorf: Privately published, 1946).
Bölscher Bernd, *Hitlers Marine im Landkriegseinsatz 1939–1945* (Norderstedt: Books on Demand, 2015).
Borthwick, Alastair, *Battalion* (London: Bâton Wicks Publications, 1994).
Brett, Lt Col GA, *History of the South Wales Borderers and the Monmouthshire Regiment, Part III, The Second Battalion the Monmouthshire Regiment, 1933–1952* (Pontypool: Hughes & Sons, 1953–1954).
Buchwald, Wolfgang, *Endkampf – Das Schicksal des Ausbildungs-und-Ersatz-Bataillons „Kampfgruppe Panzerteufel" der 12. SS-Panzer-Division "Hitlerjugend"* (Privately published, 1977).
Buckley, John, *British Armour in the Normandy Campaign 1944* (Abingdon: Frank Cass, 2004).
Buckley, John, *Monty's Men, The British Army and the Liberation of Europe* (London: Yale University Press, 2014).
Burden, Brig, *History of the East Lancashire Regiment in the War, 1939–1945* (Manchester: H Rawson & Co, 1953).
Caldwell, Donald, *The JG 26 War Diary, Volume Two 1943–1945* (London: Grub Street, 2007).

Carruthers, R, (ed.) *Handbook on German Military Forces* (Barnsley: Pen & Sword, 2013).
Carver, Michael, FM, Lord, *Out of Step: The Memoirs of Field Marshal Lord Carver* (London: Hutchinson, 1989).
Carver, Michael, Lt Col, *Second to None. The Royal Scots Greys 1918–1945* (Glasgow: Messrs McCorquodale & Co, 1954).
Carver, Michael, *The History of 4th Armoured Brigade* (Aldershot: Gale & Polden, 1945).
Clausewitz, Carl von, *On War* (Michael Howard/Peter Paret translation, Princeton University Press, 1976/84).
Close, Maj Bill, *A View from the Turret* (Tewkesbury: Dell & Bredon, 2002).
Cooper, Matthew, *The German Army 1933–1945* (London: Macdonald and Jane's, 1978).
Courage, Maj G, *History of 15th/19th Hussars 1939–1945* (Aldershot: Gale & Polden, 1949).
Coutts, Brig Frank, *One Blue Bonnet. A Scottish Soldier Looks Back* (Edinburgh: B+W Publishing, 1991).
Cowburn, PM, *Welsh Spearhead, A History of the 53rd Reconnaissance Regiment 1940–1946* (Solingen Ohligs: Wilhelm Müller jr, 1946).
Crew, Francis, *Official History of the Second World War, The Army Medical Services, Campaigns, Volume IV: North-West Europe* (HMSO: 1962).
Crookenden, A, *The History of the Cheshire Regiment in the Second World War* (Chester: WH Evans Sons & Coy, 1949).
Crow, Duncan (ed.), *Armoured Fighting Vehicles of the World, Volume 3, British and Commonwealth AFVs 1940–1946* (Windsor: Profile Publications, 1971).
Crow, Duncan (ed.), *Armoured Fighting Vehicles of the World, Volume 5, German AFVs of World War II* (Windsor: Profile Publications, 1973).
D'Arcy-Dawson, John, *European Victory* (London: Macdonald & Co, 1945).
Day, John, *A Plain Russet-Coated Captain* (Dorking: Self-published, 1993).
De Zeng, Henry and Stankey, Douglas, *Bomber Units of the Luftwaffe 1933–1945, Volume 2* (London: Ian Allan, 2008).
Dear, Ian, *Ten Commando, 1942–1945* (London: Leo Cooper, 1987).
Delaforce, Patrick, *Churchill's Desert Rats in North-West Europe* (Barnsley: Pen & Sword, 2010).
Delaforce, Patrick, *Red Crown and Dragon. 53rd Welsh Division in North-West Europe, 1944–1945* (Brighton: Tom Donovan Publishing, 1996).
Delaforce, Patrick, *Taming the Panzers, 3 RTR at War* (Stroud: Sutton Publishing, 2000).
Delaforce, Patrick, *The Black Bull. From Normandy to the Baltic with the 11th Armoured Division* (Stroud: Sutton Publishing, 1993).
Dungan, TD, *V-2. A Combat History of the First Ballistic Missile* (Yardley: Westholme Publishing, 2005).
Durnford-Slater, Brig John, *Commando* (William Kimber, 1953).
Eisenhower, Dwight D, *Crusade in Europe* (London: William Heinemann, 1948).
Ellis, Maj LF, *Victory in the West* (HMSO, 1968).
Ellis, Maj LF, *Welsh Guards at War* (Aldershot: Gale & Polden, 1946).
Erskine, D, *The Scots Guards 1919–1955* (London: William Clowes & Sons, 1956).
Essame, H, *The Battle for Germany* (London: BT Batsford, 1969).
Essame, H, and Belfield, EMG, *The North-West Europe Campaign 1944–1945* (Aldershot: Gale & Polden, 1962).
Farrar-Hockley, AH, *Student* (New York: Ballantyne Books, 1973).
Fitzroy, Olivia, *Men of Valour, History of the 8th King's Royal Irish Hussars* (Liverpool: Tinling & Co, 1961).
Forty, George, *British Army Handbook 1939–1945* (Stroud: Sutton Publishing, 1998).
Forty, George (ed.), *Tanks Across the Desert* (London: William Kimber, 1981).

Foster, Maj RCG, *History of the Queen's Royal Regiment, Volume 8, 1924–1945* (Aldershot: Gale & Polden, 1961).
Fraser, Gen Sir David, *And We Shall Shock Them* (London: Hodder & Stoughton, 1983).
Fraser, Gen Sir David, *Wars and Shadows* (London: Allen Lane, 2002).
Gerwarth, Robert, *The Vanquished. Why the First World War Failed to End, 1917–1923* (London: Allen Lane, 2016).
Goebbels, Joseph, *The Goebbels Diaries – The Last Days* (London: Secker & Warburg, 1978).
Graham, Col A, *Sharpshooters at War; the 3rd, 4th and 3rd/4th County of London Yeomanry 1939 to 1945* (London: Sharpshooters Regimental Association, 1964).
Gunston, Bill, *British Fighters of World War II* (London: Aerospace Publishing, 1982).
Hamilton, Nigel, *Monty, The Field Marshal 1944–1976* (London: Hamish Hamilton, 1976).
Harclerode, Peter, *Go To It! The Illustrated History of the 6th Airborne Division* (London: Bloomsbury, 1990).
Harrison Place, T, *Military Training in the British Army, 1940–1944* (London: Frank Cass Publishers, 2000).
Hastings, Maj RHWS, *The Rifle Brigade in the Second World War 1939–1945* (Aldershot: Gale & Polden, 1950).
Haynes, Lt George, *11th Cavalry Group from the Roer to the Elbe, 1944–1945* (Nuremburg: Entwurf, Druck Union-Werk, 1945).
Hinsley, FH, *British Intelligence in the Second World War, Volume 3, Part 2* (HMSO, 1988).
Hogg, Ian, *German Artillery of World War Two* (London: Arms & Armour Press, 1975).
Hooton, ER, *The Luftwaffe, A Study in Air Power 1933–1945* (Classic Publications, 2010).
Huett, Denis, *The Long Drive* (Pearlbay UK Ltd, 2004).
Hutchinson, James Lee, *The Boys in the B-17* (Bloomington: AuthorHouse, 2011).
Jewell, Brian, *Over the Rhine* (Staplehurst: Spellmount, 1975).
Kemp, Lt Cdr PK, *4th Battalion King's Shropshire Light Infantry 1745–1945* (Shrewsbury: Wilding & Son, 1953).
Kemp and Graves, *The Red Dragon – The History of the Royal Welch Fusiliers 1919–1946* (Aldershot: Gale & Polden, 1960).
Kemsley and Riesco, *Scottish Lion on Patrol* (Bristol: White Swan Press, 1950).
Kershaw, Ian, *The End* (London: Allen Lane, 2011).
Kershaw, Ian, *Hitler. Nemesis 1936–1945* (London: Allen Lane, 2000).
Kesselring, Albert, *The Memoirs of Field Marshal Kesselring* (London: Greenhill Books, 1988).
Klapproth, Willy, *Kriegschronik 1945 der Stadt Soltau und Umgebung* (Soltau: Mundschenk, 1955).
Kleinebenne, Hermann, *Kriegstage in Petershagen April 1945* (Stolzenau: Weserdruckerei Oesselmann, 1994).
Kleinebenne, Hermann, *Die Weserlinie – Kreigsende 1945* (Stolzenau: Weserdruckerei Oesselmann, 2011).
Kunz, Andreas, *Wehrmacht und Niederlage*, (München: R. Oldenbourg, 2007).
Langdon, John, *The Sharp End – A Personal Account of Life in a Tank Regiment in the Second World War*, (Monmouth: Stationery Kate, 2003).
Lewin, Ronald, *Ultra Goes to War – The Secret Story*, (London: Hutchinson & Co Ltd, 1978).
Lomax, Maj Gen CEN, *The History of the Welch Regiment, 1919–1951* (Cardiff: Western Mail and Echo, 1952).
Longden, Sean, *To the Victor the Spoils*, (London: Constable & Robinson, 2007).
Lucas, James, *Last Days of the Reich* (London: Arms & Armour Press, 1986).
Macdonald, Charles B, *US Army in World War II, European Theatre of Operations, The Last Offensive* (Washington DC: US Government Printing Office, 1973).

Madej, Victor W, *German Army Order of Battle, The Replacement Army 1939–1945* (Allentown: Game Publishing, 1984).
Mason, Francis, *German Warplanes of World War II* (London: Aerospace Publishing, 1983).
Mehner, Kurt, *Die Deutsche Wehrmacht 1939–1945, Führung und Truppe* (Rinteln: Privately published, 1990).
Mercer, John, *Mike Target* (Lewes: The Book Guild, 1990).
Meyer, Heinz, *Von der Invasion bis zur Kapitulation* (Preußisch Oldendorf: Verlag KW Schütz, 1987).
Meyer, Hubert, *The 12th SS. The History of the Hitler Youth Panzer Division: Volumes One and Two* (Mechanicsburg: Stackpole Books, 2005).
Middlebrook, Martin and Everitt, Chris, *The Bomber Command War Diaries, An Operational Reference Book* (Harmondsworth: Penguin Books, 1985).
Mills, Maj Gen GH, *The Annals of The King's Royal Rifle Corps, Volume VII, 1943–1965* (Winchester: Leo Cooper/Celer et Audax Club, 1971).
Mills-Roberts, Brig Derek, *Clash by Night – A Commando Chronicle* (London: William Kimber, 1956).
Montgomery of Alamein, *Normandy to the Baltic* (London: Hutchinson, 1949).
Moorehead, Alan, *Eclipse* (London: Hamish Hamilton, 1945).
Mortimer, Gavin, *The SAS in World War II* (Oxford: Osprey Publishing, 2011).
Muir, A, *The First of Foot, The History of The Royal Scots* (London: Blackwood & Sons, 1961).
Myatt, Maj F, *The British Infantry 1660–1945* (Poole: Blandford Press, 1983).
Neillands, Robin, *The Raiders. The Army Commandos 1940–46* (London: Weidenfeld & Nicholson).
Neitzel, Sönke and Welzer, Harald, *Soldaten, On Fighting, Killing and Dying* (London: Simon & Schuster UK, 2012).
Neitzel, Sönke, *Tapping Hitler's Generals, Transcripts of Secret Conversations* (Barnsley: Frontline Books, 2007).
Neville, Lt Col Sir JEH, Bt, (ed.), *The Record of the 43rd in the Second German War, Volume 4, June 1944–December 1945* (Aldershot: Gale & Polden, 1952).
North, John, *North-West Europe 1944–1945* (HMSO, 1953).
Oatts, Lewis Balfour, *Proud Heritage – The Story of the Highland Light Infantry, Vol 4, 1919–1959* (Glasgow: Thomas Nelson & Sons, 1963).
Padfield, Peter, *Dönitz – The Last Führer* (London: Victor Gollancz, 1984).
Price, Dr Alfred, *Luftwaffe Handbook, 1939–1945* (London: Ian Allan, 1986).
Price, Dr Alfred, *The Last Year of the Luftwaffe, May 1944 to May 1945* (London: Arms & Armour Press, 1991).
Price, Robert Stanley, *Just a Walk in the Sun* (London: Nivelo, 2011).
Randel, Maj PB, *A Short History of 30 Corps in the European Campaign* (BAOR, 1945).
Rosse, Capt The Earl of, and Hill, Col ER, *The Story of the Guards Armoured Division* (London: Geoffrey Bles, 1956).
Rottman, Gordon L, *Victory 1945: Western Allied Troops in Northwest Europe* (Oxford: Osprey Publishing, 2015).
Russell, John, *No Triumphant Procession* (London: Arms & Armour Press, 1994).
Saft, Ulrich, *Krieg in der Heimat* (Walsrode: Druckerei Gronemann, 1988).
Sajer, Guy, *The Forgotten Soldier* (London: Cassell, 1999).
Samain, B, *Commando Men. The Story of a Royal Marine Commando (45) in North-West Europe* (London: Stevens & Sons, 1948).
Sandars, John, *British 7th Armoured Division, 1940–45* (London: Osprey Publishing, 1977).
Saunders, Hilary St George, *The Green Beret* (London: Michael Joseph, 1949).

Schramm, Percy, *Die Niederlage 1945. Aus dem Kriegstagebuch des Oberkommandos der Wehrmacht* (München: Deutscher Taschenbuch Verlag, 1962).

Schwarzwälder, Herbert, *Bremen und Nordwestdeutschland am Kriegsende 1945 (Teil II)* (Bremen: Carl Schünemann Verlag, 1973).

Scott, A, Packer, C, and Groves, J, *Record of a Reconnaissance Regiment, History of the 43rd Reconnaissance Regiment 1939–1945* (Bristol: White Swan Press, 1949).

Seaton, Albert, *The Fall of Fortress Europe* (London: BT Batsford, 1981).

Seaton, Albert, *The German Army 1933–1945* (London: Weidenfeld & Nicholson, 1982).

Sellar, RJB, *The Fife and Forfar Yeomanry 1919–1956* (Edinburgh and London: William Blackwood & Sons,1960).

Showell, Jak (Foreword), *Führer Conferences on Naval Affairs, 1939–1945* (London: Chatham Publishing, 2005).

Shulman, Milton, *Defeat in the West* (London: Secker & Warburg, 1947).

Speer, Albert, *Spandau – The Secret Diaries* (London: Macmillan Publishing, 1976).

Taylor, AW, *Shine Like a Glow-Worm* (Darlington: Serendipity, 2002).

Tessin, Georg, *Verbände und Truppen der Deutschen Wehrmacht und der Waffen-SS im Zweiten Weltkrieg 1939–1945* (Bissendorf: Biblio Verlag).

Thompson, Julian, *Imperial War Museum Book of Victory in Europe. The North-West European Campaign 1944–1945* (London: Sidgwick & Jackson, 1994).

Thornburn, Maj 'Ned', *After Antwerp – The Long Haul to Victory* (Shrewsbury: 4th King's Shropshire Light Infantry Museum Trust, 1993).

Trevor-Roper, Hugh, *Hitler's War Directives 1939–1945* (London: Sidgwick & Jackson, 1964).

Trevor-Roper, Hugh (ed.) *The Goebbels Diaries – The Last Days* (London: Secker & Warburg, 1978).

Tudor, Geoffrey, *Hoofprints in the Clouds – Jeep Tracks in the Mud* (Brighton: Pen Press Publishers, 2008).

Verney, Maj Gen GL, *The Desert Rats* (London: Hutchinson, 1954).

Wake, Maj Gen Sir H, Bt., and Deedes, Maj WD, *Swift and Bold. The Story of the King's Royal Rifle Corps in the Second World War, 1939–1945* (Aldershot: Gale & Polden, 1949).

Warlimont, Walter, *Inside Hitler's Headquarters 1939–1945* (London: Weidenfeld & Nicholson, 1964).

Wegmann, Günter, *Das Kriegsende Zwischen Ems und Weser 1945* (Osnabrück: Kommissionsverlag Wenner, 1982).

Wegmann, Günter (ed.), *"Das Oberkommando der Wehrmacht gibt bekannt...". Der deutsche Wehrmachtbericht, Band 3, 1944–1945* (Osnabrück: Biblio Verlag, 1982).

Weir, Adrian, *The Last Flight of the Luftwaffe* (London: Cassell & Co, 1997).

Westerman, Edward A, *Flak. German Anti-Aircraft Defenses 1941–1945* (University of Kansas Press, 2001).

White, Peter, *With the Jocks* (Stroud: Sutton Publishing, 2001).

Wilson, Edward, *Press on Regardless. The Story of the Fifth Royal Tank Regiment in World War Two* (Staplehurst: Spellmount, 2003).

Wolff, Cpl Perry S, *Fortune Favored the Brave, History of the 334th Infantry* (Mannheim: Mannheimer Großdruckerei, 1945).

Woolhouse, Andrew, *13 – Lucky for Some. The History of the 13th Parachute (Lancashire) Parachute Battalion* (Amazon Createspace, 2013).

Wray, Maj Timothy A, *Standing Fast: German Defensive Doctrine on the Russian Front during World War II* (University Press of the Pacific, 2004).

Young, David, *Four-Five, 45 Commando 1943–71* (London: Leo Cooper, 1972).

Other Published Works

Convention Relative to the Treatment of Prisoners of War, Geneva, 27 July 1929.
The Times, 17 April 1945.
After the Battle magazine (Battle of Britain International Ltd).

Unpublished Works – British

Forrester, Charles James, '"Montgomery and his Legions": A Study of Operational Development, Innovation and Command in 21st Army Group, North-West Europe, 1944-1945' (PhD Thesis, University of Leeds, 2010).
Peaty, John, 'British Army Manpower Crisis 1944' (DPhil Thesis, King's College, University of London, 2000).
Hart, Stephen, 'Field Marshal Montgomery, 21st Army Group and North-West Europe, 1944–1945' (PhD Thesis, King's College, University of London, 1995).
Rae, Colin, 'Playing at Soldiers, 1939–1946'.
Rait, Wg Cdr, P, 'Me, myself and I: How important were personality, ego and personal relationships to British Air Land Integration in the Western Desert and Normandy?' (Essay, Advanced Command and Staff Course, 2014).
Steel Brownlie, William, 'And Came Safe Home', (Unpublished private memoir, Tank Museum Archive).
Ward, Lt Col, DCR, 'My Time with 45 RM Commando' (King's Own Scottish Borderers Regimental Museum, T1.36).
4th Armoured Brigade, 'Operations East of the River Aller, 14–19 April 1945'.

Unpublished Works – German

Gefechtsbericht der 4./117 und 4./162, 2 Mai 1945.
Gefechtsbericht des Flakregiments 122(E), 14 April 1945.
Gen.Kdo. Ems A.K. Korps Befehl Nr.3, 5 April 1945.
Tagesstärke der dem Korps Ems Unterstellten Truppen, Stand 21.4.1945.
Gedenkfeier und Steinweihe auf dem Ehrenfriedhof Essel, 16 April 1950.
OKW/WFSt Op Nr. 88745/45 v. 2. April.
Offiziersstellenbesetzung Mar.Gren.Rgt.6 am 3. April 1945 bei der Verladung in Husum.
Einsatzbereitschaft der flg.Verbände im Bereich Lfl.Kdo.Reich. Stand. 12.4.1945, abends.
Richter, Wilhelm, *Aufzeichnungen zu den Kriegsereignissen im April 1945 an Weser, Aller und im westlichen Teil der Lüneburger-Heide unter besonderer Berücksichtigung der Kampfhandlungen im Gebiet von Rethem/Aller* (1967).

War Diaries and Archives

The National Archives, Kew
The first time significant mention is made in the narrative of a British organisation, the archival reference to the organisation's war diary held by The National Archives, Kew is provided as a footnote; thereafter war diary references are made by exception.

Foreign Military Studies, Historical Division, US Army Europe (accessed through http://www.sturmpanzer.com)

B-147   Heeresgruppe 'H' (November 1944–March 45), Oberst Geyer.
B-354   1. Fallschirmjäger-Armee (March–April 1945), General Blumentritt.
B-361   Final Operations of Armee Blumentritt (10 April–5 May 1945), General Blumentritt.
B-414   Heeresgruppe 'H' (March–May 1945), Oberst Geyer.
B-665   Wehrkeise VI and XII (September 1944–March 1945), Generalleutnant Faeckenstedt

Internet

http://romanoarchives.altervista.org, *1945 Last Film from the Oder Front*.
http://ww2talk.com – British Army operations and establishments (Trux).
http://www.sturmpanzer.com – contemporary German manuscripts.
http://www.lexikon-der-wehrmacht.de – German organisations.
https://www.uboat.net – German U-boat commanders.
https://forum.axishistory.com – German organisations.
http://forum.12oclockhigh.net – *Luftwaffe* organisations and operations.
http://www.5ad.org – US 5th Armored Division operations.
https://www.8thafhs.org – US 8th Air Force operations.
http://www.pegasusarchive.org – 6th Airborne Division war diaries.
http://www.ww2.dk/Airfields – *Luftwaffe* operations and bases.
https://en.wikipedia.org – Miscellany.

Letters

Cannon
Gibbs
Huett
Leakey
Lewis
Wilde
Wilson
Stimpson
Sutton

Assistance

Nick Beale
Anthony Biggs
Phil Buss
Philip Graham
Marcel van Heijkop
Mike Jelf
Phil Jones
Hermann Kleinbenne
Dr Steve Pannell
Michaël SES Svejgaard

Index

People

Allied

Adair, Maj Gen 133
Adams, Capt 272
Adkins, Capt 322
Alderson, Capt 203
Allen, Lt Col 336, 418, 422
Anderson, Cpl (12 Devon) 162–165
Anderson, Cpl (23 Hussars) 225
Andrews, Lt 404–405
Anstey, Lt 427
Ap Evans, Capt 285
Ardizzone, Edward 411–413
Astles, Maj 176
Axtell, LCpl 149

Baker, WO2 212
Balharrie, Maj 227
Barker, Lt Gen 123, 141, 442
Barnard, Lt 185
Bartholomew, Lt Col 203
Baxter, Capt 377
Beadle, Maj 172, 303
Beard, Tpr 197
Beckenham, Capt (padre) 192
Bell, Maj xiii; Weser crossing 152; 153, 198, 223
Bellamy, Brig 129, 162
Bellamy, Lt 449
Blake, Maj 174, 174n67, 199
Bligh, Tpr 315
Blythe, Pte 385–386
Bolling, Maj Gen 220
Bols, Maj Gen 127
Borthwick, Capt 434
Bourne, LCpl 297, 299
Bowker, Maj/Lt Col 247, 248, 251, 252, 328, 401, 418
Boyes, Tpr 299
Bradley, Gen 33
Brecknell, 2Lt 214, 216
Brett-Smith, Lt 446–448
Briggs, Lt 407
Brindle, Cpl 296, 297, 301
Broadhurst, AVM 138
Brock, Pte 345
Brockbank, Capt 294
Brooke, Lt Col 336, 346, 379
Buck, Lt 217–219
Bulloch, Lt 306, 315
Burgess, Sgt 325
Burrows, Lt 303
Burton, Sgt 324, 324n17
Byles, Pte 416, 418

Cagle, 1st Lt 184, 185
Calder, Lt 184

Cannon, Tpr 342, 345
Carver, Brig 137, 391, 395, 398, 405, 408, 423–424
Caspar, Lt 175
Castles, Lt 256
Chambers, LCpl 197, 325
Charlton VC, Gdsmn 441
Charlton, Tpr 214, 297, 299, 317
Churcher, Brig 126, 450
Churchill, Winston 38, 129
Clegg-Hill, Maj the Hon 318
Clift, Lt 144
Close, Maj 285–287, 450
Cockbaine, Maj 337
Cohen, Capt 281
Coleman, Brig xviii, 136, 238, 239
Collie, Lt 306, 311, 316
Coningham, AM 137, 156
Connolly, Capt 283
Cooke-Hurle, Maj 324
Cooper, Flt Lt 177
Cooper, Sgt 304, 304n1
Corbett, Capt 211–212, 213–214, 215–216
Court, Cpl 203
Coventry, Capt 173
Cranston, Sgt 285–288
Creed, Cpl 279
Crerar, Gen 103
Crickmay, Maj 349
Crocker, Lt 253
Crozier, Lt Col 372
Cruden, Capt 202
Crump, Sgt 197
Cundall, Mne 295
Cunnigham, Lt 314

D'Arcy-Dawson, John 27
Dalton, Pte 215–216, 311
Darell-Brown, Lt Col 159
Darling, Lt Col 188–189
Davies, Capt 248
Davies, WO 303
Dawson, LCpl 347
Day, Capt 175
de Grineau, Capt 332
de Warrenne Warren 377
Deakin, Sgt 321
Deaves, Rfn 402
Dempsey, Gen 103, 106, 239, 361, 434, 446
Dennis, FO 177
Dibble, Sgt 325
Dixon, Capt 349–350
Downing, Rfn 402
Draper, Pte 190
Duff, Sgt 212

Dufty, Lt 241
Dunne, Capt 175

Easton, Capt 304
Edwards, Maj 210, 214, 216
Edwards, Sgt 445
Egerton, Lt 325
Eisenhower, Gen 32, 33; revised strategy 38; 39, 103, 390
Ellis, Maj 318
Elrington, Brig 136, 370, 386, 422; death 441
Elstob, Sgt 214, 297, 297n43, 301, 315
Elvin, Cpl 212
Emery, Capt 283
Enever, Tpr 297, 317
Evans, Lt 345
Evans, Tpr 196

Fairclough, Maj 279
Ferguson, Lt 384
Finlinson, LCpl 324, 324n17
Forrest, Tpr 259
Francis, Capt 324
Franks, Lt Col 113
Fraser, Lt/Gen 44, 284–285, 448, 453–454
Frazer, Lt 321
Freeland, Lt Col 427
Freeman, WO 177
Frisby, Lt Col 251, 364
Fuller, Lt 148–150, 156, 156n37

George, Cpl 330, 333, 335
Gibbs, Maj 394–395, 394n9, 399
Giles, Pte 190
Gilmour, Maj 272
Gleadell, Lt Col 144
Goldsmid, Maj 379, 383–384
Gore, Lt Col 338
Gosse, Maj 402–403
Graham, Capt 360–361
Grant, Sgt 289
Gray, Lt Col 293
Green, Tpr 418
Greenacre, Brig 129
Greenaway, Maj 385
Griffin, Maj 364
Griffith, Capt 274–275, 274n10, 279
Grossmith, LCpl 149
Gush, Lt 191
Gwatkin, Brig 134
Gwilliam, Lt 350–351, 351n23

Haldane, Capt 325
Haley, Fus 256
Hancox, Lt 271
Hanmer, Lt Col 372,
Harding, Sgt 306, 467
Hargreaves, Lt (12 Devon) 168
Hargreaves, Lt (5 RTR) 348
Harper-Gow, Maj 279
Harrington, Lt The Earl of 321
Hargreaves, Lt 168, 348
Harper-Gow, Maj 279
Harris, Cpl (Hans Hajós) 198-199
Hartland, Capt 160
Harvey, Brig 126

Hawley, Capt 377
Hayhoe, Tpr 325
Hearn, Sgt 412
Hedges, Lt 377
Hehir, Capt 322
Hemelryk, Maj 385, 385n27, 386–387
Henderson, Cpl (3 Cdo) 285
Henderson, Cpl (53rd Recce Regiment) 383–384
Hennessey, Tpr 259
Hewson, LCpl 402
Heywood, Lt 386
Hide, Tpr 325
Hill, Brig 128, 142
Hill, LSgt 295
Hobart, Lt Col 413
Hopson, Maj 200, 278, 279
Horrocks, Lt Gen 443
Howard, Lt Col 371–372, 371n11
Huett, Tpr 346
Hughes, Maj 338
Humphreys, Lt 402
Hunter, Lt Col 152
Hurley, Capt 324
Hutchinson, Lt Col 243, 259
Hutchinson, Sgt 184

Ireland, LCpl 344

Jepson, Maj 446
Johnson, Brig 134
Jones, Lt 375

Kent, Maj 239, 301
Kershaw, Lt 366
Killeen, Sgt 316
Kindersley, Lt Col 372
Kreyer, Lt Col 321, 324

Langdon, Lt 214; loss of Comets at Essel 286–289; crossing the Aller 296; action with F01 297–301, 306; action in Essel forest 305–318, 321–322; 311, action on the moor 315–318; 321–322
Lawrence, Capt 279
Le Neve, Sgt 184
Leakey, Lt Col 337, 349–351
Lemon, Maj 250, 374
Lewis, Capt 404–405
Lewis, Lt Col 200, 282–284, 28
Lewis, Maj 374
Lewis, Rfn 311
Lilley, Cpl 379
Lines, Sgt 349, 361
Lomas, 2Lt 285–288
Long, Lt 379
Loram, Maj 196, 212
Lord, WO1 429, 429n55, 430, 431
Loynes, LCpl 299
Lucas, Capt 179
Lyne, Maj Gen 44, 131, 237, 408, 414

MacHenry, Capt 241
Mackenzie, Lt 344–345, 347
MacKichan, Sqn Ldr 177, 178, 198
Mackie, Sqn Ldr 177, 295
Macnaughton, WO2 295

INDEX 487

Mallorie, WO2 304n1
Manning, Tpr 286
Marris, LCpl 149
Martin, Tpr 325
Matthews, Rfn 403
Matthews, Sgt 217
May, Capt 151
McBeath, Capt 176
McIver, Sgt 191
McLaren, Brig 133
McPhilbin, Mne 295
Meeks, Pte 162–163
Mercer, LBdr 421
Merrills, Lt 366
Mildmay, Capt The Hon 438
Miles, Cpl 208
Miller, Lt 210, 278
Mills-Roberts, Brig 130, 158, 173, 175, 197, 200, 202, 273, 277, 278, 279, 280, 282, 289
Milne, Capt 279
Minnette-Lucas, Lt 142
Mitchell, Tpr 142, 368, 379
Mitford, Lt Col 211, 285, 289
Montgomery, FM 32, 36, 37, 38; Eisenhower strategy change 39; 44, 106; universal tank 108; relationship with RAF 137–138; 141, 156, 282, 390; post-surrender tasks 449–450; 451
Mooney, Capt 168
Moorehead, Alan 44, 199, 285
Morrish, Sig 277, 279, 279n17
Morrison, Lt 399
Morrison-Jones, Lt Col 247
Moses, Sgt 248
Mulhearn, Cpl 245–246
Muncaster, Sgt 305, 307
Mundy, LCpl 189

Nash, Cpl 403n19
Newman, Pte 212
Norris, 2Lt 377

O'Brian, Tpr 299
Oram, Sgt 385
Oxley, Tpr 149

Palmer, Maj 160, 162, 164
Pannell, Tpr 301n47
Pape, Lt 189
Parry, Cpl 416, 418
Parry, Pte 332, 333, 335
Pearson, 2Lt 285, 286, 289
Pearson, Tpr 349
Pembleton, Cpl 214, 216
Pender, Capt 385
Phelps, Maj 418
Pierce, Capt 303
Pierson, Capt 427–430, 431
Pine-Coffin, Lt Col 189, 192
Poat, Maj 125, 208–209
Poett, Brig 128, 190
Pollard, Lt 275
Potts, WO2 366
Powell, Tpr 197
Price, Capt 284n25
Price, Pte 196, 209, 271, 272–273

Probert, Sgt 311

Rae, Capt 274–275, 275–277, 280, 289
Ralph, Cpl 318
Ramsay, Capt 378, 385, 387
Randall, Lt 302
Reakes, Lt 162, 169
Redpath, Cpl 214
Reid, Maj 190, 191
Rhodes, 2Lt 422
Rice, Tpr 297, 299
Richardson, Cpl 253, 259n45
Ritchie, Lt Gen 44, 130, 238, 390, 393, 409
Roberts, Maj Gen 125, 175, 193, 221, 228, 272
Roberts, Pte 314
Robins, Capt 176
Robinson, Lt Col 297, 314
Rokossovsky, Marshal 59, 445
Rolt, Capt 176
Ross, FO 179
Ross, Maj Gen 136, 238, 347, 364–365, 372, 391
Rowe, Tpr 286
Russell, Lt 291n39
Ruston, Maj 200, 278, 278n14, 279, 280
Ryde, Capt 271

Sarginson, Cpl 321
Sayers, Tpr 147
Scott, Capt 315
Scott, Lt Col 148, 210
Sheddan, FO 178–179
Shipley, Tpr 286
Simpson, Gen 38
Smith, Cpl 174, 279
Smith, FO 177
Smith, Lt 318
Smith, Pte 250
Smith, Tpr 272
Smyth-Osbourne, Maj 314
Spencer, Cpl 427–429
Spencer, Sgt 412
Spurling, Brig 133, 446
Steel Brownlie, Capt 44, 148, 194
Stewart, Lt Col 406, 408
Stimpson, Sgt 253, 348, 361
Stone, Cpl 324
Storey, Maj 366
Strudwick, Pte 190
Sullivan, Lt 215, 306, 311, 316
Sutton, Lt 366, 368

Taylor, Maj 189
Taylor, Pte 144–147, 163, 164–165, 168–169
Taylor-Balfour, Brig 302
Templeton, Lt 184
Thornburn, Maj 216–217, 305
Tighe, Tpr 324, 324n17
Timson, LCpl 402
Tod, Lt Col 126
Tomlinson, Sgt 347
Tudor, Capt 273, 280
Turnbull, LCpl 286, 288
Turner-Cain, Lt Col 157
Tyler, Lt Col 399–400, 423

Unthank, Mne 290, 293–294

Vickers, Lt 227
Virgo, Sgt 284

Wagstaff, Capt 192
Walker, Cpl 208
Walkley, Cpl 174
Walpole, Sgt 215
Ward, Lt 172–173, 179, 198–199, 203, 277–278, 290, 293–294
Wardle, Lt 275
Wardrop, Sgt 253–259, 253n40
Webb, Wg Cdr 339, 339n9
Webster, Tpr 299
Wellsted, Capt 208
Welsh, Capt (padre) 156
Wentzell, Sgt 408
West, Lt 215
Wheeldon, LCpl 318
Whistler, Maj Gen 335
White, Lt 414, 416–418, 449, 467
Whitehouse, Capt 286, 301
Whiteside, Maj 366, 422
Wild, Pte 347
Wilde, Capt 346, 356
Williams, Sgt (2 Mons) 345
Williams, Sgt (Welsh Gds) 437
Wilsey, Brig 136, 244, 251, 328, 336, 364, 367, 401, 418
Wilson, Capt (padre) 449
Wilson, Lt 341, 347, 467
Wiltshire, Lt 215
Wingfield, Brig 132, 408–409
Wood, WO2 301
Woodman, Capt 191
Wyatt, Tpr 286

Yeomans, Sgt 320–321
Yetman, Lt 226

Zhukov, Marshal 56, 450

German
Abraham, Gen 36
Albrecht, Matrose 443
Axmann, Reichsjugendführer 72
Bässmann family 356
Becker, GenLt 443
Bellof, Fw 164
Blaskowitz, GenOb 35, 36, 37, 39, 40, 47, 49, 64, 291
Bleckwenn, GenMaj 56
Blumentritt, Gen 36, 37, 39, 47, 49, 260–261, 302, 321
Bohnekamp, Olt 302
Bormann, Reichsleiter 372-373, 432, 445, 462
Burgdorf, Gen 49
Burkel, KKpt 235, 236
Busch, GenFeldm 48, 49, 435, 460
Chales de Beaulieu, Uscha 224, 311–312
Dahlmann, Maj 92
Dargel, Oscha 211, 221
Deichen, Maj 86
Döll, Maj 233
Dönitz, Gr.Adm 54, formation of marine divisions 55–57, deployment of marine division 62–64, 372, 389, 435, 444, Hitler's successor 445–446; surrender 448–450; personality 462–465

Engelhardt, Oberfeldartz 79
Fehrmann, Olt 84, 159, 160, 163, 168, 293, 301
Ferber, Maj 77, 158, 159
Förste, Adm 56
Forster, Albert 59, 59n33
Franzen, Uffz 169, 293, 297, 301, 306–307
Franzisket, Maj 93
Fries, Ustuf 312, 414
Früh, Ustuf 441
Fuchs, Mtr 241
Fuchs, OLtzS 241, 377
Gallhof, Oblt 400
George, Otto 306-307
Gering, Lt 178
Gern, Lt 444
Geyer, Obst xvi, 40
Gilbert, GenLt 54
Goebbels, Joseph 96, 187, 462
Göller, Marine-Oberstabsrichter 444
Gördes, KKpt 60, 66, 86, 262, 266, 272; death 281; 291, 465, 467
Göring, Reichsmarschall 55, 56, 61, 88, 95, 187, 445
Götz, Maj 92
Grabher-Meyer, Stschf 70, 311-312
Greim, GenFeldm 88
Greiners, Ustuf 72, 215
Grosan, Obst 82, 267, 291, 302, 318; surrender 441
Guderian, GenOb 81–82
Hache, Maj 85–86
Hahnke, Obst 43
Harries, Obst 302
Hartmann, KzS 59, 66, 67, 205, 238, 435
Hassel, Fhn 178
Hausser, Gen 47
Heck, Olt 58
Heinemann, Obst 90
Heinrici, GenOb 260
Held, Ogfr 166
Helmig, Maj 75, 101
Herbst, OLtzS 388–389, 393
Herrmann, Obst 95–96, 95n89, 182, 183
Himmler, Reichsführer-SS 51, 54, 57, 62, 75, 86, 302, 432, 434, 445, 462
Hitler, Adolf 31, 33; 'Shackling' order 34; 35, 37, 39, 40, 47, 48, 49, 51; formation of marine divisions 55–56, 58, 63, 64, 65, 81–82, 88, 260, 434, 435, 444, 445, 455; oath to 457, 457n11; 458, 459, 460, 461–463, 466
Hitzfeld, Gen 53
Hoffmeyer, Dr 348
Hornemann 364
Horner, Uffz 177
Horthy, Adm 369n8
Jäckle, LtzS 235, 246
Jodl, GenOb 34, 40, 56, 450, 460
Jordan, KzS 59, 66, 233, 235, 236, 244, 260, 348, 356, 359, 361, 406, 435, 438
Kahle, Maj 82, 267
Kammler, Ogruf 86–87, 86n80
Keitel, GenFeldm 34, 56, 63, 432, 446, 450, 460
Kessel, Hptm 380, 405–406
Kesselring, GenFeldm challenges on West Front 33, 48, 240, 435, 461
Kinzel, Gen 449
Kleffel, Gen 37
Knaust, Olt 43

INDEX

Köhler, Lt 179
Köhler, Maj 82
Köhnke, Maj 95
Komische, Oscha 216
Kopp, KKapt 291
Koslowski, Uscha 75
Kowalewski, Obstlt 93
Krafft, Stubaf 68
Krebs, Gen 82
Krieg, Mtr 403–404
Kummetz, Adm 49
Lange, Hptm 368
Last, Hans (James) 79n71
Lichel, Gen 77
Lichtschlag, Obst 66, 101
Lier, Obstlt 43
Linka, Dr 226
Lüttwitz, Gen 36, 37
Mahler, Oblt 388
Majewski, Maj 98, 101, 151, 236
Manthey, Maj 302
Marhenke, LtzS 378
Markert, LtzS 393–394
Marsen, Ostuf 70, 209, 312
Meincke, KKapt 370, 380, 385, 388
Meindl, Gen 36, 37
Meinecke, Ortsgruppenleiter 237, 237n11
Melzer, K.Kapt 370, 388
Meyer, Hubert 70, 70n57
Model, GenFeldm 37, 38, 47, 260, 442
Mohnke, Ostubaf 69n54
Müller, Olt 378
Müller-Broders, Hptmn 91
Munzel, GenMaj 82,
Nagel, Lt 184, 186, 186n9, 467
Najork, Erika and Ursula 192
Neitzel, KzS 59, 65, 362, 373, 384, 399, 432
Nicolussi-Leck, Hstuf 219
Otto, Obstlt 77
Peinemann, Hstuf 71, 205, 215
Pesch, Hptm 182, 186
Petermann, Obstlt 79
Peters, OLtzS 388
Pfaffelhuber, Ogfr 306
Picht, Maj 79
Pieper, Mtr 260
Polzer, Oscha 211
Prüm, Maj 85, 320
Rasp, Gen 54, 443
Ratzinger, Joseph (Pope Benedict XVI) 101n107
Rödel, Obst 94
Sahlberger 232
Sajer, Guy 150-151, 458
Scherer, Obst 80
Scheurlen, VAdm 58, 65, 67, 238, 238n13, 261, 413
Scheurlen, LtzS 58

Schilffarth, GenLt 98
Schlageter, Albert 92–93
Schlemm, Gen 36, 37
Schmidt, Maj 94
Schmidt, Obst 302
Schmidt, Uffz 178
Schneider, Uffz 177
Schroers, Flak-v 411–412
Schulze, Maj 83, 158
Schwalbe, Gen 40
Schwerin, GenLt 54
Shrickel, OLtzS 402
Siebken, Ostubaf 69, 69n54
Siegel, Maj 61
Söffing, Lt 156
Spahr, Ernst 306
Speer, Albert 56, 88, 450, 461–462
Sprecht, Karl 299, 307
Stange, Adm 48
Stephan, Ostuf 269
Stiehler, Obgren 148, 150
Stimmler, Uffz 178
Straube, Gen 36
Stroh, Obst 79
Student, GenOb 36, 39; Haltern counter-attack 40; 49, 50, 77, 79; change of command 260
Stumpff, GenOb 89
Szalasi 369n8
Szvdlowski, StaOJkr 224, 224n61
Tesch, Hptm 409
Thomale, GenLt 82
Thören, Kaptlt 236, 388
Tischler, Ostuf 158
Totzeck, Obst 321, 326
Tzschökell, GenMaj 80
Unrein, GenLt 442
Viedebantt, Maj 92
Volker, Obst 82
Vollmers, Oblt 258
von Bassewitz-Levetzow, Obst/KzS 238, 362
von Friedeburg, GenAdm 449
von der Kammer 237
von Kluge, GenFeldm 260
von Runstedt, GenFeldm 33, 260
von Schwerin, GenLt 54
Wagner, Kadm 62, 63, 372
Warlimont, Gen 35
Wechsmann, Maj 238
Wenck, Gen 261, 442
Westphal, Gen 48, 48n4
Wilke, Ostuf 75, 312
Winkelmann 389
Wohlke, Heinrich 236
Wolff, Ogruf 446
Wolz, Gen 446
Zeidler, Ustuf 208

Geography

Countries and Regions
Alsace 36, 54
Ardennes 125, 127, 128, 135

Bavaria 88, 445
Belgium 31, 43, 68, 127, 130, 131, 451

Crete 260
Crimea 58
Cuxhaven peninsula 434, 439, 451
Czechoslovakia 89

Denmark 39, 48, 55, 56, 93, 94, 104, 390, 434, 444, 449, 459

East Anglia 182
East Pomerania 60
East Prussia 233, 429
Egypt 136
Eifel 87

France 31, 68, 89, 130, 131, 133, 185, 231, 260

Harz Mountains 93, 183, 442
Heligoland 449
Hungary 71, 89

Italy 89, 107, 133, 137, 253, 446

Kuban 58

Lithuania 190

Low Countries 88, 89
Lower Silesia 238

Mecklenburg 233, 260
Netherlands 35, 36, 47, 48, 55, 64, 67, 87, 98, 127, 128, 139, 156, 199, 260, 339, 446, 449

Nordrhein-Westphalia 451
Normandy 31, 32, 67, 72, 107, 110, 112, 117, 124, 126, 127, 128, 130, 131, 132, 133, 135, 136, 138, 216, 260, 316, 349, 421
North Africa 107, 131, 132, 133, 253
North German Plain 23, 26, 32, 47
North Germany 94, 98, 156, 420
North Sea 182, 446
Northern Ireland 134
Norway 104, 390, 434, 444, 459

Odon Valley 130

Poland 52, 231
Pomerania 55
Pommern 233
Prussia 229

Rhineland 32, 36, 125, 135
Ruhr 32, 37, 39, 51, 420, 442

Saarland 68
Scandinavia 63, 390

Schleswig-Holstein 39, 50, 56, 60, 61, 62, 67, 98, 229, 236, 260, 404, 434, 439, 443, 448, 449, 451
Sicily 136
Sweden 390

Teutoburger Wald 38, 39, 44

Vosges 36

Weser-Aller Plain 23, 26, 30
Wesergebirge 77, 79

Places
Aachen 260
Achim 443
Achum 169
Ahlden 205, 209
Ahnebergen 373, 380
Alexanderplatz 266, 282
Altenboitzen 402, 405, 411, 414
Altenbücken 239
Altenwahlingen 370, 375–380, 381, 385, 387, 388–389, 391, 394–395, 398, 399, 402, 414, 452
Alperstedt airfield 229
Amsterdam 182
Anderten 252, 259, 336
Angermünde 62
Antwerp 31, 67, 87, 88
Armsen 379, 401, 406, 418
Arnhem 31, 67, 68, 130, 429
Artlenburg 445
Aurich 60
Averhoy 228

Bad Oeynhausen 451
Bad Segeberg 445, 450
Bannetze 320–321, 326
Banseeberg 278, 293, 303, 305,
Barnstedt 66, 348, 364, 373–374, 380
Bassum 44, 68
Becklingen 471
Bendingbostel 420, 423–424
Bentheim 47
Berchtesgaden 445
Bergen-Belsen 80, 82, 85, 86, 266, 267, 269, 285, 302, 312, 322, 324, 327
Berkhof 186
Berlin 31, 32, 38, 77, 80, 184, 267, 273, 435, 444, 445, 450, 465
Bevensen 221
Beverlo 67, 72
Bierde 158, 159, 165, 404, 452
Bleckede 445
Böhme 66, 378, 389, 394, 398, 414
Bomlitz 413, 414
Bommelsen 41
Bordenau 180, 187, 188, 217, 220, 221
Borken 43
Bothmer 193, 227, 228, 264, 266, 267, 271
Brase 223
Bremen 23, 39, 40, 44, 48, 49, 50, 73, 98, 141, 232, 237, 239, 260, 335, 362, 390–391, 424, 434, 442
Bremerhaven 23, 446

Bremervörde 390, 446
Brunswick 66, 99, 177
Buchholz 302
Bückeburg 79, 169
Bühren 199
Bulford 451
Büren 208
Buxtehude 441

Caen 132
Celle 23, 66, 221, 260, 261, 266, 267, 390
Celle airfield 92, 154, 221
Cologne 71, 77
Cuxhaven 58

Danzig 52, 59
Darchau 434
Dedelstorf airfield 92, 177, 420
Deipholz 68
Delmenhorst 443
Demouville 421
Dessau-Roßlau 77
Diepenau 148
Diepholz 237
Dieppe 129
Dobbin-Linstow 445
Dorfmark 431
Dörverden 251
Drakenburg 240, 240n22
Dresden 466
Dudensen 208, 209, 221
Dunkirk 134
Düshorn 413

Ebbingen 67
Eckernförde 60, 65
Eggebek airfield 94
Eickeloh 228, 268, 269, 291, 305, 327
Eiderstedt 451
Eilte 348, 370
Eilvese 206, 208
Eitze 401, 423
Elfriede' 236, 238, 247, 328, 330, 332, 333
Elsdorf 439, 441
Emden 48, 60, 63, 443, 446
Emmerich 32, 36
Empede 208
Emsdetten 43
Engehausen 267, 290, 296, 301, 302, 306, 320
Enschede airfield (B.106) 139
Erfurt 229
Erichshagen 66, 72, 205
Esbjerg 56
Esperke 269
Essel/Essel bridgehead xiv, 65, 86, 193, 261, 262, 264, 266, 267, 269, 272, 285–286, 288, 290, 303, 305, 318, 327, 362, 390, 404, 452, 453, 465, 467
Evensen 208
Eystrup 233, 235, 245, 253

Falaise 130
Fallingbostel xiv, 80, 83, 87, 158, 169, 209, 266, 268, 293, 424, 426, 431–432
Fassberg airfield 93, 94
Flensburg 450

Flushing (Vlissingen) 130
Frille 101, 144, 147, 159, 168
Friller Brink 159, 168. 220
Fulda 82
Fulde 413–414

Gadebusch 446
Gardelegen airfield 95
Geestefeld 66, 373–374
Geesthacht 446
Gifhorn 229
Gitter airfield 93
Glissen 148, 149, 156
Glückstadt 56, 60, 61, 65
Gnarrenburg 446
Goch airfield (B.100) 139
Goslar airfield 93
Gotenhafen (Gdynia) 56, 59
Grabow 445
Griefenhagen 62
Grindau 264, 266, 268, 269, 271–272
Gr. Eilstorf 388, 394, 395, 398, 402–404, 405, 406, 407, 414
Gr. Häuslingen 66, 356, 370–371, 375–377, 379, 381, 395
Grove airfield 94

Hademstorf 228, 262, 264, 266, 267, 268, 288, 291, 295, 303–305, 466
Hagen 206
Hagenow airfield 92
Hahnenberg Forest 87, 203
Halbe 461
Halen 44, 237
Haltern 39
Hamburg xiv, 38, 40, 50, 89, 93, 94, 98, 238, 266, 267, 336, 390–391, 414, 432, 434, 441, 444, 446, 451
Hamburg-Fuhlsbüttel airfield 94
Hamelin 49, 51
Hämelheide 233, 245
Hämelhausen 244, 250, 359, 364
Hämelsee 237
Hamminkeln 159, 163, 170
Hamwiede 405, 424
Hannover xiv, 23, 39, 49, 80, 98, 178, 182, 183, 187, 203, 217, 219, 232, 471
Harburg 414, 441
Harrienstedt 148, 156, 180
Hassel 101, 235, 241, 244, 250, 251, 262
Haßbergen 72, 245
Hedern 351
Heimsen 77, 196, 197
Heisterholz Forest 144
Helmstedt airfield 93
Helstorf 210, 221, 228, 269, 453
Hingste 239
Hirschbergin 238, 238n14
Hodenhagen 67, 291
Hohenaverbergen 368, 379, 400, 418
Hohenholz 240
Hollige 411
Holzhausen II 101, 142
Hoya 64, 65, 98, 101, 229, 233, 235, 237, 239, 241, 245, 250, 260, 338, 370, 453
Hoya airfield 229, 243
Hülsen 67, 232, 236, 250, 259, 260, 362, 364, 372, 471

Hünzingen 414
Hustedt airfield 92
Husum (Schleswig-Holstein) 56, 59, 65, 66
Husum (Schleswig-Holstein) airfield 94
Husum (Nienburg) 211, 213, 214, 215, 216, 268

Ibbenbüren 39, 43, 44, 77, 80, 125, 141, 237, 336, 357,
Idsingen 405, 408, 423–424
Itzehoe 56, 60, 372

Jarlingen 411
Jeddingen 432, 435, 438

Kaiserslautern 68,
Kaltenkirchen airfield 93, 186
Karlsruhe 32
Kassel 23, 38, 53
Kettenburg 435, 437, 465
Kiel. Mutiny 38, 60, 209, 266, 390, 435
Kirchboitzen 380, 388, 398, 402, 404–405, 409, 411, 413, 418
Kirchlinteln 399, 401–402, 418, 420, 422–423
Kirchwahlingen 356, 378–379, 388-389, 391, 393–394, 395, 398
Kl. Häuslingen 370, 372, 379, 381
Kröpke inn 312
Kükenmoor 420
Kutenhausen 144
Kyritz 55

Lachendorf 80
Laderholz 209
Lahde 77, 147, 147n15, 159, 164, 165, 467
Landesbergen 74, 157, 205
Langendamm 69, 73, 75, 205, 227
Langern 157
Lauenburg 66, 442
Leck airfield 448
Leese 73, 74, 82, 99, 151, 158, 172, 175, 179, 197, 198, 202, 203, 208, 245, 268, 453, 470
Leeseringen 157,
Leipzig 38, 77
Lemke 199
Lengerich 141
Leuna 97
Libau 59, 60n34
Lichtenhorst 223, 228
Lichten Moor 210, 221, 228, 233
Liebenau 75, 87, 157, 199
Lindsburg 215, 216, 223, 227, 268
Lindwedel 233
Lingen 40, 47
Loccum 82, 152, 193, 194, 196, 205, 206, 210, 217
Lofoten Islands 129
Löningen 64
Lübeck 390, 445
Lübeck-Blankensee airfield 92, 420
Lübbecke 141
Ludwigslust (Aller) 370–372, 381, 386
Ludwigslust (Mecklenburg-Vorpommern) 445
Lüneburg 229, 408, 432, 442
Lüneburg airfield 92
Lüneburg Heath 26, 80, 449
Luthe 217
Luttum 401, 418, 423

Magdeburg 23, 38
Magdeburg airfield 95
Mainz 32
Mandelsloh 180, 193, 210
Mardorf 206
Mariensee 208
Marklendorf 278
Marx airfield 93
Masloh 158, 159, 162, 168, 188
Mehlbergen 73, 75
Meinkingsburg 215, 216, 217, 223, 268
Merville (B–53) 185, 185n7
Metz 31
Milowitz 61
Minden 23, 50, 75, 77, 79, 86, 141, 156, 451
Moordorf 190, 191
Moscow 94
Münster 37, 39
Münchehagen 192
Mürwik 450

Neddenaverbergen 379, 401
Neunkirchen 435, 437, 439
Neu-Roofen 445
Neustadt 445
Neustadt (am Rübenberge) 69, 180, 187, 188, 189, 208, 217, 220, 228, 269, 285, 453
Neuwinsen 272
Niedernstöcken 180, 193, 210, 228, 267
Nienburg 27, 43, 44, 51, 64, 65, 66, 67, 68, 71, 72, 73, 75, 87, 98, 101, 141, 157, 158, 183, 199, 205, 227, 229, 233, 239, 251, 260, 267, 268, 336, 372, 390, 413, 453
Nienburg Forest 208, 228, 267
Niendorf 198
Nijmegen 130
Norddrebber 227, 266, 268
Nordkampen 348, 405, 406, 408
Nuremburg 260

Ochtrup 247
Oksbøl 56
Oldenburg airfield 92, 98
Oldenzaal 40
Oranienburg 55
Örbke 80, 83–84
Osnabrück 43, 63, 92, 130, 141, 158, 187
Ostenholz 86, 264, 266, 267, 268, 272, 291, 293, 296, 306, 312, 327
Osterholz-Scharmbeck 444
Otersen 364, 366, 368–369, 379–380, 381, 384–385
Ottersberg 73
Ottingen 38, 435–437

Paderborn 38
Parchim airfield 184
Petershagen xiv, 77, 141, 157, 158, 159, 179, 180, 188, 193, 197, 203, 205, 206, 217, 453
Plön 444
Putlos 83, 297n44

Quassel 89
Quetzen 158, 159, 165, 188

Rees 32, 37
Rehburg 206, 208, 210, 211, 216, 217, 220

Rehburg Moor 212
Reims 450
Remagen 32, 33, 77, 87, 93
Rethem 64, 65, 66, 101, 158, 205, 221, 228, 229–233, 237, 238, 244, 245, battle of 247–xxx, 260, 261, 266, 268, 293, attacks 11 april 328–335, attack 12 April 336–361, 362, 368, 370, 377, 379, 384, 391, 395, 404, 409, 414, 420, 421, 442, 443, 453, 465, 467, 471
Rethemer Fähre 351, 377, 391, 471
Rethemer Moor 212, 235, 237, 252, 339
Rheine 39, 43,
Ricklingen 188, 217, 219–220
Rieda 373, 380
Riede 239
Riepholm 435
Rinteln 79
Rodewald 209, 210, 221, 227, 268
Roermond 127
Rotenburg 238, 367, 405, 424, 439, 441, 443
Rotenburg airfield 94
Rusben 169

s'Hertogenbosch 135, 359
Sachau airfield 95
Salamis 60
Salzgitter 93
Salzwedel airfield 95
Sande 101, 144
Schaumburg Forest 85, 157, 158, 159, 168, 169, 220
Schleswig airfield 94
Schlüsselburg 157, 158, 179, 180
Schneeren 206, 217
Schneeheide 241, 409, 411–412
Schneverdingen 306
Schumann Mill 236, 247, 328, 330, 356,
Schwarmstedt 51, 65, 66, 186, 187, 221, 227, 233, 262, 266, 268, 269, 271, 272, 274, 278, 286, 288, 289, 453
Schwarzenbek 229
Schweinfurt 187
Schweinebarth' 235, 246, 251, 328, 330
Schwerin 92, 445
Schweringen 239
Sidi Rezegh 430
Siedenburg 338
Sieverdingen 424
Sindorf 409
Soltau 229, 302, 347, 390, 414, 432, 441
Specken 418, 420, 422
Spiekerberg 158, 159, 168
St Nazaire 129
Stade 390
Stade airfield 92, 94
Stadthagen 50
Stadtlohn 43,
Stapelburg 89
Stargard 55
Stedebergen 380
Stedorf 251, 373-374
Steimbke 216, action at 223–226, 227, 228, 268
Stellichte 424
Stemmen 379–380, 383–384, 401, 406
Stendal 95, 182
Stendal airfield 95, 182
Stendern 239
Stettin 55, 62

Steyerberg 87, 199
Stöcken 235, 237, 241, 252, 259, 330, 338–339, 347, 380, 395
Stöckse 216
Stolzenau xiv, 51, 67, 73, 75, 77, 86, 87, 98, 141, 148, 152, 154, 156, 158, 173, 175, 177, 180, 197, 228, 466
Südkampen 348, 405–406, 407, 414
Sulingen 44, 68, 73
Sülte airfield 92
Suroide 441
Swinemünde 55
Syke 239

The Hague 88
Thetford 26
Thören 320,
Timpen 160, 162
Timpenberg 241, 378, 381, 395, 409
Todtenhausen 144, 144n9, 158
Torgau 445
Tostedt 238
Travemünde 445
Tutow airfield 94, 421
Twente airfield (B.106) 339

Ubbendorf 239
Uchte 75, 151
Uelzen 266, 269, 390; battle of 442–443
Uetersen airfield 92

Vahrendorf 441–442
Venlo 127
Verden 23, 44, 50, 54, 64, 65, 229, 233, 237, 362, 368, 373, 379–380, 388, 390–391, 399, 402, 405, 418, 420, 422–424; capture of 432–433; 443, 453
Vesbeck 228
Vethem 405, 406–407, 408, 423
Villers-Bocage 131, 132
Vilsen 253
Visselhövede 390, 432, battle for 435–441, 465
Vlotho 79,
Volkel airfield (B.80) 139, 177, 178
Völkenrode airfield 93
Völkersen 73
von der Kammer farm 236, 248, 328, 330
Vörden airfield 92

Wahnebergen 233
Walcheren 31
Walsrode 67, 86, 99, 205, 223, 238, 241, 266, 268, 293, 305, 312, 334, 348, 359, 390, 391, 405, 409, capture of 412–413, 424, 432
Wasserstrasse 196, 197
Waterloo 406
Wehsen 435
Weisser Berg 408
Weitzmühlen 401–402, 418, 423
Wenden 223, 228
Wesel 32, 36, 37, 130, 131
Wesergebirge 77, 79
Westen 67, 236, 251, 260, 336, 347–348, 362, 364, 367, 368, 370, 372, 373, 379–380, 384, 399, 401, 453
Westerkapeln 238
Wiebusch Wood 210
Wienbergen 239

Wietersheim 101, 144
Wietzendorf 82
Wilhelmshaven 48, 60, 446
Winsen (Aller) xiv, 80, 86, 261, 266, 267, 269, 272, 302, 318, 320, 322, 326, 327
Winsen (Elbe) 441
Wismar 221, 434, 446
Wistedt 441
Wittlohe 367, 369, 374, 379–380, 381, 384–385
Wohlendorf 233, 235, 236, 248, 251, 367
Wolterdingen 302
Wulfelade 208
Wunstorf 69, 75, 90, 92, 180, 189
Wunstorf airfield 180, 188, 190, 191

Xanten 131

Zehden 60
Zeven 390, 441
Zossen 444

Transportation
Alte Celler Heerstraße 210
Allertalbahn 229, 229n3, 232, 264, 467

Kreisstrasse 149/Ostenholz road 266, 278, 281, 291, 297, 301, 305–307, 311, 318, 321–322, 452

Landesstrasse 159 371, 375–377, 381, 398
Landesstrasse 160 399
Landesstrasse 171 435
Landesstrasse 180 266, 267, 291, 306, 318, 320, 325
Landesstrasse 190 266, 267, 275, 285, 288, 293

Railway network 65
Reichsstrasse 209 66, 67, 209, 235, 236, 241, 252, 259, 336, 351, 356–357, 362, 370, 377–378, 388, 389, 391, 394, 395, 398, 402, 405, 409, 411–413, 414, 416, 424, 427
Reichsstrasse 214 66, 210, 213, 217, 233, 264

Steinhuder Meerbahn 75, 206

Waterways, Seas, Rivers and Canals
Aller/Aller crossing/Aller bridgehead xiv; character of 23; 26, 27, 44, 47, 51, 53, 65, 66, 67, 86, 99, 141, 205, 209, 216, 221, 223, 228, 229, 232, 236, 241, 243, 244, 250, 251, 252, 259, 260, 261; at Essel 262–264; 266, 267, 269; assault crossing at Essel 272–274; 285, 290, 291, 302, 318, 321, 325, 327, 335, 338, 348, 351, 356, 364; crossing at Westen 364–367; 370, 372–373, 379, 386, 390–391, 399, 404, 405, 406, 413, 414, 420–421, 432, 433, 452, 466, 467
Alpe stream 238, 248, 349
Aue stream 164

Baltic Sea 56, 220, 434, 445, 446

Black Sea 58
Böhme 412, 427
Bruchgraben stream 317

Caen Canal 128

Dortmund-Ems canal 23, 37, 43, 44, 420
Drebber stream 297, 321
Dummer See 177, 178, 237

Elbe 38, 39, 40, 66, 131, 238, 239, 266, 327, 390, 413, 414, 434, 439, 441, 442, 443; crossing of 445
Elbe-Havel Canal 23
Ems 39, 43, 63, 420
Esseler Kanal 264, 267, 278, 281, 282, 291, 295

Fähresee 232

Gehle stream 168

Ijssel 40

Jordanbach stream 405, 409, 413

Lehrde stream 423
Leine 23, 39, 44, 141, 158, 180, 187, 191, 193, 210, 216, 217, 219, 220, 221, 261, 262, 266, 267, 272, 285, 291
Lippe 37

Maas 32, 127, 128, 129, 131
Meiße stream 317
Mittelland Canal 23, 44, 77, 102, 147, 169, 180, 442

Neisse 94
North Sea 59

Oder 38, 60, 62, 94, 260
Orne 128
Osnabrück Canal 44, 237

Rhine/Rhine crossing 31, 37, 43, 51, 72, 77, 87, 89, 110, 124, 127, 138, 156, 188, 198, 429, 467

Scheldt 31, 94, 133
Seine 127, 131
Steinhuder Meer 177, 178, 179, 180, 184, 187, 188

Vethbach stream 406–407

Weser xiv, 23, 44, 47, 48, 49, 64, 66, 73, 75, 77, 82, 85, 92, 98, 101–102, 141, 142-148; VIII Corps crossing of 142–158; 170, 177, 179, 182, 192, 197, 198, 200, 205, 210, 216, 221, 229, 233, 235, 237, 239, 240; assault crossing at Hoya 241–244, 293, 370, 413, 420, 441, 443, 453, 466, 467
Wölpe stream 328, 330

INDEX

General

Aktion Leuthen 53, 77, 79, 236

BBC 243
Bletchley Park 187; Ultra urgency rating 357
British Army state of 103–104; approach to European campaign 104; manning 104; corps 106; structure of divisions 106; armour development 107–109; tank types 109–110; armoured brigade HQ 110–111; armoured regiment structure 111–112; APC regiment 112; reconnaissance 112–113; state of infantry 114–115, 360–361; infantry brigade HQ 115; types of battalion 115–118; artillery 119–120, 360; employment of artillery 119–120; types of regiment 120–122; engineers 122; communications 122–123; transport 123; supply 123; medical 123; maintenance 123; minor services 123; strengths and weaknesses 451–452, 452–454

CANLOAN 168, 214n47, 385, 385n27
Clausewitz 458, 461, 464

D-Day xiii, 63, 104, 128, 132, 135, 136, 198, 253, 429; British Army's development since 452–453
Die Deutsche Wochenschau 59

Flak provision by Göring 56; support to Weser Line 97–102; guns 99
Führer Conferences on Naval Affairs 54, 55, 56; deployment of marine division 62–64; 372, 389

Geneva Conventions 1929 196, 284, 334, 451
Germany links to Britain 23; state of agriculture 26; war industries 30; execution of civilians 75, 227, 432; pre-war strategic plan 88; state in 1945 435; state at surrender 451
German Army state of army 33–34; strategic direction 34–36; deployments 36; withdrawal from Rhine 36–40; situation early April 47–49; defence of Weser 49–53; Ersatz Heer 51–53; Infanterie-Division 45 57, 60; advisers 62; positional defence doctrine 65; motivation 454

Hitler Youth 59; fitness of 70; in Volkssturm 83; in Flak 97; 198, 232, 456

Kriegsmarine/German Navy Libau massacre 60n34; naval conferences 62-64; awards 457; motivation of 463, 464, 465

Luftwaffe state of 87–88; organisation 88–89; bases North Germany 91; ordnance 96; attacks on Stolzenau 153–157, 176–179; Schulungslehrgang Elbe 182–187; attack on Rethem bridge 420–422, 433; surrender 448; award system 457; motivation 466–467

National Redoubt 38
National Socialism/Nazi/Nazification awareness of terror system 45; Nazification of Germany 455–456; elite 458–460; 461

Normandy campaign use of armour 108; reconnaissance experience 112; VIII Corps 124; 11th Armoured Division 125; 7th Armoured Division 131; 53rd Welsh 135

Royal Air Force raid on Kaiserslautern 68; relationships with Montgomery 137; speed of ground advance 156–157; patrols over Weser 177; effectiveness of rocket projectiles 339

Soviet Union/Soviet Army Germany's strategic plan 88; threat to Denmark 390; prisoners 424–425, 431; meeting Western Allies 445; 459, 461

The Times newspaper 332

Ultra/Ultra decrypts 35, 47, 48, 61; FORTITUDE NORTH 63; 64, 72, 77–78, 101, 154, 156, 180, 187, 229, 240; warning of marine division 357; urgency ratings 357; product dissemination 357; 406, 420, 422, 462
US Eighth Air Force raid on Kaiserslautern 68, 88, 139, 182, 229

Versailles Treaty 464
Völkischer Beobachter 59

Waffen-SS 54, 62, 68, 69, 70, 70n57, 75; V-weapon programme 86–87; 219; British attitude to 226; 232; Rethem massacre allegation 332–334; alleged presence in Rethem 359; 466, 448, 450; post-war imprisonment 451
Weimar Republic 464
Wehrkreis functions of 52–53
Wehrmacht 26, 33n11, 47–48, 231, 435; oath 446, 457n11; 451; motivation 455–462; nazification 456, 459
Wehrmachtbericht 186n10, 432, 433

Yalta Conference 38

Operations
ARCHWAY 113
BLACKCOCK 130, 133
BLOCKBUSTER 32
BLUECOAT 124
BODENPLATTE 88
ENTERPRISE 221, 442, 445
FORTITUDE NORTH 63
GOODWOOD 124, 130, 131, 217, 317, 317n12
GRENADE 32
HATTON fire plan 337–338, 339
JUPITER 124
MARKET GARDEN 31, 125
NORDWIND 36
OVERLORD 129, 137
PLUNDER 32, 36, 130
VARSITY 37, 113, 127, 128
VERITABLE 32, 135
VOLCANO 445
WACHT AM RHEIN/HERBSTNEBEL 32, 32n4, 94

Formations and Units

Allied
SHAEF Eisenhower strategy change 38; 39
12th Army Group 32, 33, 38
21st Army Group casualties xiv, 31, 32–33, 36, 38, 39; structure 103; air support 137; 141; Rethem 'massacre' 332; 359, 434, 441, 446, 449
Canadian First Army 31–32, 103, 105, 138, 446

British Second Army
Second Army Rhine crossing 32–33; 38, 40, 43–44; characteristics 103–104; structure 105–106; 121; air support 138, 156; 141, 180, 217, 227, 269, 357, 361, 390, 434, 441, 442, 446, 452
GHQ Liaison Regiment (Phantom) 105

Corps
I Corps tasks 105, 451
VIII Corps xiv, 40; advance from the Rhine 43–44; 47, 105; structure 124–125; Weser bridgeheads 141–180; 158, 182, 187, 220, 228, 269; Belsen 302; 327, 390, 441; battle for Uelzen 442; Elbe crossing 445; 451
XII Corps xiv, 36, 40; advance from the Rhine 43–47; 105, structure 130–131, 182, 221, 227, 228, Weser bridgehead 229–244; 237, 239, 244, 260, 269, 327; failure to provide Crocodiles 338, 359; 369, 389; breakout plan 390; 405, 433; final advances 435–442; 439; Elbe 446; 451
XXX Corps 36; advance from Rhine 40–44; 47; 130; Bremen objective 239; 260, 390, 441, capture of Bremen 442–443; 446, 451

Divisions
1st Airborne 63, 128, 429
3rd Infantry 239, 336, 443
5th Infantry 442, 445
6th Airborne xiv, 37, 43, 113, 124; structure 127; 129, 141, Weser crossing 142–148; Schulze counter-attack 158–170; 181; advance to the Leine 187–193; 217, 220, 227, 269, 390, 442, 445, 446, 451
7th Armoured 43, 44, 111; structure 131; advance to Weser 237; 238, 239, 243, 251. Rethem 'massacre' 333–334; 336, 347; plan from Aller 390-391; 405, 408, 414, 433, 441, 446
11th Armoured xiv, 43, 44, 111, 124; structure 125–126; 130, 136, 138, 141, 158, 170, 171, 180; breakout from Petershagen bridgehead 193–197; 205; advance to Leine 205–217; 216, 221, 227, 228, 237, 262, 269, 289, 293, 302, 311, 327, 390, 391, 441, 442, 445, 452, 466
Guards Armoured 111; structure 133; 390, 433, 438–439, 441, 443
15th Scottish 37, 43, 124, 131, 141, 158, 180, 181, 220, 269, 390, 441, 442, 445, 446
38th Welsh 134
43rd Wessex 443, 446
49th West Riding 124
51st Highland 36, 429, 443
52nd Lowland 43, 133, 237, 338, 390, 424, 443, 446
53rd Welsh xiv, 43, 44, 133; structure 134-136; losses 135; 237, 238, 243, 244, 251, 252, 327, 333; plans for Rethem 335; 339, 349; losses Rethem 356; 357; perfomance at Rethem 358–361; 390, 391, 399, 405, 433, 441, 446, 453, 467
79th Armoured 106n9, 110, 112

Brigades
1st Commando 36, 43, 70, 124; structure 129; 131, 141, 158, 180, 197; attack on Leese 200–205; 227, 228, 261, 266; assault crossing of Aller 272–275; Essel forest battle 275–285; 281, 286, 289, 291, 293, 305, 327, 445, 452, 453, 466
3rd Parachute 127; structure 128; 142; capture of Minden 142; 170, 188, 192, 217, 220, 446
4th Armoured 111, 131, 136; structure 136; 379, 390-391, 405, 406, 408, 409, 413, 414, 420, 423–424, 452
5th Guards Armoured 133, 134
5th Parachute 127; structure 128; 142, 181, 187, 192, 217, 219
6th Airlanding 127; structure 128; 142, 158, 162, 165, 187, 188
6th Guards Armoured 37, 43, 111, 113, 124, 127; structure 129; 181
22nd Armoured 44, 132, structure 132, 237, 239, 244, 405, 408, 413, 414, 424
29th Armoured 125; structure 126; 148, 151, 157, 175, 181, 193, 197, 205, 206, 210, 211, 212, 223, 272, 285, 288, 289, 305, 312, 318, 322, 327, 445, 452
32nd Guards 133, 134, 435-437
71st Infantry 44; structure 136; 239, 244, 335, 370, 372, 377, 380–381, 385, 387, 391, 399, 420, 423, 432, 441, 446, 452
131st Infantry 44, 132, 133, 239, 408
115th Infantry 44
155th Infantry 133, 408, 414, 432, 441
158th Infantry structure 136; 238, 244, 248, 250, 335, 336, 339, 369, 370, 372; German counter-attacks 379–381; 391, 395, 398, 399, 418, 420, 423
159th Infantry 125; structure 126; 136, 148, 157, 180, 181, 193, 197, 205, 206, 211, 221, 269, 272, 302, 318, 322, 450, 452
160th Infantry structure 136; 237, assault crossing of Weser 238–243; 335; attack on Rethem 336; 347, 370, 379, 399, 418, 420; and Grosan pocket 441

Armoured Units
Inns of Court 125, 157, 193, 199, 206, 208, 228
Scots Greys/Scots Greys Group 137, 391, 395, 398, 402, 404–405, 406, 408, 409, 413, 420, 423, 452
1 (Armoured) Coldm Gds 134
1 RTR/1 RTR Group 132, 237, 239, 405, 409, 413, 414, 424, 431
2 FF Yeo/2 FF Yeo Group 44, 126, 148, 157, 193, 196, 197, 206, 208, 209, 210, 213, 221, 269, 271, 273, 289
2 (Armoured) Gren Gds 134, 448
2 HAC 133
2 (Armoured) Irish Gds 134
2 (Armoured Recce) Welsh Gds 133, 134
3 RTR/3 RTR Group 126, 151, 210, 211, 212, 214, 215, 216, 217, 223, 226, 227, 251, 278, advance from Essel 285–289, 296, 303, battle on the Ostenholz road 305–322, 307, 312, 321, 327, 450, 452
3 (Armoured) Scots Gds 129
3/4 CLY 136, 137, 391, 395, 401, 418, 422–423
4 (Armoured) Coldm Gds 129
4 (Armoured) Gren Gds 129, 142, 187
5 Innis DG 132, 133, 417, 441
5 RTR 132, 133, 136, 244, 251, Wardrop ambush 252–259, 336–337, 339, attack on Rethem 336–351; 373; Geestefeld action 375

INDEX 497

6th Airborne Armoured Recce Regiment 113, 127, 142, 188
7 RTR 338, 391, 399
8 Hussars/8 Hussars Group 132, 133, 237, 409, 411–413, 424–425, 430, 431, 449
10 Hussars 126
11 Hussars 132, 337, 447
15th Recce Regiment 169, 188, 217–220
15/19 Hussars/15/19Hussars Group 125, 126, 148, 156, 157, 180, 197, 206, 208, 209, 211, 213, 221, 278, 318; advance to Winsen 320–326; 327, 450
23 Hussars/23 Hussars Group 126, 150, 151, 176, 203, 206, 217, 223; Steimbke action 224–226; 227, 266, 327
44 RTR/44 RTR Group 108n18, 137, 391, 393–394, 395, 398, 402, 405, 407–408, 414, 424
49th APC Regiment 112, 137, 380
53rd Recce Regiment 136, 239, 240, 253, 368, 370, 379, 381, 382–383, 387, 441

Infantry Units
1 CAN Para 128, 142, 169, 188, 217, 219–220
1 Cheshire 126, 180, 197, 206, 208, 213, 221, 278, 290, 296, 301, 302; advance to Winsen 320–326; 327, 450
1 Coldm Gds/Coldstream Group 134, 437–438
1 E Lancs 136, 244, 250, 328, 336, 359; crossing of Aller 364–369; 379, 381, 384, 399, 401–402, 418, 420, 422–423
1 Gren Gds 134
1 Hereford 126, 150; Schlüsselburg bridgehead 157, 179; 193, 196, 210, 221; Schwarmstedt action 271; 272; capture of Winsen 326; 450
1 HLI 136; operations on Aller right bank 372, 377–388; 391, 394, 395, 409, 432–433
1 Manchester 136, 328; support to Aller right bank 372; 377, 401
1 Oxf Bucks LI 136, operations on Aller right bank 370–388, 375–377, 381, 388, 432–433
1 RB 133, 244, 409, 411, 413, 426
1 RUR 129, 147, 159
1/5 Queens xiv, 133, 409, 413; capture of Fallingbostel 426; 442
1/5 Welch 136, 245; attacks on Rethem 247–250; coup de main 248; Rethem night attack 328–331; alleged massacre 332–335; losses 335; 336, 359, 361, 368, 379, 381, 399, 401–402, 418, 422–423
2 Devon 133, 237, 402, 427, 442
2 KRRC 137, 391, 393, 394, 394n10, 398; action at Gr Eilstorf 402–404
2 Mons 136, 239, 240, 262; attack on Rethem 336–361; 372, 377, 379, 384, 399, 401, 420, 453
2 Oxf Bucks LI 129, 142, 144, 159, 169, 220
2 Scots Gds/Scots/Welsh Group 134, 435–438
3 Cdo 130, 180, 197, 198, 199; Leese action 203; 228, assault crossing of Aller 273–277; 278, 279, 282, 289, 295, 467
3 Irish Gds 134
3 Mons 126, 180, 251, 336
4 KOSB 133, wood clearance 414–418
4 KSLI 126, 151, 210, 211, 212, 213, 215, 216, 290, 293; battles on Ostenholz road 297–301; 299, 301; battle on Ostenholz road 305–311; 307, 311, 312, 315, 318, 321, 327, 449
4 RWF 136, 336, 370, 375; at Altenwahlinegn 377–378; 381, 385, 387, 388, 389, 391, 393, 467
4 Welch 136, 239, 240, 244, 245, 251, 335, 348, 364; Geestefeld action 373–375; 380, 399, 420
5 Coldm Gds 134
6 Cdo. 130; attack on Leese 200, 202; 228, 273, 278, 281; charge to the Essel bridge 282–285; 289, 290, 296, 452
6 HLI 133, 372, 414
6 RWF 136, 239, 241, 243, 244, 252; B Company ambush 252–259; 338, 359, 368, 379, 391, 395, 404, 405, 406–407, 408, 420, 452
7 Para 128, 188, 189; disaster at Neustadt 190–192
7 RWF 135, 136, 244, 245, 250; capture of Hülsen 259–260; 328, 335, 367, 368, 379, 381–382, 384, 399, 401, 418, 423
7/9 Scots 133, 414, 441
8 Para 128, 142
8 RB 126; at Stolzenau 151–154 158, 170, 171, 173, 175, 197, 217; Steimbke action 224–226; 227, 266, 327
9 DLI 133
9 Para 128, 142
12 Devon 129; Weser crossing 144–147; 159, 160; Schulze counter-attack 160–169; casualties 170; 188, 220, 293, 452
12 Para 128, 188, 189
13 Para 128, 188, 189, 190
45 (RM) Cdo 130, 158; crossing Weser 172, 173; 174, 179, 180; Stolzenau bridgehead 197–199; attack on Leese 202; 228, 273; crossing Aller 277–278; 281, 290; Essel forest action 293–294; 303
46 (RM) Cdo 130, 198; attack on Leese 200, 202; 205, 228, 273, 278, 279, 282, 285; Essel forest action 293–294; 303

Royal Artillery Regiments
AGRAs 121, 131
1st Mountain 121, 130, 173, 273, 277, 279, 280, 295, 304, 453
2nd Airlanding Anti-Tank 128, 170
3 RHA 132, 337
4 RHA 137, 404, 405
5 RHA 132, 409, 411, 427
6th Field 124, 128, 165
13 (HAC) RHA 126, 151, 171, 224, 273, 314
13th Medium 131
15th LAA 132
21st Anti-Tank 133
25th Field 124, 128, 168
25th LAA 136, 240, 402, 421
53rd Airlanding Light 128, 144, 165
55th Field 133
58th LAA 126, 154, 156, 176, 322
59th Heavy 131
61st Medium 124, 165
63rd Anti-Tank 124, 128, 165, 302
63rd Medium 124, 128
64th Medium 133
65th Anti-Tank 132, 421
67th Medium 131
71st Anti-Tank 136
72nd Medium 131, 240, 259, 338, 347, 376
75th Anti-Tank 126, 296, 303
77th Medium 124, 141
80th Field 133
81st Field 136, 259, 388
83rd Field 136, 240, 259, 330, 338
86th Field 133
94th LAA 133
109th LAA 124

112th LAA 131
121st LAA 124
133rd Field 136, 240, 245, 338, 360
146th Medium 124, 126, 173, 197, 273, 281
151st Field 126, 157, 171, 179, 197, 325
153rd Field 133

Royal Engineer Companies & Squadrons
4 Field 132
13 Field 126, 152, 175, 221
14 Field 133
100 Field 124, 148, 159, 180
147 Field Park 295
224 Field 152, 175
244 Field 136, 356, 377, 393
249 (Airborne) Field 128, 129, 147, 162, 170
257 Field 290, 303
279 Field 180
282 Field 136, 239
555 Field 136, 367, 377, 422
591 Para Field 128, 144, 147
612 Field 126, 152; Stolzenau 175–176; 221, 290
615 Field 133
621 Field 132

Miscellaneous
1st Independent Machine-Gun Company 134
2nd Independent Machine-Gun Company 126, 157, 196
3rd Independent Machine-Gun Company 132
No. 2 Forward Observation Unit 128, 165, 168
No. 2 Operational Research Section 150n23, 339
No. 4 War Material Recce Team 241
No. 5 Army Film and Photographic Unit 87, 289
344 Searchlight Battery 398
British Army of the Rhine 451
Control Commission Germany 451
Frankforce 113, 125, 193; Nienburg forest action 208–209; Belsen 302
GHQ Liaison Regiment (Phantom) 105
Special Liaison Unit (Ultra) 357
Todforce 126, 199

Royal Air Force
Army Co-operation Command 137
Second Tactical Air Force 32, 137; structure 138; tasks 138, 156
Bomber Command 32, 137
Fighter Command 137
No. 2 Group 138, 335
No. 83 Group 138, 156
No. 84 Group 138
122 Wing 139
137 Wing 351
139 Wing 351
56 Squadron 139, 177, 198
80 Squadron 139, 177, 295, 311
137 Squadron 139, 339
175 Squadron 398
181 Squadron 139
182 Squadron 139, 339
184 Squadron 139, 377, 395
486 Squadron 139, 178
617 Squadron 141, 141n2
653 (AOP) Squadron 251, 421

Canadian Army
9th Infantry Brigade 36

Russian Army
1st Belorussian Front 56

US Army
9th Army 32, 38, 43, 142, 217, 220, 269, 442
XIII Corps 36, 79
XVI Corps 37
XVIII Airborne Corps 40, 43, 442, 445, 446
5th Armored Division 142, 169, 442
7th Armored Division 445
8th Infantry Division 445
17th Airborne Division 37, 40, 127
21st Airborne Division 63
30th Infantry Division 37
79th Infantry Division 37
82nd Airborne Division 445
84th Infantry Division 169, 220
11th Cavalry Group 220
27th Armored Infantry Battalion 32
334th Infantry Regiment 169
638th Tank Destroyer Battalion 169

US 8th Air Force
1st Air Division 139
2nd Air Division 140, 182
3rd Air Division 139, 182
93rd Bombardment Group 184
100th Bombardment Group 184
490th Bombardment Group 184
418th Bomb Squadron 184

Wehrmacht HQs, Formations & Units
OKH 34-35, 80, 85
OKL 88, 89, 154
OKM/'Koralle'/Seekriegsleitung 59, 63–64, 444, 449
OKW 34–35, 37, 39, 47, 48, 49, 63, 87, 432, 442, 444, 445
OB West 33, 40; command difficulties 48; 180
OB Niederlande 49
OB Nordwest formation 48; structure 49; 89, 444
Ersatz Heer 51, 80
Führer-Reserve OKH 36, 39
Führungsstab Nord 445, 449
Führungsstab Nordküste 48, 49, 63, 73, 180
Führungsstab Süd 445
Reichsluftschutzbund 232
Reichsarbeitsdienst 69, 83, 97, 231, 451
Seekriegsleitung 63

Heeresgruppe
Heeresgruppe 'B' 37, 38, 40, 47, 47n1, 90, 442
Heeresgruppe 'C' 33
Heeresgruppe 'D' 260
Heeresgruppe 'G' 36, 47
Heeresgruppe 'H' 35, 36, 39, 40, 47, 48, 50, 51, 64, 67, 90, 98, 180, 357, 446
Heeresgruppe 'Mitte' 49
Heeresgruppe 'Weichsel' 55, 62, 260, 439, 443, 444

Armee
1. Fallschirm 32, 36, 37, 39, 47, 48, 237, 260, 443
4. Armee 260

INDEX

5. Panzer 31
6. Panzer 31, 71
9. Armee 461
11. Armee 53
12. Armee 261, 442
15. Armee 31
17. Armee 58
19. Armee 54
25. Armee 36, 37, 48, 55, 260, 443

Armeegruppe Student/Blumentritt
Armeegruppe Blumentritt change of command 260; Belsen negotiations 302; 327, 443; surrender 446; 454
Armeegruppe Student (31 March–6 April 1945) 40, 40n25, 48, 65
Armeegruppe Student (6 April–10 April 1945) formation 49; structure 50; deployment 50–51; right flank 53–54; centre on the Aller 54–67; centre on the Weser 67–79, 86–87; left flank (Aller) 79–86; 98; change of command 260

Korps
II. Fallschirm-Korps 36, 37, 40, 64
XI. Armee-Korps 40,
XLVII. Panzer-Korps 37, 39
LXIII. Armee-Korps 36, 37
LXXXVI. Armee-Korps 36, 37, 39, 43, 53, 77
LXXXVIII. Armee-Korps 40, 48
Korps Ems/XXXI Armee-Korps z.b.V. 50; structure 53–54; 73, 260, 435, 441, 443
Korps Hannover 50, 51; structure 77–79; 67, 77, 85, 101
Armee-Korps z.V./Division z.V. 51, 86–87

Divisions
1. Marine-Infanterie 55, 56, 60
2. Fallschirmjäger 36
2. Marine-Infanterie xiv, 50, 53; origins 54; structure 57–59, 62; equipment 60–61; deployment 62–67; defensive layout 65; 85, 223, 226, 229, 236; death of commander 238; 260–261, 262; new commander 291; losses at Rethem 356; 362, 370, 372, 388, 389, 406, 409, 432; final battle 435–439; 443, 444; power of camaraderie 457; 464, 467, 471
3. Marine-Infanterie 55
6. Fallschirmjäger 36
7. Fallschirmjäger 36
8. Fallschirmjäger 36, 450
11. Marine-Infanterie 55
15. Panzergrenadier 36, 37, 39, 43, 73
16. Marine-Infanterie 55
84. Infanterie 36, 37, 47
116. Panzer 36, 37
163. Infanterie 55
180. Infanterie 36
190. Infanterie 36
245. Infanterie 64
324. Infanterie 36
325. Infanterie/Infanterie-Division 'Jütland' 39, 77, 141, 206
Division Nr.180 54
Division Nr.471 39, 43, 47, 53, 77, 80
Division Nr.480/Division z.b.V. Gilbert 53, 73, 362, 367, 443
Division Nr.490 39, 47, 52, 420
Divison Stab z.b.V. Nr.172 54

Panzer-Division 'Clausewitz' 82, 85; at Uelzen 442
Panzer-Lehr-Division 80
Volksgrenadier 31, 57

Units
Artillerie-A.u.E. Regiment 16 61
Artillerie-A.u.E. Regiment 22/Regiment Schaffer 54, 236, 362, 368, 420
Artillerie-Ersatz-Abteilung 58 420
Artillerie-Regiment z.V. 902 87
Aufstellungsstab-Lehrtruppe 84
Bataillon Blinzler 362
Bataillon Lotze 82, 86, 267, 291, 312, 316, 321
Bataillon Sperling 82, 86, 267
Division Stab z.b.V. Nr.172 54
Divisionsführer-Lehrgang 238
Fallschirm-Sturmgeschütz-Brigade 12 442
Feldjäger/Feldjägerkommando I 240, 444, 451
Führer-Reserve OKH 36, 39
Grenadier-Ausbildungs-Bataillon 16 367, 420
Grenadier-Ausbildungs-Bataillon 47 367, 420
Grenadier-Ausbildungs-Bataillon 65 367, 420, 424
Grenadier-A.u.E. Bataillon 159 77, 79
Grenadier-Ausbildungs-Bataillon 280 (M) 54
Grenadier-Ausbildungs-Bataillon 489 367, 420, 422
Grenadier-A.u.E. Regiment 22 54, 367, 420, 423
Grenadier-A.u.E. Regiment 269 54, 235, 367, 420, 424
Grenadier-Ersatz-Bataillon 376 54, 235, 367, 420, 424
Grenadier-Regiment I./590 159
Gruppe Grosan structure 79–85; deployment 85; 209, 261; support to marine division 267; Tigers 291–293; Belsen negotiations 302; 318, 320, 322, 327; surrender 441
Gruppe Nord 87, 101, 199
Gruppe Süd 87
Heeres-Gasschutz-Schule 1 Celle 80
Heeresmusikschule I 79
Heeres-Unteroffiziers-Schule 11 Hannover 43, 43n28, 53
Heeres-Unteroffiziers-Schule für Nebeltruppen Celle 43, 43n28, 80
Jagdpanzer-Kompanie 1199 61
Kampfgruppe Aller 362, 365, 370
Kampfgruppe Hartmann 385, 387
Kampfgruppe Hornemann/Abteilung 22 362, 364, 367, 384, 399, 401, 418
Kampfgruppe Jordan 380, 385
Kampfgruppe Kahle 291
Kampfgruppe Köhler 82
Kampfgruppe Scherer structure 79–80, 221
Kampfgruppe Schulze structure 83–85; deployment 85; 157, counter-attack 158–170; end of 169; 188, 219, 233, 293
Kampfgruppe Tebener/Abteilung 11 362, 367, 368, 380, 399, 401
Kampfgruppe Totzeck structure 79–80, 261, 267, 320, 322, 326, 327
Kampfgruppe Verden 362, 399
Kampfgruppe Volker 82, 193, 196
Kampfgruppe Wiking 219
Kampfkommandant Bremen 54, 443
Kampfkommandant Celle and Uelzen 80
Kampfkommandant Nienburg 101
Kampfkommandant Wesel 36
Landesschützen-Abteilung 'Wietzendorf' 82, 86, 267, 318
Landesschützen-Bataillon 1020 67, 101
Lehrkompanie für Panzer-Fahrlehrer 84

Marine-Artillerie-Regiment 2 61, 67, 98, 236, 388, 399, 404, 406, 408, 424
Marine-Feldersatz-Bataillon 2 62, deployment 67, 205, 291, 295, 404, 435–438, 439
Marine-Füsilier-Bataillon 2 command 60; deployment 66; 86, 205, 227; defence of Aller 262–267; Waffen-SS companies with 268; battle at Schwarmstedt 271–272, 273; battles in forest 291–301; 305; on the Winsen road 318; 359; last action 435–437; 444
Marine-Grenadier-Regiment 5 command 59; deployment 66; at Hoya 229; defence of Rethem 233–236; action at Hoya 241–244; battle for Rethem 246–248, 251–252, 260, 328–348; Rethem 'massacre' 333; 339, 370; counter-attacks 380–388; 385, 402, 406, 414, 435, 438, 443
Marine-Grenadier-Regiment 6 command 59; deployment 66; withdrawal from Nienburg 205; 233, 251; defence of Aller right bank 370-371, 375; Altenwahlingen 377–378; counter-attacks 380–388; 385, 387, 388, 394, 395, 398, 402, 404, 409, 413–414. 435, 437, 453
Marine-Grenadier-Regiment 7 command 59; deployment 65; 348, 362, 367, 373, 374; counter-attacks 380–388; 384, 399, 400–401, 407, 418, 435, 438, 439
Marine-Kampfschule deployment 67
Marine-Kraftfahrzeug-Abteilung 232, 260
Marine-Küsten-Polizei 62
Marine-Panzerjäger-Abteilung 2 61, 67, 235, 236, 266
Marine-Pionier-Bataillon 2 61, deployment 67
Marine-Schützen-Brigade Nord 55
Marine-Versorgungs-Regiment 200 62, 439
Nebeltruppenschule Celle 79,
Oflag 79 291n39
Oflag 83 82
Panzer-Abteilung 21 83
Panzer-Ausbildungs-Verband 'Grossdeutschland' 39, 73, 237, 439
Panzer-Ausbildungs-Verband 'Thüringen' 82
Panzer-Ersatz-Abteilung 11 79
Panzerjagdverband 'Großer Kurfürst' 77, 86–87, 144, 147, 148, 159, 165, 196, 197
Panzerjäger-Lehrgänge 85, 267, 320
Panzerjäger-Lehr und Versuchs Kompanie 85
Panzer-Lehr-Regiment 130 83
II./Panzer-Regiment 21 83
Panzertruppenschule Bergen I and II 80, 82–83, 85, 86
Panzertruppenschule Krampnitz 80
Panzertruppenschule I Wünsdorf 80
Panzer-Pionier-A.u.E. Bataillon 16 144
Pionier-A.u.E. Bataillon 22 420
Pionier-A.u.E. Bataillon 26 83
Pionier-A.u.E. Bataillon 30 54
Pionier-A.u.E. Bataillon 34 54, 367, 420
Pionier-Brücken A.u.E. Btl.2 77
Pionier-Ersatz-Bataillon 6 77, 83, 141, 142
Pionier-Kompanie Golde 83
Pionier-Reserve-Offizier-Bewerber Bataillon Nienburg 67, 380, 384, 388, 405–406
Pionierschule II 77
Pionier-Sperr-Brigade 1100 77, 141, 158, 172, 197
Polizei-Bataillon 'Ottersberg' 54
Schwere Heeres-Panzerjäger-Abteilung 661 85, 85n78, 267, 278, 288, 291, 305
Stalag XIB xiv, 257; relief of 424–432; 431, 470
Stalag XID 425
Stalag 321 425

Stalag 357 233; relief of 424–425; 430, 431, 470
Stellvertretendes General-Kommando 50–53
Ungarisch Artillerie-Ausbildung-Bataillon 7/Bataillon Kolotay 236, 251, 362, 364–367, 369, 399
Volks-Artillerie-Korps 402 54, 420, 424, 439
Volkssturm 83, 233, 267, 451
Volkssturm-Bataillon 'Lüneburg' 82–83, 86, 267, 318, 321
Wehrkreis-Kommando 52
4. Alarm-Bataillon 'Wesermünde' 54
6. Lehrgruppe 83
9. Marine-Flak-Regiment 56
11./101 Festungs-Pak-E.u.A. Abteilung 266, 291
II./Werfer-Lehr Regiment 80

Wehrkreis
Wehrkreis VI 51, 180
Wehrkreis X 48, 50, 53, 67, 77
Wehrkreis XI 50, 67, 77, 82

Luftwaffe
Gefechtsverband Kowalewski 93
Gefechtsverband Helbig 94
Küstenfliegergruppe 106 59
Luftflotte Reich 48, 89, 90, 98, 154, 156
Luftflotte 3 89
Luftflotte 6 89, 94
Luftgau XI 49, 98
Lufthauptmunitionsanstalt 3/XI 69, 227
Luftwaffenkommando West 89
Nahaufklärungsgruppe 6 93, 156
2. Jagd-Division 94, 156
3. Jagd-Division 94
Nachtjagdgeschwader 1 94
9. Flieger-Division (Jagd) 95
14. Flieger-Division 89; structure 90; 94; attacks at Stolzenau 154–156; 420, 422
15. Flieger-Division 89, 90, 93
16. Flieger-Division 89
II. Jagd-Korps 90
IX. Flieger-Korps (Jagd) 94
JG 7 95, 183, 184
JG 11 94
JG 26 92, 156, 177, 466–467
JG 27 92, 156, 176
KG 76 93, 156, 186, 402, 433
NAGr. 6 93
NSGr. 1 (Nord) 91, 154, 176, 177, 178–179, 221
NSGr. 20 92, 156, 177, 372
I./KG (J) 54 95, 183
I./KG 66 94, 420, 422
I./Schlachtgeschwader 5 92
II./KG 200 156, 178
III./KG 200 92, 156, 176, 372, 420
5./KG 200 96
IV./JG 300 229, 229n1
Schulungslehrgang Elbe 95–96, 95n90, 182–187, 466, 467

Flak
Flak organisation 97–98, railway Flak 98
II. Flak-Korps 439
VI. Flak-Korps 98
3. Flak-Division 98
5. Flak-Division (W) 87
8. Flak-Division 98, 443
14. Flak-Division 97

INDEX

8. Flak-Brigade 98
Artillerie-Regiment 902 z.V. 101
Flak-Abteilung 263(E) 101
Flak-Regiment 122(E) structure 98–99; guns 99; 202, 205, 223, 233
4./434 Flak-Abteilung 101, 142
Leichte-Flak-Abteilung 859(E) 101
RAD Flak-Abteilung 366 409
II./RAD Flak-Regiment 36 101
4./117 and 4./162 (gem.) Batterien 99, 235, 241, 388, 409, 411
1. u. 4./125(E) Batterien 101, 236, 246
4./132 RAD Batterie 99, 152, 196, 206, 223
2./137 Batterie 101
5./280 RAD Batterie 99, 101, 202, 235, 241, 243
1./521 RAD Batterie 101, 101n104, 205, 267, 285, 291
2./604 (gem.) RAD Batterie 99, 235, 241, 246, 339, 388, 409
3./607 Batterie 101, 205
2./859(E) Batterie 99
4./871 Batterie 99, 202
2./902 Batterie 101
6969 z.b.V. Batterie 101, 101n105

Kriegsmarine
Kaiserliche Marine 464
Küstenbefehlshaber Deutsche Bucht 58
Marine-Einsatzstabes Kertsch 58
Marine-Oberkommando Nordsee 48, 56, 63
Marine-Oberkommando Ostsee 48
Marine-Schule Mürwik 450
Marine-Schützen-Brigade Nord 55
2. Admiral Nordsee/Ostsee 441
9. Marine-Flak-Regiment 56
24. U-Bootsflottille 60
25. U-Bootsflottille 59
Admiral Graf Spee (ship) 463
U-37 59, 59n30
U-198 59, 59n30
U-469 58
U-510 59

Waffen-SS
XII. SS-Armeekorps 260
1. SS-Panzerdivision 'Leibstandarte Adolf Hitler' 72
5. SS-Panzerdivision 'Wiking' 219
12. SS-Panzerdivision 'Hitlerjugend' 67, 70
SS-A.u.E. Btl.12 'HJ' xiv; origins 67–68; structure 68–69, 72; equipping and training 69–71, 72; deployment 72–75; 87, 99, 101, 157; action at Leese 170–179, 197–205; withdrawal battles 205–217, 221–222; 180; alleged massacre of 212–213; 221; action at Steimbke 223–226; 227, 228, 245, 261; defence of Essel forest 267–269; action at Schwarmstedt 269–272; action in Essel forest 291–301, 303–305, 311, 312; 334; suggested presence in Rethem 359, 359n31; 413; dismissal of under–18s 414; action at Fallingbostel 424, 427; 441; action at Vahrendorf 442–443; 451, 453, 454, 462; motivation 466–467
Kampfgruppe Tischler 158, 170; attack 171–172; 179, 197, 205, 206, 453
SS-A.u.E. Bataillon 16 'Reichsführer SS' 68
SS-A.u.E. Bataillon 18 'Horst Wessel' 54
SS-Führungshauptamt 73
SS-Panzer-Grenadier-Regiment 25 72
SS-Panzer-Grenadier-Regiment 26 68, 69
SS-Werfer-Lehr-Abteilung 80,
SS-Werfer-Abteilung 500 86–87
SS- und Polizeiführer 240

Miscellaneous
Arbeitserziehungslager Lahde 147n15
Beetenbrück ammo site 412
Belsen concentration camp 209, 267, 302, 327, 442
Brigitta oil facility 228
Danzig-West Prussia Volkssturm 59
Deurag-Nerag refinery 26, 203, 267
Eibia GmbH/Wolff 75n66, 406, 414
Gestapo 451
Kampfstoffabrik Leese 87, 180, 203, 470
Karl' 75, 75n65, 157, 199
Loccum fuel depot 203
Misburg concentration camp 267
Neuengamme concentration camp 267
Organisation Todt 409
Sanitätsdienst 301
Wehrmachtbericht 186
Werwolf 434

Aircraft, Equipment, Vehicles and Weapons

British
Achilles 110, 121, 126, 128, 132, 133, 303
AEC armoured command vehicle 106
Archer 121, 391
Armoured cars 112–113, 387
Auster 137, 251, 421
Bailey bridging 44, 122, 148, 159, 180, 188, 210, 220, 221, 221n57, 240, 243, 244, 251, 269, 290, 303, 320, 321, 327, 336, 367, 377, 379, 391, 395, 413, 420–421, 423, 443, 445, 453
Bailey raft 122, 295, 453
Besa machine-gun 108, 109, 189, 208, 224, 269, 297, 312, 317, 321, 325, 405, 412, 438
Boeing B-17 Flying Fortress 140, 182, 185, 229
Bren 116, 117, 219, 256, 257, 279, 325, 344
Buffalo 37, 443
Centurion 110
Chaffee 132
Challenger 108, 111, 125, 132, 133
Churchill 108, 110, 111, 127, 142, 144, 188, 190, 219, 406
Churchill ARV 111
Churchill bridgelayer 423
Comet 43, 107, 109–110, 121, 125, 126, 148, 194, 203, 208, 210, 212, 224, 225, 227, 269, 278, 285, 288, 289, 301, 306, 315, 315n9, 324, 325, 327, 452
Consolidated B-24J Liberator 140, 182, 183
Crocodile 110, 335, 337, 347, 359, 391, 399, 401, 418, 422, 433
Cromwell 108, 111, 125, 131, 132, 133, 142, 197, 251, 253, 258, 321, 341–344, 345, 348, 395, 412, 417, 437–438
Folding Boat Equipment 122, 147, 162, 165, 170, 180, 192, 335, 368, 370, 379, 384, 391, 445
International Harvester M14 112–113, 117
Kangaroo 112, 133, 380, 391, 395, 398, 404, 409, 411, 427, 452
Lancaster bomber 37

Locust 113
Loyd carrier 116, 117, 245
Meteor 93, 170, 170n60
Mustang 140
PIAT 116, 117, 162, 216, 218, 278, 281, 305, 314, 385
Rocket projectiles 138–139, 453
Sexton 120, 133
Sherman 107, 108, 111, 133, 137, 214, 398, 401, 418, 423–424
Sherman Firefly 108, 111, 121, 131, 137, 253, 254, 258, 341–344, 346, 348, 401, 422
Sherman ARV 111
Sherman V 111, 137
Sexton 126, 132, 409
Spitfire 138
Staghound 106, 112
Sten 116, 117, 197, 219, 246, 386
Stuart/Honey 111–112, 132, 406, 412, 430
Tempest V 138, 177, 198, 295, 311
Thunderbolt 140
Typhoon 1B 138, 168, 315, 336, attack on Rethem 339, 348, 360, 377, 395, 398, 404, 423, 453
Universal carrier 113, 347, 377
Valentine 111, 408
Vickers machine-gun 113, 117, 126, 132, 136, 147, 157, 283, 305, 372, 401
Vickers K machine-gun 113
Wasp 116, 215, 248, 297, 301, 367, 378, 393, 395
White armoured truck 112, 113, 117
.303-in rifle 116
.50-in Browning quad 114, 421
2-in mortar 116, 416
3-in mortar 117
3.7-in howitzer 121, 280, 283
4.2-in mortar 113, 117, 126, 132, 136, 157, 328, 339, 372, 377, 401
4.5/5.5 field gun 121, 133, 240, 280, 347, 417
6-pdr anti-tank gun 116–117, 128, 159, 219, 305
17-pdr tank gun 107, 108, 408
17-pdr towed gun 128
25-pdr field gun 120, 132, 133, 136, 245, 417, 452, 453
40mm Bofors 122, 156, 241, 421
75mm pack howitzer 121
75mm tank gun 108, 321, 408
76.2mm tankgun 107, 108, 209
155mm M2 121

German

Ar 234 B-2 93, 156, 186, 322, 402, 422, 433
Bachem 349 88
Bf 109 G and K-4 87, 93, 93n87, 95, 156, 176, 182, 185, 190, 229, 322, 422, 448
Bf 110 G 94
Dornier 335 88
Fiesler 156 'Storch' 190
Fw 190 A-3/U4 93
Fw 190 F/G 92, 93, 156, 176, 177, 178, 190, 243, 322, 372, 420–422, 448
Fw 190 D-9 92, 156, 177
He 162 448
He 219 A 94
Hetzer 61
Infra-red 85
Jagdpanther 219
Ju 52 243

Ju 87 D-5 91, 153, 176, 178, 190, 322
Ju 88 G 94, 156, 190, 420–422
Ju 88 S 94, 420,
Ju 188 94, 156, 420
Jumo 004 93
Kar 98k 60, 70
Luftwaffe ordnance 96–97
Me 108 444
Me 163 B 88
Me 262 93, 95, 183, 322, 448
Me 262 A-1/U3 93
MG 42 60, 65, 70, 236, 252, 293–294, 305, 346, 374, 386, 467
MP 40 374, 375
Nebelwerfer 144, 267, 320, 321, 324
Panzerfaust 44, 61, 70, 85, 86, 144, 148, 149, 150–151, 157, 189, 197, 210, 215, 225, 227, 235, 236, 248, 251, 256, 266, 267, 269, 271, 283, 286, 293–294, 305, 306, 320, 321, 322, 324, 328, 342, 345–346, 348, 371, 374, 377, 388, 393, 394, 395, 400, 405, 407, 408, 411, 413, 422–423, 438, 452
Panzerschreck 61
Panther 84–85, 108, 109, 159, Schulze counter-attack 165–168, 217, 219, 267, 301
Panzer Mk IV 267
Panzer IV/70 79, 85, 220, 267, 279, 281, 288
PWK 8H63 85–86, 267, 320, 324
Renault FT-17 406
SdKfz. 4/1 80
SdKfz. 184 (Ferdinand) 170, 170n58, 219
SdKfz. 222/223 85, 86, 209, 267
SdKfz. 251 73, 75, 159, 165, 171, 205, 208, 219, 223, 267, 268, 281, 312
SdKfz. 251/20 85
Siebel 204 190
StG 44 60, 70, 86, 116, 374, 467
StuG III 442
StuG IV 79, 168
Teller mine 236
Tiger I 84–85, 108, 110, 116, 158, Schulze counter-attack 159–169, 218–219, 267, 288, 291, 293, 297, 299, 301, 305, 306, 314–316, 318, 322
Tiger F01 163, 170, 293, 297, 297n44, 299, 306, 307, 311, 452, 467
Tiger II 84
V-1 75, 75n67, 87, 88, 139, 199, 460
V-2 73, 75, 75n67, 86–87, 88, 199, 203, 205, 401n17, 460, 468
Walther P38 375
2cm Flak 83, 99, 152, 196, 202, 235, 241, 339, 345, 351, 362, 409, 412
3.7cm Flak 61, 83, 99, 152, 202
7.5cm le. IG18 60, 85, 266
7.5cm FK 18 420
7.5cm Pak 40 61, 65, 85, 227, 235, 236, 248, 266, 345
8.8cm Flak 36/37 99, 152, 196, 202, 205, 223, 235, 241, 259, 339, 362, 399, 401, 409, 418, 423, 424, 432
8.8cm Flak 41 83, 99, 321, 325
8.8cm Pak 43 85–86, 267, 285, 288, 289, 303–304, 305
10.5cm Flak 39 99, 144, 159, 205, 235, 236, 241, 267, 285, 339, 341, 351, 424, 433
10.5cm le. FH 61, 267, 285, 399, 406, 408, 420
15cm s. IG33 60
15.2cm 433 (r) 420